WHITGIFT SCHOOL

A HISTORY

Whitgift School, Croydon, like most other schools of ancient foundation, has experienced periods of obscurity as well as of success. One hundred and twenty years ago, when it was reconstructed after years of oblivion, so little of its earlier existence was known that the School was generally regarded as a completely new venture.

F. H. G. Percy, an Old Whitgiftian, a former master at the School, and, since his retirement from teaching, the School's archivist, has been able, however, to reconstruct the story of the School in considerable detail. After many years of research in ancient and more recent records, his *History of Whitgift School* was published in 1976, and the present book is a revised and much expanded edition of that work. Mr Percy has continued to gather information from an increasingly wide range of sources, and has thus been able to include much new material relating to the School from its earliest days onwards, as well as giving a full account of Whitgift in the 1970s and 1980s to bring the history up to date.

The excellence of the text has been further enhanced by the addition of almost 200 illustrations, in which portraits, prints, plans, photographs and printed material of various kinds are reproduced, often in full colour.

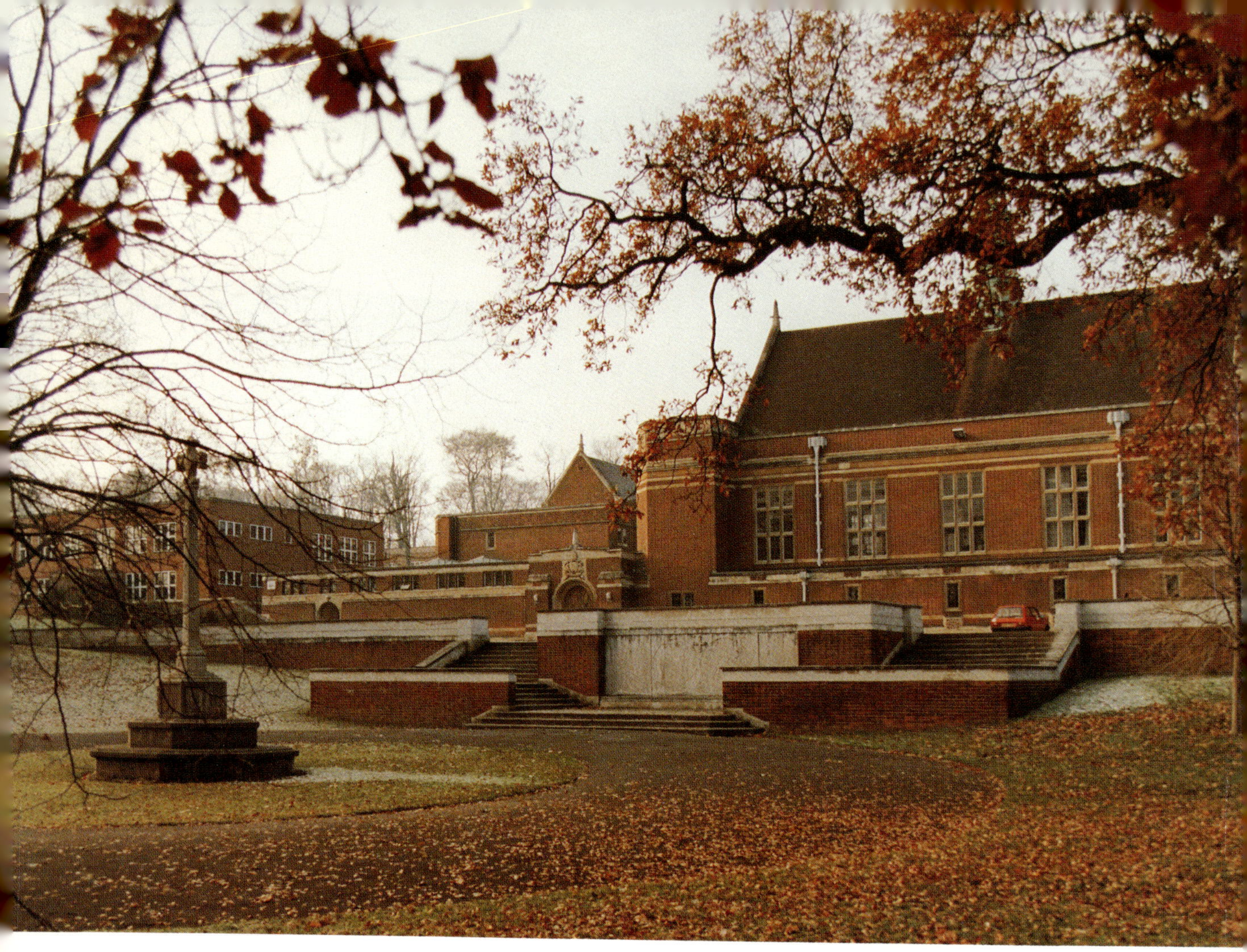

F.H.G. PERCY

WHITGIFT SCHOOL

A HISTORY

THE WHITGIFT FOUNDATION

WHITGIFT SCHOOL
A HISTORY

A new, revised and expanded edition of
History of Whitgift School (1976).
This edition first published in Great Britain by
The Whitgift Foundation
North End, Croydon, Surrey CR9 1SS

Designed by Michael Legat

Copyright © The Whitgift Foundation 1991

All rights reserved. No part of this publication
may be reproduced, stored in a retrieval system, or
transmitted, in any form or by any means, electronic,
mechanical, photocopying, recording or otherwise
without the prior permission of the Copyright owner

ISBN: 0 9517320 0 5 cased edition
ISBN: 0 9517320 1 3 paperbound edition

Printed and bound in Great Britain by
Burgess & Son (Abingdon) Limited
Thames View, Abingdon, Oxfordshire OX14 3LE

Contents

Acknowledgements		vi
Preface		9
Preface to Second Edition		11
1.	The Founder	13
2.	Foundation	31
3.	The Seventeenth-Century Grammar School	45
4.	Henry Mills, 1712–1742	77
5.	Decline, 1742–1843	94
6.	The Struggle for Reconstruction, 1843–1871	110
7.	The Reconstructed School Under Robert Brodie, 1871–1902	129
8.	S. O. Andrew, 1903–1927	162
9.	Ronald Gurner and Haling Park	193
10.	G. E. H. Ellis and World War II	213
11.	E. A. G. Marlar and Post-War Opportunities	223
12.	M. J. Hugill	240
13.	David Raeburn and Great Expectations 1970–1990 A Headmaster's Personal Retrospect (by David Raeburn)	256
About the Author		295
Appendices		308
I	Schoolmasters and Head Masters	309
II	Alumni 1600–1800	314
III	A Select and Varied List of 100 OWs since 1871	320
IV	Chairmen of the Governors	323
V	Benefactors	325
VI	Whitgift Heraldry	328
VII	Summary of Developments at Haling Park 1921–1990	330
VIII	The Old Whitgiftian Association and affiliated Clubs and Societies	334
IX	Bibliography	336
Index		343

Acknowledgements (First Edition)

To scholars, archivists, librarians and others in many places I am grateful for their advice and professional skill, and for their help in locating material and making it available. I apologise to anyone whose name has been inadvertently omitted from this list.

Mr. M.L. Barnes, Clerk to the Whitgift Foundation, Dr. G.R. Batho, Mr. E.G.W. Bill, Librarian of Lambeth Palace, the Rev. P.E. Blagdon-Gamlen (OW), Vicar of Leysdown, Kent, Dr. H.F. Brooks, the late John Carleton, Dr. Patrick Collinson, Mr. W.R.B. Cross, Mr. P.S. Crowson (OW), Mr. H.A.C. Evans, the late J.L. Fanner (OW), Mr. J. Foster White (OW), Mr. A.P. Glover, Reference Librarian, London Borough of Croydon, The Rev. G.P. Gordon Clark, Rector of Keston, Kent, Mr. Leonard Green, Mr. A.G. Hawkes, Mr. R.E. Latham, Mr. R. Lovatt, Keeper of Archives, Peterhouse, Cambridge, Sir James Marshall (OW), Mr. H.G.F. Micklewright, the Rev. N.A.L. Miller (OW), Mr. W. O'Sullivan, Keeper of MSS., Trinity College, Dublin, Mr. M.H. Ouseley, Mr. H.E. Parr, Miss Alicia C. Percival, Sir David Pitblado, the late Miss Dorothy Pullinger, Mr. G.F. Pullinger (OW), Dr. J.W. Roche, the late A.P. Ryan (OW), Mr. H.B. Shaw, Mr. I.P. Shaw (OW), Dr. Brian Simon, Mr. R.E. Smith, the Rev. W.J.T. Smith, Vicar of Boreham, Essex, the late A. Talbot Smith (OW), Dr. R.S. Tompson, Mr. A.A. Williams, Bursar, Queen's College, Oxford, Mr. J.M. Woolley, Clerk of the Merchant Taylors Company; the Registrar, National Register of Archives, the Librarian, Caius College, Cambridge, the County Record Officer, Chelmsford, Essex, the Archivist, Borough of Grimsby, the Librarian, Guildhall Library, London, the Librarian, Sheffield City Library, the Clerk, Stationers' Company.

I am particularly indebted to Mrs. Joan Simon for reading part of an earlier draft of the book and for making invaluable criticisms and suggestions.

To my former colleague and fellow-Whitgiftian, Mr. W.D. Hussey, I owe far more than I can express. It is he who from the outset has given me the greatest encouragement by his interest and sound advice. He has himself done a great deal of research, now inextricably mixed with my own. This would have been a better book if he had written it, but his other historical interests did not allow him to undertake more than he was already committed to.

I am very grateful to two Head Masters of Whitgift, Messrs. M.J. Hugill and D.A. Raeburn, and to the Governors of the Whitgift Foundation, for granting me two periods of sabbatical leave to complete research and writing, which have occupied much of my leisure time over twenty years, and which could not have been concluded without a long period of freedom from other daily responsibilies. The publication of this book would have been impossible had it not been financed by the Governors of the Foundation. The selection and interpretation of evidence and any expression of opinion are the author's own, and do not necessarily reflect the opinions and policy of the Governors and Head Masters.

I also wish to thank the following for permission to quote from unpublished material: the Archivist, City of Bristol, the Keeper of MSS., British Library, the Chief Librarian, Croydon Public Libraries, the Kent County Archivist, Maidstone, the Librarian, Lambeth Palace Library, the Keeper of Archives, Leicester Records, the Keeper of Western MSS., Bodleian

Library, Oxford, the Librarian of Christ Church, Oxford, on behalf of the Wake Trustees, the President and Fellows of Corpus Christi College, Oxford.

Transcripts of Crown-copyright records in the Public Record office appear by permission of the Controller of H.M. Stationery Office.

Above all, I wish to thank my wife, who has not only endured for many years an involvement on my part that has often kept me unsociably preoccupied, but has also given me her unstinted help in preparing this book for publication.

F.H.G. Percy

Haling Park Cottage
South Croydon
December 1975

Further Acknowledgements (Revised Edition)

I am indebted to many more informants, scholars, librarians and archivists in many places, among them: Miss Janet Arnold, the late R. L. Arrowsmith of Charterhouse, Mr. Anton Bantock, Mr. D. J. Bell, Librarian of Ashridge Management College, Canon G. H. Brown, Rector of Great Grimsby, Miss H. Brooks, The Earl of Cawdor, Dr. Hugh Cecil, Mr. L. Colchester, Ms M. P. G. Draper, Archivist of the Bedford Estates, Mr. Jack Farley, Ms Catherine Hall, Archivist of Gonville and Caius College, Cambridge, Revd. Philip Ireson, Vicar of Swinefleet, Miss A. C. James, Assistant Librarian, Society of Antiquaries, Miss. P. A. Jenkins of the Government Art Collection, Dr. John Lipscombe, Mr. Theodore Mallinson and Mr. Sam Eideman of Highgate School, the late Sir William Maycock, Mrs. B. Parry-Jones, Archivist of Magdalen College, Oxford, Mr. Edmor Phillips, Principal, Carmarthen Technical and Agricultural College, Miss Mary L. Robertson, Curator of MSS, Henry E. Huntington Library, San Marino, California, Mr. Malcolm Rogers, Head of the Archive, National Portrait Gallery, Mr. Stephen Roud, Croydon Public Library, Mr. W.B. Rymer, Solicitor to The Whitgift Foundation, Mr. R. Stepney-Gulston, Mr. Paul Thompson, Mrs. Lilian Thornhill, Mr. J. P. Threlfell, Mr. P. S. Trevis, Mr. Jason Wilcox, whose researches into the identity of early members of the Whitgift staff have been very valuable; the Librarian, Folger Shakespeare Library, Washington DC; the Archivist, Herts Record Office; the Librarian, National Maritime Museum; the Archivist, Northants Record Office; the Librarian, Pembroke College, Oxford; the Librarian, National Library of Wales.

I very warmly acknowledge the contribution made by David Raeburn, Headmaster 1970–91, to the final chapter, which records his own régime. No previous headmaster has left an account of his aims and struggles during his period of office. Because the conclusion of Mr. Raeburn's lengthy headmastership coincides with the publication of this book, I invited him to summarise his 21 years of direction of the School's affairs. Any other survey could only be the work of a bystander, such as I am myself, and I am glad to have the collaboration of one supremely qualified to conclude this account of a most important era in the School's evolution, culminating in the occupation of the splendid new building, itself a symbol of Mr. Raeburn's devoted service, distinguished achievement and imaginative foresight.

For the production of this second, expanded account of the School's history, I am much indebted to Mrs. Ann Higgins, who has patiently typed many pages of additional copy and combined it with the version published fifteen years ago.

I am particularly grateful to Michael Legat, OW, who has supervised every stage of the new book's design and production. He has drawn upon his own experience as a publisher in designing its format and appearance to suit modern taste, taking advantage of up-to-date methods of book production, and encouraging me to provide a wider range of illustrations. The Governors have again decided to support its publication by underwriting the expenses of the venture, and to them also I express my appreciation.

F.H.G. Percy

Whitgift School
March 1991

Acknowledgements - Illustrations

Gratitude is expressed for the kind permission to reproduce the copyright portraits, prints, photographs, plans, manuscripts and pages from books, granted by:

Aerofilms Ltd.: North End (p.246); Trinity School (p.251); Whitgift Centre (p.252); Haling Park (p. 203). The Society of Antiquaries: Funeral Procession of Queen Elizabeth I (p.25). The Keeper of the Western MSS, Bodleian Library, Oxford: Two Latin Exercises [Rawl. Poet. 123] (p.68). City of Bristol Museum and Art Gallery: Sir John Smyth, Bt. (p.80). The British Library: William Crowe's *Elenchus* (p.62); Brodeus (p.55). Miss Helen Brooks: Revd. George Coles (p.111). Syndics of Cambridge University Library: Hammond's Plan of Cambridge (p.19); John Whitgift (p.26). Governing Body of Peterhouse, Cambridge: John Whitgift (p.16). His Grace the Archbishop of Canterbury and the Church Commissioners: Ralph Snow (p.75). Carmarthen Museum: Richard Vaughan, Earl of Carbery (p.53). Messrs. Chorley and Handford: Music School (p.244); Language Laboratory (p.245); Croham Hurst (p.261); A series of photographs of the new buildings (pp.285, 288, 289, 292, 293, 300, 301). The Courtauld Institute: Ralph Snow (p.75). The Croydon Advertiser: Demolition at North End (p.247). The Chief Librarian, Croydon Public Library: Sir Frederick Edridge (p.93); Haling House in the Eighteenth Century (p.95); *Verses on the Peace* (p.79). The Croydon Times: OWA Day 1958 (p.231); Unveiling of Andrew Memorial (p.236); Martin Jarvis (p.250). Jack Farley FPS: Tomb of William Nicolson (p.54). Fox Photos: Lord Diplock (p.211). The Vicar of Grimsby: St James's Church, Grimsby (p.14). G. Hana, Ltd.: Building under Construction (p.284). Harold Hore, Esq.: Lord Trend (p.210); Hockey XI 1989 (p.276); Fencing 1989 (p.277). Kent County Council Record Office: John Dalyson's School Bill (p.57). The Curator, Temple Newsam House, Leeds: Whitgift's Shoe (p.30). the Rt. Hon. the Earl of Liverpool: C. C. C. Jenkinson, 3rd Earl of Liverpool (p.100). The Keeper of the National Portrait Gallery: Lord Burleigh (p.17); Lord Howard of Effingham (p.21); John Whitgift (p.28); William Camden (p.49). Ken Simmons FPS: Sir Daniel Harvey (p.56). South Thames Studios: Unveiling of War Memorial (p.232). Sport and General: Prize-giving 1947 (p.225); Public Schools Sevens (p.247). His Grace the Duke of Sutherland: Duke of Bridgewater (p.73). Bonar Sykes, Esquire: Sir Frederick Sykes (p.178). The Keeper of the Tate Gallery, London: Thomas Law Hodges (p.98).

Preface

Like that of any other ancient school, the history of Whitgift is both typical and unique. So little used to be known about the School's first two hundred years of existence, which were followed by a long period of almost complete suspension, that a common belief arose that there was nothing to be discovered. Indeed, the conviction that there had really been no school of any consequence whatever before 1871 was so strongly held, that in March 1871 *The Croydon Chronicle* referred regretfully but confidently to 'three hundred years of nothingness'. Nevertheless, it can now be safely said that more has come to light about Whitgift than is known about most schools of similar antiquity. Even so, the first two hundred years remain a period of comparative obscurity.

In this account I have tried to set the story of the School's foundation, development, decline, revival and expansion against the background of prevailing views on education and of social influences over the centuries. Yet the success or otherwise of the School has depended so much on the character of the various Schoolmasters and their successors, the Head Masters, that I have followed the quite usual course of basing the narrative upon these central personages. The Schoolmasters, moreover, have had an influence on the amount of source material available, not merely because they were responsible for maintaining the Foundation's records, but also because, if they were enterprising men, references to their activities would collect and sometimes survive.

Unfortunately, the Foundation's early records give very little information about the life of the School itself, although they provide valuable material for students of local, economic and social history. I have made little use of this material to illustrate the administration of the Hospital and the life of its inmates, except where the School and the Schoolmaster have been involved, although the temptation to digress from my central theme has sometimes been hard to resist.

Because John Whitgift placed his foundation under the surveillance of his successors as Archbishops of Canterbury, their archives at Lambeth Palace should provide a further reliable source of information, but here again what records survive (for obsolete papers were not systematically preserved) deal mainly with the administration of the Hospital and its estates. What has been discovered about the School's earlier history has been through the chance survival, and even more accidental coming to light, of documents, records, private letters and papers in many places. There remain large gaps in the story that may never be filled without the help of further lucky finds such as have so much helped already to illuminate it. But material relating to the last hundred years exists in overwhelming quantities; ruthless elimination of much possibly interesting matter has been necessary to avoid a mere recital of names and events that are easily traceable in the School records.

All historians are interested in policy. School policy has been largely in the hands of the Archbishops of Canterbury, including the Founder, the Governors, and the Schoolmasters and their successors. There have been times when these policy-makers have been directed or over-ruled by Parliament (during the Interregnum) and its deputed authorities, such as the Charity Commissioners (1853), the Endowed Schools Commissioners (1869–74), and the Board of Education (1902) and its various successors. Policy has also been influenced by the wishes of parents and even the expressed needs of pupils, by the requirements of universities, of employers and of professional bodies. It has been my endeavour to follow these threads of policy throughout this history, but the texture they have woven is sometimes complex, the pattern confused for lack of evidence, and occasionally only shreds are left.

Preface to the Second Edition

In preparing a revised edition of *The History of Whitgift School* I have had the following ends in view; firstly, to correct errors in the original text, a few being the result of oversights in proof-reading or in alterations by the printer after that stage, others being due to my own lapses in accuracy, none of them, however, grossly distorting fact; secondly, to introduce new material that has recently been discovered or that has become available after being regarded as confidential or personal; thirdly, to extend the account as far as the present time (still with certain strictures already referred to); and fourthly, to provide more plentiful illustrations than could be printed at the time of the first edition.

I have sometimes been reproached for not mentioning certain people, usually long-serving masters or prominent old boys. It has been impossible to do justice to the many members of the staff who have so greatly contributed in their various ways to the School's life and to their pupils' success and well-being. To mention only a few of these men must be to deny recognition of many others equally deserving. An unwieldy catalogue of names might go some way towards fuller acknowledgement of teaching ability, academic distinction, initiative, devotion to duty, long service, personality and even eccentricity - all of which qualities have been shared in abundance by my former mentors and colleagues. Some members of the staff who strongly influenced their pupils were birds of passage only, moving on to other fields. But whom to include by name? Whom to leave out? In my long association with Whitgift I am inevitably swayed by my personal memories, friendships, enthusiasms and experiences. The problem is not only taxing; it is also embarrassing. I have had to adopt a principle of selection. Where a clear and original contribution in some important area has been made to the School's progress, effectiveness or reputation - it may be the organisation of a department, or the introduction of new methods of teaching, or instruction of excellence in music, games or sport - I have thought it proper to attribute responsibility and accord praise. To those whose names could also have been included for many reasons, were it not for the demands upon space, I can only apologise. Their names and achievements, however, are not overlooked, for they are recorded in the pages of *The Whitgiftian*, and live for a while at least in the memories of hundreds of their pupils.

It is a similar case with Old Boys. The roll of pupils between 1600 and 1860 must have amounted to several thousands; of these we know the names of barely a hundred, but their identity is part of the historical evidence. A good proportion of these were men of distinction; that is mainly how we come to know of them. Since 1871 over 15,000 names have been inscribed in the Admission Registers. It is difficult to select whom to mention from the most eminent of this great number. We are proud of our distinguished members in the services, in politics, in scholarship, in science and the law, our international representatives in various games and sports, but who are to receive acknowledgement, who are to be omitted? I can only quote from the invitation inscribed on the frame of the Founder's portrait: 'Feci quod potui . . . fac melius si potes'.

1. The Founder

Family Origins

The family name of Whitgift derives from the village of that name on the southern bank of the River Ouse five miles from Goole. The locality had possibly formed dowry-land presented by or to a person named White in pre-Conquest times. Although the place-name is recorded in a Charter of 1070 whereby William I granted fishing rights at Wytegift to the Abbot of Selby, the first mention of anyone bearing the name appears to have been in the Calendar of Close Rolls of Edward II, when on 12 July 1308 the Sheriff of York was authorised to release twenty-three men, including John de Whitgift and Adam his brother, who had been imprisoned at Lincoln for divers trespasses committed upon one Ranulph de Otteby. It may be this John de Whitgift who is referred to in the Calendar of Patent Rolls on 3 December 1322, when John, son of Richard de Whitegift, was granted a commission to maintain the banks of the River Ouse in the parts of Marshland between the River Aire and Trentfall, Co. York, a stretch of the river about midway along which the village of Whitgift is situated. There are a few other references to members of the family before the sixteenth century, but they appear never to have been very numerous, although there must have been others not referred to, who lived in obscurity. In spite of claims that were made later, it seems that the family was never armigerous, but some of its members were ecclesiastics or prosperous tradesmen; in February 1346/7 Sir Walter de Whytegift was a party to a grant of land at Burton Constable, eight miles NE of Hull (the appellative 'Sir' was commonly accorded to priests in the Middle Ages), and this man may have been the same who held the Rectory of Vange in Essex from 1336 to 1352. Beween 1377 and 1404 three Whitgifts, a Thomas and two Williams, were tapestry-makers, and a John Whitgifte was a mercer, in York, where another John Whitgifte made his will in 1440.

After this there is a gap, however, and we are unable to trace any definite connection between these Whitgifts and the Founder's grandfather, John Whitgift of York, who had two sons, Robert and Henry, and a daughter, Isobel. Although Sir George Paule, the Founder's Steward and first biographer, to whom we are indebted for almost everything in the way of personal memories and comments, says, '...he had many children, some whereof he made scholars, others he placed abroad in several Courses of Life', no record has come to light of any other children than these. Robert, the eldest, was in October 1525 elected Abbot of the Augustinian Monastery of Wellow, very near Great Grimsby, in Lincolnshire, where he had for several years already been serving as a member of his order. Henry, the Founder's father, may well have come to that town at his brother's suggestion; he married Anne Dynewell of Grimsby and was a merchant and property-owner there when their children were born. He was an important figure in the town, being an alderman in 1550 and having held a number of responsible offices in the dozen years preceding; he owned several houses in the market place and by the town gates.

The young John Whitgift

Henry's eldest son, John, was born between 1530 and 1534, before the introduction of parish registers in 1538, so no record exists of the date of his birth or baptism. He himself declared in 1590 that he was then aged 60, and Paule gives

The Church of St Mary Magdalene in the village of Whitgift

1530; a portrait at Lambeth Palace, dated 1602, gives his age as 68, and other evidence has been adduced supporting 1532 and 1534; but he should perhaps be relied upon to know his own age better than others might. He had five brothers: William, Philip, George, Richard and Geoffrey, and a sister, Alice; of all these, only William left any children: two sons and four daughters. These daughters were fairly prolific, but only one of the sons married and he, in his turn, left but a son and a daughter, so it is small wonder that the family name died out in the early eighteenth century, as far as we have been able to discover. Dr. Alex Comfort has said: 'It had for thousands of years been necessary, if one wished to ensure the continuance of one's name and descent, to have six or seven children.'

Robert Whitgift was dispossessed of his abbey at the Dissolution in 1536, but he had already sworn the oath of allegiance to Henry VIII, imposed by the Act of Supremacy, and was granted a fairly generous life pension which he supplemented by conducting a school for a while; it was at this time that he established an influence over his eldest nephew, and seeing that the latter showed intellectual promise, persuaded his father to let him go and live in London with his aunt Isobel, who had married Michael Shaller, a verger of St. Paul's Cathedral; thus he was able to attend St. Anthony's School half a mile away in the direction of Bishopsgate. (The occasion of his leaving his uncle's tuition may have been the latter's appointment in May 1538, when John was only eight, to the prebendal church of Ketton in Rutland.) It is uncertain if there was a grammar school in Grimsby at that time, unless it was where Robert taught, although in 1547 the town was enabled by royal licence to convert a chantry into a school. But why, since he had a relative closely connected with the Cathedral of St. Paul's did he not attend Colet's foundation that had absorbed the old cathedral school? St. Paul's and St. Anthony's were the great rival schools of London at that time, but St. Paul's had an inadequate High Master who did not teach Greek, the importance of which in the eyes of scholars was expanding and which John Whitgift either wished or was encouraged to learn. John Stow in

Commemorative window, St James's Church, Grimsby

his *Survey of London* recalled that scholars from the two schools when they met called each other 'Anthonie pigs' or 'pigeons of Paules'; 'they usually fall from words to blows, with their satchels full of books, many times in great heaps that they trouble the streets and passengers'. Although there were two hundred boys at St. Anthony's in 1560, a hundred years later it was in decline and so closed, the competition from the wealthier, more recently founded London schools, Westminster, Merchant Taylors', Charterhouse and Mercers', proving too strong.

Cambridge

John Whitgift did not get on well with his aunt, whom he displeased by refusing to attend mass, so she turned him out, saying that whereas at first she thought she had received a saint into her house, she now perceived he was a devil; the incident is clear evidence of the Protestant beliefs he had absorbed perhaps from his uncle Robert, or from those he had come in contact with in London. Upon his return home he was advised by his uncle to go to Cambridge, so in 1548 or 1549 he went up to Queens', but in May 1549 transferred to Pembroke, where Ridley, then Bishop of Rochester, was Master, and Grindal, later Archbishop of Canterbury, was President. His tutor was another heroic reformer and martyr, John Bradford, who obtained him a bible-clerkship, giving him much-needed financial help, for at about this time his father sustained mercantile losses at sea.

His father died before John had taken his first degree, leaving in his will dated 9 June 1550 and proved on 7 October 1552 an estate that seems not to have suffered any crippling blow from his recent misfortunes. Indeed, it reveals that the Whitgifts were in quite comfortable circumstances. Henry gave a bequest to charity in the form of 40 pence to the poor man's chest in the church and also another 12 pence for tithes. To his wife he left £15 in cash and the use of his house and its furnishings so long as she remained unmarried; to his daughter, who was as yet not married to one Henry Cookson, he left a dowry of £6. 13s. 4d., while most of his property was to be held in trust for his six sons when they came of age, each to receive an equal share. To John, his eldest son, however, he left the special gift of 'my best gowne and my best Dublytt of Taffataye' (a silk doublet). His wife and Robert were to be executors, and Robert was to receive a house 'for his labour', and the residue of his goods.

John Whitgift was now presumably of age and with his uncle Robert was responsible for his younger brothers, except Philip, who had died in the same year as his father, at the age of 12. In addition to these family responsibilities, he was faced with troubles of a political, religious and academic nature, the accession of Mary in 1553 introducing a time of great difficulty for those who held the Protestant belief. Whitgift had adopted the religious views that his uncle had acceded to and which Bradford had supported, but he kept them much to himself, so that he was able to remain at Cambridge and take his BA degree in 1553/4. When in 1555 he was elected to a fellowship at Peterhouse, he found in the Master, Andrew Perne, another sympathetic friend, who helped him to escape the awkward investigations of Mary's Visitors, so that he was able to maintain an unbroken residence in Cambridge and study for further degrees. But for the intercession of Perne, who was Vice-Chancellor of the University, he might have felt it necessary to withdraw, like many others, to the Continent to avoid any violation of his conscience under questioning. He proceeded MA in 1557 and after ordination in 1560 was inducted to the rectory of Teversham, a convenient if not very profitable benefice, whose position just outside Cambridge enabled him to continue to play a full part in University affairs. He seems already to have become more than just a man of promise and after taking his BD in 1562 he was elected Lady Margaret Professor of Divinity. His position in the University was now, in spite of his youth, an important and influential one, and he was already showing a taste and talent for administration, which earned him the approval of the Heads of Colleges.

After Elizabeth I's accession to the throne in 1558 there was a violent reaction against the papism of Mary's reign. The return from Geneva of those extremists who had sought asylum there was followed by a conflicting variety of Presbyterian doctrines, which was leading to confusion in the Anglican Church; many disputes arose over liturgical, vestiarian and ecclesiologi-

John Whitgift as Fellow of Peterhouse (1555–67)

cal matters, which could be settled only by a strong authoritarian lead from the Queen and her archbishop, Parker. At Cambridge Whitgift himself had seemed to favour Puritan views and had at first protested against the too rigid insistence by the Church upon the traditional forms, but wearied perhaps by the disputatious element that, by their extreme opinions, threatened to disrupt the religious and, in consequence, the political and academic life of the country, he came out strongly in support of uniformity, for which he was constantly attacked by many who regarded him as an apostate. Whitgift saw the efforts of the non-conformists as a gigantic conspiracy against the law and order that he respected. For the next few years he consolidated his position in Cambridge in the forefront of those who supported the authority of the established Church.

Although, then, in November 1565 he had been one of those, heads of houses in the main, who had pleaded with Sir William Cecil, Principal Secretary of State and Chancellor of the University, not to impose too rigorously the vestiarian regulations that had greatly angered the Puritan element so strongly entrenched in the University, within eighteen months he was safely established on the side of authority and uniformity. The intervening time had been a difficult one for the Anglican Church, which was looking for men of firm will and purpose to be appointed to positions of authority, and it may be significant that in January 1565/6 when one of Cecil's men visited the University for the purpose of enlisting suitable entrants to Cecil's service, he did not find any of 'years and gravity'; he nevertheless reported that there were 'divers young men in the university, learned and honest, the which would gladly serve your Honour, with whom I will talk concerning that matter when I know your further pleasure'. One of these young men could have been John Whitgift, then aged 35.

When, on 25 January 1566/7, Robert Horne, Bishop of Winchester, wrote to Sir William Cecil recommending 'Mr Whitgift, a man honest and well learned', to be promoted to the Deanery of Canterbury, or some other preferment of the late Dr. Wotton, John Whitgift did not receive this appointment, but he was elected Master of Pembroke Hall on 21 April, his predecessor, Matthew Hutton, having been preferred to another of Dr Wotton's benefices, the Deanery of York. Cecil had not forgotten him, however, for a few weeks later he was offered the Mastership of Trinity, which was in the gift of the Queen, whose father had founded the College in 1546. This appointment was not altogether favoured in Cambridge, for on 17 June he wrote to Cecil vindicating himself against false reports upon his qualifications for the Mastership:

. . . It is not unknown unto me, what is reported of me to your Honour, while you intend . . . to place me in Trinity College . . .

For God's Sake, Right Honourable, let it be judged what I am by my doings, and not by the report of those, who do not to me, as they would themselves be done unto. As touching my Notconformity (which is one thing laid against me), I dare be judged by my Lord of Canterbury his

Teversham Church. John Whitgift Rector 1560–71

William Cecil, Lord Burghley (1520–98)

Grace, your Honour, or my Lord of London, or Master Dean of York: who knoweth more of my mind in this matter than any man doth beside. I never encouraged any to withstand the Queen's Majesty's laws in that behalf; but I both have, and do by all means I may, seek to persuade men to conform themselves; for it grieveth me, that any man should cease from preaching, for the use of these things, being of themselves indifferent . . . That preferment that I have, whatsoever it is, I have it of your Honour his means. And therefore I owe myself wholly unto you. But it is not so much as it is reported. The Mastership of Pembroke Hall is but £4 the year and 18d in the week for commons. My benefice is one of the least in all the diocese [*the Rectory of Teversham*]. My Lecture is the whole stay of my living. My debts are more than I shall ever, being in the state I am, be able to discharge. And extreme necessity, not any prodigality, hath brought me unto them . . .

If this letter can be interpreted aright, it reveals much of Whitgift's character and temperament.

Dr. Patrick Collinson has suggested that instead of vindicating his integrity, this letter attempts an elaborate self-justification against attacks that have much truth in them; we know that he had somewhat shifted his ground concerning 'these things' that were 'indifferent', but to imply that he had deviated in order to gain advancement overlooks the direct honesty with which he admits that his finances are desperate.

He never did become inured to attack by enemies, who tried to confuse him by accusing him of inconsistency in his conduct, with the result that he grew indignant and angry, leaping into self-defence and counter-accusation, instead of ignoring the calculated provocations of lesser men. When he refers to the 'use of these things, being of themselves indifferent', he is thinking of, for example, the strong objection of non-conformists to the wearing of certain vestments that, although a survival from Catholic times, represented the uniformity and stability of the established Church; to him non-conformity was at best a vanity, at the worst, indiscipline. Several modern historians have compared Whitgift with a schoolmaster—sometimes a Victorian Headmaster-Bishop—and it is this sense he displays of always being in the right against petty-minded opposition that supports this comparison.

Why should he have been hard up? The emolument he received from the Lady Margaret Professorship in Divinity had been increased the previous year by 50 per cent from 20 marks to £20 a year and he must have had other income from pupils; he had no wife or children to support; why his debts and necessity should have been so burdensome is uncertain, but after his father died, Whitgift does seem to have made himself responsible for the upbringing of his younger brothers, two of whom were admitted to Peterhouse in 1560 and 1561. If he undertook to see them through university, his means may have been stretched. In January 1564/5, however, his uncle Robert had died and although his will has not been discovered, it appears likely that John was his heir, for in 1565 he bought a house called Curles at Clavering in Essex, about eighteen miles from Cambridge, where his eldest brother, William, went to live after his marriage. Beside providing a permanent home for his brother, he had now established a convenient retreat for himself when the responsibilities of his position at Cambridge demanded relaxation. In conjunction with the former owner, Margaret Fulnetby, he established a charge on the property to the value of 4 marks a year to support a bible-clerkship at Peterhouse, in recognition, no doubt, of the help he had received as an undergraduate at Pembroke Hall; this payment, which was to begin in 1572, continued until about 1940. His debts do not seem to have been due to self-indulgence but to generosity. Although himself a man of simple tastes, he seems always to have had a financier's interest in money and he kept a close eye on his accounts, especially when he had a large income at his disposal; as we shall see later, he did not like to feel he was being imposed upon.

Master of Trinity

In July he was inducted Master of Trinity. He never lost the favour of the Queen, who after first hearing him preach declared, 'He hath a white gift indeed', and made him a Royal Chaplain. 1567 had been a wonderful year for him, for he had also been made Regius Professor of Divinity. Yet the following year brought him further advantages, for he was made Chaplain to the Bishop of Ely and a few months after this appointment he was given a prebend and made a Canon of Ely.

After a rather lax predecessor, Whitgift established at Trinity a stern and paternal rule, very much in keeping with his schoolmasterly character. It must be remembered that many of the undergraduates were in their early teens (for instance, Anthony and Francis Bacon were admitted Fellow-Commoners in 1573 at the ages of fifteen and twelve respectively) and the functions of the Master of any college were those of, as it were, the Housemaster of 'School' House, looking after the welfare of the pupils committed to his charge. Whitgift enjoyed a reputation as a trustworthy tutor; several of his pupils at Peterhouse migrated with him to Trinity. Mention has already been made of his attention to financial detail; an account book in which he has recorded expenditure made on behalf of some fifty of his pupils shows the close supervision he exerted over their studies, their pastimes, their health, their apparel and indeed every aspect of their existence while away from home. It is kept in great detail so that he can render an exact account to their parents or guardians. One of his most illustrious pupils was George Clifford, third Earl of Cumberland, who had succeeded his father at the age of eleven and who was thirteen when Whitgift recorded these expenses on his behalf in May and June, 1571:

'Dominus georgius comes cumbreland'

to the carier	iiijs.
to an other brought hys .l. stuff from the cariers to the college	iiijd.
paper	iiijd.
a pen knyfe	iiijd.
an ower glasse	vjd.
a zithern lute	xs.
matriculation	ijs.
one dosen of sylk poynts	vid.
mendyng hosse	iiijd.
a come	jd.
tutor att mydsom	xs.
lawndres	ijs. vjd.
hys brekfasts to the .22. of June	xvs.
a bowe	xvjd.
a paper boke	vjd.
to the carer for hys gowne	vjd.
colloquiū erasmi [*a text-book*]	xxd.
for a key to a privy dore	xijd.
shoeing of hys horsse	xijd.

(These few items have been selected for their variety and for ease of comprehension, Whitgift's spelling being largely idiosyncratic. From the complete accounts a good picture of life at Cambridge and the responsibilities of a tutor can be formed.)

Trinity soon came to rival St. John's as the largest and most fashionable college; certainly it contained a large number of aristocratic fellow-

Trinity College, Cambridge, as it was when John Whitgift was Master, 1567–77

Whitgift School

commoners, while the fact that young noblemen such as Cumberland, Lord Zouche, the Earl of Worcester, Lord Dunboy, and Anthony and Francis, the sons of Sir Nicholas Bacon, were at Trinity in Whitgift's time reflects the confidence reposed in him. His interest in the more material aspects of their welfare has been illustrated above, but he paid close personal attention to their courses of study and was, to quote Paule once again, 'always severely punishing . . . omissions and negligence.'

He usually dined and supped in the Common-Hall, as well to have a watchful eye over the scholars, and to keep them in a mannerly and awful obedience, as by his example, to teach them to be contented with a scholar-like college diet.

He served two terms as Vice-Chancellor of the University—the chief administrative post—in 1570–1 and 1573–4, and it was while he held this office that he took up the suggestion of reforming the University Statutes; he was always anxious that clear and reasonable regulations should be established and followed at all the institutions with which he was connected, and he was always ready to have them amended if changing circumstances made it desirable. At about the same time he was involved in a most

Titlepage of *An Answere to a certen Libell*, 1572

troublesome dispute with the Puritan faction at Trinity, headed by Thomas Cartwright, who had defied his regulations about the wearing of certain vestments such as the surplice, then detested by the Puritans as the survival of an unholy romish practice. Cartwright eventually attacked boldly the constitution of the Church of England, and was dismissed from the Lady Margaret Chair of Divinity. Whitgift and Cartwright were later involved in the polemical disputes contained in the *Admonition to Parliament* and the *Reply to the Admonition*, which cannot receive attention in this brief notice, although they involved principles of vital importance to the security and development of the Anglican Church.

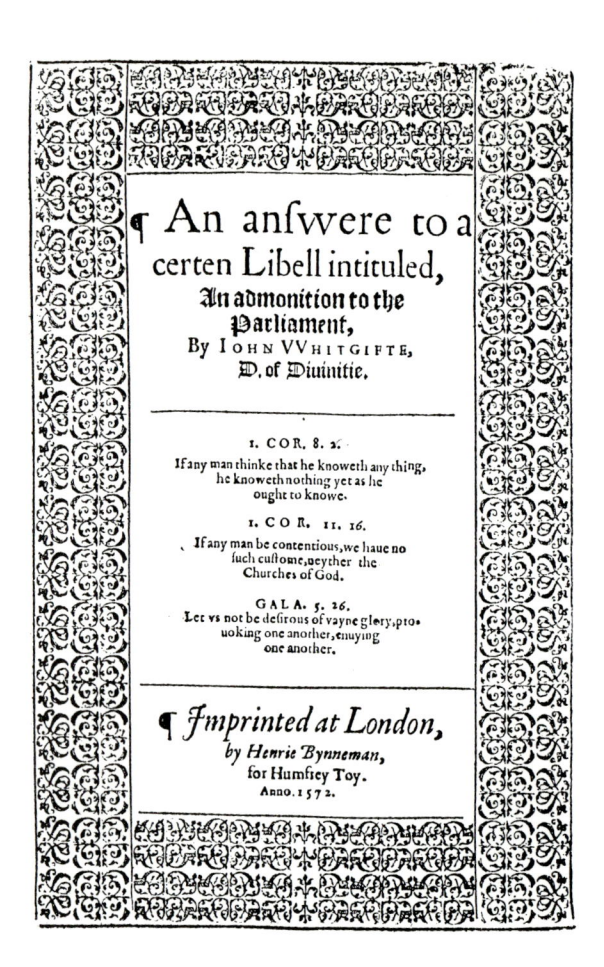

His opposition to Puritan doctrines at Cambridge, his success in raising Trinity's reputation, his ability as an administrator and the Queen's approval of him, together with the notice that had been taken of him by Cecil and others

Thomas Cartwright (1535–1603)

powerful in the government of the country, brought promotion to a bishopric, and in 1577 he was consecrated Bishop of Worcester.

Worcester

At Worcester he found much to occupy him. He had to adapt himself to a new way of life, in which display and entertainment played an important part, and where civil crimes and disputes often impinged upon ecclesiastical duties. He preached regularly and dealt with recusants and Puritans with equal firmness; he was responsible to the Privy Council for matters both vital and trivial. Thus, although Whitgift's diocese was a comparatively quiet one, possibly owing to his own firm methods of control, problems existed for him in plenty. Among his responsibilities was the settling of disputes at the neighbouring cathedrals of Lichfield and Hereford; with Whitgift's support and interest, a new grammar school in Hereford Cathedral was set up as a successor to the ancient school that had expired after the Reformation, and new statutes for the Cathedral there were drawn up. Meanwhile, the Church of England under Archbishop Grindal seemed to be losing ground to a surge of enthusiasm for papism; a large number of the most powerful families in the land were still professing catholics; many recusant priests and missionaries were executed on the grounds that they were traitors to the Queen in that they owed allegiance to the Pope. The Puritans, on the other hand, received less discouragement from Grindal; he wanted to direct their zeal towards the full support of the established Church, a doubtful course that did not recommend itself to Elizabeth. His refusal to put down 'prophesyings', private meetings of clergy, especially those with Puritan leanings, to study the Scriptures, led her to sequestrate him in 1577 until his death, with the result that the Church was under no effective leadership for six years.

Canterbury

Upon Grindal's death in July 1583 Elizabeth nominated Whitgift to succeed him at Canterbury, where he was enthroned on October 23. It has been said that Grindal himself wished Whitgift to be his successor, and that Elizabeth had contemplated persuading Grindal to resign in Whitgift's favour, but the latter refused the appointment so long as the other was alive.

The new Archbishop now had a much harder task than before; the Privy Council had taken over much of his predecessor's authority, and Whitgift set out to restore the power in ecclesiastical matters that should have been his. When the Council began by requiring the Archbishop to justify himself in certain actions, he firmly but with dignity declined, and thereafter the Council treated him with greater respect. Yet many powerful members, including the Earl of Leicester, Knollys, Treasurer of the Queen's Household, Mildmay, Chancellor of the Exchequer, and Secretary Walsingham, were sympathetically inclined to the Puritans. The

Lord Howard of Effingham, Earl of Nottingham (1536–1624)

danger, as they saw it, came from Rome and from Spain, where Philip was already preparing his attempt at invasion. Since the Privy Council were adopting measures to oppose the papist faction, Whitgift drew up and issued to the bishops rigid articles for the conduct of the Church's affairs, designed to limit the freedom of the Puritans, who might have set up their own independent congregationalist churches. Other opposition he had to contend with was the determined assault made in Parliament on the Book of Common Prayer and the power of the bishops. However, during these early months of office he had the Queen's support for his actions, which gave him confidence to pursue policies that made him distinctly unpopular with many honest and conscientious members of church and state. When in February 1585/6 the Queen made him a member of her Privy Council, the first cleric to be appointed since Cardinal Pole in Mary's reign, for it was not an *ex officio* appointment, he was able to express directly his own views and listen to those of the other members of the Council, who varied in their estimates of him. Although animosity existed between him and Leicester and particularly Robert Beale, the Clerk, there were several who had links of friendship with him. Burghley had continued to be a good friend ever since the time when Whitgift had been picked out for promotion nearly twenty years before; they had their differences, but they enjoyed each other's respect and confidence. A constant supporter of his was Sir Christopher Hatton, appointed Lord Chancellor a little later, and the latter's two successors, John Puckering and Thomas Egerton who, together with Robert Cecil, were also sympathisers. Lord Howard of Effingham, Lord High Admiral at the time of the Spanish Armada, came to live at Haling Manor in the parish of Croydon in 1592 and thus became Whitgift's close neighbour, but he may not have taken much interest in Church affairs, and indeed little is known of the association between the two men.

Whitgift's chief concern, indeed the duty laid upon him, was now to impose discipline upon *all* the clergy of the realm, some of whom asserted that the services and by implication the beliefs of the Church of England were founded on romish practices, so they themselves were not prepared to submit to episcopal authority or, on the other hand, to resign the benefices they enjoyed in the church they rejected. Puritan opposition became furious at Whitgift's attempts at suppression, culminating in 1588 in the notorious and frequently scurrilous *Martin Marprelate* pamphlets of which Whitgift was the chief victim, often assailed with ribald and contemptuous abuse.

When in due course his policy of enforcing conformity met with increasing success, he turned his attention towards the betterment of the clergy, their status, their emoluments and their qualifications; he realised how important to the stability of the Church it was that the clergy should be well educated and able to wield authority in their parishes through their superiority of knowledge and behaviour. Most parish priests were poorly paid; Whitgift had personal experience of this situation and sought to improve their lot by recovering church property that had been concealed or misappropriated, or even by allowing some to hold benefices in plurality. The disciplining of the Puritans he left increasingly to his chaplain and lieutenant, Richard Bancroft, who was made Bishop of London in 1597 and who was to succeed him at Canterbury. Bancroft was a harder and less sensitive man than Whitgift, and much of the opprobrium that was later directed against the latter seems to have been better deserved by Bancroft.

Whitgift's reputation in non-conformist circles has naturally always been low; many of their attacks and accusations in his own lifetime were offensive, personal exaggerations; in the time of the Commonwealth this invective was raised to a fresh height of fury. Historians with non-conformist sympathies have usually execrated him, describing him as a narrow-minded, merciless inquisitor, but Macaulay's famous judgment of him as 'a mean and tyrannical priest, who gained power by servility and adulation' is not borne out by contemporary evidence which, less biased in his support than are the attacks in his disparagement, refers to his lengthy patience and even sympathy with the recalcitrant ministers he was with reasoned argument trying to persuade, and we know he was not a man well endowed by nature with patience. It must be remembered that religious tolerance was a concept alien to all parties in these disputes, and the laws of libel did not exist; moreover, the Puritans, able men of unselfish character and loyal to their principles, were no less ruthless when in power than their opponents had been. Several recent historians have acknowledged Whitgift's services in stabilising the Anglican Church and his ability not only as an ecclesiastic but also as a powerful and shrewd statesman.

Whitgift's wealth

Whitgift's enemies did not hesitate to attack him in any way to which he might be vulnerable. One point of weakness, they thought, was the vast income he enjoyed as Archbishop. Even before he became Bishop of Worcester he was criticised for enjoying rich pluralities; although he resigned the Professorship of Divinity in 1569, he had been appointed to several benefices by the Bishop of Ely the year before. These appointments were superseded, however, by still richer ones in the Diocese of Lincoln, and in 1575 his income from the Deanery, a prebend and the Rectory of Laceby amounted to over £250, in addition to his emolument as Master of Trinity. What did he need this money for? By all accounts his life in college was a model of austerity to his pupils; the debts he spoke of to Cecil in June 1567 would now presumably have been paid off (the postponement to 1572 of the rent charge on Curles at Clavering presupposes some expected solution of financial difficulties); his brothers William, George and Richard were now in their thirties and no longer a responsibility to him, although there is no record of their being gainfully employed; the youngest brother, Geoffrey, had been admitted scholar at Trinity in 1570 and could have been still something of a liability, but William's numerous progeny had not yet all been born. It seems likely that he was generous to the deserving, especially those at Trinity; a number of pupils from Grimsby figure in the lists of the time. These and other promising young men could have been the recipients of unobtrusive and unrecorded help. The Head of an Oxford or Cambridge College, if he can afford it, has often been a liberal benefactor. Paule refers to his maintaining scholars in the University at his own charge, although this was at the time he was Archbishop.

Upon his translation to Worcester his income was nominally much increased. It is well known how Elizabeth, in spite of her professed care for the Church of which she was the head, was quite unscrupulous in her veiled annexations of bishops' lands, carried out by unequal exchanges, yet she forwent her rights to the first-fruits of Whitgift's office and in other ways helped him towards financial stability at Worcester.

An Elizabethan bishop was a great but not an hereditary landowner, with accompanying responsibilities; he was also a local administrator responsible to the Privy Council and had to support a retinue of servants and officials. Bishops and more particularly archbishops were expected to maintain a considerable household and show a lavishness commensurate with their position; such a demonstration of his authority Whitgift was not unwilling to undertake immediately upon arrival at Worcester. Some bishops of Elizabeth's reign were notorious for the wealth that they accumulated and the manner in which they oppressed their tenants and clergy in order to acquire it, but Whitgift cannot be classed with such men. Many bishops were married men with families, who would quite naturally have to be provided for; relatives and retainers had to be looked after to ensure their loyalty during times when loyalty was often merely a commodity. Among those to whom Whitgift granted leases of property belonging to the See of Canterbury appear the names, not only of his brothers, but also of a number of retainers, who were able to gain a steady income by sub-letting at a profit.

Whitgift was fully conscious of the importance of his position in the state; he is reported to have said that he would be beholding to never a nobleman in the land, since he was the second person in it. He maintained a small force of fighting men, who were placed at the Queen's service against the Spaniards in 1588 and who actually helped in the suppression of Essex's rebellion in 1601. He often entertained the Queen at Lambeth or Croydon, and it is well known how some rich men were ruined by such hospitality. In his case things were different; she had a good idea of his means and his manner of spending, and he had many times warned her of the danger of stripping the Church of its wealth, a procedure which at the time had many influential advocates among the laity.

After his benefactions at Croydon had been criticised by his opponents for being the conscience-offerings of greed, he made a statement in November 1599:

The Archbishopric is no better to me than it was to my predecessors: Who died not very wealthy, for any thing I can learn: And I hope I bestow it as well as they did. But whosoever saith that this Archbishopric is yearly worth £6000 or worth in any Way, in Ordinaries or Extraordinaries, £3000, must answer to God, at the least for vain Speeches, that I term them no worse. And yet out of that which any Way I receive, there goeth in Annuities, Pensions, Subsidies, and other Duties to her Majesty, £800 at the least. And then what remaineth is soon known.

Any other ways I receive not one Penny. The Land which I had before mine Advancement, and which I have purchased since, my Brethren have. Those excepted which I have bestowed upon mine Hospital.

(Whitgift's own accounts for 1587 show his receipts totalling £2215; another record for 1600, which may not be complete, gives a total of less than £2000; to these figures would have to be added the value of fines on the renewal of leases, which would not be brought to book, but which might have amounted to several hundred pounds.) He supplies details of the lands he purchased since he became Bishop of Worcester, not including the Manor of Curles, bought in 1565.

One Farm, called Chamberlayns, in Clavering, in the County of Essex. For my Brother William Whitgift. Which cost me £470.

(Curles, a moated house, and Chamberlayns still stand, although much altered externally.)

Toward the purchasing of a piece of land in Kent, for my Brother George Whitgift. I gave to him £400.

(This land was at Tounge and was bequeathed by George to his brother William's grandson.)

One House in Shorne in Kent, with two Acres of ground, which cost me £100 and the Reversion of a Lease.

Two Tenements in Shorne, and some three Acres belonging which cost me £121. 2s. Rent £8.10s.

One Cottage and fifty Acres of Marsh Land in Kent, for my Nephew John Whitgift, which cost £432. Rent £24.

Compared with the expenditure on the buildings of his Hospital and School, and the endowment thereof, these amounts, although generous enough, are by no means extravagant.

Having devolved many of his official duties upon Bancroft, Whitgift was able to devote time to the great interest of his latter years, the foundation of his Hospital and School of the Holy Trinity in Croydon, where he spent more of his time than ever before, although his main place of residence remained Lambeth, for he was still involved with the business of government. From the records of the Privy Council, it can be seen that he was always one of the most regular in attendance, but he was less inclined than before to get involved in religious controversy, although he maintained his close watch on all aspects of Church affairs.

A Relaxation of Responsibilities

Although he never revisited Cambridge after he resigned the Mastership of Trinity, his determination to suppress dissent, coupled with his concern for academic standards and for the education of the rising generation, ensured his continuing interest in university affairs. He was not easily satisfied that his successors in office were exercising their authority with the strictness that he would himself have imposed. In 1602 his complaints to Sir Robert Cecil, Chancellor of the University as well as Secretary of State, resulted in a peremptory reminder to the Vice-chancellor and the college heads that the Statutes were to be faithfully observed. Failure to attend lectures, negligence in wearing academical dress and the decline in the use of the Latin tongue in college and elsewhere were all condemned. The rebuke: 'The negligence, dissoluteness and boyishness of many tutors is the undoing of many youths, both in learning and manners' surely quotes Whitgift's own words.

Death of Elizabeth I

Elizabeth died on 24 March 1602/3; she had called Whitgift to her bedside, where he remained comforting her and praying for her until she became unconscious. There had long been a firm bond between them; ever since she had heard him preach in 1567, she had been aware of his loyalty to her political aims; by his outspokenness he had on occasion been out of favour, but she perhaps regarded his friendship as more genuine than that of many of her courtiers, who were expected to play the game of being in love with her; her appellation for him of 'little black husband' shows her confidence in him and her deference to his rigidly

Funeral Procession of Queen Elizabeth I, 28 April 1603, supposedly drawn by William Camden
John Whitgift in the centre of the bottom row

held principles; she liked to be entertained by him, she approved of the members of his household, and she held a favourable view of unmarried bishops. On Hatton's death in 1591 she wanted Whitgift to succeed him as Lord Chancellor, but he wisely declined. After his prompt action in countering Essex's rebellion she and he relied on each other more than ever before. In April 1602 a domestic tragedy occurred at Lambeth: two young members of the Archbishop's household quarrelled while playing bowls, and one of them, a page, the son of Sir Thomas Wilford, stabbed and killed the other. Whitgift was so grieved that the Queen came across the river to comfort him at Lambeth.

Death of John Whitgift

When, within three months of his accession, James I endeavoured to squeeze money out of the universities, Whitgift, already practised in defending the Church's interest against royal cupidity, protested to him against this action which would 'overthrow learning'. After the coronation, performed by Whitgift on 25 July, there was a feeling in some quarters that religious tolerance would increase, but James soon made it clear that things would go on much as before. Although many of his archiepiscopal functions were now in Bancroft's hands, Whitgift was still spiritual head and took part in the Hampton Court Conference in January 1603/4 when, however, he was a sick man. On his return to Lambeth he was rowed over each day in the wintry weather to the other side of the river to attend at Whitehall in spite of suffering from a heavy cold; on Sunday, 26 February, after a full morning's attendance, he was about to go into dinner when he had a stroke that paralysed one side and impaired his speech. He lingered until Wednesday the 29th, dying at about eight o'clock at night, when after many vain attempts to speak, he managed to utter three times: 'Pro Ecclesia Dei'. He was 73.

Two days later he was buried in Croydon, according to the request in his will: 'in the Chapel there within the parish Church which I have appointed for my poor and Scholars to sit in at the time of divine Service'. This was the Chapel of St. Nicholas, where later his memorial was erected in a style closely copied by its designer from that of Whitgift's predecessor as Archbishop, Edmund Grindal. The church was destroyed by fire in 1867, and the monument gravely damaged, but the present restoration is a faithful copy. The funeral service was not conducted until 27 March; two of his noble pupils, the Earl of Worcester and Lord Zouche attended, and another pupil of his at Trinity, Gervase Babington, Bishop of Worcester, preached the funeral sermon.

Whitgift's Will

The provisions of his will (PCC Harte 45), which he signed on 27 October 1602, reveal a good deal of the man and his interests, and of his concern for all his successors, temporal and spiritual. The first bequest of all was made to his successor as Archbishop: '... the Organs remaining in the Chapels at Lambeth and Croydon and also the musical instrument in the Chamber at Lambeth called the Presence Chamber and the instrument of musick in the lobby or entrance into the same Chamber and all the pictures upon tables and the Maps being in my gallery at Lambeth. ...' He next ensured that all household chattels within his Hospital at Croydon should be indisputably the property of his alms-people. Then follow the various bequests to his brothers, nephew and nieces. Of his brothers, only William and George survived him, but they had already been generously provided for. To William he left one of his best horses with its harness, and all the plate he used at Lambeth when he dined in private. George, who like Richard—who had died in 1597—had acted in some capacity in the Lambeth household, was made executor, together with Bancroft; he received a quarter of the residue of the estate and the right to use the rooms set aside for the Founder's own use in the Hospital. His nephew

John Whitgift, Archbishop of Cantebury 1583–1604

John was his heir and received the house and appurtenances at Shorne and elsewhere in Kent that had been referred to in the statement of November 1599, and 'all such my implements household stuff furniture plate ready money books movables and utensils whatsoever as shall remain ... in Shorne'. Shorne seems to have been a private residence, although we have no record of his having lived there. The younger John Whitgift had married in May 1601, and the Clavering property had all been settled on him by an agreement made between the Whitgift brothers. Two of his nieces had already received marriage portions; Bridget, the youngest and as yet unmarried, was left £200 and 50 oz of gilt plate; the three shared the residue of the estate with their uncle George. Trinity College, Cambridge, received most of his 'written parchment books', and Peterhouse and Pembroke also received a gift of books. To Bancroft he left 'all my written books in paper touching matters of learning or any way concerning matters of the Church'; these manuscripts, which include a volume of records and accounts of the building of his Hospital (MS 275), together with printed books that Bancroft bought from legatees, formed part of Lambeth Palace Library, established by Bancroft in his will in 1610.

Whitgift's Character

What sort of man was John Whitgift? Several contemporary painted portraits survive, but the very crudity of their technique impairs any subtlety of character that they may have been intended to convey; that in the National Portrait Gallery seems to be painted with the greatest sympathy and insight, revealing melancholy eyes and a sensitive mouth, far different from the stern, aloof expression and rigid attitude of the portrait in the Hospital Chapel. The representations of the portraits may be amplified by Paule's description of his appearance: 'He was of middle Stature, of a grave Countenance, and brown complexion, black Hair and Eyes, he wore his Beard neither long nor thick. For his small timber, he was of a good quick strength, straight and well shaped in all his limbs, to the habit of his Body; which began somewhat to burnish towards his latter years.'

None of those who knew him well has left any account of him or of his conversation as a private man in the company of friends. Apart from the fact that his public image—the stern upholder of the Church of England's authority—was the one that most of his contemporaries were aware of, at that time candid personal memoirs of national figures were extremely rare. The only detailed description again comes from Paule, who naturally dwelt on the more conventional virtues; we may expand it to a slight extent with impressions gained from other sources.

It is not only Paule, however, who refers to his 'good resolution and courage' in his dealings, and his 'most mild and moderate hand' in the treatment of his opponents; his forbearance extended to intercession on behalf of his former adversaries when they were receiving harsh treatment at the hands of others, and he would rather persuade than coerce. Nevertheless, Paule says: 'It may be confessed . . . that the greatest, or rather the only fault known in him was Choler.' In one of the last letters that Whitgift wrote—to his old friend Gilbert Talbot, Earl of Shrewsbury, from Croydon on 12 December 1603, only a few weeks before he died—he says: 'I thank God I go on as I was wont to do, altho' at this present I am tainted with my old Disease, the Jaundice.' Jaundice may account to some extent for his testiness; many have referred to the patience with which he listened to those he was in dispute with; others, however, have recorded how this patience could become exhausted, and his schoolmasterly ire break forth. There are references to 'angry words', 'bitterness and vehemency'. In 1584 a group of dissenting Kentish clergy were called 'boys, babes, princocks, unlearned sots', and 'vainglorious fools, asses, dolts'; one of these was addressed: 'Thou boy, beardless boy, yesterday bird, new out of shell.' Some years later, when examining Henry Barrow, he burst forth with: 'Where is his keeper? You shall not prattle here. Away with him. Clap him up, close, close. I will make him tell another tale ere I have done with him.' These, in their context, however, are the words of a man who, having been prepared to listen to reason, has become exasperated by the

Tomb of John Whitgift, Croydon Parish Church, drawn by J. Corbet Anderson

Whitgift School

John Whitgift

wilful refusal on the part of others to talk reason as he saw it. But such abusive and intemperate language was a commonplace in Elizabethan times, even among men of breeding.

Paule makes much of his generosity as a host; his entertainment of Queen Elizabeth at least once a year was the highlight of his social life, but he kept a 'bountiful house' and often feasted the clergy, gentry and nobility of his diocese and neighbourhood at Lambeth and Croydon; he was generous and affable with the members of his household and he took a number of young gentlemen to teach them the liberal arts, mathematics and languages, 'insomuch as his House, for the Lectures and Scholastic Exercises therein performed, might be accounted a little Academy'; some of the young men he would then send on to university. (At this time sons of the nobility and gentry were seldom educated in schools, but more often in small groups by tutors in noble households; many others were sent abroad.) He maintained a kind of militia, training his gentlemen and servants in military discipline, so that he had a hundred foot soldiers and fifty horsemen prepared for emergency, and Paule speaks with approval of his progress in his triennial journeys through Kent to Canterbury; a display which was food for criticism from those who regarded it as personal ostentation rather than an invitation to respect due to the leader of the Church.

His closest friends included several of his old pupils from Cambridge, and of his Chaplains, a number of whom became bishops. He would dine with them at Lambeth or Croydon, and even welcome them to his Hospital when, as was his custom, he was living there in simplicity and contemplation.

Although we know of his interest in music, we must guess at other ways in which he entertained his friends; they would not be above laughing at a Fool or Jester, and even the outwardly solemn Archbishop employed one of these, if not for his own delight, for that of his guests; he was 'Ned, my Lord of Canterbury's fool'. His interests were surely more intellectual, but were not narrowly confined to theological and ecclesiastical controversy; we have seen evidence of his interest in geography and in painting. In May 1596 he was president of 'a very great society of Antiquaries' founded by Archbishop Parker some twenty-five years before; Paule refers to

Old Palace, Croydon. The Hall on the left, the Chapel on the right

the 'fair Library he left behind him', not all of which was acquired by Bancroft, by any means. Containing about 6000 volumes of manuscripts and printed books, it was one of the greatest private libraries of the time and comprised a wide range of general works. While there were many lexicons, books of theology and ecclesiastical argument, sermons and bibles in many languages, there were also numerous classical texts, including Aristotle, Virgil, Thucydides and Xenophon. His interest in history extended to Persia and China, and in foreign literature to Dante. There was a wide range of works of English authors: Thomas More's *Utopia* and other works, Chaucer, Elyot's *Governour*, Ascham's *Scholemaster*, Gerard's *Great Herball*, all of them standard works of the time. Besides a keen interest in history (apart from the works already mentioned, he had Holinshed,

Old Palace, Croydon. The Hall in the 18th century

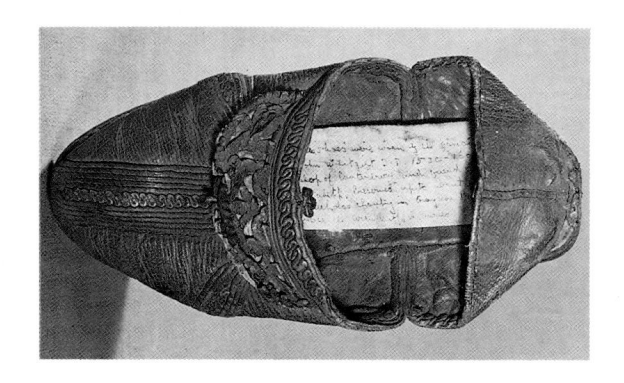

Shoe once worn by John Whitgift

North's *Plutarch* and a *History of Scotland*) he evidently had a great curiosity, as any educated Elizabethan could be expected to have, in geography, travel and discovery. He possessed many maps and atlases and the well-known books in this field, such as Hakluyt, Lindschoten, Camden's *Britannia* and Stow's *Survey of London*. On the other hand, he owned no volumes of plays and few other works of secular imagination. (Such books would be out of place in the Library of a leader of the Church, although he was responsible for licensing the printing of all books, including plays.) Neither is the first collection of Francis Bacon's *Essays* (1597) in his catalogue; one gathers that he and his former pupil had later little in common.

His childlessness he must have regretted but not bemoaned; his brother William's children took to a certain extent the place of any of his own. He had given no hostages to fortune, and Bacon's aphorism* was strangely echoed; when friends made some observation upon his courage and steadfastness, he said that there were two things that did much to make a man confident in good causes, namely, 'Orbitas et Senectus', and 'they steed me both'. (Here it seems that 'orbitas' should be rendered not in its usual sense of being bereft of wife and children, but of never having had them.)

Whitgift turns out to have had a more amiable character than many who have studied his public life have given him credit for; the conventional picture of the cold, stern, calculating and ruthless persecutor of the Puritans is one-sided; he followed a path of duty that required an unwavering persistence in the face of much exaggerated vituperation; in the main his polemical works are restrained and closely reasoned; his recorded utterances are persuasive rather than authoritative, but with occasional outbursts of vexatious anger, which are not, however the gathered spleen of a vicious and uncontrollable temper. He was given a position of authority and, judged by the standards of the age, he seems to have exercised his power with clemency and impartiality.

It is by his great acts of benevolence that he is now chiefly remembered, and those who have cause to be grateful therefor will continue to honour his name.

* "He that hath wife and children hath given hostages to fortune; for they are impediments to great enterprises, either of virtue or mischief."

Francis Bacon: 'Of Marriage and Single Life' in *Essays*, edition of 1625.

2. Foundation

Whitgift's concern for the Poor

During Elizabeth I's reign several enactments were passed to relieve the lot of the poor. Whitgift had always had compassion for their sufferings; the theme of the first sermon that he preached at St Paul's Cross in 1565 was the parable of Dives and Lazarus, which was to be the chief feature of his Hospital's seal.

Before the Reformation, concern for the 'impotent, aged and needy' had been largely the business of the Church, and the dissolution of the monasteries and chantries had resulted in the closure of a number of institutions whose purpose it had been to help the needy traveller or to succour the sick. In addition to these places there existed hundreds of hospitals and almshouses throughout the country, some founded for a particular purpose, such as the reception of lepers (lazar-houses) or for local elderly folk. The latter type of hospital, sometimes adapted from older buildings perhaps of monastic origin, and sometimes of completely new construction, was a customary object of philanthropy in Elizabethan times. In addition there were many centres for the regular distribution of 'doles', including food, one such being the Palace of Lambeth.

When in the middle 'nineties there were widespread shortages of food, and many died from starvation, Whitgift recommended to the Council steps to combat the situation, by urging moderation and forbearance on the part of those who were in an easier position (Register, 10 August 1596). He was a member of a committee of the House of Lords that was set up to consider the Commons' proposal for the Charities Bill of 1597/8, that encouraged the establishment of hospitals and almshouses, but by this time he had already made great progress in planning his own foundation in which the School was eventually to play so important a part.

Education in Elizabethan Times

Before the circumstances of the School's origin are related, it is necessary to give an outline of the educational system in England in the sixteenth century, and show how Croydon was in need of a school when Whitgift decided to establish his foundation.

The grammar schools of England existed to produce 'scholars', that is, boys or young men with enough Latin to proceed to the Universities of Oxford or Cambridge or to one of the Inns of Court in order to study to become priests, lawyers, men of learning, teachers, functionaries of the State and so on. The term 'grammar' meant the study of the Latin tongue and its literature, for learning knew no national bounds, and 'scholars' communicated through Latin, which was the medium of the dissemination of knowledge through books and lectures. All lectures at the universities were given in Latin; in the 1670s Isaac Newton delivered his lectures on optics and mathematics in Latin.

Greek, too, had become increasingly important as a subject in schools following a greater interest in biblical studies after the Reformation. The medieval churches had sporadically supported many grammar schools, held perhaps in an aisle, a chapel, a room over the porch, or sometimes in a separate building; some schools, such as Winchester, Eton and St. Paul's and a number of town schools were independent of church control. A school existed in Croydon in

Whitgift School

the fourteenth century, for on 5 April 1393, Archbishop Courtney ordained deacon one 'magister John Makheyt, magister scolarium grammaticalium de Croydon'—John Makheyt, master of the grammar scholars in Croydon. A.F. Leach, in the *Victoria County History of Surrey*, Vol., II, 1905, has suggested that this school was maintained in the Parish Church in connection with St. Nicholas Chantry, which was dissolved in 1548.

With the dissolution of the monasteries and chantries at the Reformation some grammar schools were closed; no further record of a school in Croydon has been found between 1393 and 1582, when a licence was granted by Archbishop Grindal to Ralph Betham, MA, to teach grammar in the town of Croydon. That Betham's school was a private one of small account may be a correct inference if Whitgift within twenty years founded another; in any case, Betham was not there long, being appointed to a Yorkshire living in 1588.

The loss to education by the closure of schools connected with the monasteries and chantries has in the past been exaggerated, for many of them were in fact re-founded on a much sounder basis with part of the endowments from the religious establishments. Some towns re-established schools through collective local action; the foundation of these schools and others which had been granted some of the ancient endowments was sometimes attributed to Henry VIII or Edward VI, although neither king can be given much credit for the schools that now bear his name. It was, however, by private benefactors mainly that gaps were filled and the age's expanding requirements for education were met. In Elizabeth I's time hundreds of grammar schools were founded by City livery companies, successful merchants, statesmen and churchmen, either in their place of birth or in the town where they had settled. Queen Elizabeth herself took the credit for refounding Westminster in 1561, the same year as the Merchant Taylors' Company founded their school. Felsted was founded by Lord Chancellor Riche in 1564, Rugby by Lawrence Sheriff in 1567, Uppingham by Archdeacon Johnson in 1584.

Letters Patent from Elizabeth I, 25 November 1595

Whitgift's interest in Education

Whitgift had had a long experience of educational administration. As a Fellow and later Master of a Cambridge college, he could well judge the adequacy of the grammar schools by the products they sent up to the University; one of his differences with the Queen arose over the right of Westminster School to send half-a-dozen scholars yearly to Trinity, a drain on the College's resources that aroused him to protest to the royal foundress. When Bishop of Worcester he was associated with a petition to Lord Chancellor Burghley to re-establish the grammar school at Hereford. As Archbishop of Canterbury he took a keen interest in the numerous charitable institutions—schools and hospitals—that came under his survey. He had new statutes drawn up for Eastbridge Hospital, Canterbury, and provided for a schoolmaster there to teach twenty poor children to read, write and 'cast accompt'; and he revised the statutes of the Hospitals of St. John and of St. Nicholas, Harbledown, at Canterbury. In 1592 he supported the protest made by John Harrison, High Master of St. Paul's School, to the Mercers' Company against the abuse of Colet's ordinances, and in the same year succeeded in getting Harrison's stipend increased. Mention has already been made of his concern for the quality of many of the clergy, who were frequently ignorant and ill-qualified for their office.

Benevolent intentions

Like many other successful men, Whitgift felt that his wealth, acquired in the normal course of his duties, should be put to good use, for he said: 'It is much safer for a man to do good and charitable deeds by himself, while he liveth, than to hope that others will do the same for him after his death.' He much enjoyed those occasions when he could retreat to Croydon Palace, which afforded him relaxation from the responsibilities of office, Croydon then being a pleasant little town of perhaps two thousand inhabitants, surrounded by country estates belonging to statesmen, court officials and merchants, who valued the easy access to London. In spite of his generosity to his brothers, nephew and nieces, and the pomp and circumstance that attended him, his modest personal tastes enabled him to consider in what charitable manner he could dispose of his wealth. He felt an obligation to those who were in his service and to the aged whose remaining days would be far less comfortable than his own. Although he admitted that Grimsby was 'a Corporation which Nature tendeth me to favour and to wish well unto', he seems not to have felt any great interest in his birthplace, and it was at Croydon that he decided to found a hospital, buying on 14 February 1594/5, for £200, an old inn, the Checquer, at the corner of George Street and North End, whose site he intended to build on; he chose a healthy position, almost on the outskirts of the town, a quarter of mile from the church and his palace in the low-lying centre.

(There were already two almshouses in Croydon, both on a modest scale; the older, founded by Ellis Davy in 1447 for seven old people and called 'The Great Almshouse', and another, of unknown date and foundation, called 'The Little Almshouse', but accommodating nine persons.)

Together with the Checquer were included several other small properties amounting to thirteen acres in all in various parts of the parish of Croydon, which afterwards became part of the Hospital's endowment. Just a fortnight later Whitgift bought for £30 a house adjoining to the north of the Checquer, and six weeks after that, for £80, the Swan Inn that stood yet further to the north, and four acres of land in Croydon.

The Letters Patent

Having bought a site adequate for the erection of buildings, Whitgift next applied for a licence to found his Hospital, which was granted to him by Letters Patent from the Queen on 22 November 1595. This beautiful document, the first of several valuable and richly decorated deeds, authorised him to found a hospital or almshouse in Croydon for the maintenance of certain poor Christians, to be called the Hospital of the Holy Trinity in Croydon, and to consist of a warden and poor to any number under forty. The first seven members, all from his household, were named, incorporated and enabled to hold property given to them by the Archbishop or any other benefactor for the maintenance of the Hospital to an annual value not exceeding £200. Undoubtedly he was inspired to dedicate his foundation to the Holy Trinity by the

Deed of Foundation, 22 August 1599. Signed by the Founder 'Jo. Cantuar' (John of Canterbury)

example of the college whose Master he had been at Cambridge. The limit of £200 was imposed by the Statute of Mortmain, which restricted the amount of property a charitable corporation might hold, for, existing in perpetuity, it would not be subject to the taxes levied on the estates of private citizens when they died. The restrictions of this statute and the means taken to avoid them gave rise to much trouble during subsequent centuries.

The Hospital of the Holy Trinity

There is no reference to a school, which was seemingly an afterthought, for the first mention thereof appears in an early draft of the Founder's Statutes (BL Sloane MS 27), which bears considerable alterations in the Founder's hand and which was drawn up perhaps early in 1596. No school building is referred to, but there is provision for two schoolmasters to teach in Croydon and in Lambeth. On 6 October 1596, however, the purchase for £80 of a tenement and one and a half acres of land called Staycross, adjoining the Checquer Inn in George Street, provided the site for school buildings, and it is from this year that the School's foundation is dated. Three months later, on 10 January, demolition of the Checquer began and within another four weeks work on the foundations of the Hospital of the Holy Trinity was started. Whitgift entrusted the supervision of the building works to Samuel Finche, the Vicar of Croydon, who regularly reported progress to him and to his steward at Lambeth, Christopher Wormeall. Finche kept an exact record of expenditure on material and wages, which is preserved in Lambeth Palace Library (MS 275).

Finche had also the responsibility of bargaining with the various craftsmen for their rates of pay and of agreeing with the freemason for the supply and erection of the stonework. For instance, William Hyllarie, the carpenter, was to receive 21d. the day, and his workmen 13d.; the bricklayers, John Greene and John Nortup, received only 14d. the day, and their labourers 10d. The sawyers, William Buckminster and George Carles, were paid by piece-work, receiving 2s. the hundred feet for board work and 2s.2d. the hundred feet for slitting work.

The plan and arrangement of the Hospital were to resemble those of a Cambridge college (until the 1920s, the building was frequently referred to as 'The College'), with staircases giving access to rooms on two floors. There were to be a chapel and a hall, and a suite of rooms for the Warden. Like Cambridge, the vicinity of Croydon is deficient in good building-stone, so the construc-

The Common Seal, showing the story of Dives and Lazarus

The Hospital of the Holy Trinity, 1755

tion was mainly of brick with stone dressings to the doors, windows and gables, while the plinth was faced with knapped flints. The greater part of the brickwork remains, but successive restorations, particularly one carried out in the 1840s, have much altered the chimneys, windows and doorways. The present entrance to the Chapel bears no resemblance to the original, and there is none of the old stone anywhere visible. After the Second World War the roof had to be almost completely retiled, and two gables were rebuilt. In June 1983, after several years' work of restoration and adaptation to modern standards of comfort and amenities had been completed, the Hospital was visited by Queen Elizabeth II.

The foundations were well laid, four feet deep and packed with greate flinte and small stone, and brickbatts, and rubbushe, not confusedly, but orderlye layed in, and rammed stronglye, course upon course, stronge and sure so that after nearly four hundred years and the reverberation of much heavy modern traffic the walls still stand secure.

During the excavations four skeletons were dug up which, after John Outred, the former tenant of the Checquer, had denied any knowledge of them, were thought by Finche to have been buried 'in the tyme of some mortalitye'. The weather then delayed progress so that the foundation stones at the north and south corners of the Hospital could not be laid until 22 March, the date that is commemorated as Founder's Day. From the first Finche had trouble with the men and their materials; incompetent workmen and a cheating foreman had to be dismissed; the first batch of bricks, made at Park-hill (the Archbishops' park), was found to be defective, so 'to the lome pitts beyond Dubbers-hill we came, neere Halinge-gate (where bricks had bene made in tyme past)', and it was there that was found such earth as satisfied the brickmaker.

Whitgift School

At about this time there occurred the death of Whitgift's brother, Richard, who in 1593 had purchased a field of one acre called Clot Mead, which was in the mid-nineteenth century to become the site of the 'Poor' School; at some time before or after his brother's death John Whitgift bought this piece of land for what his brother had paid for it—£14—and followed this purchase on 13 April 1597 with a much larger one—that of Christian Fields and Ryecrofts, seventy-seven acres in all, in the northern extremity of the parish, for £375, these purchases being intended for the endowment of his Hospital.

The Schoolhouse

Building went on well for the rest of the year, and on 24 September Finche reported that the structural work had been finished at a cost of £1238.12s.7d., although much remained to be done in the way of carpenter's and glazier's work. In the following January (1597/8) work was started on the Schoolhouse and the Schoolmaster's House which, though being of very similar design and construction, were yet not planned as an architectural group with the Hospital, confirming that the Founder had not contemplated the whole scope of his foundation at the outset. By this time it is apparent that he had reconsidered his early version of the Statutes, in which he had made provision for two schoolmasters; the Lambeth master is now eliminated,

The Common Hall, 1810

The Courtyard, 1839

The western front, 1840

and at the same time the importance of the Croydon master is greatly increased in the scheme of things. Another purchase in April 1598 of eighty-seven acres near Stroud Green in the eastern part of the parish was followed by slower progress in building, for the Schoolmaster's House was not finished until June 1600.

The Deed of Foundation

Meanwhile, however, Whitgift was steadily progressing with his arrangements to set up his corporation of brethren and sisters, although they are not yet called such in the legal documents prepared by his instructions; except in the more familiar language of the Statutes they are known as 'poor people' or 'the poor'. On 25 June he signed his Deed of Foundation to establish 'an hospitall and abiding-place for the finding, sustentation, and relief of certen maymed, poore, needie or impotent people . . . called by the name of the Hospitall of the Holye Trinitie in Croydon of the foundation of John Whitgift Archbishop of Canterbury'.

There is still no mention of a school or a schoolmaster, but he appointed as head a Warden, Philip Jenkins, and twelve men, the majority, if not all of them, servants in his household at Lambeth, to be the first inmates. He gave as a first endowment the lands of Christian Fields and Ryecrofts, that brought in an income of £10 a year, but having made provision for the Hospital to be legally capable of holding property up to the value of £200 a year, he had in mind a considerable extension of his generosity. On 10 July 1599 the Chapel was consecrated by Richard Bancroft, and on 22 August, in a Deed of Endowment, Whitgift made over to the Hospital all the property in Croydon that he had bought, confirming the endowment he had already made. At the end of the same month he purchased, for £1400, various farms at Woodside, Shirley and Addiscombe, amounting to a further 194 acres in all. The first inmates, some but not all of them already named in the Letters Patent and the Foundation Deed, were admitted to the now completed Hospital in October 1599. During the next two years further purchases of property, including the extensive Croham Manor estate, were made by the Founder and conveyed, together with the Woodside, Shirley and Addiscombe lands, to the Hospital in another Deed of Endowment.

Early Benefactors

Many of Whitgift's retinue and household wished to be associated with his benevolence and contributed in various ways to the Hospital's construction and equipment, their names being recorded by Samuel Finche.

Among these benefactors are William Myll, who 'was at the Charge of the Force (pump) for Leade, Soader, Brassworke & Workmanship, whiche coste hym xlviii£ xviis xid'; William Thornehill, one of his Grace's chaplains, at whose cost 'the greate Windoe in the Chapple' was constructed, was a Yorkshireman, as a stone above the window records: 'Eboracensis hanc fenestram fieri fecit 1597'; Edward Aylworth, one of his Grace's lawyers, who paid for the stained glass windows in the Hall; John Boys, Steward at Canterbury, who paid for the windows of the Schoolhouse. Others who contributed included Abraham Hartwell, Whitgift's secretary, who presented a Bible to the Chapel, the 'Treacle' Bible that remains in the Hospital's possession: Christopher Wormeall, who gave 'the Table of the X Commaundements in the Chapple'; and Dr. Thomas Neville, Dean of Canterbury and Master of Trinity College, Cambridge, who gave a silver cup which is now on loan to the Victoria and Albert Museum.

Apart from these and many other gifts towards

the furnishing and equipment of the Hospital, several benefactions were made to the endowment. Dr. William Prithergh, whose connection with Whitgift and his Hospital is unknown, in 1600 left a reversion, after the death of himself and his wife, of two houses in the Market Square at Northampton, which remained the property of the Foundation until 1920. Edward Barker and his wife gave a rent charge of twenty nobles (£6.13s.4d.) a year for 1000 years upon the site of Lancaster College in St. Paul's Churchyard, together with forty nobles to purchase land; this they did in honour of John Whitgift and in expiation of the assassination of St. Thomas à Becket, one of whose murderers, Sir William Tracy, was an ancestor of Mrs. Susan Barker. The deed making this gift is one of the most historically valuable of the Foundation's possessions, being richly decorated with coats of arms and with seals that are attached by silk threaded through a gold coin, an 'angel'.

The Founder himself made one or two further important purchases; in October 1601 he bought the Manor of Croham, consisting of 340 acres, for £740, and in July 1603 three houses in the older part of the town. This purchase was the last he made, for he died in the following February, leaving the control of his Hospital and its endowments in the hands of Samuel Finche.

While Finche was in command, the brethren and sisters were unable to exert the power over their affairs that they later enjoyed; surplus income (which later was usually divided among them) was saved and in June 1614 invested in the purchase of several properties in different parts of the town. At the same time another benefactor, Richard Stockdale, who later became one of the poor brethren, gave the Hospital a house in Butcher Row, now known as Surrey Street. Finally, in August 1618, the ancient endowment was completed at the order of Archbishop Abbot, Finche now being dead, by the purchase out of accumulated funds of a house in High Street and a meadow in Scarbrook Road.

Statutes and Ordinances

Whereas the School has figured little in this account of the establishment of the Hospital of the Holy Trinity, the Founder's Statutes and Ordinances give a clear indication of its status and of that of the Schoolmaster. The Statutes were drawn up in their final form probably in 1602, but the Schoolmaster was not paid his quarterly stipend at the full stipulated rate of £5.0s.0d. until shortly after Whitgift's death, and had been receiving the amount provided for in the early draft already referred to. Whitgift's experience of the difficulties in administering the Hospitals at Canterbury had convinced him of the necessity of ordering very carefully the management of his own foundation, and his Statutes were based on those of the Canterbury Hospitals which had been drawn up by Archbishop Parker in 1560 and 1569, and modified in 1584 and 1591 by Whitgift himself.

Several early manuscript copies of the Statutes in their final form exist in various places, there being two at Lambeth Palace, two in the British Library (in addition to Sloane 27), one in possession of the Foundation, one in the School Library (the Schoolmaster's own copy), and one in the Library of Caius College, Cambridge. The most authoritative is one of those at Lambeth, found among some miscellaneous papers there about 1840, and since kept with the accounts of the building of the Hospital in MS 275; the second

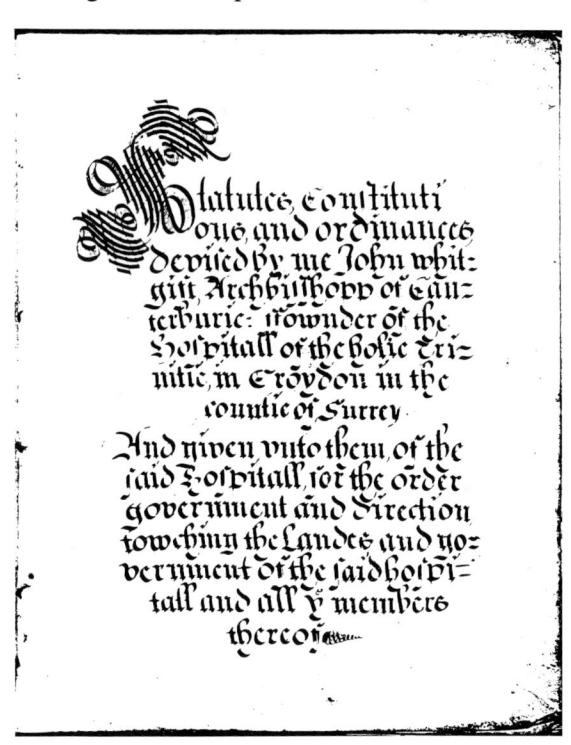

Titlepage of Statutes

copy at Lambeth and the others are clearly derived from it. This definitive version of the Statutes consists of twenty-one chapters and amounts in all to nearly seven thousand words, so only those clauses relating to the School and the Schoolmaster will be quoted here in detail.

Chapter One deals with the number of those that are to be maintained in or by the Hospital:

First I doe ordeyne that the number of the Brethren and Sisters of the said Hospitall shalbee ever thirtie at the least, and soe many moe (under Fortie in all) as the Revennues . . . may beare. . . . Of the which number of Brethren, one shall teache a Grammar Schoole in Croydon in the Schoolehouse there by me buylded and perform such other duties as is appoynted unto him in theis Ordinaunces and Statutes.

Chapter Two ordains that women shall not outnumber men in the Hospital, and Chapter Three that inmates shall not have members of their family living with them unless they have already been themselves admitted as inmates. Chapter Four deals with the appointment of members, the Warden and the Schoolmaster:

I doe ordeyne that within one moneth (yf conveniently it may be) after yt shalbee notified . . . that the place of the Schoolemaster, or of any other of the poore Brethren or Systers . . . is anywaie become voide the Archbysshoppe of Canterbury for the tyme being . . . shall nomynate & place someone qualyfied according to theis ordinaunces under . . . his hand and seale. . . .

Item I ordeyne and appoynt that the poore Brother appoynted to be the Schoolemaster shalbee a person well qualyfied for that function (that is to saie) an honest man, learned in the Greeke and Latine tongues, a good versifier in bothe the foresaid languages, and able to wryte well (yf possible it maybe): Which poore Brother appoynted to that office, & quallified and placed as afore, shall have for his lodging and dwelling place, during the tyme that he contynueth Schoolemaster that house which I have buylded for that purpose, adioyning to the said Hospitall and neere unto the Schoolehouse, together with such backsides and groundes, as I have appoynted to be annexed to the said house, and which the present Schoolemaster now enioyeth. And shall have the some of Twenty Poundes yerelie for his Stipend, to be payed quarterlie together with other furder commodities of corne and wood as hereafter shall happen to be allotted unto other of the poore Brethren . . . I doe likewise ordeyne & appoynt that the house which I have buylded for the said Schoolehouse, and also the house which I have buylded for the Schoolemaster, shalbee forever ymployed to that use onlie and to none other.

Chapter Five lays down the qualifications of those to be chosen into the Hospital, there being three degrees: in the first place, those who are akin to the Founder or who have served in his household, or who, after his death, will have served the Archbishop of Canterbury; in the second, such honest men and women of the Parishes of Croydon and Lambeth who, being over the age of sixty, are of the poorest sort and unable to get their living; and in the third, such men and women as above, but coming from certain parishes in the See of Canterbury. The Schoolmaster is specifically exempt from any of these conditions. Chapter Six gives the terms of the oath to be sworn by all admitted members of the Hospital.

Chapter Seven defines the Schoolmaster's duties:

The Schoolemaster shall freelie teache such of the Children* of the Parryshe of Croydon (without exacting any thing for theire teachinge) as are of the poorer sorte, such as shalbee accounted by the Vicar or Curate of Croydon and two of the better sorte of the inhabitants in Croydon: But yet it shalbee lawfull to and for the said Schoolemaster to receive that which is voluntarily bestowed uppon him by any of the said poorer sorte of paryshioners. And for the children of such as bee of the better sorte of the paryshe of Croydon, yf the said Schoolemaster shall exacte too much for theire teaching or refuse to teache them, the same shalbee ordered and moderated by the Archbisshopp of Canterbury for the tyme being.

Bothe the sayd Schoolemaster and Schollars shall from tyme to tyme be ordered, governed, and directed by such prescriptions and Ordinaunces in all poynts, as by mee the Founder of the said Hospitall shalbee in my life tyme devysed, And after by my successors Archbishopps of Canterbury. Soe that allwaies the said ordinaunces of my Successors be not contrary to my ordinaunces.

---

*The Founder's use of the term 'children' does not imply that the School was open to girls. John Lyon's regulations regarding his foundation at Harrow (1591) contains the provision "that no girls be received, to be taught in the school", but this limitation was generally regarded as superfluous, for no one considered it either desirable or seemly that girls should receive the same sort of education as their brothers. Evidence can be produced that on rare occasions the daughters of a schoolmaster may have attended their father's school, but learned women of the time—the daughters of Sir Thomas More, for example—had been taught by private tutors.

Amended draft of Statutes, Chapter VII: the Duties of the Schoolmaster

Chapter Eight lays down the stipends for the Brethren and Sisters. The Warden is to receive £6.13s.4d. and the rest £5 yearly, to be paid in quarterly instalments from the rents received from the lands with which the Hospital was endowed. Chapter Nine provides for three Ledger Books to be maintained by the Schoolmaster and kept locked in a Chest. In these books are to be recorded such items as the admittance and departure of every member, copies of leases, inventories of property, records of benefactions, and the quarterly accounts of payments and disbursements. In point of fact, it seems that only two books were kept to begin with, and of these the one containing the particulars of leases was lost a hundred years later.

Chapter Ten imposes strict attention to religious observance:

The Schoolemaister besides teaching of his Scholle and making of entries into the Lydger bookes and doeing other duties appoynted unto him . . . shall saye publique praiers Mornynge and Evenyng in the Chappell of the Hospitall to the Brethren and Sisters on all daies (beeing working daies) except Wednesdaies and Fridaies in the forenoone, and Satterdaies in the afternoone.

Chapter Eleven authorises the Warden to appoint a Porter from among the Brethren, whose duty it will be to open and close the Hospital gates in the morning and at night respectively. Chapter Twelve allows the Brethren and Sisters to work at such trades as they may still be capable of to get some part of their living, but forbids them to beg; there is provision, however, for an almsbox for voluntary offerings. Chapter Thirteen warns against crimes that must be avoided, such as 'Incontynencie, Forgerie, Periurie, Obstinacie in Heresye, Sorcerye or any kind of Charmyng or Witchcrafte', all punishable by expulsion; any Brother or Sister found guilty of being a Blasphemer, a Swearer, a Gamester, a Drunkard, or a Haunter of Taverns or Alehouses, a Brawler, Fighter, Contentious Person, Scold or Sower of Discord is subject to a system of admonitions, fines and, in the event of repetition, expulsion.

Chapter Fourteen provides for the care of the sick or impotent, and Chapter Fifteen ordains the careful preservation in a special room in the Gatehouse of the Evidences (Deeds), the Common Seal, and a stock of ready money. Chapter Sixteen lays down the method of granting leases and of disposing of the money derived from fines and the sale of timber, and Chapter Seventeen gives instructions for the receipt and distribution of the Hospital revenues among the members. It is the Schoolmaster's responsibility to present his account every year on 4 December for the satisfaction of the others.

Chapter Eighteen allows for repairs to the fabric of the Hospital and the Schoolhouse to be paid for out of the Hospital funds, but

> The house allotted for the Schoolemaster to dwell in, shalbee repayred at the Costes and charges of the Schoolemaster uppon such penaltyes as the Archbysshopp of Canterbury for the tyme being shall thinke convenyent.

Chapter Nineteen provides for any negligence on the part of the Schoolmaster or of the Warden to be punished at the discretion of the Archbishop.

In Chapter Twenty Whitgift reserves to himself the use of the Audience Chamber over the Common Hall and of the two rooms over the Inner Gatehouse. It was his pleasure to go and live with the members of his Hospital and to share their life. After his death these apartments were to be reserved for the use of his brother George, and then of the Warden. Paule says:

> ... the Archbishop had ever a great affection to lie at his Mansion house at Croydon, for the sweetness of the place, especially in Summer time ... yet, after he had built his Hospital, and his School, he was further in love with the Place than before. The chief comfort of repose or solace that he took, was in often dining at the Hospital among his poor Brethren, as he called them: There he was often visited by his entire and honourable friends, the Earls of Shrewsbury, Worcester, and Cumberland, the Lord Zouch, the Bishop of London, and others of near place about her Majesty, in whose company he chiefly delighted.

Chapter Twenty-one orders the administration of the Hospital after the Founder's death. The Archbishop of Canterbury is given full authority as Visitor, Patron and Governor of the Hospital to interpret and enforce, but not alter, the Statutes, and the Vicar of Croydon is appointed overseer with the power of directing the Warden and Brethren in their conduct and in the observance of the Statutes. The chapter concludes with the wish that Samuel Finche should continue to take the same great care and pains in supervising the Hospital's affairs that he has already taken about its building, and he is rewarded with a payment of £6.13s.4d. a year until his death. Finche had been keeping the Ledger Books, although the Schoolmaster was nominally responsible, but he now handed over these duties, continuing to act as Overseer and signing the accounts 'Samuell Fynche, Governour'. Without knowing precisely when the Statutes were finally approved, one may think it possible that the Schoolmaster and the Warden (who now also for the first time was paid at the full rate) were not deemed to earn their full stipends until Finche handed over to the others the responsibilities that he had until then undertaken.

(Although most ancient schools were managed by a governing body consisting of a number of feoffees or trustees appointed according to terms laid down by the founder, the only immediate supervisor of the Hospital's—and consequently of the School's—affairs was the Vicar of Croydon, whose responsibilities extended little beyond the selection of pupils to be educated free and support for the Schoolmaster in his disciplinary control of the old people. Successive Archbishops of Canterbury, who did not always consult the Vicars, were sometimes unable or unwilling to ensure that the Statutes were being observed. One consequence of this slack administration is the absence of records of the management and administration of the School before its reconstruction in 1871.)

School Ordinances

In Chapter Seven of the Statutes reference is made to ordinances for the governance of the Schoolmaster and Scholars, which ordinances had not apparently been drawn up at the time of Whitgift's death; certainly, if any were framed they have not survived, but they would have followed a standard pattern which included qualifications for admission such as literacy in English and knowledge of the Latin accidence; the daily hours of attendance, the length of terms and of holidays, the curriculum, perhaps in some detail of authors to be studied; discipline; extra payments ('free' normally applying only to teaching) for pens, ink, paper, books, candles, cleaning, heating and repairs.

A comparison with the regulations and provisions of other foundations shows a resemblance in many important points that would have been repeated in others. The dimensions of the Schoolhouse, 50 feet by 21, were just a little smaller than, for example, Oundle, but a little larger than Tonbridge and Uppingham. The Schoolmaster's stipend—£20—was an almost standard figure in the upper bracket, the same as at Aldenham, Blundell's (Tiverton) and Banbury, schools founded in the same decade. The Schoolmaster's qualifications, too, were phrased much after a pattern, exemplified in 'a good understanding in the Greek and Latin tongues', 'well skilled in Latin and Greek', and 'well instructed and skilled in Latin and Greek literature', to quote other statutes, so it is clear that Whitgift intended his Grammar School to be on a par with the best foundations of the age. It is impossible to apportion the value of the endowments between the Hospital and the School, beyond observing that after all stipends were paid, the income, if well managed, would be ample for the good upkeep of the building. Many grammar schools of contemporary date were but poorly endowed, and managed by local feoffees who also appointed the Schoolmaster. Chapter Seven is more liberally drawn in respect of the charging of fees than are most statutes; in some schools free teaching was limited to a certain number of pupils, perhaps ten or twenty, or all teaching restricted to boys from a certain parish or parishes; the schoolmaster was sometimes not allowed to take any private or fee-paying pupils at all, it being assumed by the founders that conditions would remain static for ever, and a salary of £20 sufficient for all time. Whitgift's Statutes, although including a provision for 'poor' boys, encouraged the Schoolmaster to accept pupils from well-off families within or outside the parish of Croydon, and indeed it is clear that the Schoolmaster was expected to augment his stipend by taking in paying pupils. After all, the Schoolhouse could easily hold at least eighty boys, and that number wishing to receive a classical education could not then be found from the population of Croydon alone. Moreover, the fact that the Schoolmaster was made responsible for the maintenance and repair of his house indicates the Founder's expectation that such a responsi-

The Schoolhouse and Schoolmaster's House as in 1600

Courtyard of the Schoolmaster's House in 1897

the Board of Education in 1939, which may be regarded as authoritative in this matter:

> The scholars, usually described in the school statutes as 'children' or 'youth' for whom the Grammar Schools were intended, were of no one class in particular. The school was to be for such as required an education in grammar, and among them would be boys of all classes, but many more of those above the labouring class than of those in that class. The 'poor' are frequently named in the school statutes, but rather in a way indicating a desire to keep the school available for them, than in expectation that they would in fact form the majority of the scholars.

Even this statement requires some modification. To assume that in 1600 any children at all of 'the labouring class' in any particular locality would 'require an education in grammar' may be wide of the mark. Their aspirations would be those of their parents, who might be illiterate; there was little reason for their being taught to read, let alone write, and the study of Latin would be unavailing. There were a good many people who could read; they taught their own children—and others—at home, who would then read whatever they could

bility would not be unreasonable. The house and School are referred to by John Stow in his *Survey of London* under the date 1600:

> This yeare the most Reverend father, John Whitgift, Archbishop of Canterbury, did finish that notable and memorable monument of our time, to wit, his Hospital of the Holy Trinitie in Croydon, in the county of Surrey, by him there founded and builded of stone and brick for the reliefe and sustentation of certain poor people; As also a fair Schoolhouse for the increase of literature, together with a large dwelling house for the Schoolmaster his use.

This description indicates respect for the importance of the new foundation.

An explanation of the provision for free teaching of the 'poorer sorte' has been given in the *Report of the Consultative Committee on Secondary Education* (The 'Spens' Report), published by H.M. Stationery Office on behalf of

Coat of Arms above the Fireplace in the Audience Chamber, 1600

get hold of; the Bible, chap-books and stories that would be passed round. Writing was a different matter; it was a manual skill, often despised by the educated classes, whose writing was frequently illegible. The ability to write presupposed some purpose in learning. Other children might have attended a 'petty' school—if there was one—and would achieve their ambitions by becoming apprenticed to a trade. To aspire any higher through the study of Latin would be exceptional. Sometimes a boy employed in an educated household or one picked out from his congregation by a zealous vicar might reveal potential talent that was deemed worthy of development by attendance at a grammar school, perhaps with the idea that he might be employed in some administrative capacity, or even be sent to university to train for the church. Other openings were rare. Whitgift's reference to 'the poorer sorte' must be understood against the background of society at the time. And throughout history there has been a reluctance among many parents of the poorest classes to give up their children to be educated 'beyond their station' so that they became lost to their families.

It was not very usual for a hospital for the aged and a school to be founded together, although a famous earlier example exists at Ewelme, Oxfordshire, and we have seen how Whitgift's conception of a separate school developed from his first idea of a single building in which no special accommodation was provided for scholars. To begin with, he thought that the Vicar or Curate of Croydon might combine his pastoral duties with those of Schoolmaster, in which case the spacious parish church might have provided accommodation, although the Audience Chamber at the Hospital would have made a useful, if small schoolroom. A few other examples of hospital and school combined exist, such as Sutton's Charterhouse, and Alleyn's Dulwich College, founded in 1611 and 1619 respectively, both on a more impressive scale. Perhaps their founders gained an idea from Whitgift's precedent.

3. The Seventeenth-Century Grammar School, 1600–1712

The Importance of Croydon in 1600

Croydon enjoyed many advantages for the successful establishment there of a grammar school: (i) It benefited from a healthy, well-drained position, with a pure water supply, on the line of springs at the foot of the North Downs. (ii) A market-town that attracted traders and customers from miles around, it was prosperous and well known to many people coming from some distance. (iii) It was a social focal point in an area where numerous members of the nobility, of the Court and of Parliament had chosen to set up a country home within easy reach of the capital; they were joined by lawyers, merchants and wealthy tradesmen, who settled their families in the towns and villages along the spring-line. In Croydon itself the Archbishop's Palace, Lord Nottingham's house at Haling, and Addiscombe Place, the property of Sir John Tonstall, gentleman-Usher to Queen Anne, James I's consort, were the most important; there were also several gentlemen's houses. Other residential villages and small towns within an eight-mile radius included Epsom, Sutton, Carshalton, Mitcham, Beddington, Addington, Beckenham, Bromley, Farnborough and Chislehurst, all of which were associated with important statesmen and courtiers of the time: for instance, Lord Hunsdon, of the Privy Council, and the Carew family, at Beddington; Sir Julius Caesar, Chancellor of the Exchequer, at Mitcham; the Leighs of Addington; Sir John Heydon, Lieutenant-general of the Royal Ordnance, of Addington, the Lennards, of West Wickham, to mention only a few. (iv) Communications were for the time good; roads led from Westminster and the City of London to Croydon, to Bromley (where the Bishop of Rochester had his palace), to Mitcham and to the royal palace of Nonsuch at Ewell. Another road linking the villages of the spring-line was used by Queen Elizabeth I to reach Nonsuch after being entertained by Whitgift at Croydon or Sir Julius Caesar at Mitcham. (v) There were no other grammar schools within ten miles. Just outside this radius were Kingston-upon-Thames Grammar School (founded in 1561) on the west, and St. Saviour's (1599) and St. Olave's (1561) in Southwark. On the other side of the Thames were the great schools of London, but Londoners themselves frequently sent their children to be educated in a healthier locality, where perhaps they lived in a second home, rather than expose them to the infections of the city. And it was not unusual for parents to make use of a good local school rather than a London one. At this time the only other Surrey school apart from those mentioned was at Guildford (1509), twenty-five miles away, and the nearest in Kent was at Sevenoaks (1418) about sixteen miles. It is difficult to say what limit of travel could be set for a day-boy, who might come on foot or on horse-back (perhaps riding behind a groom until he was old enough to ride his own horse or pony), but a daily journey of up to six miles each way may be surmised. Boarders would likewise attend the most accessible school if it was a reputable one. (vi) The interest of the chief local resident—the Archbishop and 'Visitor'—ensured the appointment of a well-qualified and efficient Schoolmaster and the proper supervision of the School.

Schools in similarly favoured places, such as Hampton, Middlesex, and Barnet, Herts, also enjoyed a marked prosperity at this time.

Croydon and its surroundings in the early 17th century

Ambrose Brygges

It was not until June 1600 that the Schoolmaster's House was finished, the court paved, and the gates hung, but the first Schoolmaster had already been appointed on 31 March. he was 'Ambrose Brygges, Mr. of Artes and qualified according to his Gr. Constitutions in that case provided, maried and of the age of xlviii yeres', and was the eighth poor brother to be admitted. Chosen by the Founder himself, he should have been a man of experience and proven ability, but as no mention of him occurs in the published records of the Universities of Oxford or Cambridge, he is difficult to identify. Brygges was paid at the rate of £13.6s.8d. per annum, the salary ordained by the Founder in his first draft of statutes. Whether Brygges was unsatisfactory or whether he was not content with his salary is not known, but he lasted less than fifteen months, and the only other reference to him in the Ledger Book, apart from the record of payments of salary, is that recording his departure: 'Ambrose Brygs, Scholemaister, Departed the xxiiiith day of June 1601'. At this time he may have had no scholars to teach, although it seems unlikely that a brand-new school, established by the chief ecclesiastic of the time and the principal inhabitant of the town, should not have attracted immediately a number of the youth of Croydon, but his may have been merely a 'caretaking' capacity, until a more suitable man, whom Whitgift already had in view, could be appointed. This conjecture is supported by the fact that Brygges was collated Rector of Sutton (in the gift of Sir Francis Carew) on 29 December 1600.

John Ireland

The second schoolmaster, John Ireland, was appointed before the departure of his predecessor, for he is recorded in the Ledger Book as: 'Mr of Arts & Student of Christ-Churche in the Universitie of Oxforde, sole, And of the age of xxvi years, entred Scholemaister the xxiiith [*sic*] day of June 1601', the same day that Brygges departed. He had been educated at Westminster, where he was a Queen's Scholar, and was elected a Student of Christ Church in 1591.

For his first quarter's stipend, Ireland was paid £3.6s.8d., the same rate as Brygges, but after the Founder's death he was paid £5 a quarter, the rate laid down in the Statutes.

Soon the School was in full operation, but no record of its scholars has been preserved. The Hospital Statutes provide for the names of all poor brethren and sisters to be recorded, and these lists were usually faithfully kept as a check against the correct payment of stipends, but no roll of boys was required; even the hypothetical School Ordinances might not have demanded such a record. It was a practice at some grammar schools to maintain lists of boys 'on the Foundation', although they have in only a few cases been preserved. The fee-payers were the concern of the Schoolmaster alone, for he augmented his income from the fees he charged, and out of these fees he had to pay his ushers. No particular number of scholars was envisaged by the Founder, and no Foundation income was devoted to their support, so no records were kept.

With so little firm knowledge of the identity of the boys who attended the School in its early days, we can yet infer that those we do know of were not untypical. The Statutes set no limitations on the locality or class that the pupils came from, and the Schoolmaster's House had ample room for boarders. It is clear that a number of boys were the sons of the nobility and gentry, not always locally resident; the assumption is justified that others came from similar families in the vicinity, especially if they were recorded among the increasing number of admissions to Oxford and Cambridge Colleges, which had been recently enlarged in number and size by benefactions.

University pupils came from schools all over the country during the first half of the 17th century, showing the good use that was made of these Elizabethan educational foundations. Croydon and its environs follow this trend very markedly, and it is reasonable to suppose that here, as elsewhere, most local boys, if they attended a grammar school at all, would attend their local one, especially as it possessed great advantages. There is, for example, no formal evidence that William Shakespeare attended Stratford-upon-Avon Grammar School, but the assumption that he did has come to be almost universally accepted as a certainty.

The Working of a Grammar School

In the absence of School Ordinances, we have no direct information about the manner in which the School was conducted, but it can be safely assumed that it followed the general pattern of the time. If Whitgift had been thinking primarily of providing an education for potential clergy, by the end of the century the need was being well met, but an education in Latin was useful for every kind of professional man, be he scholar, lawyer, physician or statesman, and indeed for a merchant, too. Although, ideally, a boy's career at grammar school would lead to the university, only a small proportion of pupils found their way there, depending on their intelligence and diligence, the competence of the schoolmaster, the ambition, resources or social status of the parents, the availability of scholarships, and so on. (The Founder's disapproval of the Westminster scholarships at Trinity may account for the fact that he rather surprisingly made no provision for scholarships to his old college or to the university, although many schools were generously endowed in this respect.) There were soon to be thousands of educated men in the country who, although they did not 'use' their training, nevertheless contributed largely to the culture of their age; recent research indicates that the proportion of the male population in the first half of the seventeenth century that received a higher education up to university standard was not equalled for nearly three hundred years. At this time a thousand undergraduates were admitted yearly to the two universities, three times as many as a hundred years before. Not all of these graduated, for the universities, like the Inns of Court, now provided social opportunities as attractive as the educational ones, so that to many young men a degree was superfluous.

Francis Bacon, who opposed the foundation of Charterhouse and of Dulwich College '. . . (subscribed) to the opinion that, for grammar schools, there are already too many, and therefore no providence to add where there is excess . . .; there being more scholars bred than the state can prefer or employ, . . . it must needs fall out, that many persons will be bred unfit for their vocation.' But a grammar school education was now regarded as an extremely desirable attainment by all who could afford it. No longer did the clergy retain a monopoly of learning; the culture of the ruling classes had advanced from a merely crude stage of self-indulgence to an appreciation of the humanist arts, classical literature, music, architecture, poetry, drama and other writings in the native tongue, and the concept of what a gentleman should be was emulated by the rising middle classes.

Normally, before a boy was admitted to grammar school at the age of at least seven or eight he was expected to know the Lord's Prayer, the Creed and the Ten Commandments (for religious observance was a regular feature of the school day), and be able to read and write in his mother tongue. In addition he was required to know some of the accidence of Latin nouns and verbs; this learning he would gain in the 'petty' school. Many boys, however, especially boarders, might not join the School until they were ten or eleven, having been educated at home under a tutor. The usher, living perhaps with the Schoolmaster's family and paid at the rate of £10 a year out of the fees collected from the 'better sort', would drill the boys in their grammar, which they learnt from the approved textbook of the time, Lily's *Grammar*. They would practise construing and making 'Latins' or 'Vulgars' and would read the simple metrical moral precepts that went under the name of 'Cato', or a Latin version of Aesop's Fables. Not merely for light relief, but in order to acquire a useful conversational Latin, for the boys were forbidden to speak their native tongue in school, they might read a few pages from the comic playwright Terence. The younger boys would continue to receive tuition in penmanship—not from the learned Schoolmaster, who scorned to perform such manual instruction—but from a local or itinerant writing-master, such as Nicholas Rowed, who was established in that capacity in Croydon in the early 1600s; for this 'extra', performed after normal school hours, a special fee would be paid. Alternatively, the usher might undertake this instruction.

The Schoolmaster himself would take the higher forms, instructing them in the art of composition based on the examples provided by the classical authors they had studied, such as Cicero and, later, Virgil and Horace. The brighter boys, destined for Oxford or Cambridge, might start Greek at fourteen, using Camden's *Grammar*, published in 1597, and studying the New Testament; they would also compose Latin verses. A generation earlier, some boys were ready to go to university at this age, but during the seventeenth century the age of admission was rising. Many of the less ambitious would be ready to leave at thirteen or fourteen, some, especially if they were younger sons, being put into apprenticeship.

Library Books

An inventory in the Ledger Book 'of such things that belonge at this present to the Schole and Hospitall, 1602', begins: 'Imprimis there belonge to the Schole as yet 4 books, viz. A Coper's Dictionarie and Barret's Dictionarie and two Lexicons bothe of Scapula'. This first brief library list is identifiable as follows:

Coper: Sir Thomas Elyot's Latin Dictionary, 1538, improved and revised by Thomas Cooper, Master of Magdalen School, Oxford, in 1552 and later, was a standard reference dictionary of the time. It seems to have been presented by Richard Massinger, a member of Whitgift's household and a beneficiary in his will, for inside the cover of the copy of the Statutes in

William Camden (1551–1623), scholar, historian, antiquary

Lambeth Palace Library (MS 275) is stuck a printed slip:

> Quam Non-dividuae Triadis fundavit honori
> Whytgifti pietas Praesulis alma Scholam,
> Huic Massingerus (tanti devotus Alumnus
> Patris) Cooperi dedicat istud opus.
> 1599.

(The School that the benevolent piety of the Primate Whitgift founded in honour of the undivided Trinity; to this Massinger (the devoted pupil of such a father) dedicates this work of Cooper 1599.)

The printed slip could be a duplicate of that inserted in the book presented to the School, of which no further record exists.

Barret: An Alvearie or Triple Dictionarie in English, Latin and French, 1573, by John Baret, Fellow of Trinity College, Cambridge.

Scapula: Lexicon, Graeco–Latinum, Basle 1579, and various reprints; the standard school dictionary.

The possession of these books indicates that high standards were expected in both the classical languages, for there were few schools that owned such expensive and comprehensive works of reference.*

The Seventeenth-Century Grammar School, 1600–1712

School Life

In 1604 Samuel Finche, although he continued to witness admonitions and other entries in the Ledger Book in his capacity of overseer or 'Gouvernoure', as he describes himself, relinquished the maintenance of the records, which was now undertaken by Ireland, and the following extract from the 'Yearely Disbursements of money for the uses of the Hospitall of the Holy Trinitye, beginninge from the Feaste of St. Michaell Ano Dmi 1604', shows something of the life of the Hospital and the School:

Given to Mr Aylworthe for a Fee of his Counsayle about the lettinge of Christen Feilde & Ricrofte Woodes	10s.
For the hiring of two horses the same time for my selfe & Francis Beste one eveninge the same buysines	2s.
For going by water to & froe to the Temple & back to Lambeth	9d.
Given to Mr Thomas Woode for drawinge a copy of the same lease	3s. 6d.
For mendinge the Glasse of the Schoole	2s. 6d.
For mendinge a windowe at the upper end of the schole	2d.
For mendinge the claspes of the Schoole bookes	2d.
Pd to Father Feilde [*a poor brother*] for mendinge the Rope of the Sanctus Bell	6d.
Pd to Goodman Blease for mendinge the iron Staple of the Schoole doore locke & fasteninge the stones of the streete doore cheekes	10d.
To the Tincker for mendinge a kettle	2s. 4d.
Pd to the Glasier for mendinge the Schoole windowes agayne	9d.

(The total expenditure of this nature for the year came to £4.0s.1d.)

There was plenty of wear and tear of the School premises, and vulnerability of the windows to damage created a constantly recurring charge on

---

* In 1585 Sir John Deane's School, Northwich, bought copies of Baret's and of Cooper's for 8s.10d., a very considerable outlay. In 1645 Thomas Fuller, describing "The Good Schoolmaster", says: 'Some men had as well be schoolboys as schoolmasters, to be tied to the school, as Cooper's Dictionary and Scapula's Lexicon are chained to the desk therein.'

49

the Hospital income. Whereas poor brothers and sisters were responsible for the repair of damage to their rooms, responsibility for broken School windows was evidently more difficult to apportion, and glass was an expensive material.

Ireland's tenure of office was not a long one. The Ledger Book shows that 'Mr Irelande Schoolemayster relinquished his place the iiiith day of julye, Ano Dmi 1606'. He may have resigned because of ill-health, for he was buried at St. Margaret's Westminster, on 27 September 1607. In his will he left £3 to be divided equally among the poor of the Hospital.

Until this time at least, the influence of Westminster School appears to have been strong. Under the particular patronage of the Queen, Westminster was the most celebrated and fashionable, but not the largest, school in London; even Eton and Winchester were regarded as provincial. Between 1575 and 1593 William Camden was Under-Master at Westminster, becoming Master in the latter year. Camden was a distinguished antiquarian whose interests were shared by the Founder. He was also the author of the *Greek Grammar* which was an obvious textbook to be adopted at Whitgift.

Camden's own knowledge of the School is revealed in his *Britannia* (translated into English from the Latin in 1610):

And neere unto Croidon, the right reverend father in God, Doctor John Whitgift, Archbishop of Canterburie, of most praiseworthy Memorie in his pious Affection founded, and endowed with living a very faire Hospitall for the releefe of poore people, and a schoole for the furtherance of learning.

Whitgift's nephew, another John, was a pupil at Westminster, leaving in 1590 with a scholarship to Trinity, Cambridge. His contemporaries included Richard and John Ireland, who both proceeded to Christ Church. Richard succeeded Camden as Master of Westminster in 1599. John came to Whitgift two years later.

John Ireland's resignation was followed by the immediate appointment by Archbishop Bancroft of Robert Davies, another Christ Church man, who had been serving as an usher at Westminster for four years. It is more than likely that the Westminster Statutes, following chiefly the general pattern, were adopted by the Founder and by his designated 'Governor', Samuel Finche, as a model for the running of the School.

Robert Davies

To begin with, Robert Davies conducted the School in a satisfactory manner. The names of two of his pupils—the first in the School's history that can be established—are recorded in the Admissions Register of Caius College, Cambridge. They are Thomas Jenney, son of Ambrose Jenney, gentleman, of Eltham, Kent, and Henry Dalendar, son of Sir William Dalendar, of Buckland, Surrey. They must have been boarders with Davies.

At this time the School of the Hospital of the Holy Trinity was known as Croydon School or the Free-School at Croydon. The names of the founders of mediaeval and Elizabethan schools are rarely, if ever, incorporated in the titles and, where they do appear, the schools have usually been reconstructed in the nineteenth century. References to 'Croydon School' in the seventeenth and eighteenth centuries allude to Whitgift's foundation.

Acknowledgment must be made to the usefulness of the records of certain Cambridge colleges in furnishing the names of former members of the School. Several colleges, notably Caius, St. John's and Sidney Sussex, have preserved since the late sixteenth century in their Registers of Admissions not only the place of birth and parentage of some of their members, but also the schools they attended. Thus a number of pupils have been traced, and it is interesting to see that a high proportion of them were not local boys. Unfortunately, not all colleges, and most regrettably none of the Oxford colleges, kept a record of this kind; indeed, those that did were not always consistent in this respect. The number of boys from Croydon and its environs going to Oxford was greater than the number going to Cambridge, and of the latter only a small proportion are definitely identifiable through the college registers as coming from the School. The Cambridge evidence that there was a strong boarding element supports the belief that the School was held in high regard by many families beyond the immediate area of Croydon.

As the names of so few Old Boys during the seventeenth and eighteenth centuries have come down to us, it seems all the more important to make a brief reference to the more interesting of them, as they appear, and thereby give an indication of the type of boy who attended the School and of its success in its task of educating him. Further notes on these and other alumni will be found in Appendix II.

The care with which the Schoolmaster was selected, and the promptitude with which he was dismissed when necessary encouraged confidence in the education given there. In 1616 Davies got into trouble with the Archbishop, who held an enquiry into the conduct of members of the Hospital.

By the most reverend father in God George Abbot Archbishop of Canterbury was holden a visitation in the chapell of the Hospital of the holye Trinitye by his Commissioners Dr Ridleye & Dr Haywarde, & prorogued untill the 25 of June following to Bow Church in London, & then to the 28 of the same moneth at wch time Robert Davies Schoolemaister & Nicholas Feild poore brother were expelled.

It has been hinted (in the 1892 History of the School) that Davies was expelled for embezzling funds from the poor-box, but examination of the Hospital accounts reveals no grounds for this suspicion, and A.F. Leach has suggested that the expulsions were due to some religious or internal dissension. Feild had already received a number of admonitions from Davies, and it seems that they were not confederates in any misdemeanour. Indeed, in view of Feild's history of unsocial conduct, his expulsion resulted probably from the culmination of a series of misdeeds that the Archbishop would at length not tolerate. Light upon Davies's expulsion is shed by Anthony à Wood, who in his *Athenae Oxonienses* says that Davies's successor, William Nicolson, 'was made master of the Free-School at Croydon, in Surrey, in the place of one Robert Davis, Bachelor of Arts of Oxon, then displaced for his frequent hunting with Dogs, and neglecting the School'. It may be significant that Henry Dalendar was removed in 1616, after four years under Davies, to attend a school in Charlwood for a year before going up to Cambridge in 1617.

William Nicolson

Nicolson was appointed within a week of Davies's dismissal. A married man of 24, he had been educated at one of the most reputable schools of the time, Magdalen College School, Oxford, where he was a chorister. He graduated from Magdalen in 1611 and, besides being Chaplain, he received in 1614 the college living of New Shoreham, Sussex. Although he appears to have been held in high esteem by his college, in that year he had been admonished by the Vice-President 'de negligentia in Divinis et Cantu'; Magdalen at this time was a 'very nursery of Puritans', with whom Nicolson was not in sympathy.

He proceeded MA in 1615, 'at which time, I conceive,' says Anthony à Wood, 'he was Chaplain to Henry, Earl of Northumberland, then a prisoner in the Tower of London, and Tutor to his son the Lord Percy. But his chief delight being exercised in the faculty of Grammar and therefore noted by many for it, he was made Master of the Free-School at Croydon. . . . From that time to the beginning of 1629 he continued there, doing great benefit by his instruction. . . . He was a right learned

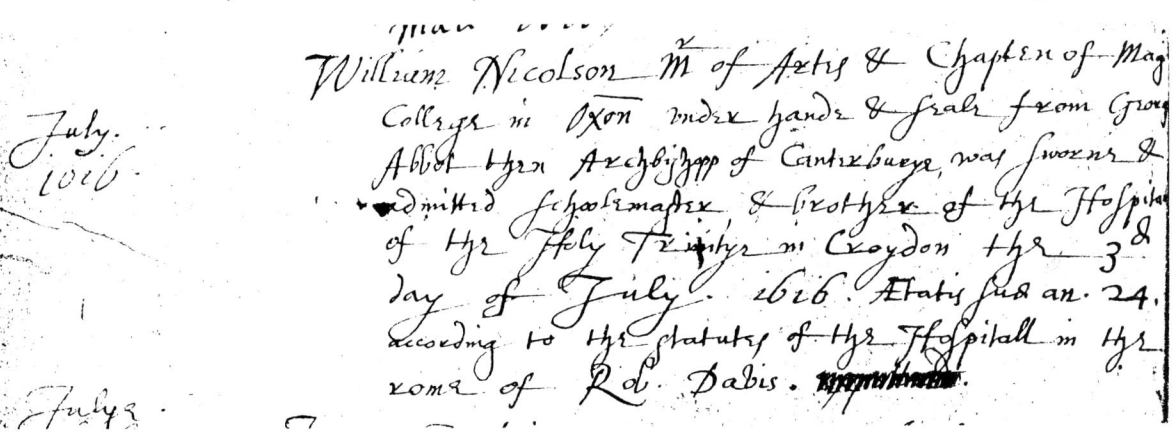

William Nicolson signs in to replace Robert Davies, 1616

divine, well read and seen in the Fathers and Schoolmen, but above all, most excellent he was in the critical part of Grammar, in which faculty none in his time, or perhaps before, went beyond him. His writings . . . shew him to be a person of great erudition, prudence, modesty and of a moderate mind.'

Anthony à Wood's statements are not invariably reliable, some of them being derived from hearsay, but it is sometimes possible to check them. In the case of Nicolson's relationships with the family of Percy, there are some conflicts of evidence with Wood's account. In the Northumberland papers there are no references to Nicolson either as a chaplain or as a tutor to Algernon, Lord Percy, who proceeded to Christ Church, Oxford, no later than October 1615, at which time Nicolson may still have been at Magdalen. But the ninth Earl's papers reveal that between February 1615/16 and February 1616/17 'Mr. Nicolson, Schoolmaster', was paid £8 for teaching Mr. Henry Percy (Algernon's younger brother) for a quarter of a year and two months; during the following twelve months a further £5 was paid to him 'not paid last year'. In that year (1618) a Mr. Willis of Isleworth who had recently established a school which he successfully conducted for half a century was paid £25 for a whole year's teaching, as against Nicolson's rate of £20 per annum. It is conceivable that Nicolson went to Syon early in 1616, took Henry Percy, aged eleven, to Croydon, but returned him to Isleworth, which is very near Syon, in 1617. Conjectural reasons for his leaving the School are manifold, but one could be Nicolson's reluctance to continue with a pupil whose fees were not being paid. The Earl's imprisonment on suspicion of involvement in the Gunpowder Plot, and his having to pay a vast fine, together with the extravagance of supporting his heir at Oxford in the manner of life deemed suitable for a nobleman, left the family in straightened circumstances. Henry followed his elder brother to Christ Church; in 1643 he was created Baron Percy of Alnwick (See Appendix II).

Davies's neglect of the School had included inattention to repairs to the fabric, for soon after his arrival Nicolson recorded in the accounts several items of necessary work such as:

At the schoole payde for repairing 3 casements	is vid
for 72 quarrels [*tiles*]	vid
for repairing the armes	id
Pd for mending the bucket of the well of the Schoolehouse	viiid

Under Nicolson the School greatly enhanced its already growing reputation, despite its setback through Davies's neglect, and within a few years a steady stream of boys was proceeding from Croydon to the universities and the Inns of Court. His success is attested by his taking in 1618 a lease from the Hospital of the 'Swan' Inn next door, in order to use it as a boarding-house, but there are tantalisingly few records of the boys he boarded there.

Among those who can with absolute certainty be attributed as pupils of Nicolson, there is Richard Vaughan, second Earl of Carbery, of whom more will be heard later; another is Richard Hatton, son of Sir Robert, Knight, born at Tottenham, Middlesex, in 1608. Sir Robert was an official in the Archbishop's household and had among his duties the surveillance of the Hospital, as the Ledger Book shows:

March 3rd 1617. Maurice Powell was convented before my Lords Grace of Canterbury at the place of Croydon, Sr Robert Hatton steward, Mr Scott Treasurer & divers others of his Graces gentlemen then present for the like disorder, viz. gaming, drinking & rayling, & was there lessoned, persuaded, & threatened by his Grace himselfe to amend his disordered life. . . .

Powell had already been twice admonished during the previous month for 'calling Goodwife Scroobye old whore in the streets' and for 'rayling, gaming & Frequenting of alehouses'. As a young schoolmaster, Nicolson, and for that matter, his predecessors and successors, must have found it a burdensome responsibility to discipline their often unruly Brethren and Sisters of the Hospital, some of whom, in the unaccustomed possession of a regular unearned income, found the temptations of the numerous inns and taverns of Croydon more than they could resist. In 1605 the constables reported to the magistrates that the number of inns and alehouses, thirty in all, was excessive.

Richard Vaughan, Earl of Carbery (1604?–86)

In 1620 Nicolson married as his second wife Elizabeth, the widow of Robert Brigstocke, a member of a long-established family of Croydon yeomen. She was a good many years older than her second husband, and her son, John, baptised in 1604 is more than likely to have been at the School under Nicolson.

Nicolson's departure

Already mentioned as a pupil has been Richard Vaughan, who succeeded his father as Earl of Carbery in 1634. When Richard was at school, his father was Comptroller of the Household to the Prince of Wales (the future Charles I), and in 1620 MP for Carmarthenshire, in which county the family seat, Golden Grove, was situated, in the parish of Llandeilo-vawr. Richard Vaughan followed his father to Parliament in 1624. In 1624 Nicolson was persuaded by Richard to accept the living of Llandeilo, but he did not leave Croydon until the spring of 1629. It was already policy to encourage clergy to accept preferment in Wales in order to support the established church and thereby the belief in the divine right of monarchy. In 1625 Nicolson's stepson, John Brigstocke, had married a Carmarthenshire girl, Mary Bowen, of Llechdwny, Kidwelly, whom he may have met through friendship with Richard Vaughan, and bought the Llechdwny estate from her father. One senses a strong bond between the two pupils and their schoolmaster; years later, Nicolson dedicated a volume of sermons to Carbery, and John Brigstocke's son, Owen, married a cousin of Carbery's. Advancement came to Nicolson in 1644, when he was made Archdeacon of Brecon, but in 1648 royalist resistance in Wales ceased (Carbery having been its ineffectual leader), and he was dispossessed of his preferments. With William Wyatt, the incumbent of a neighbouring parish, he started a successful scholastic venture; they were shortly after joined in this by Dr. Jeremy Taylor, the author of *Holy Living* and *Holy Dying*. Taylor lived for years at Golden Grove, where he was Carbery's chaplain, and which provided a title for another manual of devotions, also dedicated to his patron. Newton Hall, the 'college' they established nearby, with Taylor as its spiritual head, and Nicolson and Wyatt as experienced teachers, became celebrated as a private seminary.

At the Restoration, Nicolson regained his preferments and in 1661 was consecrated Bishop of Gloucester, an office he retained until his death in 1671. Although no portrait of him has been discovered, he is commemorated by a splendid memorial tablet in Gloucester Cathedral, erected by his step-grandson, Owen Brigstocke, who had been educated under Nicolson at Newton Hall, just as his father had been at Croydon. Carbery's sons were similarly taught.

Like his colleague, Jeremy Taylor, Nicolson published a number of religious works. One of them, *The Plain Exposition of the Church Catechism of the Church of England . . .*, was reprinted several times and was prescribed for study in many grammar schools. Another, *An Exposition of the Apostles' Creed, delivered in several Sermons*, was dedicated to Richard, Earl of Carbery, and his wife; Nicolson acknowledges his pupil's influence in bringing him to Wales and refers to his interest in his endeavours. 'The seeds of these were first sown in you and other hopeful fresh earth at Croydon, which there was committed to my husbandry . . .'.

Monument to William Nicolson, Gloucester Cathedral

Nicolson's was the sort of school that Ben Jonson (who had been under Camden at Westminster) had in mind when he wrote 'Of Public Schools' in his *Discoveries*:

'A Youth should not be made to hate study before he know the causes to love it: . . . but called on, and allured, entreated, and praised: . . . For which cause I wish them sent to the best school, and a publike, which I think the best. Your Lordship I fear hardly hears of that, as willing to breed them in your eye, and at home; and doubting their manners may be corrupted abroad. They are in more danger in your own Family, among ill servants (allowing they be safe in their Schoolmaster), than amongst a thousand boys . . . To breed them at home is to breed them in a shade; where in a school they have the light and heat of the Sun. They are used and accustomed to things and men . . . They hear what is commanded to others as well as themselves. Much approved; much corrected; Therefore I like no private breeding . . .'

John Webb

Nicolson was succeeded by John Webb, of Magdalen Hall, Oxford, and evidence all points to his being a former pupil of Nicolson's, and thus the first and only OW to be appointed Schoolmaster. He may even have served under Nicolson as usher. The son of Thomas Webb, of Wallington, Surrey, he would naturally have attended the local school under a master who was clearly making a success of things there, subsequently going up to Magdalen Hall (at the time closely associated with Magdalen College itself) at Nicolson's recommendation. Thus Nicolson had personal knowledge of his successor, who came to be appointed to a successful school at the early age of twenty-six. Under Webb this success was maintained, and many of his pupils went to university, a number of them being of more than passing interest.

Henry Tubbe, who left in 1635, is memorable as the first OW benefactor, for when he died in 1655 he left forty shillings to buy books for the School. His legacy is recorded in the Ledger Book:

Mr Henry Tubbe, Master of Arts, sometime Schollar of this School, gave 40s. which was paid by Dr Samuel Bernard [*formerly Vicar of Croydon*] for the buying of books for the use of the School about the year 1655, and with that moneys was bought Brodeus upon the Greek Anthologies, Ruderus upon Martiall, and a Poetical Dictionarie: which are still in the School 1658.

The first two books are commentaries, of use for advanced study in the Classical literatures, and the fact that Greek was still an important feature of the curriculum proves that the Schoolmaster of the time was directing the courses of study desired by the Founder. (An article on Tubbe by Mr. W.D. Hussey from which the above facts are drawn appeared in *The Whitgiftian* of December 1955.)

A more distinguished alumnus of Webb's era was Sir Daniel Harvey, a member of a family of Turkey merchants who had settled at Coombe in Croydon, and nephew of William Harvey, the discoverer of the circulation of the blood. Daniel Harvey became Ambassador to the Sultan of Turkey in 1668 and died four years later at the age of only forty.

Laud's Visitation

In Chapter 21 of his Statutes Whitgift had thus commended the supervision of his foundation to his successors:

I doe ordeyne, that my Successors Archbisshopps of Canterburie shalbee the contynuall Patrons, Governors and Visitors, of the said Hospitall, Earnestlie requesting them in the Bowells of Chryste, to have from tyme to tyme a fatherlie and Compassionate care of theire good estate, and of the poore members thereof, And that they would be pleased from tyme to tyme (as occasion shalbee offered) to compose theire Controversies, to protect, advise, order, governe, and direct them, and when neede shall requier, by themselves, or by such discreete persons, as they shall thinke fytt, in person freelie to visitt the said Hospitall; and to enquier both of the publique state of yt, and also of the private demeanor of everie particular member thereof, by such course as the Lawes doe allowe. Which visitation I would hartelye wish, might at the leaste everie Third yeare bee performed, whether there seeme any necessary occasion thereof, or noe.

Since the Archbishops continued to be frequently in residence at Croydon Palace, they were able to give close supervision to this charge, and the occasions that are recorded in the Ledger Book when admonitions were given by officers of their household may be interpreted as 'visitations'. If, indeed, these formal inspections were ever performed with the frequency enjoined by the Founder, which is doubtful, few of them have been recorded in any detail, but in August 1634, in the year after his translation, Archbishop Laud ordered the Hospital to be visited. To this end fifteen interrogatory articles were drawn up, most of them enquiring into the administration of the endowments and revenues, the upkeep of the records and the observance of the Statutes. Two of these questions refer directly to the Schoolmaster:

13. Item, Whether the master, warden, schoolmaster, usher, or any of the almsmen or officers of the said hospital, have offended against the statutes and ordinances of the said hospital; and when, and wherein?

14. Item, Whether the schoolmaster and the usher perform their duties, in instructing the youth committed to their charge? and whether is the schoolmaster's house kept in such repair as is fitting? and whether do the schoolmaster and the usher carry themselves sober and free from scandal as the statutes require? and whether doth the schoolmaster duly read divine prayers in the hospital chapel as is required?

These extracts come from Archbishop Laud's Register at Lambeth Palace, but unfortunately no answers were preserved, and we can only surmise that they were satisfactory.

(Laud had been educated at Reading School, in which he maintained an interest. Soon after he received the Visitation report he was writing to the Mayor of Reading, advising him that £10 p.a. stipend, without a house, was insufficient to attract a good schoolmaster; but a fortnight later

Titlepage of 'Brodeus' as presented by Henry Tubbe

Sir Daniel Harvey (1631–72), Ambassador to Turkey

he wrote again, having heard that the stipend was intended to be increased, and recommended a candidate for the vacant post. In his will he left provision for a stipend of £20 p.a. for the Schoolmaster of Reading; but it was still too small a sum to manage on without augmentation from fee-payers and boarders.)

There are other indications, however, that under Webb the School was prosperous. Apart from records of boys proceeding to University, two pieces of evidence throw a light upon the economics of sending a boy to the School at this time.

School bills

In February 1634 Aaron Best of Croydon made his will by which his executors were instructed to allow his son Henry £16 a year for his upkeep 'until he is seventeen years old or is to go to the University', when he was to have another £14, but out of consideration for his daughters Best stipulated 'as long as he shall continue with his mother and be taught Grammar at Croydon, if a less allowance shall serve for his maintenance than £16 a year, I will it be lessened.' Henry Best proceeded to Emmanuel College, Cambridge, in 1642.

These figures may be compared with the more detailed accounts of money laid out on behalf of John and Spencer Dalyson, sons of Sir Maximilian Dalyson, of Hallinge, Kent, by the latter's executors, Sir Moulton Lamberd of Greenwich and Sir Edward Hales:

[from Michaelmas 1633 to Lady Day 1634]

	£.	s.	d.
Shirts 24s.; a coat 17s. hatt and gloves 9s	2	10	0
Sendinge horse and man seuerall tymes to Islington [*where he had been at school before*]		4	0
Tronke carredge and other things from Islington		2	0
Stockings, bands, coffes, handkershers, shooes, and gloues	1	4	0
Garters and shoe strings		3	4
Bringinge a tronke and other things from London to Grenewich; and seruants charges in byinge theise things		3	6
Carredge of them from Grenewich to Croydon and a mans and horse hire to goe with it		3	0
Giuen him at seuerall tymes		5	0
A dosen of napkins, towells, capps and makinge	1	5	0
His parte in a syluer boule giuen Mrs Webb	1	10	0
Sendinge for them from Croydon and giuen the seruants		4	0
Payd Mr Webb monye layd out for mending his clothes, bookes, and school dutyes	1	3	0
His part in a yard ½ of laune for Mrs Webb		5	3
A sute of aparrell	2	15	0
His halfe yeares dyett due at the Annunciation 1634	8	0	0
	19	17	1

[other items later in 1634 included:]

	£	s	d
Pd Mr Webb mony disbursed for Mr John For 2 qtrs dyet & schoolinge to be ended at Christmas 1634	8	0	0
For expence money at seuerall tymes		5	0
For a Red flanell wastcoate		2	6
For mendinge his breeches			6
For footinge a pair of Stockings			4
For a Camdens Gramer		1	1
Mendinge his Coate			2
For a Waxe Candle			2
paper			2
2 pair of Shoes		4	0
mendinge his breeches			3
For a Waxe Candle			4
left unpd formerly		1	5

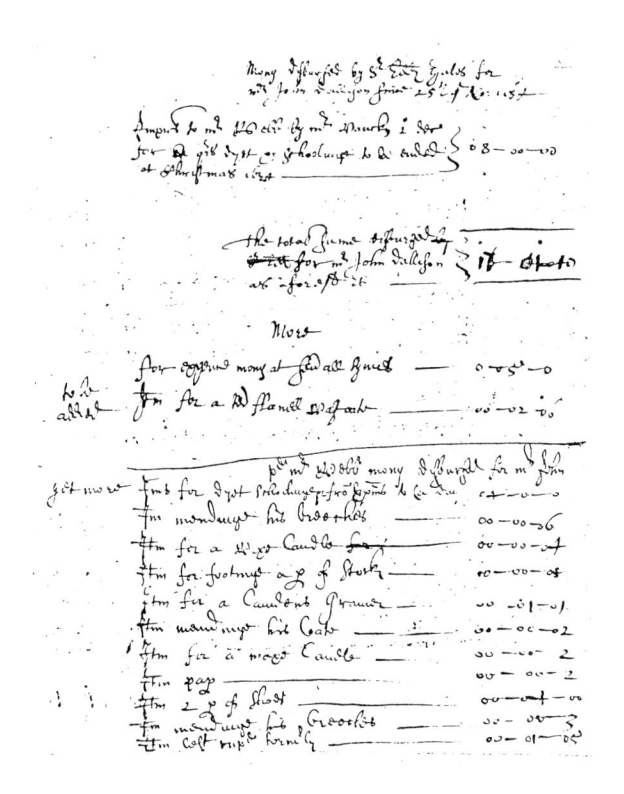

John Dalyson's School bill, 1634

The items show the responsibilities assumed by the Schoolmaster and his wife. School fees of £16 a year with board is a figure in line with the charges at many other reputable schools at the time and compares with the allowance provided by Aaron Best for his son. The boys were closely supervised by Mrs. Webb, who seems to have been generously rewarded by the joint gift of a silver bowl and a length of linen. Candles, paper and books (it is confirmed that Camden's *Grammar* was used) were comparatively expensive items that had to be carefully guarded.

The Civil War

The Civil War brought much misery to Croydon which, with the rest of Surrey, was quickly overrun by parliamentary troops, although strong royalist supporters resided there and in the neighbourhood. After 1642 many ministers and schoolmasters who were deemed to be 'ill-affected to the Parliament' were ejected from their places. John Webb may have been content to pursue a submissive course, for he remained in office until his death in 1648.

With Laud's impeachment and the abolition of bishops in 1644, the School was left to the surveillance of the minister of Croydon, Dr. Samuel Bernard, who had been Vicar since 1624, was himself displaced in 1643, but was not hindered from setting up a school of sorts at Waddon in competition with Webb and his successors. There was now, of course, no question of a bishop's licence.

In 1643 Sir Richard Onslow, of the Surrey County Committee appointed by Parliament to raise money for their cause, wrote:

I am informed that some scattering of troops of the King's are up and down the county.... One of them that was at Guildford was one Mr. Christopher Gardiner. I believe there may be some news of him at Lady Heydon's, but I believe that his brother that lives in Halyng knows not of him, for he has been from Oxford once before in these parts and robbed his own brother of all his horses in the night; if you carry the enquiry handsomely, you may probably find him out. He is there in a dangerous corner of malignants and may with his company much prejudice the county.

His brother Onslow Gardiner no doubt professed his ignorance not only out of brotherly loyalty, but also out of prudence, as any admission of complicity with the King's party would have cost him a heavy fine for 'malignancy'.

Onslow and Christopher Gardiner were the sons of Christopher Gardiner, who after the death of the Earl of Nottingham bought the Manor of Haling. He was a man of scientific interests and conducted a number of alchemical experiments at Haling House which he reported to his brother-in-law Sir John Heydon, Master of the Ordnance to King Charles I, who was then living in Sanderstead. In 1638, at the age of eighteen, Onslow Gardiner went up from the School to his father's old college, Sidney Sussex; his younger brother, Christopher, matriculated from Magdalen Hall (Webb's old college) two years later. Christopher Gardiner, senior, had married Elizabeth Onslow, a connection of Sir Richard's, and his elder son was named after his mother's family. Such family division of loyalty was not uncommon during the Civil War.

Gowns and Windows

Many hospitals provided a kind of uniform for their inmates, but the statutes do not stipulate any sort of costume to be worn. However, Edward Aylworth, who had paid for the casements and glazing of the Hall, left at his death 'xxvi rugg gownes' for the use of the poor; and Archbishop Abbot converted the yearly allowances of three members of the hospital into 'gowne money', allowing the members to renew their gowns every two years, although this money had to be supplemented on occasion from fines on the renewal of leases. The Schoolmaster, though not obliged to wear such uniform himself, was pleased enough to receive in ready money the equivalent, as the following entry shows:

Laid aside for the yeare 1645 toward gownes—15£ out of the years rents which funde was disposed of as followeth

Mr Webb the Schol^{mr} and Mrs Bradbury the Founders kinswoman had each of them twenty shillings instead of Cloth: eight and twenty pounds bought fourscore and three yards of Broadcloth which at six shillings and four^d a yard came to 26£ 5s 8d the odd 8d was abated by the Draper: of the 35s which was left every brother and sister had twenty pence toward the making of their gownes: the cloth bringing home cost 3s 2d the remainder being 3s 10d was put into the poores box.

[signed] John Webb.

In the quarterly accounts of the Hospital there continue to be regular references to repairs at the School carried out by local craftsmen or by brethren of the Hospital themselves, for among the poor there were nearly always a few aged but still skilful craftsmen. In 1645 there seems to have been some kind of disturbance or outbreak of high spirits, for in that year appears the entry:

Paide for mending the Schole windows 17s
whereof there was gathered of the boyes in the
schole 4s 9d   12s 3d

That Webb had to make a levy on the boys' pockets indicates that this large expenditure on window repairs was not due to the ordinary wear and tear on the building.

Noris Wood

Webb died on 16 April 1648, but his successor, a Puritan non-conformist, was not appointed until two months later. There being now no Archbishop of Canterbury, the affairs of the Hospital had been temporarily placed in the hands of the incumbents of Croydon and Lambeth who, 'the See being void', were authorised by the Founder in Chapter Four of his Statutes to appoint a Schoolmaster thus:

June 14, 1648. Noris Wood, M.A. sometime of Trinity Colledge in Cambridge under the Hande and seale of E. Corbitt Minister of Croydon and John Rawlinson Rector and Parson of Lambeth was sworne and admitted Schoolemaster and Brother of the Hospitall of the Holy Trinity in Croydon the 14 daye of June aetatis suae 30 according to the statutes of the Hospitall in the roome of John Webbe deceased the 16 day of April.

Wood was an Old Carthusian who, after taking his degree, returned to Charterhouse as an usher in January 1643/4, remaining there for four years until his marriage, which necessitated his resignation in December 1647. It had taken him six months to obtain a satisfactory post, but he took over a flourishing concern. (Admittedly, the sudden death of the previous Schoolmaster may

Facsimile of a Latin exercise, c. 1650

Henry Tubbe: Letter to Dr. Bernard, c. 1635

have resulted in the withdrawal of many of the pupils, but the School could have continued temporarily under an usher.)

Relics of Wood's time were discovered about 1890, when in the course of repairs to the Schoolmaster's House, there were found under some floorboards a pocket diary and almanack for 1650, a Latin exercise and a sermon in manuscript. The almanack must have belonged to Wood or to one of his pupils boarding with him. Robert Brodie (Headmaster in 1890 and also a Carthusian, but unaware of this connection with his predecessor) offered a prize to the boy who could make the most exact copy in modern writing of the English and Latin of the exercise; the prize was won by A.R. Neligan, and the winning version was published in the School Magazine of 1896. Most regrettably, none of these interesting relics has survived. A facsimile of the Latin exercise was published in the Magazine but the sermon was illegible. Brodie cautiously described it as 'probably the oldest Whitgift Latin exercise in existence', and it does indeed antedate by some thirty years the next oldest survival, discovered since Brodie's time. (There exists, however, an earlier piece of formal writing in Latin from the hand of Henry Tubbe, the donor of books to the Library, in the form of a letter of *c.* 1635 to his guardian, the Rev. Samuel Bernard (BL Harleian MS 4126), describing his pleasure at the prospect of proceeding to Cambridge.)

In 1651 Wood obtained the post of Master of the Free Grammar School of Leicester, which for some time had been looking for an experienced man. He quickly established himself there, being in sympathy with the Puritan atmosphere of Leicester, and later in the year, in accordance with common policy, which he must have followed when he was in Croydon, he substituted Christian authors in Greek and Latin for the traditional Classical texts, 'full of fables, vanities, filthiness, lasciviousness, idolatries and wickedness of the heathen', as the then Master of Caius described them. With a stipend of £32 per annum, supplemented by a collection of up to £18, Wood might have thought himself better off than when he was at Croydon but at Leicester he missed the lucrative profits from private pupils, and he was still not satisfied; a letter from Richard Lee, Master of the New Hospital at Leicester, to the Mayor, supports his application for more generous treatment:

> Sir, [1652/3] March
> I humbly desire that it may be offered to Mr Mayor and the rest of the brethren, That I have been the occasion of Mr Woods leaving Croydon, where I am informed he had betwixt £200 and £300 per annum by boarders, besides the benefit of Town boys, and £20 salary with his share in all leases belonging to the Hospital there; a fair house with a convenient orchard and garden, where for his accommodation he laid out betwixt £20 and £30: all which he loseth by coming to Leicester.
> My request is he may not be reduced to a worse condition than he was in. Sir, the work is good and will become you to move in it.
> Your ready friend and servant,
> Richard Lee.

If the figures quoted in this letter are only approximately true, and Wood may have allowed Lee to gain a somewhat extravagant idea of the prosperity of his school at Croydon, the importance of the boarding element in those days reveals the high reputation the School enjoyed. A.F. Leach, who brought this letter to the notice of the Editors of *The Whitgiftian* in June 1908, commented on the size and status of the School, for the Headmaster of Winchester only twenty years before was estimated to receive £300 from boarders, representing perhaps 20 boys.

At Whitgift's School, unhampered by restrictive statutes regarding the number and origin of its scholars, the Schoolmaster was able to develop its course just as far as his own drive, capabilities and esteem with parents would allow him to.

In 1654 Wood achieved another ambition and returned to Charterhouse as Head Master, staying there until his resignation in June 1662.

Thomas Day signs in, 1651

Thomas Day

The power of appointment of the next Schoolmaster had devolved, not upon the Ministers of Croydon and Lambeth but, ironically enough, upon Laud's successor as occupant of Croydon Palace, Sir William Brereton, baronet, a general who had formerly been in command of the Parliamentarian forces in Cheshire. Croydon Palace and other lands, which had been sequestrated from Archbishop Laud and the See of Canterbury in 1643, were bought by Brereton in 1647; he later usurped the Archbishop's responsibility for the affairs of the Hospital. Unfortunately, there is no indication of the reasons for his appointment of Thomas Day, MA of Christ's College, Cambridge, on 24 March 1651, beyond his academic qualifications. He was now aged 36, but nothing is known of his previous experience and little more of his régime.

The former local gentry with their Royalist sympathies were either under a cloud or had removed elsewhere, and new families were moving into the ascendant, but the School continued in its former manner, if offering us now very little evidence of how it was conducted and with what success, except that wear and tear was a constant minor charge on funds, For example, repairs in 1655 include:

For mending the formes in the schoolehowse	6d
For mending the boards in the Schoolehowse in Carpenters worke	6s 4d

The School seems to have maintained a fair reputation, however, for Thomas Fuller in his *Church History of Britain*, published in 1656, referring to Archbishop Whitgift, says:

> Nor was his liberality only a cistern for the present age, but a running river from a fresh fountain to water posterity in that school of Croydon which he hath beautifully built and bountifully endowed.

Fuller writes as if the School was now the more important part of the Foundation, but his fondness for alliteration may have betrayed him into exaggerating the architectural virtues of a building which he possibly never set eyes on.

During the middle years of the century, the Bishop's licence having been suspended, at least another eighteen schools were established in Surrey but a number of these were modest private and temporary concerns conducted by local clergymen, like Samuel Bernard, ejected from their livings by the Parliamentary Commissioners. A notably successful one was set up in Cheam in 1645 by George Aldwich, whose school flourished in the time of the Plague, when boys were sent into the country to avoid infection in the towns. It later became the distinguished preparatory school.

This competition may account for an apparent decline in the School's importance after Wood's departure, but the grammar schools were at this time beyond their peak of success, and many of them had already lost status. Charles Hoole, in his *New Discovery of the Old Art of Teaching*

Schoole (1659) describes schools that 'very seldom or never improve Scholars further than to teach them to read and write and learne some little . . . in the common Grammar, partly because the Master is overburdened with many petty Scholars, and partly because many parents will not spare their children to learne, if they can but finde them any employment about their domestick or rureall affairs.'

One of Day's boarding pupils was John Price of Esher, who was admitted Fellow-commoner at St. John's College, Cambridge, in April 1657 at the age of sixteen. Six years later he was a party to the sale of his father's property, the Manor of Esher, so it seems that Day continued the practice of drawing pupils from the land-owning families in various parts of the county. By now the universities, too, were less populous, and references to Croydon students are very few.

The occasion of Day's departure must have been the Act of Uniformity of May 1662, which required all Schoolmasters to take the Oath of Non-resistance and to renounce the Covenant of 1643, with the consequence that on 24 August two thousand beneficed clergymen resigned, Thomas Day being apparently one of their number, for his successor was appointed a month later. No record of Day's departure appears in the Ledger Book.

John Philips

John Philips Mr of Arts sometime of New Colledge in Oxon nominated by the most reverend father in God William Juxon Lord archbishop of Canterbury . . . entred scholemaster . . . the 29th day of September 1662 and took the oaths injoyned by the Founder.

A Schoolroom of the mid-17th century

1668 Mr John Philips Schoolmaster of the free Schoole in Croydon deceased August the 6th.

These two entries in the Ledger Book constitute virtually all that is known about the School and its Schoolmaster during the six years of Philips's term of office, and no Old Boys of his have been traced. John Phillips, of Middlesex, pleb., matriculated at New College in October 1621 at the age of nineteen, taking the degree of BA three years later and proceeding MA in June 1627, but beyond these facts, college and university records are silent.

His appointment was the first to be made of a man manifestly too old for the post: he was over sixty in 1662, and in a lawsuit of 1672 the Hospital taxed a tenant with 'taking advantage of the weakness, neglect and great infirmities of the late Schoolmaster'. The fact that his patron, William Juxon, himself in his dotage, had been educated at Merchant Taylors' School leads to the conjecture that some connection between the two may already have existed. Examination of the Merchant Taylors' Company records reveals that John Philips had been appointed First Under-Master in November 1627, his identity being confirmed by his very distinctive signature. He would have expected to succeed in the course of time to the post of Headmaster, who was traditionally promoted from this direction, but Philips was disappointed in this respect on no fewer than three occasions, with the result that he became the centre of subversion, being 'ill-disposed to live on friendly terms with his superior'. His behaviour became so intolerable that in January 1638 he was dismissed from his office, albeit with a parting gift, in view of his long service, of forty marks. A man of this name was Master of St. Saviour's Grammar School, Southwark, from June 1638 until late 1643, but otherwise for the next twenty-four years he disappears into limbo; he may have joined Juxon in exile.

17th Century Grammar Schools

It can be confidently asserted that men successfully educated at 16th and 17th century grammar schools, universities and the Inns of Court enjoyed reading. Their reading matter, by our standards very limited, was chiefly the Bible in English, together with poetry, narrative prose, plays, sermons and works of religious and political argument. Translations into English from the other literary languages of Europe, Italian, French and Spanish, were becoming available in increasing numbers. They could also choose to read history, mythology and poetry in Latin and Greek, and if disposed to, could read works of international learning which were still written in Latin. Such men were keen that their sons should be educated in the same way for very good reasons: (a) to be able to wield authority effectively, even if only over their own estates, through a knowledge of law and with confidence in their superior education, (b) to pursue literary interests as a leisure occupation, (c) to enjoy membership of a society that shared a common culture.

Few young men of this kind took holy orders; those who did frequently came of more plebeian stock and at university were scholars or of servitor status. Their ambition was to acquire a parish living through patronage, possibly by connections made during their years at school or university.

Other men might send their sons to university or the Inns of Court for ambitious reasons—to mix with the sons of the influential. John Brigstocke's association with Richard Vaughan may have been unpremeditated, but the outcome was significant.

It must be assumed that few grammar schools could draw upon a cultured clientèle; small schools in rural districts might at times find it very difficult to attract any pupils at all who aspired to a thorough training in Latin. Some schools such as Tonbridge, Repton, Sherborne and Bury St. Edmund's, for example, gained a high reputation among the gentry of a large and prosperous area, and under vigorous headmasters flourished for several decades. These were schools unhampered by any subordination to superior interests, such as parish, borough or city control, or those who shared the endowment.

At Whitgift the dominating interest was that of the brethren and sisters, who had command of all income including casual windfalls in the form of fines. When an ineffective master such as Philips was appointed, the School collapsed and was difficult to revive.

So Philips seems to have been a failure from the first, yet his time at Croydon was one of great opportunity, with the Restoration of the old order in Church and State, and even the disasters of the Plague and the Great Fire of London to give further scope; Croydon had long been a retreat for the families of London citizens and the town received many refugees from the congestion and hazards of the City, but it was not immune to the Plague, among whose victims in Croydon were three of Philips's family, or at least of his name.

It was during Philips's régime that Izaak Walton published his *Life of Richard Hooker* (1663), in which he said that Whitgift 'built a fair free-school, with a good accommodation and maintenance for the master and scholars'. That Walton had first-hand knowledge may be doubtful; he could have been paraphrasing what he had found in Stow (1600), Camden (1610), Paule (1612) or Fuller (1655).

Titlepage of Crowe's *Elenchus*, 1672

William Crowe

Philips's successor was a man of thwarted ambition, under whose direction the School's course remains conjectural. There was a gap of four months before William Crowe was appointed by Gilbert Sheldon, during which time the School may have lapsed into complete inanition, if it was not already in that state by the time the ineffective Philips died. Crowe is dignified by an entry in the *Dictionary of National Biography*, although his fame is somewhat tarnished. He graduated from Caius in 1637 and from 1648 until 1654 he was Vicar of Mudford, Suffolk, which had been his father's living. During this period and later he spent much time in Cambridge studying the books and manuscripts of the Lambeth Palace Library, which had been removed to the University Library in the Interregnum. He was an enthusiastic cataloguer and compiled a catalogue to the University's Holdsworth Collection. Having been nominated for the University Librarianship, he was disappointed not to be elected, but he was awarded in consolation the Mastership at Croydon on 4 December 1668 when he was fifty-two.

He is unkindly spoken of by Anthony à Wood in *Athenae Oxonienses*, which remains almost the sole source of comment on his life, and is accused of about the worst sin a scholar can commit, that of theft of another man's work. A certain John Osborne had taken great pains in making *A Catalogue of Our English Writers on the Old and New Testament* and had printed eight sheets of it, 'but William Crowe of Suffolk, Schoolmaster of Croydon in Surrey . . . coming out before him on the same subject in 1659, prevented him from going any farther. His Catalogue, which hath several times since been printed, is called by some Osborne's, but by the generality, Crowe's Catalogue.' Wood was always biased against a Cambridge man, but the unfortunate Crowe can hardly be blamed for producing the fruits of his labours before his rival. The disparaged work, entitled *An Exact Collection or Catalogue of our English Writers on the Old and New Testament*, does not bear Crowe's name on the title-page. It was a useful work for theological students and for clergymen in preparing their sermons, as it listed writers and commentators according to the books of the Bible they had commented on, in some cases chapter by chapter.

Crowe completed his next book, *Elenchus Scriptorum in Sacram Scripturam tam Graecorum quam Latinorum*, a similar compilation of writers in Latin and Greek, while he was at Croydon, for it was published in 1672. On this occasion his name does appear on the title-page: 'Opera & Industria Guil. Crowaei, Sudovolgiensis, Ludimagistri Croydoniensis'. Material for this book, too, Wood accuses Crowe of filching from another scholar's work: *Foelix Consortium; or a Fit Conjuncture of Religion and Learning*, by Edward Leigh, published in 1656.

The dedication of this volume to the author's patron, Archbishop Sheldon, reminds us that the latter's chief task was the restoration of the Anglican Church; even before Juxon's death in 1663 he had taken an important part in the Church's re-establishment. His appointment of Crowe shows concern for one who had been faithful and assiduous in his self-imposed guardianship of the Lambeth Library, by this time returned to its former home.

In 1665 Sheldon had instructed his bishops to furnish him with information about all the schools and schoolmasters in their dioceses, paying particular attention to their diligence in religious observance and their loyalty to the government. He emphasised the Bishops' duties of issuing licences to teach, and was determined that the Act of Uniformity of 1662 should be rigorously enforced. Sheldon was well satisfied, of course, with Crowe's qualifications as a scholar and his habits as a clergyman, but Crowe had no experience, as far as has been discovered, of teaching a school or of controlling such an institution as the Hospital.

After Sheldon had held a Visitation in 1671 he issued a severe rebuke to Crowe and the Warden for offences in leasing Hospital property and in felling and selling timber without authority, but in this case it appears probable that Crowe was the dupe of a cunning group of Brethren. The circumstances of the management of the Hospital did allow the Schoolmaster and Warden to undertake in collusion certain underhand and private deals with their tenants, and the knowledge of this possibility was a constant encouragement to the Brethren and Sisters to make accusations, often wildly and vigorously sustained, but sometimes quite justifiably, of corruption on the part of the Schoolmaster in particular.

The Restoration and Christopher Wase

The Restoration coincided with a decline in the reputation and popularity of the grammar schools. This decline, which had already been noted by Hoole in 1659, has been partly attributed to the disfavour with which the restored royalists viewed the schools' success in breeding radical parliamentarians, especially at social levels below the gentry. There was jealousy, too, of the success with which those educated gratuitously at the schools were competing for the jobs available to the educated minority. But dissatisfaction with the methods of education was more widely spread. For other reasons, according to Anthony à Wood, the universities were also declining in favour. The narrow attention to religious orthodoxy that was imposed upon them excluded those who, whether non-conformists or papists, were of independent principles and views. Another group was discouraged by the 'low breeding' that pervaded the universities. Thus the lack of confidence both in schools and in universities resulted in the choice by many families of an alternative education, which could be obtained only from tutors at home or at schools abroad.

The many endowed schools which were now failing to perform the functions they had been designed for were criticised by many would-be reformers. What seems to be the first systematic attempt to gather historical details about the grammar schools of England and Wales was undertaken by Christopher Wase, Schoolmaster of Tonbridge School 1662–8. Wase who, like Francis Bacon sixty years before, thought there were too many schools, sent out a questionnaire in 1673 to all the free schools in England and Wales, asking for the name of the founder, details of endowments, the succession of masters, exhibitions to the universities and details of school libraries. After collating the information he had received, Wase intended to publish his findings in detail, but gave up this idea and instead produced *Considerations regarding Free Schools as Settled in England* (Oxford 1678 and 1687), which is a general review of education in England and Wales at the time. His manuscripts in Bodley comprise the returns made from schools throughout the country. Surrey schools that sent information were Bletchingly, Kingston, Guildford and St. Saviour's, Southwark. No return came from Crowe, but a correspondent of Wase's, referring to schools at Newdigate, Reigate (recently founded but not yet endowed), Camberwell and Croydon, promised to obtain information for him. Crowe's reluctance to comply with the request prompted another correspondent to help:

> That of Moulton in dorso will, I hope, satisfy: that of Croydon infra is the best I could get of the Master in the short time I stayed there, most exact in the succession of Masters.....

Some inaccurate information is given, carelessly taken from the Ledger Books, and Crowe's works are described.

On 9 November 1674 the correspondent wrote again, this time giving short notes on the constitution of the Hospital of the Holy Trinity, apparently compiled after an examination of the Statutes. There is no new information, but he concludes:

> The poor people have five pounds p.a. apiece. All payd quarterly by the School Mr out of the Revenue, wch is two hundred pd. so that no Salary properly belongs to the School & none are taught free though (says Mr Crow and present Master) I have understood there ought to have beene by the Founder's intention both salary, and free teaching.

Crowe's remark indicates that he was then taking pupils but hints that free pupils had never been numerous. Furthermore, what seventy years before had been a customary stipend for a schoolmaster was now regarded as payment only for his duties as Chaplain. The Founder's failure to lay down statutes for the conduct of the School and to anticipate the fall in the value of money resulted in few of 'the poorer sorte' taking advantage of the opportunities for free education, and the Schoolmaster's liberty in building up a school profitable to himself if he had the ability and ambition to do so is once more illustrated.

Although Crowe's reputation as a biblical scholar and a learned classic might have obtained him pupils at the School, he had a difficult time. The rebuke from Sheldon was followed by a costly lawsuit with the tenant of the Addiscombe lands, but his main troubles arose from the character of the then Vicar of Croydon, Dr. William Clewer, a notorious evil-liver who brought such distress to the town that in 1672 the inhabitants petitioned the King to have him removed: their statement declared that 'he hath caused the gentry to leave the town, to the ruin thereof; spoiled the school, so that no gentlemen's sons come at it'. This imputation is partly justified by the Hearth-Tax returns for the County of Surrey in 1673–4, which show that several of the bigger houses were now lying empty. Clewer was at last deprived in 1684, but on James II's accession the following February he attempted unavailingly to get restored. Although no evidence exists that Clewer was in any way responsible, Crowe committed suicide, allegedly out of despair; according to the parish register:

1675, April 11. William Crowe that was skoolmaster of the Free Skool, who hanged himself in the windo of one of his chambers in his dwelin house, was buried in the church.

As a suicide, Crowe was not entitled to burial in sanctified ground, but it may have been Clewer himself who, with characteristic truculent contrariness, allowed Crowe's body to rest in the church itself.

John Shepheard

On 17 April, only a week after Crowe's death, John Shepheard, MA, sometime of Wadham College, Oxford, was appointed Schoolmaster by Archbishop Sheldon. Five months later he married the niece of the owner of Sanderstead Court, Harman Atwood, whose great-nephew and heir, also named Harman, was in all probability a pupil at the School and the means of acquaintance between Shepheard and the Atwood family. Three years later Shepheard was inducted Rector of Sanderstead, the advowson being in the gift of the Atwoods.

During Shepheard's time some of the problems due to the very care with which the Founder framed his Statutes came to a head. Chapter Sixteen laid down certain conditions upon which leases were granted, designed by the Founder to preserve the interests of the members, not only in the ordinary course of law, but also against combination between the Schoolmaster and tenants; leases were to be granted for not more than twenty-one years, tenants were required to maintain all buildings, hedges, fences and ditches in good order, and they were not allowed to fell trees or sell any timber. By the Statute of Mortmain, and also by a clause in Chapter Sixteen, the rents were limited to the figure established at the end of the sixteenth century; the increase in the actual value of the lands leased, however, could be tapped by means of a system of fines, or premiums, levied when the leases were granted or renewed. It came to be that leases were not always allowed to run their full term, but were renewed at irregular intervals at a fine, to the advantage of both parties, a practice that was to become common by the early eighteenth century.

The Founder made provision for the disposal of these fines and of the receipts from the sale of timber, etc., which

shalbee layed up in their Common Tresorie, and kept together, untill it ryse or shall amownte unto the some of one hundreth powndes. And then the overplus of that some of one hundreth powndes shalbee equally devyded by the Warden & Schoolemaster for the tyme being ... amongst all the poore Brethren and Systers of the said Hospitall, and they to have theire equal portions with the rest....

Now whereas the agreements recited quite clearly all the conditions of lease and the rents payable, and the Ledger Book recorded the rents as they were received, these leases were renewed only 'upon payment of a competent fine'. For a good many years the fines and their distribution among the members were carefully recorded in the Ledger Book, but towards the end of the seventeenth century the references become less explicit and then vanish altogether. There were several unsatisfactory elements in this system: (a) the fines came in at irregular intervals, so that a number of windfalls might accrue within a short while to the members, although years might pass without any payment; for instance, during the two years 1604–5 £84.11s.6d. was received and distributed, but over the next five years only £6 was forthcoming; (b) many of the old people had no good use for this money; with no family responsibilities, used to a simple diet partly provided free from their rights of corn and their coney warrens, and supplied regularly with fuel and plain but adequate clothing, they often turned for entertainment to the inns of Croydon and to the voicing among themselves of their discontent; (c) the money could thus frequently have been put to better use, such as the more careful repair and improvement of the Hospital premises; and (d) it allowed clandestine arrangements to be made whereby the true amount of the fines was concealed by the Schoolmaster—with or without the connivance of the Warden—from the others. The Schoolmaster by virtue of his superior education and experience could easily contrive, if he had a mind to, an understanding with a tenant to withhold a portion of the sum privately agreed upon, to the advantage of both; and suspicion of this possible manipulation was undoubtedly a main cause of the poor people's prejudice against the Schoolmaster, who might justify his action to himself on the grounds that by equal share-out his own inadequate basic salary would not be increased in the same proportion as the stipends of the inmates, in spite of his having to do the work of negotiation. A consequence of such collusion, evidence of which at this stage is impossible to produce, could be that a tenant might obtain a moral hold over the Schoolmaster, who would be reduced to further shifts in case anything should be found out by the members.

Both Philips and Crowe had had disputes with Sir Purbeck Temple, owner of Addiscombe Place and leaseholder of the Hospital's 'Messuage and Lands at Adgercombe [Addiscombe]' of one hundred and twenty-three acres at a rent of £28.10s. per annum. The Hospital attempted to evict Temple, whom they accused of destroying the timber and otherwise spoiling the estate, but were eventually involved in defending a lawsuit that cost them over £200 in legal charges to maintain their own rights. Shepheard, 'a person being well esteemed of' by his Grace, was appointed with a view to establishing a better order of affairs after the inefficiency of Philips and Crowe. He found there was much to do, and reported regularly to Dr. Robert Thompson, Secretary at Lambeth to Sheldon and also to Sancroft who, succeeding Sheldon in 1678, took a particularly keen interest in the Hospital's affairs. A visit to Sir Purbeck, who continued to prove awkward, enabled Shepheard quickly to get the other's measure; the latter had, in fact, improperly used timber on the estate, had sublet parts of it at great profit to himself (which he denied) and had refused to meet the Hospital over the question of fines, but until the twenty-one-year lease expired, little could be done to rectify these abuses without expensive recourse to law.

Another source of anxiety for Shepheard was the Northampton property. In September 1675 a disastrous fire had laid waste the centre of that town, including one of the Hospital's two houses there; the tenant, with the support of local magistrates, was demanding what appeared to be unreasonably generous treatment, and in March 1677 Shepheard went to Northampton 'through the worst of Ways and weather I have ever yet Experienced'. (The 1892 History comments on his 'audacity to charge the Foundation £5.10s. for riding his own horse eleven days', as if his visits to Northampton and elsewhere were made for his own pleasure.)

Yet another worry for him was Lancaster College, the property in St. Paul's Churchyard on which there was an annual rent charge of £6.13s.4d.; in the Great Fire of 1666 the building was destroyed, and the Hospital had waived the rent for some years; however, the owner had rebuilt, and Shepheard thought some of the arrears should now be paid, so he and the Warden attended the Court of the Commissioners for Charitable Uses at Guildhall to get some of the money owed.

Shepheard's actions on their behalf did not dispel the suspicions of the Brethren and Sisters that he was withholding from them a good deal of what was their due, even if it was put in the Chest against future contingencies. After a further Injunction from Sheldon there was no diminution of their spite against him and the Warden. Early in December 1679, just after his wife's death, at a time when he was much disturbed in spirit, he wrote to Dr. Thompson: ''Tis of late reported that my great end of raising the fines of the Hospital is mainly to engrosse the best leases for my own use.' Three weeks later, after the yearly audit had been presented in the Hall, he wrote again:

Their Chancellor made a noise & uproare among the Dissatisfy'd for Grievances, which they could not fix nor find. You can't imagine the Injurys they have done me by their Falshood and Malice. There are more

Poore than Rich, more Fools than Wise, & the major party, which is theirs, damnes a mans Reputation by Noise & Clamour.

John Oldham, usher

But Shepheard's régime is chiefly of interest through an usher in his employment, John Oldham, a minor poet whose works, although now but little read, were greatly esteemed in his own day for their coarse satirical wit. Pope summed him up well: 'Oldham is a very indelicate writer; he has a strong rage, but it is too much like Billingsgate.' Oldham, born at Shipton Moyne in Gloucestershire in 1653, was admitted to St. Edmund Hall, Oxford, in 1670, where he was 'soon observed to be a good Latinist, and chiefly to addict himself to the Study of Poetry and other Polite Acquirements'. He graduated in 1674 and for a time lived with his father, the Rector of Tetbury, Gloucestershire, but as his life there proved dull and restricted, he was glad to accept the post of usher offered to him by Shepheard, the relative of a college friend. He arrived in Croydon some time before July 1676 and remained until the end of February 1678/9. An usher's job was a lowly and ill-paid one involving a good deal of drudgery, and in his *Satyr addressed to a Friend that is about to leave the University, and come abroad in the World* he expresses dissatisfaction with the occupation he had been compelled to adopt:

> For want of better opportunity
> A School must your next Sanctuary be.
> Go, wed some Grammar-Bridewell, and a Wife,
> And there beat Greek, and Latin for your Life:
> With birchen Sceptre, there command at Will,
> Greater than Busby's self, or Doctor Gill.*
> But who would be to the vile Drudg'ry bound,
> Where there so small encouragement is found?
> Where you for recompense for all your pains
> Shall hardly reach a common Fidler's gains?
> For when you've toil'd, and labour'd all you can,
> To dung, and cultivate a barren Brain;
> A Dancing-Master shall be better paid,
> Tho' he instructs the Heels, and you the Head:
> To such Indulgence are kind Parents grown,
> That nought costs less in breeding than a Son:
> Nor is it hard to find a Father now,
> Shall more upon a Setting-dog allow:
> And with a freer hand reward the Care
> Of training up his Spaniel, than his Heir.

In the Bodleian Library there is a collection of many of Oldham's poems in draft or final form (MS Rawlinson Poet. 123), some of which he had written on the back of boys' exercises or of draft letters. Their chief interest to us lies not so much in what they reveal of the development of his poetic inspiration, but in that we are given a view of a couple of dozen pieces of school work of the time, of which a few, a very few unfortunately, bear the names of the boys whose work they are. There are simple Latin renderings of fables and like pieces, a number of 'similitudes' and other examples for composition, some long-division sums and even pages of hand-writing exercises, including the alphabet, showing the lowliness of some of the usher's duties. He encouraged his pupils to write English verses themselves, and a number of boys have turned

John Oldham (1653–83), Usher 1676–79

---

* Richard Busby, Head Master of Westminster 1640 to 1695, was notable for his learning and his addiction to the birch; Dr Gill was High Master of St. Paul's 1635 to 1640, when he was dismissed for excessive cruelty.

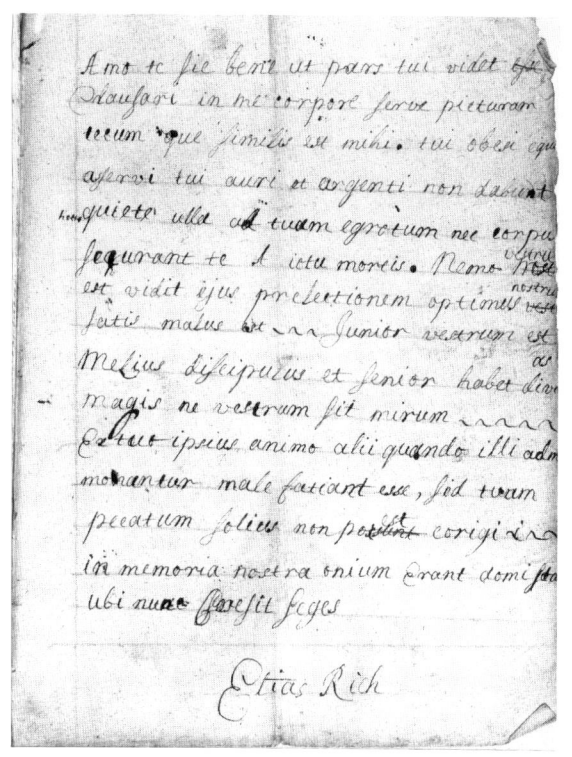

Elias Rich: Latin exercise, c. 1679

Another exercise by an unknown

their hand to lamentable doggerel on the theme of 'The Gunpowder Plot', not of 1605 but the Popish Plot of 1678.

> Curst't and fore'er curst be the day wherein
> Those Rebels first their lives they did begin,
> 'Gainst her Majesty and the Parliament
> Thinking to have putt down all Government
> First blowing up his Sacred Majesty
> Then cutting of alth' Royall Progeny.

and

> I thought that those dam'd Rogues had done their worst
> And to rebel again they ne'er againe had durst
> And that they all thoughts of the former plot
> Meant everlastingly to have forgot
> But now I have cause my mind to alter
> And think them not worthy of a halter.

On these scraps of paper there are the names of only three boys: Harry (?) Blese, Ed. More and Elias Rich. There was a prominent family named variously Blease, Bleaze and Bliss in Croydon at that time. Edward More has not yet been identified. Elias Rich, an example of whose work is illustrated above, was the son of Sir Peter Rich, an Alderman and Sheriff of the City of London, whose interest in local affairs is shown by his setting his signature to the first petition for the incorporation of Croydon in 1691.

Oldham had enough leisure to continue writing poetry, and copies of his work came to the notice of the Earl of Rochester, the Earl of Dorset and Sir Charles Sedley, celebrated poets of the day. There is a story that these noblemen came to Croydon to visit the author of the poems that had attracted their attention.

Mr Shepherd, the worthy master of the School, seeing Lord Rochester's card, and thinking it quite impossible that such a mark of distinction could be intended for his obscure assistant, took the whole credit of the compliment to himself, and, after carefully arranging his toilet, went to receive his visitors. . . . The old gentleman had prepared a speech for the occasion, expressing his high sense of the honour conferred upon him, and modestly deprecating his claims to so extraordinary a condescension; when Lord Dorset good-naturedly interposed, and informed him that the motive of his visit was to see the usher. By this time Mr Shepherd had got into a little confusion in his speech and was probably not unwilling to make his retreat, confessing, frankly enough, that he had neither wit nor learning to qualify him for such fine company.

This ridiculous Victorian elaboration of the simple yet remarkable fact of Rochester's visit contains so many absurdities introduced for dramatic effect that there is little need to analyse its falsity, beyond commenting on the glaring anachronism of the visiting-card and the foresight 'the old gentleman' (now in his early thirties) displayed in preparing a speech for an occasion that he had no foreknowledge of. Nevertheless, there was some such visit, and thereby Oldham was introduced to the literary life of London.

He left Croydon at the end of February 1678/9, having obtained the post of tutor to the eight-year-old grandson of Sir Edward Thurland, a baron of the Exchequer, who lived at Reigate. This position he probably owed to the Atwoods or the Carews of Beddington, whose acquaintance he made through Shepheard. There is a draft of a letter by Oldham in the Bodley volume referred to:

From Rygate March 2 1678[9]

Honoured Sr,
I am at length removed to my new place of residence; I left Croydon on Saturday with as much concern allmost as ever I left any place. Most of my boys cried at my departure. I cant yet give you an account of how I like it here. I am not settled yet. I find all the people mighty civil courteous and obliging, the family sober and well governed. My business is easy enough, the care of only one lad, so that (thank God) I see nothing yet but a prospect of living to my satisfaction & content....

This draft may have been intended by Oldham for his father or for Harman Atwood. The letter does not support the idea that he was completely unhappy at the School, or that he always regarded it as a 'Grammar-Bridewell'.

When Harman Atwood shortly afterwards died, Oldham wrote a panegyrical ode to him, whom he regarded as a benefactor. After remaining at Reigate until 1681, he entered the service of the Earl of Kingston, at whose house at Holme Pierrepont in Nottinghamshire he died of smallpox on 9 December 1683. He was described as 'tall of stature, the make of his body very thin, his face long, his nose prominent, his aspect unpromising, but satire was in his eye. His constitution was very tender, and inclined to a consumption, and it was not a little injured by his intense application to his studies' (although another authority refers to his application to the bottle).

Much disenchanted after six years of office, the responsibilities of which had brought him little but anxiety and unpopularity, Shepheard must have felt much relieved when he retired on 11 June 1681. Archbishop Sancroft, determined to pursue the reformation of the Hospital's affairs, may have been equally glad to see him go, so that he could appoint a man of only twenty-six, especially chosen to manage the Hospital according to the Founder's Statutes.

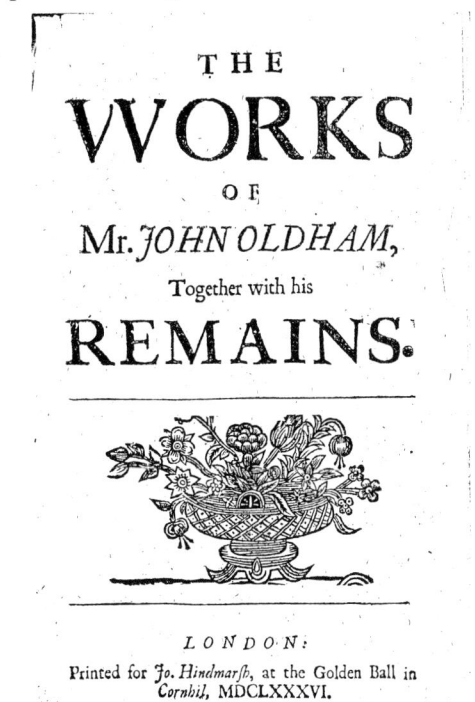

Titlepage of John Oldham's *Works*, 1686

John Caesar

John Caesar, who replaced Shepheard on the day of the latter's resignation, had come from Christ's College, Cambridge. Ordained priest in September 1677, he probably held a curacy somewhere or was an usher at another school before coming to Croydon. Bringing fresh vigour and method to the conduct of the Hospital's affairs, he reorganised the system of accounting and bought new books to supersede the old Ledger Books that had been in use for eighty years and were now in a state of congested confusion, for Shepheard in particular neglected many of the Founder's instructions for maintaining them. Caesar's records of receipts and disbursements are more tidily and methodically kept than at any other time since Samuel Finche was responsible. The Archbishop reposed considerable confidence in Caesar, and a few months after the latter's appointment Dr. Robert Thompson wrote from Lambeth to convey instructions from Sancroft about certain observances in the Hospital that had been allowed to lapse.

Archbishop Sancroft's zeal

The Archbishop was particularly anxious that the old custom of wearing gowns should be maintained by the old people, especially when attending church, and he imposed fines upon those who should fail to conform. The custom is observed to this day by the residents of a number of hospital almshouses, such as St Cross, Winchester, Abbot's, Guildford, and the Royal Hospital, Chelsea. Sancroft, who had called for a copy of the Statutes from the Schoolmaster, which he then compared minutely with the definitive version at Lambeth, was determined that in the conduct of the Hospital there should be no departure from the Founder's Ordinances, but he was willing to impose further obligations upon the Brethren and Sisters, quite in contradiction to these same Statutes, which while authorising the Founder's successors as Archbishops to *interpret* the Statutes, did not permit any alteration or addition. Sancroft was able to impose these conditions without being challenged, but a hundred and fifty years later, when the Brethren and Sisters were more sophisticated, and the authority of an Archbishop less dominant, such an assumption of prerogative would have met with outright rejection.

Among Sancroft's papers in the Tanner Collection in the Bodleian Library, there are many relating to the Hospital's affairs, some of them being returns required from the Schoolmaster, but Sancroft, it appears, was concerned only with the correct administration of the estates and with the appointment and control of the members; in the School as such he seems to have taken no interest whatsoever—a sufficient indication that he regarded it as a minor feature and the personal responsibility of the Schoolmaster alone. But he studied deeply the history of the foundation, not only by perusing Finche's records and the Statutes at Lambeth, but also by getting Caesar to copy out entries from the Ledger Books, especially those that referred to additions to the endowment after Whitgift's time, to customs, and to injunctions made by other Archbishops.

The buildings of the Hospital and School had now been in use for over eighty years without any major repairs. The quarterly accounts show that the urgent replacement of tiles, window-panes, bell-ropes, hinges, floor-boards, etc. was regularly performed, but the policy of distributing all income among the members after 'necessary' disbursements had been made did not encourage those members—whose tenure of their position was in the nature of things only transitory—to build up any reserve for future dilapidations. One hundred pounds had to be kept in the Chest, specifically against actions in law, but the Statutes did not make any allowance for rebuilding or improvements to the School and Hospital premises. Indeed, the repair of the Schoolmaster's House being the responsibility of the incumbent for the time being, it is small wonder that the Schoolmasters had tended to neglect this requirement, especially if they felt that any improvements they might make would be chiefly for the benefit of their successors. Caesar found the buildings in very poor shape and he was not slow to bring to Sancroft's notice the desirability of a complete restoration. Fortunately, financial resources were soon to be at hand.

In 1683 Sir Purbeck Temple's lease of the Addiscombe lands fell in, and before the Hospital would allow him to renew it he had to pay a fine of no less than £294, a sum that it would have been absurd to distribute among a couple of dozen old people. Sancroft was most willing for the money to be put to more practical use and he not only ordered the Hospital and Schoolhouse to be fully repaired, but also allowed Caesar £40 to repair the Schoolmaster's House; after all this expenditure there was still over one hundred pounds for distribution among the Brethren and Sisters.

Extensive repairs

A summary of the accounts for this full-scale restoration of the building exists, although greater detail would have shed an interesting light upon the capacity and fittings of the School and Schoolmaster's House.

	£	s	d
The Bricklayer's Bill for Hospitall & Schoole	45	0	5
The Carpenter's bill for the Hospitall	13	18	4
The Carpenter's bill for the Schoole	21	19	0
Another bill for the Schoole	1	9	2
The Joyners bill for wainscotting the School	8	19	6
The Glaziers bill:– For Hospitall Windows & Schoole Windows whiting the Chappell & the Schoole & for some work laid in Oyle	6	16	9
The Wardens bill:– For what he had of the Smyth for hookes hinges nailes spikes & other Ironworke & for bread & beare for the workmen	9	2	11
Matts for the Chappell	1	4	0
Mr Edwards his bill:– For taking & writing 3 Terrars of Sir Purbeck Temples Farme everyone of which larger than the Lease itselfe,	2	6	0
For severall journeys Horse hire & expences about the business between Sir Purbeck Temple & the Hospitall	5	0	0
A Table for the Schoole		16	0
	116	12	1
More done in repairs as by other bills	12	2	6
Given to Mr Snow the Clerke for his trouble in the business of Sir Purbeck Temples Lease	1	1	6
To Dr Thompson Clerke for the like and for writing and entring Orders	2	1	6
To the Gents of the Chamber		5	0
To the porter		2	6
To the Controullors servant	1	1	6
To Mr Caesar schoolMr. Allowed by Order of his grace the Ld. ABpp. to repair his dwelling house	40	0	0
Paid in Exchange for Brassmoney, & the Brass money given to the Poor people to be sold		11	0

Tot of the Page payd – 173 17 7

(N.B. (a) The carpenter's bills for the School, significantly larger than that for the Hospital, show that the School, although a much smaller building, required more thorough repair; there had been heavy wear and tear from its occupants.

(b) There were a number of palms that had to be oiled before business could be completed.

(c) Brass-money was used for small change. The smallest coin of the realm at this time being the silver penny, local tradesmen issued their own base-metal tokens for smaller values; these tokens bore the tradesman's name, an inn-sign or name, or some other device, and were used as small currency in the locality, being redeemable in goods or at their face value. Some used to find their way into the poor box. It would appear that the workmen had received some of this small cash while they were working in Croydon and, on being paid off, were given in bulk exchange the equivalent in coins of the realm; the tokens were then distributed to the members of the Hospital for them to redeem or to spend as they pleased.)

In January 1691/2 another large fine of £60 was received from Sir Purbeck Temple, which was this time distributed, Caesar, the Warden and twenty-one resident members receiving £2 each, five non-residents £1, and the remainder, after 10 shillings had been paid to Caesar for horse hire to Lambeth about the business, going towards the reserve stock in the Chest. Caesar ruled that economy must be exercised over cutting trees for firewood, and fines would have to be used primarily for repairs in future.

In recognition of his success in the control of the Hospital's affairs, Caesar received in January 1688/9 another mark of favour from Sancroft, who collated him Vicar of Croydon. Although this was not a rich living, it enabled him to

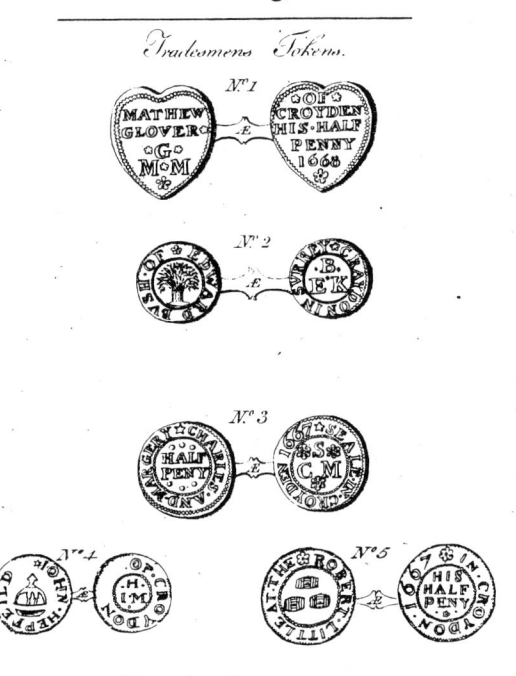

Croydon brass money

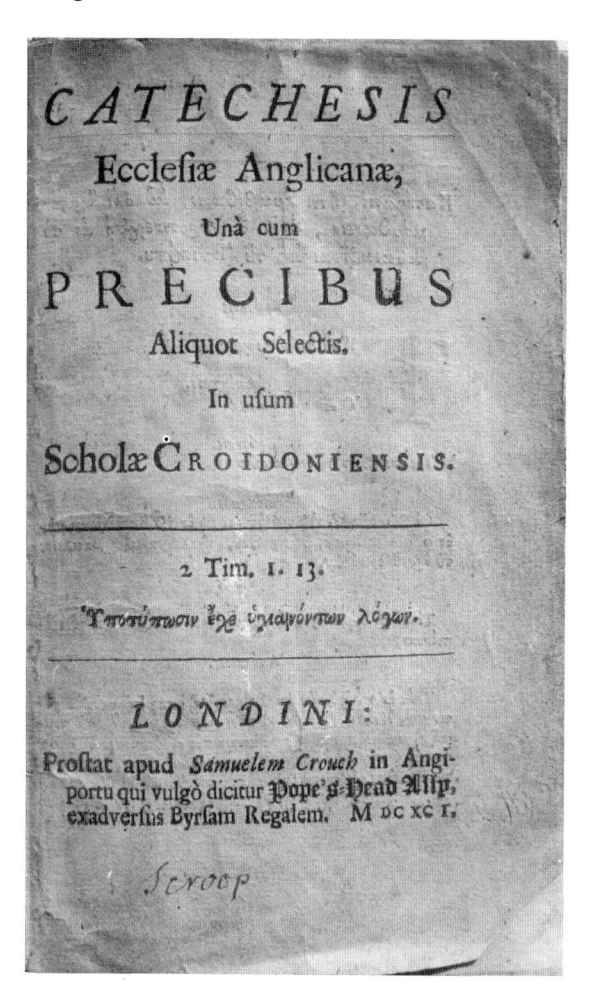

Titlepage of Scroop Egerton's Prayer Book, 1691

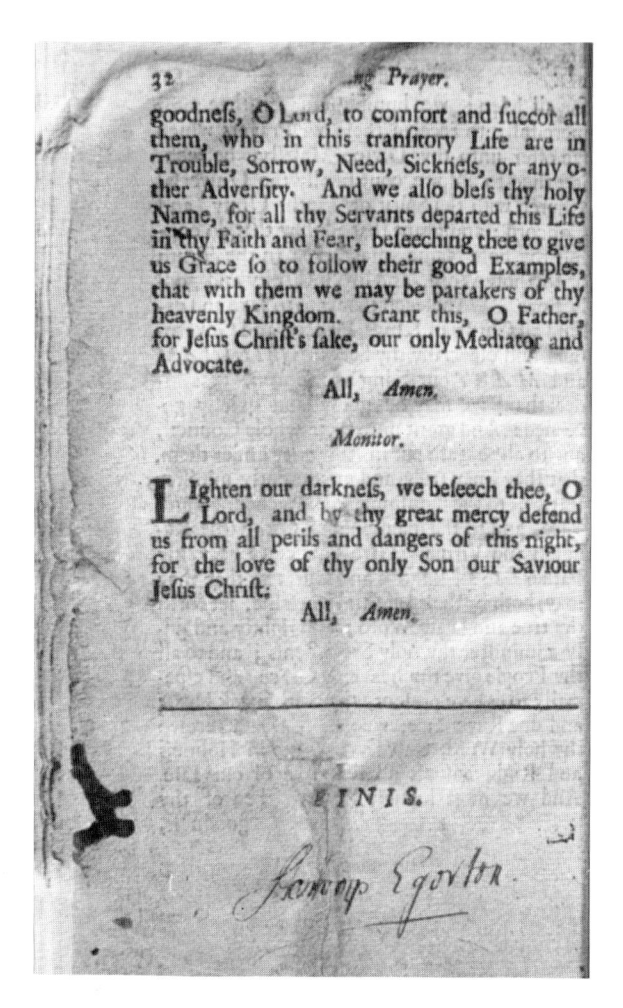

Last page of Scroop Egerton's Prayer Book

appoint a curate to help at the Parish Church and also to act as usher at the School. On the other hand, his new responsibilities involved him in anxieties such as disputes with influential local inhabitants over tithes and vicarage rights, and later with the increasingly powerful dissenting element in the town.

Egerton relics

While he was restoring the buildings, re-establishing the old customs and increasing the Hospital's income, Caesar was at the same time conducting a successful school, for whose use he ordered a prayer-book to be printed in 1691. A copy of this book came to light in 1934 and was bought by Old Whitgiftians for presentation to the School Library. It consists of the Church Catechism in Greek and Latin on opposite pages, followed by Morning and Evening Prayers in Latin and English respectively. Similar prayer-books were not uncommon at the time, and it seems that a standard text existed to which was prefixed a different title-page for whichever school wished to produce a book bearing its own name at the front. In the British Library there are three very similar school catechisms, each produced by a different printer, for Bury St. Edmund's, Ipswich, and Merchant Taylors' Schools in 1673, 1683 and 1697 respectively; these were all schools of very high reputation in the seventeenth century. The interest of the copy belonging to the School is enhanced by its bearing a boy's signature; on the title-page is the name 'Scroop', and on the last page 'Scroop Egerton', the names of Viscount Brackley, the son and heir of the third Earl of Bridgewater (grandson of Thomas Egerton, Keeper of the Great Seal and a fellow-member of the Privy Council with John Whitgift). The book, whose provenance can not now be traced with certainty, was probably sold to a dealer when the Egerton family records were dispersed after the sale of Ashridge, the Bridgewater seat in Hertfordshire, in the 1920s. The great bulk of the papers was bought by the Henry E. Huntington Library, San Marino, California.

Another important survival is one of Scroop's earlier school bills, in the possession of the Duke of Sutherland, a descendant of Scroop through his daughter Louisa.

The Right Honble Lord Brackley.
from Decemb. 13th 89 to June 13 1690

	(£. s. d)
Pockett money	00.05.00
Poll mony	00.01.00
Gram^r & constr. (construing exercises?)	00.01.06
Taylor	00.03.01
Shoemaker	00.04.04
Gloves	00.03.04
Barber	00.03.00
Writing Books, penns, &c	00.03.06
The Smith mend. Cab. (Cabinet?) locks	00.00.06
French Mr	00.10.00
Dancing Mr	01.02.00
Board & Teach	10.00.00
Receiv'd Septemb, 16th 1690 in full this Bill. paid J. Caesar.	12.17.03

Scroop Egerton (1681–1745), Duke of Bridgewater 1720

Comparison with John Dalyson's bills of nearly sixty years before (p. 56) shows that the expenses of schooling for a 'half' have remained fairly constant. Whereas board and tuition have gone up from £8 to £10, the amount of pocket money remains the same at 5s. (One wonders what there was in Croydon to spend the money on: food, no doubt.) A Camden's *Grammar* at 1s. 1d. is replaced by a *Grammar* and another book for 1s. 6d. There is little difference between the shoemakers' and tailors' bills. Egerton had regular haircuts, but Dalyson managed without, unless Mrs. Webb attended to him. Dancing and French have become important extras, illustrating the greater sophistication of the School in Caesar's time; without knowing what lessons Egerton took from each master, we can hardly judge whether one or the other was the better paid, but the entry may possibly support John Oldham's protest of 1678 (p. 67).

Born in August 1681, Scroop Egerton succeeded his father in March 1700/1. Caesar's connection with the Egertons probably originated through his family associations with Hertfordshire, where the Egertons had their seat, Ashridge. By 1707 Caesar had been appointed chaplain to his former pupil, an office that entailed few obligations and may even have provided him with a modest emolument.

Being active in the Whig interest, Scroop was created Marquess of Brackley and Duke of Bridgewater in 1720. This advancement in rank occurred only three months after Caesar's death; his pleasure and pride, had he heard the news, would have been immeasurable.

The only other pupil of the 1690s that has been traced was John Frederick, who was grandson of Sir John Frederick, Lord Mayor of London in 1662, and who was created baronet in 1723.

Whitgift School

A Jamaica connection

As has been explained, it is mainly by chance that names of Old Boys have been discovered, and an interesting find in 1927 by C.G. Paget among the Town Depositions in the Public Record Office revealed the names of several more. On 21 October 1727, Julius Caesar, of Doctors' Commons, London, gentleman, aged 37, was sworn and, in answer to a question regarding the identity of William Pusey, declared:

That this Deponent is natural and lawful son of John Caesar, clerk, late Vicar of Croydon, Surrey, who was schoolmaster of the free school of Croydon aforesaid for 25 years and upwards . . . and this Deponent well remembers William Pusey, Esq., the Complainant, to be a scholar there for five years and upwards, during which time this Deponent was intimately acquainted with him. This Deponent went from the school about nineteen years ago, and believes the Complainant left it about two years before this Deponent, but cannot set forth the exact time. That there was no other scholar of the name of Pusey there at the time. That the said Complainant came from the island of Jamaica because there were several other scholars, viz., Philip Roberts, Arthur Turner, Verney Phelps, Matthias Phelps and Edward Cooke, who all came from Jamaica and were schoolfellows with the said Complainant. . . . This Deponent well remembers that the said Complainant did, when at Croydon School, with the leave of the Deponent's father, the said master thereof, go to London to visit a Relation, and one of the Ushers (whose name was either Wotton or Gratwick, but which of them this Deponent cannot say) waited on the said Complainant to London. And further saith that he, this Deponent, with Arthur Turner, John Parker, Thomas Knaggs and Thomas Daberon and others whose names this Deponent cannot now recollect, were of the same class or form with the said Complainant at Croydon School aforesaid.

William Pusey was endeavouring to establish his right of succession to the family estates at Pusey in Berkshire. He failed, for he could produce no creditable evidence of his line of descent.

Notes on some of the other names given by Julius Caesar are given in Appendix II.

Besides providing a few names (it is a pity that the deponent could not remember more), the document is valuable in showing that the School at this time was sufficiently prosperous and well attended to have at least two ushers on the staff. Charles Gratwick signs as a witness to admonitions in 1700 as 'curate'; he graduated from St. John's College, Cambridge, in 1694, and in 1714 he was appointed Rector of Curry Mallett, Somerset, where he died in 1735. The other usher, Wotton, was one of two brothers, James and William, who graduated from Trinity College, Cambridge, in 1694 and 1698 respectively, but there is no example of his signature in the Ledger Books. Other curates and, by inference, ushers under Caesar were William Hollier, later Rector of Carshalton, John Dacie, later of Crediton, Devon, and John Evans, later Vicar of Ewell. So far, all the evidence points towards this period of Caesar's mastership as one of prosperity, and the School enjoyed a more than local reputation.

Ralph Snow, a benefactor

It was during the time that William Pusey was at the School that another generous benefaction was made to the Foundation. Ralph Snow, Treasurer and Registrar to Archbishop Sancroft when authority was granted to the Hospital to undertake repairs out of Sir Purbeck Temple's fine, died a very old man in 1707, bequeathing £300 to the Hospital of the Holy Trinity, Croydon, £200 to the Hospital of Harbledown, Canterbury, and £200 to the Hospital of St. John's Without, Canterbury. With these sums were bought a number of properties in Mitcham, which were sold in 1926 and the proceeds re-invested by the trustees in freeholds in the centre of Croydon.

Caesar in disgrace

John Caesar had carried out his duties in connection with the administration of the Hospital for close on thirty years before he was detected in a fraud, but on 23 March 1710/11 he signed a statement to the effect that he, 'Clerke, Pryor and Schoolmaster of the Hospital . . . is endebted to the public stock and Chest of the said Hospital to the extent of £184.19.0 for rents and fines received from him and not paid into the said stock', by an account exhibited to Archbishop Tenison, which 'by reason of diverse misfortunes he is not at present able to satisfye'. He agrees, in order to repay the debt, to set aside his annual stipend of £20 and other profits receivable.

Ralph Snow, Benefactor, 1707

It has been charitably suggested by A.F. Leach that Caesar had distributed these sums to the Brethren and Sisters instead of making up the reserve in the Chest contingent upon law suits. This assumption was based on a memorandum attached to the Hospital audit of December 1712:

> That his present Grace the now Lord Archbp of Canterbury hath of his own pious Charity given unto the Poor of this House the Summe of One hundred Pounds which is now locked up in the Chest, and is in lieu of as much money misapplyed by Mr. Caesar the late Schoolmaster which money is at all times to defend Law Suites.

and

> That his present Grace . . . considering the Poverty of the House hath out of his pious Charity paid the Charges of Altering and Fixing the Pump in the Hospll Yard.

Tenison's will, dated 11 April 1715, clearly shows a different picture, however, for, after reciting the provisions of Chapter Sixteen of the Statutes concerning the laying-up of a reserve of £100 in the Common Chest, it states:

> . . . whereas the Sum of One hundred Pounds, so deposited in the Chest . . . was clandestinely taken out . . . and embezzl'd, so that the poor Brethren and Sisters were deprived of their Proportions of Dividend, and thereby reduc'd to great Straits; and whereas I have deposited in the said Chest, the Sum of One hundred Pounds for remedying at present of this great Evil, there to remain until they who embezzl'd the said Sum . . . shall repay it . . .; and whereas I find small Hopes of the Recovery of the . . . sum, I do bequeath unto . . . the said Hospital the said Sum . . . to remain deposited in the said Chest, for the Uses and Ends ordained by . . . the . . . Founder.

The climax of Caesar's sorrows came when he was committed to the Fleet Prison as a debtor, and towards the end of 1711 or early in 1712 he was compelled to resign. His quarterly accounts had always been regularly audited, or at least attested, by a couple of local residents; there is a memorandum in Caesar's hand appended to the audit of 4 December 1692:

> Upon perusal of this account I find by a mistake in the casting there is 8s. 10d more due to the poore, which was this day given to them.

The inference may be drawn that Caesar was habitually neglectful, if not fraudulent, not only in his accounting, but also in his guardianship of the monies he received on behalf of the Members of the Hospital. Upon his appointment Caesar recorded the fines obtained on the renewal of leases, but in time the record of these fines becomes much slighter and then vanishes. While Sancroft was alive, Caesar had been most punctilious in his observance of the Statutes and diligent in his care of the Foundation's interests, but after Sancroft's death in 1691 there was a gradual decline in his concern. Even before Sancroft died, the Members of the Hospital were voicing grievances against Caesar for not following the ordinances in a number of respects, particularly in his method of granting leases, and for keeping the rents in his house instead of in the three-keyed Chest. During the time that Archbishops Tillotson and Tenison continued to place their confidence in him, there is no evidence that they ever investigated the Hospital's affairs as closely as Sancroft had done, until it was too late. Attempts had been made to warn Tenison of Caesar's concealing of rents and fines, but at first corrupt officials kept the informants at bay, and later, when Tenison had heard some of the complaints, he 'refused to believe that a clergyman could be so wicked'.

The reasons for Caesar's defalcations can only be guessed at: as Vicar of Croydon he had been involved in litigation over tithes, which may have drained him of his resources, and his children's education was perhaps a burden at a time when his income had diminished. The Caesar family (whose founder was Sir Julius Adelmare Caesar, Chancellor of the Exchequer, died 1636, great-grandfather of John), had established themselves as gentry in Hertfordshire, but by the fourth generation their wealth had been dissipated. In January 1683/4 John Caesar had occasion to write to Archbishop Sancroft about the desperate straits his father had been put to as a young man. An inherited habit of mismanagement, though not evident in his early years at the School, may have taken over as he grew older and more involved in debt. While he possessed the vigour of youth the School flourished; he enjoyed the confidence, and taught the sons, of the nobility and gentry, but his money troubles suggest a decline in the School's prestige; by the time of his downfall the School had also greatly sunk in reputation. He was rescued from the Fleet by his friends and in spite of his malpractices he kept his vicarage of Croydon until his death in March 1719/20. His case and that of Clewer show how difficult it was for a parish to rid itself of an unprincipled incumbent, who could be removed only by the direct intervention of the monarch, or after an ecclesiastical court, reluctant to give publicity to scandalous conduct on the part of a clergyman, had studied well-authenticated evidence of criminal or grossly immoral actions. During the rest of his life Caesar endured the contempt and distrust of his parishioners, many of whom deserted the Church and increasingly supported the Quakers and other dissenters who flourished in Croydon at this time of disgrace.

4. Henry Mills, 1712–1742

An Ambitious Schoolmaster

In Archbishop Tenison's Register at Lambeth there is a copy of the Licence of Corrody granted on 11 April 1712 to Henry Mills, admitting him a Poor Brother and Schoolmaster. This Licence was followed on 26 June by another, authorising him to teach. In both Licences the School is referred to as 'Publica sive Libera Schola infra Hospitale Sancti Trinitatis apud Croydon', in which terms the original use of the expression 'public school' is illustrated.

Tibi de cujus Fidelitate, Literarum Scientia, Conscientiae Puritate—Religionis Sinceritate et Diligentia in hac parte ... confidimus ... Licentiam et Facultatem nostras ... benigne concedimus et impertimus per praesentes.
(To you of whose Loyalty, Learning, Purity of Conscience—Sincerity in Religion and Diligence in this respect we are assured, ... our Licence and Faculty we graciously grant by these presents.)

Henry Mills was a man of vigorous personality, sanguine temperament and great ambition, accompanied by a willingness to abandon strict veracity and constancy of opinion if his objectives were aided thereby. He came from Wells, Somerset, where he had been educated at the Cathedral Grammar School before going up to Trinity College, Oxford, where he graduated in 1694. Soon afterwards he was given the job of 'settling the library books' at Wells Cathedral, and on 1 October 1696 he was given the complete custody of the Library. He may have combined this office with that of usher at the Cathedral school, for when the schoolmastership there became vacant in September 1699, Henry Mills was given the post. He made a success of the Cathedral school and increased its reputation among the local gentry. He was an enthusiastic producer of plays: in 1706 the boys did 'Hamlet', in 1708 'Julius Caesar', in 1710 'Oedipus', and in December 1711 they 'spoke speeches in Virgil's Aeneids'.

Mills had no intention of spending the rest of his life in Wells; he had had hopes of gaining further ecclesiastical preferment but by 1711, at the age of thirty-seven, he felt he would have to seek it elsewhere, and his success at the school at Wells was enough to inspire this warm testimonial from the Dean and Chapter:

... Mr. Henry Mills, M.A. ... hath by his great Industry and Learning, Prudence, decent Behaviour, Integrity and Example of his unblameable Conversation, rais'd the Reputation of his School far above what former Masters could effect these many years; and that the Children committed to his Charge have eminently improv'd under his Conduct their Genius, their Invention, and their Elocution, to the Honour of their Master, and the Satisfaction of all. And were it possible any thing could bribe us to refuse to recommend, or to do him right, it could be only our Unwillingness to part with him. In Witness thereof, we have hereunto set our Hands this 11th Day of June 1711....

With such an enthusiastic recommendation in his hands (the phraseology of which is remarkably similar to his own style of composition), Mills had hopes that his ambitions might be realised, through his appointment to some more prominent school, possibly near London. In January 1711/12 he was offered the Mastership of Highgate School, then at rather a low ebb, but before the actual election was held he had accepted a better offer at Croydon, and notified the Highgate Governors accordingly. Although the Highgate Schoolmaster's stipend was the

Whitgift School

greater, he was not to be allowed to take in paying pupils there; at Croydon they were to provide him with his main income. (It is significant that after Mills's refusal the Highgate Governors allowed the new Schoolmaster to take in not more than 15 boarders.)

Keeping the news of his appointment to himself for a while, Mills returned to Wells in order to persuade the parents of some of his pupils to allow them to continue under his tuition when he took up his new post, which he did in March, some weeks before Tenison granted him his formal licence to teach. One can imagine that Mills did not fail to stress the importance of a school so much under the especial notice of the Archbishop of Canterbury who, he hoped, could not but be impressed with his merits. In Croydon he expected to make influential friends and be provided with the opportunity of rising quickly up the ladder of academic or ecclesiastical fortune, a course that at Wells had persisted in eluding him. How this obscure provincial schoolmaster came to the Archbishop's notice is unknown, but it was possibly through the influence of George Hooper, Bishop of Bath and Wells. Mills was never reluctant to thrust himself forward, and Tenison for his part was satisfied that he had chosen a man of experience and proved ability. The Minutes of the Dean and Chapter of Wells, dated 1 April 1712, state:

Whereas Mr. Mills late master of the grammar school in Wells belonging to the Dean & Chapter hath left the same and no one to take care of it, that the said school is now actually void by the said Mr. Mills his disreliction of it and takeing to another school at Croydon in Surrey. . . .

The impression conveyed is that Mills left the school at Wells in the lurch, but the Dean and Chapter could not have been unaware that Mills wished to leave, for they had signed his testimonial ten months previously. However, his successor, Robert Creyghton, was appointed on 2 April, so the school, or what was left of it, did not remain long without instruction.

Mills's Difficulties

When he arrived at Croydon, Mills found that the School was virtually extinct and that the Hospital was seething with discontent and suspicion of authority; the inmates regarded the new Schoolmaster also with cynicism and mistrust. Immediately upon his arrival he had to admonish two of the brethren, Francis Comber and Edward Wilmot, for sowing discord, and a few months later they had to be admonished again. Wilmot had finally to go, for on 26 April 1714 he received his third admonition, as is recorded in the Ledger Book:

Edward Wilmot had his 3rd & last Admonition given him & is expell'd the House according to the Statutes for being a Common Swearer, A Drunkard, A Brawler, A contentious Person, A Sower of Discord, of Wch he was convicted by 3 credible witnesses.
Hen Mills Scholemaster
John Blake Warden

Hen Zealey
X Thos Mainard

This atmosphere of suspicion remained for many years, during which Mills was constantly at loggerheads with the Brethren and Sisters, who were supported in their enmity by some of the local residents, more especially the Dissenters and Whigs. One cannot help feeling that they had a good deal of justification for their discontent. Nevertheless, Mills was determined to make a success of his new school, which he would have to revive after its decline during Caesar's later years. Certainly he established an initial success, as this letter shows:

London, Nov 8th 1712.
. . . My nephew Smyth has bin soe oblidging to write me the pritiest letter that ever I saw he and the little Capt were both very well. Master tells me he has sence I saw him learnt all the notes and understands them very well and is very desireous to learne on the spinett he sayes he grew weary of it att Wells because he did not learn by booke but there is a Master att Croydon he writes me word that teaches very well. Mr Milles is very musickall and has a consort once a weeke and severall Masters goes thither often from London. I doe think musick a very pretty devertion for younge Gentillmen att their Leasure hours and the spinette is now as must [sic] Learnt on by younge Gentillmen of Quallities as Ladyes. I writ my Nephew word I would acquainte your Ladyship that he had a desire to Learne. he likes Miss Astryes playing very much and I believe that makes him have an inclination for it; Soe if your Ladyship does aprove of it I will endeavour to find out a good bargain of a spinett for him, indeed he

dose now by what I can find take delight in every thing that is Genteell, and I dont doubt but he will make as fine a Gentleman as any in England he is very ingenious and will be a very fine Scholar his master sayes and I doe thinke the schoole he is att much better than Eaton is now for I doe here of a great many wild sparkes that are now there. . . .*

* This letter, from the Smyth Papers in the City of Bristol Archives, was written by Mrs. Elizabeth Gernon to her sister-in-law, Lady Smyth, née Astry, wife of Sir John Smyth, Bart., of Long Ashton Court, near Bristol. 'Miss Astry' was a younger sister of Lady Smyth; 'my nephew Smyth' was John Smyth, then aged thirteen, eldest son and heir of Sir John; 'the little Capt' was his brother Hugh, then aged only six.

Verses on the Peace

Mills had brought several of his old scholars from Wells, where they had been boarding with him, and he quickly secured a number of boys from the families of the Croydon gentry and elsewhere, who were impressed with his record, his plain intention to raise the standard of the School, and the confidence that the parents in the West Country reposed in him. On 13 May 1713, in order to celebrate the Treaty of Utrecht, signed a month before, that ended the War of the Spanish Succession, he arranged for several of his boys to recite their own verses to an invited audience, and these he

[1]

THYRSIS and CORYDON, TWO SHEPHERDS.

THYRSIS.

WHY now so Blith, fond Shepherd, why so Gay?
In joyful Songs you pass the Time away.
I pitying oft, have heard you here complain
Of *coy Amynta*, and her proud Disdain.
Whence is this happy Change? You've now no Care,
No Signs of Grief, I see, or sad Despair:
The Spring's Approach sure cheers your gladsome Mind,
When all Things sport, and every Mate is kind.
The grassy Fields with smiling Verdure please,
And early Bloom adorn the budding Trees,
Vigour and Warmth have driven your Grief away;
Delights and Rural Songs take up the Day.

Cory. *Thyrsis*, 'tis not alone the Joyfull Spring
That gives me Hopes, that makes me smile and sing.
I never shall *Amynta's* Coyness mind,
Nor dread her proud Disdain, if *Cloe's* kind.
Who will not now put on a chearful Face?
For Spring is come——the Spring that bringeth Peace.
No more rude Forragers, with fearful Haste,
Shall break down Hedges, nor the Country waste;
Nor rob th' unwilling Folds, or tear the Lambs
From pensive Shepherds, and from bleating Dams.
Now in the Earth the fruitful Seeds are sown,
And Peasants call the next Year's Crop their own.

Thyr. We in a Doubt indulg'd the pleasing Thought;
At last, the Joyful News *Menaltas* brought.
Then tune your Rural Pipes, and bless that Pow'r
That cou'd such Joys bestow, in such an Hour.
Come, praise the Goddess who Protects the Plains;
Shepherds may safely sing, while *ANNA* Reigns.

WIL. DRAPER.
THO. GAY.

Thrice

VERSES
ON THE
PEACE;
BY THE
SCHOLARS of *Croyden* School, *Surry.*

Spoken in Publick *May* 13, 1713.

——*Inest sua Gratia Parvis.*

LONDON:
Printed for *A. Baldwin*, at the *Oxford Arms* in *Warwick-Lane.* MDCCXIII.

Titlepage of *Verses on the Peace*

Page 1 of *Verses on the Peace*

Sir John Smyth, Bt. (1699–1741)

published in a quarto pamphlet of twelve pages, nine of which formed the text and contained eleven poems in English, six in Latin, and a couple of Greek verses. Though of slight merit—the English poems are trite and conventional, and the other verses empty and laboured—that a handful of boys should be able to produce such work at all is a tribute to Mills's teaching and enthusiasm, or perhaps to his own polishing of their ingenuous efforts; yet they do at least reveal more poetic skill and depth of thought than the work of Oldham's pupils over thirty years before.

But it is not so much their literary interest that is of importance to us as the attribution of each set of verses to an author; we are thereby supplied with another short school list of fifteen names, many of which have been identified with their owners. These names are: William Andrews, Richard Bagg, William Bush, Thomas Bushel, William Draper, Thomas Gay, William Glynn, Randolph Greenway, Edward Biss Hale, Matthew Hale, John Heathfield, Edward King, John Smyth, Thomas Tenison and William Wigan. Appendix II gives some account of what has been discovered about these schoolboy poets. With the exception of Andrews, it seems, none of them embarked upon a literary career. It is here sufficient to say that Andrews, Bagg, Bushel, the two Hales and Smyth all came from the West Country with Mills, that Heathfield, Bush and Draper (grandson of John Evelyn, the diarist, and son of the owner of Addiscombe Place that had been inherited from Sir Purbeck Temple) were local boys, and that the remainder were probably boarders, the sons of London or county families; they were between thirteen and sixteen years of age.

Some measure of their friendship may be judged from the correspondence that at least four of them conducted among themselves after they left school. Letters between William Andrews, William Draper, Thomas Gay and John Smyth, often giving news of others, have survived and are preserved at the British Library (Liverpool Papers) and at the Bristol Record Office (Smyth Papers).

Mills's Ambition

Mills's ambition was at this time a driving force. He hoped his High Church Tory views would assure him some tangible results from the store of patronage at the disposal of the Ministers of the new Tory Government of 1710. The Whigs had supported the War of the Spanish Succession; by praising its conclusion through the Peace of Utrecht, Mills hoped not only to enhance the reputation of his School, but also to attract to himself the favourable attention of influential Tories.

With this publication also to advertise his skill and success as a teacher—and we may be sure that the collection found its way into the hands of many who might be impressed by it—Mills felt himself to be a strong candidate for the High Mastership of St. Paul's School, which fell vacant in the same year. On 10 October 1713 the Court of Assistants of the Mercers' Company that met to choose a successor to John Postlethwayte considered the qualifications of five 'divers candidates, Persons of known Abilitys now attending for the obtaining this place'. Three of them appear to have had no previous experience of teaching in a school, and

Philip Ayscough, then aged fifty-six, who was not present at the election owing to illness, but who had already spent twenty-eight years at St. Paul's as Surmaster, was elected. That Mills managed to get 'short-listed' speaks well for his own reputation and for that of the School, for St. Paul's, although not then at the very height of its fame, was one of the most celebrated London schools.

Whereas we know little otherwise about Mills's pupils, events during the next four or five years were to shed only too much light upon the School's affairs.

He had brought with him a wife and a young daughter. Not long after they arrived his daughter caught smallpox, from which she recovered, but his wife then caught the disease and died. Mills thought he would lose boarders now that there was no one to act as matron to them; in fact the Smyth boys were removed on that account, although he had expressed his intention 'to have a wife as soone as he can gett a good one', to quote Mrs. Gernon again. In April 1714 he remarried, his second wife bringing with her a marriage portion of three thousand pounds, so he was subsequently in a more comfortable position than hitherto, and able to invest in property in Croydon. He built a house on Hospital land adjacent to the Schoolmaster's house, and it seems likely that this was used for boarders' accommodation under an usher.

The house that Mills built c. 1720, showing the Schoolmaster's House on the left. Photo c. 1866

Archbishop Tenison's School

When Mills first came to Croydon, Archbishop Tenison regarded him as a far more reliable churchman than the vicar. The established Church in Croydon under the openly discredited Caesar was boycotted by his parishioners—certainly whenever he was conducting a service, although his curates enjoyed some popularity until he drove them out—so the Dissenters took advantage of this situation to increase their own congregations and to set up a school where the parish children could learn to read and write and be introduced to dissenting beliefs, which were all the more readily accepted by the parents as well, for the example of rectitude afforded by the dissenting ministers was in great contrast to that displayed by Caesar. This disturbing state of affairs prompted the Archbishop, who had already founded schools in Westminster and Lambeth, to establish a Charity School in Croydon. For the inspiration of this action Mills gave himself much of the credit.

In April 1714 Tenison conveyed a messuage at the North End of Croydon (in which his school was housed) and seventy-four acres of land at Limpsfield to found and endow a perpetual charity school for ten poor boys and ten poor girls of Croydon, Henry Mills being one of the original trustees. There was now a strong movement, initiated by the Society for Promoting Christian Knowledge, to establish charity schools all over the country, often by public subscription; such schools, intended mainly to encourage Bible-reading, were open to children of both sexes, which the grammar schools never were. Archbishop Tenison's School, providing the type of education then much in demand by 'the poorer sorte' of Croydon, remained successful at a time when Whitgift's School, in common with most other grammar schools, declined.*

Mills's Politics

National politics were also harassing the Church. Queen Anne had drawn away from her

---

* In 1955 Tenison's School, which had become a 'National School' attached to St. Peter's Church at South Croydon, was upgraded to the status of a grammar school and in 1959 was provided with new buildings on its third different site. Since 1978 it has been a comprehensive school.

Whig friends the Churchills; Tenison, no favourite at her Court, was of Tory inclinations and very anti-papist. Yet Anne wanted her half-brother, the Pretender James Stewart, to succeed her and hoped for the support of the Tories to that end. They failed her, however, and on her death the accession of the Hanoverian George I ushered in a period of Whig supremacy, under which latitudinarian views spread within the Church. Caesar, as we have seen, was a Whig; Mills held High Church Tory views, which were not only opposed to the Dissenters, but were now also repugnant to Tenison in his necessary support for the new King. Mills had the temerity to express his opinions in the hearing of some who were ready to report any indiscretion of his; his views on the legitimacy of the succession and an ill-considered remark that he would 'as soon be a papist as a presbyterian' were promptly retailed to Tenison, who towards the end of his life had become very tetchy and suspicious; he suffered acutely from gout, and his last illness kept him confined for many months to Lambeth Palace, where he listened to rumours, read anonymous letters and came to the conclusion that Mills was a strong Jacobite, a papist and a cheat. Several incidents involving Mills had given some justification for his distrust. There was the case of the unauthorised felling of the Hospital's timber, and of its disposal for cash that was somehow not all accounted for; an usher had preached a seditious sermon in the Parish Church; the ill-feeling among the Brethren and Sisters, understandable in Caesar's time, seemed undiminished; and then there was the unpleasant disturbance that took place in Croydon on Christmas Day 1714, when a number of Dissenters' children had made a mockery of the festival by dressing up 'in Merry Andrew fashion', riding an ass in the streets and 'abusing the people going to Church'. On Tenison's instructions Mills investigated, and reported in strong terms, but the Dissenters so vigorously defended themselves that Tenison was satisfied that there had been no blasphemous intent, and the excitement died down. But Mills's reputation and popularity in Croydon had suffered a blow. He wrote:

Dayly Abuses are put upon me for enquiring into the Profanation of Christmas Day.... When first the Archbp mentioned it to me his Grace express'd all the just & requisite severity that became the Head of our Church, & resolv'd to prosecute for Blasphemy. But this unhappy use is made of his Grace's Sickness that the insolent Offenders lift up their daring Head; & think that the Cause of the Church is gone....

There is reference to the publication of a book about this incident, but it remains untraced.

Having reduced Caesar to impotence, the Dissenters had now gleefully accepted Mills's challenge, ridiculing him with such lampoons as:

Some Mills there are, that by their rattling Noise
Do startle Asses, frighten tim'rous Boys.

Although he thought that 'All are so foolish & weak that they are not worth my notice', he was greatly concerned for his character with Tenison, whom he had at first regarded as a possible, sympathetic patron.

Tenison's Concern

Mills's anxiety was in no way relieved when he received a peremptory note from Tenison early in October 1715:

I would desire to know, who was your last French Usher, and whither he is gone, and why, and who is your present French Usher, and whether he is in Holy Orders. Pray do this with Speed; you shall know my Reasons afterwards.

To this Mills replied:

My last French Usher was Emanuel Decize. He is now in London, contrary to what he said; for at Whitsuntide he assur'd me that he was going away very soon to travel with a Gentleman on advantageous terms.

My present teacher of French came into England with the King; his name is Pillonnière & in Holy Orders.

I know little of him, only that he is exact in the pronunciation and lives very soberly. I shall be very thankful to know for what reasons, this enquiry is made....

Tenison's enquiry was prompted by his hearing that Pillonnière, an apostate Jesuit, was in reality still an adherent of the Roman Church, and that Mills was presumably a sympathiser. Tenison had the matter investigated and, by some accounts, was satisfied that Pillonnière's renunciation was genuine, but he remained suspicious that Mills was a Jacobite at the time of the uprising of 1715. When Tenison died in December that year, Mills was therefore much relieved to think that he would be free from the old Archbishop's penetrating enquiries, and he immediately set out to cultivate the favour of the new—William Wake. It was three weeks before he obtained an interview, but thereafter he was a regular attender at Lambeth Palace, rather more regular than the mere business of the Hospital would require. Wake, whose chief interests seem, from his diary, to have been his own ingratiation with the Royal Family and a concern for the function of his digestive system, was unwilling to get involved in local troubles, and allowed Mills greater freedom to conduct affairs at Croydon on his own responsibility.

Mills's peace was short-lived, however. The Dissenters had got their knives firmly into him since his condemnation of them after Christmas Day 1714, but, in addition, the trouble aroused by Pillonnière's presence in his household broke out in another place.

Pillonnière, the French Usher

The Schoolmaster and his French ushers never saw entirely eye to eye; at a time when religious differences were a major topic of interest, with minor points warmly debated, and loyalties and enmities largely based on sectarian prejudices, Croydon provided an example of a general disposition. That Pillonnière and Mills did not part company earlier was due to Pillonnière's difficulty in obtaining another job, and Mills's in finding a replacement for him. One of the attractions of the School was the modernity of its curriculum; while the Classics remained the basis of instruction, such refinements as French taught by a native (and this was regarded as the only effective method), for which extra would be charged, put the School on a par with the better type of private establishments that were beginning to attract the notice of gentlemen requiring something more than just Greek and Latin for their sons' education. Pillonnière stayed with Mills for another six months after Tenison's investigation. They then parted, later to accuse each other of dishonesty and unworthy behaviour, with Mills claiming to have dismissed Pillonnière, and Pillonnière claiming to have resigned in disgust.

Despite Tenison's death and Pillonnière's departure, what might have collapsed as a trifling local dispute became inflated into a controversy of almost national interest, comparable with a popular newspaper scandal of the present day.

Benjamin Hoadly, Rector of Streatham and absentee Bishop of Bangor, preached on 31 March 1717 a sermon based on the text 'My Kingdom is not of this world', in which he challenged the authority of the Church in matters of conscience and stated that sincerity was the chief part of true religion. This view met with heated attacks from the High Church party, and several pamphlets were published in refutation. Among the writers of these rejoinders was Dr. Andrew Snape, Head Master of Eton who, in condemning Hoadly's assertions, accused him of harbouring a Jesuit, namely Pillonnière, in his household, where he had taken a post as tutor in Latin, French and mathematics since leaving Croydon. It was Pillonnière who chiefly resented this attack, answering Snape's accusation with a dignified denial in a pamphlet published in August. So far Mills had not been involved, although Hoadly had suggested that he could clear up any doubts as to Pillonnière's sincerity. But Snape returned to the fray a couple of months later with a *Vindication* that included a most unwise account from Mills of his personal relationships with the usher, in which he particularly criticised the latter's attitude to the Church:

Mr Pillonnière, during his Stay here, was constantly disparaging the Articles of the Church of England, not only to me and my Wife, but to the young Gentlemen. . . .

I sent three Messages for him, on a Sunday morning, to come to Church; he at last came with Reluctance, and said, Had he known he must have undergone the Slavery of frequenting the Church, he would never have made an agreement with me.

His Behaviour during the Time of Divine Service was suitable to his Talk; for he either gaz'd about, or read some Pamphlet, but join'd not in the Publick Service.

The Bangorian Controversy

Misjudging both his adversary and the trend of the times, which was fast moving away from the fanatic zeal of 'High Church', Mills seemed now determined to associate himself with Snape and the losing side. From this point the great 'Bangorian Controversy' became a medium for personal abuse, accusation and counter-accusation, involving letters and certificates from all kinds of unreliable sources in support or denunciation of the disputants, now Mills and Pillonnière. Snape and Hoadly were almost forgotten. Attempts were made to pay off old scores; De Cize and Jean Rouire, Mills's new French usher, a moral coward singularly incapable of either telling the truth or adhering to a lie among a crowd of perjurers prepared to twist meanings in any direction that suited them, were deeply involved; the Brethren and Sisters of the Hospital were only too eager to revile Mills; the Croydon dissenters were delighted to deride him in the full publicity of the London news-sheets and in fourpenny pamphlets. He attempted to defend himself with the support of certificates of character irrelevantly supplied by Croydon tradesmen and his own parishioners in Somerset, and by attacks on Pillonnière from anonymous pupils.

The result was that Mills's conduct of his School was mercilessly laid bare. Much of the criticism is distorted or exaggerated, and Mills had to fight single-handed against adversaries determined to overlook no opportunity to discredit by fair means or foul a man whose chief offence had been to establish a successful Tory-supported school in Croydon. Many of the attacks on him make amusing reading, and there is more than an element of truth in some, even if there is much invention in others. Some idea of the way the School was run can be derived from these few examples taken from the thousands of words of vituperation printed in 1717 and 1718.

It was in his *Reply to Dr. Snape's Vindication*, published in February 1717/8, that Pillonnière gave rein to his bitterness and spite towards Mills:

I trusted Mr. Mills so much that I made no agreement with him in writing. This occasioned some dispute on his part about money matters at the end of the first quarter, so that we agreed to write down our terms. But in order to have me cheap amongst other things he told me that it was very hard that he should give me thirty pounds for an hour and a half of my time every day, whilst he allowed to the Rev. Mr. Jones, his Latin Usher, but twelve; tho' besides his spending four hours every day in the School he was obliged to say prayers twice a day every other week and to preach alternis with him three miles off, every other Sunday all the year round.

This seemed to me not only strange, but wholly incredible; and I went immediately to Mr. Jones to know the truth of the matter. He smiled and told me that Mr. Mills indeed gave him but twelve Pounds out of his pocket, but allowed him besides Eighteen Pounds from his Vicarage. Mr. Jones (who was not an enemy to Mr. Mills) added that Mr. Mills had said the reverse to serve another turn; and told one of the children's mother who had a mind to make him a present that there was no manner of need of it because he allowed Mr. Jones Fifty Pounds. . . .

At my coming hither, I was very much surprised to find a nest of young men almost all railing continually against King George, of whom one of the biggest of them when I reproved him once said 'that he was no more to him than a footman' . . . and using the most indecent language against Dissenters and even insulting their Meeting House. I confess, I thought it my duty to endeavour to assuage these animosities . . . and for that only reason I went at first under the name of a Presbyterian. . . .

After such accusations of hypocrisy, Pillonnière turns to more precise description of Mills's treatment of the boys; it must be remembered that violence and brutality in schools were only too common in those days.

One might wonder at the influence such a Master can have over his Scholars, if one did not know how he dispenses Favours to some and his Cruelties to others, in the most arbitrary manner. I myself have seen with great Heart-ake, the little ones boxed, pinched beat and kicked unmercifully and generally for Trifles. I was once by when he kicked a very good natured Boy all along the Room two or three times, before all the Scholars, only for having said, that he had smelt something amiss in this Room; and I heard the poor boy crying under the Kicks (which I also heard) and saying. Sir, If I have committed some fault, are there not more proper ways of punishing me? Mrs. Taylor, a worthy gentlewoman at Croydon who was formerly Mr. Mills friend and got him two Scholars, keeps constantly about her two Teeth, which Mr. Mills beat out of her son's mouth at one Blow, after having made his Nose bleed several times. The Mother took away her son who was of the soberest and most diligent of all and of a very bashful temper and put him under the care of Mr. Perronet of Queen's College, Oxford, who was then Tutor to a young Gentleman that went as a day Scholar to Mr. Mills School. . . .

Mills's retort took the form of *A Full Answer to Mr. Pillonniere's Reply to Dr. Snape.* Although most of his book consists of certificates and statements in his own support or by way of attack upon his detractors, he does give some attention to his methods of teaching; he defends his conduct of his school ('I should think it very honourable for a person... to rejoice that a School sunk in its reputation, nay quite gone, was risen again... and become a flourishing one') and stresses the importance of training up young people to understand their religion as well as languages. Religious instruction was of course laid down in Mills's licence to teach and was part of the ordinary curriculum in grammar schools everywhere.

> This I carefully undertake Twice every Week. The Bible, the Duty of Man are constantly read.... 'Tis and ever was my Practice, not only to teach the Words, but some plain and practical Exposition of our Church Catechism. Thus far I go with the whole School, forming and fashioning young Minds with the first plain, substantial Rudiments of Religion. But besides and after this, I do indeed, to those more advanced in years, and just going abroad into this World of Danger, teach the 39 Articles; but these are read and explained to the Seniors only.

Of Pillonnière's accusation of cruelty, Mills gives a rather feeble denial:

> As for my partiality in the School, 'tis of the same Nature with the rest; He gives an Instance of a Blow given to a Lad, the Consequence of which was hurtful. But 'tis known, that this also is as false, as 'twas designed to be injurious. The Persons then present will attest and have already given it under their Hands, that what he relates, is not true. But these and all other Objections against my Conduct, can be abundantly disprov'd by a great Number of Gentlemen gone abroad into the World, who treat me, wherever I afterwards see them, with the same Kindness and Affection, I had formerly treated them. Two flourishing Schools rais'd by me, the first from a small one, this from none at all, are a full Confutation of any Mismanagement.

Mills on the Rack

The most damaging attacks on Mills, which came from his old enemies the Dissenters, were gathered in *A Vindication of Joseph Warder, Physician at Croydon, and of Charles Bowen, Master of the Charity-School at Beddington.* Warder had gained some celebrity as the author of an early study on the habits of bees, and possessed an original mind and a racy style of writing.

Upon Mills's arrival in Croydon, Warder, so he claimed, had received him in a friendly manner and had treated his family professionally, but he had become disillusioned with Mills, and he gives an often ludicrous account of the latter's less creditable adventures in the town. Of all the outpourings in the controversy, his are the most amusing and the least bombastic; eschewing Mills's habitual orotundity, and substituting a felicity of phrase and an absurdity of illustration, he must have made Mills writhe with fury.

Titlepage of Henry Mills's *Full Answer*, 1718

Not long after we were acquainted, he told me he was unwilling to forget his preaching; and often wish'd he had some small Town within Three or Four Miles of Croydon, where he might go himself, and send his Usher to preach; by which means he design'd to save (as he hath done since) above half of his Usher's Salary.

Warder claimed that he succeeded, although a Dissenter, in obtaining him such a place at Mitcham. He also tried to get boarders for him but tried no more when he found that Mills was not loyal to the Government. It was Warder who cured Mills's daughter of smallpox, but he could not attend the mother, because she was sent away.

At his first coming to live amongst us, he told many of us, and myself in particular, that he had left £400 per annum at Wells; which we have known since to be false; and very lately, that he had Sixty Noblemen's Sons at his School there; which every Body knows to be impossible.

In order to raise the Credit of his School, which was filled every day with Fiddlers, who gather'd the Mob, and occasioned great Disturbance, about his House, as late as Ten or Twelve a clock at Night, till the late Archbishop, as I am told, reprimanded him for it, he took a fancy to have a play of his own Composure acted by his Scholars; the bright part of which was a Burial, perform'd by one of them in the Habit of a Parson, and Mr. M's own Gown on.

This play may have been 'Hamlet'; we know that Mills's boys at Wells performed it, and Warder, as a Dissenter, would be profoundly ignorant and contemptuous of the drama; his views on music are a contrast with those of the 'genteel' Mrs Gernon.

He told one of them at first, that he had a Mind to be generous, and to do the whole at his own Expence. Nevertheless he thought it adviseable afterwards to receive the Free-Gifts of the Spectators, and appointed one of the most fashionable Boys for that Purpose; and among the several Injunctions he gave to all of them behind the Scene, he gave strict Commands to him, 'above all things to mind the Plate'. But as he was conscious that this look'd a little untoward, he took care to say aloud in the Pit, 'The Boy is mad, what does he mean?' When the Play was over, Mr. M. feeling that this Begging did not quite answer his Expectation, and that it was not sufficient to make up the Charge, declared it to the Players, that they must pay so much a piece towards it.

The Tutor of that young Gentleman, who hath repeated very often to several the merry Story, Told Mr. M. that the Parents of his Pupil would be very unwilling to pay after they had been told that he expected nothing. This did not hinder Mr. M. from threatening the Boy into Payment; and as he said that he had no money, Mr. M. told him, 'Have you no Books, you Blockhead, that you can sell? Go presently and see.' The young Gentleman went accordingly; and his Tutor found him actually searching among all his Books, which he could best spare, to satisfy Mr. M.

So far, it is possible to construe everything that Warder has to say as exaggeration or misrepresentation. In most school anecdotes, a basis of truth can support a whole edifice of distortion.

Mr. Monday, who was some years ago Curate here, the same whose stupid look hath been mistaken by some for Drunkenness (tho' I must be so just to him to say, that he can drink many Full-Pots of the strongest Beer, without being in the least affected by it) and was Mr. Mills's 'fellow-Labourer', not only in the Business of the Ass, but in many others, in which the Good of the Church was concern'd; Mr. Monday, I say, happen'd to be turn'd out by Mr. Caesar, upon account of his Disaffection to the Government. Mr. Mills, in order to ingratiate himself to the Tutor of one of his Scholars, spoke to him thus about the Misfortune of his good Friend Mr. Monday: 'Indeed', said Mr. Mills, 'he is a dark hidden Fellow: he hath not taken the Oath to the King.' The next Day, another Gentleman happen'd to ask Mr. Mills, whether the common Report of the Town, viz., that Mr. Monday had not taken the Oath, was true? 'How can it be?' answered Mr. Mills, 'I have seen his Certificates.' 'How then,' reply'd the Gentleman, 'could you tell yesterday such a one, that he was a dark hidden Fellow?'

With such anecdotes the authors built up their case against Mills's veracity.

Swearing is another Perfection of this great Ornament. . . . A Man told me lately that he heard Mr. M.'s Man say, that he knew but none that would outswear his Master. He threaten'd once one of his Scholars in this Manner: 'I wish this Right-Hand of mine may rot off, if I don't whip you to Morrow Morning'; tho' he took afterwards no manner of Notice of him. And this is known to be his common Way of speaking to his Children, when he makes their Noses bleed, and their Limbs black, and beats Teeth out of their Heads.

His Tenderness . . . I cannot forbear mentioning one remarkable Instance of it; at which his very

Scholars were very much offended. An old Clergyman, who preach'd at Croyden-Church two Sermons one Sunday, which inclin'd everyone to think him a good Man, went the next Day, in a short grey Coat, and all in Rags, to beg at Croyden-School, and apply'd to Mr. Pillonnière who gave him Half-a-Crown, invited the Scholars to raise some Money for him among themselves, (which very willingly they did) and carry'd him to Mr. Mills, of whom he ask'd only some old Shirts, and an old Gown. Mr. Mills star'd upon him, and having view'd him from Head to Foot, told him: 'It seems,' said he in so many Words, 'as if you had been hir'd by the Atheists, to ridicule the Order', and added, that he must be an idle drunken Fellow; and sent him away, without giving him any Thing. This Mr. Mills's Scholars were very much offended at; and some of them made Sport with Mr. Mills's Romantick and Uncharitable Speech.

These tendentious passages are unconvincing; they both reply upon hearsay, and Mills would have known quite enough about vagrants, preaching or others.

His Diet.... The Children have been often heard at the Door, complaining that they were allowed but one Draught of Small-Beer to their Supper; which generally was a Piece of Bread and Cheese; and reckoning that, at least three times a Week, the Supper for the whole School could hardly amount to a Shilling.

Without knowing how many boys were boarding at the School, we cannot say if the shilling would have sufficed, but was there ever a time when boys were satisfied with School fare?

His overselling Books to his Scholars.... One of them, whose Name I forbear to mention, was one Day very inquisitive about the common Price of 'Boyer's French Grammar', which is two Shillings. And being asked why he was so? he answered, 'Because Mr. Mills hath made my Mother pay three for this, tho' it is a second hand Book.' I must also observe, that those second hand Books have proved sometimes to be such as had been missed by some of the Scholars, some of whom have sometimes charg'd Mr. Mills with having sold their own Books twice to themselves.

His Pride and sottish Vanity.... I have been often told that Mr. M. said, He was not inferiour to many Bishops; and that he might have been a Bishop but refused it, because there was too much Trouble in it. He hath told a worthy Gentleman, who had repeated it here very often in Company, that there was once a Report that he had been nominated to a Bishoprick, and that he received congratulatory Letters from all Parts on that Account. He also ask'd the Advice of a considerable Lady, what he should do, in case the late Queen, who, he said, had sent for him, should offer him some great Preferment, and whether he should accept of it.

It would be endless to go on telling all his Stories which have been the great and daily Entertainment of this Town, almost ever since it hath been bless'd with Mr. Mills.

There was no easy redress in those days against defamation of character.

The second half of Warder's book is taken up by letters and certificates from several other people who were at enmity with Mills, including a number of the inmates of the Hospital, who were only too happy to rake up old grievances.

The Appellations of Rogues, Whores, Villains &c are the common Treatment we meet with from him; and he told us a little while ago, that, if we concerned ourselves with him, (we suppose he meant in this Affair) he would have us all (poor Objects, some Eighty Years of Age, and would make but poor Spectacles) whipt at the Cart's Arse, if it cost him a Hundred Pounds.

If we make every allowance for misapprehension, the distortions of hearsay, prejudice, spite, and the desire for revenge, Warder's denunciation of Mills does in the end leave us with the impression of a disappointed and intolerant man with a 'Romantick' or imaginative ambition, whose impetuous and choleric nature set him at odds with everyone with whom he disagreed. Dressed in a little brief authority, he tended to be impatient and scornful of his inferiors, and jealous of others whose lack of talent was no impediment to their superiority over him—faults that are not altogether uncommon in our own day.

Mills did not venture a reply to the attacks from Warder and his circle, no doubt regretting that he had already written so much, but Pillonnière had by no means exhausted himself and in June the same year (1718) he published *A Third Defense*, consisting chiefly of denials and accusations, and elaborations of his previous attacks on Mills. But there is little that is worth quoting. Everything that Mills did was turned to his discredit. We have already seen his pleasure in music treated with contempt by

Warder, and this technique is repeated by Pillonnière:

> Mr. Mills diverted [the stories against him] from his thoughts by the Comforts he otherwise enjoy'd in his Family, his School, his Study or with some Instrument of Musick.... What Comforts he enjoyed in his School, in which he was very far from being 'daily resident' [*as Mills had averred*]. I never did perceive.... As to his Study, I can solemnly affirm, that I never say him with a Book in his Hand, except now and then by Chance, for half a quarter of an Hour, or so, all the time I was with him.... As to his Musick, I must wonder indeed if he could find any Comfort in it.

Mills Finds Support

When *A Third Defense* was published, the controversy, even that part of it that held aloof from the squabble between Mills and Pillonnière, was already on the wane. Archbishop Wake had avoided involvement; he deplored this undignified brawling between churchmen, which could only serve to bring the Church into further disrepute, but in one way at least he was sympathetic to Mills. Among the Bishop of Bangor's warmest supporters was Archdeacon Edward Tenison, the previous Archbishop's kinsman and executor, with whom Wake was involved in litigation over dilapidations at Lambeth and Croydon Palaces, and who had made derogatory remarks about Wake in the pulpit at Canterbury. Edward Tenison's son, who had recited some of the 'Verses on the Peace' in 1713, had been happy at the School under Mills, but had been removed by his father at the Archbishop's suggestion, only to run away from his next school. Wake and Mills were united against this opponent. Wake had also plenty of confidential information coming from Croydon, some of it very complimentary to Mills, supplied by an independent source, a Mrs. Mary Blanchard, one of those determined, disinterested but interfering characters who from time to time have enquired into the affairs of the Whitgift Charity in order to remedy abuses and initiate reforms.

During the dispute Dr. Snape's name had been removed from the list of the King's Chaplains, his part having given offence at Court, but he was to some extent rehabilitated in 1719 by being appointed Provost of King's College, Cambridge. He and Mills strengthened their relationship through Snape's marriage in 1721, at which Mills officiated. One would think that Mills's unhappiness resulting from their association would have discouraged him from close friendship, but the lady was the daughter of Sir John Hervey, Merchant of London, and sister of Mills's second wife.

Benjamin Hoadly was translated in 1721 to Hereford and successively to Salisbury and Winchester; he continued his defence of liberty against the Crown and the Church until his death in 1761. He had soon become disillusioned with Pillonnière, who by degrees came to lead a life of extravagant fantasy. Let Hoadly provide his obituary notice in these Johnsonian terms:

> He was very profuse in giving away to others, in appearance of want, that competency that had been most kindly provided by his friends. By this weakness he soon found himself reduced to great necessities; and then accepted from me, through a friend's hands, a small yearly allowance.... At length, from the study of the mathematical and other useful branches of learning, he suddenly departed into the golden dreams of the lowest chemical projections. This change was succeeded by a sort of religious madness, in which he was not content with his usual great temperance, but brought himself to believe that, by the promises of God in Scripture, a good man might, by degrees, come to live without taking any sustenance at all. In this attempt he went to such excess, that his condition at last could not receive any benefit from a contrary regimen. And by this management he brought himself to death, in the midst of imaginary visions and nightly conversations with Heaven.

Wake's Visitation

While Mills seemed to be fighting a losing battle against his calumniators, the Brethren and Sisters of the Hospital were encouraged to open defiance and abuse of the Schoolmaster and the Warden, even to the extent of appropriating the account books and trying to take over the business of the Hospital themselves.

In August 1718 Mills begged the Archbishop, who so far had not set foot in Croydon, although the Palace there was being repaired at his direction, to intervene with a personal Visitation. In due course, on 28 October, Wake obliged and together with a number of his officials, came to Croydon and listened to complaints and denials from both sides. He returned to Lambeth the same day, but investigations continued over many months until in July 1719 he issued instructions for the closer supervision of the Hospital's affairs by his own officials; he was quite satisfied that there was no substance in the members' accusations of falsification of the accounts and he enjoined that the members of the Hospital should in future keep silent and uncomplaining, and promised that if he was troubled again with frivolous and groundless complaints he would have the disturber of the peace punished. Wake's Injunction had some effect, and he was not now so bombarded with accusations and grievances, although the unruly element among the Members remained troublesome to Mills and the Warden. On 5 November 1719 Hannah Steward, a declared enemy of Mills, was admonished 'for beginning again, as she always has done, to be troublesome & give fresh Disturbance to the House, & was a conten-

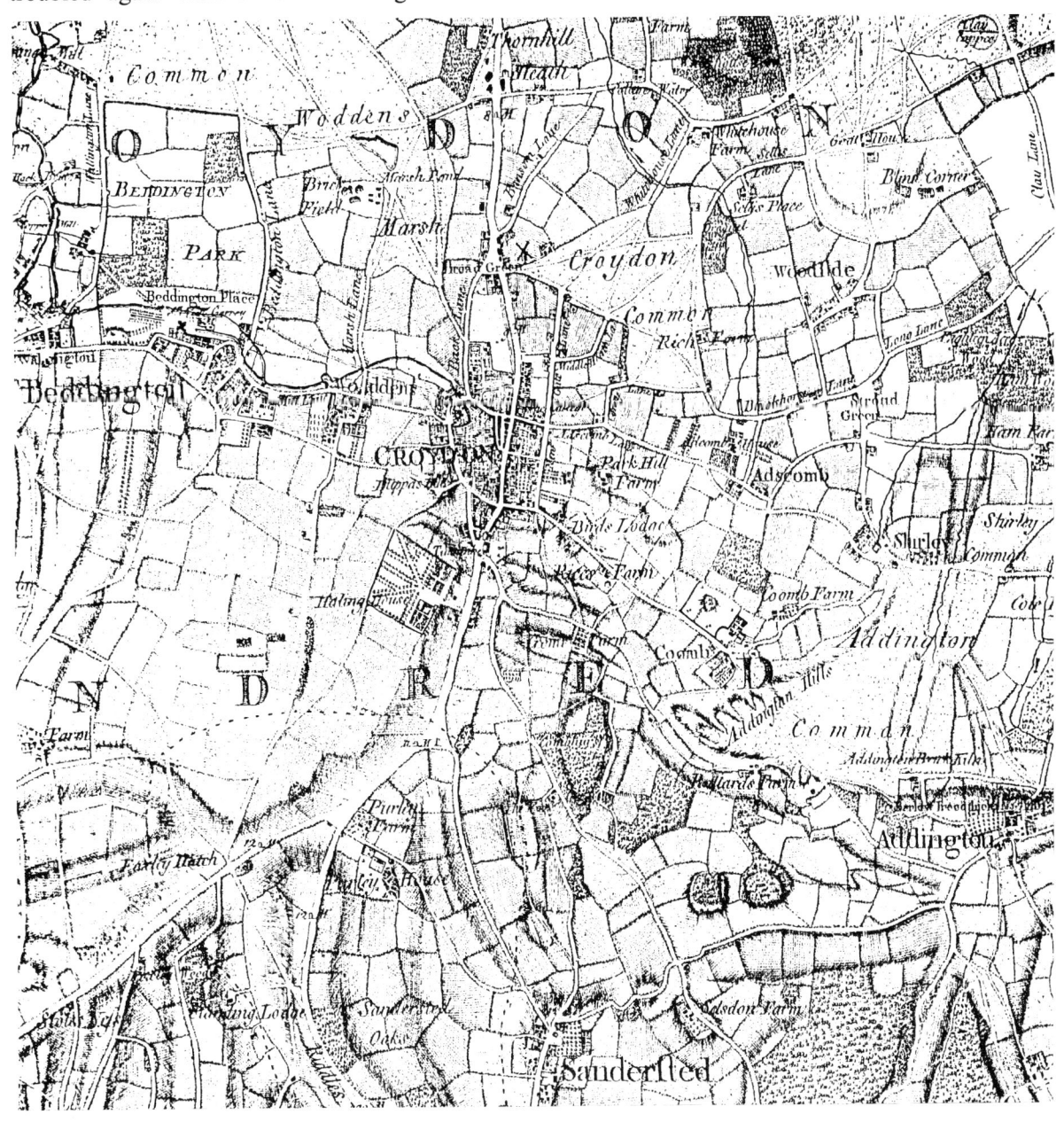

Croydon in the 18th century

tious Person & a Sower of Discord'. Four months later she was admonished again for tale-bearing:

> Elizabeth Turner affirm'd and offer'd to take her Oath that Hannah Steward declar'd, that Margaret Langrege was in the same Bed with John Strong, a Member of the House; & that Strongs Son Thomas pulled her out of the Bed; wch Accusation she cannot prove, but continued to be contentious & a Scold.

There were other Members who received admonitions, chiefly for 'Lying & making a Disturbance', but inebriety was a temptation to many of the Brethren, who frequently found in the numerous ale-houses of the town relief from the squabble-ridden atmosphere of the Hospital; for example, on 27 February 1821/2 'John Summers was admonish'd for being drunk & falling down in Prayer Time, after he was warn'd agst this Vice by Mr Trebec [*the Vicar*].'

On 23 June 1721 the Court of Assistants of the Mercers' Company met again to elect another High Master of St. Paul's. Mills, now aged 47, was once more a candidate among a very strong field, which comprised the Surmaster and a number of Headmasters of other schools, including those of Colfe's Grammar School and King's School, Worcester. The original eight candidates were reduced by ballot successively to four, to three and to two, who were Mills and Benjamin Morland, FRS, aged 64, the Headmaster of a private school of very high repute at Hackney. Age proved no bar, and in the final ballot Morland received twenty-one votes to Mills's fourteen, so he was once again disappointed. That he so nearly succeeded must indicate that his reputation and by inference that of the School remained quite high. When Morland died in 1733, Mills did not offer himself again.

Mills had been a warm favourite for the post; ten days before the election Wake had received a deputation from a number of Croydon worthies recommending the curate to succeed him if he should go.

At this time Croydon Palace was nearly ready once more for occupation, and Wake made a few visits to inspect the progress of work. When on 30 August he set off to spend his first vacation there, he was met by a large number of local people who, delighted to welcome back their chief resident after many years of absence, conducted him in triumph to the Palace where, with the exception of a few odd days, he spent the next two months with his family. Mills and his wife and other Croydon notables became frequent guests there. From now onwards the Archbishop spent some months every year at Croydon, and Mills and his wife grew to be on quite intimate terms with him.

Mills's disappointment over St. Paul's was somewhat relieved by another mark of favour from Wake, who, on 18 February 1723/4, appointed him to the Rectory of Merstham, eight miles south of Croydon, which he held until his death. This moderately valuable living enabled him to take life a little more easily; he put in a curate and he was not now so dependent on the School, which he may have conducted with less enthusiasm than hitherto. However, another entry among the admonitions provides evidence that Mills was still interested in securing boys of good family for the School:

> July 13 1723 Thomas Holloday had his third Admonition this Day for saying that if my Lady Lovelace knew so much of Mr Mills as he the said Holloday knew her Ladyship would set her Foot in his the said Mills backside and kick him out of Doors.

Lady Lovelace, who lived at Sanderstead, was the daughter of Sir John Clayton, a vastly rich financier and property-owner in Surrey, and the widow of John, fourth Baron Lovelace of Hurley, Governor of New York when he died in 1709. Their surviving son was an infant when he inherited the title. At the time of the admonition, Nevill, sixth Baron Lovelace, was fifteen years of age, so Mills's visits to the mother could well have been paid to her as a parent. Exactly a year later, Lord Lovelace and the Millses dined together with the Archbishop at Croydon Palace.

In 1732 John Pemberton, a publisher of Fleet Street, a Croydon resident and a close friend of Mills, printed an anonymous work entitled *A Journey through England, in Familiar Letters from a Gentleman here, to his Friend Abroad*. Letter VII has a local interest:

> ... I arrived at Croydon, a large Market-Town, very pleasantly situated, and well supplied with all sorts of provision. 'Tis of late very much beautified and enlarged by new buildings. There is ... a handsome

College, founded by the famous Archbishop Whitgift ...; near which is a very large Free-School, the Gift of the said worthy Prelate; ...

Near this place are many Gentlemen's Seats; at Aydgscombe there is a noble Seat belonging to William Draper, Esq.; the Paintings and Furniture of which are very grand.

The reference to the 'very large Free-School' can hardly be applied to Whitgift's old Schoolhouse alone; the writer must be thinking of the additions made by Mills and of the number of his pupils; there is more than a hint that at this time the School was still flourishing.

An Essay on Generosity

In the same year Pemberton published for Mills *An Essay on Generosity and Greatness of Spirit. The Builders of Colleges, Hospitals and Schools, Prais'd and Commended. The Invaluable Blessing of a Sound, Useful, and Pious Education; especially that of School Learning; with a Particular View to Archbp Whitgift's Foundation, in Croydon Surrey*. In spite of its title, this work seems to have been written in answer to books by another schoolmaster, John Clarke of Hull Grammar School, who had recently published *An Essay upon the Education of Youth in Grammar Schools* and *An Essay on Study*. There was at this time a great concern over the general failure of the grammar schools to perform their educational duty. Clarke complained that after six or seven years in a grammar school many boys were incapable of understanding half a dozen lines of even the easiest authors, and many went up to university quite ungrounded in grammar. He criticised the common methods of teaching, particularly those of rigid discipline and monotonous memorising, and the lack of good text-books (he condemned Lily's *Grammar* for its difficulty and complexity and for giving all explanations in Latin; he had himself compiled a simplified *Grammar* with explanations in English). He also deplored the neglect of mathematics, history, geography, French and the study of one's native tongue. A follower of Locke, he called for a study of the right methods of teaching and believed that a private education brought the best results. He denounced many country grammar schools, which were 'little more than houses of correction for the boys of the neighbourhood, where by daily confinement they are kept from tearing their Cloaths'. He disapproved too of the 'Great Schools' with their 'herds of rude, wild boys', and indeed had little to say in favour of 'publick education', which he defined as 'Education in a School where all comers were admitted'. Instead he recommended a 'private' education by a tutor under the parental eye, or in a private school containing only boarders numbering no more than thirty.

With many of Clarke's opinions Mills is prepared to agree. He too supports Locke, quoting him on the influence education has upon the development of men, and it is largely in this connection that he develops his theme. Mills favours the teaching of history, geography, mathematics and, of course, French, but he emphasizes (which Clarke does not) the importance of instruction in the Scriptures, and displays a poetic feeling for the language of the Bible. His views are more conventional than Clarke's; he compares children to empty vessels into which knowledge may be poured. Children must always be under close supervision and kept away from undesirable influences; faults and youthful follies must not be tolerated; discipline must be rigorously applied. Repressive measures clearly appealed to him. We have seen that Mills encouraged music, drama and the composition and declamation of verses; he believes that close attention should be given to leisure pursuits and that in addition to the activities mentioned, the study of globes, maps, medals and curiosities of art and nature are important. He heartily disapproves of 'vicious Romances, unchaste Songs, lewd Plays and lascivious Writings, with tales of Enchanted Castles, sumptuous Banquets and conquering Beauties'. From these restrictions he passes to the fundamental moral lessons of Sincerity, Truth, Humility, Mercy, Fortitude and Justice, and to the acquisition of social graces, such as ease of conversation, avoidance of gross language, knowledge of the Scriptures and correctness of behaviour. He is chiefly interested in the education of the nobly born, of those who may achieve high office, political or judicial, of private gentlemen and of future clergy. On these the sense and manly thoughts of the elegant classical authors will bestow judgment and eloquence. Mills stresses the importance of oratory and gives hints on dramatic eloquence. Yet all these must be subordinate to charitableness and the leading of a good and useful life, unmarred by the intemperance and prodigality that has become so prevalent. He throws a few crumbs of comfort to those not included in the social classes he has been concerned with: even tradespeople and others, who find learning perhaps not easy to acquire, can yet be taught habits of truth, honesty and justice. These rather platitudinous observations are preceded by sixty-three pages of Dedication to Archbishop Wake, who is fulsomely flattered and compared with Whitgift to the advantage of both. In this Dedication he takes a further opportunity of denying responsibility for any mismanagement of the Hospital's affairs.

Pueritiae Formandae Artifex

In 1741 Mills continued the exposition of his educational theories in *Pueritiae Formandae Artifex*—'The Craftsman on the Formation of Youth', written entirely in Latin. Dedicated to Dr. William Oliver, the physician of Bath, whose grateful patient Mills acknowledges himself to be, it contains a long preface on the general subject of education. His views are an extension of those expressed in the *Essay on Generosity* and are the result of a lifetime's experience; he bases his theories on the importance of poetry which, when learning was in its cradle, was the chief medium of instruction. Changing his simile from the 'empty vessel', he likens children to blank sheets of paper upon which anything may be written, and in disagreement with Clarke insists upon the importance of learning by heart; he strongly defends 'public' education, where strict measures and supervision under 'Censors' (by which term he may mean a sort of monitor or prefect) will control any tendency towards undesirable behaviour; he remains adamant that boys should be removed from the softening influence of indulgent parents. Far from admitting that after seven years a boy may remain almost ignorant of grammar, Mills reckons that, with his strict discipline, a boy at the end of this time should be a good Latinist. Whereas Clarke thinks that Greek is a superfluous study, Mills recommends that it should be started early and become part of the regular curriculum with Latin. In contrast with Clarke's practical and utilitarian outlook, Mills's views are those of a scholar who enjoys literature for its own sake and as an agreeable accomplishment for a gentleman of the eighteenth century. Both agree upon the importance of speaking fluent Latin in school, correct in grammar and pronunciation. But Mills will have nothing to do with Clarke's new *Grammar*; he deplores the absence of a standard Grammar used throughout the country, but Lily's, he thinks, should be used in every school to give uniformity of standards.

Mills gives his syllabus, which has changed

PUERITIÆ FORMANDÆ

ARTIFEX.

AUTHORE

HEN. MILLS,

Scholæ Croydonenfis

PRÆCEPTORE.

Omnium Populorum Felicitas, maximè vero Reipublicæ Chriſtianæ Salus, à rectà Juventutis Inſtitutione pendet.

Henricus Quartus Angliæ Rex.

LONDINI:

Apud J. Pemberton in Fleet-ſtreet.

M.DCC.XLI.

Titlepage of *The Craftsman on the Formation of Youth*, 1741 little during the past hundred years: the first two years are to be occupied in learning declensions and conjugations, with study of the Dialogues of Castalion, Phaedrus and Ovid; to these may be added Ovid's Epistles and Metamorphoses, and Terence. After these first two years a boy may start writing verses and begin Greek. Mills's interests are mainly linguistic and literary. He underlines the importance of the native tongue, and recommends an early introduction to Hebrew for those intending to enter the Church, and of course he encourages the learning of French.

His Preface serves to introduce a collection of pieces from the Latin poets arranged under different headings in alphabetical order, e.g. 'ars'; 'avaritia', 'beatitudo', etc. These were to be learnt by heart and serve as models for original versification. *Primitiae Poetices: sive Illustrium veterumque Poetarum Sententiae*... was designed as a working text-book and was presumably in use at the School and elsewhere, for he had had it printed separately some years before he wrote the Introduction, and it went through several editions. The book concludes with 'Preces Matutinae' and a hymn, 'Salvator Mundi'.

A Summing-Up

Conclusions concerning the condition of the School during Mills's last ten years are difficult to draw; his books indicate that the School may have been well frequented, but there are no firm identifications to be made of boys going up to the universities, which, however, were now out of favour with the classes that formerly sent their sons there to finish their education. Moreover, several sons of local families who did go up to Oxford or Cambridge are shown as having been to Eton or Westminster. There was also formidable competition from the many successful private schools and academies that had been set up throughout the country; an effective local rival was Cheam School, already established in 1650, which supplied a steady stream of pupils to the universities over the next 150 years.

Mills's thirty years' tenure of office was a period of varying fortunes, in which his own mercurial temperament contributed towards the School's prosperity and its later reverses, but the change in the educational climate which he himself deplored was one that was spreading throughout the country, and he could do nothing to moderate its effects.

Henry Mills died at Croydon on 11 April 1742 at the age of 68, and a week later he was buried in the chancel of his parish church at Merstham. He left his family well provided for: he was able to settle £1000 on his daughter by his previous marriage, and his widow received the balance of his estate, which included three freehold properties in Croydon as well as two leaseholds from the Hospital (one of them the house he had built next to the School). He died, then, in fairly prosperous circumstances, which cannot be attributed to any outstanding success as an author or as a schoolmaster. He has revealed himself as ready to seize his chances of success and preferment, but in the main these eluded him, with the result that he had to be satisfied with small church livings and the mastership of a minor school that he hoped might be the stepping-stone to a more important post. He was not without generosity himself, and two small gifts made by him to his church and to the Hospital are recorded in their respective Registers: in 1728 he gave a silver paten to Merstham Church, and at some time between 1735 and 1737 he entered a note in the Hospital Ledger Book:

Memorandum that Mr. Mills gave 4 new outward doors which is mentioned, lest the members shou'd make this a Precedent to oblige future Masters to be at any Expense for the Hospital.

Perhaps by this time his temper had mellowed, and the eventual removal by death of the more contentious inmates had encouraged him to regard the Hospital and its affairs with a more tolerant and compassionate eye.

5. Decline, 1742–1843

The Plight of the Grammar Schools

During the eighteenth century the universities and the grammar schools of England sank very low in efficiency and reputation. In spite of a few exceptionally enlightened men who interested themselves and their pupils in natural sciences and other 'modern' studies, both Oxford and Cambridge, but more particularly Oxford, were stifled by adherence to the mediaeval study based on the Greek conception of the liberal arts. Already by 1605 Francis Bacon in his *Advancement of Learning* had deplored the narrowness of the curriculum devoted in the main to an appreciation of style and manner rather than to invention and weight of matter, soundness of argument and depth of judgment. Throughout the seventeenth century the more advanced thinkers were endeavouring to infuse vigour and modernity of outlook into the old academic studies. Political events, wider concepts of the meaning of liberty, the increase in independent religious thought, the growing awareness of other civilisations, and the emergence of scientific method—all these great developments and many others were pressing men of original mind to question the traditional educational aims and methods. During the Interregnum there had been proposals for the reform of the universities, and even though they were dropped at the Restoration, a prolonged dispute arose between the 'ancients' and the 'moderns'. Locke's *Thoughts concerning Education*, published in 1693, was only one of many works that called for a broader intellectual training more suited to the requirements of the time.

It was not only men of learning who condemned the conservatism of the curriculum. There was among the more enlightened type of men who had formerly sent their sons to grammar schools a widespread desire for an education that would be more vocational and practical, such as could be obtained at the courtly academies established on the Continent or even at the non-conformist and other private academies that were established with varying success after 1670. The example of Cheam has already been cited. The alumni of Hackney School (whose Headmaster was Henry Mills's successful rival for the High Mastership of St. Paul's) proceeded in large numbers to university during the 18th century; several became members of the Royal Society, and many are recorded in the Dictionary of National Biography. In 1760 Joseph Priestley wrote:

> The severe and proper discipline of a grammar school is become a common topic of ridicule; and few young gentlemen, except those who are designed for some of the learned professions, are made to submit to the rigour of it.

Why, then, were these demands not met? The universities were reluctant to abandon their narrow field of study, and their graduates who went out to teach in grammar schools were so equally imbued with dead classicism, that a vicious circle was created, particularly difficult to break owing to the circumstances of the foundation of many of these schools. A large number of them, including our own, founded or re-founded in the sixteenth century to supply scholars for the universities and clergy for the Church, were forced by the terms of their statutes to perpetuate the mediaeval study of the 'trivium' (grammar, rhetoric and logic) prior to a university career. So restrictive in many cases were these statutes that not only were Latin and Greek virtually the sole subjects studied (religious doctrine was taught, often partly through the medium of the dead languages), but the schools were legally not allowed to study any others. The statutes, too, might restrict the number of scholars and disqualify any who were not born or resident in a certain parish or locality. For instance, at Harrow (founded 1571 but not constituted until 1590), which was described by its founder as a Free Grammar School, education was available free for the sons of *all* parishioners, but 'foreigners' could be admitted on the Schoolmaster's terms; similarly at Rugby (1567). At Highgate (1562, opened 1578) up to forty boys from Highgate and four adjacent parishes could be admitted, but the Master was forbidden to take any fee-payers at all. Again, statutes frequently limited the stipend of the schoolmaster to an absurdly small sum; where such a limitation could not be circumvented, the school either died, became an unimportant appendage to a more lucrative office or, as in the case of Whitgift's school in the seventeenth and eighteenth centuries, was dependent on the success that the Schoolmaster achieved in obtaining paying pupils; not in all cases where the latter course occurred were the statutes so liberally drawn in respect to the origin and status of the pupils. In yet other cases, through vagueness in the drawing up of ordinances, a school might decline into a village school where the rudiments were taught, and the pupils apprenticed to simple trades.

There were, moreover, too many small grammar schools, some of them established in districts such as East Anglia, whose former prosperity, based on the wool trade, was yielding to the growth of industrialism in the coal-fields and elsewhere. As these schools declined, supported by a merely static or even diminishing population, private venture schools, some of them remarkable for great originality of curriculum, and enlightenment in teaching method, and free to provide an education that was demanded by their patrons, were set up in the towns of newer growth. These constituted the example for the establishment throughout the country of hundreds of private schools which, even until the middle of the last century, provided instruction for the majority of the children, boys and girls, of the professional and commercial classes. It was mainly in these private schools and academies that the inventive minds received their training; even one of the Archbishops of Canterbury, Thomas Secker, 1758–68, had been brought up at a dissenters' academy.

Another important reason for the grammar schools' decline was the obsolescence and unsuitability of their buildings, often little altered since they had been built perhaps two hundred years earlier. The eighteenth century, that saw the almost universal adoption of architectural principles based on the classical orders, viewed 'gothic' as barbarous and unlearned and consequently unsuitable for educational institutions. A few grammar schools that remained successful had recently enlarged or rebuilt their ancient premises. There were yet others that, despite being only modestly endowed, were able to maintain some degree of success: they enjoyed

Haling House in the late 18th century

the advantage of closed scholarships at the universities, provided either by their founders or by benefactors who wished to favour a particular locality. In this category were, for example, Bromsgrove, Oakham and Uppingham. Unfortunately, John Whitgift had made no such provision (see p. 47).

Lastly, and as important as any other reason: whereas a grammar school had been attended by boys of all classes, a sense of class-consciousness in regard to education was growing stronger; certain schools became fashionable, retaining and indeed increasing their reputation and social status, such as Eton, Winchester, Harrow, Westminster and Rugby; others which had at times enjoyed a more than local esteem declined with the majority into complete obscurity, although the schoolmasters themselves might continue to draw a stipend for an office that was virtually a sinecure.

Even early in the seventeenth century, some ancient schools of former high repute had disappeared, such as John Whitgift's own alma mater, St. Anthony's, but a hundred years later the situation was far worse. In 1734 the grammar school at Birmingham (King Edward's) was empty of boys; at Oundle in 1762 only one boy was admitted, in 1779 there were four in the school and in 1785 none at all. It is no surprise, then, to find that at Croydon a similar state of affairs developed; the number of boys declined and eventually dropped to nil.

In broad terms there had to be a combination of some favourable circumstances for a grammar school to continue to prosper in the eighteenth century; among these were:

(i) a clear constitution for its management,
(ii) a method of electing responsible trustees or governors, who in their turn would appoint a competent and ambitious Schoolmaster, and dismiss an ineffective one,
(iii) the control of any increased income from endowments which could be applied to:
    (a) the maintenance, improvement and enlargement of buildings,
    (b) raising the salaries of the Schoolmaster and Ushers, and even superannuating a senile master,
    (c) the provision of scholarships to the universities,
(iv) some continuity of reputation,
(v) freedom to draw paying pupils from a wide field.

Of these conditions, Whitgift's School could score only with the second and the last, which were not enough.

Samuel Staveley

Such a situation may well have prevailed at the end of Mills's régime, but so little is known of the School under his next two successors that its status can only be guessed at. The Ledger Book does not record when the first, Samuel Staveley, was appointed by Archbishop Potter, but his corrody as Poor Brother was granted in May 1742, a month after Mills's death. From Sherborne he had gone to Emmanuel College, Cambridge, in 1736. Soon after graduating in 1741 he was ordained, so when he was appointed to Croydon he had had little experience. Like Mills he was a musician, having been organist of his college chapel. His lack of experience and of useful contacts with prospective parents may have discouraged confidence in him and the School, about which absolutely nothing has come to light concerning the nine years he was Schoolmaster. After his youthful appointment he would have hoped to obtain advancement and a more important living, but whether the office of Chaplain in the East India Company fulfilled his ambitions seems doubtful. Nevertheless, he left Croydon in August 1751 and immediately sailed for Madras, which he reached in June the following year.

John Taylor Lamb

Eight days after Staveley resigned, John Taylor Lamb was sworn, having been appointed by Archbishop Herring. Except for his successor Matthew Hutton, who held the primacy for less than a year, Herring was the last Archbishop to reside in the Old Palace of Croydon; from there he was able at times to keep a close eye on the Hospital and School. Lamb had graduated from St. John's College, Cambridge, and having been educated at a private school in Streatham, he seems to have made use of some local contacts. On 2 August 1751 he was appointed Usher and

A Schoolroom in Hodgson's time

Fellow of Dulwich College, but this appointment was quickly superseded by his being given the Schoolmastership at Croydon on 3 September.

As in his predecessor's time, records are now almost silent on the School's history. For the next twenty years, Lamb seems to have conducted a small school for unambitious pupils, according to the testimony of various entries in the Ledger Book for repairs to the fabric of the Schoolhouse. For instance, in December 1762, Mr. Ray, bricklayer, was 'paid 8 shillings and 10 pence for Laying of Herth & mending Plaister in School'; Mr. Matthews, carpenter, received payment for 'Work done at the School, &c.', and in 1763 there was again a considerable amount of work done with bricks, timber and nails. Occasionally, too, it was necessary to deliver admonitions for brawling and drunkenness, but not now for accusations of cheating against the officials of the Hospital.

Just before Herring died in 1757, he collated Lamb Vicar of Leysdown in the Isle of Sheppey. This remote living proved an embarrassment to him, for it brought him only a few pounds a year, and he always had difficulty in finding a curate to act on the small allowance he was prepared to pay. He was glad to relinquish this unremunerative absentee living in 1761 on being collated by Secker to the Rectory of Keston, Kent, only five miles from Croydon, which he held until his death early in 1774 and which became associated with the chaplaincy of the Hospital. He left three sons aged 14, 10 and 9, who upon their father's death were admitted to St Paul's, so they had no doubt been educated previously by him.

James Hodgson

The next Schoolmaster was James Hodgson, about whom a good deal more than conjecture has survived. From Charterhouse he went up to Christ Church and, after serving as curate in his father's parish of Humber in Herefordshire and 'being a sound Scholar and noted for impressive eloquence in the pulpit, he had not long to wait for preferment'. It was through the influence of another Carthusian, Sir Charles Jenkinson, Bart., created Baron Hawkesbury in 1786, advanced to the Earldom of Liverpool in 1796, who at the time was living at Addiscombe Place, that Archbishop Cornwallis appointed Hodgson in 1774 to Croydon; he had proceeded MA the previous year and was still in his early twenties.

Although during Hodgson's first dozen years or so there is no evidence of the way in which he conducted his school, by 1790 he was enjoying some success. However, in common with many other grammar schools that had managed to survive, Hodgson's school was now more like a preparatory school. Some local boys, such as Frederick Apthorpe, the son of the Vicar of Croydon, stayed until they went to university, but others, including boarders, would leave at an earlier age to go to their 'public school', a name that had already taken on a more limited meaning than before. For instance, Hodgson's younger son, Francis, went on to Eton after his early years under his father; he eventually became Provost and was well known in certain literary circles. A family of four boys, sons of Thomas Hallett Hodges, Sheriff of Kent in 1786, of Hempstead Place, Benenden, were under Hodgson in the 1780s; three of them went on to Harrow, but one, John, stayed on until he went to a naval academy at Chelsea. Something of their life and the precariousness of the schoolmaster's occupation is illustrated in letters they wrote to their parents (Kent County Archives: Twysden Papers, U49 C13). The eldest, Thomas, in writing from Harrow, often passed on news that he had received from his brothers in Croydon, where they seemed to be happy under Hodgson. On 2 March 1790 (?), when he was fourteen, he wrote to his mother:

> I have heard by John's letter of Mrs Hodson's (death). What a loss she will be to Mr H and the School in general. . . . I think Mr H. of all men has had his share of affliction both in his blind son [*the elder, John*] and the death of his wife. Because of her Death I hope his School will not diminish, which is very often the case. Such an untimely blow will be in some measure avoided if Mr & Miss H. join their schools, that she may take care of the House. I hear that Miss Hodson was almost always at Mrs H's during her illness, for when I was there everything was just as if she had been well. Miss Hodson I imagine then kept the House, for she gave orders for everything both for our dinner and for Frank's reception.*

On 17 May 1792 John Hodges, aged fourteen, wrote to his father from Croydon:

> Dear Papa,
> My reason for not writing to you last week was I had a very bad cold and sore throat which is now quite well. . . . Their is a French gentleman come here by Lord Hawkesbury recommending to learn English I think him a very agreeable man, he chatters French so very quick it is almost impossible to understand him, our present French Master is going to France and we agoing to have a new one who I beleive come next month. Pray tell Mama I should be much obliged to her if she would (get) me some linen waistcoats as I am in great want of them as likewise two pair of stockings for the 5 pair I have are not quite sufficient. I have received my hat and it fits very well. I have no more to say at present so Give my Love to Mama and Sister.
> I am Dear Papa
> Your Dutiful Son,
> John Hodges.

There had been some talk of Hodgson's moving into Norfolk, where he held a living; John was so attached to him that he wanted to go with him there; he was already past the age when his brothers had gone to Harrow, for he was the backward one of the family, and his letters are ill-spelt and awkwardly composed, as the above example has shown. Thomas once wrote from Harrow: 'I have had a letter from Croydon from John . . . which I could not have believed John wrote, it was so well worded.'

On 15 July 1792 John wrote to his mother:

> . . . As for the time (Mr Hodgson) intends to go into Norfolk, I cannot give you the exact time of, but I beleive it will be very early in July [*he means August*], I should be much obliged to you if you will let me know in your next if I go with Mr Hodgson which I should like much better than going to another School, If I shall have the pleasure to go, I think it will be very inconvenient for you to bring me home for so short a time as the Holidays will be so therefore I suppose I shall remain here, as it is for a very good reason I shall not be much dejected. My Knals (nails) are in very good condition and also my Teeth. . . .

Nothing came of this projected move to Norfolk, however, and a year later John was writing again in the same strain.

C. C. C. Jenkinson

Another of Hodgson's pupils had been Lord Hawkesbury's elder son, Robert Banks Jenkinson, who followed his father to Charterhouse. As the Second Earl of Liverpool, he was Prime Minister from 1812 to 1827. During his vacations from Charterhouse and Oxford, he followed a course of reading with

Thomas Law Hodges, writer of letters 1788–90

---

*Miss Ann Hodgson, the Schoolmaster's sister, seems to have kept a school of sorts in the house built by Henry Mills. Frank was the writer's youngest brother.

Hodgson, but can hardly be called a School pupil, for Robert was already at Charterhouse when the Jenkinsons moved to Addiscombe. Hawkesbury's son by his second marriage, Charles Cecil Cope Jenkinson, fourteen years younger than his half-brother, was introduced to life with the Hodgsons before he was three, for on 26 April 1787, James Hodgson wrote to Hawkesbury:

It will be a satisfaction to your Lordship and Lady Hawkesbury to hear that Masr Cecil has commenc'd his acquaintance with my family in a very pleasing manner. He has now been with us two mornings, without the least symptoms of uneasiness.... Your Lordship's Judgment as to his Temper and Disposition were perfectly correct; they are both easily directed; and therefore may either be improv'd or spoil'd, according as he is treated.

Cecil Jenkinson, after a period under Hodgson's care, was destined as a younger son for a career in the Royal Navy (perhaps his Temper and Disposition had not after all yielded to direction) and he saw action as a midshipman at the age of eleven; on 4 July 1795 he wrote to his father giving an eye-witness account of the fall of Quiberon. Within a year or two, however, Cecil persuaded his father to allow him to leave the Navy and prepare to go to university. It then fell to Hodgson to coach him up to the standard required for admission to Christ Church, for Hawkesbury (by now advanced to the title of Earl of Liverpool) wished to engage Hodgson as sole tutor to his son in this case of emergency. Lord Liverpool, who concerned himself minutely with his sons' upbringing, if not so much through personal contact, at least by means of letters of advice and admonishment and through written instructions to their mentors, was eager that the gaps in Cecil's academic training should be completely filled, and laid down a detailed course of studies for him to follow. On 2 February 1798 Cecil wrote to his father to tell him that he and Hodgson had finished Robertson's *History of Scotland* and to ask what other book they should start on. A month later he wrote again:

We have finished in the course of the week the first book of Caesar, and have read some part of the second; it becomes very easy to me, and is amusing. I am getting on with the translation of the life of Atticus but have a great deal more to do in it.

In spite of the ease with which he tackled Caesar and the amusement he derived from his reading, there seems to have been a great deal of hard work necessary before Cecil was able to compete with those whose education had followed a more orthodox course. Lord Liverpool continued to direct closely his son's reading and gave fully of his views to Hodgson on how a young nobleman should be educated, revealing a typical aristocratic bias towards the Classical tongues. On 4 January 1800 he wrote to Hodgson:

My great object, however, is that as long as he is under your tuition, he should direct his principal attention to the Greek and Latin languages. His general reading both in English and French has been so extensive ... that any further progress therein ought to give way to his improvement in the two learned languages.

By this time Hodgson was nearing the end of his term of office at Croydon. Lord Liverpool thought very highly of Hodgson's learning and capacity as a tutor, and had already indicated how he was to be rewarded, for writing from his London house in Hertford Street on 10 February 1799, he said:

I have just heard that the living of Barwick in Elmet is become vacant by the Death of Mr Deane, the late Incumbent. This Rectory is in my gift [*Liverpool was Chancellor of the Duchy of Lancaster*] and is, as I am informed, worth £1000 pr annum, in consequence of the late Inclosure. I am disposed to give you this Living, not only from Friendship but in consideration of the Care you have taken of the Education of my youngest son. But as I wish that this Education should be finished under your Care, I shall expect that you shall continue to reside in Croydon, 'till I am satisfied that his Education is finished....

Lord Liverpool's interest in his son's tutor was a genuine one, although he did not disdain the satisfaction of turning down a plea from the Archbishop of York, only two days after writing the previous letter:

... your Grace's letter, in which you recommend to me two of your sons, for the two valuable livings of Barwick in Elmet and Kirk Barwicke.... But the Obligations which I feel most sensibly are such as I owe to those who have been concerned in the Education of my Children; I consider these as debts of gratitude, which I am bound liberally to discharge.

I have given therefore to one Gentleman, who had some Share in the Education of Lord Hawkesbury, and who under my Eye, now devotes the whole of his Time to the Education of my second Son, and with great success, the Living of Barwick in Elmet.

This is an interesting example of the power and influence for personal ends then wielded by holders of office, completely without any sense of unfair discrimination; also illustrated is the begging of favours on behalf of those possibly quite undeserving of reward.

Cecil Jenkinson's career at Oxford, like his career at sea, was terminated early, and he came down without a degree, although while he was still in his second year, his father was soliciting for a Fellowship at Merton on his behalf. He then entered the diplomatic service, but having inherited an estate from a cousin, he went into Parliament in 1807. On his brother's death in 1828, he succeeded to the Earldom.

Death of James Hodgson

James Hodgson died at Barwick in 1810, and Cecil Jenkinson wrote to Francis Hodgson a letter of sympathy:

My dear Frank—

I received the melancholy news conveyed to me by your letter the day before yesterday. . . .

My obligations to your father are so well known to you that, was it not for the fear of the accusation of ingratitude it would be needless for me to mention them in this place. From the period of time that was passed by me at sea, my education would have been deplorable had I not received from him that fostering

Charles Cecil Cope Jenkinson (1784–1851), 3rd Earl of Liverpool

aid and assistance which enabled me to appear at the university little inferior in my classical studies to those whose education had been conducted by the more certain and regular process of public education. His manner of instruction was not the least part of the obligation I owe to your father; he inspired me with that desire for knowledge which alone enabled me to make the rapid progress I did. . . .

His father's death involved Francis Hodgson in considerable financial difficulty. In spite of holding a series of more or less lucrative livings in Herefordshire, Croydon (with Keston), Norfolk and Yorkshire, and enjoying a ministry at the Savoy Chapel in the Strand, and chaplaincies to Lords Liverpool and Dunmore, James Hodgson 'had long been accustomed to exercise open-handed liberality to his poorer parishioners, and in anticipation of his future ample capabilities of repayment of loans, had left out of sight the uncertainty of life'. This improvidence on the father's part did not deter the son from undertaking the discharge of his father's debts, which remained an embarrassment to him for many years until a generous gift from his friend Lord Byron released him from the burden.

Addiscombe Place, home of William Draper and of the Earl of Liverpool

The Enclosure Act

Just as Hodgson was preparing to depart, the Hospital's endowments received a large addition. The Croydon Enclosure Act of 1797, with the resulting Commissioners' Award in March 1801, gave the Foundation over 110 acres of former common land, much of it of high agricultural value in convenient allocations near property it already owned. At the same time, by means of agreement with other land-owners, small detached properties were exchanged, and the boundaries of others adjusted to mutual convenience. The existing tenants also benefited from this good fortune, but as the Hospital had been put to considerable legal expense and was required to fence and drain its new properties where necessary, it was some time before this increase in value became apparent to the Brethren and Sisters.

In contrast to this prosperity, the School was now quite empty, although there were other schools in Croydon that enjoyed some success. Archbishop Tenison's School still taught its twenty children, and certain private schools met the demands, however inadequately, for a more sophisticated education, even if the local directory of the time did describe the proprietors as 'traders'. Alexander Bisset and William Green each conducted an 'Academy for Gentlemen', whereas James Dempster and Norman Wallis were just 'Schoolmasters'. James Hodgson was referred to only as Chaplain to the Hospital and to Lord Hawkesbury.

John Rose

The appointment by Archbishop Moore of a successor to Hodgson did not result in the revival of the School; indeed it seems probable that Dr. John Rose, 1801–12, took no pupils whatever, yet the new Schoolmaster came to his post with more experience behind him than any of his predecessors. Born in Lambeth, he was sent to Merchant Taylors' School, being Head Boy there from 1770 to 1772, in which year he was elected to a scholarship at St. John's College, Oxford, at the age of seventeen. Not long after graduating he became in 1779 Third Under-Master at Merchant Taylors' and progressed to the rank of First Under-Master by 1785. A pupil of his at that school described life there in terms that indicate that the absence of pupils under Rose at Croydon was not altogether to be regretted:

> Two more cruel tyrants than Bishop (the Headmaster) and Rose never existed. . . . Rose was so great an adept at the cane, that I once saw a boy strip, after a thrashing from him, that he might expose his barbarous cruelty, when the back was actually striped with dark streaks like a zebra.
>
> Before I left the school the pupils had the satisfaction of witnessing the administration of the 'lex talionis' in a most summary and somewhat awful manner. The boy I spoke of, . . . remembering the blow, and on proceeding to college, kept up the recollection of this most gratuitous barbarity; for, shortly afterwards, he came into the cloisters during a play-hour, went to Rose's apartment, lured him to the door of it, and horse-whipped him there before the admiring and approving scholars until he roared for mercy.

An interest in the theatre acquired while he was at Merchant Taylors' resulted in his writing several plays which were produced at the Little Theatre and the King's Theatre, Haymarket. Written at a period when English theatrical standards were at a very low ebb, they offer no attraction to modern taste, and even in those days provided Rose with little gain and no fame.

However, he obtained a securer and more ample income when he was collated Rector of the Parish of St. Martin, Outwich, London, in December 1795. This church, whose patrons were the Merchant Taylors' Company, was situated in Threadneedle Street, quite near where the Company's school then stood, and was being rebuilt at the time. It provided a valuable living, with a stipend of £1000 per annum, so he resigned his place at the School. The circumstances strangely echo those of 160 years before, when John Philips, Chief Usher at MTS, had been passed over for promotion to Head Master. When Bishop, who seems, despite the above anecdote, to have enjoyed the respect of his pupils and his governors, died in 1795, Rose's hopes were dashed by the appointment of another OMT, who was already a Head Master elsewhere. But within a week the Company awarded him this generous gift in consolation.

When Rose was appointed Schoolmaster and came to live in Croydon, he gave public notice of his readiness to receive scholars on the Foundation, but as he received no applications and was either unable to obtain, or unwilling to accept, fee-paying pupils, the School remained closed.

He obtained a curacy at Addington, although he retained his living of St. Martin, Outwich, where he occasionally returned to conduct baptisms and other services. His patron, Archbishop Moore, dying in 1805, was succeeded by Manners-Sutton, who in 1808 conferred on Rose the degree of Doctor of Divinity, an honour not lightly bestowed but giving a clear indication of the esteem in which he was held by his chief parishioner at Addington Palace, where the Archbishops had now moved after selling the Old Palace in Croydon. But the following year the Archbishop, having heard worrying reports of the affairs of the Hospital, instructed his private secretary, Mr. Christopher Hodgson (no relation, as far as has been discovered, to the previous Schoolmaster) to inspect the Hospital accounts. Dr. Rose produced a statement of the year's income and expenditure on a slip of paper, showing the Hospital indebted to him to the extent of over three hundred pounds, but Mr. Hodgson, after insisting on seeing the accounts in the ledger, was not satisfied and reported to the Archbishop, who then instituted a detailed investigation of the accounts. The members of the Court of Inquiry that was set up were Dr. Vyse, Rector of Lambeth, Dr. John Ireland, Vicar of Croydon, and Mr. Hodgson. As a result an action was later brought by the Brethren and Sisters of the Hospital in their corporate capacity against Dr. Rose for restitution of monies incorrectly appropriated by him. Among the different methods of swindling his fellow-pensioners was the device of drawing, in addition to his stipend as Schoolmaster, a further £5 per annum as a Poor Brother; he also received fines on the renewal of leases, only part of which he paid into the Hospital funds, keeping the remainder, which amounted to nearly £500; and he ingeniously entered tradesmen's bills as paid twice over in the ledger. Eventually, after a long investigation, the jury found for the plaintiffs, and Rose repaid to the Members a total of £762.15s.9d, of which nearly half went to the lawyers, instead of receiving from them, as he first claimed, the sum of £302.9s.10d. Rose's position in Croydon was no longer tenable, and he resigned in April 1812. In spite of the scandal, which attracted wide publicity and execration, he remained in possession of his living at St. Martin, Outwich, until his death in May 1821.

This most disgraceful episode in the Hospital's history resulted in a more methodical conduct of its affairs; thereafter, as the old leases fell in, the estates were let out at a rack-rent, instead of being renewed after the payment of fines, and the management of the estates and the accounts was by demand of the Members removed from the Schoolmaster's responsibility and placed in professional hands. (The Statute of Mortmain was by now a dead letter, but its application to educational endowments was not legally removed until 1944.) There was thus a steady increase in the amount of income distributable among the Members, but until the expiry of all the twenty-

AN ACCOUNT
OF THE
Proceedings & Evidence,
OF A
WRIT of INQUIRY
EXECUTED
Before the SHERIFF of Middlesex,
AND A JURY,
On the First day of November 1813,
TO ASCERTAIN THE
DAMAGES
DUE FROM
The Rev. JOHN ROSE D. D.
UNTO THE
WARDEN & POOR,
OF THE
Hospital of the Holy Trinity,
IN CROYDON.

TAKEN IN SHORT HAND,
By Order of the Warden and Brethren of the Hospital.

CROYDON;
Printed by Harding Junior, at the Oracle Printing-Office.
1813.

The Reverend Doctor John Rose:
Writ of Inquiry, 1813

HOUSEHOLD Furniture,

Erections of Dairy and Coach House, Garden Engine, Cow in Calf and Effects.

GEORGE STREET, CROYDON.

To be Sold by Auction,

BY MESSRS.

BLAKE,

On Friday April 24th, 1812,---at 12 o'Clock precisely,

PART OF THE GENUINE

Household Furniture,

AND EFFECTS,

The PROPERTY of the Rev. Dr. ROSE,

(LEAVING CROYDON)

COMPRISING a general assemblage of Household Furniture, the Erection of a Dairy, fitted-up with Shelves &c. complete, a Coach House with Pantile Roof, (nearly new) several Rods of Oak Pale Fencing, Gates, a capital Lead Pump, quantity of Inch and ¾ framed Partition with Doors in ditto, Cupboards, Shelves, Stoves, Coppers, Brewing Utensils, excellent Garden Engine, (nearly new) Cucumber Boxes, Lights, and various Effects.

May be viewed the Day preceding the Sale when Catalogues may be had; at the Principal Inn's, Carshalton; Sutton; Mitcham; Tooting; Streatham; Beckenham; Bromley; the King's Arms, and of the Auctioneers, High Street, Croydon.

Harding Junior Printer, Butcher-Row, Croydon. April 16th, 1812.

Auction of Dr. John Rose's effects, 1812

one-year leases (the extreme period laid down), the old method, with its openness to fraud, existed concurrently, so that by 1818, although the estates were valued at over £2600 a year, the income had gone up only to £860; for instance, Croham Manor Farm was valued at £542 a year, but the tenant was paying a rent of £42.6s.6d., £8 more than the Founder's stipulated figure, an increase due only to the additions from the Enclosure Awards.

John Collinson Bisset

Reference has already been made to Alexander Bisset, who kept an 'Academy for Gentlemen' in Croydon in Hodgson's time. He had a son, John Collinson Bisset, who was no doubt educated under his father before going up to Oxford in 1803. He graduated in 1808, when he probably returned to assist in his father's academy, which was conducted at the old 'George' Inn on the corner opposite the Hospital. He and Rose were then on very good terms, for between 1810 and 1815 Bisset acted as curate in Rose's church of St. Martin. Certainly there was no competition between them over a school. This connection with Rose did not deter Archbishop Manners-Sutton from appointing him successor to Rose upon the latter's resignation, and Bisset conducted his school in the traditional classical manner, but not in the old Schoolhouse; he took over the boys from his father's academy and also its premises. He was now the Schoolmaster of the Hospital and his boys therefore formed the School.

During Rose's time and indeed for some years before, the old Schoolhouse had not been used for its original purpose, for it had been utilized as a storehouse for Government supplies in readiness for invasion by Napoleon in 1796. When this danger was past, and the building was derequisitioned, it was too dilapidated for Bisset to use, yet, as will be seen, it was not entirely unsuitable for teaching purposes.

Elementary Education

With the exception of Archbishop Tenison's School and the School of Industry attached to the Workhouse, the schools of Croydon did not provide for the education of the poorer classes. There were numerous private schools for young children and 'several most respectable boarding schools for young ladies and gentlemen', but organised education for the children of the artisan and the farm-labourer did not exist and in the main was not required, either for their work or for their leisure activity, although the more ambitious of these workers perceived the advantages of being able to read and even write. In general, all that was available was a 'Dame' school, run more as a child-minding service, where an old woman, perhaps barely literate herself, taught the alphabet and little more to half-a-dozen children. At this time it was not thought that the state had any obligation to provide such a private service as education, but there were enlightened members of other classes who wished to provide a cheap but effective means of teaching the children of the poor to read, mainly with the intention of instilling virtuous habits through reading the Bible and works of moral precept. One such system that had met with success in many places was that of the Sunday schools, which gave the only schooling that many children received, if they received any at all. Another was to prove far more successful, however.

The National School 1812

In the first decade of the nineteenth century Joseph Lancaster introduced the not altogether original system of instructing a number of older children, or monitors, in a lesson which they would later transmit to their juniors. This scheme, variously described as the Lancasterian, the Madras, or Dr. Bell's system (Dr. Andrew Bell, an Anglican clergyman, who was another exponent, had established such schools in Madras) had the merits of economy in employment of instructors and cheapness in operation. On 30 September 1812 a meeting was held at the 'Crown' Inn to establish in Croydon a school to be run on Lancasterian principles. It was to be supported by voluntary subscriptions and donations from local benefactors, and its benefits were to be extended to the children of all indigent parents, whatever their religious persuasions might be. The latter stipulation, for the Lancasterian Society was largely run by dissenters, presented a challenge to the Vicar of Croydon and the members of his vestry, and a month later an assembly of the parishioners under the chairmanship of Dr. Ireland instituted another school under the auspices of 'The National Society for promoting the Education of the Poor in the Principles of the Established Church of England and Wales', which, founded by Dr. Bell in 1811, set up schools attached to the local parish churches; many of these schools have survived, no longer known as 'National Schools', but maintained by the local education authority.

There remained the problem of finding premises for this new school; any appropriate building, even a barn, would do to begin with, but something far more convenient was to hand. There was the empty Schoolhouse, ample in size and convenient in location, and it was to some degree under the control of the Vicar, as the Founder's 'Governor', and of the Archbishop, as Visitor, who from the beginning had been a strong supporter of the National Society. But there were doubts as to the propriety of putting the building to such a purpose, so the supporters of the vestry scheme sought counsel's opinion, warned, no doubt, by Lord Eldon's ruling (p. 105), that their course might not be completely smooth. So a case was put, stating that

much clamour has lately prevailed in the Parish in regard to this [*Whitgift's*] school, and the Archbishop has recently been petitioned and otherwise applied to as Visitor to cause it to be opened on some other plan. A subscription has just been set on foot . . . for establishing a school on Dr Bell's principle for the teaching of reading, writing and arithmetic—and the subscribers wish . . . to consolidate the two schools if (as they believe) the Grammar School cannot be totally dropt—and it is expected the Archbishop will give his consent to the measure to permit the old School House to be so appropriated if he legally can. . . .

It is conceded that instruction at the School on the Foundation is probably confined to the learned languages, but as

the School Room . . . is of considerable magnitude and every way adapted to the purpose and there is a room adjoining most probably large enough to contain such boys as may be sent on the foundation, and if not, the subscribers would enlarge it at their own expense, so that the two Schools might be conducted in fact under the same roof though distinctly and separately managed. . . .

The questions to be asked were (a) whether the Schoolmaster could be required or allowed to teach the three Rs, or whether he could fulfil the Statutes only by giving a Classical education, and (b) whether there was any legal objection to the use of the Schoolhouse as the subscribers had indicated.

Counsel (W.D. Best, of Lincoln's Inn Fields) gave as his opinion that the Schoolmaster could, if he thought fit, teach the vernacular tongue, but he could not be compelled to teach anything but Classical learning; counsel thought that as the Schoolmaster was required to 'be able to write well', the simpler parts of education should be within his plan if he so desired. He saw no objection to allowing the Schoolhouse or part of it to be used for teaching the proposed National School if it was not required for the purpose of a Grammar School, and he saw no reason why the subscribers should not enlarge the building in the way proposed.

Thus began an association between the Schoolhouse and elementary education that was later to have a great influence upon the affairs of the Foundation. During the period of nearly fifty years that the National School was lodged in the Schoolhouse, no subsidy was granted from the funds, and no control exercised by the officials of the Hospital of the Holy Trinity. The Vicar directed the School, kept its accounts and appointed the Master, the first one being John Skelton Chapman, who has been on occasion mistakenly referred to as Master of Whitgift's School. This confusion was a not unnatural one, for in other cases, such as Aldenham and Highgate Schools, the trustees had in fact allowed the foundation Schoolmaster to establish schools of this kind, to meet a local demand and often to satisfy a statutory requirement to give free teaching to *all* children in a parish who demanded it.

Lord Eldon's Ruling

The virtual extinction of the grammar schools had not occurred without protest and attempts to remedy the lack of a system of education that would prepare boys for the universities and the learned professions. A test case, brought in 1805 by the governors of Leeds Grammar School, who wished to enlarge the old Classical curriculum by adding arithmetic, writing and modern languages, resulted in a judgment by Lord Chancellor Eldon that declared that they were not competent to modify their founder's statutes. Eldon, who had been educated at Newcastle Royal Grammar School at a time when it was enjoying a revival of reputation, maintained that Leeds School, like Newcastle, had been founded as a 'free grammar' school, whose function was to teach the Classical languages and nothing else, so that any alteration or addition to the curriculum would be a misappropriation of the endowment. Thus, all over the country, masters of ancient grammar schools were confirmed in their claims either to refuse to teach anything else or to make a charge for teaching other subjects, even if their schools had been founded as 'free' schools, entirely or in part. During his term of office, which lasted until 1827, Eldon fought hard against any kind of reform, and it was not until the Grammar Schools Act of 1840 that governors were allowed any greater freedom in the interpretation of the terms of their trust. In fairness to Eldon, it must be acknowledged that the legal principle he was defending was that no alteration to a charitable trust could be made without an Act of Parliament to authorize it. Of this ruling Bisset must have been aware and he was thus able to conduct the School on his own terms.

More than ever the success of a grammar school depended not so much on the local demand for education, which could often be better met by the wider curriculum of competing private schools, but on the vigour and quality of the schoolmaster, and especially on his power to attract boarders; he himself could vary in reputation over the years. Thus a school's popularity might rise and fall irregularly during a short time. Even a 'great' school, such as Shrewsbury, for example, according to one account, had in 1798, like Whitgift's School, but one boy; but whereas twenty years later Bisset had perhaps forty or fifty, Shrewsbury counted over three hundred. Harrow and Rugby dropped from about three hundred boys in 1818 to much less than half that number in ten years. But apart from half a dozen 'great' boarding schools and a similar number of day schools in the cities, the grammar schools of England were reduced almost to extinction.

Local indignation in many places over this situation that permitted the abuse and misuse of educational endowments gave rise to attempts to stir up interest on a national scale. In 1818 Nicholas Carlisle published his *Concise Description of the Endowed Grammar Schools of England*, which contained references to 475 old schools; he attempted to expose the inefficiency, neglect and dishonesty that existed, and called for a public investigation. It is significant that although Whitgift's School is not even mentioned, yet compared with some, it was flourishing.

Henry Brougham's Select Committee

Another man, however, was in a better position to initiate reforms, although he was concerned not so much with grammar schools as such as with the possibility of using their endowments for the elementary education of the masses. In 1816 Henry Brougham, MP (later Lord Brougham), persuaded Parliament to appoint a *Select Committee to Enquire into the Education of the Lower Orders of the Metropolis*, of which he became chairman. After amassing a great deal of evidence of poverty in London, he was disappointed by the apathy displayed on all sides towards his committee's findings, but he was allowed to continue his enquiries and to extend them to the whole of England and Wales. Brougham, who had followed Joseph Lancaster as President of the Royal Lancasterian Society, conceived the ambition of bringing to the masses of Britain the type of elementary education supplied by France, Switzerland and Holland. One way of providing the schools was to obtain control over the large number of endowed foundations throughout the country. He was determined to investigate every foundation that might be considered to have a duty towards the education of the poor, but he was baffled by the limiting conditions that no foundation with a Visitor at its head could be coerced into reformation, and that no Court of Equity could deal with any case of breach of trust, perversion of the founder's intentions or neglect of the statutes, but only with direct misappropriation of funds.

In 1818 Brougham's 'Select Committee' took evidence concerning the charities of Croydon, and on 6 June that year Mr. William Dutton Harding, another of those characters, exemplified a hundred years before by Mrs. Mary Blanchard, who took up the cause against abuses of Whitgift's charity, gave evidence. He declared that for the past eight years he had had little else to employ his time but enquiring into the state of charitable funds in Croydon, and gave an account of the way the Hospital revenues were being increased under the care of himself and others. This Mr. Harding was a man of some strength of character and bluntness of speech, as revealed in his answers to the Committee's questions:

Who is the Visitor of the Hospital?—The Archbishop of Canterbury.

Does he ever visit?—Yes, he does.

When did he last visit?—He appointed two other persons last Monday to visit it, not on account of the revenues, but on account of the misconduct as they conceived of the warden and schoolmaster; this warden I got put in; he was one of the poor brethren; he is offensive to the Archbishop and the clergy: the school is now kept open by subscription, and not according to the ordinances.

What school do you mean?—The Hospital.

Do the ordinances require it to be a free school?—Yes, for such as are of the poorer, and men of the better sort.

Are they fed or clothed?—No, neither food nor clothing are given; there was no school kept; government occupied it as a storehouse within my memory, till Joseph Lancaster came to Croydon, and then Dr. Ireland called a meeting of the inhabitants, and they established a school under Bell's system.

In what year?—In the year 1812.

Was this school established by subscription?—It was.

Does Archbishop Whitgift's Hospital subscribe to it?—No.

Is the Archbishop's school in existence at all?—No, not at all; the schoolmaster appointed on that establishment keeps a private school for his own emolument, and does no public duty as schoolmaster whatever.

Before, fifty years ago, used there to be a school in the Hospital?—Oh, yes.

How many have you heard of being there?—The old inhabitants have heard of numbers being instructed there.

Has the Archbishop, as visitor, insisted on the school being revived?—No, but I have, and he will not do it.

Harding evidently had little idea of how the School had been run during its first two hundred years. There are a number of slightly erroneous statements, and the hearsay evidence, even then second-hand, is not convincing; if any local boys had been educated there fifty years before, surely some one of them could have been found to confirm Harding's assertions.

A couple of days later two churchwardens were called and examined; they could give very little information upon Whitgift's Foundation, could not recollect the name of the master who taught in the old Schoolhouse, but knew that Mr. Bisset took in boarders.

Does he take in any free, and for nothing?—I do not think he does one.

You state that the reason why he teaches none free, is, that none have applied?—So it is said.

Why do people in Croydon wish to be taught when they pay, and not apply to be taught for nothing?—I believe the reason is from the long disuse of it; that seems to be the case.... [Application] has not been forbidden but discouraged; there has not been a school for many years.

Obstacles to Reform

Whether Bisset was not invited to give evidence or whether he declined is not known, but the publication of witnesses' statements was taken as an overt criticism not only of Bisset's conduct of his responsibilities as far as the School was concerned and the Archbishop's neglect of his duties as Visitor, but also of the Rev. John Ireland, who had now left Croydon to become Dean of Westminster. In *A Letter to Henry Brougham, Esq., MP* he states his own responsibilities in the matter and gives an account of the conditions leading to the disposal of the old Schoolhouse:

In the enquiry...in June last concerning the Hospital...you thought proper...to implicate me in a responsibility for its management. Had you asked...whether my situation as Vicar gave me any control over the Hospital, the answer must have been, no. But from this you abstained, and have left me in the unpleasant situation of which I complain.

Ireland goes on to explain in detail the circumstances of the establishment of the National School, and denies that the Archbishop ever refused to revive the original school.

(There was a general misapprehension over the purpose and history of the School since its foundation. Many local residents fully believed that all and sundry ought to receive free instruction, whether in the elements or in the classics, from a schoolmaster enjoying an emolument of little more than £20 a year; there had never been a suggestion of increasing it. Furthermore, Brougham himself, ignoring any post-Reformation custom, claimed that Latin was intended to be taught in grammar schools to enable the poor to follow the church services.)

If the funds of the Hospital had been used for this purpose, blame might still have been laid; but all was done at our own private expense. The Master of the new school was paid by the subscription of the friends of the church establishment; and the new room, adjoining to the original Grammar School was built, from the same fund, for the Grammar scholars of Archbishop Whitgift if any should choose to come; on recent enquiry, from the present schoolmaster of the foundation, it appears, that not a single proposal has been made to him for the admission of children there. One of the witnesses informs you, that the inhabitants do not know the privilege they have to send scholars. It is then their own fault. It has been repeatedly announced. Once it was done through my own advice; and notices were stuck on the church door and all the public places of the parish.

After describing his appointment to inspect the accounts during Rose's time, and explaining that he had no power to direct the Hospital's affairs, Ireland reveals that the Archbishop himself has been defied by the Members.

I am now about to add another particular which, perhaps, will surprise you: namely, not only was I excluded from the management of the property, but also the Archbishop himself. When the warden and poor brethren took the affairs of the Hospital into their own hands, the Archbishop, acting on the customary authority, sent them an injunction not to proceed with the destruction of the timber on the estates, which had already begun, without the usual reference to him. But having now the benefit of other advice, they answered his Grace, that all the power which they conceived to be given him by the Statutes was to come among them and compose their quarrels within the walls, &c., and that they would manage their own property in their own manner. Under this defiance, the Archbishop sent the case to...the late Sir Samuel Romilly. He was desired to say, whether the Archbishop had the power, not only of punishing offences and redressing grievances, but of 'interfering in the management of the Hospital, so as to be necessarily consulted in the renewal of leases, the affixing of the seal to any instrument affecting the interest of the Hospital, the cutting of timber, and the appropriation of revenues; the warden being generally an ignorant man, chosen by the poor themselves, and one of their own body.' All these powers had been exercised by former Archbishops, but the time was now come for a change; and the opinion of Sir Samuel was, that the Archbishop had no right to interfere in the cases described; that he had no other authority than that of Visitor and patron, and that the general management was with the Hospital.

(The advice taken by the Brethren and Sisters, led in defiance of the Archbishop and the Schoolmaster by an obstinate and unscrupulous Warden, was by no means gratuitous, and having entrusted their affairs to a surveyor and a solicitor in London, they were persuaded into expensive and sometimes disastrous litigation. In 1814–15 they became involved in a lawsuit in which they were committed to the extent of £410 in payment of their own costs and of those of the adverse party; in the same year they undertook another, but this time successful, claim for £484; unhappily the sum was not even enough to pay their attorney's bill for the action, quite apart from other expenses incurred for witnesses' expenses.

Whitgift School

Between 1816 and 1820 another similar sum was lost. At the end of one action in the Court of Common Pleas the Hospital's attitude was described by the judges as unjust and dishonourable. The Brethren and Sisters were eventually extricated in 1820 by a local solicitor, Patrick Drummond, whose firm and its successors have continued to act for the Foundation until the present day.)

Brougham's enquiry and Ireland's protest did not result in any reforming action for no such action was yet legally possible, so the National School continued to be conducted in the Schoolhouse, and Bisset continued to teach his own school, comprising at one time fifteen boarders and thirty day-boys. Had he ever had a genuine 'poor scholar' to teach the classics to, it seems likely that he would have taken him with his other pupils, rather than occupy the otherwise vacant room built on to the Schoolhouse, for how could he, without employing extra staff, split his school into two? One wonders what risk there was to Bisset of having to take on any such scholars.

Croydon in 1820

One of his pupils has left a description of the centre part of Croydon as it was about 1820. He was William Page, born in 1810. His recollections, written down in 1880, are the only descriptive record in any detail of the appearance of Croydon before the invention of photography; those that describe the vicinity of the Hospital are of particular interest.

The east side of North End, starting from 'The College', consisted mainly of small shops and modest private houses, many of wooden construction. The site of the former entrance to the North End School buildings and of the present entrance to the 'Whitgift Centre' was then 'a stone-mason's yard, enclosed in front by a dwarf wall and iron palisade, showing within materials for the trade, a few pieces of old statuary and tomb-stones, etc.' The north side of George Street is described:

College Corner, as it is now, also the private house now occupied by one of the masters at Whitgift [*this was a house erected by one James Lewen, a leaseholder, in about 1760*], School next, then lower School-room and the Headmaster's house, at this time kept by the Rev. John Bisset, Chaplain to the Hospital or College. I was one of his pupils but not a distinguished one, oh no, far from it. Next, the old house lately pulled down, occupied by the late Dr. Cooper [*this was the house erected by Henry Mills*].

Then McCarthy's hunting and livery stables, occupying a large frontage enclosing a quadrangle of stables and a small two-storied dwelling, occupied by the owner. Here assembled in the morning a goodly number (in the season) of the sons of sporting gents, booted and spurred, in their scarlet coats and velvet caps, mounting their horses to enjoy the day's run, perhaps to meet Lord Derby's hounds in the neighbourhood, or other parks. At the time, this quiet street (there not being a shop in it) had the appearance of a miniature Melton Mowbray. You then came to two large houses, one occupied by Col. Watts, and the other by Dr. James, then the leading and fashionable doctor of the county. I now see him in my mind's eye, a fine handsome man, buttoned up to his throat in a blue coat with metal buttons.

Bisset's school was not fashionable enough for Dr. James; his sons went to Eton.

By this time the Society of Friends, which had had for many years a Meeting-House in Croydon, had established a flourishing boarding school there, and the East India Company had their military college at Addiscombe, so Whitgift's School was completely overshadowed by establishments that already had a more than local fame and were destined to become still more celebrated, although they both vanished long before the end of the century. The prosperity of Croydon is reflected in the increasing amounts shared out among the 'poor', who were now frequently men and women drawn from the lower-middle class in indigent retirement. The old and the really destitute were being committed to the workhouses, the first of which in Croydon had been erected in 1727. In 1827 Bisset received a total of £28; the following year he received £40, and the amounts increased yearly, so that by 1842 he received £47. The extra sums above his £20 were the same as those distributed to each of the almspeople, who were beginning to do very well indeed and, within a few more years, were to receive not only free lodging but also an unearned income greater than the wage earned by an unskilled worker in regular employment.

The Charity Commission

The commotion that had been stirred up locally and nationally about abused charities seemed to have died down, but the Charity Commission established in 1818 was steadily doing its work, and on 26 July 1836 the Honourable Daniel Finch, one of his Majesty's Commissioners of Charities, visited the Hospital and for three days investigated its accounts and its management. Bisset recorded in his Ledger:

He examined the Schoolmaster upon Oath relative to the Archbishop's School and other matters, and inspected the title deeds and all papers relating to the property of the Hospital, and kindly sorted out the principal deeds and recommended them to the special care of the Warden, Schoolmaster and Claviger, (he) expressed himself as perfectly satisfied with the Prudence & discretion shewn by the Hospital in the management of their Estates and Affairs in general.

Bisset's ingenuous estimate of the Commissioner's satisfaction was not altogether reflected in what the latter had to say to his Chairman. During his three days in Croydon Daniel Finch had very shrewdly weighed up all the evidence available and on 4 February 1837 he reported his findings. Most of his report is concerned with a résumé of the history of the Hospital and a summary of its statutes, together with an account of its buildings, the management of the estates and the day-to-day conduct of the Hospital, but he has some significant remarks to make about the state of the School.

The Rev. John Bisset . . . officiates as chaplain to the hospital, and reads prayers at the chapel every day on which there is no service at the parish church. . . . With regard to the instruction of youth, he now performs no duty whatever; till within the last six years he took private scholars, as well from Croydon as from other places, for classical instruction; he had at one period from 15 to 30 pupils from Croydon under his care, but for these he made such charges as he thought proper; he states that no application was ever made to him for the admission of a free scholar, except in three instances, when finding that the object of the parents was that their sons should be taught reading, writing and accounts, his own scholars being of another class, he made an arrangement with the master of the National School to take the boys, with which the parents were perfectly satisfied.

The room built by the Founder for a school . . . is still used for the instruction of the children of the national school.

The Grammar Schools Act 1840

But nothing further could be done after Mr. Finch's report until Parliament had passed *An Act for improving the Condition and Extending the Benefits of Grammar Schools* in 1840. The Act was designed to free the governors of the ancient grammar schools from the restrictions that limited instruction to the dead languages and in some cases imposed impediments to the schools' expansion. The Act was only permissive, however, and although some schools took advantage of this freedom to re-organise, it was not for another thirteen years that the State took an active part in promoting the revival of such schools, so the condition of Whitgift's School remained unchanged.

Early in 1843 Bisset resigned his position at Croydon Hospital and his living at Addington (which had been presented to him by Manners-Sutton upon Rose's death in 1820) on being collated Vicar of Leysdown, Kent (which John Taylor Lamb had held nearly one hundred years earlier), and here he spent the rest of his life, which ended in 1852. He seems not to have taken any more pupils after Finch's visit and in the census return of 1841 he describes himself as 'Independent', so on his retirement the School had been in abeyance for a dozen years; not for another generation was it to be properly revived.

6. The Struggle for Reconstruction, 1843–1871

Archbishop Howley's Dilemma

Upon Bisset's resignation, it fell to Archbishop Howley to appoint a successor. Howley, having succeeded Manners-Sutton in 1828, had been acquainted with the Hospital's affairs for fifteen years; in 1831 he had listened sympathetically to suggestions from Bisset and the Warden concerning the distribution of their increased income; and he had also recommended that the Schoolmaster's House should in future be included with the rest of the Hospital's buildings when the cost of repairs had to be met, the charge no longer to fall upon the Schoolmaster. This recommendation, which was readily accepted by the Brethren and Sisters, seemed to be in acknowledgment that the Schoolmaster/Chaplain's stipend had not been increased in the same proportion as that of the other inmates.

One might think that, taking advantage of the Grammar Schools Act, Howley should have made some attempt to revive the School, for he was not devoid of reforming zeal. But without the co-operation of the Brethren and Sisters he would have found reform impossible, even with the support of the Charity Commissioners and the Court of Chancery, who were equally powerless to act without the good will of the trustees of any foundation under the protection of a Visitor; as yet there was no solution to this problem. Secondly, as a keen supporter of the National Society, he may have thought that the existing situation could not be improved. Thirdly, he had the opportunity of making an appointment that was convenient to the Vicar and Vestry of Croydon, although not greatly advantageous to the cause of education.

George Coles

He chose for the post a man who since 1823 had been serving as a clergyman in Croydon, first as assistant curate of the parish, and since 1829 as incumbent of St. James's Chapel, later the parish church of St. James, on Croydon Common; this was one of the first of the new districts that were carved out of the old parish in order to cater for the increasing population. George Coles was born in 1799 and educated at Eton and Peterhouse, and after ordination seems to have spent the whole of his pastoral life in Croydon.

His appointment to the Hospital in January 1843 was clearly designed to augment a small stipend and to provide him with a residence, but it does appear that he took a few pupils, in spite of what has been stated to the contrary. Twenty-five years after Coles's death a local inhabitant recalled that 'Mr Coles received four or five sons of the aristocracy, but not free scholars of Croydon according to the Founder's will'. This statement is borne out by the Census returns of 1851 and 1861, which show that among these pupils (for whom 'aristocracy' must be a misnomer) were in fact one or two who boarded with Coles.

His school was merely a small private establishment of little significance compared with several other local schools, such as Fairfield House, under Mr. Twentyman, which stood at the corner of George Street and Park Lane, where Suffolk House now stands, and which had in 1851, besides an unspecified number of dayboys, forty-one boarders, including three French boys of 17 and 18, although the other pupils were all aged between 8 and 14.

It was during Coles's time that great efforts

The Reverend George Coles, Schoolmaster 1843–65

were made to revive the School. The construction of the railway between London and West Croydon in 1839 attracted as residents prosperous professional and business men from London who could now live well away from their place of business yet still make a quick daily journey to and from town. These men required good schools for their sons. The public schools of England, of new and of old foundation, had not reached their greatest period of expansion (made possible largely by the later network of railways throughout the country) and most large and medium-sized towns were looking, albeit vainly, to their ancient grammar schools to develop, and provide a suitable education for their middle-class inhabitants. The local tradesmen, too, were greatly in favour of resuscitating such schools, which would encourage the right type of wealthy customer to settle in the district, and which might also be suitable for their own sons to attend.

The advisers to the Brethren and Sisters, whose increased income had become by now something of an embarrassment, had counselled them to provide accommodation for additional inmates, and in 1844 Archibishop Howley issued an injunction empowering them to build a block of six more rooms, which was erected between the Hospital and the Schoolhouse in 1848; the block was demolished in 1899. These additions did not suffice to allay indignation over the failure to provide education, and certain people began to examine ways and means of compelling the Hospital to re-establish the School in a permanent form. The Charitable Trusts Act of 1853 at last provided a method of legally achieving this end.

Attempts at Reform

The Statute of Charitable Uses of 1601, which probably received the Founder's particular support, and from which most legal definitions of 'charities' derive, first established that endowments devoted to education were 'charitable', and set up machinery to remedy abuses. But the method, which involved bringing a suit in the Court of Chancery, was long and costly—certainly it had become so by the end of the eighteenth century—and reformers found that litigation could swallow up the income of many years of the charity that was being investigated. Brougham himself was well aware of this drawback.

A court of equity affords most inadequate means of enquiry. No prudent man will easily be induced to involve himself in a Chancery suit, where his private interests are at stake. To expect that any one will do so from the love of justice, and a sense of duty towards the public is in all but a few extraordinary cases, truly chimerical.... Parish officers ruined by their attempts to obtain justice for the poor, a respectable solicitor and clergyman ... expending large sums of their own money in the same pious work, and rewarded by the general contempt and even hatred of their fellow citizens; a worthy inhabitant of Croydon exposed to every kind of vexation for similar exertions, and his coadjutor falsely and maliciously indicted for perjury.

In 1786 an Act was passed requiring returns to be made of all 'Charitable Donations' then in existence, but no further action was demanded. The next important Act was passed in 1812—the Charitable Procedures Act—but although Dr. Rose's defalcations might have seemed to provide an opportunity for reform, this Act referred only to disputes between trustees and beneficiaries; it might have been invoked in Rose's case, had not the court action between him and the Brethren and Sisters been settled before the Act came into force. Brougham's Commission for Charities, set up in 1818, was precluded from taking any action over a charity having a special Visitor (in the case of the Hospital, the Archbishop of Canterbury) or over universities and most of the greater schools. All these limitations were lamented by the Commission when it made its Report in 1835. Up to the time of the Charitable Trusts Act of 1853, no fewer than thirteen bills relating to the reformation of charities had failed in Parliament. This Act set up a new Charity Commission with powers, *inter alia*, to demand sight of and to enquire into accounts and other documents, to give advice and authority to trustees, to control the institution of legal proceedings (as we have seen, an often severe and unnecessary drain upon funds), to control dealings in real estate, and to act as Official Trustee of Lands and Funds.

Outside Intervention

Already, with a knowledge of the effects the Act would have upon foundations that had not adjusted themselves to the requirements of the age, some local men were taking steps to reform the administration of the Hospital's affairs. C.S. Masterman, a grocer and cheesemonger of North End, Croydon, and his son, W.S. Masterman, solicitor of Clifford's Inn, but also resident in North End, were among the first to take legal action. Early in 1853 they submitted an 'Information' to the Lord Chancellor, in which they cited the Warden, Schoolmaster and Claviger for neglect and mismanagement of the Hospital's affairs and of the School in particular; they also cited Archbishop Sumner, who had succeeded Howley in 1848, for declining to interfere as Visitor. The informants prayed that with the Attorney-General's *fiat* the Court of Chancery should settle a Scheme for managing the Hospital's estates and its affairs in general and 'particularly for conducting a grammar school or other school for the benefit of the poorer classes'. On 27 January 1853, J.P. Fearon, Solicitor to the Attorney-General, asked W.S. Masterman to see him, as the Attorney-General had directed that enquiries should be made about the Hospital. On the following day the Archbishop's secretary wrote to Fearon, stating that the Archbishop had already begun the revision of the Statutes, especially in regard to the School, so apparently Fearon had reported Masterman's actions to the Archbishop. As a consequence of this interview with Fearon, Masterman stayed his hand and did not press for the Attorney-General's *fiat*. After waiting for the best part of a year, however, he came to the conclusion that the Archbishop was indeed reluctant to interfere, so he wrote tongue in cheek to Sumner, apologising for not consulting him earlier, but suggesting that they might co-operate in their efforts to reform the Hospital's affairs and revive the School, his chief purpose being 'to see the sons of the Middle Classes receive a sound Christian education'. Sumner acknowledged Masterman's request with some asperity, but made no step to meet him half way; he said that a committee under the Vicar of Croydon (the Rev. J.G. Hodgson) had agreed upon a Scheme that would be shortly submitted to him as Visitor for his approval, and which he was sure would answer the object that Masterman had in view. Having received no encouragement from that quarter, Masterman hopefully approached the Hospital's solicitors, asking for a sight of the proposed Scheme, but here also he drew blank; he was assured that the Scheme was in its last stages of preparation, but Messrs. Drummond trusted 'you will not take so needless or so injurious a course as to move further in the proceedings in Chancery'.

Masterman waited another seven months without obtaining either the Attorney-General's *fiat* or any information about the proposed Scheme, so on 3 July 1854 he got his father to make application to the Charity Commissioners for their certificate authorising in their name the Information laid, but not 'filed' or accepted, eighteen months before. There was emphasis upon the revival of the School, among the reasons given being that the Schoolmaster no longer taught the boys of the town the Classics, and that 'the School house is used as a National School and frequented by the Poor Children, and another Master (not a clergyman) teaches them their alphabet, &c. . . . My sole object in interfering in the Charity is to get the Grammar School revived for the benefit of the Town.'

The Attorney-General's Petition

It is clear that Fearon and H.M. Vane, Secretary to the Charity Commissioners, were keeping each other informed about the progress of the Whitgift affair and that they were unwilling for any outsider to interfere; they were in touch with a number of other dissatisfied Croydon people, but wished the Hospital's reformation to come from within, or at least from those who had some hand in its management. The Vicar's committee, slowly perhaps, was in fact preparing a Scheme, whereas the Mastermans were relying upon the vaguer proposals of their Information. On 29 July Vane told Masterman that the Attorney-General was proceeding in the business. Indeed, two days before, cutting the ground from under Masterman's feet, the Attorney-General, *ex officio*, had petitioned the Master of the Rolls

> in the Matter of the Warden and Poor of the Hospital of the Holy Trinity in Croydon...
>
> to declare that it is expedient to apply the prospective increase in the rents and profits of the Estates of the said Hospital for the purposes of Education and that an enquiry may be made of what the Charity property consists and that a Scheme for the administration and management of the Charity may be settled by the Court.

This petition was granted on 31 July and 'filed' on 12 August.

Now that the preparation of a Scheme was authorised, it might be thought that the Vicar and his committee would move into action, but the Charity Commissioners, who were busy establishing order out of the chaos of the charitable trusts, had basic principles for the reconstruction of the numerous schools and other foundations that they found themselves involved with. As far as possible they consulted ancient statutes where they existed, and studied local conditions and requirements. A Scheme had to satisfy a good many conflicting opinions and interests, had to be financially workable, and in the case of a school had to provide an education suitable to the locality. In spite of the Vicar's efforts, his Scheme was either not yet available or had to be further worked on by the Commissioners before it could be put into effect.

The mythical 'Common School'

It will be remembered that the Founder, in Chapter One of his Statutes and Ordinances, laid down that one of the Brethren 'shall teach a Grammar School in Croydon in the Schoolhouse there by me builded...'. When Dr. A.C. Ducarel, in his *History of Croydon*, published in 1783, printed a transcript of the copy of Whitgift's Statutes that he had found in Lambeth Palace, where he was librarian, he allowed several mistakes to intrude that remained undiscovered until a close examination of the manuscript was made in 1958; the clause above was rendered 'shall teach a *Common* School in Croydon...', and other, less significant, mistakes had also crept in.

The Schoolhouse

Whenever the Statutes were referred to or reprinted, Ducarel's version was regarded as authentic and was adhered to; in 1810 and 1821 Croydon printers reproduced it exactly; so did D.W. Garrow and G.S. Steinman in their *Histories of Croydon*, 1818 and 1834 respectively; in 1863 and 1890 the Governors caused it to be reprinted with one or two alterations that seem to be common-sense corrections of obvious mistakes, but 'Common School' remained. All other printed versions of the Statutes, whether complete or in abstract, show the same error, which so impressed itself upon those responsible for drawing up new Schemes, that it was confidently but quite erroneously believed that:

> ... the Founder here intended to create a school in which the middle and labouring classes should be taught together; it is, in fact, an instance of a common school founded for both classes, comprising within itself the germs of both the modern primary and modern secondary schools. The school, for some time,

performed the work for which it was intended; it educated the sons of the inhabitants of Croydon of both classes. But, at last, owing to well known social and other changes, this became impossible. A system of modern education arose, and as the Schoolmaster insisted on teaching Latin and Greek and little else, to all children who came there, and also charged highly for books, the number of scholars decreased to zero, at which figure it has stood, *as I was informed*, since about 1830. The last master, who was, *if I am rightly informed*,* appointed about 1832, and who died last year, found no pupils attending when he came to the school, and never had any at all during the thirty odd years he was master.

This extract from D.R. Fearon's statement in the *Report of the Schools Inquiry Commission* of 1868, Appendix IV, p.468, shows how unreliable his local informants could be. Although Fearon may have had some doubts, which would prove to be well founded, about the reliability of what he was told, he readily accepted the false evidence about the 'common' school.

It seems unnecessary, in the light of present knowledge of how the School was anciently conducted, to draw a distinction between the purpose of a 'grammar' school and that of this 'common' school, which was a figment of the writer's imagination. Whitgift's School itself had never become an 'elementary' school, despite the use of its buildings by the National Society. In order to understand the effect of the mistake, it would be well to examine the educational needs in the fifties of the last century.

'Middle-Class' Education

Education in England was in many ways inferior to that of several Continental countries, especially those such as Germany, that were educating their young men to develop industry and trade. The functions of various types of school have already been touched upon; the labouring classes had their particular schools: the 'charity' and the 'national' schools; the middle classes had a wider choice: from private schools, day or boarding, to grammar and public schools (many of which were one and the same); and the upper classes went to the 'great' public schools or had private tutors, or sometimes went to élite private schools. All existed in generally inadequate

* Author's italics.

numbers and buildings (with the exception, perhaps, that there were far too many small, inefficient private schools). There was a need and, from enlightened quarters a demand, for a different type of school, more suited to the requirements of business, commerce and the minor professions.

The Creative Mind

If one studies the origins of a hundred men of the greatest creative and original talent – artists, writers, explorers, radicals, thinkers, scientists, industrialists – who were born between 1800 and 1845, they can be grouped according to their early education.

i. Ten per cent of them, Darwin (Shrewsbury), Lewis Carroll (Rugby), Swinburne (Eton) and Thackeray (Charterhouse) for example, were educated at one or other of the 'great' schools, as were most of the distinguished statesmen, lawyers, soldiers and high-ranking clerics, who do not rate for inclusion as 'creative'.

ii. Fifteen per cent attended the few surviving successful grammar schools such as King Edward's Birmingham (Burne-Jones, Francis Galton) or newly founded schools, such as KCS (1829) (D.G. Rossetti), Cheltenham (1841) (Lord Morley) and Marlborough (1843) (William Morris).

iii. Another ten per cent received a sound education at a good private school or at a Quaker school (Lord Lister, Alfred Waterhouse).

iv. A small but significant group of scientists and inventors came from Scotland, having attended the High Schools or Academies of Edinburgh and Glasgow (Lord Kelvin, Clerk-Maxwell).

v. But the remainder received an education that was irregular or even rudimentary, perhaps confined to parental tuition (J.S. Mill, Ruskin), but in several cases conducted partly abroad (I.K. Brunel, Lord Leighton). In this large group may be placed Dickens, Huxley, Hardy, Millais, Livingstone and Lord Armstrong. Yet they seemed none the worse for it, as far as their creativity was concerned, unstifled by the rigours and narrowness of a conventional schooling.

Nevertheless, the moribund grammar schools, if they could have been resuscitated earlier and their curriculum modernised, might have contributed vastly to the education of a more literate, more inventive and more independent-minded middle class. Whitgift, like most of the others, contributed nothing, and no man of any particular distinction seems to have emerged who was born or bred in the vicinity of Croydon during those forty-five years.

Thomas Arnold's views on the purpose of secondary education covered more than the religious and moral aspects, which have received most general attention. He divided a man's life into two callings – that of his own career or profession, and that as a citizen and a man. 'The education which fits him for the first is called professional; that which fits him for the second is called liberal.' But he had nothing to say about the imagination, which he may have regarded as vicious and distracting!

It was not thought desirable to combine these two types of education in one school. A 'liberal' education at school led preferably to the same kind of study at university, where after graduation one could become a clerk in holy orders or a teacher; no further professional training was required. After university, professional training in the law could be followed at the Inns of Court, many men being called to the Bar without any intention of practising; civil servants, writers, journalists, landowners frequently possessed this useful qualification.

One could also read for the Bar without proceeding to university, and training for minor professions could be followed by becoming articled to a solicitor, a surveyor, an architect, etc. Technical qualifications were obtainable at colleges now being established in Victorian times by charitable persons, livery companies or municipal bodies.

Middle-class Opportunities

The tremendous expansion in internal and overseas transport and trade that was now taking place provided an increasing variety of opportunities for young men with more than a primary education, but not necessarily with the Classical training that was still thought essential for the senior professions and the leisured classes.

Subordinate posts, leading later to positions of responsibility in the Civil Service, local government, public utilities, banking and insurance, as well as in commercial firms, were open to boys whose education had finished at the age of fifteen or thereabouts, but who had received instruction in more than the three Rs. Such an education, it was thought, should include the study of Latin, a foreign language, English, History, Geography, Mathematics, Book-keeping, Mensuration, Elementary Mechanics and Political Economy; in fact, a far wider and more practical curriculum than was to be found in any public or grammar school, although scientific theory had little place. There was, then, especially in the large towns, a demand for 'Middle-class Commercial Schools', following the Victorian conviction that different types of education were suitable for different strata of the population. Commercial schools were viewed as philistine and illiberal by those who had no desire or need to prepare their sons for life in the competitive world of commerce.

The Victorian 'middle-class' was a vaguely defined and constantly shifting body, ranging from shop-assistant to prosperous financier. Matthew Arnold, who was devoting much of his writing at this time to the criticism of this philistine class and to the improvement of its education, stated, 'To prevent ambiguity and confusion, I have always adopted an educational test, and by the middle class I understand those who are brought up at establishments like Salem House, and by educators like Mr Creakle.' *David Copperfield* was published in 1850; there were plenty of schools more or less like Salem House in Croydon at this time and for many years to come. They were advertised in *The Croydon Chronicle*: Croydon Grammar School, Landsowne Road, 'for the Education of Young Gentlemen—Boarders or Daily Pupils admitted at 7 years of age'; College House Boarding and Day School, George Street; The Educational Institute, Day School for Young Gentlemen, Crown Hill; Eton House School, London Road; New University School, Lower Addiscombe Road; Manor House School, North End; and many others, some very short-lived. The pretentiousness of their names disguised the paucity of their aims and the modesty of their buildings. (After the 1851 Census it was estimated that 50,000 children were receiving secondary education in grammar schools; the same number at home, and half a million at private schools.)

Croydon was mainly a middle-class town; between 1840 and 1860 many large and medium-sized suburban houses were built, some of which remain to this day. The local tradesmen were becoming more prosperous, and it was chiefly they, calling themselves the 'rate-payers of Croydon', who were clamouring for their rights to the establishment of a 'Middle-class' school that would provide a subsidised utilitarian education. A smaller, professional group wished to have the Grammar School revived, with its emphasis on the Classics and connection with the universities. Another faction, however, led by the Vicar, wished the income from the Whitgift estates to be chiefly applied to the elementary education of the very poor, of whom there were many in the older part of the town, and they quoted that article of the Statutes (Chapter 7):

> The Schoolmaster shall freely teach such of the Children of the Parish of Croydon (without exacting any thing for their teaching) as are of the poorer sort, such as shall be accounted by the Vicar or Curate of Croydon. . . .

that seemed to support their claim, although, being misled by the corrupt phrase 'common school', they ignored the requirement that the Schoolmaster should be 'learned in the Greek and Latin tongues, a good versifier in both the aforesaid languages'.

The Charity Commissioners' Scheme

At last a workable scheme, based on the principles that had been adopted by the Charity Commissioners and the Court of Chancery, was drawn up by the Vicar and his committee, and submitted to the Court in February 1855. In the main it satisfied the wishes of the Croydon reformers. A Court of Governors was to be set up to conduct the affairs of the Hospital in place of the Schoolmaster, Warden, Brethren and Sisters, and all surplus income after expenses in connection with the Almshouses had been met was to be applied to support two schools:

> There shall be two Schools of which one shall be a commercial or Middle school suited to the educational requirements of respectable tradesmen, professional men, and gentlemen of humble means, and the other a Poor school of the Class now ordinarily established by the National society, and suited to the sons of the humble or working Classes . . . to be established and conducted in the buildings occupied for that purpose.

A 'Commercial School'

The ancient Schoolhouse was at this time still occupied by the National School, which under the Scheme would continue there exactly as before, except that it would have a new name and be financed by the Whitgift Governors; a house for the National Schoolmaster was to be built nearby. The 'Commercial' School was to be built on the field belonging to the Hospital to the north of the Schoolmaster's garden, a plot of one acre that had been bought by the Founder in March 1600 and had customarily been leased to the Schoolmaster, who had either used it as an extension to his garden or had sub-let it. The Head Master of the Commercial School, who was to live in the old Schoolmaster's House, was to be regarded as one of the Brethren of the Hospital and was to carry out the duties of Chaplain and Warden in addition, so he would have to be in Holy Orders. For his services as Warden he was to receive an emolument of £100 a year, and for his services as Head Master and Chaplain a further £200. There was to be an Under-Master at £100, and assistants who would receive not more than £75. The subjects to be taught were:

> Holy Scripture, according to the Church of England, Reading, Writing, Arithmetic, English Literature and Composition, Geography, Mathematics, Algebra, Land Surveying, Book-keeping, Chemistry, Physical Science, French, and such other languages and subjects as the Governors approve.

The Governors rather than the Head Master were to run the School.

> All boys of the age of eight years and upwards being resident in the Parish of Croydon being able to read and write and having some acquaintance with the first four rules of arithmetic, and being certified to be of good moral conduct shall . . . be qualified . . . for admission. No Scholar shall remain after the age of eighteen years.

The fees payable by parents were to be not more than £4 per annum, of which one half was

North End and the School precincts in 1865

to go to the Head Master in addition to his fixed salary, one quarter to the Under-Master, and one quarter to the general funds. Clearly the intention was to encourage the Head Master to build up and maintain numbers, rather than to draw a fixed salary and be indifferent to the prosperity of the School. Equally clear was the intention to do things otherwise as cheaply as possible, without making sufficient provision for adequate payment of assistants, equipment and maintenance; nothing much could be expected as a subsidy from the Charity's funds. Not only would the assistant masters' salaries be low, but the ratio of staff to pupils, also.

A 'Poor School'

The Poor School was to be open to

> Boys resident in the Parish of Croydon of the age of seven and upwards who are able to read and are not afflicted with any infectious or noisome disease . . . no Boy shall remain therein after the age of fourteen years.

The Poor School's Head Master's salary was not to exceed £75 per annum, plus his own stipend as Poor Brother of £40. The fees were to be not more than fourpence a week, and the subjects to be taught were to be those usually taught in the national schools; there were to be scholarships available to boys promoted to the Commercial School at the age of twelve years, but there were to be no more than six such scholarship holders in the Upper School at any one time.

This Scheme was altered in one main particular before it met with the approval of the Court of Chancery on 1 August 1856: the Poor School, which would have been an embarrassing neighbour to the Head Master of the Commercial School, whose house was adjacent, was to be accommodated in a new building in Church Road, on the Charity's property known as Clot Mead, much nearer the Parish Church and Old Town, then very densely populated and from where most of the pupils would come.

Governors

An overwhelmingly important matter was the selection of governors. The Vicar's Scheme, hammered out with the help of the Charity's solicitor, John Drummond, and approved by the Archbishop, yielded no ground to the views of an increasingly vocal and influential body of critics of the Church of England, which demanded a monopoly and a privileged position for itself in regard to education. There were to be not fewer than eight or more than twelve governors: the Vicar of Croydon, *ex officio*, and eleven others appointed by the Archbishop, who would be responsible for seeing that the number never fell below eight. No concessions were to be made to any idea that some of them should be democratically elected or be representative of any learned or independent body. They were, in fact, all in the Vicar's pocket. The Rev. J.G. Hodgson (so far as has been traced, unrelated to James Hodgson, Schoolmaster, or to Christopher, Secretary to the Archbishops for many years) had been Vicar of Croydon since 1846 and was a man of dominating personality and great organising skill. The Founder's Statutes, he understood, bestowed upon him the special responsibility of choosing those boys who were to benefit from the endowments, so he had regarded the National School as his own particular property. He was determined that the Charity's surplus income should primarily support the cause, so close to his heart, of educating the poor children of his district in the established faith at the National School's successor, Whitgift's Poor School. When their needs in this respect had been met, children of other classes might be allowed to benefit. In short, his was a benevolent but narrow parochial outlook.

He had no lack of willing supporters. First and foremost was John Drummond, the Solicitor and Vestry Clerk, who had been associated with the Charity since the days of his father, Patrick Drummond. Drummond was conscientious and unselfish in his attention to the interests, and especially to the charities, of the parish, being a trustee of most of these. The rest of the Governors seem to have been nominees of the Vicar, although some must have been personally known to the Archbishop. Four of them were already trustees of Snow's Charity at Mitcham: John W. Sutherland, of Coombe, described at his death as 'one of the old school of gentry', with a son who was Captain of Cricket at Eton in 1858; Thomas Keen, the senior member of a well-known firm of mustard-merchants, and a local landowner; Charles Chatfield, a wine-merchant in the High Street; and John Budgen, clock- and watch-maker in Mint Walk, who was particularly active in parish business. Other Governors were: Robert Amadeus Heath, of Coombe Hill House, a wealthy City merchant and the son-in-law of Thomas Keen; John Wickham Flower, a well-to-do amateur geologist and archaeologist, of Park Hill; Edward Westall, a Croydon surgeon; William R. White, JP; William J. Blake, who shortly resigned upon being appointed Surveyor to the Charity; and George Price, wine-merchant, who succeeded to Chatfield's business on the latter's death more than twenty years later. These Governors deserve a little study. Several of them closely connected by family or business ties, they comprise members of the land-owning gentry, independent and professional gentlemen, and respectable tradesmen. Many gave long service to the Court of Governors, including R.A. Heath, later Baron Heath and a generous benefactor, the Vicar, George Price and John Drummond, who all served for upwards of twenty-four years.

They took their duties with high-minded seriousness, but their knowledge of educational requirements in the mid-nineteenth century seems rudimentary; they were dealing with a completely new situation, the virtual creation of a new school system, and whatever their own schooling may have been—public or private school (in all probability the latter)—their own experience could have had little relevance.

It seems that as time went by they tended to rely more and more upon the Vicar and upon John Drummond and his partner and brother, William, who was appointed Secretary, part-time at a salary of £50 a year. With their profound knowledge of the Hospital's and other local affairs, these three assumed control of the administration to the extent allowed by the Charity Commissioners, whose authority had to be obtained for any capital sale or expenditure and for any lease of property for more than twenty-one years; the Commissioners also closely scrutinised the annual accounts.

The strict control thus exercised was frequently irksome and time-consuming and, being somewhat remote, it did not always take good note of local conditions, the Commissioners often preferring to send, at the Governors' expense, an architect or surveyor of their own choice to give his views, rather than rely upon the specialised knowledge of the local man. The impression is gained, too, that the Commissioners felt that a close eye should be kept upon the actions of the Messrs. Drummond, whose positions of power as Solicitor and

Secretary gave them the opportunity, should they accept it, of personal advantage when dealing with the Hospital's property. In point of fact the Drummonds were most scrupulous in their devotion to its interests, as they conceived them, while for the enormous amount of work they had to do, much increased by the exacting requirements of the Commissioners, their rewards were slight indeed.

The 'Poor School' Premises

The newly appointed Governors firmly decided upon their course of action, which was to establish the Poor School as quickly as possible with funds available augmented by a mortgage, and then wait until their assets and income should have increased sufficiently for them to build the 'Commercial' School.

Described by the Inspector of Charities as 'well adapted', with 'the effect of the whole conveying the idea of solidarity and neatness', the 'Poor' School consisted of three main rooms with accommodation for 228 boys. Built of red bricks set in blue mortar, with windows of Bath stone and thick glass, it had been designed by M. Rhode Hawkins, Architect of the Committee for Education, but was a more pretentious structure than most schools of its type, and the Vicar in particular was very proud of it. With the Head Master's House adjoining, it was erected at a cost of nearly £3000 and was opened for use on 21 January, 1858, the boys being marched down from the old Schoolhouse in George Street under their Head Master, Mr. William Ingrams, who,

The 'Poor School', 1858–81,
Whitgift Middle School 1882–1931

having been appointed to the National School in 1850, was now invited to take over the new school which, as yet uncertain in title, quickly became a centre for social services in the poorest quarter of Croydon. In the *Croydon Chronicle* of the time there are references to the Penny Savings Bank at 'Whitgift's New Schools, Church-road', bread-tickets at 'Whitgift's school', adult school classes at 'The Whitgift School', and a conversazione at 'Whitgift's National School-room', while Messrs. Drummond refer to it as 'Croydon Hospital School'.

On being vacated, the old Schoolhouse reverted to its chequered career of fifty years before; it was variously let for casual entertainments, to the YMCA, to a carpenter and to a shopkeeper who used it as a store for musical instruments. For a while, together with the house built about 1760 between the Hospital and the Schoolhouse, it was let to a private schoolmaster, Henry Webb, MCP, 'Principal of College House Boarding and Day School', who advertised his course of instruction as including 'every branch of a complete Commercial Education, with the Classics, Mathematics, Modern Languages, Drawing and Vocal and Instrumental Music'. After five or six years Webb moved to better premises in London Road; his school's successful existence illustrates how demands for a 'commercial' education were being met.

Delay in Implementing the Scheme

The rise in value of the Hospital estates was now steady but not spectacular. Some of the house property, which had not always been maintained in good repair, became convertible to shop premises and brought in higher rents, but the majority of the farm land that was the main portion of the Founder's endowment lay in remoter parts of the parish and beyond, that were not yet ripe for development. Moreover, the National School, which up to 1857 had been no charge on the Foundation's funds, being supported by contributions from the parishioners, was now absorbing a good proportion of the revenue, although for its first year or so of new life it continued to receive support from its previous subscribers. The small surplus was invested at the direction of the Charity

Commissioners in gilt-edged stocks realisable when it should be considered timely for the Commercial School to be built.

This delay was not favoured by the large number of people in Croydon who wished to see the Commercial School started as soon as possible; there seemed no good reason for a National School to be provided for St. John's when the newer districts, all part of the ancient parish of Croydon, had to support their own schools; and there was an increasingly influential body of opinion which disapproved of the establishment of either a 'Poor' or a 'Commercial' school; such people wanted a revival in a modern form of the old 'Classical' or grammar school which, it was clear to them from such records as had survived and by comparison with other schools of similar foundation, was the type of school that had existed in previous centuries, whatever the misleading term 'common' school might imply. Thus the Governors were caught between two fires: if they regarded their trust as mainly concerned with educating the 'poor', they offended those who were pressing for more ambitious schemes; if they persisted with their plans for a well-appointed school for a higher kind of education, they were accused of diverting charity from the needy. In the end the dispute was settled for them.

During the period of waiting, ideas about educational requirements for the times were maturing. In response to wide-spread criticism of the public schools, especially Eton, a commission under the chairmanship of Lord Clarendon was appointed in 1861 to investigate the administration and in particular the use of endowments of the 'Great' schools: Eton, Winchester, Westminster, Charterhouse, Harrow, Rugby and Shrewsbury, to which were added the two London Schools, that were attended mainly by day-boys, St. Paul's and Merchant Taylors'. In their Report, published in 1864, the Public Schools, or Clarendon, Commissioners, approved of continuing with the Classics as the principal study, but advocated a widening of the curriculum to include mathematics, a modern language, history and geography, some natural science, and art or music: English was to receive closer attention, but it was thought to be most correctly acquired in combination with the study of the Classics. The utilitarian subjects were poorly thought of, and anything in the nature of 'commercial' subjects was despised. At Shrewsbury Kennedy had instituted a commercial class, but giving evidence before Lord Clarendon in May 1862 he said: 'I call it a non-collegiate class, because I have never allowed the word "commercial" to enter in among us' (Report, Vol.IV, p.320). The Victorian upper classes, themselves frequently recruited from successful commercial and industrial families, wished to emulate the patricians of ancient Greece and Rome, with the unintentional effect of impeding the successes of trade that had directly or indirectly provided them with their affluence.

This scorn for the word 'commercial' was not so evident in the town of Croydon, whose prosperity depended largely on the success in London and Croydon itself of the businessmen who now lived there, but a growing opinion existed that the new School should be modelled more upon the great metropolitan schools like Merchant Taylors' and St. Paul's, than upon the Stationers' and Coopers' Companies' Schools, which educated boys mainly for careers as clerks.

Financing the Scheme

As the Charity's reserves were not growing as fast as the Governors had hoped, and the surplus of income over expenditure in 1864 amounted to little more than £300, the Governors proposed to sell enough land to raise £10,000 to build the Commercial School. The Charity Commissioners, however, would not sanction with any promptitude the sale of land as proposed by the Governors, and it was not until May 1868, after three years of negotiation with the Commissioners, that one hundred and nineteen acres of Woodside Farm were sold for £22,500. (According to the contemporary estimate, that sum represented approximately one-tenth of the capital value of all the estates.)

Meanwhile, George Coles had been occupying the post of Chaplain to the Hospital and the house of the Schoolmaster, but no longer fulfilling the latter's functions. For his Chaplain's duties he received an emolument of £80.10s. per annum, in addition to his stipend as vicar of St. James's. He was too old to be considered for appointment as Head Master of the new School, even had he been thought otherwise suitable, and he had been offered a pension of £200 a year if he would resign his office so that the Governors could fill it in preparation for the opening of the new School. He did not accept this offer but he caused the Governors no embarrassment thereby. Because of failing health he left Croydon in the summer of 1863 to live at Dorking, where he died on 22 January 1865. His body was brought back to Croydon and lay in the Chapel of the Hospital until burial in St. James's churchyard. A man whose kindness of disposition had endeared him to his parishioners, he served Croydon as a parish priest rather than as a schoolmaster. During the period that Coles spent at Dorking a *locum tenens* occupied his place, but in April 1865 the Archbishop appointed the Rev. H.C. Watson as temporary Chaplain only, to live in the Schoolmaster's House until the official Head Master and Chaplain should be selected; he too was the incumbent of St. James's. William Ingrams, Master of the Poor School, was now in effect the only Schoolmaster of the Foundation, although not qualified according either to the Founder's Statutes or to the requirements of the Scheme.

No Schoolmaster, no School

Coles's death had provided at last, so some Croydon residents thought:

the opportunity of appointing a schoolmaster of energy and ability to the vacancy, and of establishing what is most needed—an ancient grammar school in the town. . . . . It is almost impossible to exaggerate the advantages which a well-regulated and efficient Grammar School confers on a town, especially when the charges are moderate, and the well-known examples of Bedford, Tonbridge and others, shew that such schools attract residents, and tend much to increase the prosperity and popularity of a neighbourhood. [From a letter in the *Croydon Chronicle* of 4th February, 1865.]

The Governors were not going to be rushed, but by spring 1866 they were ready to decide upon plans. After some doubts as to the architect they would employ (they first considered E.M. Barry, son of Sir Charles, but he was too expensive) and as to the suitability after all of the site in North End (the Inspector of Charities who came down to examine the area favoured at first an area of seven acres at Oakfield Lodge, now the site of Croydon General Hospital), they decided to enlarge it by various purchases of adjoining property, including a three-acre field belonging to Messrs. Drummond, and their decision was confirmed in its wisdom by the appointed architect, A.W. Blomfield (afterwards Sir Arthur), whose later designs were to include Selwyn College, Cambridge, and chapels at Malvern and Haileybury Colleges.

(Although the Governors were still legally bound by the terms of the Chancery Scheme, the status, as well as the name, of the future school was still uncertain: in this same year William Drummond referred to 'The Commercial School', Blomfield to 'The Middle School', and Messrs. Drummond to 'The Grammar School'. H.M. Vane, Secretary to the Charity Commissioners, was displeased with this departure from the official term and regularly corrected it to 'Commercial or Middle School'.)

Two years later the Governors were still pressing the Charity Commissioners to approve the architect's plans deposited with them in December 1866, which the Governors wished to put into execution, especially as the Woodside land was at last in process of sale. The Commissioners had jibbed at the cost, however; an estimated £12,000 was too high (Barry's would have cost £15,000), and Blomfield had to reduce the amount of ornamentation by £3,000. Even in its amended form the design may be considered elaborate enough, and the lowest tender submitted was for £10,271. Work started at last before the end of 1868, and on 16 March 1869,

Memorial Stone, 1869

Archbishop Tait, who had succeeded Longley the previous November, laid the Foundation Stone. Within a cavity in this stone was placed a glass bottle containing thirteen coins of the realm and a piece of vellum describing and commemorating the occasion; these mementoes, intended no doubt to be discovered at about the same time as Macaulay's traveller from New Zealand would be sketching the ruins of St. Paul's, were brought to light less than one hundred years later.

The vellum described the building as 'The Commercial or Middle-Class School of the Hospital of the Holy Trinity in Croydon of the Foundation of John Whitgift, formerly Archbishop of Canterbury'.

Archbishop Tait's Influence

At this point, with the introduction of Archbishop Tait's name, it is appropriate to mention certain aspects of his character and experience, for his interest in the Foundation and especially in the School was to have a great influence upon the latter's development. He had succeeded Arnold as Head Master of Rugby in 1842, so he had a good knowledge of public-school practice; he had succeeded Blomfield as Bishop of London in 1856, and had taught Blomfield's son Arthur, the architect, at Rugby; he was *ex officio* a Governor of Charterhouse; he believed strongly that people wanted their children to receive a Christian (which for him meant Church of England) education; he was aware that the Church could not financially support an all-inclusive system, but was optimistic about the persistence of the Church's influence even in a State system; he was an effective, regular and respected speaker in the House of Lords; he was tenacious of his authority in matters connected with endowed schools, helping to throw out from the Lords the Commissioners' Scheme for King Edward's, Birmingham, which would have severed that school's connections with the Church; he was a personal friend of Lord Clinton, a Charity Commissioner; he had taught at Rugby another Commissioner, Henry Longley, son of Archbishop Longley; his residence at Addington brought him into easy and frequent touch with Croydon people, including the Governors, and particularly the Vicar.

By this time a number of changes in the Governing Body had occurred. Archbishop Longley seems not to have taken a very keen interest in the developing affairs of the Whitgift Charity. Since the first appointment of Governors by Sumner in 1855, there had been four deaths or resignations, but the numbers did not fall below the minimum until John Budgen, the clockmaker, resigned in May 1868 at the age of 79. A few days later Longley made five appointments, all of them men who may have been well known to him. They were J.M. Eastty, gentleman, aged 48, who lived at Wellesley House, very near the site of the School, two Doctors of Medicine, (Sir) William Hood and Alfred Carpenter (the latter was medical adviser to the archbishops for many years and until Edward Westall retired in 1860 had been in partnership with him), Samuel Rymer, a dentist, and Charles Newton, stationer and local postmaster; the landed gentry were not quite so strongly represented now.

Memorial of the Inhabitants

Meanwhile, the long delay had set Croydon in a ferment, and the Governors were the target of much criticism and even abuse. John and William Drummond, in whose hands the power and responsibility increasingly lay because of their knowledge of local circumstances and procedure with the Charity Commissioners, were mistrusted both by the tradesmen and by the radical element in the town. On 3 April 1868 a Public Meeting of the Inhabitants was called in the Public Hall, and as a result a committee was appointed 'to promote the carrying out of the Middle Class School in connection with the Whitgift Hospital and to consider the condition of the Charity generally'. The chief promoter of this meeting was Mr. Michael Saward, of Leslie Lodge, Addiscombe, a retired actuary who, like Mr. Dutton Harding of fifty years before, employed his retirement in investigating and endeavouring to reform charitable abuses.* Five weeks later a *Memorial of the Inhabitants of Croydon* was drawn up and presented to the Commissioners. This lengthy document formed a round attack upon the Governors, and particularly upon Messrs. Drummond, who were criticised in detail

---

*Saward had sent his sons to Merchant Taylors' in the 1850s; the disadvantages of travelling daily to a congested site in London were all too apparent to him.

for delay and bad management of the Charity's affairs, although the Memorialists' confidently assumed superior knowledge of the Governors' business was based upon an imperfect grasp of the problems the Governors had to contend with. Their main proposals were that Governors should be democratically elected and that the new School, when it was opened, should be a 'Classical' one. The Governors also replied at length, defending themselves against what they asserted was misrepresentation, and attributing delay—quite justifiably—to the Commissioners; the Memorialists issued a *Rejoinder to the Reply*, and everything was argued to the last detail in public and in the local papers, but the dispute had little or no effect upon the immediate prospects of opening the School. The Charity Commissioners sat tight and allowed matters to go as they wished them to, for more important events were now taking place.

The Schools Inquiry Commission

One of the recommendations of the Public Schools Commission had been the investigation of those secondary schools with which the Commission was not concerned, including ancient grammar schools, private and proprietary schools. In consequence the Schools Inquiry Commission, under Lord Taunton, was set up in 1864; it reported in 1867 and 1868 upon several hundred schools of very varying standards of efficiency.

An extract from Assistant Commissioner D.R. Fearon's report on Whitgift's Foundation has already been given on pages 113–114. The Taunton Commissioners found throughout the country a deplorable state of affairs; there was an aggregate of vast endowments, most of them improperly or inadequately used. They made very comprehensive suggestions for a complete reform of secondary education, whereby a State-controlled system would be set up, divided and sub-divided into regions and local authorities, but this and other far-sighted proposals were rejected. Like the Clarendon Commissioners (indeed a number of them were identical), they believed that the schools should provide a liberal education based upon a close study of language, chiefly Latin, and they also wished to encourage the study of English and modern languages, as well as of mathematics and natural sciences based on observation. One of the most significant of their recommendations was in the grades of school they wished to see established. (It must be understood that education according to ability and aptitude had never really been considered by the Victorians; universal secondary education was not introduced until after the 'Butler' Act of 1944, and 'comprehensive' education, even if it could have been imagined, would have been impossible without a standardised system of primary schooling.)

Education beyond the elementary stage, which was also the final one for the vast majority of children, if they received any at all, was considered to be classifiable into three grades: the first grade, for those leaving school at 18 or 19 and proceeding to university (Latin and Greek would be the staple for them); the second grade, for those leaving at 16 or 17 and going into professions that did not require a university training, who would study Latin and modern languages; and the third grade, for those leaving at 14 or 15, who would study the elements of Latin and French, and subjects suitable to their entering commercial occupations. All three grades would of course follow a curriculum enlightened by the addition of subjects mentioned in the previous paragraph. The importance of Latin, not only as a means of training the mind and of helping in the study and understanding of English, but also as a mark of difference between the classes, can hardly be overstressed. Similarly, a smattering of Greek, which remained necessary for many years to obtain entrance to Oxford and Cambridge, divided the classes at a higher level.

'It is obvious,' said the Commissioners, 'that these distinctions correspond roughly, but by no means exactly, to the gradations of society. Those who can afford to pay more for their children's education will also, as a general rule, continue that education for a longer time.' They made it clear that the third grade was 'for the whole of the lowest portion of what is commonly called the middle class'. (The Commissioners were all of them public school men and of the 'upper' class, for they had also been to university; several of them were noblemen.) There was no shift in the opinion that secondary education was a service that parents were expected to pay for, although exceptionally gifted boys might be provided with the opportunity of advancement through a system of scholarships from a lower to a higher grade.

The Endowed Schools Act, 1869

This Report was followed by the Endowed Schools Act of 1869, establishing the Endowed Schools Commissioners, who took over from the Charity Commissioners the duty of providing new schemes for the management of schools, but who left them with other responsibilities, including control of endowments.

The Chairman of the Endowed Schools Commission, Lord Lyttelton, had been a member of both the Clarendon and the Taunton Commissions. In their instructons to frame new schemes for the hundreds of schools under their survey, he and his two fellow commissioners were given almost complete discretion. Having seen so much waste, decay and misappropriation during the investigations, he plainly stated that 'Governing bodies...should be fully aware...that...in very many cases the "pious founder" would go to the wall'; the popular idol, 'Founder-worship', was to be overthrown.

In support of the Schools Inquiry Report, Lyttelton declared that 'the lion's share must go to the great middle-classes' who, unable to afford unaided the higher standards of education that were now necessary, were caught in the social gap between the lower classes with their subsidised National Schools and the upper classes with their 'Great' public schools or expensive private education, either by tutors or at select academies.

Many of the endowed schools had by their statutes been compelled to give at least some 'free' education to boys from a particular locality, with the result that in many cases they had been educating freely those who could afford to pay, or those who were unable to profit, or—none at all. The Commissioners saw no reason to continue the handicap of this commitment to teach 'freely', but local opinion was often very strong to the contrary, for instance, at Rugby, Harrow and Bedford. The first two of these, founded as local grammar schools, but for many years by this time 'Great' public schools, were to be challenged in reputation, efficiency and cost, by certain of the 'first-grade' schools, just as they already were by recently founded competitors such as Cheltenham (1841) and Marlborough (1843). But the bulk of the reformed schools would be of the second or third grade.

Furnished with three basic types of scheme to be applied according to the requirements of particular localities, namely for a first-, second- or third-grade school, the Commissioners sometimes aroused fears among governing bodies and headmasters by their ruthless determination to throw over any traditions or even statutory customs that ran counter to their conception of the great work of educational reform. They were particularly anxious to break down any monolithic structure of a governing body and were mistrusted on this account especially by churchmen (not least by the Governors of the Whitgift Charity), who still dominated the social scene. The Commissioners were said to be supported by 'Political Dissenters, Philosophical Radicals (and others), who all agree in the most intense hatred of the Established Church'.

Mitchinson, Head Master of King's, Canterbury, and Thring, of Uppingham, apprehensive that schools like theirs, built up on the indoctrination of Christian belief, might be ruined, arranged in 1869 a meeting of headmasters of endowed schools that was the forerunner of the Headmasters' Conference. Yet Thring constantly expressed his confidence in the Commissioners, who held him in the highest respect as the outstanding schoolmaster of his time, and wished Uppingham to be regarded as an example for other first-grade schools. It was his governors that Thring mistrusted, for he was afraid that they might propose a scheme that would destroy all his work, carried out mostly without their approval.

In addition to this determination to break away from the limitations of tradition and to reduce the power of the Church of England as exercised through the trustees of many schools (the elimination of the Archbishop as Visitor and appointer of Governors and the Head Master would be the first step to reform of the Whitgift Charity), the Endowed Schools Commissioners followed the recommendations of the Schools Inquiry Commission that endowments should be applied to four main objects:

1. The provision of suitable school buildings. (At Croydon these were being completed and seemed adequate for a first-grade school.)

2. The payment of a minimum fixed salary to the Head Master, augmented by a proportion of the capitation (tuition) fees. (The Chancery Scheme had adopted this principle in granting the Head Master £300 a year plus a half of the capitation fees.)

3. A reduction in the cost, and an improvement in the quality, of education compared with what was available privately. (The numerous private schools of Croydon varied widely; the 1871 Census returns show that there were over five hundred boarders alone of both sexes in Croydon schools, whose tuition fees ranged between 4 and 32 guineas a year, according to their aims and pretensions.)

4. The provision of scholarships to encourage 'merit', and leaving exhibitions to the universities. But endowments were not expected to be applied on a large scale for the reduction of fees generally; the Commissioners had no intention of 'democratising' the schools; the three-tiered layer proves that. (The Chancery Scheme provided for promotion with no increase of fees of boys 'of diligence and good conduct' from the 'Poor' School to the 'Commercial' School, whose status was vague; it was to be a third-grade school where boys could stay until they were 18. There was no provision for university exhibitions; the Governors had not contemplated an education of that standard.)

It is now easy to understand how the Charity Commissioners, while making no suggestions of their own, but being well aware of what their successors, the Endowed Schools Commissioners, would be empowered to do, were content for the delay in establishing the new School at Croydon to continue until a new scheme should be drawn up in accordance with the latters' requirements, and they cleverly played off one faction against another in this local dispute. The Endowed Schools Act authorised trustees to put forward their own suggestions for new or revised schemes, and the Governors submitted the draft of a Scheme on 9 December 1869.

Appointment of a Head Master

Three weeks before, on 16 November, they had sent a copy of their Scheme to the Archbishop with a request that he should appoint a Head Master to advise on the fitting-out of the buildings, which were now almost ready for occupation. Tait had not even time to look at these matters before he was struck down by a cerebral haemorrhage resulting in partial paralysis, and a withdrawal from public affairs for the next eighteen months. His inability to make an appointment created a further delay which the Endowed Schools Commissioners were pleased to take advantage of, for the Scheme was by no means acceptable to them, and they did not yet feel that they had the Governors under their control.

The draft Scheme was but a slight modification of that of 1856, which of course had never in its main provisions, referring to the Commercial School, been in operation. The preservation intact of the clause relating to the appointment of the Governing Body—still to be entirely in the hands of the Archbishop—showed how little the new Commissioners' requirements had been understood. Virtually the only change was to create a 'Middle-Class' School instead of a 'Commercial' School, impossibly split into two divisions but three grades. There was to be an 'Upper School' comprising 75 boys aged 8 to 18 of the first grade, and 75 boys aged 8 to 18 of the second, at fees of 12 and 8 guineas respectively; and there was to be a 'Lower School' of the third grade with 150 boys aged 8 to 14 and fees of 4 guineas. The subjects of instruction remained almost unaltered for all, but Latin had been firmly reintroduced. The 'Poor' School was to be continued as before.

This was no way to accelerate the opening of the School. The Commissioners were very patient, however, and explained in detail how the Scheme must be altered to meet their general and minimum requirements. The appointment of the Governing Body could no longer be the prerogative of one man, however eminent and highly qualified he might be, but it must be elected on some democratic principle. It was undesirable to have three grades in one school, so it would be better to establish a separate third-grade school, by converting the Poor School. Elementary schools, it was made clear, were to receive adequate assistance from government grants and other sources, and they could not be maintained out of endowments, which were to be directed to the support of secondary education.

To begin with, the Governors were adamant that the Archbishop should continue to exert his undiminished authority and patronage in appointing both Governors and Head Master. It was the Founder's clearly expressed intention; the Archbishop's position, his character, his peculiar associations with Croydon, the distinction his patronage would confer upon to the School, the avoidance of evils arising from party spirit; all these they viewed as advantages to the Charity. Neither would they agree to the admission of boys from outside Croydon, certainly not as boarders. This they saw as contrary to the Founder's wishes when the population was very much smaller than it now was. They wished for no change either in the status of the Poor School, which was so much the Vicar's own creation and concern that it had come to be regarded by the remainder of the Governors as something they could not interfere with. They also adhered firmly to their interpretation (*via* Ducarel) of the Statutes and fully believed that to abolish the Poor School would be to disregard the Founder's firmest intentions.

They were in a quandary. If they could get a Head Master appointed they might open the School and run it according to the 1856 Scheme, as they were still fully authorised to, but this Scheme, they realised, was not only unacceptable to the public of Croydon and the Commissioners; it was also impracticable, with its low fees and masters' salaries, and a good Head Master willing to undertake the organisation of a merely temporary Scheme might be hard to find. Moreover, they did not now desire this type of school themselves. So they proposed to the Charity Commissioners that they should themselves be allowed this once, with the help of the Bishop of London, Tait's deputy, to appoint a Head Master who would run the School for the time being according to the terms of their draft Scheme until a new one should be agreed upon, perhaps within a year. They were told in reply that they would not be justified in this course, and in any case all these matters were within the jurisdiction of the Endowed Schools Commissioners, so they had once more to acquiesce in delay. The Endowed Schools Commissioners, who 'felt considerable embarrassment on the subject', decided to send an assistant commissioner, James Bryce, to confer with the Governors. He paid three visits to Croydon between April and June 1870 and, after making thorough investigations and consulting all shades of opinion in Croydon, he reported back in great detail.

James Bryce's Reports

He said after his first visit that there was in Croydon a great want of facilities for education of the second and third grades, although there were many private day and boarding schools. Secondary education of the first grade was provided by boarding schools (but not markedly those of Croydon) or by day schools in London (St. Paul's, then still by the Cathedral, Merchant Taylors', which had not yet moved to Charterhouse Square from Suffolk Lane, King's College and University College Schools, then situated in the buildings of their respective colleges, and City of London), which also catered for a good deal of the demand for second-grade education, and which were easily reached by train.

The Commissioners thus thought that it was desirable that the School should be of the second and third grades and that the Poor School should be disposed of for use as an elementary school, but Bryce was sent down again to Croydon to make further investigations; this time he received some very cogent proposals from Saward's Committee. These proposals recommended (a) the diminution of the Archbishop's powers of appointment, (b) the establishment of an all-grade local day-school with Greek in the curriculum, but one which would allow easy transfer between the grades, (c) that the Head Master need not be in Holy Orders, (d) the closure of the Poor School, and (e) the early provision of a school for girls.

Bryce's second report took notice of these proposals, with the details of which he was not entirely in agreement, but he was able to announce that the Governors seemed quite aware that they would have to yield and were not disposed to prolong a fruitless resistance, and that a spirit of compromise, if not of conciliation, had been produced, so that they and Saward's committee of malcontents were prepared to concede much which would otherwise have been bitterly fought over. He now produced figures to show that the population of Croydon was in large measure composed of well-to-do people, living in houses of high rental value, 'professional men, retired military men in easy circumstances, and commercial people, bankers and merchants, wealthy enough to keep their sons at school until eighteen and send them to the universities, many of whom do now send their sons to the great boarding-schools or to the great day-schools of London.' But the Governors still wanted nothing higher than the second grade if they were not to be allowed to cover the whole range of education. Their opponents, especially those of the advanced Liberal Party, averred that Messrs. Drummond, who virtually ruled the town, wished to maintain a hold over the tradespeople, whose sons they could admit or not to the School as they pleased. There was also, said Bryce, a profound need in the town for a good school for girls.

Meanwhile, seventy-three parents of prospective pupils had submitted a memorial to the Governors, complaining that the delay was preventing their settling upon any arrangements for the education of their sons, and urging that a Head Master should be appointed forthwith. These parents were prepared to accept a rise in fees and pledged their support to a Head Master willing to accept the responsibility with its attendant uncertainties.

The Governors had already made several further attempts to persuade Tait to find a Head Master. He had sufficiently recovered to give a private interview to the Vicar and some other Governors, but it seems that he may have received from someone else the suggestion that the appointment was best delayed.

The Commissioners now took things firmly into their own hands and produced in August 1870 a Scheme which was as extreme as they could make it, reducing the Archbishop's power almost to nothing, merely allowing him to appoint the first Head Master, who could be a layman, but no Governors at all. The School was to be of first and second grades combined, with fees of up to thirty guineas (placing it in the same category as Tonbridge and Uppingham, and above Dulwich and King's, Canterbury, for which schools Schemes were also being prepared), and taking boarders, but not teaching Greek, as it was to be a 'Modern' school. The Poor School was to be converted to the third grade.

These proposals, put forward partly, no doubt, to warn the Governors that they must be prepared to concede much more than they had hitherto been prepared to, aroused opposition, not only from this quarter, but also from the other interested parties, who did not desire a superior school from which the majority of Croydon boys would be excluded, however many others might wish to receive an expensive, first-grade education. Saward's committee tore it to pieces in detail, and the Governors produced in November an Alternative Draft Scheme which proposed little more than their previous one: there were to be two sets of Governors, one for the Almshouses, appointed by the Archbishop, and one for the educational branch of the Foundation, only a quarter of which would be the Archbishop's nominees; there would be a 'Middle-Class' School of indeterminate grade, but allowing for the teaching of Greek, of two divisions, with fees of not more than 15 guineas, and restricted to day-boys from Croydon. The Poor School was still to be preserved.

In submitting this Scheme the Governors reported that they had again requested the Archbishop to appoint a Head Master and that Tait had invited the Rev. George Blore, then Head Master of Bromsgrove, Worcestershire, but he had declined, having decided, after a visit to Croydon, not to leave his school which was in full operation and progress under his care. But they were confident that Tait would shortly find someone suitable. Blore's name had been suggested to Tait by the latter's commissary, the Rev. C.W. Sandford, who had been under Tait at Rugby and who until a few months before had been Censor of Christ Church, where Blore, an Old Carthusian, had been an undergraduate and Senior Student.

Robert Brodie

But now Tait went off to winter and recuperate at San Remo for six months. The weeks went by, but fortunately Sandford had matters in hand. The proviso that the Head Master should be a clergyman was a hindrance but would be removed in any future Scheme, according to Section 18 of the Endowed Schools Act. Sandford now had someone else in mind; could the Charity Commissioners remove this condition and allow a layman to be appointed? They could, and there was a lengthy exchange of letters between Lambeth and San Remo. On 28 December 1870, Tait was able to write and confirm the offer of the post of Head Master to Robert Brodie who, like Blore, had been at Charterhouse and was a Senior Student of Christ Church. The world of ecclesiastical and scholastic appointments was a small one.

My dear Mr. Brodie,

I learn that the difficulties in the way of the appointment of a layman to the Headmastership of the Croydon School are now removed by the action of the Charity Commissioners. I have therefore great pleasure in offering to nominate you to the post should you find it such as you desire . . . I shall think we are fortunate if we secure your services. . . .

At this time Brodie had not been to Croydon; some years later he recalled:

On a certain Monday morning in January 1871 I came down to West Croydon and walked along North End, and I determined not to ask anyone where the School was, because I knew I should recognize it directly I came upon it, and a thrill of delight passed through me when I found the place so much better than I had expected. I felt that if a great school were not established here it would not be the fault of the site or of the buildings, but of myself.

Because of the need for equipping the buildings and engaging staff, the date of opening was still uncertain, but that January, when Brodie had accepted, the Governors announced that the School would open in the first week of May, without waiting for Parliament to approve a new Scheme. The Commissioners had sanctioned the opening, and their guidance had had to be followed in many particulars, although not in all—the Governors had set themselves against accepting any boys from outside Croydon and

ARCHBISHOP WHITGIFT'S SCHOOL.

THE MIDDLE CLASS SCHOOL of ARCHBISHOP WHITGIFT, at North End, Croydon, will be OPENED in the FIRST WEEK of MAY NEXT, for the reception of Pupils whose Parents or Guardians reside in the Parish of Croydon.

Parents or Guardians desirous to place Children in the School, are requested to send applications, stating the Name and Age of each Child, to Mr. WILLIAM DRUMMOND, (Clerk to the Governors,) at NORTH END, CROYDON, on or before the 28th day of FEBRUARY NEXT.

The School Fees will be Nine Guineas a Year for the Lower School, and Fifteen Guineas a Year for the Upper School—the distinction to depend on the qualification of the Pupil, to be ascertained by a preliminary Examination.

There will be Three Terms in each Year; and each Term is to be paid for in advance.

An Entrance Fee is to be paid, on admission, of One Guinea for the Lower, and One Guinea and a Half for the Upper School.

The ARCHBISHOP OF CANTERBURY has signified his intention to appoint ROBERT BRODIE, Esq., M.A., late Senior Student and Tutor at Christchurch College, Oxford, as Head Master of the School.

The intended subjects of Instruction (subject to alterations by the Scheme now under consideration) are—Religious Knowledge (any Parent or Guardian having power, by written application, to withdraw a Boy from all Lessons on Religious subjects), English Literature & Composition, History, Geography, Writing, Arithmetic, Mathematics, Latin, Greek (when required by Parents), French, German, Natural Science, Drawing, Vocal Music, and Drilling.

(By Order)

WILLIAM DRUMMOND,

Croydon, 13th January, 1871.

Clerk to the Governors.

S. CLOUTER, PRINTER, CROYDON.

Poster, 1871

they were determined to make it clear that they wanted a School not of the highest grade, for they prepared a prospectus entitled 'Archbishop Whitgift's Middle-Class Day-School'. In its final form the prospectus has been mercifully amended, no doubt at the instance of the Head Master, and is headed simply 'Whitgift School, Croydon'.

7. The Reconstructed School under Robert Brodie, 1871–1902

Whitgift School

Robert Brodie was thirty years of age when he was appointed to the Head Mastership. A member of a prominent professional and learned family, he had been a Gownboy at Charterhouse, which had already provided two former Schoolmasters (Noris Wood and James Hodgson). He went up to Oxford in 1859, matriculating from Balliol, but he removed to Trinity when that college awarded him a scholarship. After gaining first-class honours in Moderations he spent a term teaching at his old school before returning to Oxford and taking 'Greats', in which also he gained a first class. He then taught for a short time at Sherborne before obtaining a Senior Studentship at Christ Church, where he remained as a tutor until his appointment to Whitgift. At this time fellows of colleges had to resign if they wished to marry, so it seems that one reason for his leaving Oxford was his hope of marriage, which took place in February 1871. His bride was the same age as himself, so they had probably been waiting many years for this opportunity.

Brodie had time to select his staff, acquaint himself with the local atmosphere, obtain the equipment he needed, and consider in which ways he wanted his school to develop. He had ambitions for it to be established among the ranks of the public schools, of which he regarded Charterhouse, then still in the City, as the model in many ways. He had been a frequent prize-winner and an exemplary pupil of the Head Master, Richard Elwyn. In December 1862, as an undergraduate, he had given evidence before Lord Clarendon. His replies to provocative questions about conditions at his old school indicate an almost uncritical approval of the *status quo*. When it was put to him that Charterhouse had a bad reputation for excessive flogging and fagging, and that conditions were unduly oppressive, he could not agree; and indeed he had nothing to suggest in the way of improvement. He had a great admiration for his former head masters, and especially for Elwyn, with whom he remained on friendly terms for many years. Elwyn had to resign in 1863 owing to ill-health, and he was succeeded by William Haig-Brown, an Old Boy of Christ's Hospital; could Brodie have been hoping to take Elwyn's place if the latter had run his complete, normal course? He had clearly been happy at Charterhouse, but even if he had wanted to, he would not have been able to establish a similar organization at Croydon. Certainly he had not been brutalised by his schooldays, for he was always reluctant to give corporal punishment, although he did not shirk it, at a time when it was taken for granted as the proper and indispensable form of correction.

Opening of the School

He was himself the embodiment of the public-school ideal: a man of sound scholarship, good breeding and Christian beliefs and possessing the manly virtues of fortitude, moral courage and purposeful energy. A good sportsman, who had played three years in the Charterhouse cricket eleven, for Trinity and Christ Church, and on occasion for Warwickshire, he saw the advantages to be gained from encouraging boys to take part in competitive games and other activities. His objects were expounded in his address to the School and the assembled company at the opening ceremony on 4 May 1871:

> ... The object, as I conceive it, is to give to every boy who comes here a sound liberal education. By

Robert Brodie, MA

education I mean no mere cramming of facts and theories—no mere teaching of accomplishments, but such a course of discipline and instruction, both in school and out of school, as will make the best which can be made of every boy, morally, intellectually, and physically. Under 'sound' I include all that is genuine, honest, thorough—the opposite of cram, smattering, and humbug. By 'liberal' I mean such a training as will develop a boy's powers to the greatest extent of which they are capable, and which will make him able, when he has left school, to master readily and thoroughly any kind of learning or business which he may wish. . . .

No amount of buildings, no amount of books, no amount of cricket-grounds will make a good school; the only thing that can make a good school is good boys—boys good in conduct, good in learning, good in all kinds of healthy games, boys, in short, who are possessed of what is called the public school spirit. Now what that is I cannot define, but I can tell you some of the signs by which you may know that it exists. Where you can find a school in which the boys are honest and truthful, in which they work with a will and play with a will, in which every boy tries to excel, not only to gain praise for himself but to win honour and glory for the school; in which the boys regard their masters, not as their natural enemies and tormentors, but as their real friends; whenever you find a school which the boys who have left it think the best school in the country, there you will find the public school spirit in its best form. It rests entirely with you whether this shall be a large private or a small public school.

In spite of the unexceptionable terms of Brodie's address, local opinion, although much appeased by the overdue opening of the School, was by no means unanimous in its approval, and *The Croydon Chronicle*, the organ of the extreme liberal party, could find little in its favour:

> . . . We can turn to the educational establishment in North End and behold in its presence advantageous means for monopolising, at a remunerative rate, the education of boys who would otherwise be taught in one or more of the excellent schools at present existing and admirably conducted in the town. . . . Obliterating from our memories the long years of unrealised expectancy, we can appreciate the presence of an establishment which is, of course, a valuable addition to the town. But beyond this expression of thankfulness public opinion does not emerge.

This disapprobation was somewhat mollified by the Governors' statement that followed the Elementary Education Act of 1870, setting up local School Boards, whose duties chiefly involved the provision of elementary education for the masses. In due course, when accommodation had been provided by the building of a Board School for the boys then attending the Poor School, the Governors intended to replace the latter with a Middle-Class School of the third grade, where the fees would be no more than five pounds a year at the outside, and which would satisfy the requirements of the lower-middle classes of Croydon.

The new Building

The new building was regarded variously as a distinguished ornament to the town or as an ostentatious and palatial edifice, according to the eye and inclination of the beholder. Designed in 'the

The Reconstructed School under Robert Brodie, 1871–1902

popular Perpendicular Gothic Collegiate style', it comprised Big School, 85 by 35 feet, with clouded glass windows, a hammer-beam roof and bare brick walls above a five-foot wainscotting; a Library 43 by 22 feet, six classrooms, a Head Master's Room, a Waiting-room, a Tower, and Cloisters affording a dry playing-space in wet weather. In many ways a conventional building designed for the kind of teaching that had been in use for centuries, it was said to be capable of accommodating three hundred boys, a capacity that Bryce had already expressed his doubts about, but even with Big School used for three or perhaps four classes, and the Library for another, the number of boys in each form would be excessive for anything higher than a third-grade school. The view persisted in the 'Great Schools' that the traditional use of the main schoolroom was a valuable one, not only enabling the Head Master to keep a close eye on all that was going on, but also compelling boys, amidst the hubbub, to learn to ignore distractions and concentrate on their work. The Schools Inquiry Commissioners had stated in their Report (Vol.I, p.276) that

> the minimum requirements ought to consist of a good and well ventilated schoolroom with convenient desks and other furniture, at least one good classroom and decent offices, a good master's house, a grass playground and a site healthy and readily available.

These modest requirements were amply met, and despite the absence of such up-to-date desiderata as a masters' common-room, a laboratory, a gymnasium and changing-rooms, the buildings may have seemed quite adequate before they came to be occupied. The cost of the land and the buildings having come to £40,000, there was little money left for anything more than the barest essentials in the way of equipment, but many local people generously provided such appointments as pictures, books for the Library, a globe, a telescope and microscopes.

Meanwhile, the original Schoolhouse continued in use as a store-house at a trifling weekly

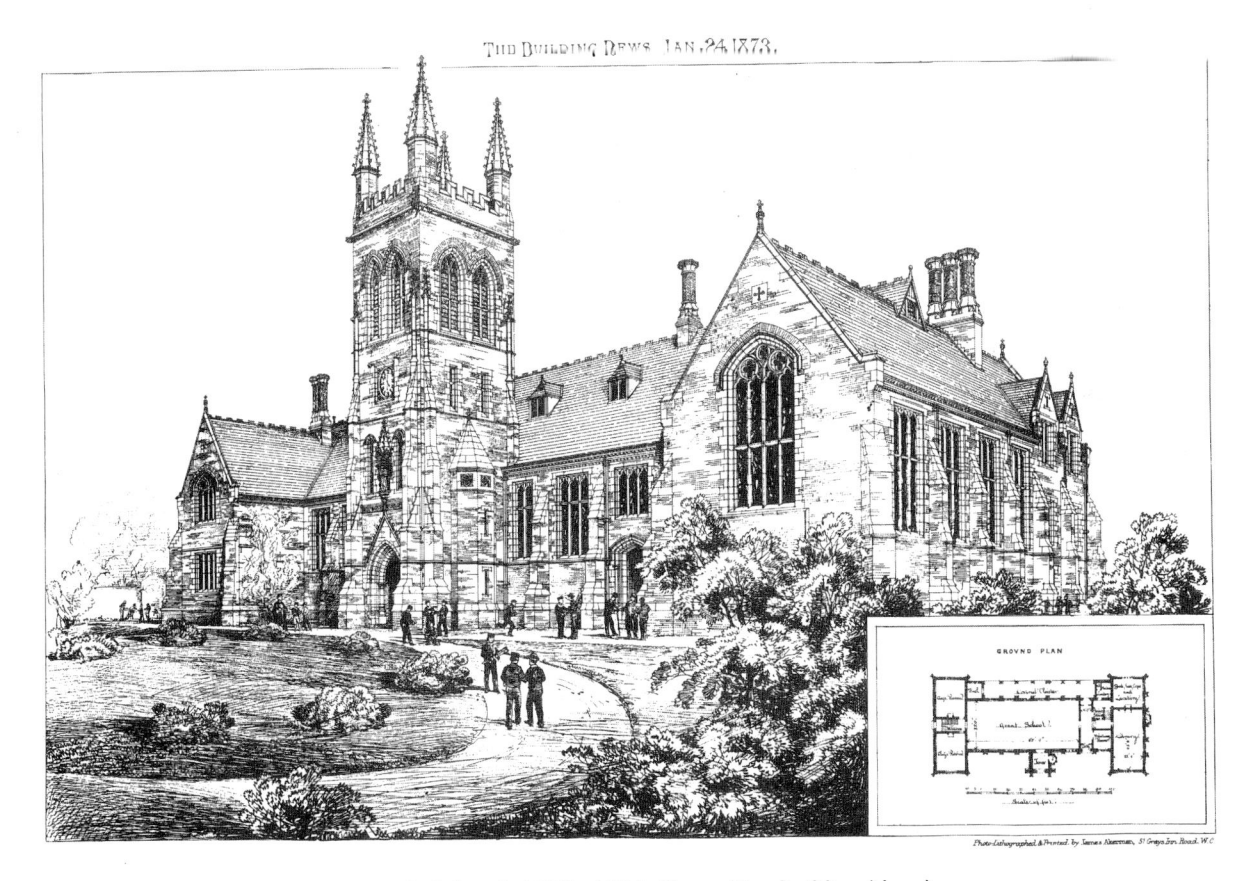

Whitgift School, 1871–1931 (from *The Building News*)

Whitgift School

The Library

The Library Staircase

The Founder's Statuette and the Memorial Stone in the Tower

rent. It was in a dilapidated condition, but Brodie wished to have it restored and used as classrooms for the junior part of the School, thus relieving pressure on space in the new building whenever it should come to be fully occupied, as he and the Governors hoped it soon would be. The restoration of the Schoolhouse, which came to be called 'The Nursery', and of the adjacent house on its western side was completed in September 1872.

The Boys

Under the provisional arrangements agreed upon after much discussion and compromise between the Governors and the Commissioners, only boys resident in Croydon with their parents or guardians were at first to be admitted; the curriculum had been designed with 'commercial' careers in view, and the fees were fixed at only half the upper limit of thirty guineas that the Commissioners had suggested. The Governors could not imagine that a successful school, attracting both day-boys and boarders from outside Croydon, would increase in size and reputation and even become financially profitable, to the educational advantage of the inhabitants of the town. The result was that the ambitions and achievements of the early pupils were mainly unaspiring, for the boys came largely from that section of the population that desired an education of the second or third grade, while their standard of attainment on admission was poor indeed. A survey of the occupations of the fathers of the first two hundred and thirty-two boys admitted (the four terms' entry between

May 1871 and May 1872) shows that one hundred and twenty described themselves as merchants, retail traders, innkeepers, clerks, etc., seventy as professional men: ministers of religion, medical practitioners, solicitors, officers in the services, etc., while the remainder are variously and imprecisely described as 'gentlemen' (which distinction applied to a Croydon resident might indicate a London retailer), manufacturers, artists, etc; the mothers of 18 boys were widows.

It is clear that these early pupils came from a wide spectrum of those who looked for a 'middle-class' education. The local private schools lost a good many of their boys at one fell swoop, and within a few years some of them had closed, although those that remained did not compete much with the new school, but concentrated on providing a 'commercial' education with no frills at a cheap rate. Not all boys had received their education at local schools, however; fifteen had had governesses at home, and over fifty had been at boarding-schools, either public or private. The general standard of preparatory education was extremely low; the best-prepared were probably those who had been taught at home by their parents, by governesses or by tutors. A number of parents waited to see how the School would develop; they had no intention of allowing their sons to act as guinea-pigs, but were ready to give their support when success seemed probable.

The Staff

On the first day Brodie had three assistants, only one of whom, the Rev. H.W. Turner, lasted more than a few terms, but after initial difficulty in finding suitable staff, being handicapped by not being able to offer really attractive salaries for men with good degrees, Brodie did manage to find a few well-qualified masters, among them E.H. Genge, a Wrangler, who was appointed 'Mathematical' Master in January 1872 and provided with the renovated house between the Schoolhouse and the Hospital. He enjoyed a higher status and a higher salary than any other assistant, but he seems never to have received any designation of superior rank, such as Deputy Head Master, or to have taken on any responsibility to match, yet his name always followed Brodie's in the School Roll.

The School was a 'semi-Classical' one in that every boy was taught Latin (as will be explained later, the embargo on Greek was ignored whenever a boy wished to learn it); the usual system prevailed whereby the form-master taught his form most subjects, including Latin, English, History and Geography, but not Mathematics or Modern Languages, although he might be expected to teach some French or German grammar. The whole School was setted for Mathematics, so the form-masters might enjoy the relief of taking an almost totally different group of boys for one period a day; the top two sets were taught by the best-paid and qualified specialists (Genge and Turner). If possible, form-masters would be recruited from graduates of Oxford or Cambridge, but perhaps only with pass degrees; men such as these with but a poor mastery of the Classical languages were fairly easy to come by and were good enough for most forms in the School. Other specialists were scarce but not yet highly thought of; the system of form-master teaching did not permit a diversification of talent among the members of the staff. Modern Languages were taught by visiting part-time native 'lecturers', whose discipline was usually poor and who were treated with the contempt with which the English boy of the time only too often regarded foreigners. The German lecturer, Dr. Weil, had been a visiting master at Charterhouse in Brodie's time. Not for many years would enough Englishmen well qualified to teach foreign languages become available in the schools. Drawing and Singing were also taught by visiting masters to such boys as were judged to have ability.

The visiting masters, as a rule, had little understanding of their pupils and no sympathy with them, or any interest in the School as such. An exception must be made in the case of Edward Griffith, the Singing and Music Master and the composer of the School *Carmen*; his success in producing the annual Concert in Big School was the climax of the interest he aroused in the classes he took. (There used to be a tradition, fostered by Griffith himself, and encouraged in the *History of Whitgift Grammar School*, 1892, that the Founder in his will had made provision for a 'Song Master' at the School. This tradition was quite unwarranted, there being no such reference in the will, the Statutes or any other document relating to the foundation of the School.)

There was then no system of teacher-training for public and grammar schools, and the form-master more often than not regarded the routine subjects of his syllabus—English (with a strong emphasis on grammar and spelling), History and Geography—as best taught by the same method as Latin, with plenty of learning by heart of lists of words, names or dates, with subsequent tests and exercises.

Salaries

Classes were fairly small, ranging from a dozen or so to a maximum of about twenty-five, for the total number long remained well below capacity. The pupil-master ratio compared quite well with most public schools. Salaries varied considerably; there was no national scale, for it was half a century before the appointment of the Burnham Committee, and there were no regular increments. In some cases assistant staff came to personal arrangements with the Head Master who distributed such additions and bonuses as he could persuade the Governors to provide. There was some kind of basic scale at Whitgift; a non-graduate teaching in the Lower School, whose own education had probably finished in the sixth form of a grammar school, would be appointed at a starting salary of £90 a year, subsequently increased by £10 or so from time to time; a young graduate was paid £150 but was accommodated with other bachelor masters in a furnished house in North End that belonged to the School, where he and his colleagues were looked after by a small domestic staff. This was called by Brodie 'the monastic system' and was copied also from Charterhouse. Until it collapsed through the dissatisfaction of its members, it was reckoned by him to contribute greatly to the well-being of the School, quite apart from being in theory economical for the Governors. The value of these 'fringe' benefits was thought to be £50 a year, but when one of the bachelors, who wished to get married and set up his own home, requested that sum in lieu of the accommodation, his request was turned down, so he remained single.*

Three years after the re-opening, the staff as a body applied for a general rise in salaries; the Governors regretted that finances did not yet permit any increase, but they offered their sympathy. They had calculated that it might be five years before the School could cease running at a loss, which they were not prepared to increase through any unnecessary expenditure.

Some members of the staff were much better off, however. The Head and Genge received salaries based partly on the number of boys at the School. Brodie received a fixed sum of £200 a year, plus a capitation payment of £3 per boy on the Roll; thus with a full complement of three hundred boys he would have £1100 a year in addition to a house free of rent, rates and expenses for repairs; Genge also had a house, a salary of £100 and a capitation payment of £1 per boy. There was, then, a great difference between the incomes of those at the top and those at the bottom, but Brodie's salary was regarded by the Endowed Schools Commissioners as in line with what the Heads of public schools could expect. (There was at least one Head of an Oxford College who relinquished his office to become a Head Master.) In the twenty years following the Report of the 'Taunton' Commission, hundreds of old schools were either reconstituted or extended, and the Commissioners regarded it as their responsibility to get and keep these schools filled; this could best be done, they thought, by making the Head Masters' salaries dependent upon their success in the recruitment of pupils and upon their ability in keeping them. It had, too, the effect of numbers being enlisted at all costs, without concern for quality.

The Teaching of Science

Although provided for in the 1856 Scheme and in all subsequent Draft Schemes, Science was a much neglected subject. Brodie's attitude to it was ambivalent: he spoke of it on occasion in a patronising manner; to him Science as a school subject meant chiefly Chemistry – 'stinks' – an inappropriate study for a gentleman, but he realised it was important to a proportion of boys who would need to study it for a profession, and he frequently pressed its claim upon the Governors. At Charterhouse there had been voluntary lectures and demonstrations which were popular and which he may have attended, and he could, of course, have attended lectures in

---

*He was aged 34 at this time; eight years later he resigned. In 1906 he died destitute and still unmarried.

Natural Science while he was up at Oxford. Shortly after his appointment Brodie became a member of the recently formed Croydon Microscopical Society, in which he was joined by William Ingrams, Head Master of the 'Poor' School. The microscope was a favourite scientific toy enabling gentlemen to admire in detail 'the wonders of nature' rather than to study the systematic structure of natural objects. Brodie no doubt felt able to make a distinction between the humdrum occupation of the scientist and the liberal avocation of the amateur enthusiast. Ingrams taught himself a good deal of botany. Yet Brodie's family were no strangers to scientific study; his uncle, Sir Benjamin Brodie, Bart., had been President of the Royal Society and also of the Royal College of Surgeons, and his cousin, Sir Benjamin, 2nd Bart., was a Fellow of the Royal Society, President of the Chemical Society, and Professor of Chemistry at Oxford.

In 1870 the Royal Commission on Scientific Instruction and the Advancement of Science was appointed under the chairmanship of the Duke of Devonshire. In its Sixth Report, published in 1875, which concerned the teaching of Science in public and endowed schools, a deplorable state of neglect was described. Two hundred and five Headmasters had been invited in 1871 to answer questions on the teaching of Natural Science in their schools; only sixty-three of those who bothered to reply could say that there was any Science teaching at all, and only thirteen of these had a laboratory. Brodie explained that the School had just been opened, but he hoped that the following year instruction in some branches of Science might be given. Three years later, at the end of 1874, replies to a further questionnaire showed some improvement in the general situation, but all that Brodie could say was that half the School was learning Physical Geography, Elementary Geology or Physics for between half an hour and two hours a week, but there was no practical work.

No doubt in an attempt to lend respectability to the subject, the following February he delivered a public lecture in Big School on 'Ancient and Modern Science', so it was a theme he professed to have at least some theoretical knowledge of. He read a paper on the same theme to the Microscopical and Natural History Club in 1889.

Apart from the problems of expense in providing apparatus and materials, and of finding a room that could be used for lectures and demonstrations, there was the difficulty of finding a teacher. The Devonshire Commission had recommended that there should be at least one Science Master for every two hundred boys, but such men were almost impossible to find. Visiting lecturers, who would come down from London for an hour or so each week, could cost as much as a full-time junior master, and while Science was still regarded as an 'extra' or was not required by the majority of pupils, a full-time scientist would be a superfluous luxury. Even if a qualified man were found, 'a mere chemist, geologist or naturalist', according to the Report, 'however eminent in his own special department, would hardly be able to take his place among University men.... The men from Dublin, London and Scottish Universities would not find themselves in sympathy with Public School teaching.' This suggestion of a cool welcome from colleagues would surely not have applied at Whitgift, where men with Dublin degrees—or none—were not unknown. But it was not until the next century that a full-time scientist was appointed to the Whitgift staff.

When in 1875 Brodie was invited by the Governors to report on the practicability of introducing the teaching of Chemistry, his reply indicated that it would involve too much expense for the small number who wished to study it, and the matter was dropped. However, one of his staff, W.S. Ingrams (the eldest son of the Head Master of the Poor School), undertook in 1876 to give 'extra' lessons to voluntary pupils, using his own chemicals and apparatus, and Brodie had a small room in the 'Nursery' set aside for the purpose. When Ingrams left at the end of 1878 to go to Oxford, later becoming Science Master at Shrewsbury, a part-time lecturer was engaged to visit twice a week for a guinea or so each time, but the Governors were not yet willing to make Science a part of the regular curriculum. In January 1882, Brodie appointed a cousin of his, Douglas Brodie, as an assistant master, who undertook the Science-teaching as well as his ordinary duties, and became 'Chemistry Master' a year later. The 'malodorous cupboard', as the room in the 'Nursery' was termed by Brodie, continued in use until the Chemistry Laboratory

Whitgift School

and Lecture-Room were opened in January 1888, but these were empty of boys for most of the day until the end of Brodie's time. Science was still an 'extra', like Shorthand, or Electricity, which could be studied after school hours, and by many parents it was regarded as a waste of time and money, or subversive of religion, or educationally superfluous, or not genteel, yet it might be necessary for certain careers. Even before the Laboratory was built, nearly one hundred boys had left to take up scientific careers, including one astronomer, forty doctors, dentists or veterinary surgeons, and forty-five engineers; there were even four analytical chemists. But few schools were yet enlightened enough to make Science a subject of the curriculum for every boy at some stage in his school career.

The 1870s

One of the ninety-one boys who presented themselves at the School at its re-opening has left an account of life there. He was the youngest of the seven that formed the Upper School, where no entrant was older than fifteen and a half. His sounds an authentic voice and deserves to be heard:

The Upper School ... wore the school cap with blue stripes, red being the corresponding colour for the Lower School.... The top form was then called the Fourth, consisting at first exclusively of the seven Upper boys, afterwards the Fifth, and finally the Sixth when the School had grown sufficiently large for five classes or more to be formed beneath and, what is more important, when the members of this top class were judiciously considered by the Head Master to be worthy of the dignity thus conferred upon them. Even then, as was inevitable, his optimism was by no means immediately justified; but it could only have been eventually realized by a preliminary course of make-believe. When in 1876 the office of prefect was created, it proved very unpopular; 'Those beastly prefects!' was the comment made by a quite well-behaved boy even before the first four prefects had entered into office; and a test case occurred on the very first occasion when one of them exerted his newly acquired authority. The Head Master of course supported him, but refrained from increasing the imposition to which by making an appeal the offender was liable ..., who, it may be added, was one of a group of boys of good social position, who were doing the School a lot of harm by standing aloof from it outside, even to the extent of divesting themselves of the School colours.

At first, of course, the senior boys were not only too young for their position at the head of a public school, but they were also without experience or training, not having the example of any seniors to follow, and no discipline imposed upon them from the same quarter; consequently there was an almost total lack of institutions managed by the boys themselves of any educational value in promoting *esprit de corps*. The only two boys to show signs of possessing it were Charles Rogers, the first captain of cricket, and Alexander Freeland, who followed him as captain. Though a short, spare boy, Rogers was a fine all-round athlete, who won nearly every event in the Sports; and having previously spent a few terms at a public school, he rendered good service at Whitgift by asserting boys' rights to manage their own affairs independently of any master who might presume unduly to interfere. Moreover, he was smart and well-mannered; but for all that a dunce, not from lack of ability, but from distaste of sedentary occupations; and his school career came prematurely to an end. Freeland unfortunately had a cold, official manner, which did not conduce to popularity; but his merits were amply recognized when, on leaving, he was presented with a gold chain as a testimonial, the only one given to a boy in the early days of the School at any rate; and the Head Master did him the great honour of publicly bewailing his departure at the Prize-giving soon after.

(The writer of the above, the Rev. W.F. Pelton, was a member of a class that largely made use of the School in its early years. He was the son of John Pelton, a prosperous and very respectable grocer in the town, whose elder son, too old to have been admitted to the School, was educated privately, joined his father in business, and later became Mayor of Croydon and a Governor of the Whitgift Foundation. W.F. gained a Scholarship in Mathematics at Caius College, Cambridge, and held posts as a university lecturer before taking holy orders. The lives of these two members of an intelligent middle-class Victorian family provide an interesting illustration of the social effects of the revived grammar schools. Other significant names in early School Rolls are Allder, Batchelar, Courlander, Ebbutt and Kennard; in these cases the sons mostly joined the family retail business; perhaps their education contributed in some degree towards the firms' prosperity.)

The Governors' narrow regard for the middle

The Reconstructed School under Robert Brodie, 1871–1902

WHITGIFT SCHOOL.

Report of _Moss_   Aug. 1871

would have been higher if he had not lost all his Repetition marks for prompting.

PLACE.—In General Subjects ..... For Term: 4   For Exam: 10   from Top in 11   Form of 13 Boys.
In Mathematics .... For Term: 5   For Exam: 6   from Top in B   Form of 13 Boys.

Subject	Very Good	Good	Fair	Not Good	Bad	Very Bad	REMARKS.	Master's Sig.
Latin		—						RB.
French			—					EJ.
German		—						RB.
Greek								
English	—						Takes great pains with Exercises, and sometimes writes better History than any boy in Forms IV & V.	RB.
Arithmetic				—			Rather backward, but improving.	HWS.
Euclid				—			Not at all accurate.	HWS.
Algebra			—				Has made a very fair start in this subject.	HWS.
Higher Mathematics								
Natural Science								
Writing				—				RB.
Spelling		—						RB.
Drawing				—				RB.
Singing							Cannot Sing. Devotes his time to other subjects.	
Drilling		—						RB.
Conduct	RB	HWS						RB

General Remarks:— _Takes great pains and improves satisfactorily._ RB.

All Boys are required to be in School at 9 o'Clock on _Monday_ the 25th of _September_
Leave of absence can be granted only in case of illness or other unavoidable hindrance.

An early Report, August 1871

classes imposed another handicap upon the School during these early days of reconstruction. The School was divided into 'Upper' and 'Lower' divisions; Brodie had adopted these terms 'in accordance with the usage at all the public schools with which I am acquainted and because I thought them more convenient than "Senior and Junior Departments".' In the former the fees were fifteen guineas, and in the latter, nine guineas a year. The Lower School, comprising at first the forms below the Fourths and taught in the main by non-graduates, did not represent solely the younger part of the School, for it became the custom for some boys to linger there for a while in order to avoid the higher fees of the Upper School. Thus it was not unusual for boys of fifteen or even sixteen to remain in the Lower School, while the higher forms contained some boys a couple of years younger. The sudden jump in fees meant, moreover, that parents were inclined to remove their sons, regardless of their aptitude, when they had completed the Lower School course. Some went on to other schools after using the lower forms as a preparatory school, but there were others who took up the modest kinds of employment in business and commerce that were then open in London and Croydon to boys of quite tender years, and which sometimes led to positions of responsibility and affluence. The Lower School contained a considerable number of boys who were there to obtain a third-grade education of a superior kind to that provided by many private schools, and they would be withdrawn whenever a suitable clerk's job could be found for them.

Of the first two hundred and thirty-two boys on the Roll, seventy left before they were fourteen, although most of them must have gone to other schools; it was with some boys a custom to make a steady progression through different schools, spending a couple of terms in each and trying unsuccessfully to find a congenial place which would suit their talents or the lack thereof. Of the remainder, eighty-four left before they were sixteen, and only nine stayed on until the age of eighteen or nineteen.

Brodie knew that the success of the School as he wished it to develop would largely depend upon establishing a sound academic reputation by sending boys to university, and despite the official restriction against Greek, he had no compunction in teaching it to those who required it for passing 'Responsions' for Oxford and 'Little-go' for Cambridge. Among the very first boys to be admitted on 4 May were two who gained Scholarships in Classics and in Mathematics at Oxford and Cambridge respectively; neither, however, achieved particular distinction at university or in later life. The Oxford man, H.E. Rose, died before he was thirty; W.F. Pelton was the other. Rose, whose mother was a widow, needed further financial help to get to Oxford; Brodie proposed to the Governors that they should award him a Leaving Exhibition. Such exhibitions were not allowed for in the 1856 Scheme, but were to be included in any scheme authorised by the Endowed Schools or the Charity Commissioners. The Governors declined, however; the School was not yet paying its way, and they were not yet committed to the idea of a first-grade school; happily, a generous Governor of the School, R.A. Heath, added to his many other benefactions by providing Rose with £40 a year for three years.

These successes were followed by others at London; for example, the record of the three brothers Berry, who were admitted in May 1872, may be quoted. The eldest, James, gained a Scholarship to St. Bartholomew's Hospital, where he had an exceptionally brilliant career; he became a distinguished surgeon, receiving a knighthood in 1925 and being elected President of the Royal Society of Medicine in the following year; the next brother, Edward, won a Scholarship to University College, London, and but for ill-health would, it seems, have had a successful career as a research chemist; the third, Arthur, after gaining a series of awards that took him to King's College, Cambridge, became Senior Wrangler in 1885 and later Vice-Provost of King's. None of these, however, proceeded to university straight from school, and the reasons are not far to seek: the Sixth Form was not developed to cater for boys of such high promise, who found few to challenge and stimulate them in intellectual effort, with the result that they left at the age of sixteen to be coached privately; indeed Arthur Berry spent a year at another school before going to university. A further reason was that there were as yet no scholarships or exhibitions in the gift of the Governors, so it became a fairly common practice for promising boys to go off to other schools of high academic reputation, such as St. Paul's, whence after a couple of years they could proceed to university with the additional help of endowed exhibitions.

Brodie was not satisfied with the way things were developing. The townspeople of Croydon made it plain that the sort of school he wished to establish was not in accordance with their aspirations. He valued the benefits of a boarding-school, but he was forbidden to accept any boarders, and at the Prize-Giving ceremony in August 1873, when the Archbishop gave away the prizes, he complained that when boys went home at the end of school, the schoolmaster had no control over their idleness and could not be sure that sufficient time was given to the preparation of their work; he mentioned also the difficulty of controlling their behaviour between school and home, and of stimulating a pride in their school, but he did acknowledge that there had been an improvement in that respect. In endeavouring to establish standards of behaviour, Brodie gained a reputation for harshness; no fewer than four of the first two hundred and thirty-two boys were expelled, and although corporal punishment was repellent to him, he administered public canings for misdemeanours that were sometimes less than grave. He also had to dismiss three of the first ten of the assistant masters he appointed. Another difficulty that beset him was the strong Victorian class-consciousness, evidenced by an editorial in *The Croydon Guardian*:

In Croydon there exists . . . a condition of *caste* which is an insurmountable obstacle to anything like social equality. We need not mince the matter. Parents have withdrawn their children from the Middle-Class School, simply because it was too middle-class to suit them. The fees were too high, and yet not high enough, and the consequence has been an admixture of boys which, to the sensitive, has not been palatable.

Brodie attempted in many ways to foster pride in institutions and activities that he hoped would come to be accepted and perpetuated by future generations. For instance, in July 1872 he obtained permission from the Governors for boys leaving the upper forms to have their names carved on the stonework surrounding the windows in Big School, 'the practice of old Schools such as Harrow and Eton' (and of

Robert Brodie and Staff, 1877

Charterhouse, too). (The name 'Big School' must have been chosen by Brodie for its associations with the Great Schools.) Before long these names had to be restricted to those of Sixth Formers, and before the end of the century the practice had to cease for lack of space.

Games

Perhaps the greatest factor in stimulating pride in the School was Brodie's encouragement of games. Still a keen cricketer himself, he recruited a number of players among the early members of his staff, and they, by playing with and against the boys, did much to develop the 'public-school spirit' he set such store by. In 1874 a professional was engaged. This was the time when the public schools were developing their particular ethos of athletic excellence, which was to result in the spread of organised games and sport not only in England but also throughout the world. Pelton describes how

in dealing with the part which the masters took in the game to the great advantage of the School in those early days, the first place must be assigned to Robert Brodie, whose influence, personal and impersonal, was of the most valuable kind. He thoroughly understood the game [*of cricket*] from a scientific point of view, besides being an accomplished batsman and a good change bowler. So also did the Rev. H.W. Turner, another accomplished batsman, but far more than that, a bowler of medium pace and wily, reckoned by many to be the best amateur bowler in Croydon. . . .

139

For the first few seasons the match-team, except when chosen to meet other schools, always included four, and sometimes five, masters; and twenty-two boys received their annual drubbing at the hands of an eleven composed of masters, the annual examiner and the drill-sergeant. It was, of course, a most undesirable necessity for young boys to be sent in to face the bowling of men, for matches with other schools were very few; and the ambition of each of these immature batsmen was limited to 'cracking his duck' by means of one desperate slog to the boundary, or a lucky tip through the slips. Soon a professional coach was appointed, and an improvement was at once effected from the mere fact of comparatively young boys ceasing to be scared when facing an adult bowler. . . . What was sadly needed was a Sportsmaster; but such an institution was unknown anywhere in those days. Some of the masters who were cricketers took a lively interest in the game, and even gave some coaching; but as a whole they certainly might have done more.

Although a Carthusian, Brodie encouraged rugby football from the beginning, a game that has without a break been the principal winter-season sport. In this game, too, there was an early willingness among the staff to instruct; that it was rugby that was played is perhaps due to one man in particular, who had already in the first summer term encouraged young cricketers—the genial Thomas Southey Baker, who started to teach boys the game in September 1871; his enthusiasm was boundless, but his departure at the end of the same term might have been disastrous to the game's popularity at the School if other masters had not been willing to take his place on the field. The game was still in its infancy, with twenty players a side, the Rugby Union having been formed no earlier than 1870, but although there were few neighbouring schools that played the game or, for that matter, association football, there were several local clubs. Rugby fives and lawn tennis were taken up quite early, the former in 1872, three courts having been built, and the latter in 1882; athletic sports, in the form of competitive races and jumping, were started in 1872. An account of the early phases of all these games may be found in the *History of Whitgift Grammar School* (1892).

The first inter-school cricket match was played against Epsom College in 1871, both sides being assisted by masters, and Whitgift winning by eighteen runs. It was not until 1874 that any matches were played without masters in the side; in that year, of seventeen matches played, there were only four against schools, including Epsom and two games against lower sides from Dulwich. Within ten years, however, the fixture list included King's College School, Hurstpierpoint, Cranleigh and St. John's, Leatherhead; most of these schools are still opponents at the present time.

The record of rugby matches does not go so far back; it is certain that to begin with the disparity in size and age could not well permit masters and boys to play together in teams. Although the lists of teams go back to 1871, the first recorded game against another school took place in 1875, when Dulwich 2nd XV were defeated by three tries to one. During the next ten years the game achieved wider popularity, and fixtures were arranged against King's College School, St. John's, Leatherhead, and City of London (all of which schools later gave up playing rugby for a while), Mill Hill, and Merchant Taylors' and Christ's Hospital 2nd XVs. Overall, a good many more games were lost than won; despite Whitgift's advantage in having a playing-field adjacent to the School, the London schools had many older boys.

The Cadet Corps

Yet another encouragement towards self-respect was the formation in 1874 of the Cadet Corps, attached to the 1st Volunteer Battalion of The Queen's Regiment:

It seemed good that boys should learn habits of implicit obedience and of self-control, and acquire an appearance of smartness; that they should learn how to handle and become familiar with the use of firearms; and that they should be prepared for entering, in after-life, either the army or the auxiliary forces.

With the Corps, shooting was introduced, and in 1878 the School first entered a team in the Ashburton Shield Competition, then held at Wimbledon. Out of a field of thirteen, the team came eleventh, but three years later they were third, a position that has so far been several times equalled, but never surpassed.

The Magazine

In December 1879 the first issue of *The Whitgift Magazine*, now known as *The*

Whitgiftian, appeared, and although there was little enough in the way of School activities to report, it provided a medium for disseminating knowledge of School affairs among the boys and their parents, and offered encouragement to boys with literary ambitions; in fact, the amount of space devoted to what is now called 'expression' was greater in proportion than that of today.

Old Boys' Clubs

One advantage that a day-school should possess is the active interest and support of its Old Boys, many of whom remain for some years in the locality, preserving close contact with the School and with each other. In 1876 a Rugby Football Club was formed, called the North Park Whitgift FC which, however, after a couple of seasons found it necessary to open its ranks to strangers; it came to be known later as the Croydon FC, but OWs continued to form the majority of its strength until the formation of the OWFC in 1901 led directly to its demise. The Whitgift Wanderers Cricket Club, formed in 1878, and the teams that entered for the Public Schools Veterans Shooting Trophy (The Whitgift Veterans Rifle Club, although operating in 1886, was not formally constituted until 1896) also contributed to the School's repute and self-esteem, whilst the first Annual OW Dinner, held under Brodie's chairmanship in Big School in December 1884, made manifest the respect and affection in which he was held by many of his Old Boys. At the Dinner, Brodie expressed the thought that it was the final institution the School required to make it complete, yet the School had by no means reached maturity, especially intellectual, and it was during the next ten years that were founded the Musical, the Debating, the Natural History and Scientific, and other Societies that catered for the enquiring mind.

There was also *Carmen*, with words by Brodie himself, and music by Edward Griffith, which was published and first sung in 1889. The verse-form, described by Brodie as monkish rhyming Latin, was clearly inspired by the Charterhouse *Carmen*, by Haig-Brown. It needs to be very well sung for it to be truly effective. It has continued to be rendered on official occasions, although attempts have been made to drop it.

Revised Schemes

The Governors had opened the School without having any new Scheme approved, and only with the grudging consent of the Charity Commissioners, who permitted a number of departures from the sole official Scheme of 1856, such as in subjects taught, the scale of fees, and the emoluments of Head and Assistant Masters. The Endowed Schools Commissioners could not object to the Governors' action because their authority over the educational side of the foundation would not become absolute until a Scheme of their own had been given the royal assent.

Messrs. Drummond now discovered a delaying tactic of their own. Having got the School open at last and conducted more or less on the lines they desired, they cast doubts, through their interpretation of Section 24 of the Endowed Schools Act, on the power of the Commissioners to reconstruct the Governing Body in the manner they had proposed. Drummonds claimed that the proportion of endowments hitherto available for education in the case of the Whitgift Charity did not amount to the minimum required for the Commissioners to be empowered to act. There followed a triangular exchange of legal argument between Drummonds, H.J. Roby, Secretary of the Endowed Schools Commissioners, and H.M. Vane, Secretary of the Charity Commissioners, which was at last concluded by the recognition that it was (a) the responsibility of the Charity Commissioners to determine the apportionment of the endowment between the eleemosynary and the educational purposes, and (b) they who, in the event of dispute, were the only judges of their own jurisdiction. This legal tangle had so exhausted the Endowed Schools Commissioners' patience that when in 1872 the Governors submitted further detailed proposals for amending the Commissioners' draft Scheme, the latter left it on the table for over a year, and concentrated their efforts on foundations that were not so intractable.

But by 1874 the Commissioners returned to action with a 'Revised' Scheme which went a substantial way to meet the Governors' views. They had withdrawn their complete opposition to the Archbishop's power of appointment of the Governors, four of whom out of a total of twelve would still be nominated by him, although the Vicar was no longer one of them *ex officio*, but the appointment of the Head Master was to be firmly vested in the Governors once Tait was no longer Archbishop. The Middle-Class School received sanction in much of its organisation, the fees proposed were to be reduced to not less than £15 or more than £25 in the Upper School, and not less than £9 or more than £15 in the Lower School. It was to be a day-school only, but boys from outside Croydon were to be admissible. Greek could be taught as an extra, and boys could remain until nineteen. Although the Commissioners had somewhat lowered their requirements for the Middle-Class School, they had repeated almost exactly their proposals to replace the Poor School with Whitgift 'New' School, of the third grade and open to day-boys of seven to fifteen years at fees of not less than £5 or more than £7. The Governors, as we have seen, were not now averse to this proposal.

During the next few months the Governors examined this revised Scheme in detail, still finding objections to its full acceptance, and made further amendments before submitting it to the Archbishop, but progress was halted by the Endowed Schools Act of 7 August 1874, by which the Endowed Schools Commission was to be dissolved at the end of the year. The Commissioners had made themselves so unpopular through the dictatorial exercise of their comprehensive powers that Disraeli's new administration removed them from office, and their responsibilities were resumed by the Charity Commission. There followed a period of inaction while the latter gathered up the threads again and adapted themselves to a less ruthless control of the schools under their survey.

In September the same year Michael Saward died, and his committee also lapsed into quiescence.

The Charity Commissioners had taken over not only the case-histories and files of their predecessors, but also a number of their staff, who applied themselves to easier problems than those besetting the Whitgift Schools. Thus two years passed, allowing the Governors time to consolidate the School's success; the numbers were steadily rising, and Trinity Term of 1876 opened with two hundred and ninety-one boys on the Roll, only nine short of the theoretical maximum.

During the first five years of the School's revival, Brodie had earned a high reputation socially and academically; he was held in respect by the people of Croydon who knew him, and in high esteem by the Governors, even if he was having some difficulty in converting them to his way of thinking, for they had not always the courage of their convictions in the face of a good deal of local opposition. They listened to his advice and acquiesced in his requirements as far as funds would permit, but they had no experience of the administration of a public school and were indeed uncertain whether a public school was what they or Croydon wanted. The Vicar, in particular, who was Chairman of the Governing Body, was wedded to the principle of providing a popularly based education.

In 1874 boys from outside Croydon were admitted for the first time. Brodie instanced schools that had achieved great celebrity through developing the boarding side, but the Governors thought local opinion would be against it, and resolved to go no further, in spite of acknowledging that boarders would swell the numbers, retain masters longer, raise the tone, ease financial difficulties, and increase the efficiency of the School, but 'it would become less available to inhabitants of Croydon for whom it was originally intended'.

Local Dissatisfaction with the Scheme

After this short period of consolidation, however, 1877 saw the resurgence of local dissatisfaction. This time complaints were first voiced by John Corbet Anderson, an artist who had been living in Croydon for twenty years and had taken a great interest in local history and antiquities, which had led him on to a study of the Whitgift Charity in particular. To him, a man of great ability and resourceful enthusiasm, yet lacking in subtlety and judgment, much is owed for his investigations into Croydon's past, but his part in the forthcoming disputes was played with an extravagance and importunity that at last alienated his associates.

In January 1877 he attacked the Governors for not conducting the School according to the terms of the 1856 Scheme. After writing to the editors of the local papers, he visited uninvited the office of the Charity Commission, demanding a sight of the Foundation's records, which he was denied, and in March he and a few supporters called a public meeting, from which resulted another 'Memorial of the Inhabitants' and a deputation to the Commissioners. Lord Clinton made it clear that the Governors were operating the School on a temporary basis with the Commissioners' approval; a new Scheme, however, would have to be prepared, and a public inquiry, conducted by an Assistant Commissioner, would perhaps be held.

For the next few months Corbet Anderson devoted much of his time to preparing his case and writing scurrilous pamphlets in criticism of the Governors. The chief of his complaints, apart from accusing the Governors of maladministration of their trust, was that the Schools did not fulfil the intentions of their Founder, who, he claimed, had founded 'a free grammar-school, wherein sons of tradesmen and struggling rate-payers of the parish might obtain a good education'. He was one of a vocal, but comparatively small, group of the lower middle classes which claimed to represent 'the rate-payers of Croydon'; this group consisted of superior artisans, small shopkeepers and clerks who, while scorning to patronise the public elementary schools that were frequented only by the lower classes, could not afford the fees charged at the Middle-Class School. They did not require a first- or even a second-grade school, but a cheap, subsidised education of the third grade that would enable their children to become rather more prosperous in the sort of occupations that their fathers followed. To this, they felt, they were entitled as being 'of the poorer sort' (but not the poorest) and so particularly designated by the Founder for his benevolence. Upward mobility in a time of great social insecurity was possible by much determination allied with ruthlessness or self-denial, as well as by ability and good fortune, being easiest through the numerous strata of the middle classes for those equipped with a modicum of education. Such men could not afford to be greatly ambitious for their children, who had to be put to work as soon as they were old enough, especially if they were the oldest of a family. A young clerk with a basis of elementary education could begin as a 'penman' at the age of thirteen or fourteen at, say, £20 a year; in an office he could pick up a far more useful education than would be provided by the study at school of Latin, French, History and Geography, for example. These refinements, however, if they had been studied for a year or so at a private or endowed third-grade school, were not to be despised as an additional qualification.

In October 1877 a further claim on the Charity's bounty was made. The Chairman and Clerk of the Croydon School Board, now responsible for the provision of elementary education under the Act of 1870, complained that the poorest inhabitants of the town were not reaping much educational advantage from the endowments. When the Poor School had been opened twenty years before, it catered for the whole of the parish, but with the growth of the town's population (during this time it had nearly trebled), many other elementary schools had had to be established, and the Poor School was now serving only a very limited area. The Board proposed to the Governors and the Charity Commissioners that the Poor School should be converted to an Advanced (or Higher) Elementary School, such as had been set up in Bradford and other industrial towns, to which boys from all over the parish could be sent.

In December 1877, Corbet Anderson's group, 'The Whitgift Hospital and Croydon Charities Committee, appointed by the Croydon Vestry' (which it had managed to pack, much to the Vicar's disgust), produced yet another Draft Scheme, which it submitted to the Commissioners. This scheme removed nearly all power from the Archbishop and placed it in the hands of Governors elected mainly by local bodies. There would be two schools: the School in North End would become the 'Upper' School for 1000 boys of eight to eighteen with fees of not more than £4.10s. a year, rather on the model of some Scottish schools or of the Central Foundation School in Cooper Street, Finsbury; and the School in Church Road would become the 'Lower' School for boys of seven to fifteen at fees of not more than 30s. They would be satisfied with an education of the flimsiest and cheapest quality, conducted in large classes by badly paid teachers; at this time even elementary schools cost between 30s. and £2 per head to run.

It is not surprising that another group, consisting largely of parents of pupils and prospective pupils at the Middle-Class School, issued their

Whitgift School

own Memorial prepared by John Flower, a solicitor, disassociating them from such opinions and asking for a full investigation and discussion of the problem.

The Governors, until then reluctant to subject themselves to the rigours of an inquiry, now formally made a request for one to be held. In February 1878 Assistant Commissioner Fearon, who ten years before had reported to the Schools Inquiry Commission on the Whitgift Foundation, was instructed to arrange for an inquiry to be held in Croydon with the purpose of formulating a Scheme.

Tait's Intervention

Such a Scheme would have to receive the attention of the Archbishop, who had continued his very active interest in the School; although unable to be present at the opening, he had presented the prizes at the first four annual Speech Days, and had declared himself proud of its promise of great achievement. He now turned to the defence of his position as Visitor of the Foundation. Being well acquainted with two of the Commissioners, Lord Clinton and Henry Longley, he was able to press his views on these younger men, who held him in personal as well as official respect. Speaking for his successors as Archbishops, Tait told Clinton privately at the House of Lords that although he was willing to surrender his power of nominating the whole of the Governing Body, he still wished to be able to appoint half of them; he also wished to remain as Visitor and to keep the power of appointing the Head Master. These terms would have been quite unacceptable to the Endowed Schools Commissioners, but the Charity Commissioners were willing to concede much, although Fearon (who had been also an Assistant Endowed Schools Commissioner) had doubts as to the propriety of so doing, it being 'the Commissioners' ... invariable practice to place the appointment and removal of the Head Master in the hands of the Governing Body, and ... their ordinary practice to provide that the Visitorship ... should be transferred to Her Majesty'. The Commissioners hoped that Tait would reconsider his proposals, but 'should this not be the case, the Commissioners being very sensible of your Grace's authority and experience in educational matters, and being desirous of having the good will and co-operation of your Grace, ... we are willing to make an exception in this case'. But Tait was adamant and followed up his insistence by requiring not only that the Archbishop should appoint the Head Master, after being given a short list of three candidates by the Governors, but also that the Head Master, although not necessarily in Orders, must be a member of the Church of England. (These conditions remain to the present day.) Tait's position in the case was a strong one; he was held in great respect for his liberal views; he had already realistically conceded much of the Church's traditional control over education, fully aware that its authority and financial power were no longer strong enough to overrule the public desire for secularly controlled education. But Whitgift School had a closer connection with the Church than most; no other Archbishop of Canterbury except Grindal (St. Bees) had founded a public school. (Tenison's Schools were in a different category.) His appointment of Brodie had received more than local acclaim; *The Daily News*, a Liberal paper, had welcomed the appointment, which had 'more significance than appeared on the surface', and recommended 'this example to the Trustees of other schools. The Archbishop has done a service to education by this authoritative practical protest against the superstition which requires that teachers of boys should be clergymen. . . . It dates from the times when none but clerics were scholars.'

When Tait distributed the Prizes at the School in 1873 he made it clear that he accepted the necessity of change according to the wants of the age, including the provision of a 'conscience clause' for those who wished not to receive instruction in Church of England doctrine, but he stipulated the continuance of Christian teaching in accordance with the intentions of the Founder.

The Inquiry of 1878

At last, in May 1878, the Inquiry took place in the Town Hall, and Fearon spent five days in hearing evidence from all shades of local opinion, listening with equal attention to those whose ideas were based on reasoned argument and to those who revealed prejudice and ignorance, although the latter were corrected and rebuked; among these was Corbet Anderson, who ruined his case by his absurdities, which were repudiated by the members of his own committee.

Another year had to pass before Fearon's Report was ready, for he had many other investigations to pursue elsewhere. One can only marvel that he managed to combine his other work with the production in eighty-four closely printed foolscap pages of a survey of the Foundation's history, an analysis of its finances, a summary of the evidence taken, and his conclusions and proposals.

In the meantime, uncertainty about the School's future was proving injurious. The numbers dropped to two hundred and twenty-seven; many parents of boys then in the School feared a decline in its aims and reputation and removed their sons, while parents of prospective pupils decided on other schools, but the eventual publication of the Report encouraged a renewed confidence, and numbers started climbing again in September 1879, although they continued to fluctuate until the Scheme was promulgated in July 1881.

In his Report Fearon devoted most of his attention to the conduct and organisation of the School, which he considered very satisfactory, with high standards of instruction, attested by examinations conducted by independent examiners. He found Brodie's staff well qualified and not too numerous, but certainly not overpaid, with a pupil-staff ratio of twenty-two to one, exclusive of the several visiting masters for French, German, Singing and Art; the subjects taught covered a suitable range, with Latin as the main subject, and twelve boys taking Greek as an extra. Such a school did not conform with the Court of Chancery Scheme of 1856, but it was a school of a type much needed in Croydon and one that had approached the recommendations of the Endowed Schools Commissioners.

The Poor School he described as performing very adequately the functions of a local elementary school, and he praised William Ingrams for his success in conducting it.

In conclusion, Fearon drew up in outline his proposals for a new Scheme, of which only a few can be commented on here. He recommended that a Governing Body of thirteen persons, comprising the Vicar of Croydon *ex officio*, six Governors appointed by the Archbishop, two elected by the Justices of the Peace for Surrey of the Hundred of Wallington, two by the local Board of Health and two by the local School Board, should administer the Whitgift Foundation, now to be established in replacement of the corporation of the Warden and Poor of the Hospital of the Holy Trinity, which was to be dissolved, and its endowments vested in the Official Trustee of Charitable Lands and Funds. This reconstruction duly took place, but some of his other proposals were either discarded or modified before being accepted by Tait and the existing Governors.

Fearon's most controversial proposal, to convert in due course all the Brethren and Sisters to out-pensioners, to pull down the Hospital buildings and develop the site in order to increase the income of the Foundation, met with the strongest opposition from the Governors and, in particular, from Tait, who addressed in very plain terms Fearon, D.C. Richmond (Secretary to the Commissioners) and Henry Longley, the last of whom, on account of Lord Clinton's imminent retirement, had taken over the case from the latter. Tait strongly deprecated the discontinuance of the old people's collegiate life (both he and Mrs Tait were frequent visitors to the Hospital and took an interest in the inmates' well-being), although he seems not to have expressed any views upon the destruction of a building of historic and architectural importance.

Before making his proposals for the future of the two Schools, Fearon closely investigated the Vestry Committee's plan for a school of 1000 pupils; this he regarded as quite impracticable, for he doubted in the first place whether that number of boys whose parents were desirous of this kind of secondary education could be found in Croydon. He also dismissed the School Board's plans for a Higher Elementary School, on the grounds that such education should rightly be supplied out of the rates by the School Board itself, and that there would remain a large group of pupils unprovided for if two secondary schools were not established. All parties were agreed that the Poor School should not be continued as an elementary school.

Whitgift School

The Scheme of 1881

Fearon recommended, then, that there should be two schools of the type envisaged by the Endowed Schools Commissioners in their Draft Schemes, namely a combined first- and second-grade school in the North End buildings, open to all boys without local restriction and making provision for boarders; and a third-grade school in the Church Road buildings, with provision for scholarships to the first-grade school. The latter was of course already in operation as the Middle-Class School, still referred to sometimes as such if a distinction had to be made clear, but known generally as Whitgift School.

Names of the Schools

Fearon accepted a suggestion from Dr. H.J. Strong of the local Board of Health, that the first-grade school should be called 'Whitgift Grammar School', for 'there are many boys who go from Croydon to London to King's College and the Merchant Taylors' Schools, who would go to the Whitgift School if it had another name'. Fearon did not agree with Strong's other suggestion that the third-grade school should be called 'Whitgift Commercial School'; instead he preferred 'Whitgift Modern School'.

Provision was allowed for a Girls' School to be established when the funds of the Foundation should permit.

Although Fearon's proposals did not meet with universal approval, the Report showed that he had fully and impartially studied all the evidence and had acquired an excellent understanding of local conditions and requirements, and had produced a workable scheme that met to some degree the wishes of most interested parties. There were naturally objections, and suggestions for amendment, but the air had been so much cleared that the parties were inclined to compromise on most issues, allowing their warmth of principle to dissipate in argument on comparatively minor points. After discussion about the merits of 'Croydon Commercial School', 'Croydon Middle School' and 'Croydon Intermediate School' on the part of the School Board, and doubts about the suitability of 'Modern' on the part of the Vestry Committee, both bodies approved of the 'Modern School' and its name, which largely answered their demands; they almost ignored the Grammar School in putting forward their further recommendations. They both disapproved of the Head Mastership of the Modern School being offered to William Ingrams who, they maintained, however respected and successful he might be as Master of the Poor School, was insufficiently qualified to hold a higher post; he held a first-class certificate from the Education Department, but they thought the new post should be held by a graduate. But the Governors, supported by the former Vicar (recently retired and now Canon Hodgson) and the Archbishop, were in favour of Ingrams, who was to take over and conduct the School with great success.

The Governors were so relieved that the Report should go so far in meeting their own views upon the Schools (and with the Vicar out of the way they felt somewhat freer), that they had little to offer in the way of further criticism. Certain details involving matters of administration they wished to have settled in a slightly different form, but their chief objection was to the term 'Modern'; they preferred 'Middle'. There was Bedford Modern School, which was of a different grade, and the term had a distinct meaning when applied to a department of a school such as Marlborough or Cheltenham, but it was not applicable in this case, they maintained, for ' "Middle School" expresses precisely the character of the proposed new School as being in a middle position between the Grammar School and the voluntary and School Board Elementary Schools', so 'Middle' it became.

On 15 July 1881 the Queen in Council gave her assent to the Scheme which, amended in minor details from time to time, remained in force until it was repealed, and a new Scheme, devised by the Board of Education, was sealed in 1915.

On 9 November 1881 six new Governors, appointed by the new electoral bodies, joined the survivors from the earlier Scheme. They showed themselves eager to co-operate. Indeed, William Drummond wrote to Fearon with great satisfaction: 'The new Governors are men of business and would be very glad to be initiated into all the particulars of the Foundation. I am glad to say (they) will make very good Governors and are not at all likely to disagree with their older colleagues.' Whereas some infusion of educational experience might have brought with it a more liberal and ambitious outlook, the old régime was in fact perpetuated, and existing attitudes were frozen. The two new Governors who showed an enlightened interest in the educational side of the Foundation, Dr. Strong of the Board of Health, and W.T. Malleson, of the School Board, who had been a member of the Vestry Committee, were very much in the minority.

Whitgift Grammar School

In the main the Governors continued their parochial view of their duties, jealously guarding places in the School from encroachment by too many competitors from outside Croydon, and even discouraging candidates from entering for the Scholarship examinations unless they came from the Middle School. Their sanction was required for any attempt to set up a boarding-house, which the Scheme now permitted, but they never contemplated providing premises themselves.

There was now an increasing demand throughout the country for first-grade boarding education, which was being met by the expansion of some schools of old foundation, such as Uppingham, Sherborne and Tonbridge, and the foundation of yet more proprietary schools, such as Malvern (1865) and Eastbourne (1867). The general view among the prosperous professional classes and people of independent means was that sending a boy away to boarding-school encouraged him to stand on his own feet; he was also removed to a homogeneous social group, which was uncharacteristic of most day-schools, whose aims were set at a lower level, academically and socially. Thring had explained his own success at Uppingham: 'Wherever a foundation can supply boarding-houses and a small annual income for exhibitions to attract boarders, a large self-supporting school can be established, which shall entirely maintain itself in an efficient working state out of its own earnings' (Schools Inquiry Report, Vol.V, Pt.ii, p.92). But the boarding-houses at Uppingham and elsewhere were built, not by the Governors, whose endowment income was frequently minute, but by the Head Masters and 'Housemasters', who brought capital with them and derived a handsome return from their investment, which could be profitably realised upon their retirement.

During the next dozen years, seven masters opened small establishments in their own homes, the first being the Rev. J.W. Thomas, during the first term of the new Scheme; of them all only the Rev. M.H.H. Mason made anything like a success out of his venture, and 'Pa' Mason's House continued in Dingwall Road until the move to Haling Park in 1931. There were never

View from the cricket field

more than two or three boys in most of them; the houses were not big enough, being merely suburban residences; they were not immediately adjacent to the School; no one had sufficient capital to set up on any economic scale; only for very personal reasons would parents contemplate boarding of this kind, there being plenty of other schools where accommodation was as cheap but much better; the Governors were never more than mildly tolerant of the situation, and without their active encouragement any such project was risky indeed. With a family of four sons and a daughter and, it would appear, no private means to speak of, Brodie had no room for any more residents, and could not establish a 'School House', although, as we have seen, he was, until he came to terms with the Governors' views, very anxious to develop a strong boarding side.

The name 'Whitgift Grammar School' was at first popular with members of the School and with their parents alike. The official status of the School was now at least unequivocal, and it was no longer believed by anyone to be intended for the third grade of secondary education. Apart from this change of name, there was little alteration in the School itself, although there was a considerable increase in the number of boys on the Roll, which after the fluctuations of the previous six years, now climbed steadily to the figure of three hundred and ten in 1885.

That the School was still not able to compete strongly with other first-grade schools in London and elsewhere was partly due to the Governors' determination to keep the fees low, and consequently to the lack of first-class amenities, including university exhibitions. Higher fees would have made it possible to obtain better-qualified staff and more adequate equipment; they would have eliminated, too, that element whose lack of 'tone' so much embarrassed the professional class and the gentry who wished their sons to proceed to university, but who persisted in sending them to other schools, especially, those that had dropped the word 'grammar' from their name. 'Grammar' schools were likely to be large day schools in industrial towns—Manchester, Bristol, Leeds and Bedford. (The school of the last-named town was perhaps the most socially prestigious; it dropped 'Grammar' soon after it moved to new buildings in 1892.) On the other hand, higher fees would have eliminated a large number of hard-working boys of character and promise.*

Whitgift Middle School

At the end of 1881 the Poor School was closed, and its pupils dispersed among the various new schools that had been opened since 1870, but mainly to two Church schools, the Parish Church (St. John's) and St. Andrew's. The buildings were re-opened on 12 January 1882 with fifty boys under the same Head Master, William Ingrams, as a new school of the third grade with the name of Whitgift Middle School. A handful of Ingrams's former pupils stayed on with him but now paid the fee of £2.5s. per term instead of 3d. per week.

In the main the new Scheme gave satisfaction. The closure of the Poor School created no hardship, as there was now adequate provision of elementary education by denominational bodies and by the new Board Schools; in the Middle School the Vestry Committee had the type of school they wanted at a price they were willing to pay; and those who wanted a first-grade school also had one. It was towards this direction that the Commissioners had been persuading the Governors over the past fifteen years, but it was the Vestry Committee who gave themselves credit for the changes, which were in reality now closer to the Governors' wishes than to those the Committee had expressed as their own.

Baron Heath

Only a few months after the implementation of the new Scheme there occurred the death of one who, with the exception of Robert Brodie himself, had done more than anyone else to bring the School to its successful condition. The only survivor of the first group of Governors appointed in 1855, Robert Amadeus Heath, later known as Baron Heath on succeeding to his father's Italian title in 1879, died suddenly in

---

*Lest the impression should be given that the School was only moderately successful, it must be said that a number of other schools in course of foundation or reorganisation had sought advice from Brodie; the Head Master of Rugby, Jex-Blake, who had consulted him over the establishment of the Sir Lawrence Sheriff School, said he considered the Grammar School to be the most successful of its kind in the country.

June 1882 at the age of sixty-three, after twenty-seven years as a Whitgift Governor. He had been a great benefactor to the School, even before its re-opening, by his presentation of a hundred and fifty valuable books. He had a profound respect and affection for Brodie and would respond most promptly and generously to any of the Head Master's requirements that could not be met from Foundation funds. His personal benefactions were numberless; he helped several boys to go to university, he subsidised the concerts, gave large sums to support the Corps and to supplement the Library, and together with Stephenson Clarke, another generous Governor, he defrayed the cost of additions to the Head Master's House. His philanthropy was not confined to the School; he was well known for his generosity towards any good cause in the town. Brodie paid tribute to him in the following terms:

> Everybody who knows anything of Whitgift knows that there is no institution connected with it that has not had good cause to remember with gratitude the extraordinary generosity of Baron Heath, that he devoted a great deal of time and thought to making this school successful, and that nothing gave him greater pleasure than to hear that his labours in that direction had not been without effect. Our library, our cadets, our exhibitions, our tennis-courts, are witness to his thoughtfulness for our welfare, and to his splendid munificence in securing it. Whenever anything was needed for which the funds of the Foundation were not sufficient, he never failed to volunteer to supply it himself; and by his help we have been enabled to do many things which without him must have been altogether left undone. We miss him on Prize Day; we shall miss him at our concerts; we shall miss him on many occasions when his clear head and generous heart would have been of the greatest service to us. The present and past generations will need no external sign to keep alive in their hearts the feeling of love and gratitude to him who, since the time of our Founder, has been the greatest benefactor that the School has ever had.

A more tangible tribute to his memory was paid when a public subscription, to which many Governors, parents and boys contributed, raised over £1000 to provide a university exhibition fund.

The 'Educational Ladder'

The Scheme of 1881 made possible the fulfilment of an educational ideal that had been among the Governors' hopes ever since the re-opening of the School in 1871, namely, to provide a ladder by which a poor boy from Croydon could advance by means of scholarships from a national or public elementary school to the university. The Scheme of 1856 allowed the Governors to promote a boy from the Poor School to the proposed 'Commercial' School without any increase of fee, but no boy seems to have been promoted in this way. Under the new Scheme the Governors were to provide a number of exhibitions, open to boys from the public elementary schools, for admission into the Middle School, and also a number of exhibitions for boys from the Middle School to the Grammar School; furthermore, they were authorised to provide, if funds permitted, exhibitions from the Grammar School to the universities. Thus, in theory at least, the ladder was there to be used, but in practice full advantage was rarely taken of it, the successive rungs becoming more and more difficult to negotiate as one ascended. Only too frequently boys gaining awards from the Middle School to the Grammar School at the age of thirteen or so spent only a few terms there before leaving at the same age at which they would have left if they had stayed where they were; it is small wonder that Ingrams was reluctant to lose his best boys in this way. But there were others whose parents could not accept the place without some kind of subsistence allowance that the Governors were not authorised to provide, and not for another thirty years did any elementary schoolboy make his way through the two Whitgift Schools into the university. A tradition of this kind of educational climbing was very difficult to establish; to none but a minute proportion of boys at elementary schools would the idea of a university career have occurred; this was a privilege of the upper classes, and there had been no means of achieving it. Now that it was becoming theoretically possible, the practical difficulties remained insurmountable: a knowledge of Latin *and* Greek for Oxford or Cambridge; the freedom from any necessity to earn a living during adolescence—a period when parents would expect to receive from a son a contribution towards his support, rather than to continue maintaining him entirely; the association with a superior social class whose mode of life was in sharp contrast with one's own; the intense competition for university schol-

Whitgift School

The Cadet Corps, 1888
Members of the Shooting VIII in the rear rank are proudly displaying their colours; the rifles are Sniders

arships. And when one got to university, what was the outcome to be? Without further means to prepare for a profession, the only thing to do, unless one had a call to the Church, was to take up the unambitious occupation of teaching. No, far better to leave school at fourteen, go into 'business', take what opportunities were offered, and achieve prosperity in middle life. And this argument applied equally well to those in much easier circumstances.

School Life

The ordinary boy's school career was in great measure undirected; if he had the university in view he had something definite to work for, and certain professional bodies had established preliminary examinations which could be taken by boys while they were at school. Entry to the clerical grades of the Civil Service was now achieved through competitive examination and was the aim of many of the brighter pupils at some second-grade schools, who also entered boys for the Oxford and Cambridge Local Examinations established in the 1850s. These examinations were taken by individual pupils, however, and no external system existed, comparable to the General Certificate of Education, whereby all boys of a uniform age were methodically tested by an independent body. At Whitgift the Oxford and Cambridge Local Examinations were regarded as rather out of keeping with the dignity of the School, but a number of boys were entered yearly for the external examinations held by the Department of Science and Art at South Kensington; the occasional boy might take London Matriculation before he left School, but rather for the purpose of gaining entrance to the university than of acquiring a certificate of achievement. The culmination of the school year was the annual summer examination of the whole school, conducted by tutors and lecturers from various colleges and institutions in return for a suitable fee. Thus there developed a friendly connection between the members of the staff and the gentlemen who came down regularly each year to set and mark the papers, with the result that no really adverse criticism of the teaching was offered to the Governors, who were presented each year with a soothing, if never enthusiastic, comment on the School's attainment. Upon the results of this examination the Prizes were awarded.

After the first four occasions when Tait gave away the Prizes, it became the custom to invite some other man of public distinction, including several connections of Brodie's from Charterhouse or Christ Church. Since then nearly every Archbishop has on some occasion presented the Prizes.

Another Old Boy has left an account of the School's administration as it affected a pupil in the 'eighties:

The School hours were from 9 a.m. to 12.30 p.m. and from 2 p.m. to 4 p.m., except on Wednesdays and Saturdays, when the hours were 9 a.m. to 1 p.m. On half-holidays the last hour was devoted to drilling for the majority of the boys. The cadets formed one company, the remaining boys being divided into several companies. . . . Drilling was conducted by Sgt-Major Burke, a big man with a big Voice. . . .

(Before the almost universal spread of Cadet Corps and organised games, 'Drilling' was an important part of physical training in many schools, especially those deficient in recreational space. It 'set one up', improved one's bearing, inculcated habits of obedience and a sense of corporate unity, gave opportunities for older boys to give words of command, and provided a certain amount of exercise in the open air.)

I don't think that we can have done much work on Saturdays, as before Drilling there was the ceremony of Weekly Call-over. On Saturdays each form-master made up the total of marks gained by each boy during the week, and announced the results, placing the boys in the order of their marks. Then all the School, except the Nursery, assembled in Big School, occupying the same places that they did for prayers, but sitting in the order of their marks. The Head Master and his staff assembled on the dais, and each form was called out in turn and formed a crescent in front of the dais. The Head then read the form-master's report, naming each boy in turn. If I remember rightly, the boys at the top would be simply 'very good', and similar brief comments would follow on the other boys; but some of those at the bottom would be told off severely.

Speech Day was always the last day of the summer term. . . . Printed lists were distributed which set out in full the names of the boys in each form in order resulting from the examinations, also the boys in each mathematics set. . . . It must have been a rush to get this made up and printed in time, as the examinations were held right at the end of the term. . . .

I have heard complaints from Old Boys that although boys who wanted to learn could do so, it was not particularly difficult for boys who did not wish to learn to avoid doing so. . . . I may close by saying that I never suffered from any master who was unjust, or who bullied his boys, or showed favouritism or was incapable of keeping order.

Additions at North End

During the twenty years after the re-opening, the Governors took opportunities of buying pieces of land adjoining the School fields, including the Wellesley House estate of about seven acres to the north, purchased in 1878, and two acres, part of the Dingwalls estate to the south, purchased in 1883. (Dr. Strong's proposal that the remainder of Dingwalls—the site of the present Dingwall Avenue properties—should be purchased was defeated.) The two purchases made were invaluable, but the failure to obtain the whole of the Dingwalls property has ever remained to be deplored. The area of the School's playing-fields was gradually enlarged but never to an extent sufficient for its growing needs, and for as long as it remained at North End space for games was so restricted that only boys who showed marked keenness or aptitude could be adequately catered for. The capital was found from mortgages and sales of property, including those to railway companies, which paid high prices for land that might be unproductive of good rents or far from ripe for development. Although the Dingwalls land was incorporated into the School grounds soon after its purchase, the Wellesley estate was bought mainly as an investment, with the idea of future development, not as an addition to the School premises and certainly not, as the Governors had to affirm, as a site for a new lower-grade school; indeed it was nearly thirty years before any part of the grounds was used as an extension to the playing-fields.

Still separated by fields and woodlands from London, the town of Croydon was now, in the 'eighties, an important dormitory for workers in the City; well served by train services to and from a number of London termini, it was a popular locality for families who wished to live on the fringe of the country. The re-development of the narrow streets in the centre, and the demand for building sites on the outskirts, especially if they were close to a railway station, enabled the Governors by degrees to dispose of parts of their property for building purposes, so that a great increase in their resources was in prospect. Nevertheless, the Charity Commissioners kept a rigid supervision over the Foundation's finances and would not allow the Governors to interpret the terms of their trust in any manner that they, the Commissioners, considered liberal or inconsistent with a narrow interpretation of the Scheme of 1881. Indeed, any evidence of independence of action would bring a sharp rebuke or even some penalty.

The Founder's Tomb

In 1867 the Parish Church had been almost destroyed by fire, and Whitgift's tomb in St. Nicholas's Chapel was badly damaged. The Church was in due course rebuilt, and the Governors received sanction to give £250 towards the restoration (in a personal capacity they gave nearly £2500 between them). When, however, in 1888 they made a donation of £200 towards the restoration of the Founder's monument, which cost in all about £700, the Commissioners ruled that, despite the Hospital's care of the tomb during the centuries, the payment was an improper one, and declared that the Scheme, which did not allow for such *pietas*, had to be observed 'to the exclusion of any previous Instrument or Usage'. They even suggested that Whitgift should have made express provision for the upkeep of his own tomb, which was erected and paid for by his friends after his death. The outcome was that after questions in the Commons and the issue of a White Paper, the Governors between them refunded the £200 from their own pockets, under threat of legal action. This kind of treatment, meted out mainly because the Governors had not sought the Commissioners' prior permission for the donation, could have lent little encouragement to men who gave gratuitously of their time and on occasion generously of their substance in the service of the Foundation.

After 21 Years

In 1892 the School celebrated the twenty-first anniversary of its re-opening by the publication of its *History* under the editorship of Sir Henry Berney (OW 1874–79), architect and surveyor to the Foundation. Although dismissing the period of nearly three hundred years before the reconstitution as insignificant,* this work provides an invaluable record of those twenty-one years, for it comprises a Register of all boys who had attended the School since 1871, and very detailed chapters on all aspects of School life, except those of the class-room. For a thorough knowledge of which boys did what at games, in concerts, in societies, in the Corps, etc., this work is indispensable, but it gives little insight into personalities or the background of Foundation politics.

At the time of publication of the *History*, while the School was still struggling hard to gain greater reputation and recognition inside and outside Croydon, many of its alumni were laying the foundation of successful careers, especially if they had enjoyed the benefits of further education after leaving. Of the 1600

The Founder's Tomb, 1869

---

*Even the writer of the 'Historical Introduction' accepted the corrupt version of the Statutes, containing the term 'common school', without consulting the original document or accurate copies in the Foundation's possession.

boys who had passed through the School during those years, seventy were known to be dead and as many as one hundred and ninety more had been lost sight of; of the remainder one in seven had emigrated or taken a position abroad during this period of imperial expansion, nearly two-thirds were in business, one hundred and thirty were following the professions of the law, medicine, the church, teaching, etc., sixty were accountants, surveyors, civil servants, etc., fifty were engineers, twenty were in the services, and forty were at university, either as students or teachers. Two of this period became Senior Wranglers, two were elected Fellows of the Royal Society, four were knighted, and many became distinguished in their particular occupations, so that at least twenty-five came to figure in *Who's Who*, although none achieved really national fame. The large number of boys who passed through the School during these years is attributable to the early leaving age and to the persistent tendency for some to go on to other schools.

Vicissitudes of the 1890s

The early 'nineties were a period of some success and expansion; the publicity arising from the coming-of-age of the School in its new constitution helped to increase its attraction so that numbers grew in 1893 to the record total of three hundred and forty-seven. Although numbers had tended to fluctuate considerably, a trend attributed by Brodie to the vicissitudes of local trade and agriculture, the revived success of the School encouraged the Governors to regard it as permanent and to think of building extra class-rooms, so in November 1894 it was proposed to demolish the Elizabethan Schoolhouse and Schoolmaster's House in George Street, accept compensation from the Corporation for giving up a strip of land required for road-widening, and to negotiate a building-lease upon the site thus set free for development. The capital made available would go a very small way towards the cost of the construction of additional class-rooms, a new Head Master's House in the grounds of Wellesley House, and the provision of a new Middle School, the old premises in Church Road, in spite of enlargement in 1885, never having been

Head Master's House, 1897–1931

adequate for the purpose that School was now fulfilling. Henry Berney's block of eight class-rooms at the end of the Schoolmaster's garden was opened by Lord Chancellor Halsbury in July 1897. The demolition of the old buildings took place unhonoured and unregretted at the time; no one even thought it worth while to make a photographic record or a measured survey of the premises that for nearly three hundred years had housed a multitude of boys who owed their education to the munificence of the Founder. Apart from a couple of snapshot photographs taken by one of the masters, and the very vague recollections left by a few Old Boys, little has survived to help our imagination to reconstruct the appearance of the original Schoolhouse.

The Schoolhouse, known as 'The Nursery', 1600–1897

Archbishop Benson, envisaging 'the expansion of the School under the circumstances of another century', deplored the intrusion of commercial development within 'an area contiguous to the School', merely to acquire a small balance of rent. He doubted 'if it was proper to destroy a beautiful and well-known house (the Schoolmaster's, which had been considerably altered and enlarged at different times), almost co-eval with the old College', but he expressed no such doubts concerning the Schoolhouse, which William Drummond in 1871 had described as 'old, unsightly and inconvenient.'

'.... There it stands, just as the founder built it. The room 50 feet by 21, with four walls and a roof, was the area of this so-called "grammar school".'

His contempt reveals the general ignorance of the history and function of the School and other schools of similar origin. Fortunately, some photographs of the Schoolmaster's House were taken for the Surrey Buildings Record.*

There was more than the celebrations of 1892 to contribute to the School's success during the 'nineties; in 1891 F. L. Banks won the Spencer Cup at Bisley, while E.T. Warner gained an Open Scholarship in Mathematics at Christ Church and A.R. Hinks a Sizarship at Trinity Hall. But it was on the cricket field that Whitgift gained its greatest fame. Up to 1891 masters had figured in the teams when clubs were played, but ever after the opening game of the 1892 season between Boys and Masters, which the former won by 102 for 5 declared against 38, the boys were justified in relying upon their own resources. There were many excellent cricketers during the 'nineties, and a series of very successful seasons. In 1894, for the first time, all matches against other schools were won; these were Blackheath Proprietary School, City of London, Cranleigh,

*Although the Hospital was at this time not apparently under threat, twenty years before there had already been proposals to demolish it. A few years later the Corporation of Croydon and some of the Governors wanted to pull it down in order to widen the street, remove an anachronism and obstruction, and develop a valuable site. After years of dispute in which many preservationist and learned societies became involved, the question was settled in April 1923 by the House of Lords, who removed from the Croydon Corporation's Development Bill all powers to interfere with the Whitgift Hospital, which is now scheduled as a Class I protected building.

First Eleven, 1894

Eastbourne, Hurstpierpoint, KCS, Merchant Taylors', Mill Hill, St Dunstan's and UCS. Almost similar results were obtained in the following two seasons. In 1895 five centuries were scored, shared between three batsmen. The 1895 Eleven included a future Cambridge Blue, two others who were to play for the Gentlemen of England, and two who were to play for Surrey 2nd XI (H.H.B. Hawkins of Cambridge, V.F.S. Crawford of Surrey and Leicester, R.A. Sheppard of Surrey, G.U.B. Roose and W.H. Sandell). Crawford had the rare distinction of being invited to play for Surrey and for the Gentlemen against the Players while he was still at School. At a time when there were fewer means of entertainment, cricket was of wide interest, and matches at the School ground in North End sometimes attracted well over a thousand spectators.

Rugby football, too, was flourishing. The rather haphazard methods of the times, the dearth of good coaching, the inadequacy of the playing-fields, the purely voluntary principle, not only of playing, but also of attending practices, and the very varying standards from year to year of the School side and its opponents alike, together with a strong wish among a few boys to play association, did not lead to any consistent development of the game; however, 1896 was a very good season, the XV scoring 236 points to 33 in its eleven matches against other schools. Rugby had lost some of its former popularity, and few accessible schools now played; among those that did were St. Paul's, Dulwich and Merchant Taylors', but Whitgift did not then aspire so high.

Most of the fixtures were arranged on a home and away basis, and in that year the only losses sustained were against Christ's Hospital and University College School, but revenge was gained in the return matches.

The Tercentenary

In October 1895 the Governors decided that Founder's Day 1896 must commemorate in an exceptionally impressive way John Whitgift's foundation of his Hospital and School of the Holy Trinity three hundred years before. The Tercentenary could be linked with an appeal to the inhabitants of Croydon to honour the town's greatest benefactor. It was resolved that a suitable object of such an appeal should be the establishment of a fund to provide exhibitions for boys leaving Whitgift School to go to university. This was a need constantly invoked by Robert Brodie and on many occasions liberally responded to by individual Governors, including Baron Heath, in whose memory the Heath Exhibition was set up. Two other benefactors, Stephenson Clarke and John Spurrier Wright, had recently made bequests for this purpose, but the number of pupils who could benefit was still very limited, and additional funds would immediately be made good use of. College open scholarships in those days were very few, and no help from public funds was available.

The sum aimed at was £2000 which, invested in government stock at 3%, would bring in £60 per annum, a figure equal to about one-third of an undergraduate's minimum yearly expenses at Oxford or Cambridge. There was a good initial response, £1300 being subscribed within a couple of months of the issue of the appeal but this was not greatly exceeded. The first recipient of an award from the fund was J.H.G. Grattan, who was granted £35 p.a. for three years as a student at University College, London. He became Professor of English at Liverpool University, and bequeathed £300 to buy books for the School Library in recognition of the help he had received.

As the 22nd March 1896 fell on a Sunday, the following day was designated Founder's Day. A 'Festival Service' was held at the Parish Church, based on the annual Commemoration Service to benefactors at Trinity College, Cambridge, probably introduced there when Whitgift himself was Master. The service, which was attended by many members of the public, began with a processional hymn written by Robert Brodie and set to music by Edward Griffith, the composer of *Carmen*; the words but not the music have survived. God was invited to look down on 'Whitgift's sons':

> And if on them Thy Scourge, O God,
> Thou in Thy love dost send,
> Teach them to bear Thy chastening rod
> And conquer in the end.

This clear reference to the Whitgiftian motto 'Vincit qui Patitur' may have eased also the thought of chastisement applied more literally by members of the staff. Not content merely with writing a hymn applicable to Whitgift boys, Brodie also wrote a hymn of praise on behalf of the brethren and sisters, but it is not clear whether this was sung at the service.

Archbishop Benson preached the sermon, in which he praised the tolerance and munificence of the Founder. He also took the opportunity of dwelling upon the threat of demolition that hung over the Whitgift Hospital, for he was addressing a congregation with divided opinions on this question.

The solemnity of the occasion was regrettably marred just as his Grace was leaving the pulpit, when 'a discordant voice . . . from the west end of the nave exclaimed "I protest against this celebration; Archbishop Whitgift was not a tolerant man; he was an ecclesiastical tyrant." The individual . . . was quickly seen outside the sacred edifice, and came perilously near the condemnation and fate of a brawler.' (*The Croydon Chronicle*)

The day's celebrations were continued with the customary Dinner for the old people in their Hall, and concluded with a concert in Big School. Robert Brodie had persuaded his old friend Dr. Haig-Brown, Head Master of Charterhouse, to compose a Tercentenary Commemoration Ode, set to music by H. Leslie Smith, OW; there were two versions, in Latin and in English, in which the Founder's benevolence was praised, but which version was sung – 'very finely' – has not been recorded.

The date of foundation, from which Founder's Day has been adopted, was taken to be 22nd

March 1596, when John Whitgift laid the two corner-stones of his Hospital in North End. This date was recorded according to the 'old style' or Julian calendar in which the year ended on 24 March. However, with the introduction of the the 'new style' or Gregorian calendar in 1752 to accord with European practice, the New Year was officially declared to start on 1 January, so 22 March 1896 occurred only 299 years after 22 March 1596. The Tercentenary by this reckoning should have been held in 1897. Some difficult decision may have to be made before the time comes to celebrate the Quater-centenary in 1996 – or 1997.

Matters for Concern

It was all the more disquieting then, at a time when the School appeared to be riding on a tide of success, that there should be a good deal of criticism of the way it was conducted. Within a year the numbers had dropped from three hundred and thirty to two hundred and seventy, the Upper School being the chief sufferer. In 1897 one of the Governors, Sir Frederick Edridge, discussed with Brodie how the efficiency of the School could be improved; Brodie agreed to the establishment of a 'commercial' class, but his own views upon the steep rise in fees when a boy left the Lower to move into the Upper School met with no sympathy from the Governors, and no alteration was made. Less than a year later the Governors told Brodie that the much increased expenditure at the School had not met with correspondingly improved results, but Brodie, expressing himself satisfied with his staff and the way the School was run, was hopeful of the future, for already there were thirty more pupils on the Roll since the opening of the new buildings. At the end of 1898, however, following 'outside rumours of an unpopular nature', a special committee was appointed by the Governors 'to examine the curriculum and general tone of the School ... and to ascertain any grounds that may have given rise to criticisms'. In July 1899 this committee reported that the School did not compare favourably with schools of similar foundation throughout the country, the evidence given being that many private schools flourished, and many pupils came from outside the town. The unpopularity of the

The Junior School, opened 1897

School, they felt, was due to defective organisation on the part of the Head Master and to poor discipline and lack of good tone, qualifications, and interest in their pupils on the part of some of the masters; from this criticism R.J. Cheyne was notably excepted.

The Governors next asked the Archbishop (Frederick Temple, who thirty years before had, like Tait, been Headmaster of Rugby but, unlike Tait, had not been deeply involved in disputes over the School's organisation) to appoint an independent inspector to report on the School. F.E. Kitchener, Senior Examiner of the Oxford and Cambridge Joint Examination Board, spent two days at the School and reported in the first place to the Archbishop. He wrote favourably of the buildings, the grounds, the vigour of school life, and the proportion of masters to boys. The qualifications of some of the masters, however, drew adverse comment, for two of them had no degrees, another had been an undergraduate at London, but had not yet proceeded to a degree, and three others had taken the external BA degree of Irish Universities, a qualification which in the eyes of the Examiner was almost as good as none. He criticised the form-master system, the old-fashioned language-teaching and the minute proportion of boys learning Science, there being only twenty boys who studied it at all, and then but twice a week. The form-masters arranged their own syllabus and time-table, but frequently did not adhere to them. The most significant symptom of ill-health was the degree to which boys left School early, often to go on to other schools, while few stayed on in the Sixth Form with the intention of going to university or other place of higher education. By this time two of the London day-schools that attracted boys from the suburbs, namely St. Paul's and King's College School, had moved farther out, yet in spite of reduced competition, there seemed no tendency for the Sixth Form to increase in numbers.

When the Archbishop had read this report, he expressed himself willing to discuss suggestions for improvement with Brodie. After an interview Brodie reported to the Governors that he had gathered from his Grace that improvement could be effected (a) by obtaining better qualified men through offering better salaries, and (b) by the Head Master's more frequent visiting of classrooms. He attempted unconvincingly to repudiate the strong criticisms made by certain parents, but when invited to account for the increasing trend for boys to leave early, he could only 'express himself unable to shed any light on the subject', it being 'only a very small number of our parents who wish their sons to go to the university'. (There had been a noticeable falling-off in this respect.) The Governors agreed to appoint another man to take the Sixth Form in order to allow Brodie more time for administration and for supervision of his staff.

Apart from this weakness in the organisation of the School, there was at least one other ready explanation of its decline. At this time the boarding public schools were at the height of their success and reputation, which was to be maintained until after the First World War. During the last thirty years of the century, many of them, through generous benefactions or by the shrewd use of increasingly valuable endowments, had added to their buildings and amenities and had improved the quality of their staffs, attracting boys from the local grammar schools which, although they might have been reconstituted under Endowed Schools Act Schemes, were unable to provide comparable facilities, instruction or status. In the main, the public schools of England were now of three kinds: firstly, those that for centuries had enjoyed a fairly consistent reputation, such as those that were the subject of the Clarendon Commission; secondly, schools founded earlier in Victoria's reign, run to begin with on economical lines as private or proprietary foundations, that provided a chapel-centred, traditional education for the upper middle classes,

such as Brighton, Cheltenham, Marlborough, Lancing, etc. (schools in this category were particularly numerous in Kent, Surrey and Sussex), and thirdly, schools of ancient foundation that under Charity Commission Schemes had acquired a new prosperity, sometimes by attracting financial support from individuals or from the surplus funds of rich city companies; this wealth, ably administered by enlightened Governors, attracted exceptionally gifted and enthusiastic Head Masters. Among such schools may be considered Aldenham, Oundle, Repton and Tonbridge. Few schools of this type existed in south-eastern England (the Endowed Schools Commissioners would have been quite prepared for Whitgift to become one), a state of affairs which accounts partly for the success of the numerous proprietary schools.

It was to these types of school, then, that boys of prosperous families were attracted, rather than stay on at a school where methods and equipment were little better than they had been thirty years before, although the Lower School, providing an adequate course for junior boys, was regarded as a suitable day preparatory school. There was also the very sound reason, advanced by Lord Snow in the more recent case of his own family, that if

Monsieur d'Autier de la Rochebriant, B ès L, Chev. de la L. d'H, by a. Talbot Smith
(*Fun*, October 1899)

one is living in prosperous circumstances it is a mistake to educate one's own children differently from those of their acquaintance; such opinions were as current in Croydon as elsewhere.

The fact of the matter is that Brodie's capacity for administration and organisation had never been as great as his academic abilities. Of profound learning and general culture, he was happiest in the class-room, being an impressive teacher of those who could respond intellectually, and inspiring loyalty, admiration and affection among those who were admitted to his closer acquaintance; yet to the majority of the School and to their parents he was remote and unapproachable. Moreover, his early enthusiasm for establishing his new school was not matched by an interest in the new ideas and methods that progressive schools were now adopting; after the death of Baron Heath and certain others who had shared with him during the first few years the responsibility of moulding the character of the School, he had not much confidence in his Governors who, representing mainly commercial interests he was not in sympathy with, had set a brake on the kind of development he would have liked to see. His cultural values were those of a leisured gentleman; his scholastic ideals were still those of Charterhouse forty years before. He had at heart a low regard for Science, which he thought worthy of study only by mechanics or potential medicos. As he approached sixty years of age, all he wanted was to guide the School calmly as he had guided it for the previous dozen or fifteen years. He was supported by an ageing, ill-paid and never very effective staff. The more vigorous and better-qualified among youthful new-comers that he recruited saw that their ambitions must be fulfilled elsewhere, and they who remained had no pension to look forward to when they would become too old to teach.

There was no pension in prospect for Brodie, either. The Scheme of 1881 provided for a Superannuation Fund for the Head Master to be established by contributions made jointly by him and by the Governors, if the latter thought fit and the income sufficed, but they had taken no action. In November 1889 Brodie had approached the Governors about the matter, but this was a time when the numbers had fallen again, and the School was already running at a loss, so the Governors declined to make the necessary contribution, amounting to £150 a year. Twelve months after his first application Brodie tried again, and the matter was referred to a committee, which never reported back. From these circumstances there developed in him a resentment that partly explains his attitude to the Governors' suggestions for reform.

By the time of the investigation, however, the establishment of a pension fund was quite out of the question if Brodie was to retire soon after the age of sixty, and the unsatisfactory situation dragged on for another two and a half years. In January 1902 the numbers were still around two hundred and forty, with as few as twenty-five over the age of fifteen; in ten years the receipts from fees had dropped by over a quarter, but the salaries of the staff had increased by over a fifth; only the Foundation's increasing income saved the situation from financial disaster. The position could be regarded as all the more disquieting in that the population of Croydon had grown from 56,000 in 1871 to 134,000 in 1901, and the adjacent areas had experienced a similar degree of expansion. From this great increase in population the School should have attracted a corresponding increase in its numbers, especially as the growth of the local railway network and of the horse-tram system had made the centre of Croydon easily accessible to these developing areas. The remarkably small number of boys in the Fifth and Sixth Forms is significant; this was the result of the fees structure, which did not favour the development of a first-grade school. At £10 per annum, the fees for the Lower School (Fourth Forms and below) were only £3.5s. more than those of Whitgift Middle School, so that for a small extra outlay a boy could be sent for a second-grade education to the Grammar School, where the standard of the premises, the social tone and reputation, and the qualifications of the masters, if not the quality of the teaching, were a great deal higher than those of the Middle School, which nevertheless was full to overflowing, being much in demand by the numerous clerks and small tradesmen who formed a substantial proportion of the town's increased population. This type of parent would see no advantage in their sons' remaining at school beyond the age of fourteen (by which age most children were at work, anyway), especially when, as was the case at the Grammar School, a considerable jump in fees—now from £10 to £16 per annum—would be incurred, so the boys were withdrawn to take up the jobs in business that formed the limit of their immediate ambitions, and for which no qualifying examination was required. And the more boys of this type there were in the School, the less those parents wishing to provide their sons with a first-grade education were prepared to keep them at a school which was increasingly failing to meet requirements; so more and more boys were withdrawn early in order to complete their education at other schools. A further result of these circumstances was to deter the better-off or the more discerning parents from sending their sons to the Grammar School at all.

Brodie now had more definite suggestions to offer. He was prepared not only to make concessions to the modern view of education, but also to recommend that certain practical studies should be provided for. He asked for a full-time Science Master instead of the lecturer who attended a mere three afternoons a week. He made this proposal, not with the idea that Science should be taught to all, or nearly all, the School, but to allow boys whose parents did not wish them to continue with Latin to give to Science the time that would thus be made available. His other requests included the provision of a manual workshop and a miniature range, and the enlargement of the playing-fields. His only suggestion that penetrated to basic troubles was the re-iterated one that the fees structure should be made uniform throughout the School, in order to discourage the removal of boys when they should be about to proceed to the Upper School. Of these requests, the Governors agreed only to the construction of a miniature range, showing by their decision that the blame for stagnation was not Brodie's alone.

But they saw that their ultimate solution was to persuade Brodie to retire, for they were not prepared to dismiss him out of hand as they were entitled to. On 2 March 1902 the Commissioners were informed:

... The Governors are forced to the conclusion that a radical change is needful unless the School is to be allowed to continue its increasing drain upon the income of the Charity. The most practical form of change ... is that of a change of Head Master. For Mr. Brodie all the Governors have the highest personal regard, and would much regret causing him any pain. ...

The letter went on to ask for authority to grant him a pension out of the Foundation's income.

The Governors having asked the Archbishop for his support in their application, Temple wrote to the Commissioners on 13 March:

... The result of (the) inquiry was to show that the Head Master, though an excellent Teacher, was not a good organizer of the work of the School and was not likely to adapt it to the present need of the parents. But he had certainly at one time been a fairly good Head and had undeniably worked hard in the discharge of his duties. And it is no new nor rare thing that a man should be a good Head Master for a time and yet not able as years went on to adapt himself and his methods to the inevitable changes that in these days affect all education very seriously.

To dismiss the Head Master with no provision would be very unjust and yet there appears to be no power to award him any retiring pension.

If it be possible to remedy this defect in the constitution of the School I submit to the judgment of the Commissioners that it should be remedied. ...

Brodie's Retirement

The Commissioners' first reaction was to remind the Governors that the Head Master was dismissible at pleasure, at six months' notice, but as it was clear that they would not take this step, the Board on 4 May sanctioned the offer of a pension to Brodie of £400 a year. It did not take him long to accept and he tendered his resignation to take effect at the end of the Michaelmas Term. He was sixty-two and had completed thirty-two years' service, a longer period than any of his predecessors.

The boys of the School had little knowledge of the dissension between their Head Master and the Governors, and the regret at his departure and the appreciation of his services that were expressed in the Magazine reveal the respect held for him. After his retirement he continued to live in Croydon until his death in December 1925; he was survived by his wife, who had given him unfailing encouragement by her interest in the School and who must be remembered for the faithful copy she made of the Founder's portrait, which used to hang in Big School at North End and now hangs in North Entrance. The original, after being displayed for some years previously in the School, was returned to its former position in the Chapel of the Hospital.

Staff 1888

L. to r., Back row: D. Brodie, Watson, Griffith, Mason, Cheyne, RSM Burke, Dodd, Balley,
Front row: Huddlestone, Genge, R. Brodie, Bentham, Capt. Collins

In an obituary notice, Geoffrey Marks, one of his Old Boys who were in closest friendship with him, wrote:

To his classical learning, as sound as it was brilliant, and as deep as it was wide, he added an extensive and accurate knowledge of English and French literature and of the philology of both languages. His lessons were never merely lessons, and when he took the Sixth there was no subject which came up which he did not make interesting, even to the less intelligent, by some striking comparison or contrast, or by some comment, serious or humorous, which compelled attention or excited curiosity. His mind was as orderly as it was well-stored, and from it he could produce at will an apt analogy or apposite illustration to any matter in discussion. Yet he was not in the least pedantic, and intellectual arrogance was as foreign to him as intellectual snobbery.

Before this chapter is concluded, and lest the impression be given that any general reflection upon assistant masters should be applied to them all, acknowledgment must be made of the services rendered by many members of the Staff, whose pupils have remembered them with gratitude and affection. At the very beginning of Brodie's time the Rev. E.H. Genge proved himself to be an outstanding teacher of Mathematics, who continued for thirty years to train scholars for the universities; unhappily, there were too few pupils of the necessary calibre to take advantage of his talents. His pleasure in seeing two of his former pupils become Senior Wranglers must have been sharply diminished by the fact that they had gone on to other schools before proceeding to university. Others of the early days who wielded influence were the Rev. H.W. Turner and John Wheatcroft, both of whom were good cricketers; Turner spent fifteen years at the School before becoming Rector of Sutton; the latter became a Headmaster in Australia. Edward Griffith, the 'Song Master', has already been referred to. All who knew him have spoken with respect of R.J. Cheyne, who was among the very first boys to be admitted to the School in 1871 and who returned as a member of the Staff in 1877; he died suddenly in 1899 and is commemorated by a plaque that used to be in the Dining Hall; more than any other master of his time he devoted himself to out-of-school activities—most games, the cadets—and in other ways that a modern schoolmaster takes as a matter of course; he was a good teacher and a good disciplinarian at a time when most discipline was either lax or over-strict. Sergeant-Major Burke (1874–99) was a much respected figure, W.H. Collins (1882–95), Captain of the Cadets before Cheyne took over, and Douglas Brodie (1882–94) were popular. Among those who arrived later in the Brodie era, A.E. Watson (1881–1920), E.J. Balley (1883–1919), W.H. Dodd (1886–1921), M.H.H. Mason (1887–1922) and E.W. Tate (1899–1923) all left their distinct marks. Watson, who died in a bicycle accident, made a bequest to the School to provide the Watson Divinity Prizes; a man of handsome presence and devout Christian principles, he had a strong moral influence on many junior boys. Balley, diminutive in stature, but gigantic in personality, lived to the age of ninety-six, having attended his last OW Dinner two years before his death; he is also remembered as the author of a previous attempt at a History of the School: *Whitgift School and its Evolution*, published in 1937. The names of Dodd, Mason and Tate are perpetuated by the Houses named after them that they used to control, and they all three took a lively interest in many aspects of school life; they were mainly concerned with teaching the middle part of the School, where their experience and understanding of boys enabled them to create an abiding impression upon their pupils.

Mention must not be omitted of the boys, most of whom were proud of being Whitgiftians both during their schooldays and long afterwards.

In the closing years of the nineteenth century a high proportion of public-school men sought a career overseas, mainly in the territories that made up the British Empire. It has already been mentioned that at least one in seven OWs was resident abroad in 1892, but as many as 25% of old boys of such schools as Marlborough, Cheltenham and Uppingham emigrated. A few of these were employed in the diplomatic or colonial services, which were chiefly the preserve of the 'great' schools and of those like the above-mentioned, including Wellington and Haileybury, which also officered the army and developed strong traditions of military sacrifice and of empire-building. But the great majority of these emigrants, unqualified to take up any professional or skilled career at home, yet unwilling to lose caste by adopting jobs in industry, commerce and trade, followed the hazardous occupations of tea-planting, sheep-farming, cattle-raising, mining and agriculture in newly exploited areas. There were many OWs in these categories.

In spite of the difficult times, many of those who were at School in the last ten years of Brodie's régime achieved distinction; among them may be mentioned such diverse characters as the Right Honorable Major-General Sir Frederick Sykes, Whitgift's first Chief of Air Staff and Governor of Bombay in 1928, Sir Newman Flower, Chairman of Cassell's the publishers, Leon and Charles Quartermaine and Harcourt Williams, Shakespearean actors well known to a previous generation, Air Vice-Marshal Sir Alfred Iredell and H.E. Evans, QC, Solicitor-General of New Zealand, yet few of them, if any, could attribute their success to their academic training at the School. But Brodie's influence was well summed up by Geoffrey Marks when he wrote of the 'high ideals of citizenship which he held and constantly impressed upon his boys. His whole outlook on life was unselfish, and his best endeavours were devoted to the making of good men and citizens who could do some service to the State.'

8. S.O. Andrew, 1903–1927

The Education Act of 1902

While conditions at the School were giving concern to the Head Master, the Governors and the parents, Parliament had been considering the whole question of secondary education on a national scale. The Taunton Commission's recommendations for a system of secondary education under a central government office had been premature, but educational thought had recently been moving towards assent. In 1895 the Report of the Bryce Commission on Secondary Education, set up to find the best methods of establishing a national system, recommended the co-ordination of the numerous bodies responsible for education. The School Boards formed as a result of the 1870 Elementary Education Act, the Science and Art Department of the Board of Trade, and the Charity Commissioners, who controlled most of the endowed schools, were those chiefly concerned, and it was proposed that county councils and county borough councils should be given powers of control, under a Minister of Education. Such a minister was not appointed for many years, but the Board of Education was set up by Act of Parliament in 1899, absorbing in due course the educational responsibilities of the Charity Commissioners. The Education Act of 1902 established the Local Education Authorities (LEAs), who were empowered to set up their own secondary schools. Thus the County Borough of Croydon (incorporated since 1883) became responsible for its own system of both elementary and secondary education.

The effects of the 1899 Act upon the Whitgift Foundation were not immediately apparent, for some years elapsed before the Charity Commissioners handed over their own responsibilities to the Board of Education. One necessary piece of reconstruction was the division of the Foundation into two parts, for although the Board was to assume responsibility for supervising the control of the Schools, it could not be made responsible for the Almshouses and their inmates. The result was an Order of 12 February 1904 establishing two separate but closely linked trusts, the Whitgift Almshouse and Pension Foundation and the Whitgift Educational Foundation. The latter was responsible for the general administration of the estates and for the management of the Schools, and disposed of the remainder of the endowment income after expenses incurred by the former had been met. Both Foundations were to be controlled by the same Governing Body as provided for by the Scheme of 1881 and its amendments.

Whitgift Middle School, 1882

At this point it is appropriate to review the fortunes of the Middle School since its establishment in 1882. It had met with immediate success; it was the type of school that had been clamoured for by those townspeople who were eager to pay for their sons to be given a sound practical education leading to jobs in commerce and trade. For twenty years it had been overfull while the numbers in the Grammar School were fluctuating and later declining. Its status was that of a second- and third-grade school according to the recommendations of the Taunton Commission, but although the normal age limit was sixteen, few boys remained there even to the age of fifteen. It was performing excellent service in inadequate buildings that had received few additions or improvements since they had been opened in 1858 for the Poor School.

Until 1902 no provision for secondary education could legally be met out of local rates, so schools of the 'middle' type were in increasing demand. Such schools, which accepted boys from the age of seven, were the only alternative to private schools for parents who could not afford, or did not aspire to, a first-grade school, but who would scorn to send their sons to an urban public elementary school, not so much for educational reasons, as out of concern for hygiene and social caste.

Already, long before 1882, the Governors had become aware that the upgrading of the School in Church Road would necessitate better accommodation. With the steadily increasing assets of the Foundation they intended not only to enlarge the Grammar School, but also to rebuild the Middle School. In consequence of the continued expansion of Croydon and with the improved methods of transport, including the tram and the safety-bicycle, boys were travelling greater distances to get to school; a large number who attended the Middle School lived in North Croydon (South Norwood, Selhurst and Thornton Heath), so the Governors decided to look for a suitable piece of land in that area where either an additional school, or a larger school to replace the buildings in Church Road, could be erected. In December 1894 they selected a site of nearly seven acres in The Crescent, Selhurst, and the Charity Commissioners, who had for a long time been urging such a move, gave their sanction to the purchase for £4144. Sufficient funds were not yet available for building, but it was thought likely that by about 1902 work might start. Berney drew up plans for a new Middle School for five hundred boys to cost about £30,000 and to include a swimming-bath, a rifle-range and a dining-hall, amenities that did not yet exist at the Grammar School. After a builder's tender had been accepted and authority given for the sale of government stock to meet the cost, the Governors resolved in April 1902 to proceed no further, for the Croydon Council now had the power to introduce competition with new secondary schools of their own, and the Governors wished to wait until the Council's intentions were known. This decision gave the Governors some relief while they were dealing with the problems of Brodie's departure and the appointment of his successor, but it was a great disappointment to a large number of Croydon residents, for not only had the existing Middle School been far more *popular* than the Grammar School, but the proposed one promised also to provide on a much more generous scale the type of education that the new local authority schools would be designed to cater for.

S.O. Andrew

Having considered sixty applications for the Head Mastership, many of them from Heads of other schools, the Governors selected the names of three applicants for submission to Archbishop Temple. They were: S.O. Andrew, Head Master of Hulme Grammar School, Oldham, H. Bompas Smith, Head Master of Queen Mary's Grammar School, Walsall, and W.H. Wagstaff, Assistant

S.O. Andrew, MA

Master at Wellington College. On 23 October 1902 Temple appointed Andrew as Brodie's successor.

Educated at Manchester Grammar School and Oriel College, Oxford, Samuel Ogden Andrew, like his predecessor, had taken a first class in Classical Moderations and in Greats; in 1892, after a year at German universities, he became sixth-form master at Llandovery College; three years later he was appointed to Oldham which, being a newly opened school, gave him opportunities to organise from its inception.

He was aged thirty-five, with much useful experience behind him, when he took up his duties at Whitgift in time for the opening of the Lent term on 19 January 1903. Ten days later the Schools Committee of the Court of Governors received from him a report that revealed how complete a grasp of the situation he had already acquired. He began by stating that the School suffered from the lack of any guiding conception of the aims of a curriculum, and he deplored the haphazard allocation of subjects in the Upper School; the methods of teaching and the textbooks were out of date; the visiting masters he regarded as inefficient, out of touch and expensive to employ; the standards achieved were too low, and the buildings and equipment were inadequate. He therefore proposed to the Governors that they should apply for the School to be inspected by the Board of Education's Inspectors:

> I cannot but think that it would be well to have an authoritative, expert and impartial judgment on the teaching, the curriculum, the discipline, and the standards of this School before I lay my hands upon it.

The Governors, deeply impressed, immediately made application to the Board, and an inspection took place during the first three days of April.

HMI Report 1903

In July the Inspectors' Report was presented to the Governors, whom they had already informed that a thorough reorganisation of the School in regard to teaching, staff and buildings was necessary. The Inspectors had judged the School by a high standard, according to its situation, its endowment, the Scheme under which it was governed, and its more than local importance, and they found it deficient in many particulars. They considered the buildings to be unsuitably designed, inadequate and ill-equipped for good work. Among the additions that they declared were essential were a new Head Master's room, a common-room for Assistant Masters, new laboratories, a gymnasium, art-rooms, changing-rooms and a dining-hall. The installation of electric light instead of gas, and complete redecoration were also imperative. About Andrew himself they were most complimentary and enthusiastic, emphasizing his wide and profound scholarship and his interest in modern educational developments; he had already drawn up a syllabus for each subject and was evolving order out of chaos. His assistants, however, received but slight commendation; there were too many old men among them, whose teaching was inefficient, who had pastoral or coaching work outside the School and who regarded their duties as ended with the close of teaching hours. There were also too many visiting masters, who were expensive to hire, and whose interest in the School was slighter even than that of their regular colleagues. Youthful vigour and concentrated interest were sadly needed.

In the teaching itself they found little to approve of; textbooks were old-fashioned, and the methods and techniques were in general dispiriting; Latin was particularly badly taught by masters with a very imperfect grasp of the language; English lessons were dull and mechanical; the teaching of modern languages was shared between visiting masters and form-masters without a competent knowledge, neither party knowing what the other was doing; Science was not regarded as a serious matter and was taught as an extra by a visiting master to those who fancied it, whereas it should have been an essential part of the regular curriculum.

The Inspectors were critical of the manner in which scholarships were awarded for a period of one year only, instead of being offered upon undertakings that promising boys should stay on long enough to do more advanced work. They denounced too the sudden rise in fees when a boy entered the Upper School, which discouraged parents from allowing their sons to follow a systematically designed school course, even if such had existed. All these points had already been subjects of criticism by Andrew.

The general conclusion was that 'the efficiency, discipline and organisation of the School leave much to be desired'.

Before the Report had been placed before the Governors, Andrew, foreseeing many of its recommendations, had given notice to most of the visiting, and to a number of the regular, staff. They were replaced by eight young men of excellent qualifications, six of them with first-class degrees; among them were W.E. Cross, who had been under Andrew at Oldham and was appointed Senior Science Master, A.H. Smith (with a degree from the Sorbonne, and the first full-time French Master), G.E.H. Ellis (middle-school Classics), R.B. Morgan (Junior School) and E.M. Carter (the first full-time Art Master). Joined within a very few years by H.G.F. Micklewright (Chemistry), E.E. Kitchener (Junior School), C.J. Fisher (Geography and Mathematics), Ll.J. Jones (French) and E.W. Snell (Junior School), they formed the nucleus of a loyal and distinguished staff, qualified to give specialist teaching in all subjects. These men gave an aggregate of many years' service to the School. There were several others who did not stay so long but who increased the School's prestige by obtaining head masterships or university lectureships. Andrew always encouraged ambition in his staff, knowing that if the School gained a reputation for being a good jumping-off ground, it would attract ambitious young men eager to serve under him and learn from him at the low rates of salary that still prevailed, although he never ceased to battle with the Governors for an adequate salary scale.

The Inspectors' Report, carrying an overwhelming vote of confidence in the new Head Master, confirmed the wisdom of the choice of the Governors and the late Archbishop (Temple had been succeeded by Randall Davidson even before Andrew took office), so Andrew was not slow to follow up the advantages he had gained, and bombarded the Governors with requests and proposals; he demanded—and obtained—new maps, models, books, desks, lockers, and more stationery, laboratory apparatus and other equipment.

Reorganisation under Andrew

With a well-qualified full-time staff, Andrew was able to reorganise the teaching even if space and equipment were still insufficient. In June 1903 he told the parents of his immediate plans, the chief of which were: all boys would in future be taught science, and the laboratory fee would be abolished; all below the Sixth would be taught drawing; the library fee would be abolished, and form libraries instituted; the Fifths and Sixths would be divided into Classical and Modern sides, the boys in the Classical Sixth being prepared for University Scholarships, and those in the Modern Sixth for business, the Civil Service, London matriculation, and entrance to university if they wished to study Mathematics or Science, including medicine.

To provide these integrated courses and to pay his staff more generously would mean finding more money from fees. Andrew was of the same mind as Brodie and the Inspectors about the jump in fees from the Lower to the Upper School, for he found forty per cent of boys had been leaving before reaching the Fifth Form. Not only were too many parents using the School for a second-grade education (the lack of a progressively planned curriculum had in fact discouraged any serious view of the School as a first-grade one), but there were also some who had sent their sons to inferior private schools for most of their education, before getting them into the Grammar School for a 'finishing' year, which would give them a cachet they could make use of in seeking employment.

At first Andrew hoped to cover the extra expenditure on Science by putting the School on a grant-earning basis, a proposal he quickly abandoned on learning from other Head Masters that it would involve undesirable external control. His proposal to increase fees was not warmly received by the Governors. Although they now desired a well-equipped and efficient first-grade school, they had difficulty in understanding that this could be achieved only if they discouraged the intake of pupils who had no intention of staying on beyond the age of fifteen. They were afraid that numbers would fall if the fees were raised, not being confident that the request for higher fees would be tolerated even by parents who had greater ambitions for their sons and who would feel that they were getting value for money. Indeed, the Governors were not greatly troubled that boys were leaving from the Lower School, for they were still possessed with the idea that they must provide a *cheap* education available to all. The criticism they most resented was that the Grammar School fees were too high for many parents to buy the education offered. At this time, in point of fact, the parents who desired a first-grade education for their sons were mainly those who *could* afford it, but for those who desired a second-grade education there were not enough places available at the Middle School; moreover, the Grammar School gave a better social label.

During the next school year, some compromise was reached over an increase. The numbers were now rising rapidly, and quite a few among the new boys had come from public boarding schools which they had previously attended in preference to Whitgift. Reassured that a modest increase would not jeopardise the prospects of success, the Governors allowed a new scale to be introduced in September 1905. Boys were now encouraged to stay on by being charged the same fee throughout their school career according to their age at admission: those entering under the age of twelve would now pay £13.10s.; between twelve and fifteen £16.10s.; and over the age of fifteen, £19.10s.

At the same time the opportunity was taken to remove the distinction between the 'Upper' and 'Lower' Schools. Instead, a dividing line was drawn at the age of thirteen or thereabouts between 'Senior' and 'Junior' Schools, the latter, up to the Third Forms, being conveniently accommodated in the separate building erected in 1897; the division was only nominal, for Andrew designed the curriculum to be fully integrated.

The next great problem was the inadequacy of the buildings, upon which the Inspectors had made some of their most scathing comments. Apart from the shortcomings referred to, they had found few virtues in Blomfield's principles of design, which were now quite unfashionable and indeed obsolete. Admittedly, the neglect of thirty years had contributed to the pervading gloom to which the Inspectors frequently alluded, but the buildings were 'unsuitable', showing 'serious defects'; the Head Master's Room was 'inconveniently situated'; Big School was 'gloomy and singularly unbeautiful', the classrooms 'ill-lighted, -warmed, -ventilated and -equipped', and they were 'seriously prejudicial to good health and work'. But it was additions, chiefly for science and other specialised teaching, together with more space for an increase in numbers, that Andrew wanted, and by the end of July 1903 he and Berney had roughed out plans for extensions. Andrew provided the layout, Berney the architectural expertise and the trimmings. The new buildings were to harmonise with the old, so Berney's design included plenty of stone bosses, pinnacles, copings and mouldings, while gables and buttresses abounded.

Building Extensions 1906

Once approved, the extensions were quickly put in hand and were opened by Archbishop Davidson on Founder's Day, 22 March, 1906. They doubled the accommodation for teaching and were tightly fitted in behind Blomfield's block in such a way that there was little encroachment upon the very limited playing-field space. The new buildings consisted of nine classrooms (but four classrooms in the old building had to be sacrificed), cloakrooms, three laboratories and a lecture-room, with store, preparation-room, etc., and a large drawing-school; the old laboratory was converted into a manual workshop. Unfortunately, Andrew did not get all he had hoped for; Berney's estimate of the cost (£13,000) was so much below the lowest tender (£18,000) that many important features had to be omitted, including a dining-hall under the Library, a Masters' common-room, changing-rooms and new fives-courts (the old ones having been demolished during the redevelopment of North End). A swimming-bath and new pavilion had also been proposed, but had not gone beyond discussion. The finance for this project came from the reserves earmarked for the new Middle School, now indefinitely postponed, and from the sale of parts of the Addiscombe and Croham estates for building development.

But before these buildings were completed, other means towards efficiency had been introduced: the remainder of the Wellesley House grounds were incorporated in the School precincts; Andrew undertook to prepare a yearly financial estimate of school requirements; a

S.O. Andrew, 1903–1927

The Cloisters, 1904

The Extensions of 1906

superannuation scheme for the staff was set up; improvements were made to the lighting, heating and ventilation, although he could not persuade the Governors to install electric light in any part of the previously existing buildings. Other reforms included the resuscitation of old, and the foundation of new, school societies, and the redesigning and renaming of the School Magazine, henceforth to be called *The Whitgiftian*.*

For nearly twenty-five years *The Whitgift Magazine* had recorded the annals of the School without any alteration in its paper, type-face or layout; its pages were now to be enlivened with modern type, illustrations, photographs, original articles, and more news of Old Boys. These improvements were accompanied by an obvious surge in morale and pride, evidenced by many of the contributions, some of which came from the hand of Robert Keable, later to become famous as a best-selling novelist and honoured as a benefactor.

The Houses

In 1904 Andrew established the House system, one of the first in a day-school, with four senior houses under Cross, Dodd, Mason and Tate. Dodd was appointed Second Master in 1907

when Genge retired that year. By enlisting the support of three of the younger men from Brodie's staff in the new organisation, Andrew was able to consolidate his own position at the head of a loyal and enthusiastic band of assistants. Three junior houses were established at the same time, named merely 'A', 'B' and 'C'.

But the first few years had not by any means been a period of easy popularity and general support. To many—especially to those OWs who held Brodie in high esteem—Andrew was a brash newcomer from the North, with a Lancashire accent that Oxford had not succeeded in completely smoothing; some even said he was a 'bounder'. He may not have enjoyed Brodie's easy and confident manner before an audience— he was pedantic yet hesitant in speech—but his

---

*This word, noun or adjective, seems to have gained currency only slowly, possibly because as a neologism it was cumbersome and slightly absurd. There had been 'Whitgift Old Boys', the 'Old Whitgift Dinner' and, among the learnedly facetious, 'Whitgiftienses', but after it appeared in the Magazine of December 1880 the term gained in popularity, and Andrew encouraged its official use. It has been used in print in other contexts relating to the Founder and is included in Volume IV of the Supplement to the Oxford English Dictionary.

Whitgiftian (hwitgi·ftiăn), *sb.* and *a.* [f. *Whitgift* + -IAN.] **A.** *sb.* A pupil or former pupil of Whitgift School, Croydon. **B.** *adj.* Of, pertaining to, or characteristic of John Whitgift (c 1530–1604), Archbishop of Canterbury and founder of Whitgift School.
    1880 *Whitgift Mag.* Jan. 13/2 We were glad to notice among the Chorus several 'Old Whitgiftians'. **1905** (*title*) The Whitgiftian. [*Previously* The Whitgift Magazine.] **1962** *Hist. Mag. Protestant Episcopal Church U.S.* XXXI. 128 The picturesquely rhetorical phrase of F. W. Maitland has been considered the most decent dismissal of the whole Whitgiftian flavour: 'a remorseless predestinarian'. **1967** P. COLLISON *Elizabethan Puritan Movem.* v. i. 245 Of this generation of clergy, few with minds of their own would subscribe to the Whitgiftian formula without a qualm. **1977** P. CLARK *Eng. Provincial Soc. from Reformation to Revolution* v. 184 In the county [of Kent]..the Whitgiftian reaction caused a marked polarisation between moderate Puritans and conformist Presbyterians on the one hand, and less respectable radicals and separatists on the other.

Extract from Supplement (Vol. IV) to
The Oxford English Dictionary, 1986

profound learning and comprehensive grasp of contemporary educational theory and practice soon convinced everyone genuinely solicitous of the School's progress that the right man had been chosen.

Staff Problems

The most difficult and distasteful task of all for him was the dismissal of most of Brodie's staff, many of whom were quite unadaptable to Andrew's new ways. Mostly poorly qualified and now elderly, they were an impediment to progress, so for the sake of the School and its pupils they had to go. For those in holy orders the Archbishop helped to find country livings; the part-timers had to find other part-time jobs; but there were some for whom the future was bleak indeed, and their position was little alleviated by the Board of Education's grudging permission to the Governors to allow them a term's salary by way of a gratuity.

The situation had not been altogether unforeseen, for in 1899 the assistant staff had requested the Governors to consider the provision of a superannuation fund as urgent. The Governors replied that they were unable to accede; superannuation of assistant masters could not be entertained under the authority of the Scheme.

The circumstances at Whitgift, which were of course not unique, prompted A.F. Leach to write an interesting minute at the Board of Education (PRO. ED35/2396), in which he studied the legal and financial possibility, rather than the moral obligation, of establishing pension funds for assistant masters who were dismissible by the Head Master at pleasure. He said:

Endowments which were originally given and were adequate for the support of two Masters, teaching the Classics only to large Classes of boys of forty or even more, have proved in most cases utterly inadequate for the large staff now required when Mathematics, Modern Languages, and various branches of Natural Science, Music, and Physical exercises have been superadded to the curriculum ... The imposition ... and the raising of fees has to some extent relieved the financial strain ... but the fees ... have, in deference to the pressure of the ratepayers ... been fixed at a point far below the cost of the education given.... In the majority of Secondary Schools ... the salaries paid to Assistant Masters are so inadequate that the Schools present a melancholy procession of untrained and inefficient young men perpetually on the move from School to School. Good men are only retained in the profession because, owing to the incessant creation of new Schools, there has been a continual stream of promotion to Head Masterships.... If in these circumstances it is now proposed to impose on the foundations the additional burden of pensions or leaving gratuities, the money available for active maintenance will be further trenched upon....

According to the report of the recent inspection, the Grammar School also needs a large teaching staff and a considerable addition to the annual outlay for upkeep of the School buildings, plant and apparatus, and these wants are likely for some time to come to make a heavy call on any increased revenue which may accrue from the future development of the estates.

Turning to the legal aspect, he could find little in the Scheme that without straining would enable the Governors to make an *ex-gratia* payment to retiring masters, but under a clause that permitted expenses incurred 'generally in extending or otherwise promoting the ... efficiency of the School', he suggested that such payments might in exceptional circumstances be justified. Therefore, Leach recommended to the President of the Board that the Governors should be allowed to pay to two retiring masters who had served for thirty-two and twenty-two years respectively, a term's extra salary.

The recommendation received the strong support of Randall Davidson, and the accompanying publicity, together with the intervention of the Assistant Masters' Association and the Bishop of Hereford, who was going to ask a question in the House of Lords, helped to establish the regular system of superannuation schemes in all types of schools, at first voluntarily through joint contributions by teachers and governors or LEAs to life assurance societies, but later, in 1918, compulsorily through the Board of Education's scheme.

The Old Whitgiftian Association

Yet another project that owed much to Andrew for its inception was the formation of the Old Whitgiftian Association. Although the Whitgift Wanderers Cricket Club, the Whitgift

Veterans Rifle Club and the Old Whitgiftian Football Club had all been founded in Brodie's time, and Old Boys had been able to keep in touch with each other through these Clubs, at the Annual Dinners, and by subscribing to the *Magazine*, there was no club or society which could be joined by a Whitgiftian who had no particular interest in any of the established sporting clubs.

Since 1889, if not earlier, a wish had been expressed from time to time for some unifying club or association, but little general support resulted. Andrew's encouragement, however, coupled with pride in the School's rising reputation under him, led to the formation of the OWA in 1907, its modest initial aim being to maintain an address-list of OWs wishing to keep up their connections with each other and with the School. From this inconsiderable beginning, with Robert Brodie as Honorary Treasurer and M.R. Atkins (OW) as Honorary Secretary, the present strength of the Association stems. The significance of Brodie's acceptance of this office should not be overlooked.

Academic Successes

Involved as he was with such a tremendous task of creation and regeneration, Andrew might well have found little time for teaching, but already in May 1904 he had coached his first university scholar, William Paton, who gained an Open Scholarship in Classics at Pembroke College, Oxford. Paton, who became a distinguished figure in the Presbyterian Church, but died in his fifties, was the first of a long list of university scholars who brought renown to the School during Andrew's Head Mastership. During the next few years more and more boys, encouraged by the success of their fellows, stayed on in the Sixth Form with the hope of gaining university awards, and many others went up as commoners and to London colleges and hospital schools. Moreover, a larger, more responsible and harder-working Sixth Form raised the general tone of the School, which acquired a new self-respect and a desire to excel in other fields of endeavour; so that there was a noticeable improvement in the standard of games and in the results of matches against other schools.

Provision of Secondary Education by LEAs

These developments were taking place at a critical time, when a deeper interest in obtaining more and better secondary education was being shown by all responsible sections of the public. This interest can be traced to multiple origins: the elementary system set up by the Forster Act of 1870 was now well established, and the early generations of pupils were looking for even greater opportunities for their own children; the Bryce Report of 1895 had revealed gross deficiencies as well as great achievements; the Education Acts of 1899 and 1902 had introduced means of fulfilment of hopes and needs; there was a growing realisation that the nation could not afford to neglect the intelligence that reposed untrained in all classes of the community, but especially in those that could not afford to pay for their own education. This realisation was coupled with another—that many other nations were better organised in this respect. There were demands from many radical groups for free secondary education for all and, until this could be achieved, at least opportunity for all. There also existed a desire to emulate the public schools and other schools that had developed successfully during the previous thirty years, partly as a result of the findings of the Taunton Commission.

All these forces were present in Croydon; but Croydon possessed a potential such as few others enjoyed. The Whitgift Foundation had until this time been responsible for all secondary education for Croydon boys, apart from what was provided by private schools (which have continued to play an important part until the present day). The Governors had not been able to keep pace with requirements, however; there were no more boys in the two Schools combined than there had been twenty years before, when the population was half as numerous. Their capital assets were steadily increasing in value, but much of the increase had been used for enlargement of the Schools and other building developments, and the income necessary to subsidise larger numbers of pupils was not yet available. The Governors' power to direct their own affairs was by no means absolute; neither were their resolutions unanimous.

There were numerous and sometimes conflicting interests ready to exert pressure upon them: (a) The Church was still predominant; the Governors appointed by the Archbishop, but chosen by the Vicar primarily for their assiduous support of the Church, enjoyed a clear majority over their colleagues appointed by local authorities (four by the Borough of Croydon, two by the magistrates), and the Church party were determined to preserve the denominational bias that had made it difficult for outsiders to intervene. (b) The Council very much wanted to increase its representation on the Governing Body and indeed to acquire control. (c) The Board of Education, with its responsibility for organising an effective educational system (short of university) throughout the country, but without being at all committed to municipalisation, had the duty of directing the resources of the Foundation towards approved ends, and took a more than local view of the Foundation's place in the system. (d) Local opinion was very varied and depended on what different sections of the community hoped to get out of the Foundation, so that it was by no means always identical with that of its elected representatives on the Council or in Parliament. (e) The Head Master and his staff were determined on doing their best to give the School high rank and prestige, but held themselves aloof from local affairs. (f) There were also the Old Boys of the School, whose views might not coincide precisely with any of the foregoing; their opinions and objectives were uncertain and unco-ordinated, for there was as yet no Old Boys' Association to give them coherence.

Upon being given responsibility under the 1902 Act for 'higher' (than elementary) education in the Borough, a responsibility which included the organisation of evening classes, the training of teachers in elementary schools, the provision of secondary education or aid therein, the provision of scholarships and payment of fees of students at college, etc., the Council engaged Professor Walter Ripman of London University to examine the educational facilities in the Borough. He reported that, with Whitgift Grammar School and the Girls' High School, the supply of first-grade schools appeared adequate, but there was a dearth of schools with low fees for boys and girls from twelve to sixteen. Whitgift Middle School had for many years done useful work in adverse conditions in a building little suited to it, with three hundred and fifty boys crowded into rooms that should have held not more than half that number. There was a pressing need for a Croydon Borough School which would give secondary education to boys and girls who should then be receiving it but who were leaving their elementary schools at the age of thirteen or fourteen; such a school would also serve as a pupil-teacher centre for training elementary-school teachers. Ripman thought that the Selhurst site was admirable for the erection of schools of this kind.*

The Council was embarrassed by its new obligations, being already committed to a large capital outlay for other purposes. The road improvements, still in progress, had not yet resulted in a large increase in rateable values; it had become necessary to spend a quarter of a million pounds on a better water-supply, and seventy thousand pounds on sewerage; there would be an outcry from the ratepayers if they were required to find further thousands for education, for they were paying out large sums in interest on loans for these projects. There was little prospect of providing permanent secondary schools in the next five or six years.

So the Council were looking elsewhere. The Act did not *compel* the LEA to provide secondary education. In some places provision was already adequate through endowed foundations; some authorities virtually took these over, lock, stock and barrel, providing themselves at no cost with a ready-made system as, for example, at Leicester, with Wyggeston's Foundation. This was what many councillors wanted to do with the Whitgift Foundation, but it was impossible without the Governors' consent, so attention was turned to other ways of controlling the Foundation's resources. These members of the Council wanted stronger representation on the Governing Body, and they thought that boys from outside Croydon should pay higher fees, for it was not right that they should benefit from what ought to be the privilege of Croydonians alone. They wanted the schools to be placed on the grant-earning list which had been set up in 1902. Schools on this list – the forerunner of the

---

*Just as the term 'elementary school' came to be associated only with provided and/or maintained primary schools, so 'secondary school' was applied to LEA schools, although technically any school higher than a primary one is a secondary school.

Direct Grant – received a *per capita* subsidy from the Treasury through their Governing Body or the LEA, in exchange for which they were required to provide a free education for a proportion, from 10% to 25%, of pupils from elementary schools. Governing Bodies had to admit a stronger representation of local government membership. The list quickly came to comprise most of the large town grammar schools, such as Manchester, Bristol and Leeds, but a few country boarding-schools, such as Berkhamsted, Blundell's and Oakham also recognised a means of gaining financial security. The latter group, obtaining their pupils from a wider area, and admitting only 10% as free scholars, did not fall so much under the control of local interests, the danger from which Andrew continued to be wary of. All the schools mentioned in this paragraph had been represented on the Headmasters' Conference since the earliest years of its foundation in 1869. This fact sets in perspective the delays that beset Whitgift's reconstruction after the Chancery Scheme of 1855.

But neither the Council nor the Governors were prepared to make definite plans for their own contribution to local education until they knew what the other party intended to do. An attempt to break the deadlock was made in a joint conference with officials of the Board, where the Permanent Secretary, W.N. Bruce, and A.F. Leach, R.L. Morant and R.E. Mitcheson became particularly interested in the Whitgift case. These gentlemen, already aware of how successfully Andrew was giving new life to the School, commended the Governors for not proceeding with the building of a new Middle School at Selhurst, and advised them to give up the Middle School altogether and concentrate their resources on the Grammar School, for the Governors could not be expected to be responsible for the whole of subsidised education in Croydon. The Council should provide its own secondary schools of a lower grade, with a proportion of free places from the elementary schools, and scholarships to the Grammar School and the Girls' High School. (As a temporary measure the Council had formed a fee-paying Boys' Secondary School in the Polytechnic buildings situated almost opposite the Middle School. It seemed to the Board foolish to have two competing schools doing exactly the same work.) Such secondary schools should in no way compete with the first-grade schools. But as a help to the Council, the Governors might well make over the Selhurst site as a gift or let it at a nominal rent. This proposal was naturally very well received by the Council, who would in that case be eager to co-operate with the Governors and even allow them to be represented on the governing body of the schools to be erected there—which could, they thought, be called 'Whitgift Borough Schools'—but the Governors were not disposed to comply. Firstly, they had received legal advice that they could not alienate any of their real estate for less than its full value; secondly, their endowments could be used for the support of their own schools alone; thirdly, they had no intention of abandoning the Middle School, whose great merit in the eyes of the Vicar's party was the effective instruction it gave in Church of England doctrine, far superior to what was given at the Grammar School. Neither did they wish to claim grants for the Middle School as a recognised secondary school or as a pupil-teacher centre, the acceptance of such grants requiring a surrender of the School's denominational character, and they certainly had no intention of handing over the School as it stood to the Council. Indeed, they still hoped to build a new school at Selhurst or elsewhere in a dozen years' time.

To these decisions Randall Davidson gave his support; he was very conscious of the benefits gained by the Church from the position and influence of the Foundation. Son-in-law of Archbishop Tait, whose chaplain and secretary he had also been for six years, he was well acquainted with the previous history of the

Big School, 1907

Whitgift School

A Junior School Classroom, 1906

Foundation and, although he had no local residence, Addington Palace having been given up by Temple in 1897, he maintained a close contact with Croydon through the officials of the Foundation. He had trust in the Vicar's local knowledge and in the Bishop of Croydon's longer experience of its inhabitants; he took a keen interest in Andrew's efforts at the Grammar School, backing him up in a dispute with a parent who had complained directly to Davidson, and he was very pleased to be invited to open the new school buildings.

Local opinion found expression in the local newspapers; in the main it reflected the views of the more radical of the councillors, whose present hopes were impossible of fulfilment. In November 1906 members of the Fabian Society organised a public meeting at which Sydney Webb was the principal speaker. The main concern of the meeting was to promote the education of poor children with brains, by means of the scholarship 'ladder' from the elementary school to university; by giving up the Middle School the Governors could afford to be generous with such scholarships. The Governors retorted that if they continued to maintain the Middle School, the Council should then be able to support a scholarship scheme.

In 1908 the Council offered an annual scholarship to the Grammar School open for competition to boys who had attended an elementary school for at least two years. This scholarship was usually taken by boys from the Borough Secondary School who, having made good progress there, were to be encouraged to proceed to university, but few suitable candidates offered themselves. For really poor children to take advantage of the 'educational ladder', maintenance allowances were necessary, but these were not yet available. There was also reluctance among working-class parents to send their children to be educated 'beyond their station'. Although there was great competition to gain scholarships to the Middle School in order to obtain a second-grade education, the result was that many boys of 'merit', who were being sought for selection, went without the education they could have made good use of.

Settlement of the conflict over the future of the Middle School, which lasted for over five years, was aided by the general recognition that the Grammar School had achieved a status that put it beyond the grasp of a local authority, and the Governors were able to dictate their own terms: they would after all allow the Borough to buy the Selhurst land either at a valuation or at the price they had given for it in 1896. The Borough was glad to settle for the latter figure, and upon the site built Selhurst Grammar Schools for Boys and Girls, into which the Borough Secondary Schools moved in due course.

Teaching Methods

Having well consolidated his curricular aims for the School by drawing up a syllabus for each subject and by appointing a first-rate staff,

Drawing School, 1907

Andrew devoted much attention to improved methods of teaching. It was said that he could quite happily teach a sixth form in most of its specialist subjects, whether they were the Classics, Ancient or Modern History, Mathematics, French and German, or English Language and Literature (one of his pupils who read English at Cambridge had a poor opinion of his tutor in comparison with Andrew), so he had complete confidence in directing his staff in the syllabus, the methods and the text-books they used. It was a time of experiment in some schools, and Andrew himself was in the forefront as an innovator, but there was a great shortage of text-books of the kind that Andrew required. He had a remedy at hand: he and his colleagues would write them. He had already published a *Greek Prose Composition* before coming to Whitgift, and his next books were a *Geometry* and a *Practical Arithmetic*. The former of these, designed to render Euclidian geometry in more modern terms, was forty years ahead of its time, anticipating in some ways the Jeffery Report of 1943 on the teaching of Mathematics.

Encouraged to know that their text-books would be used not only at Whitgift but also, more probably, in many other schools to which Andrew's reputation had already spread, several of his staff produced works in their own specialist fields. In conformity with Andrew's views on the teaching of history, N.L. Frazer compiled a collection of important historical documents—primary sources for historians—half a century in advance of what is now common practice. Morgan and Kitchener published *English Grammar* and *English Composition for Junior Forms* respectively. It was in the field of language teaching, however, that his influence was most marked. The Direct (oral) Method of teaching modern languages was ousting the old formal, obscure and literary approach based on the conventional methods of teaching the Classics, which were quite inappropriate for living languages that should primarily be learned as spoken tongues. Andrew's appointment in 1910 of Marc Ceppi, whose name was to become known throughout the country as the author or editor of innumerable French text-books, and his insistence that other teachers of French should be trained in phonetic methods, introduced at Whitgift a system that came to be applied also to the teaching of Latin.

Andrew and W.H.D. Rouse, of the Perse School, Cambridge, another great innovating Head Master of Edwardian times, were the joint general editors of the text-book series 'Lingua Latina', to which two of the Whitgift staff, W.L. Paine and C.L. Mainwaring, contributed *Primus Annus* and *Secundus Annus*. Unhappily, both these men lost their lives in the First World War, and their dedication and skill died with them, although their books and their methods, somewhat modified, survived until the end of Andrew's time.

Since western civilisation owed so much to the legacies of Greece and Rome, the study of their literatures remained for Andrew the basis of culture. In Andrew's early days at Whitgift, an able boy who had already decided to specialise in Science could spend a year in company with his Classical schoolfellows before being transferred to the Science Sixth. The older universities, at least, were looking more for promise than for achievement in scholarship candidates, for quality rather than quantity of knowledge. Archbishop Davidson, coming to open the new buildings in 1906, was greeted with a fluent oration in Latin from the Captain of the School, D.Ll. Hammick, who had already gained a Science scholarship to Oxford.

After reading a pamphlet on 'Science for All', Andrew described to his Chief Science Master the kind of Science which he deemed desirable in advanced courses and which was needed on the Arts side as well as on the Science side, possibly more so. 'Natural Science was one of the avenues along which man had adventured in order to gain intellectual control of his environment, so as to feel at home in the world. In the Sixth Form, boys should learn about the history of man's attempts to understand the structure of the universe, the constitution of matter, and the evolution of living organisms.'

In 1907 Andrew was elected to membership of the Headmasters' Conference, which then consisted of members from one hundred and twenty schools. It was characteristic of him to refer to this recognition of the School's improved status (one qualification for membership being the number of former pupils at Oxford and Cambridge) merely by a casual remark in his annual report to the Governors; no other mention of his election was made, even in *The Whitgiftian*, which was usually ready to record

Whitgift School

Domini XI 1910
L. to r., Back row: Revd. M.H.H. Mason, Revd. W. Burton, W.L. Paine, A.H. Smith, J.H. Stevens, C.A. Howse, E.W. Snell, Front row: R.B. Morgan, E.W. Tate, S.O. Andrew, G.E.H. Ellis, Seated: Ll. J. Jones

any advantageous news. Perhaps this omission reflects Andrew's rather low opinion of the Conference's activities; he is not recorded as a regular attender of their annual meetings. In the following year another Inspection took place, not on this occasion by the Board of Education, but by the Oxford Local Examining Board. By this time the numbers had increased from two hundred and thirty, when Andrew took over, to three hundred and ninety, and the Inspectors gave unqualified approbation to the way the School was conducted.

The discipline, vigour and spirit of the School seemed to be excellent, and I noticed a loyalty among the Masters to the Head, which is one of the most important conditions of the real success of a school.

It is plain . . . that as far as the teaching and the general arrangement of the studies is concerned, the work of the School in its general lines, in its aims, and in its character, is such as to deserve the confidence of the Governors and the parents.

Five years later, six of His Majesty's Inspectors from the Board of Education paid, at the Board's suggestion, a four-day visit to the School and reported on the developments that had taken place since their previous inspection ten years before. By now the numbers had risen to four hundred and seventy-one. The proportion of boys coming from villages and small towns outside the borough was increasing. These places were enjoying the prosperity of the Edwardian era by providing new homes for commuters. Better communications included the railway line to Kingswood, opened in 1897, the motor-bus and the motor-car.

The Inspectors examined very thoroughly the teaching of all subjects and took great interest in the organisation of the School, particularly the streaming of the forms, the selection of boys to study extra languages besides French and Latin, the experimental Direct Method, and the divisions of the Sixth Form, where Andrew's experiments in working out a course to include History and Modern Languages were found especially notable. They made many useful suggestions, mainly in the teaching of English, History and Geography, for neither the organisation nor the curriculum was beyond criticism, and they also made useful proposals which, in conjunction with Andrew's own expression of requirements, helped to convince the Governors that there was still much more in the way of buildings and equipment that should be provided. They concluded by saying:

... Improvements have been accompanied by an advance in the standard of work and the efficiency of the teaching of so striking a character that it is difficult to believe that this is the same institution that was reported on in 1903. And the whole constitutes a record of progress for which it would not be easy to find a parallel.

... The effectiveness of this organisation and the special character of its work in more than one subject of the curriculum—features which it owes to the initiative and inspiration of an exceptionally capable and hardworking Head Master—give to it much more than a local interest. In certain directions its work is of an importance sufficient to demand the attention of all who are concerned with modern developments in Secondary School teaching and organisation; while the actual measure of success which it has attained as an educational institution, and its possibilities of future development, fully entitle it to a place among the leading Secondary Day Schools in the country.

Sir Frederick Edridge

The flourishing state of the school at this time inspired several acts of great generosity on the part of Sir Frederick Edridge who, first appointed a Governor in February 1892, was elected Chairman of the Court in July 1909, a position he held until his retirement in September 1919. His keen interest in the School was so sharpened by its success, academic and otherwise, that he supplied several of the deficiencies that remained after the new buildings were opened in 1906. In March 1910 he offered to erect a new pavilion on the First XI cricket ground, and no sooner was that building completed than he paid for the fives-courts to be reconstructed on the ground behind the range of shops in North End. Less than two years later, at the beginning of 1913, another gap in the School's amenities was filled

Sir Frederick Edridge, DL. JP, 1843–1921

by the construction of changing-rooms and the Orderly Room. In the same year he endowed a Leaving Exhibition and Prizes, and in March 1914 he contributed the greater part of the cost of building a gallery in Big School and of equipping the room on the first floor of the Tower as a Prefects' Common Room. The War brought a

Assault-at-Arms 1911
L. to r.: Major S.D. Roper (OW), Lt. Col. M.H. Cutler (OW), General Sir Edward Elles, Sir Frederick Edridge

halt to this generous series of gifts, but many years after his death, which occurred in 1921, the School received another unexpected benefaction from his trustees. In his will he had left £5000 to the Croydon General Hospital for as long as that hospital should be supported to the extent of fifty per cent by voluntary contributions; in the event of that ceasing to be the case, as it did in consequence of the National Health Act of July 1948, the capital was to be transferred to new trustees to assist young men proceeding from Whitgift to the university with the intention of taking Holy Orders. His generosity places Sir Frederick Edridge second only to the Founder in the magnitude of his benefactions, and his name is perpetuated, not only in his Exhibitions and Prizes, but also in that part of the playing-fields at Haling Park called after him, which is situated opposite the house, Bramley Croft, in Haling Park Road, where he lived for many years.

World War 1

The outbreak of the First World War in August 1914 resulted in an immediate drop in the number of pupils. Several masters and senior boys who had expected to return to School in September had enlisted in the Army instead. By November at least 360 OWs were serving in the forces; six had been killed.

The OTC

The parliamentary Army Bill of 1907 had made provision for military preparations in anticipation of an inevitable war. These included the establishment in 1908 of the Territorial Army to replace the 'Volunteers', and of the Public Schools Officers' Training Corps, to which Whitgift's Cadet branch of the 1st Volunteer Battalion of the 1st Queen's Regiment was promptly transferred. The Certificate 'A' examination, taken after three or four years' training in the OTC, qualified a cadet for a commission in the Supplementary Reserve of Officers. By the time war was declared numerous OWs had joined Territorial Army units; many others promptly volunteered for Kitchener's New Army.

The strength of the OTC had been steadily increasing, for it enjoyed a high reputation and received support from public funds. By October 1914 it was only those few who, being old enough, were quite unfit that had not joined.

Founder's Day Parade 1914
The leading four are: Under Officer E.S. Underhill (Capt., killed October 1916), CSM A.B. Frost (Capt., MC, killed March 1918), Colour Sergeant W. West (2nd Lt., killed August 1915), Sergeant R.A.G. Taylor (Capt., MC, 1916; Brigadier, killed 1942)

Military training occupied much time during and after school hours; more frequent field-days, night operations, intensive shooting practice, preparation for Certificate 'A', a course for NCOs during the Christmas holidays, the formation of an Army Class (for those aspiring to RMC Sandhurst or RMA Woolwich) exemplify the enthusiasm with which the School was taking up the challenge.

School Life in Wartime

The Whitgiftian reflected the attitudes and demands of the time. By general agreement all prize-moneys were devoted to war charities, such as the Red Cross. In 1914 there was no award of prizes at all, although in following years certificates were given instead of books; no Concert was held; the Literary and Debating Society folded; editorials, poems and articles in *The Whitgiftian* extolled the military virtues; there was much patriotic zeal; any tendency to slackness (such as a reluctance to play fives in the new courts) was condemned. The Concert was revived in February 1915 with martial fervour; Part II opened with the national anthems of Belgium, Japan and Russia ('the Japanese was notable for the clever harmony'), followed by the *Marseillaise*; there were also a few songs of Elgar's, although *Pomp and Circumstance* was not included.

In the OW News pages, sporting activities no longer held a place, for the rugby and cricket clubs and the golfing society had suspended all activity *sine die*; the Veterans Rifle Club offered facilities for practice to all OWs, but within a short time all able-bodied men had 'joined the colours'. Instead, many pages were devoted to extracts from letters written by OWs in the trenches or on active service elsewhere throughout the world, and to news of those who had enlisted, or had been commissioned, promoted, decorated, wounded, made prisoner or, alas, lost their lives.

The severity of the fighting in 1915 impressed upon everyone the likelihood of a long and exhausting conflict. Boys who might have stayed on at school to prepare for university tended at first to leave earlier – at 16 or 17, which was anyway the usual age for many – so that they could help the war effort by working for a while before they were old enough to enlist at 18.

Andrew predicted that this tendency would continue, but by 1916 a new pattern emerged. More boys now wished to stay on to take Certificate 'A', join the Army Class and proceed to Sandhurst, Woolwich or RNC Dartmouth, thinking of the Army or Navy as a profession, should they survive. Others wished to study science, which was likely to provide them with a qualification when at last the war should be over. Medical students in limited numbers were encouraged at the teaching hospitals and gained practical experience on the battle-fields. In September 1916 the Sixth had nearly doubled its pre-war size, and Andrew was hard put to find accommodation for them all, especially the Science side, whose numbers had to be strictly limited to the laboratory space available. There was also increasing pressure from below, and a greater proportion of applicants failed to gain places. At this time the government ordained that any boy at school over 18 was obliged to do a minimum of fifteen hours of military training per week, before he was compelled to leave at $18\frac{1}{2}$. The last requirement somewhat relieved pressure on the Sixth.

In the summers of 1917 and 1918, instead of a training camp with other OTC contingents, harvest camps were arranged in the Lake District and in Devon, at which 120 boys spent some weeks of their holidays at work on the land, for there was a great shortage of able-bodied men to gather the harvest. On both occasions the weather was terrible.

By January 1918, out of 1400 OWs known to have been on active service, 180 had lost their lives, and news of fatalities continued to pour in. Victory was uncertain. The success of unrestricted U-Boat warfare had rendered food scarce, and rationing was imposed. Supplies of all materials were short. Paper was of poor quality and difficult to obtain. *The Whitgiftian* was reduced not only in size but also in the number of issues per year: three instead of the customary six.

In March 1918 Andrew reported 'a thinning out of middle (i.e. 4th, Remove and 5th) forms, owing to withdrawals due to the air-raid menace'. Croydon had suffered several deaths from a Zeppelin bomb-attack on 13 October 1915. Whereas it had been proved that airships could be destroyed, recent air attacks were made by bomber-planes, against which there was little defence; night-fighters were as yet inadequately equipped, and only weak retaliation was effected by anti-aircraft guns assisted by searchlights. Croydon received no more direct hits, for raids were concentrated upon industrial areas. It was the noise of the guns and their exploding shrapnel, together with the throb of aircraft engines, that drove away residents who could manage to find a quieter place to live in.

Yet by July the same year spirits had risen, for the prospect of victory was brighter. Andrew proposed that a small committee should be formed to discuss the form that a War Memorial should take.

The Armistice

The signing of the Armistice in November 1918 prepared the world for the counting of the cost. More than 250 OWs and Masters had lost their lives. To Andrew the increasingly long lists of casualties that he read out in Big School on Wednesday mornings had given pangs of deep sorrow. Many of his university scholars, his prefects, his Captains of the School and of Games, together with others of promise who had occupied less eminent positions in the School, failed to return. Of the 1913-14 First XV, nine were killed; the remainder all survived service in the forces, but one of these, a regular soldier in the Indian Army, was killed in action in World War II. It was not just a pitiful waste of life, but a destruction of men of talent and a sense of duty, who would have served the community as they had served their school and country, and they would have brought distinction to the name of Whitgift. Happily the majority survived, among them Lieutenant Colonel A.W. Tedder, RFC, who became Marshal of the RAF Lord Tedder, Deputy Supreme Commander of Allied Forces in the invasion of Europe in 1944.

The 1914-18 War Memorial

The War Memorial took the form of a column surmounted by the Whitgift cross, carved in Hopton Wood Stone, upon a two-platform base, and erected on the lawn in front of the Tower. A memorial tablet consisting of six panels, with the names of the dead inscribed on illuminated vellum, was placed on a wall in Big School. Both the cross and tablet, which were dedicated by Archbishop Davidson on 11 March 1922, were removed to their present positions at Haling Park in 1931. Perhaps the most moving tribute of all is *The Book of Remembrance*, devotedly compiled by the Rev. M.H.H. Mason. It contains detailed particulars of all who gave their lives, with photographs of most of them, and lists of all OWs known to have served in the Forces, of decorations won and mentions gained. In his Preface Andrew wrote:

As one reads through the names of the Dead, they gradually, I find, fall out of their accidental alphabetical order into well-remembered groups: the goodly host of those leaving school full of hope in July, 1914, who mostly went off to become soldiers, the members of this or that Form or team, more intimate bands of bosom friends, University men with whom one had breakfast or tea on fleeting visits, little groups of athletic or city friends, outer Britons from the ends of the earth who came home, and finally, a gallant company of older Old Boys, men of character and public spirit and hard-won positions, who were looked upon everywhere as part of Whitgift's elect. We shall not easily forget any of them.

Major-General the Rt. Hon. Sir Frederick Sykes, GCSI, GCIE, GBE, KCB, CMG, MP. (Whitgift 1889-91) Chief of the Air Staff 1918–19, Governor of Bombay 1928–33

Post-War Problems

The end of the War brought many opportunities for educational reform but it also brought problems that largely nullified them. The 'Fisher' Education Act of August 1918 gave increased powers and responsibilities to the Local Education Authorities, but the 'Geddes axe' was soon to fall and cut down the money necessary to implement them. Thus the Croydon Council, instead of being able to expand its own system of secondary education, had to look more closely than ever towards organisations that could help to supply the deficiencies in school places. First-grade education was available at Whitgift Grammar School and the Girls' High School with 550 and 400 places respectively. For second-grade education there were 700 places for boys at Whitgift Middle and the Borough Secondary Schools, and 1050 places for girls at the Borough Secondary, Coloma and Old Palace Schools; in addition, at three private schools there were places for 170 boys (Croydon High School for Boys, of the second-grade) and 300 girls (Woodford House and Croham Hurst Schools, with high fees, but not catering for the academically ambitious). Thus the accommodation for girls was about one-fifth more than that available for boys. There were also no fewer than fifty-nine other private schools in Croydon, catering for nearly 4000 children. Most of these were described as 'preparatory schools', but contained between them some hundreds of pupils, mostly boys, over the age of fourteen, so the balance was to some extent redressed. In addition there were probably some hundreds of boys who attended boarding schools or who travelled daily to London schools. The great need seemed to be for still more places for boys at schools of the second grade. The Council, hard-pressed financially, were hoping they might find more places for Croydon boys in the Whitgift Schools, which were attracting an increasing number of pupils from outside the Borough.

The requirement (Clause 88 in the Scheme of 1881) that, when funds might permit, the Foundation should provide education for girls had already been rendered less urgent by the foundation of the Girls' High School in 1884 and of the Old Palace as a secondary school in 1904, followed by the establishment of the Girls' Borough Secondary School (later Selhurst Grammar School for Girls) in the same year. The implication that school places for girls were adequately provided led the Governors to continue to concentrate their traditional attention upon boys' education.

The Schools themselves had their own problems. Expenses had risen, repairs and replacements, neglected during the War, as well as additional buildings, were urgently needed; masters' salaries had not kept pace with the cost of living (the Whitgift scales were actually below the Croydon scale); new advanced courses should now be provided. In January 1919 Andrew reported that he thought the Grammar School could meet all these expenses by a fairly modest increase in fees, but rebuilding the Middle School would involve the raising of loans that could be repaid only with the help of a Treasury grant. Although the Foundation's gross annual income from endowments had nearly doubled since the beginning of the century (it was now about £10,000), heavy subsidies to the two schools were not covering large deficits.

The Governors were unwilling for both Schools to become grant-aided, for denominational provisos and control would have to be relaxed, but Andrew was now reconsidering the matter and in March he made the following points in favour of the step: (a) there was no finality in the steady rise of salaries; (b) the Staff, who were justifiably dissatisfied with their position, would be placated; (c) they could participate in the national pension scheme on advantageous terms; (d) the expansion of the advanced courses would be greatly assisted; (e) the present small proportion of public elementary schoolboys in the School, which would not meet with the Board's approval anyway, could well be increased; (f) more Leaving Exhibitions would be needed, requiring greater support from Foundation funds; (g) parents hard hit by inflation and taxation could not be expected to meet any large rise in fees with equanimity. He concluded:

> We are on the threshold of a new era, and I believe that the School is at a critical point of its history. Unless the Foundation has, or is likely to have, far greater resources than I have been led to understand, I am forced to the conclusion that we must become a Grant-aided School under the Board of Education.

The alternative, I am afraid, is to reconcile ourselves to become a second-rate school.

The Direct Grant

After some hesitation the Governors unanimously resolved in June 1919 to apply for both Schools to be given a government grant with effect from the following September, on these conditions: (a) one third of the Governing Body must be nominated by the LEA (the appointment of one more Archbishop's Governor and one more representative Governor adjusted this proportion, so that there would be: the Vicar of Croydon, *ex officio*; seven Governors appointed by the Archbishop; five by the LEA; two by the Justices of the Peace); (b) the Grammar School would accept ten per cent of its admissions from the Croydon public elementary schools without payment of fees; the Middle School would accept twenty-five per cent; (c) in return there would be *per capita* grants for all boys in the Schools over the age of eleven, with extra grants for those following approved advanced courses.

The net value of the grants to each school, after allowance was made for the loss of fees from boys occupying 'free places', was to be about £2000, so that it was possible to postpone a rise in fees until September 1922, when a flat rate of £30 per annum became payable at the Grammar School, and £12 at the Middle School.

A number of similarly placed schools accepted the grant at this time, e.g. Bedford, Taunton and University College School; King's College School had been placed on the list in 1912. Among the Schools that did not feel the necessity to join this group were St. Paul's, Merchant Taylors', Dulwich and City of London. These were all well endowed and offered generous entrance scholarships. They wished to avoid too close a contact with the LEA, were able to set their fees at an adequate level and they continued to flourish.

The Board of Education were very accommodating in their dealings with the Foundation, being fully alive to the difficulties the Governors were faced with in dealing with their two schools. The Middle School, the Board had made clear, would have to be rebuilt if it was to continue to receive the grant. They would have continued to recommend its disposal to the LEA, had the Governors not shown that they were adamant against this course. There was no pressure upon them to take the grant for either school. The Board were anxious, especially in the absence of better provision of secondary education by the LEA, that the benefits derived from the Foundation's income should be available to poorer pupils. Their 'doctrine of ransom' was applicable to a school where parents were for the most part able to pay the whole cost of education, and where income from endowment should go to enable poorer boys to attend. Where, however, most parents would find some difficulty in sending their boys, the ransom principle might well take the form of reducing the general fee. Thus in a case where a high proportion of parents could afford to pay the whole fee, the correct procedure would be for Governors to charge a fee to cover the whole cost of education but reserve power to give exemption or allowances to meet the case of parents who could not afford the cost. 'But this, however correct in the abstract, is a very difficult thing to work in practice, and . . . involves a very careful investigation and valuation of the financial circumstances of each parent' (PRO ED35/6051, Minute Paper of 28 April 1921). Such a policy, in fact, had never been considered by the Governors, who had assumed that all parents should receive a share of the subsidy, and that the type of education that their sons received would be appropriate to the fees they could afford when they made their choice of school. This principle applied also at the LEA secondary schools, where the free places were available only to pupils from elementary schools; the fee-paying places were filled by those from private schools or by those who had failed to pass the qualifying test; and of course these places were subsidised from the rates.

The elementary schools, especially those newly built in favoured residential areas such as Norbury and Addiscombe, were being increasingly patronised by a higher social class than formerly. These schools were better designed, equipped and staffed than the private schools that had provided the middle classes with primary education. The possibility of gaining 'free places' at either a direct-grant or a secondary school was an added attraction. Some of these elementary schools gained a high reputation for their success in coaching their brighter pupils to pass the qualifying test.

In 1926 a simplified system was adopted whereby 'a secondary school conducted by a voluntary body' could draw its grant directly from central government. Schools in this category were said to be placed on the Direct Grant list. LEAs received block grants and could also support non-provided, but what became known as 'grant-aided', schools.

Limitations Set by the Governors

One outcome of the Schools' altered status was the greater influence now exerted by the LEA representatives on the Governing Body, who seized the opportunity to insist on the admission of a higher proportion of boys living in the Borough of Croydon, at the expense of cleverer boys from outside, the result being that a large number were admitted who were capable only of following sluggishly behind the others. The resultant disparity between the top and bottom streams was such that in December 1923 Andrew reported in protest to the Governors that 'the lower form in each group . . . , instead of being a transition form through which the new boys pass into an A or B Form, is becoming a refuge for the incompetent, and most of the Croydon boys who go into these forms never get out of them'. The justness of Andrew's complaint is confirmed by the figures of the following year, when Croydon boys formed only one-third of the candidates but four-fifths of the number admitted.

There had been steady building development, not only in many parts of Croydon, but also in what had been local villages, such as Purley, Wallington, Sutton, Caterham, Sanderstead, Warlingham, Coulsdon, Woldingham and Chipstead, and an increasing number of good quality candidates from these areas were anxious to be admitted to the School, but the Governors laid great stress upon Clause 35 of the Scheme drawn up by the Board of Education in 1915 (largely to incorporate minor amendments that had accumulated over the years), which stated: 'If there is not room for all boys found fit for admission . . . , preference shall be given to such of them as are resident in the Ancient Parish of Croydon'. Some Governors remained strongly in favour of demanding a much higher fee from pupils admitted from outside the borough, a policy that would have further diluted the quality of admissions.

Continued pressure, in particular from Alderman T.W. Wood Roberts, compelled Andrew to submit to this directive, although there were good reasons for challenging it. His Majesty's Inspectors, who paid another visit to the School in 1921, condemned the situation that permitted a Croydon boy to enter the School with a mere 48 per cent of marks in the Entrance Examination while one from outside with 79 per cent had been rejected. 'The position is a most serious one for the surrounding district; it mainly affects the adjacent populous areas of Surrey which have in the past looked naturally to Croydon for their first-grade education.' As a general principle, the Board of Education required the same minimum standard from fee-payers as from free-placers in Direct Grant schools. It seems strange that Clause 35 should have been so narrowly interpreted when Clause 39 clearly permitted the Head Master to require a reasonably high standard of attainment at the Entrance Examination: 'No boy shall be admitted to the School except after being found fit for admission in an examination under the direction of the Head Master graduated according to the age of the boy. Those who are found so fit, if there is room for them, shall be admitted in order according to the date of their application.' (This last condition seems never to have been adhered to.) The only concession granted by the Governors was to require *all* candidates to achieve 50% marks in the examination.

In 1913 40% of admissions had come from the villages and the towns beyond, such as Reigate and Sutton; these boys formed the main academic, athletic and social strength of the School. Twelve years later the proportion had dropped by half; of the remaining 80% from Croydon, which contained only a small number of very gifted boys, about half were now of lower-middle class origin from the northern side of Croydon, able to afford the subsidised fees, but with ambitions that matched their limited talents. Many of these left young before they could even attempt the General Schools Certificate Examination, leaving places that might have been taken up by stronger candidates from outside. The position was becoming dangerously like that found by Andrew on his arrival. There followed another decline in the School's reputation among the better class of Croydon's population and among those living further afield, many of whom had themselves moved out from the older property near the centre of the town. Unhappy about these changes and unwilling, moreover, to submit their sons under handicap to the Whitgift entrance examination, such parents who might have hoped to send their sons there now made certain of Common Entrance to other schools at the age of 13.

The restrictions imposed by the Governors mainly to allow the LEA to evade responsibility for providing secondary education of a character lower than the first grade, had a number of other damaging effects upon the School. The Sixth Form, although still expanding, did not develop as it could have done; and not least important, relations between Andrew and his Governors, formerly so harmonious, now became very strained. Before the War, men of culture such as Sir Frederick Edridge, Dr. Strong, Dr. Newnham and Edward Grimwade were the dominant members of the Court, but now many of the Governors – even some of those appointed by the Archbishop on the recommendation of the Vicar, (Canon W.P. McCormick) – were deficient in education and refinement, and were guided by a narrow parochial attitude towards the educational functions of the Foundation. Jealous in fact of the School's achievements, they believed that in diminishing its status they were performing the duty committed to them.

It was now ironically evident that if Andrew had not applied for the School to be put on the direct-grant list it might, despite a further increase in fees, have attracted more boys, whether from Croydon or outside, who wanted a first-grade education up to the age of eighteen or nineteen.

School Leaving Certificate

For most boys the Fifth Form was still the limit of their school career. The introduction in 1917 of the School Leaving Certificate Examinations, conducted by University Boards, was an important step in that it gave a specific objective for school work. Designed to be a proof of achievement in a varied range of subjects within reach of an intelligent pupil of sixteen, the Certificate was additionally a means by which exemption from university matriculation could be gained. But it also became a certificate of competence to employers, especially concerns such as banks, insurance companies and commercial firms, who were now recruiting steadily in order to expand their business. These posts were greatly sought after, offering security as well as good prospects, and attracted many boys who in other circumstances might have tried for a university scholarship, but this risk was considerable, and the chance of a good job could not be neglected.

The examination for Higher Certificate, taken two years later, gave recognition of ability to follow an honours course, and could also give exemption from some university and professional intermediate examinations. From 1920 onwards a distinguished performance in this examination could earn a 'State' scholarship, tenable at any university; two of the two hundred awarded in the first year were gained by Whitgiftians. It also gave a purpose to the last two years of school life for those who regarded the age of eighteen as the leaving-age, but who did not intend to go to university. Specialised sixth-form courses were designed for these clearly defined objectives; there were now three sides to the Sixth Form: Classical, Science and Modern Studies, but further expansion without more accommodation would have been impossible. Moreover, if still more subjects were to be studied in the Sixth, there would have to be provision of expensive extra staff to teach them. The three existing advanced courses were already attracting the maximum sum in Treasury Grant, with the result that resources would become dangerously strained.

With more financial aid available to students (including 'Kitchener' Scholarships for the sons of those who had served in the War, and a larger number of exhibitions awarded by local authorities), the universities were attracting more candidates for admission. Although ordinary entrance standards were not high, and most students were still dependent on their own family resources, there was increasing competition for open scholarships. The colleges of London University and the teaching hospitals attracted many boys in the

Science Sixth, whose teaching resources became tightly stretched. Oxford and Cambridge, considerably liberalised since the end of the War, when an influx of ex-servicemen had loosened the hold of the leisured type of undergraduate, attracted in greater numbers not only the academically ambitious, but also those who could afford to go up as commoners. In the 1920s there was an arousal of evangelical religious feeling in the School, fostered by the formation of the Christian Union, many members of which went up to university with the intention of entering the Church, becoming missionaries, or taking up teaching. Most of these were assisted by exhibitions from the Foundation or from the local authority.

Shortages

These increased numbers in the Sixth Form imposed great demands that failed to be met, and the inconvenience became greater each year. A Classical Sixth division made regular use of the Headmaster's Study; the Modern Sixth were compelled to take over the Library, denying it to those who needed it for private study, and even overflowed into a corner of Big School; one Science Sixth division had to use any room in the School that happened to be vacant, carrying with them their books and apparatus. In 1921 the Inspectors had emphasized the need for additional laboratories for chemistry, physics and biology, and rooms for the expanding arts Sixths; at the same time they deplored the absence of a gymnasium and a dining-room; they also declared the Masters' Common Room to be quite inadequate.

These deficiencies were brought repeatedly to the attention of the Governors, who from time to time would accept a recommendation from Andrew, debate it, pass a resolution to instruct the architect, consider his report, call for a modification, and then defer the matter. After Andrew had renewed in June 1923 a request for a room to be constructed in the roof-space, there was silence for nearly twelve months before the Chairman surprised him with the information that the Governors could now afford to implement the Inspectors' recommendations, which had until then been postponed owing to lack of funds. The architect (still Sir Henry Berney) was

The Staff, 1914
L. to r., Back row: Abrams, Jones, Balfour, Tolmie, Ceppi, *Middle row*: Watson, Bracchi, Mainwaring, Paine, Micklewright, Snell, Fisher, Wyke-Bayliss, Woodgate, Kitchener, *Front row*: Carter, Mayo, Tate, Mason, Burton, Andrew, Dodd, Ellis, Balley, Smith, Morgan

instructed to prepare outline plans and was given the go-ahead for most of the minor extensions, but not for the Gymnasium or the Dining Hall, which were postponed. In November 1924, he reported that the plans were well advanced, but no further action took place, for there was now the prospect of a different kind of development, upon which all available funds would be concentrated.

A little less than a year later, Andrew ventured to beg for temporary accommodation for forty boys in the form of a two-roomed hut. This request was also examined, investigated, referred back, deferred, taken up again and then quietly buried, all in the space of eight months, so that Andrew never got those few extra teaching spaces that he had been striving for over a period of seven years.

Games

During the 1920s public-school sport quickly recovered its high reputation of pre-war days, and in this era of the *cultus athleticus* the ranking of public schools depended very largely upon the achievements of their football and cricket teams and of their old boys in the university matches at Twickenham or Lord's. The day-schools, with the exception of St. Paul's, Dulwich and Merchant Taylors', found it difficult to gain this utterly desirable publicity. The Whitgift teams found it hard enough to hold their own, even with the other minor public schools which formed the backbone of their fixture-lists.* The only game that had really flourished – and then only intermittently – had been cricket, for the ground at North End was level and of a good size, with a first-rate square (although there was only one), but rugby had always been played under the handicap of a very limited number of small pitches that did not offer sufficient opportunity for practice or for encouraging open play; consequently, the fifteens were often out-manoeuvred when they played matches 'away'; in addition,

*This was at a time when the back pages of *The Observer* and *The Sunday Times* were filled with short reports of inter-school matches. The secretary of rugby was required to send to an agency immediately after a home game a shilling telegram giving the score and a sentence of two about the play. Nowadays the Sunday papers are silent upon such matters.

The First XI, 1913

The Corps of Drums with the Prince of Wales, 1921

the First XV were usually much younger than their opponents. Nevertheless, many players achieved success after leaving School, some thirty who had learnt the game at North End representing their county. The first OW rugby blue and international, the Rev. P.W.P. Brook (Cambridge and England), and G.P. Goodwin, who played cricket several times for Cambridge, but without getting his blue, for he had to put his medical studies before the game, were at School in the mid-twenties.

In addition, there were several others who either represented their university on occasion at a major game or were awarded blues for some minor one, helping to give an impetus to ambition and to bring the name of the School to the attention of those who followed public-school sport.

The Purchase of Haling Park

At the end of the War Whitgift Middle School was still housed in its unworthy buildings in Church Road. Under William Ingrams's successor as Head Master, the Rev. G.A. Jones, it had been performing good service in these cramped and ill-adapted premises, enlarged once more in 1907 by some temporary corrugated-iron classrooms. The leaving age had then been raised by an amendment of the Scheme to a permissive seventeen, enabling an advanced course in Science to be followed, and the need for rebuilding was more urgent than ever. The further raising of the leaving age in 1921 to eighteen gave better opportunities for advanced-course teaching, and members of the Sixth Form were now able to aspire to university awards, which were gained with increasing frequency. The problems of accommodation, however, were vastly intensified. The Governors were looking for a suitable site for a new Middle School when they learnt that the trustees of the late Colonel James Watney intended to sell Haling Park, only a mile south of the centre of the town. In 1920 a contract to purchase an area of about five and a half acres with a frontage to the Brighton Road was signed, the cost being met out of accumulated funds and the proceeds from the sale of portions of the Foundation's estates at Addiscombe and Croham, but when the Board of Education pronounced the site to be too small, a further purchase, which included Haling Cottage, was contracted for, making a total area of twelve acres of fairly level land which would provide a convenient site for a new Middle School with useful playing-field space. In July 1922, shortly after this purchase had been concluded, the remainder of the estate that had not already been disposed of privately was offered for sale by auction in building lots. The reserve prices were not reached, however, but one lot, containing the remainder of the Brighton Road frontage, includ-

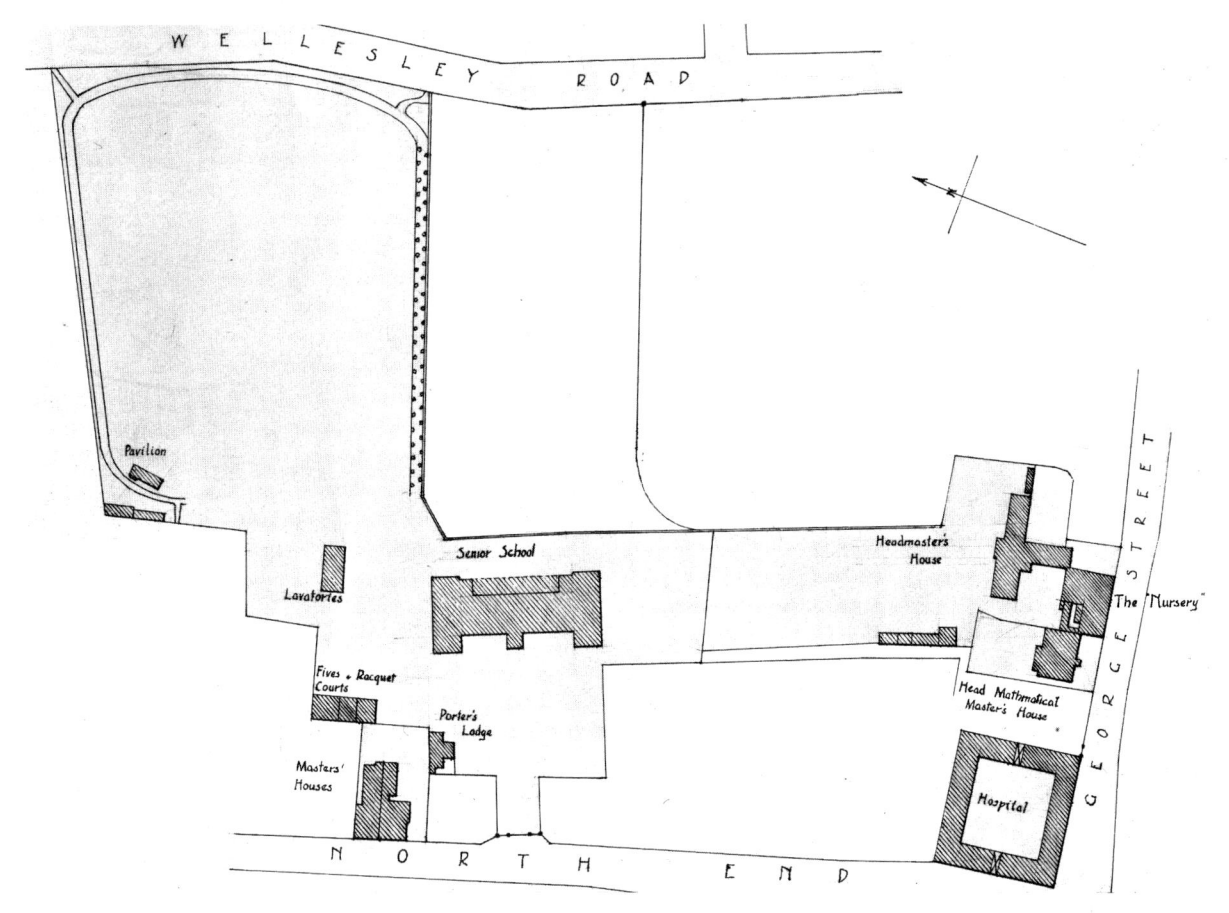

Plan of Whitgift School 1871

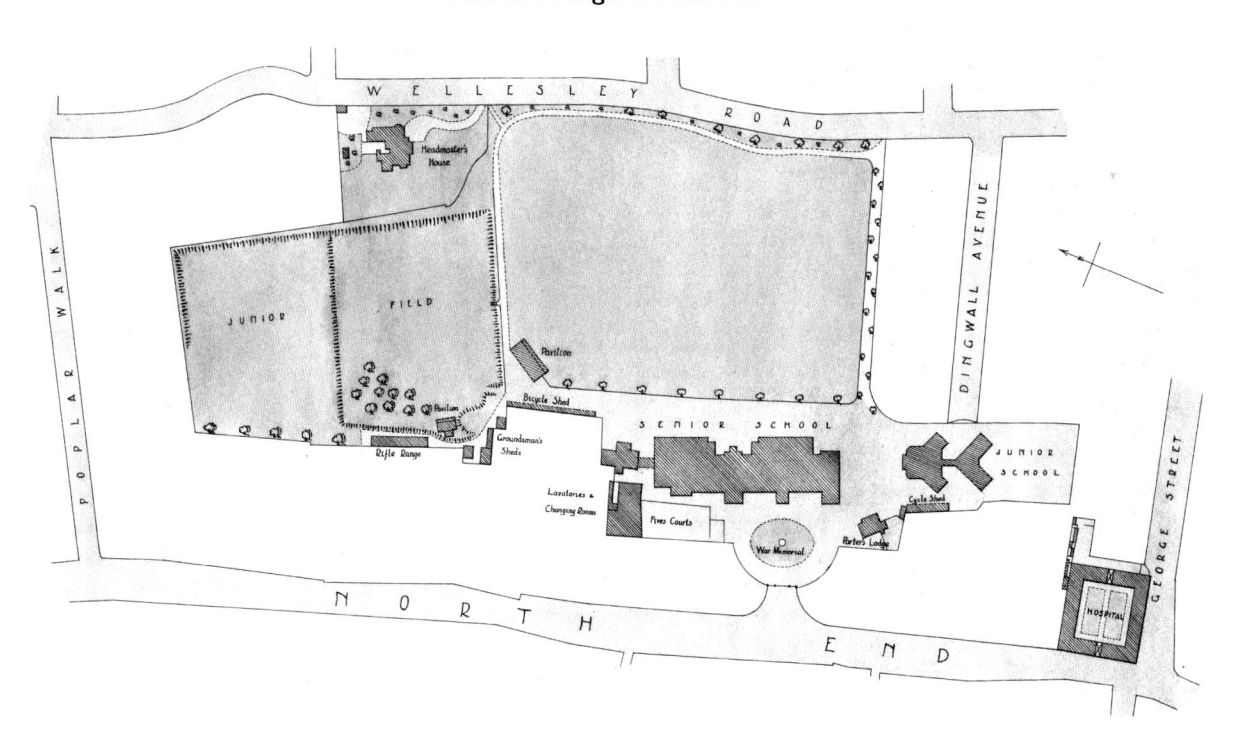

Plan of Whitgift Grammar School 1928

ing Haling Park Cottage, was seen by the Governors to be a very valuable addition to their other land. It was bought jointly by the Clerk (John Jones) and the Surveyor to the Foundation, under private instruction from the Governors, whose decision to proceed had been reached without the formality of a full Court meeting.

They had now acquired an area of approximately fifteen and a half acres at a cost of £13,500. The purchase was not immediately followed by plans for building. The Croydon Education Committee and the Board of Education were both anxious that the Governors' intentions should be closely watched and, if necessary, guided. The Borough Secondary School had moved to Selhurst, assuming the name of Selhurst Grammar School, and the Council saw the Middle School on its proposed site as no longer in competition with their own school, but in a complementary position to it, at the other end of the Borough, and with the added advantage of continuing to act as a blessed relief to the rates. In fact, they were quite prepared to give it a subsidy, without requiring any further degree of control than that which already existed through their representation on the Court of Governors, but they wished to be consulted over all the proposals.

In October 1924 the surveyors to the Foundation reported on the difficulty of finding land on the Foundation estates that would be suitable for use as additional playing-fields by the Grammar School, whose grounds at North End, never by any reckoning enough, were quite inadequate for the five hundred and seventy boys now in the School. They recommended for this purpose the purchase of the remaining unsold portion of Haling Park, an area of twenty acres that six months before had again been offered for sale by auction with no result. In the same month the Governors, who had been advised that the new Middle School should accommodate between five hundred and six hundred boys, resolved to invite architects to submit preliminary plans. The further purchase at Haling Park, however, had prompted one of the Archbishop's Governors, Mr. Bryan Harland, to propose that consideration should be given to building a new Grammar School, instead of a new Middle School, there, and that the Middle School should take over the premises consequently to be vacated in North End. Attention was given to this

Officers of the OTC 1922
L to r.: Under Officer B.O. Massé, Lt. W.A.H. Lewis, Lt. R.F. Parr, Major Ll. J. Jones, Capt. H.G.F. Micklewright, Lt. E.W. Tate, Lt. H.G. Woodgate

proposal, but two months later, in January 1925, Mr. William Peet and Mr. Wood Roberts, representative Governors of the LEA, moved that the Court should give consideration to the erection of one school at Haling Park to replace the two existing schools. Further consultation with representatives of the Croydon Education Committee resulted in the approval of this proposal by a large majority of the Court in June 1925. The proposed new School was to contain one thousand boys, who would be admitted on two different scales of fees and would be committed to two correspondingly different curricula. The Governors who were in favour of this scheme seem to have been moved more by considerations of ease of administration and of the high development value of the sites of the two schools in the centre of the town, than by any educational advantages.

Meanwhile, these intentions having been made public, a body of opposition had arisen, led by the Old Boys of the Middle School, who feared the eventual dissolution of their own school. Andrew added the weight of his own experience and prestige, to be followed by that of Robert Brodie, the Committee of the Old Whitgiftian Association, and Mr. H.S. Clayton, who had been appointed Head Master of the Middle School in 1919. Soon there was no one actively connected with either School who favoured the proposal.

Andrew's criticism was largely based on 'the present day tendency . . . to differentiate education whenever possible, and to provide for the different types in separate institutions, giving us homogeneous schools and so economising effort and simplifying the aims and task of the

Haling House in the early 1920s

educator'. These arguments he supported by figures of the steady growth in the number of boys taking advanced courses, and the limited accommodation Haling Park offered for playing-fields for one thousand boys.

Local opinion was also warmly expressed against the merger, which to many people foreshadowed the extinction by absorption of a school (Whitgift Middle) that had with great success provided a mainly practical and commercial education; this process of absorption, however much it might be countered by the Governors' assurances concerning fees and curricula, was regarded by many people as inevitable, and it would throw the responsibility for providing this type of secondary education upon the ratepayer through the consequent necessity of building more local secondary schools, especially as there would be hardly any increase in the total number of boys. There were others, including Andrew, who feared that this new Whitgift School would earn a lower reputation than that enjoyed by the Grammar School, if the latter's aims were to be so curtailed. The Croydon Education Committee, a number of whom, it must be remembered, were also Governors, were not of this mind, however; they regarded the proposed amalgamation as a valuable relief to the rates, provided that the new school were large enough and reserved almost entirely for the sons of Croydon residents, but after a number of public meetings, in which only a few voices were heard in approval of the proposal, the Council in July 1925 withdrew its support and referred the scheme back to the Court of Governors to reconsider.

'Jack' Robinson and 'Sid' Moss, with their first motorised mower, 1924

A hurried consultation between the Governors and the Board of Education officials brought little satisfaction. The Board had never been more than lukewarm over the scheme and advised further discussions with the Education Committee and the Old Boys' Associations of both Schools. Fearing that such discussions would fail to break the deadlock, the Governors decided to restrict argument to themselves and in January 1926 they met to consider no fewer than four schemes put up by various members of the Court. The majority were still wedded to a one-school scheme, and in June a special sub-committee produced a proposal for a first-class Grammar School for 900 boys at Haling Park, with two different scales of fees—at £12 and £30—according to a parents' means test, and free places for twenty-five cent of admissions; Whitgift Middle School would be closed and its site sold, while the premises in North End would be offered for sale to the Croydon Corporation for educational purposes. But this proposal, details of which were never released to the public, was defeated by one vote, and Walton F. Turner undertook to provide a scheme for building a new Grammar School for 700 boys at Haling Park and for accommodating the Middle School, with 450 boys, at North End.

The Approved Scheme for Haling Park

It was this scheme, subsequently modified in some particulars, such as numbers, curriculum and details of finance, that was decided upon and eventually put into practice. Even so, in February 1928, Turner and William Peet, who had joined forces with him, wished to have this proposal of theirs withdrawn for further consideration, but the remainder of the Court would not countenance any further deliberation and delay.

Andrew was not well satisfied with these plans. To the Governors' second proposal for a one-school scheme he had lent his qualified support, for his concept of what a new Whitgift School should be would be better realised by this scheme than by the first. But if the Middle School were to move to North End, it would naturally wish to make use of the better facilities there, expand and become another 'grammar' school in competition, which would be wasteful of resources. He did not approve of the system of education given at the Middle School, which was then geared chiefly to Science, while humane studies were neglected. In fact there was no possibility of a Middle School boy following a bent for anything else but Science unless he gained a scholarship to the Grammar School, a course that Clayton did not encourage. Andrew's solution would be to terminate the Middle School course at School Leaving Certificate level (which sufficed for most boys, anyway) and encourage those who wished to follow an advanced course to proceed to the Grammar School at no increase in fees; this, he maintained, would be educationally and financially sound. Clayton, naturally, could not agree. He was ambitious for his own School, wished to introduce another advanced course— in Economics and Commerce—and emphasised the disruption in a boy's career if he were transferred to another school at sixteen, an age when he might expect to achieve a position of responsibility and status if he could remain at his present school. The Governors were disposed to agree with Andrew, for they had always wished to see a more frequent progress of boys from the lower to the upper School, but the Board of Education supported the reasonableness of Clayton's view and pointed out that the local authority secondary schools were themselves developing their own advanced courses; the Middle School should be encouraged to stand upon its own feet if it was to be allowed to continue in existence.

Andrew's Resignation

But long before the Court gave their approval to Turner's scheme in September 1927, Andrew had resigned. His mistrust of his Governors, in so far as their sympathy with his aims was concerned, had been confirmed. His main desire had been to train the intellect of selected promising pupils and to extend the benefits of university education to all who could profit therefrom. It was apparent to him that a large proportion of the Governing Body were incapable of understanding these objectives, which he would not have given up fighting for, had not the delayed decision over the new school placed him in a dilemma. He would be sixty in 1928. According to the terms of the Board of Education Scheme he was dismissible by the Governors at pleasure although, unlike Brodie, he would have an assured pension. If he continued in office he would have the intolerable burden for a man of his age of organising the move to Haling Park; even if he stayed until he was sixty he would be involved to some extent in the new plans; but if he were to resign a year before, a successor could be appointed who would delight in the challenge that these responsibilities for organisation would present to him. The impression is gained that the Governors' delays were partly due to their wish to have a new man better prepared to fall in with their intentions. They were pleased to receive Andrew's letter of resignation of 28 February 1927, in which he said, '. . . The Governors will, I am sure, realise what a wrench it will be to leave my work at Whitgift, which has been one of the great happinesses of my life, but the physical strain of the present conditions at the School are considerable. . .'. The Court made no attempt to dissuade him, but warmly thanked him for the valuable services he had rendered to the Foundation.

Andrew had no intention of leaving the School in the lurch. Archbishop Davidson had written to him expressing surprise and sorrow at hearing of his resignation. He expressed also his gratitude for Andrew's admirable work at the School and invited his private advice regarding his (Davidson's) responsibilities in connection with the appointment of a successor. On 10 June Andrew replied, revealing his anxiety over the way decisions were arrived at by the Governors:

> . . . It is natural that the judgment of the Representative [i.e. the Croydon Council] Governors should be coloured by their views of the interests of the Educational Authority or the ratepayers; even when there is no difference of interests, real or apparent, it will often happen that they do not see eye to eye with 'good Whitgiftians', e.g. they do not always distinguish between the work and tone of the Grammar School and those of an ordinary Secondary School, or see the advantage to the Grammar School of its now very strong connections with the older universities. The Governors' Scheme in 1925 would have completely changed the character of the School, and in the opinion of good judges, would have been disastrous financially and would have ultimately destroyed the independence of the Foundation. It is a very disquieting thought that this Scheme after being passed by the Governors was only defeated by a small majority of the Town Council on grounds quite unconnected with the merits of the case.

He goes on to recommend the appointment by the Archbishop of a really representative Old Boy and of one or more men with an intimate knowledge of education in its broadest aspects. It would not be difficult to find men of these kinds.

The Archbishop himself had been aware of the problems outlined by Andrew and in reply he said that he had just appointed one such Old Boy, Mr. Geoffrey Marks. He concluded by saying: 'I shall not scruple to trouble you further if it seems to me that counsel from you would aid me in deciding any question in which my opinion is asked.'

The appointment of Geoffrey Marks (1873-82) came rather late. In July 1909 the Rev. M.H.H. Mason, Secretary of the Old Whitgiftian Association, had spoken to the Archbishop about the desirability of having an Old Boy on the Governing Body, and had been encouraged to make a recommendation. The following October the Committee of the Association nominated Geoffrey Marks as a suitable candidate for the next vacancy. He had had a distinguished career under Brodie, being Captain of the School and Captain of Games; he went into business and achieved distinction and respect as an actuary. He was one of the first OWs that Andrew came to know, and they enjoyed a warm friendship. Marks was a man of culture and they discussed matters of the mind, including questions of philosophy. But Davidson sought advice from the Bishop of Croydon (H.H. Pereira), who in turn obtained confidential information from the Secretary to the Foundation (John Jones) that Marks was only a 'nominal' churchman and therefore unsuitable, and that his appointment might not be sympathetic with 'the present independent and strong administration'. Jones indicated, too, that Marks stood for the 'Brodie element', which many people wished to get represented on the Governing Body. It seems that Jones was mistaken in this judgment and deflected a good man from an office in which he could have given useful service for a much longer period.

An outstanding Headmaster

Enough has been said of Andrew's work at Whitgift to show that he was one of the outstanding Head Masters of his time. If he had been given after the First World War a Governing Body more sympathetic to his aims and more willing to provide him with adequate staff, buildings and equipment, his achievements would have been surpassing.

He never sought the public eye by such devices as writing letters to *The Times* or by speaking from a platform, but his reputation as an educationalist (a term he would have deprecated, preferring to be known as an 'educator') was fittingly acknowledged by his being invited in 1919 to serve on the Prime Minister's Committee to enquire into the position of Classics in the educational system and to advise as to the means by which their study might be maintained and improved. Among the members were many distinguished Classicists, including Professors Gilbert Murray and W.P. Ker, Dr. Cyril Alington (Head Master of Eton), Cyril Norwood (Master of Marlborough, later Head Master of Harrow) and Sir Richard Livingstone. He was next invited to serve on the Consultative Committee of the Board of Education that in 1926 produced the 'Hadow' Report on 'The Education of the Adolescent'.* He served on these and on other Committees while involved in the struggle to reorganise after the War, battling with the Governors, devising syllabuses and plans for extensions which were never proceeded with, interviewing candidates for positions on the staff, and conducting much official correspondence in his own hand, for he was without a personal secretary. With it all he was a teaching Head Master; not only did he prepare his Upper Classical Sixth in their scholarship work, but he also took some of the lower forms in English and Divinity, for one of his aims was to get to know every boy in the School. Indeed, like so many other vigorous men of outstanding capabilities, he could be criticised (as he was in 1920 by an HMI) for not delegating sufficiently, for he also kept the organisation of several departments closely in his own hands.

Most of his boys had to make their own way in the world, unassisted by parental wealth, influence or professional tradition; they had their education and their character mainly to rely upon. He was confident that many of them would achieve success in business or professional life, so he encouraged the talented boy to set his sights high. During the twenty-five years he spent at the School, professional careers were opening wider to men of talent who could not expect full parental support during their years of training; careers in the universities, the diplomatic, consular, civil and colonial services, at the Bar and on the Bench, in the armed forces and in politics. Many Whitgiftians distinguished themselves in these fields—for example, D.Ll. Hammick, FRS (1900–6), Vice-Provost of Andrew's old college, Oriel, Lord Diplock (1916-25), a Lord of Appeal in Ordinary, Sir Bernard Carr (1903-7), of the Colonial Service, Sir Gordon Whitteridge, KCMG (1925–7), H.M. Ambassador to Burma and to Afghanistan, Sir Walter Chiesman, MD (1911–18), Medical Adviser to the Treasury, Instructor Rear-Admiral Sir William Bishop (1910–17), T.C. Skeat, FBA (1918–26), Keeper of the Manuscripts at the British Museum, in addition to those already mentioned in passing. Over forty of his Old Boys achieved a place in *Who's Who*, a number very similar to that of Brodie's time, but later it was becoming harder to qualify, and a fifth of Brodie's pupils in this category had gone on to other schools.

Several of the men that Andrew had appointed to the staff during his first ten years remained after his departure. Chief among them was G.E.H. Ellis, who had been appointed Second Master a year after Dodd's retirement in 1921; it was Ellis who had been mainly responsible under Andrew for the teaching of Classics, and his work must not go unacknowledged; he continued, even more successfully in the years to come, to prepare university scholars. H.G.F. Micklewright, as Head of Science, building on the foundations laid by his predecessors, W.E. Cross and the Rev. W. Burton, contributed greatly to the successful expansion of the Science Sixth and remained until his retirement in 1944,

---

*The Hadow Report recommended *inter alia* that secondary education should be available to all, and reorganised along tripartite lines as formulated in the 'Butler' Act of 1944. One incidental proposal was that existing schools of the LEA 'secondary' type should be known as 'Grammar Schools.' Some of these schools were already named in this way, for example, Selhurst Grammar School.

having had a hand in the training of five Fellows of the Royal Society. There was H.G. Woodgate, Head of History, whose scorn for pretentiousness and intellectual flabbiness corrected many a superficial idealism; there was C.J. Fisher, not by any means an experimental teacher, but one whose unruffled calm and ruthless pressure urged on everyone who sat before him; E.E. Kitchener carried the Junior School with him for many more years; C.S. Musgrave, who founded the advanced course in German after the First World War, continued after the Second as the chief exponent of the Direct Method until his retirement in 1946.

Andrew's favourite definition of 'the aim of Education' was Herbert Spencer's: 'to prepare us for complete living'; he would have agreed again with Spencer that education has also for its object the formation of character. Several OWs who knew him well contributed their memories of him, in honour of the centenary of his birth:

He was an awesome and formidable man and so far as we could tell . . . he wielded immense power. He was austere and remote and certainly a figure of massive integrity and moral uprightness. That, I believe, was the general impression he gave, and an OW well past middle age said that even now when he thought of SOA his knees began to tremble . . . (Rev. N.A.L. Miller (1919—25)).

He had brought with him from his native Lancashire a directness of approach, an integrity of character and a broad humanity that influenced every boy under his charge. Even when, as happened to most of us, we had little day-to-day working contact with him, he powerfully influenced our lives.

A sense of personal responsibility was the first thing we learnt from him. We knew that he did not expect us all to be good scholars or to get into the XV and the XI, but that he would be down upon us like a ton of bricks if we did less than our best at work or play . . . .

He was a great headmaster. Talking to men from other schools, some of whose headmasters were famous national figures as Mr. Andrew was not, confirms this high estimate of his excellence. Those who sat under him in the Sixth, especially if they had a bent for the Classics and, above all, for Greek, learnt to know something at least of the profound scholarship and the wide humanism from which he drew strength. He inspired this happy few with his love of and zest for all the good things of the mind—literature and music, history and travel. A visit to the Opera at Covent Garden with him in term time was a delicious piece of truancy . . .

(A.P. Ryan (1913–18)).

In his retirement he addressed himself to the intellectual interests he must so much have missed during the last twenty years. Chief of these were the translation of Homer into an English metre of his own invention, a textual criticism of *Beowulf*, and a translation into modern English of *Gawain and the Green Knight*. All these and other works were published, possibly in the main as an act of *pietas*, by E.F. Bozman (1907–14), of Messrs. J.M. Dent.

Although continuing to take a keen interest in the School and especially in the fortunes of his Old Boys, he did not in his retirement feel it appropriate to pay a visit to the School—except on one occasion, when he took the Chair at the Annual OW Dinner held, for the last time in Big School, in 1931. During his last years he was bed-ridden, being crippled with arthritis, a disease he bore with characteristic stoicism. He died in April 1952 at the age of eighty-four and is commemorated by the fountain and quadrangle named after him.

9. Ronald Gurner and Haling Park

Ronald Gurner

Archbishop Davidson chose as Andrew's successor a man of very different temperament and personality. He had in fact recommended to the Governors a candidate of his own for them to put forward for his consideration. The name of Ronald Gurner had been in the public eye on account of a dispute he had been involved in with the Education Committee of Sheffield, where he was Head Master of King Edward VII School, a local secondary school over which the recently elected Council wished to extend a much closer control.

Born in 1890, Stanley Ronald Kershaw Gurner attended Merchant Taylors' School in Charterhouse Square, London (two of his predecessors, John Philips and John Rose, it will be remembered, were also OMTs), where he markedly distinguished himself. Besides winning several academic prizes, he was for three years a robust forward in the First XV and a member of the Fives IV; he was good at jumping and putting the shot, and won the trophy for 'the best all-round athlete' in his last year at school. He was a Monitor, and the culmination of his career was the ward of the 'Gilpin' prize 'for the boy of the best conduct during the year'. In 1908 he proceeded with a Sir Thomas White Scholarship to St. John's College, Oxford. He obtained a First Class in Honour Moderations and had prospects of a good degree in 1912 but after a nervous breakdown just before taking 'Greats' he was awarded an *aegrotat*. Having considered but rejected the idea of sitting for the Indian or Home Civil Service examination, he took a temporary post at Haileybury, followed by another at Clifton; while he was there he decided that teaching was to be his career. There followed a permanent appointment at Marlborough as a form-master in the middle part of the school teaching general subjects. Then, having been commissioned there in the Officers' Training Corps, he was gazetted after four terms to the Rifle Brigade, for the outbreak of War in 1914 had supervened. By May 1915 he was in France.

His front-line service was terminated in April 1916, when he was seriously wounded at Arras and at which time he was awarded the Military Cross. After a further period of mental illness and convalescence he served in Military Intelligence and the Propaganda Department of the War Office before returning in September 1918 to Marlborough, where he was promptly offered a Housemastership.

His experiences during the War had disillusioned him, however, and he now found Marlborough uncongenial. Wishing to marry, he decided that he must obtain a post in which he could support a wife, and in 1920 he applied for and was appointed to the Head Mastership of Strand School, Brixton, a London County Council secondary school. Here he quickly found that his sympathies lay with the boys from modest homes who, with their native abilities as their sole resource, were striving to equip themselves with an education that would qualify them for the promising jobs that were becoming once more available. His work at this school, where he stayed six years, and at his next school, at Sheffield, is described in his autobiography, *I Chose Teaching*. During these seven years of Head Mastership he had impressed both schools with his vigorous and dominating personality and had acquired a more than local reputation as an educational reformer, who wished to break the strangle-hold that the public boarding-schools held on the professions and the senior universi-

Ronald Gurner, MC, MA, 1926

ties, and so to enable boys of talent who were passing through the day-schools, whether they were independent, like Merchant Taylors', direct grant, like Whitgift, or municipal secondary, like Strand, to prove their worth and serve the community. Many of them responded wholeheartedly, inspired by his teaching and his sympathetic understanding of their characters and abilities. Former pupils of his have spoken of him with deep affection and respect; old Strandians in particular regarded him as one of the gods: 'Julius Caesar and Hadrian rolled into one'.

His choice of career and its subsequent course were greatly influenced by another Old Merchant Taylor, Dr. Cyril Norwood, successively Head Master of Bristol Grammar School, Marlborough and Harrow. It was while Gurner was at Clifton that he first met Norwood who, fifteen years his senior, became to him an exemplar, a preceptor, an object of reverence, to whom he dedicated his autobiography with its declaration of faith. Gurner, in his turn, became something of a protégé to Norwood, who sympathised with his wish to take a headship (by this time both were at Marlborough), helped him to obtain the post at Strand, and supported him in a dispute at Sheffield.

The circumstances of Gurner's appointment to Whitgift provide an interesting study. His application was endorsed by Norwood, by now Headmaster of Harrow, who wrote a testimonial in the warmest terms, and also by Sir Ernest Barker, another distinguished educationist, who had tutored Gurner at Oxford, had been Chairman of the Governors at Strand School when Gurner was there, and was now Principal of King's College, London. For reasons unknown Gurner later withdrew his application. In June 1927, upon reviewing the short list of candidates submitted by the Governors for his selection, Archbishop Davidson expressed himself dissatisfied with their choice and asked for Gurner's name to be restored to the list. Davidson, who was Visitor not only to the Whitgift Foundation but also to Harrow, as well as being an Old Harrovian, had already intervened in 1926 to get Norwood appointed there, where he was now successfully imposing higher standards after the relaxed régime of his predecessor. The inference is obvious: with backing from three such patrons, Gurner's appointment was not only inevitable but also manifestly acceptable. Norwood's friendship was further cemented thereby, and in 1928 he became the first man to be invited by Gurner as Guest of Honour at the annual Prize-Giving; he was followed the next year by Archbishop Davidson himself.

Andrew's resignation had been given too late for his successor to take up his appointment at the beginning of the school year at Michaelmas 1927, so G.E.H. Ellis was appointed Acting Head Master for a term. Having been so closely involved with Andrew's organisation for a quarter of a century and Second Master since 1922, Ellis found few difficulties in guiding the School for this short period.

An impressive start

When he took up his new post in January 1928, one of Gurner's first concerns was to establish a good relationship with his Governors, who were impressed by his enlightened views on secondary education, and whose confidence he quickly gained; they were also impressed by his ready exposition of his point of view and by the absence of any aloofness such as that which had put them ill at ease when dealing with Andrew. He also undertook the task of winning over the Staff, which was made easier by Andrew's own reaction to the appointment, expressed in a telegram sent to the Officer Commanding the OTC contingent, which was at camp at Tidworth Park, 'Gurner appointed. The right man'. The loyalty of the boys had also to be captured. Having been deprived of a real Head Master for a term, they were looking forward with some excitement to the novelty of fresh authority. His impact was immediate; whereas Andrew had always avoided any emotional appeal to the School, Gurner turned his extrovert personality upon the boys, preaching to them, exhorting them, scolding them, confiding in them. He sought familiar terms with the younger masters and with the senior boys, gave the prefects greater responsibility, and quickly introduced minor but popular reforms, such as permanent seating in Big School,* stricter regulations regarding school uniform (which during the War had been much relaxed and had not afterwards been reimposed by Andrew), the teaching of civics and other social studies to all members of the Sixth and, long overdue, a modernisation of the administration of the School, with the employment of a full-time secretary in place of the part-time services of two members of the teaching staff.

Although his plans for the future were mainly bound up with what was to be provided at Haling Park, he did not intend to let the grass grow under his feet while the School was still at North End. His requirements could not be met without some immediate extra expenditure, which he felt should not be unfairly withheld, for while the Middle School was receiving a Foundation bounty of four thousand pounds a year, the Grammar School was being subsidised by only a few hundred. Expansion, rather than retrenchment, even during this period of waiting, should be the aim.

Difficulties

Unhappily, Gurner's arrival was quickly followed by the early stages of the economic recession that blighted the first half of the nineteen-thirties. Whereas 1927, the last year of Andrew's régime, had yielded success in many fields, particularly the academic, the following few years were lean ones. Parents were finding it hard enough to support their sons at school, while three years at university seemed an expensive luxury at a time when a degree was too often of little value when a job was sought; in consequence the tendency for more boys to follow a sixth-form course was halted. It now seemed far better to parents that their sons should meet earlier the stiff competition for employment and, with the sound backing of a matriculation certificate, look for a secure post in a bank, an insurance office or a safe business firm, while those who wished to become solicitors, accountants, architects, surveyors, etc. could take up articles with merely that same useful qualification. The Governors' policy of admitting a preponderance of Croydon boys was also being felt, and the proportion of boys who could not achieve qualifications necessary to follow a sixth-form course was increasing. One result was that boys who had seemed destined for authority as prefects were no longer there when they were needed; another was a temporary decline in intellectual determination and stimulus in the Sixth Form, which now consisted of two more or less distinct groups—the serious workers, and the athletic triflers with their hangers-on; the generation immediately preceding had successfully combined athletic with academic endeavour.

There was another disadvantage that impaired effective teaching throughout the School: an inadequate staffing ratio, worse than that which had existed under Andrew in 1913 and 1920, when the Inspectors had strongly urged the appointment of two or three more masters. Many forms contained 30 boys or even more, and large groups made up some of the various sides of the Sixth Form; indeed it was common for boys

---

* That most of these folding seats remain in constant and heavy use after sixty years proves the wisdom of choice from six different styles; their cost was 42 pence each and they were made of solid oak. But for their durability they would have been replaced with something more comfortable many years ago. (The School, standing during the whole of morning Assembly, had not been used to any lengthy address or lecture; on occasions such as Speech Day, chairs had been hired).

entering the Classical and Modern Sixths to join those who had preceded them a year – or even two years – before. This situation meant that these new arrivals were hard pressed and yet neglected at the same time, while the older hands were held back by attempts to accommodate the interests of the neophytes. By emphasising the difference between the Whitgift staffing ratio and that of similar schools, Gurner was able to persuade the Governors – still reluctant to encourage expansion and progress – to allow him to engage additional staff. These men and others appointed in replacement of older men as they moved on or retired were to form the core of his team designed to give new vigour to all aspects of School life after the move to Haling Park.

An impression may have been gained that now Andrew had gone, academic success was more difficult to achieve, but this idea was a mistaken one, for Ellis remained as an excellent Classics coach (Gurner had been for too long out of touch with scholarship work and was, by some accounts, too impetuous and grandiloquent to be a sound classic), while the very strong Science department was ably led by H.G.F. Micklewright. Whereas Andrew's unwillingness to delegate responsibility to some of his heads of departments had resulted in their reluctance to experiment or develop a strong line of their own, Gurner encouraged his staff to pursue an individual inclination, although he too gave useful help and direction to younger, inexperienced masters.

During the next few years he was able to make a number of appointments that strengthened all departments and established new ones. The mathematical and English sides, which had been languishing for some time and in which there had been no full sixth-form courses (partly, no doubt, because of the limitation of government grants to three advanced courses), were greatly reinforced. Two young men, A.H.G. Palmer and H.E. Parr, were mainly charged with raising standards in mathematics to a hitherto unachieved level of excellence. History and Biology were also given greater prominence in the Sixth, but this expansion came about mainly on account of the broader opportunities that became available after the move to Haling Park.

Gurner had found a rather dull school, lacking in intellectual liveliness, in vigour of literary and artistic expression and in corporate spirit. There was a handful of not very active societies; the Literary and Debating, the Photographic, and the Scientific and Wireless, together with the Christian Union, provided some intellectual stimulus, with opportunity for boys to practise administration and oratory after school hours.

At this time whatever activities took place were organised and conducted almost entirely by the boys. Young masters were in great demand to help and participate, but with the exception of games coaching, officering the OTC and the, in some cases, supine control of the Houses, few members of the ageing staff before Gurner's time had taken any initiative in encouraging interests outside the classroom.

Innovations

Gurner decided that deficiencies could be partly met by greater attention to the arts, music, drama and extra-mural activities. Under Frank Potter, appointed in 1930, the Art Department was stimulated to high achievement in a variety of fields, although music, under the conventional restrictions of the time, could not for years be given the time and attention it deserved.

Drama

Before Andrew's time, the performance of dramatic pieces had been a regular undertaking, but in 1908 he seemed to be glad to take the opportunity offered by an outbreak of bad behaviour by OWs in the audience to dispense with this activity, which he thought was distracting to those who should be applying themselves to their more serious studies. With the exception of *The Frogs* of Aristophanes done in Gilbert Murray's translation in 1910, no more school plays were put on in Andrew's time. There was a strong desire in the School, already expressed in 1924 by the Literary and Debating Society, for a revival of drama.

Gurner was keenly interested in the theatre (he became a vice-president of the Croydon Repertory Theatre on its inauguration in 1932) and gave every encouragement to this enthusiam. In March 1928 the Literary and Debating Society presented two short plays – *A Night at an Inn*, by Lord Dunsany, and *The Ghost of Jerry Bundler*,

'Saint Joan', 1932

by W.W. Jacobs. A.H. Ewen was the producer, making the best of a very inadequate stage in Big School, and of the absence of any experience on the part of the cast. Since then there has been a series of annual or even more frequent stage productions, broken only during the second world war. The first full-scale production took the stage at Haling Park in 1932, when Ewen and John Garrett shared the direction of Shaw's *Saint Joan*. They followed with *Peer Gynt* and *Cyrano de Bergerac*, establishing a consistent series of ambitious but successful productions of modern plays.

Societies

The existing Societies were encouraged to expand their scope and interest, and several more were promptly formed. By 1937 there was a score of them, a few of which were quite short lived. A number of projects had to wait until the move to Haling Park, which allowed further expansion of the staff. The new men were well disposed to give up part of their leisure hours to support Gurner's plans for increased and varied activity. Ewen had already been much involved with the Literary and Debating Society, in which his sceptical rationalism and deep interest in contemporary literature, art, music and even science provoked intellectual challenge and discussion.

Contact with the outside world was encouraged, and the social life of the School was expanded. Visits to the theatre, art galleries and exhibitions were arranged, an annual dance for the Sixth Form was instituted, and closer links with girls' schools were forged through the Debating Society in particular. Frank Potter and others took parties of boys abroad; in 1932 E.S. Roberts and D.R. Wigram conducted sixty boys on the first of a series of Mediterranean cruises. Cecil Prime led biological and botanical study courses in the field. Roberts formed a scout troop.

The Fanatics

A sophisticated debating club for senior boys known as 'The Fanatics', was founded by John Garrett (later Headmaster of Bristol Grammar School), and figures of the literary and artistic world of London, such as John Gielgud, A.L. Rowse and R.C. Sherriff, were invited to the School to speak.

These fresh opportunities attracted the attention of a new generation of sixth-formers, who found that their intellectual and creative interests were being understood, stimulated and encouraged. Notable among the earliest to respond were Burke Trend (Secretary of the Cabinet and Rector of Lincoln College, Oxford), Frederick Tomlin (philosophical writer, member of the British Council and friend of T.S. Eliot), Peter Shaw (Secretary and Fellow of King's College, London, and a Whitgift Governor), Philip Martin (Chancellor of Wells Cathedral), and Paul Crowson (Sub-Warden of Radley).

Music

The annual December concert had declined in popularity. Performed for many years in the North End Hall, for there was no seating in Big School, it was given 'by the Boys of the Singing Classes, kindly assisted by the following gentlemen:' This considerable number, chiefly masters and OWs, comprised the body of the orchestra and the majority of the bass and tenor voices. The programme concentrated on choral works, usually of a 'sacred' nature, relieved by instrumental and vocal solos and duets, glees, madrigals and part-songs. H.L. Balfour, who had been Song Master since 1899, attending no more than two days a week, had gained a high reputation for his training of choirs, but he had to rely upon casual talent among boys and OWs for instrumentalists, there being no provision for instruction within the School. For some years performances were given on two successive nights, so popular had the concert become, and on occasion gate-crashers had over filled the Hall. By the late nineteen-twenties, however, enthusiasm had diminished; the greatest applause was accorded to the rousing finale, provided by the Drums and Fifes of the OTC, under George Etches, who would conduct his own arrangements of, for example, the overture to *Poet and Peasant*, or a selection from *Faust*, followed by a March. This extraordinary volume of sound, played mainly *fortissimo*, shook the rafters and consoled those members of the audience whose musical fervour had not been stimulated by the earlier, subdued part of the programme. By this time boys' voices had become less enchanting, for orchestral music, classical and jazz, could now be heard in rivalry on the radio and gramophone.

In 1931 the Concert was given for the first time in Big School at Haling Park. Gurner wished it to be a completely domestic affair, so the boys were now on their own; there was no orchestra. The songs were reduced in number, and two one-act plays were put on to give variety. The Drums and Fifes gave a spirited rendering from *Il Trovatore*.

After some discussion among the Governors whether the teaching of singing was after all worthy of a place in the curriculum, George Oldroyd was appointed to succeed Balfour, who retired in 1933. With the help of John Newbold, a teacher of French, a school orchestra was formed. There was still no means of learning an orchestral instrument within the School, but those who learned outside welcomed the opportunity to play with fellow-musicians. From small beginnings, and after meeting for regular practices, the orchestra was by 1936 playing well enough to perform once a week at Assembly and annually at the Concert in Big School. In March 1937 it tackled the first movement of *The Unfinished Symphony*.

Although it has been stated that no boy could yet learn an instrument on the School premises, the important exception must be made of the drums and fifes – and bugles – of the Officers' Training Corps (from 1940 until 1948 named the Junior Training Corps), under the instruction of George Etches, who combined his duties of Laboratory Assistant with those of Band Instructor. His record of success and popularity was formidable, and from the time he took over the Corps of Drums in 1905 until his retirement in 1946, their reputation, especially at the annual Public Schools OTC camps, was high indeed.

Social Awareness

A very different venture was the formation of a Boys' Club in one of the poorer parts of Croydon, supported by the School Mission collections and proceeds from special functions, and organised and staffed by prefects and other senior boys. This Club, which performed in Croydon useful service similar to that of the Public School Missions in the East End of London, was also helpful in bringing to the notice of Whitgift boys social conditions they might otherwise have been unaware of. Gurner had a strong social conscience and was a keen reformer, but he was no 'leveller'. He wanted to help the socially and educationally disadvantaged, as the phrase now has it, but he still envisaged academic excellence as attainable solely by a small minority and then only by their being caught young. The talented among the poorer classes must be identified and helped to achieve their potential.

Games

In regard to games, Gurner saw that there were three main difficulties: a lack of good grounds at North End, which would soon be remedied; a drop in the age of the School teams due to the tendency for boys to leave earlier; and a poverty of coaching talent. Having been a rugby-player at School and College, and a keen fives-player, Gurner continued to take an interest in these two games and did his best to encourage them, turning out in practices with the First XV and, although handicapped by his war wound, playing in the courts.

Site of School at Haling Park as it was in 1920

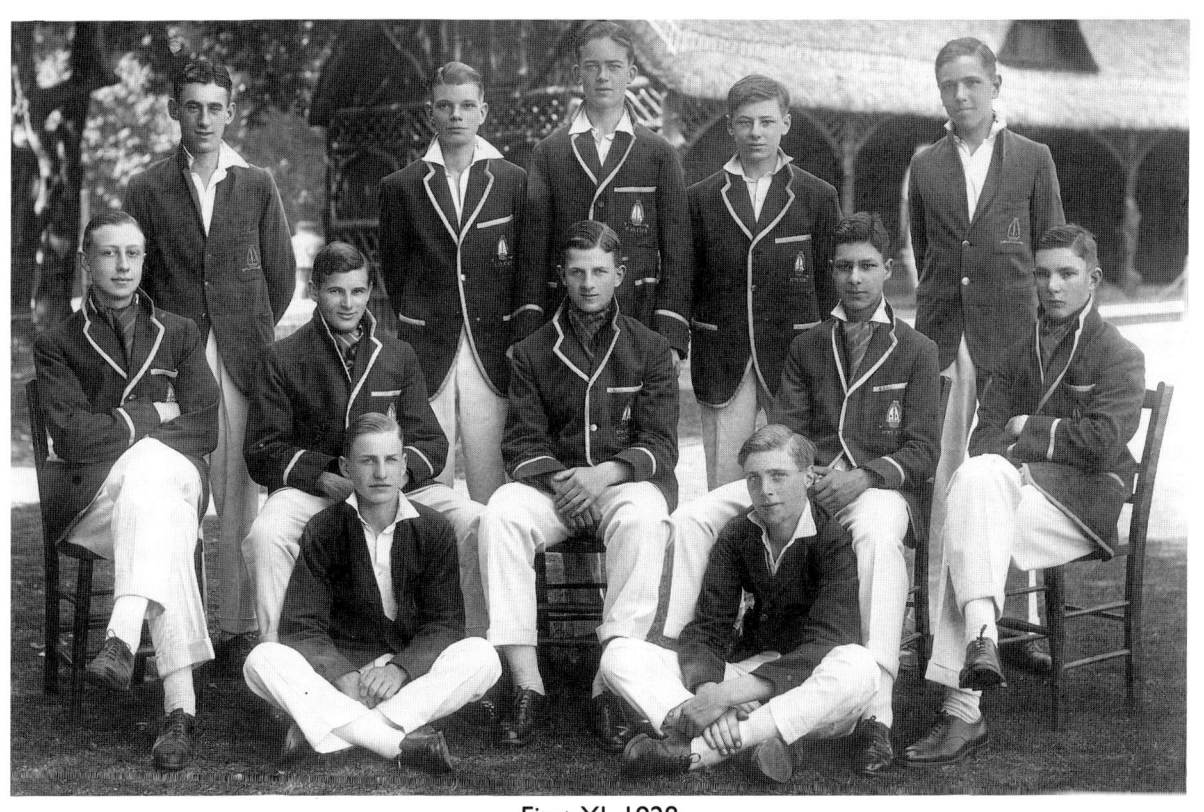

First XI, 1928
L. to r., *Back row*: Neville, Merrett, Dubois, Seear, Diplock, *Middle row*: Ling, Peart, Stutchbury (Capt.), Ewing, Thompson, *Front row*: Sykes, Hughes

Haling Park Plans

The plans for removal were dominating the attention of Governors and Head Master alike. In 1928, although the precise site of the new buildings had already been decided upon, little progress was being made at Haling Park except in the levelling and landscaping of the grounds, where good use was being made of the newly laid-out playing-fields to supplement the very limited space at North End. There were several reasons for delay: the Governors' desire to consult authorities, including the Board of Education and the new Head Master, upon the effectiveness of their scheme and upon the requirements of the new school; the need to collect sufficient capital through the sale of land for building, and through the accumulation of annual surpluses; and the fact that no architect had yet been appointed. Walton Turner's outline scheme became the subject of a special committee that took over a year to work out its not very complicated details; eventually it was decided that the School at Haling Park should accommodate 750 boys, and the Middle School in North End 500, a total increase of nearly 400 boys.

At last the decision was taken to appoint an architect, a step that had been postponed through many misgivings. Although at first the Governors had contemplated throwing the design open to competition, with Sir Banister Fletcher as assessor, they came to the conclusion that time was now so pressing that quicker action was desirable, and they therefore invited applications for the post. They selected in December 1927 the partnership of Messrs. Leathart and Granger, of John Street, Adelphi, London, who had recently completed a new school at Southport, Lancashire. The Governors were contemplating a cost of £160 per place for the bare shell of the building, which was considered by the Board to be unnecessarily high; £130, or even £120, should be nearer the mark. The Governors maintained that although they could get down to a lower figure, 'it would mean that they would have to curtail their expenditure in decorative work, and they thought that a school of this kind ought to be housed in buildings that had some nobility of character'. Against the Board's advice, they were also contemplating the possible future enlargement of the School to hold one thousand boys, for whom they wanted to provide in advance a large enough Assembly Hall and other accommodation that would avoid the necessity of making later structural alterations. They were persuaded to reconsider this idea of enlargement, however, for they found few to agree with them that a school of such a size was not too large; there would also inevitably be unforeseen additions and adaptations to pay for. In the event, the cost worked out at about £140 per place, which was much increased in due course by such additions. With the price of the land, and fittings and furniture, the total cost per head, reckoned within three years of opening, advanced to well over £200.

Gurner zealously joined the Governors in scrutinising the plans, the preparation of which proceeded swiftly enough for a contractor (E.H. Smith, Ltd., of Croydon) to be appointed in January 1930. A considerable work-force, including many highly skilled men, was quickly engaged, for it was a time of severe depression in the building trade, and such employment was eagerly sought. Work was immediately started, so that most of the foundations had been laid and many walls partially erected, when arrangements were made for the ceremony of laying the Foundation Stone to take place on 31 May. Cosmo Gordon Lang, who had succeeded Archbishop Davidson upon the latter's retirement in 1928 and had already acquainted himself with the School by giving away the Prizes the

Bishop Woods lays the Foundation Stone, 31 May 1930

previous December, had intended to officiate but was prevented by illness. The duty was performed by his proxy, the Bishop and Vicar of Croydon, the Rt. Rev. E.S. Woods. The inscription on the Stone was never corrected and declares that the Archbishop laid it himself. Only fourteen months elapsed before the buildings were complete enough for the official opening ceremony to be performed on 8 July 1931 by H.R.H. Prince George (later the Duke of Kent), but the School did not assemble there for the first time until 22 September.

Haling Park: The Buildings

Whereas the main architectural feature at North End had been Big School with its Tower, the main one at Haling Park was the Quadrangle, 176 feet by 144, around which were planned Big School, twenty-eight classrooms, the Library and administrative accommodation; behind this quad-

Prince George reviews the OTC at the opening of the School at Haling Park, 8 July 1931
L. to r.: A. J. Camden Field (Chairman of the Governors), The Mayor of Croydon, Capt. F. H. Potter, Lord Ashcombe (Lord Lieutenant of the County of Surrey), HRH Prince George

The Terrace in 1931

rangle was a smaller one which housed the Science and Art departments, the Dining Hall and the Gymnasium. Unfortunately, all the buildings except those forming the Main Quadrangle were planned on one floor, which necessitated various excrescent wings and a great deal of sprawl. It seems strange too, that in the provision of accommodation in which North End itself had been deficient, the architects were so sparing that alterations and additions became urgent within a very short time. The changing-rooms were absurdly inadequate, the gymnasium was too small; so was the Masters' Common Room (it was also inconveniently placed, a defect remarked upon by officials of the Board when they examined the plans). The kitchen was also too small, so that a portion of the dining-hall itself had to be given up for store-rooms and pantries. The stage in Big School was badly planned for dramatic presentations, and no provision was made for blacking-out; the cinematograph projection-room (a great novelty at the time) has in consequence only recently been provided with a projector. Several desirable features were omitted altogether: there was no provision for music-teaching at all, apart from three small practice-rooms, which were shown on the plans but which were never constructed; there was no swimming-bath; there was no medium-sized room suitable for lectures or for gatherings of two or three hundred people.

In some respects what was provided was actually inferior to North End: the Library was even smaller, so was the single Art-room; the corridors were too narrow, especially in the Science wings; there were no fives-courts to replace Sir Frederick Edridge's benefaction. However, the very defects of the layout (which seemed to show that after planning a noble quadrangle, the architects had been baffled by the problems of fitting in all the other requirements) later enabled many additions to the original design to be made without much difficulty.

The architectural style, which is impossible to define, was an invention of the architects, who claimed to have designed the building 'to accord with the Elizabethan associations of the Whitgift Foundation' and to 'have drawn freely on the examples of that period for their inspiration.'* The building is of steel-frame construction with brick and stone walls. The 'examples of that period' are rather difficult to trace. The windows certainly have stone transoms and mullions, and the casements and other lights are leaded; there is a fine oriel window to the Library; there are a few stone pinnacles; and over the copper-clad belfry above Big School there is a weather-vane in the form of a sixteenth-century ship.** Beyond these elements, Elizabethan architectural influences are not readily apparent. The main doorways are Romanesque in style, and the decorative motifs of the internal metal-work and plaster-work are 1920s 'art deco'. Despite these criticisms, the masses of the main quadrangle are well-proportioned and satisfying, while the brick and the stone (much of the latter has had to be restored) have matured to an agreeable mellowness.

Another Missed Opportunity

A deficiency that was harder to make good was the shortage of playing-fields, already commented on by Andrew. The contours of the site, and the situation of woods and belts of trees that it would have been a shame to fell, made full use for playing-space of the area in the Governors' possession impossible to achieve. There remained, however, adjacent to the

The Library, 1931

* At this time school architecture was dominated by the 'Queen Anne' or the 'neo-Georgian' style, with symmetrical facades and sash windows.
** This ship has been described as a Spanish Galleon (to commemorate Lord Howard of Effingham's defeat of the Armada), but it is more probably intended to represent either the man-of-war shown on the Admiral's seal of 1585, or his flag-ship 'The Ark', which was launched in 1587.

The Woodwork Shop, 1931

buildings themselves, a stretch of parkland of approximately eighteen acres that the Foundation had been unable to acquire, for it had been bought from the Watney trustees before the Governors became interested in buying any part of Haling Park. When they decided to build the new School, they hoped to secure this land, which was being used for the grounds of a country club, if ever it was offered for sale. It was offered to them in March 1931; the price asked was a high one, for the construction of the School had increased the

The Fountain, moved from the cloisters at North End to Haling Park in 1931

Aerial View, 1931

The Parade Ground, 1931

value of developable land in the vicinity, and the Governors had to obtain authority from the Board before negotiation. Unwilling to submit to delay, for which the Board and the Foundation in conjunction were notorious, the owner arranged for the property to be auctioned. If they had agreed to treat with the owner privately, the Governors could have obtained the land without much difficulty, but two days before the auction was to take place it was snatched from their grasp by a pre-emptive offer only slightly in excess of what they were officially prepared to pay.

They were now faced with the prospect of a housing estate within the closest proximity of the School itself and of being deprived of a most desirable addition to the grounds. In the end a compromise was reached, and half the area was acquired, but the remainder, comprising some of the most level and, for playing-fields, most suitable land in the whole Haling Park estate, was taken by the developers of Whitgift Avenue.

The Gymnasium (now the Drama Studio)

This lack of foresight and acumen must ever remain a sad reflection upon the Governors of the time, whose actions, once they had decided to buy the first small portion of Haling Park in 1920, were characterised by a combination of obstinacy and timidity when they were confronted by opportunities that were really beyond the grasp of their imagination. It was a saddening echo of their predecessors' failure to acquire the remainder of the Dingwalls property in Wellesley Road in 1884.

The move to Haling Park was nevertheless made with the highest hopes and enthusiasm. Five years of impatient expectation had allayed criticism of what was clearly to be a great improvement on existing conditions, which for so many years had been patently unsatisfactory. Opportunities were suddenly expanded, and ambitions fulfilled.

Grammar Schools

Advantage was taken of a change in location to make a slight change in name. The word 'Grammar' in the School's title, which had been introduced fifty years before to distinguish it from the Middle School, had become an embarrassment, for it was now almost exclusively associated with 'maintained' and 'provided' schools under local authorities.* Most other schools that had been referred to in a similar way at one time, such as Bedford and Tonbridge, had long ago abandoned this description, although the great Grammar Schools of Manchester, Bristol and Leeds continued to use it. In future the School would be known as 'Whitgift School', as it had mainly been between 1871 and 1881. Gurner was not satisfied with this simplification alone, and decided that he should be called the 'Master' of Whitgift (Cyril Norwood had been 'Master' of Marlborough). Ellis, until now 'Second Master', was also to be given another title, but he declined Gurner's suggestion of 'Vice-Master' and settled, after some discussion, for 'Deputy Master'.

To some a less welcome coincidence with the move was the economy measure adopted by the

---

* The use of the term 'grammar' in this context reflected the views of the officials of the Board of Education who, out of their respect for the humane studies, regarded secondary schools to some extent as successors of the traditional Classical school, with Latin as a basis of study for everyone—for a while at least.

Treasury in reducing the direct grant and compelling schools to cut the salaries of their staffs by ten per cent. In its prosperous state the Foundation could have afforded to forgo this economy, but after making a protest, the Governors had to submit. As a result of this saving, so the staff used to aver, the Foundation was enabled to install the oak panelling that so handsomely surrounds the corridors. A certain member of the staff claimed to have calculated the length of panelling outside his classroom that his own 'cut' in salary had provided.

The immediate increase in numbers by one hundred boys was due mainly to a much larger intake, but partly also to a natural desire of many boys to stay on for a term at least in order to enjoy the experience of the new buildings and their amenities. Having been once reminded by the Governors that it was imperative to reserve the majority of places for Croydon boys, Gurner, like Andrew, had regretfully but obediently excluded many candidates of good quality who came from outside. However, the report of an Inspection held under the direction of the Board of Education in December 1930 had reiterated the criticism of 1921 in expressing the hope that with increased accommodation the admission of a larger proportion of boys from outside Croydon would be possible.

Social Changes in Croydon

The greatest building development in Croydon during the nineteen-twenties had occurred in its northern area of Norbury and new Thornton Heath, filling the gap that had separated the town from built-up London. There had also been considerable expansion in the Addiscombe area to the east and some to a lesser extent in South Croydon. But for these additions, which accommodated middle-class 'dormitory' residents, the proportion of Croydon families with sons to send to Whitgift might have dropped quite sharply. The Victorian houses near the centre of the town were now obsolete; with the reduction in the size of families and in the number of servants employed, they were too large and inconvenient. There had been considerable development of industry in many parts of the town, together with municipal housing, but the older middle-class property, most of it rented or leased, as was then the custom, yet unimproved to meet rising standards, had been taken over by the manual working classes.

It was outside the confines of the Borough that most building development was now proceeding. The electrification of the Southern Railway encouraged the expansion of towns and villages within a radius of twenty-five miles of London, and Haling Park was conveniently accessible by this means, and by the extended country bus services, from Caterham, Reigate, Tadworth, etc. as well as from the closer former villages of Coulsdon, Purley, Sanderstead and Warlingham. Candidates from these places outnumbered increasingly those from Croydon and took up by degrees a larger percentage of places until after half a dozen years the restriction was tacitly removed, and places went to those who did best in the entrance examination, irrespective of where they lived. The Governors appointed by the Croydon Education Committee were themselves less insistent, for they were pleased to see the Middle School enlarged and housed in better premises, and they were coming to realise more keenly the true function of a school whose curriculum was designed to culminate in advanced courses. They were also far more deeply interested in the schools under their immediate control, for further education after minimum school leaving age (raised to fourteen in 1918) was now increasingly supported by government grants, to the partial relief of local rates. Whitgift was no longer the only school in Croydon through which entrance to university could normally be gained, and both the Middle School and Selhurst Grammar School were sending boys to London and occasionally to Cambridge.

External Examinations

This increase in numbers and in academic quality made itself felt when the newcomers came to prove themselves, first at School Certificate level and later in the Sixth Form. But already by 1936 university scholarship successes, by which the rating of big day-schools has come to be judged—for good or ill—had become even more numerous than ten years before. Whereas in the past the great majority of awards had been given in Classics and Science, Oxford, Cambridge and London were now offering more in Mathematics, History and Modern Languages. There was now a greater incentive to stay on to follow a university career, for the State scholarship system had been expanded, and borough and county local authority awards were more generous and more numerous, so that those who had missed winning a university award might yet hope for some other financial help. There were not many parents who could pay for a university course out of income alone.

With the Heads of Departments now having greater control over their syllabuses and over the men under them, there was an improvement in subject-teaching. This improvement was also partly due to the institution of annual subject conferences, to which members of the staff contributed their own reports, and which enabled the Heads of Departments to diagnose and deal with weaknesses as they became apparent.

The normal seven-year course that started for a boy of eleven resulted in his taking the General Schools Certificate at sixteen and the Higher Schools Certificate two years later, by which time few boys had the opportunity of a further year in the Sixth Form to take Oxbridge scholarships unless they were prepared to leave at nineteen (but it must be remembered that a matriculation certificate entitled a boy to apply for a place at university, which a good many did after a year or less in the Sixth Form). The cleverer boys did not need all this time and could well manage the same course in six, rather than seven, years. In fact it was not uncommon for some boys to pass through the lower forms more speedily than others. To accommodate such boys in a more regular style, Gurner made a selection of the most promising at the age of twelve, and two new forms—IV Special and Remove Special—were hastened through the curriculum in order to take the Schools Certificate at the age of fifteen or even less. Interest, ambition and competitiveness were encouraged by this means, and very successful results were achieved. Although such concentration on a few pupils, with undesirably early specialisation and a narrowing of the curriculum, would now be regarded as educationally unsound, not much harm seems to have been done to those who underwent the experience which, although long abandoned at Whitgift, continued to be followed at some other schools that wished to achieve a good scholarship record at all costs. One unfortunate result, at least, was that some boys who had not been selected in this way became inclined to underestimate their own abilities and did not contemplate undertaking an advanced course that would have been well within their power. Another unplanned result was that a few boys regarded the early acquisition of a Certificate as a justification for leaving.

The middle classes were becoming increasingly aware of the advantages of higher education. By the late thirties a graduate had no fear of being unemployed; there was prosperity in the south, and the professional and managerial families who were tending to establish their homes in the outer suburbs found it possible and at the same time desirable to allow their sons to pursue a course at school that would lead to a professional qualification through full-time study after their school career. Thus a matriculation certificate was increasingly regarded, not as the conclusion of a boy's school course, but as an encouragement for staying on to take Higher Certificate and to go on to university or some other place of higher education. There was also a growing tendency to stay on beyond the Fifths for a few terms without any intention of following an advanced course to Higher Certificate level. But without this goal before them, boys could find the normal Sixth Form courses irrelevant and discouraging. Gurner wished not only to keep at School those who had much to offer by their example and service as seniors in authority, but also to give them a greater purpose in their studies. He therefore established two new forms, Transitus and Middle General Sixth. Transitus enabled some who had failed General Schools Certificate or Matriculation to take the examination again without the indignity of remaining in the Fifth form. For others, in Middle General, he devised a less academic syllabus, including Civics, Economics and modern English studies.

Games

The very limited accommodation for rugby and cricket at North End and the absence of amenities for any other games, with the exception of fives, had prevented the majority of boys from taking much part in organised sport, but with the far more ample opportunities offered at Haling Park, not only did the two major games become more successful, but also others were introduced and soon flourished.

As a rule, any consistent success of a school activity is in proportion to the talent and enthusiasm of the men who act as coaches and instructors; their names, then, must not be altogether omitted, although with so many contributing in various capacities, it may appear invidious to make distinctions. At North End after World War I, M.G. Arnett, assisted by professionals, had been responsible for the cricket revival, and C.E. Loving had made the best of the limited facilities for rugby; his experience of the game as played in Wales was passed on to many of his pupils, including B.E. Nicholson, who played for England in 1937. The increase in numbers following the move to Haling Park and the retirement of several members of the Staff at this period enabled Gurner to appoint a number of young men with good academic qualifications accompanied by a prowess in games. These reinforced other young men from North End who were encouraged by the better facilities to do more than they had been able to do before. Thus for the first time systematic coaching in games, on a House as well as a team basis, for all boys throughout the School became a possibility. In the Junior School I.A. Evans and M. Etherington laid foundations that were well built upon by J. Cummings (rugby) and M.V. Lockett (cricket) and many others in the Senior School.

These policies resulted in the development of a considerable number of talented players, many of whom later played for the Old Whitgiftian Cricket and Rugby Clubs, which in the 1930s acquired a great reputation over the whole of the London area. This reputation was to be renewed and enhanced after World War II. Undoubtedly the greatest all-rounder of the period was Martin Turner, who left in 1940, and who gained a Cambridge rugby blue and England caps after a distinguished career in the RNAS; he became an inspiring captain of both the OWCC and the OWRFC.

A full-time PT Instructor was appointed for the first time. The Gymnasium, even if it was manifestly inadequate, at least made this appointment imperative, and in H. Bennett, of the Army Physical Training Corps, the School found an all-rounder of great coaching ability. Whereas gymnastics had for many years figured in the House Championship, the small number of competitors had had to undergo their training in a privately owned and poorly equipped building a quarter of a mile from the School. Now there was every inducement for the enthusiast, as well as regular physical education—instead of 'drilling'—for all boys. Fencing was introduced and quickly flourished; at this sport two boys coached by Bennett later represented England (A.R. Smith and P.G. Williams). Inter-school athletic matches were arranged, and Whitgift boys competed more regularly and more successfully at the Public School Sports at the White City. Cross-country could be trained for, and even run, in the School's own grounds, so that this became a sport that was no longer restricted to the annual House competition over Farthing Downs, but one followed by a number of boys from choice in competition with other schools or at open meetings. For the first two years at Haling Park there were no fives-courts. Sir Frederick Edridge's gift at North End was now being made use of by the Middle School, and the game could have been allowed to die, had there not been a determined move, led by Geoffrey Marks and the Bishop of Croydon, and well supported by Gurner, to have the game reinstated, with the result that four standard covered courts were opened in 1933. Another successful sporting activity was shooting. With a much better miniature range, an enthusiastic Musketry Officer (R.F. Hobbs) and a patient, experienced coach (E. Lazenby) on the open ranges, the VIII improved their performances at Bisley, achieving third place in the Ashburton in 1932 and 1935, their best since 1912.

There were notable shortages, however. Lawn tennis, a game that was becoming popular in the schools and which was a favourite with Gurner, remained unprovided for, but the main deficiency was still a swimming-pool. There had usually been a handful of enthusiasts who gave up much time, perhaps daily before school, to training, taking advantage of the nearness of the Croydon Central Baths and the excellent instruction there of Ross Eagle, who had been one of the first coaches in England to teach the Australian 'crawl' stroke. They were able to give a good

Captain Hobbs addresses his troops, 1933

account of themselves, the peak of their achievements being the winning of the Public Schools Relay Competition (The Bath Cup) in 1924 and 1925. The Governors were sympathetic to the sport and had from the outset contemplated in their plans for Haling Park the eventual construction of a pool when finances should permit. At the end of 1934 they approved plans for an open-air, unheated pool to be excavated in the Junior School playground. They had no intention that it should be used for regular instruction in swimming as part of the School physical education programme, but wished merely to provide a bathing-place. These plans were fortunately rejected by the Board of Education on the grounds of the unsuitability of the whole project, which was abandoned. The Board strongly recommended a covered, heated pool, where all boys in the School could be taught to swim, but the Governors would on no account entertain such a proposal, for reasons that have not been left on record, although at the time large surpluses were being accumulated, and the capital cost could have been paid off within a few years.

Gurner and Day Schools

The background of his earlier experience is of importance in understanding Ronald Gurner's aims and outlook when he came to Whitgift.

During the previous fifty years the term 'public school', although no longer limited in anyone's view to the schools of the Clarendon Commission, had come to denote, despite the mixed constitution of the Headmasters' Conference, a boarding-school specifically. There was a strong tendency to place day-schools in a lower category altogether, and at Oxford before the War, Gurner, like the author of *Sinister Street*, had felt himself at some disadvantage through having been at one himself. The old endowed grammar schools, if they had not become 'public schools', such as Oundle, Repton and Uppingham, had either been taken over by local authorities or had been placed on the direct-grant list. Many such provincial schools had been reconstructed after 1870 to accommodate a proportion of boarders, but these diminished in number as the bigger schools, on the one hand, achieved a higher reputation, and as the new municipal and county schools, on the other, filled the educational gaps that had hitherto resulted in boys being sent away to board at minor, cheaper schools. One result of this classification was to give some boarding-schools a spurious exclusiveness that discouraged many parents from sending their sons to a well-equipped local day-school of academic distinction, that suffered, however, from a distasteful social admixture and from the lack of a thorough-going commitment to the public-school *ethos*.

It was to the cause of the day-boy that Gurner applied himself and his very real persuasive powers. Whitgift approximated more nearly to Merchant Taylors' than did either King Edward VII or Strand. He had before him the wonderfully stimulating opportunity to reconstruct a school within new walls and among beautiful surroundings. Everything pointed towards the fulfilment of a dream. He had not the least doubt that with these splendid advantages to support him he

Fives Courts, 1935

could create the greatest day-school in England. He took as his starting-point an axiom of Cyril Norwood's: 'A school must, if it is fully to justify its existence, aim at the inculcation of religion, discipline, culture, the team spirit as taught upon the playing-fields, and the spirit of service.' These were the five essentials that were associated in the public mind with a boarding-school, and Gurner believe that in them the day-school, too, need not fail. Indeed, since they were not so rigorously imposed upon him, the day-boy had the advantage of being able to accept their validity critically, not blindly. Secondly, in the curriculum and in the preparation for careers, the day-boy enjoyed at least equal opportunities. Lastly, but most importantly, the day-boy derived from his school and home life certain advantages over the boarding-school boy, such as self-reliance, initiative, the power of acting in accordance with his own unaided judgment, independence of mind and spirit, and a realistic attitude to life.

Another point, expressed by Norwood as long before as 1909, but not laboured by Gurner, was the anti-intellectualism of many public boarding-schools, whose academic achievement was notoriously meagre, being confined largely to a small number of boys who carried off most of the classical (there were few other) awards at Oxford and Cambridge. Too many of the other boys remained obdurately barbarian, ignorant and uninstructed in other subjects, their lives being dominated by games, school routine and the inculcation of conventional behaviour and attitudes. Already then, before the 1914-18 war, this state of affairs was being attacked; and it was being challenged by the more ambitious and enlightened of the day-schools. In the 1920s and 1930s this criticism and this challenge were intensified.

His understanding and mistrust of the public-school system were curiously allied with his desire to compete with and surpass it in what the schools held as their prerogative—the 'five essentials'. To a large extent he succeeded, fighting hard to spread the fame of his school, and encouraging individuals in personal ambitions, so long as they did not stray too far from the public-school image; he deplored the fate of Shelley at Eton, but he would have been unwilling to harbour a Shelley at Whitgift. In his view the duty of the public schools was to be the breeding-place of a new race of Samurai, who should be at one with the millions that they were to lead. Because the day-boy was likely to possess more of the common touch, and because day-schools were always more likely to contain boys from a wider social range, he believed the future to lie in their hands. He believed, too, that the suppression of individuality and personality, together with the worship of convention, were the public-school system's greatest failures. The future leaders must learn to think for themselves while still at school, and to do that they must have a wider experience of the world than could be enjoyed by boys at a boarding-school. His radical way of thinking may have been ahead of his own time, but it was, of course, mainly concerned with the education of a small section of the community, i.e., the brighter children of the urban middle-class—his own kind of people, whom he regarded as the salt of the earth.

Gurner had already written a number of novels in which his favourite theme of educational progress was expounded; one, *For Sons of Gentlemen*, was written under the pseudonym of 'Kerr Shaw' (adapted from his mother's maiden name), and others, *The Day-Boy* and *C3*, under his own name. He was at the time of his appointment preparing the first formal statement of his educational principles, which appeared in 1930 as *The Day Schools of England*. He also wrote occasional articles in newspapers and periodicals on this favourite theme, and three more novels were to follow in as many years.

Gurner's Health

While these abundant developments were successfully in progress, a tragic deterioration in Gurner's mental health was taking place. Having already been the victim of two nervous breakdowns while he was under stress, he attempted in May 1939 to flee from a Nemesis that appeared to be overtaking him, but there was no escape, and he committed suicide. This time the trouble was more deep-seated than could be explained by a nervous breakdown, and the causes remain obscure. He was in debt and he was drinking hard; these weaknesses were no doubt the outcome of his psychotic disturbance, rather than its cause, but his self-destruction seems to have been the culmination of a growing self-disgust which proved too much for him to endure. For some years his actions had been subject to ever wilder impulse, and he had made it only too clear that he was in financial difficulties. The Governors had become aware of certain malpractices with the accounts under his control and had offered to help him to put matters straight, but he had denied culpability and had refused assistance, both from them and from a psychiatrist. He should have been given compulsory leave of absence, for his behaviour was doing no good to the School's reputation, and the Governors wished to get rid of him, but instead a close watch was placed upon him in order to gather evidence; of this he must have been aware, and it may well have contributed to his fatal decision. If he had had the will, or the opportunity, to confide in some stronger influence, a course that he, in his position of authority, would have found difficult to take, his life might have been saved. He could not humble himself before any of his Governors, or even his old friend Cyril Norwood, to whom by this time he had become something of an embarrassment, partly because of his attacks upon boarding-schools, to which Norwood was of course committed. The tragic event occurred at a time when the School was at a flowing tide of success, yet subject to the unpredictable personality of its Master.

His Influence

Ronald Gurner was Master of Whitgift for eleven and a half years. The imprint he left on the School was less enduring than that of Brodie or of Andrew, partly because of his own superficiality, partly because of the war that followed, which suddenly put an end to much that was new and vigorous in school life. He was a much more efficient delegator than either of his predecessors and, although ambitious and self-centred, he identified himself even more closely with all aspects of the School's existence. He mistakenly regarded the School as a thing almost of his own creation, that had been of negligible repute before his arrival, and that was at times of disappointment still unworthy of him, but one felt that Whitgift genuinely meant much to him, while his interest and pride in its achievements generated similar feelings among his colleagues and his pupils. He encouraged his subordinates to develop their own specialities and enthusiasms, but he expected a high level of performance leading to good publicity, in which he was a great believer. Success of this kind would be rewarded by a note of personal thanks and a public acknowledgment whenever the latter appeared appropriate. This appreciation meant much to men whose unobtrusive work might easily have gone unremarked upon.

His personal impact upon senior boys was a variable one; many would find him an embarrassment, inconsistent and transparently insincere in much of what he said, making extravagant promises that would quickly be forgotten, or affecting a knowledge of circumstances in which he was in fact unversed. These faults, however, were much more evident in the later stages of his illness. There were many boys that he knew very well; his own weaknesses enabled him to detect and understand weaknesses in others, but he did not condone them. He was interested in boys of promise, encouraging them and keeping in touch with them during their adult careers. Many of the most promising, like Andrew's earlier generation, lost their lives in warfare, but a large number of others achieved success, especially in

Lord Trend, PC, GCB

academic spheres; among these may be mentioned Lord Trend and Professor David Whitteridge, FRS; the Rt. Hon. Sir Reginald Prentice reached Cabinet rank, becoming responsible for, inter alia, the Department of Education and Science under Labour governments.*

But, overall, Gurner's was a flawed performance. He lacked the qualities of a great Head Master and never earned the full respect of those who worked under him. Sadly missing from his make-up were intellectual integrity, dignity, and honesty in personal relationships, and he never learnt to subordinate self-esteem, which was all the more necessary to him because of his own self-doubts, to the responsibilities of his office.

Some clues to his character may be discovered in his writings. His autobiography, *I Chose Teaching* (1937), setting out his views on education, is not so much an account of his life as a development of the *Day Schools of England* (1930) and articles in various journals. His views on education were regarded as significant and received attention from experts of the time, especially by Professor Edward C. Mack, in *Public Schools and British Opinion*, 1941.

In his introduction to *I Chose Teaching*, Gurner declares his sincerity in writing about his life and work, but confesses to being something of a poseur, one given to platitude, convention and rationalisation of motive:

> These poses come easily to me, . . . but the door is closed now, I am alone, and there is nobody to admire the attitudinising figure. I will not explain away hypocrisy or failure . . . If I find I have truckled before authority, or served tables for my own ends, I will admit it. If I have sinned against the light, moral or intellectual, I will say so . . .

In spite of these high-minded promises, Gurner reveals little of his inmost self or of any shameful experience or secret. On the contrary he becomes more self-confident as he writes, more scornful of the views of others, particularly if they speak

---

* The School Certificate forms of which Trend and Prentice were members in 1929 and 1938 respectively produced an exceptional flowering of diverse talent, for both contained five or six boys whose names were to be recorded in *Who's Who*; those with Prentice were: Professor J. Heyman, Fellow of Peterhouse; Rear-Admiral A.J. Monk, CBE; Sir Bryan Roberts KCMG, QC: ; Professor J.P. Wild, FRS.

Lord Diplock, Lord Justice of Appeal in Ordinary

for boarding-schools or support out-moded methods of teaching and discipline.

He possesses a fluent and rhetorical style suited more to exhortation than to intellectual analysis. He echoes the influences of his youth, when he was ambitious, starry-eyed, spontaneous, progressive and even reasonable: Fabian Socialism, Syndicalism, William Morris, Shaw, Wells. Much of his writing is allusive to his earlier reading and he tends to use old-fashioned colloquialisms. His experiences during World War I had disturbed the never easy balance of his mind, but he derived comfort from religion, which was dominated for him by Christ's sufferings. He frequently employs phrases from the New Testament, which he knew thoroughly.

Gurner was a Christian adherent and drew up his own syllabus of religious instruction, which was normally conducted by form-masters throughout the School. He involved himself in some of this teaching, chiefly of the Lower Sixth forms, whom he taught through a dramatic representation of Christ's life as it might have been recorded by a committee of Jewish elders; this he called the 'Sanhedrin'. He published an example of these records: *We Crucify!*, prefaced by an account of his method, part of which follows:

At the beginning of the school year we imagine ourselves to be the Sanhedrin, assembled at its first meeting. I assume, at this meeting, the post of President or High Priest, and the secretary is a boy who has been through the course during the previous year, and has volunteered to fill the office. The remainder of us are ordinary members of Sanhedrin, bearing names chosen in almost all cases at random. The chief officials are elected, and the year begins in the usual way. The drama ends with the presentation of a report, thirty-three years after, of the finding of an open tomb. Between these two dates the business of Sanhedrin, in so far as it deals with the story of the Founder of Christianity, is recorded as one imagines that it may well have been recorded at the time. Every scene is acted, usually though not always in council chamber, and the sequence of events is portrayed by a series of reports made by various members of Sanhedrin, and by interviews between ourselves and representative, though always imaginary, characters.

His extrovert personality, his fondness for drama, his egotism and his position of authority, which was rarely – if ever – challenged, enabled him to conduct these lessons with supreme confidence. Some of the other participants also became deeply involved in the Sanhedrin. Several of his pupils have acknowledged the influence of these lessons; others were less impressed.

His novels can be more revealing. They are all concerned with ideals, the ideals of young men involved in either overturning an old and effete order, particularly in education (e.g. the public schools again), or in reconstructing it. His war novel, *Pass Guard at Ypres*, 1930, his 'answer to *All Quiet on the Western Front*', echoes his own experience of war, but unlike the hopeless disillusionment of *All Quiet*, conveys a message of consolation for the loss of illusions.

Similarly, the last of his novels, *Reconstruction* (1931), reflects much of his experience, this time in teaching. It chronicles the return of a schoolmaster from the war, embittered by the sacrifice of lives, and determined to reimpose his own standards upon a slack and selfish generation, as he sees it. But he lacks sympathy and understanding with his pupils and colleagues; a rival proves to be more acceptable and consequently successful.

There seems to have been no guilty secret, beyond that of a man who came to realise that he had failed to live up to his ideals, who was too prone to indulge in extravagance of thought and action, and who early in life had fallen into debt and had drifted deeper and deeper until it was impossible for him to extricate himself. One is overwhelmed with pity at the decline and eventual suicide of a man who in his youth had shown much moral courage and promise of distinction.*

---

* I am indebted to Dr. Hugh Cecil of the Department of History, University of Leeds, for being allowed to read, before publication, his chapter on Ronald Gurner that forms part of his *Twelve British Novelists of the First World War*. I have drawn upon Dr. Cecil's thorough research into Gurner's life and associations in making my own assessment.

10. G.E.H. Ellis and World War II

G.E.H. Ellis

Even before the initial shock of Gurner's death had abated and the notoriety subsided, the Governors discovered with embarrassment and indignation the true extent of the late Master's defalcations with the School's affairs whose control he had assumed. But his death provided a prompt solution to many problems. The Governors' first action was to announce that Ellis would once again become Acting Head Master (he would have no truck with what he regarded as the affectation of 'Master', preferring 'Headmaster'; the one-world title has continued in use), and they then invited Archbishop Lang to appoint him substantively, without further ado. Lang was very willing, but the Board of Education pointed out that he did not possess such peremptory powers, and that the Scheme required the post to be advertised. This was done, although it was made pretty clear that, since Ellis was a candidate, it would be vain for others to apply. The announcement of his appointment was made on the last day of the summer term. Ll. J. Jones, Chief French Master and House master of Mason's, had already been appointed Second Master in anticipation of this news. By appointing Ellis, not only would the Governors avoid the disclosure to an outsider of many secrets they preferred to keep hidden, but also they would have in charge a man whose loyalty and devotion to the School were unquestioned, and whose esteem among parents, staff, Old Boys and present boys was of the highest. Now, at the age of sixty, he conceived it his duty to see the School through its difficulties for a few years, until the affair had blown over, and a younger man had been chosen. Ironically, when Andrew had retired twelve years before, Ellis had applied to be his successor, but was deemed to be too old. Despite their feelings of relief in relying upon Ellis to carry the heavy burden of succession, the Governors had no compunction in making a large reduction in the rate of salary offered to the new Headmaster.

Ellis had taken a First Class in Honour Moderations at Oxford, and it is perhaps surprising that he had never sought a headmastership, for which he was amply qualified (there was a strong tradition that he had declined offers of this kind). Not only had he substantial academic qualifications and proved ability as a teacher of the Classics, but he had also served under Andrew, in itself a high recommendation; he was a man of wide culture and profound intellect, being particularly interested in music and the arts; he was a keen naturalist; and he had displayed great versatility on the games-field as a track-athlete, a cricketer, and a player of rugby, hockey and lawn tennis. He had played chess for Oxford against Cambridge and had represented the two universities in their annual match against American universities. An Admirable Crichton, he had outshone his predecessor. At Whitgift he had coached the First XV for more than a dozen years and as Housemaster of Cross's since 1908 had identified himself closely with games generally. As Second Master for nearly twenty years and as Senior Classics Master under Gurner, he had borne a heavy responsibility, but his calm, equable temperament, though much strained over the past ten years, had enabled him to undertake the duties of administration that Gurner was impatient of, with an efficiency that had become a matter of dutiful pride with him.

Ellis's loyalty to Gurner had often been strained just short of its limits. Their disparate characters, temperaments, outlooks, principles,

G.E.H. Ellis, BA

abilities and backgrounds made them uneasy colleagues. Gurner was a man Ellis could not look up to; Ellis was a man Gurner could not dispense with. Although he could already have retired, Ellis had sufficient concern for the School, and sufficient obstinacy of spirit, to endure this almost intolerable situation.

Preparations for War

Gurner had devoted so much of his time to writing, travelling and taking part in conferences and social occasions that his Deputy had been compelled to take over virtually all the daily administration of the School. This he controlled so efficiently that the machine now continued to operate without disruption; indeed, with greater smoothness, for Ellis was now fully responsible, *de jure et de facto*. But the introduction of any administrative reforms that he may have wished to make had to give way to the needs of defence. Because of its international airport and its nearness to London, Croydon, it was predicted, would become an early target for German aerial attack, and had been declared an 'evacuation area'; this classification meant that in the event of war all schools in the town would be closed, and LEA school-children and others who wished to accompany them would be sent away to safer places in the country. Many public and independent schools in similar areas had already made arrangements to be accommodated elsewhere, either in large country mansions or by doubling up with boarding-schools.

The Governors had not really contemplated the possibility of such a move but had rather belatedly decided that the construction of blast-proof underground shelters at some distance from the buildings would afford sufficient protection. A year earlier, at the time of the Munich crises, Gurner, who was more alive to the need for air-raid precautions, had ordered the boys of the OTC to dig slit-trenches (which would have been useless for any prolonged occupation for shelter against air-raids), but had pressed for more effective measures. After the usual delays occasioned by seeking the approval of the Board of Education, September 1939 arrived with shelter accommodation for only three hundred and fifty boys. As usual, the Governors had been reluctant to commit themselves to a full course of action, and deferred ordering greater accommodation until developing emergency compelled them to. This deficiency was of little immediate importance, however, for war had been declared on 3 September, and in anticipation of air attacks all schools in 'evacuation areas' were kept closed by order of the Government.

Outbreak of War 1939

Many boys who had been expected to return to or to join the School had been evacuated at the outbreak of war to attend schools in Wales, on the South coast, or elsewhere, under local authority arrangements; others had been withdrawn and sent to boarding-schools or to America, and many families, including those whose head had been mobilised in the forces or who belonged to a firm that had been evacuated, left Croydon or its vicinity, not to return.

There had been no rush of young volunteers to enlist, as in 1914, for such action was discouraged by the government, which had already established a form of conscription, so that training units were fully occupied.

The War after all being stagnant, the Governors made several attempts to persuade the Board to allow both Schools to re-open, but it was not until 10 October that Whitgift was permitted to start its new term with three hundred and thirty-five boys, instead of the record number of eight hundred that only a few months before had been expected. By degrees, as more shelters were completed, more boys were enabled to attend, and as the re-opening of the School, together with the continued absence of aerial attack, encouraged the return of many boys from 'evacuation', there were by the end of November over five hundred on the Roll. (The Middle School, situated in a more closely built-up, and therefore more vulnerable, area, was not permitted to open until the middle of November.)

Archbishop Lang continued to take an interest in the School's progress and in January 1940 he wrote to Ellis congratulating him on the way he had 'been able to pull the School together'. In spite of difficulties, the roll of scholarships gained at Oxford and Cambridge before Christmas had struck Lang as 'most remarkable'.

After a very cautious beginning, for Ellis was not disposed to take risks if they could be avoided, School life returned to an almost normal routine within three months, and numbers rose to six hundred and sixty. To begin with, lessons had been restricted to the mornings only, so that games and other activities could take place in the afternoons, and most boys could be sent home before the early winter blackout descended, but later a rather more adventurous programme came to be followed; rugby fixtures that had been cancelled were renewed and, as the days grew longer, society meetings were allowed to take place, but for the duration of the War, any large assembly of boys in Big School or elsewhere was avoided, and loitering on the premises was strictly forbidden.

The evacuation from Dunkirk in May 1940 and the consequent fear of invasion caused some precautionary removals, and the summer term closed early. Yet the great aerial bombardment during the Battle of Britain, which opened during the summer holidays, deterred only a few from attending at the beginning of the next term.

War-time Restrictions

For the only time during the whole course of the War except for the few weeks while the shelters were being built, numbers fell below five hundred. During the winter of 1940-41 half the school day was spent in the shelters, which a year before had been used only for the occasional practice or on account of a false alarm. Lessons went on as best they could, in a chill and vitiated atmosphere, and at the end of the afternoon the decision had frequently to be taken whether to send boys home and beat the blackout, or to keep them in some degree of safety until the 'all-clear' sounded, and accept the risks of the blackout. It fortunately never happened that any boys were trapped in a shelter for the whole night as well.

The impracticability of effectively blacking-out all the School windows, so that no light should shine through during the hours of darkness and thus present a target for bombers, made it necessary for the building to be vacated at nightfall. Thereafter the only occupants were the groups of 'fire-watchers' – members of the staff who by rota kept a look-out for incendiary bombs with which they were prepared to deal by means of the primitive implements issued for the purpose: long-handled shovels and sand, buckets of water and stirrup-pumps. Fortunately they never had to take direct action with these. Their headquarters was the Art-room, one of the few places completely fitted up with black-out material; another stronghold was the Headmaster's Study – temporarily located between the Dining Hall and the Elementary Science Laboratory – which had been heavily protected with sandbags.

A sense of earnest purpose developed, work was taken seriously, and there were few disciplinary problems. As the War went on, and boys were called up for National Service immediately after their eighteenth birthday, the age at the top of the School declined. Potential scholars still worked successfully for university awards, but fewer boys decided to follow two-year advanced courses leading implicitly to university unless they were scientists, for whom alone there was some accommodation. Others might hope to attend university after the war—if they were alive, and if universities still existed. There developed a tendency for more to leave after

The Staff, 1940

L. to r., Back row: Shaw, Holden, Bennett, Potter, Labram, Stothard, Etherington, Rutherford, Newbold, Ewen, Shotton, *Middle row*: Bentley, Twiselton, Tolmie, Robinson, Hobbs, Porter, Cummings, Percy, H.A.C. Evans, Broadbent, Kelly, Deacock, I.A. Evans, Prime, *Front row*: Lockett, Fisher, Woodgate, Kitchener, Jones, Ellis, Micklewright, Musgrave, Lewis, Loving, Arnett

matriculation, in order to experience something of life outside school—and to reap the benefits of a short period of employment—before being called up.

But the abatement of aerial attack in 1941 allowed concerts, Prize-Givings and other social occasions to be revived, although if they were held at School, it was during the day. At the end of 1941 a School dance was even held, but not at the School. Speech Day now attracted no distinguished guest, and the prizes were distributed by one or other of the Governors. In April 1942 a performance of Handel's 'Messiah' was rendered in the Parish Church by a combined choir of Whitgift and Whitgift Middle boys.

The enforced shortages and limitations to free movement were educationally, as well as socially, frustrating. By 1942 text-books and stationery, when they were obtainable, were of very poor quality materials, *The Whitgiftian* had to be limited to a fifth of its normal size; sport and games equipment had to be hoarded; clothing was passed down. Unnecessary journeys (such as team visits to other schools at some distance) were unpatriotic and had consequently to be cancelled.

Despite being exposed to so much intermittent but concentrated aerial attack, including in 1944 and 1945 the assaults by the devastating V1 and V2 weapons, the School buildings sustained little damage. Ellis was himself the victim of a raid in August 1940, fortunately without suffering any serious injury, when his house was badly damaged, and he had to move out. Many houses in the vicinity were destroyed, and many of the School windows shattered; the roofs were damaged by blast and anti-aircraft shell fragments (before rugby could be played the teams would scour the pitches to pick up scraps of metal), and a high-explosive bomb was dropped on South Field, but the only direct hit that the main buildings received was from an incendiary bomb that pierced the ceiling of the Chemistry Laboratory, fortunately without exploding. The worst damage was sustained by the fives courts, which were put out of action by incendiary bombs. In January 1941 the beginning of term was delayed while attempts were made to locate and defuse a number of bombs that had fallen nearby but had failed to explode. Bomb blast was the chief cause of damage, especially after V1 and V2 raids, which damaged tiles and blew in many windows. Temporary repairs involved the replacement of the leaded lights with plain glass or by sheets of three-ply wood or of cardboard. A casualty that was only indirectly due to enemy action was the length of railing along Nottingham and Brighton Roads, which was removed in 1942 to supply seven and a half tons of iron for the war effort, and which has only recently been replaced. (It was not until 45 years later that a start was made to restore the railings by degrees; before completion the great storm of 15th October 1987 blew down, together with many other great trees, several limes, which crushed a number of lengths of the replacement.)

Notwithstanding the disruption caused by shortened terms and reduced hours, air-raid warnings and inactivity during the wait for 'all-clear' signals, external examination results maintained a reasonably high level. General Schools Certificates achieved in proportion to the number of candidates entered showed a not surprising decline, but Higher Certificate candidates actually increased in number, with a comparable pass rate. More pupils were coming to realise the need for qualifications in what would be a competitive post-war existence.

Happily, no Whitgift boy was even slightly injured as the result of enemy action, either while he was on the premises or outside, a fact that fully vindicated the Governors' decision not to move the School in 1939.* But the casualties among Old Boys in the forces were severe indeed, although not so numerous as in the First World War. The first to lose his life was Lt.-Com. S.D. Roper, R.N., who was on the battleship *Royal Oak* when it was torpedoed at Scapa Flow on 14 October 1939. His death was followed by that of one hundred and eighty-eight others who died for their country and in defence of freedom.

Reform of State Education

Ever since the implementation of the Balfour Education Act of 1902, secondary education in England had flourished only in a very restricted field, and although the grammar schools under Local Education Authorities had achieved a high reputation by 1939, the hope that secondary education worthy of the name should be extended to all the adolescent population (as was expressed in the Bryce Report of 1895) had not by that date been realised. In 1926 the Consultative Committee of the Board of Education, under the chairmanship of Sir William Hadow, of which S.O. Andrew was a member, had recommended in their *Report on the Education of the Adolescent* the introduction of secondary education for all, according to their needs. Some reorganisation along the lines suggested took place in the nineteen-thirties, but it was not until the publication of the 'Spens' *Report on Secondary Education* in 1939 that the tripartite system of grammar, technical and modern secondary schools, each to enjoy parity of esteem, was formulated.

The Butler Act

The interruption of the War prevented the proposals from being implemented, but during the course of the War itself the shortcomings of the existing system were so much exposed that all parties represented in the 'National' Government combined to produce the 'Butler' Education Act of 1944. This Act adopted many of the recommendations of the Spens Report and provided for the division of education into three grades: primary, secondary and further (now called tertiary). The term 'elementary' was abandoned; primary education would be given up to the age of eleven plus, at which age children would be selected according to their aptitude and ability to

Group-Captain John Cunningham, CBE, DSO, DFC, DL

---

* Information has recently been received that a boy lost part of a hand in picking up a 'butterfly' bomb.

proceed to one of the three types of secondary school outlined in the Report; these schools would be free to all their pupils. The leaving age would be raised to fifteen as soon as possible, and further education, it was intended, should become available to all, if not at university, training college or technical college, etc., then at part-time day-continuation schools.

When the Labour Government came to power in July 1945 they joined their predecessors in establishing the system that the Act provided for and which had come into force the previous April. This legislation had given a great deal of concern to the secondary schools outside the State system that provided courses similar to those at the maintained grammar schools, i.e. private schools, public schools and direct-grant schools (some being classifiable in both the last two categories). The public schools had first felt concern for their future independence when the Liberal Party, allied with Labour, came to office in 1906, but at this time schools of the first grade were not yet under any acquisitive eye. They survived another threat after the First World War. Some, mostly day-schools, were glad to accept the direct grant – with fears perhaps of some decline in their status but often, as was proved, with advantage to their academic standards. During the 'twenties and 'thirties a few boarding-schools had to close or amalgamate, and several had to close a boarding-house or two, but the Second World War brought the schools a renewed prosperity. Many of them were situated in 'safe' areas; mass evacuation did not make for ideal conditions of education; with fathers in the forces and mothers working, it was convenient to send children to boarding-school; while accepting the austerity of war-time, parents found they could afford to invest in education money that otherwise might have been hard to spend.

The Fleming Report

In 1943 and 1944 the two parts of the 'Fleming' Report were published by the Committee on Public Schools appointed by the President of the Board of Education (R.A. Butler) in 1942 to examine how the schools represented on the Headmasters' Conference could become more closely associated with the general educational system. Their recommendations included the abolition of fees in all grant-aided schools, and the reservation of places, day or boarding, at other schools, by LEAs, who would negotiate terms with the schools they favoured, so that a greater proportion of those classes who could not otherwise afford such an education could be accommodated. All independent schools of standing, it was hoped, would be willing to co-operate in such a scheme, but the emphasis was so much given to the benefits obtainable through the experience of boarding-school life, that it looked as if day-schools might be cast away as ballast to enable the others to soar. For various reasons the proposals failed, and in any case, one common view expressed just after the War was that the state system would become so efficient and highly esteemed that the public schools would either inevitably decline or would willingly agree to be taken over by the state.

The Fleming Report came too late to allow the Butler Act to incorporate any of its recommendations. By the Act R.A. Butler (Conservative) became the first Minister of Education; J. Chuter Ede (Labour) was Parliamentary Secretary for Education. Chuter Ede was a Governor of the Whitgift Foundation, to which he had been appointed by the Justices of the Peace for the Croydon Division in August 1944, in the place of Walton F. Turner. He took a keen interest in the affairs of the Foundation and was pleased to serve on the Schools Committee. His detailed knowledge of the Act was of great value to the Court, but it was his desire for both Schools to become absorbed in the State system. Having been a teacher in elementary schools and a prominent member of the National Union of Teachers, he could hardly have been expected to be sympathetic to the aspirations of the independent day-school, which he hoped would accept the new conditions laid down by the amended Direct Grant Regulations. Those who had been responsible for framing the Act (of which he was one) had been aware of the way the Fleming Committee was thinking, but did not altogether approve of the solutions offered.

The Direct Grant

In summer 1945, the war in Europe being over and peace-time conditions being at last in prospect, those schools that had been in receipt of the direct grant were being offered the opportunity of choosing between three courses: (i) voluntary absorption into the LEA, renouncing autonomy and the right to charge fees; (ii) independence, with a consequent increase of fees by about two thirds; (iii) the continuance of receipt of the direct grant, but with stricter reservations. Whereas, ever since the Foundation had accepted the grant for the two schools in 1919, Whitgift School had admitted ten per cent of its intake for Free Places from Croydon elementary schools, and the Middle School twenty-five per cent, the new (draft) Regulations stipulated, in return for a grant of £16 per head, the acceptance, with no increase in fees, of (a) twenty-five per cent of the entry as 'special places' from the primary schools of Croydon, paid at the full rate by the LEA, *if they should wish to take them up*, (b) twenty-five per cent 'reserved places', open to be taken up, as above, by the LEA, but with no restriction as to former place of education and (c) fifty per cent 'residuary places' at full fees or at reduced fees according to a means test, the difference between the reduced fee and the full fee being met by a further government grant.

These conditions would apparently have altered very greatly the standing and freedom of some of the schools which were confronted with the choice, and several very quickly decided to revert to independence. The Whitgift Governors, having studied Part I of the Fleming Report, which dealt with Direct Grant schools, strongly supported the minority group, led by Lord Fleming himself, which advocated that for certain schools the *status quo* should be maintained. However, they examined very closely the financial position that each choice offered would place them in. They found that if both schools were to adopt an independent status, with an increase of fees in each case of approximately two thirds, there would be a resultant deficit of £1500 per annum; if both schools were to accept the new conditions of the direct grant *and* if the Croydon Council supported them, there would be a deficit of £700; if Whitgift were to relinquish the grant and the Middle School were to retain it, there would be a surplus of £1800. It was clear that with so much in the way of repairs and restoration to attend to after the War, a budget surplus was essential, and on 3 May 1945 The Governors resolved by a considerable majority upon this last course. They were not entirely guided by the financial aspects, however, but also by the desire to maintain the positions of the two Schools in the general estimation, and by their wish not to sacrifice their Church of England connections, which might have been further weakened by legislative requirements over the teaching of religious doctrine.

This decision to revert to independence did not please Chuter Ede, who claimed to see in the Direct Grant Regulations a reflection of the Founder's intentions as expressed in the Statutes. On 11 June 1945, in the House of Commons, he pronounced his strong disapproval of his colleagues on the Governing Body: 'I would not have believed that any troglodytes so deep in the cave remained in the world . . .'. Nevertheless, he was somewhat mollified by the Governors' further proposals. Thinking it would be wrong to deny boys from the primary schools the same opportunity they had formerly been entitled to by gaining 'free places', the Governors offered the Croydon Council the right to pay for the same proportion of boys who had previously attended without payment, and after negotiation with the Minister of Education (Miss Florence Horsburgh) they allocated out of their calculated surplus a sum of £1500 yearly towards further concessionary fees.

The Governors subsequently received a strong request from the Chief Education Officer of Surrey (R. Beloe) to be allotted ten places for boys from his area, which the Court would not agree to, for they were unwilling to admit any more boys from primary schools on such terms. This decision may have been misguided. It seems not to have been so much an objection to Surrey, although the Governors were of the opinion that it was Croydon boys only who should be thus admitted (even then there remained a strictly parochial view of the Foundation's purpose), as a reluctance to accept more boys from LEA primary schools.

At this time these schools were increasing their reputation for good teaching; the war had helped to reduce class-distinctions; there existed a greater willingness after shared adversity to co-operate in the development of a more opportunistic social order (although the recommendations of the Fleming Report had not met with general acclaim); many parents, after the hardships of war and the burdens of taxation, had no course but to use the primary schools; others yet might rather send their children to the local primary school than pay for them to attend such private preparatory schools as had with difficulty survived the war and whose prospects were at best uncertain. Boys selected from Surrey would have been much above the average in ability, and the larger area would have produced many candidates; in the end they were accepted by other schools, including Dulwich and KCS, who cast their net wider than their immediate parish. Indeed there were numerous cases of Surrey boys being offered fee-paying places at Whitgift, which were turned down because of more attractive offers elsewhere.

In all these negotiations and decisions, James Marshall (OW) (Chairman of the Court of Governors from January 1945 to March 1970), took the leading part, in which he was constantly supported by the majority of the Governors, by Ellis and the majority of his Staff, and by such members of the Committee of the Old Whitgiftian Association as were then available to do so.

The Common Room

In January 1945 a Common Room Society was formed. No such organisation had previously existed, and there had been little shared social activity. The Staff, though not unfriendly, were divided by age and outlook, and felt little sense of community. The older men were deferred to; they expected to exercise certain privileges or powers, as departmental heads or house-masters; most people went their own ways. The young men appointed by Gurner were nearly all on active service, but a group of men in their thirties, some of them of recent appointment, decided that barriers should be broken down and a sense of comradeship promoted, at least among those whose careers lay before them, especially now that the end of the war was in prospect. A Committee, with Chairman, Secretary and Treasurer, was elected.

The proponents of the Society had also their own interests in view. There had been no easy way of gathering Staff opinion or of laying corporate views before the Headmaster and the Governors; indeed such action would have been regarded on all sides as inexpedient. But the provisions of the Education Act of 1944, whether they might be advantageous or not to the interests of the School, could certainly jeopardise the salaries and the conditions of service of the Staff. Some members were unenthusiastic for change, because under the published terms for reversion to independent status, they would stand to lose in superannuation benefits. (This hazard was removed within a couple of years.)

The Chairman (E.E. Kitchener) very properly reported the formation of the Society to the Headmaster, who was reluctant to pass on the news to the Governors, for he considered 'that as the relationship of the Governing Body and the Staff was at present very friendly, he did not think that now was the correct moment to inform them ... of the organisation, but he would inform them at an opportune moment.'

At the few events, such as Prize-Giving and Founder's Day, when Governors and Staff were both present, the two parties were certainly on good, but necessarily remote, terms; during wartime these functions allowed little opportunity for personal contact or communication. Indeed, association between Governors and Staff had never been customary, and 'friendly relationships' was something of an over-statement, Ellis alone having occasion to meet the Governors when they discussed school affairs. Francis Allen, Chairman of the Court from January 1937 until his resignation in January 1945 shortly before his death, had taken a paternal interest in the School while he was living at Haling Cottage, but had for some while allowed much of his responsibility to devolve upon the man who was to become his successor (James Marshall). It seems that Ellis, who enjoyed little compatability with many members of the Governing Body, wished to avoid displeasing the new Chairman, who was a determined autocrat.

End of the War: Ellis's Resignation

The end of the War was so promptly followed by the steady return of boys and their families, by members of the Staff who had been on active service, and by a gradual approximation to peace-time conditions, that in January 1946 Ellis felt that he could give notice of his wish to retire in the summer. In sending in his resignation to

Presentation to G.E.H. Ellis on his retirement, July, 1946
L. to r.: M. F. Adams, D.S. Anderson (Second Prefect), G.E.H. Ellis, D.N. Richmond (Head Prefect),
R.W. Ferrier (Head Prefect, September 1946)

the Chairman of the Governors, he confessed to no feeling of diminution of his faculties, and indeed none was evident, but he thought it 'right to make way for fresh blood to cope with the changing conditions of the immediate future'.

Ellis's great work of directing smoothly the School during the War could well have taxed the energies of a much younger man, who would not have enjoyed, however, the advantages of the local knowledge and long experience possessed by Ellis. He was now sixty-seven and had carried heavy responsibilities with courage and without complaint. Although something of a valetudinarian before the War, he gave in to no pressures upon his health during it, but seemed to derive strength, determination and obstinacy in the face of difficulties, his behaviour being indeed characteristic of the British nation at the time. He was inclined to be cautious whenever any decision concerning school activities was involved, for he felt himself personally responsible for every boy who might be on the school premises. Like Andrew he was loath to delegate, and until the end remained Housemaster of Cross's, with which he had been identified for thirty-seven years, and also Editor-in-Chief of *The Whitgiftian*, an office he had held for almost as long. But many of his heads of departments were almost equally experienced and they too, years after their entitlement to retire, continued until younger men, returned from war service, could take over from them. Thus at the end of 1946, Ellis was joined in retirement by C.J. Fisher, E.E. Kitchener and C.S. Musgrave, each well advanced towards his seventieth birthday.

Ellis's philosophy of education followed, quite understandably, that of Andrew. He too believed in a broadly based general curriculum without specialisation up to School Certificate standard in a profounder academic training for the brightest boys after that time, and in the pre-eminent value of the Classics, but he was sympathetic to those who did not wish to follow an advanced course of that kind but required a more vocational training. In these views he did not differ greatly from Gurner or most of the educationists of the day, but although he encouraged interest in the arts and similar serious pleasures and occupations, he admitted, 'valuable as these subsidiary subjects are and much to be encouraged for developing boys' individuality, they should not be allowed to encroach on the main task of a school, which is work and games'. This apparent approval of old-fashioned 'athleticism' is perhaps understandable when his own particular gifts are considered. The great enjoyment and comradeship that he himself derived from games he always wanted to be experienced by others, and he encouraged the boy who was not greatly gifted athletically to take part in House and School games, so that there occurred to many boys the opportunity to perform useful service of this kind, especially in their last year or so at School, when they enjoyed the extra confidence that experience and maturity could give. Like Andrew, he did not deeply regret the discontinuance of dramatic representations, or of expeditions, trips and outings which provided, he thought, experiences of only limited true cultural value. Although reluctant to sacrifice his own modest comforts, he was quite convinced that youth needed to learn how much discomfort and hardship it could endure without complaining, a not unrealistic attitude during war-time.

Like other men who had served the same school for four decades he was known and remembered by most of his pupils as a senior and authoritative figure, but in his youth – before the First World War – his athletic interests and capacities were self-evident; he coached the First XV for fifteen years and although seldom appearing on the cricket field, except in the annual match between the First XI and the Masters, he continued to play tennis for many years more. Even before Andrew's retirement he was responsible for much of the Classical Sixth's teaching and until his retirement he committed himself to coaching the Classics Scholarship candidates.

A member of his Classical Sixth has written of him:

By temperament he always appeared calm and equable, firm but not stern and never sarcastic. He was a good teacher, scholarly, clear and painstaking. By his own example he set a goal before us towards which we seemed to be impelled more by our own striving than by being driven. He was essentially conservative by nature and experience, and life taught him no other creed. He did not create affairs or allow himself to become involved in the partisan stresses and enthusiasms of the life of the Staff of a great School. At the same time his great love for Whitgift and his dedication to boys' education kept him fresh throughout the decades of his teaching life, and he was always sympathetic towards the new outlooks and needs of succeeding generations of boys, from the youngest to the oldest. (G.W. Labram, 1925-34).

He survived more than twenty years of retirement, mainly in the company of his wife whose death, three years before his own, was a great shock to him. They had no children, and his years of solitude were not happy ones. He had developed no personal ties with other members of his staff, and as a retired Headmaster, he naturally kept aloof from any suspicion of interference with the affairs of the School he had served for so long.

11. E.A.G. Marlar and Post-War Opportunities

E.A.G. Marlar

The Governors decided that they must have, as a successor to Ellis, a man already experienced in the running of a school, and one whose career had not been interrupted by war service, so their choice of candidates to recommend to Archbishop Fisher was to some extent limited to those in their early forties. (Fisher, it should be remembered, had himself been a distinguished Headmaster, having succeeded William Temple, not only in 1945 as Archbishop, but also, in 1915, as Head Master of Repton; he was well experienced in selecting men for scholastic posts.) The selection by the Governors and the Archbishop was made easier by the interest shown by the Rt. Rev. E.S. Woods, Bishop of Lichfield, who, as Vicar and Bishop of Croydon, had been a Governor of the Whitgift Foundation from 1927 to 1937. Without his persuasion, the Headmaster of King Edward VI School, Lichfield, might not have applied for the post, and the School would have missed the leadership of E.A.G. Marlar, who was already 45 at this time.

Geoffrey Marlar had been educated at Brighton College under Canon W.R. Dawson, and at Selwyn College, Cambridge, where, after taking the History Tripos, he took a further degree in law. However, on coming down from Cambridge, he engaged in teaching; his experience included the post of Sixth Form Master at Worksop under F.J. Shirley (later the celebrated Head Master of King's School, Canterbury), followed by the Head Mastership of Moulton Grammar School, Lincolnshire. He had considerable knowledge of boarding-schools, for his last two posts had involved also the personal responsibility for conducting the 'School' boarding-house.

He was also accustomed to living in school premises, a mode of life he thought right and proper for a Headmaster and which he was anxious to continue when he should come to Whitgift. Haling Cottage seemed to him admirably suited for a Headmaster's residence, but it had never been occupied as such, for it had been declined by Gurner, and Ellis had never thought of moving from his own house. After its purchase by the Foundation in 1920 Haling Cottage had been occupied by a series of tenants, including Francis Allen, Chairman of the Governors, who died early in 1945. Thereafter, the house had been let to the Corporation as an old people's club, the lease of which would not expire until summer 1948. In the Michaelmas Term of that year Marlar and his family moved in, having spent the previous two years in some discomfort in a flat at the earlier Head Master's House, built for Brodie in Wellesley Road, and last occupied in that capacity by Gurner.

When he arrived to take up his duties at Whitgift, Marlar found a school that was eager to recover its former vigour and to expand its activities after the restrictions of the war years. Although the period of austerity was not entirely over, there were now plenty of opportunities for boys and young masters to grasp. All the members of the Staff who had been serving in the forces had now returned, the temporary staff had departed, and the over-age men were being replaced by young men whose teaching careers had started no earlier than just before the War. Yet there remained a solid core of men of middle age, now to be heads of departments, who added a valuable stability and helped to maintain creditable academic standards. Among them were W. Clifford Lewis (Physics), J.H. Newbold (French), A.H. Ewen (who was promptly appointed by

E.A.G. Marlar, MBE, MA

Marlar to the post of Careers Master), A.H. Holden (Classics), H.E. Parr (Mathematics), W.D. Hussey (History), Dr. C.T. Prime (Biology) and R. Morris Thomas (Chemistry).

There was also Ll.J. Jones who, having been Ellis's deputy, was in a position to give valuable service in advising the new Headmaster in some of the difficulties that confronted him, but after being unwell for some months he fell severely ill early in 1947 and died during the summer term. Ewen was appointed to succeed him and supported Marlar most efficiently and loyally during the rest of the latter's régime; his advice was sound and was always listened to, for Ewen had a particular interest in educational theory and practice, and an understanding of Sixth Form requirements which perhaps extended beyond Marlar's own compass.

Thus Marlar was in the fortunate position of finding a community responsive to stimulus. The ease with which he got to know the people connected with the School—boys, staff, parents, Old Boys and Governors—was increased by his interest in sport, for he was a keen and knowledgeable player of team games. This interest, which extended to all School activities, was genuine and undisguised, and he was respected for it. He was anxious not only to improve the standard of games, but also to expand other out-of-school activities, such as drama, societies, travel abroad and particularly music, just as soon as conditions should permit. With this expansion in view, he sought a lively balance between academic qualifications, athletic talent, and social qualities in the assistants he appointed, many of whom continued to serve the School vigorously for the rest of their teaching careers.

One of Marlar's first actions was to consult the heads of departments about their requirements for staffing, equipment and accommodation, whose provision he hoped might not be long delayed. But at this time priority was given to the restoration of war-damaged buildings and to the replacement of destroyed housing and factories; additional buildings for an independent school that had suffered little damage must wait until the Ministry of Works would grant a licence. Maintenance licences were obtainable from the Borough Valuer for essential repairs and redecoration to the fabric, which had been neglected for many years; only a small part of this cost was reclaimable from the War Damage Commission. Certain internal adaptations were possible, including the relocation of the Headmaster's Study to the room designated for this purpose by the architects.* Other improvements necessary for the School's better administration included the provision of a First Aid Room (non-existent even during war-time!) by dividing up the Waiting Room, permanent stage fittings in Big School, better equipment in the kitchens, the

---

* Gurner had preferred to use the room at the NE end of the upper corridor, now used by the Classical Sixth. (That accounts for its panelling – so noticeably absent from the walls of the Headmaster's present study.) Its position – with a view over the approach drive – was supposed to render him less accessible to casual callers, including Governors; it also enabled him, unannounced, to walk about the School and see what was going on. Ellis had chosen to set up permanently in the room he had taken as Deputy Head's office in 1931, which had been intended for a musical practice area, but never used for this purpose. He stayed there throughout the War, for it was more easily given protection against bomb-blast and similar damage. When Marlar moved out after a few uncomfortable months, it was converted to a biological lecture room, which was in turn absorbed into the approach to the Masters' Dining Room when that was built in 1967.

conversion of an air-raid shelter into additional premises for the CCF, an extended telephone system and room for extra staff in the office.

Another of Marlar's innovations was the personal record card, maintained since 1947 for every boy in the School. Until that year the only records of a Whitgiftian's career maintained by the School were his entries in the Admission Register, the printed School Rolls and the Valete pages of *The Whitgiftian* showing his form on leaving, his sporting achievements, career in the OTC and any university award gained. There was no reference to any university entrance or to a career taken up, although some details might be gleaned from the perusal of magazines. The record-cards provided a helpful reference to a boy's career, so that his progress through the School could be monitored, and an interest in him encouraged among the members of the Staff who became responsible for him in various ways at different times.

In the same year an improved service for Founder's Day was instituted, whereby members of the School became more involved, an annual service sheet was issued, and the Captains of the two Schools laid their commemorative wreaths against the Founder's Tomb.

Games Organisation

With the post-war return to normal activities, it became necessary to codify in detail the sports and games coming under the control of the Games Committee, which since the institution of the House system in 1905 had regulated the fixture lists for inter-school and inter-house events, and had settled the principles of the inter-house competition. The Committee comprised, under the Headmaster (or the Second Master, when Ellis held this post), the Housemasters and House Captains, the Officer Commanding OTC, the masters in charge of rugby, cricket and fives, and the captains of the two 'major' sports – rugby and cricket (some of these offices were held in plurality). The 'major' sports and the 'minor' sports – athletics, fives, shooting and swimming – were the only inter-school games for which school colours were awarded. The prestigious first XV and first XI blazers, caps and ties were keenly competed for; of the minor sports, each had its distinctive colour as a background to a badge, which was also greatly valued.

The inter-house championship gave rise to intense rivalry, and the 'cock' House would display in its House-room a large framed photograph inscribed with the achievements of its victorious members, and would hold a celebratory dinner. This custom, like many others, fell into disuse during World War I, although there were several occasions in the 1920s and 1930s when it was revived by some successful house.

Marlar was a great supporter of the House system, which had enabled boys who were not chosen for a School team to have the opportunity to represent their House, to gain House colours and sometimes to display promise that was to lead to selection for the School. Marlar expanded the competition to include hockey when it became a recognised school game, house relays, CCF participation, musical performance, and achievement in the class-room, judged by the results in internal and external examinations and of scholarships gained to the universities.

Later, fencing and other sports were included. The addition of an element of academic competition was rewarded with the 'Bragg' Trophy, presented in 1949 by R.S. and M.W. Bragg in memory of their brothers, Lt. E.W. Bragg, RNVR and Lt. Col. H.V. Bragg, M.C., who lost their lives in World War I and II respectively. It was a large piece of Victorian silverware originally won by a racing Bragg at Goodwood in 1888; unhappily it was burgled from the School in 1955.

Lord Tedder presents the Prizes, March 1947
L. to r.: J.D. Lovis, Professor of Botany, University of Christchurch, NZ; Marshal of the RAF Lord Tedder (OW); A.H. Ewen (Second Master)

Sporting Successes

The late 1940s were a time of much great accomplishment. Success in the academic field (ten open awards at Oxford and Cambridge and three at London) in 1949 was matched by good results in games, which were echoed by achievements after boys had left school. Over the three years 1947 to 1949 there were in the School many exceptionally gifted games-players who later made their mark in many fields, by no means limited to sport. Besides a Captain of Cambridge rugby and International (I.D.S. Beer), a Cambridge Cricket Blue and Test Cricketer (R. Subba Row), an English Amateur Golf Champion and Walker Cup player (I. Caldwell), a British chess Champion (L.W. Barden) and an Olympic rifleman (S.B.O. Cranmer), there were more than a dozen who became county rugby players, a dozen others who won blues or half-blues for rugby fives, boxing, fencing, athletics, swimming, chess and lawn-tennis, with several others who represented their county or university at various sports.

It seems only natural that games in which boys and young men can display a healthy prowess and achieve a very high degree of skill at an early age should receive general acclaim. In all other pursuits mastery comes at a later age, after a long period of training and varied experience. The danger of games-worship may not be a very real one at a day-school, but the remedy in any such case lies in the provision, in addition, of amenities for other worth-while pursuits, and the granting of status to senior boys for achievement at other activities, academic, musical, artistic and social.

There was no doubt an unusual coincidence of talent, fostered by the young men in charge of games and by Marlar's interest and encouragement, but there was also in the School at that time a profound sense of comradeship, illustrated by the regular well-attended reunions of the former prefects of 1948-9 under the then Captain of the School, I.D.S. Beer.

Domini C.C.

A new sense of corporate spirit was also in evidence in the Masters' Common Room. The Society held meetings, both business and social, several times a term, and matters of direct or indirect interest to the School were discussed. In 1949 the first of many Christmas parties was held, and in May 1950, M. Etherington being the main instigator, the Domini Cricket Club was founded, to play evening matches during the summer term in preparation for the revived Masters' Match (soon to involve two elevens) against the School. These activities increased in the Staff a

Prefects 1948–49
L. to r., *Back row*: Newton, Johnson, Stokes, Chitty, Lovis, *Middle row*: Kidwell, Walsh, Harrison, Black, Lewis, Priest, Subba Row, *Front row*: Marsh, Tilly, Lindblom, Beer, E.A.G. Marlar Esq, Harris, Price, Holmes, Forrest

sense of involvement in the life and purpose of the School.

The following year saw the introduction of hockey as a first-choice game during the Lent term, but it was not until the appointment of R.C. Schad, an Oxford blue and England International, to the Staff that hockey came to enjoy any consistent reputation. The game was becoming popular in the schools, for not only did its skills provide an opportunity for those who did not shine at rugby, but it also came as a welcome relief to many rugby players whose hard training during the previous term had been relaxed at Christmas. For many years rugby during the Lent term internal game had been an entirely and had given way in mid-February to athletics and fives; indeed, during a bad winter there may have been no rugby played at all during the Lent term. With hockey, hard grounds were but a slight problem, and because many of the School's traditional opponents at other games had also taken up hockey, external fixtures were not difficult to arrange.*

Consequences of the 'Butler' Act

The abolition of fees in local grammar schools empowered by the Act of 1944 took place in 1947. Thereby all state school education became free, and one obstacle to parity of esteem among the schools in the tripartite system was removed. Yet the grammar schools now enjoyed an increasing reputation for academic achievement.

The prospects for independent education were hard to forecast, but they seemed not to be favourable. After the war, the reconstruction of buildings damaged or destroyed was a drain upon resources; all schools had to make shift to some extent. Income Tax remained high during an extended period of austerity. Fewer parents, it seemed, would be able to afford the independent education that they might have experienced themselves or that they aspired to for their children. To impecunious parents it now seemed extravagant to turn down opportunities at good provided schools, whose reputation was increasing, and for which new buildings and extensions were now being lavishly constructed or planned. Indeed, it was put about that these schools would become so efficient that the public school system would vanish through inability to compete. In fact they obtained an increasing proportion of university places, now available with state financial help.

Many minor public schools did find themselves in difficulties. Those in places of safety had maintained numbers during the war, but some others were closing boarding-houses and selling off property to make ends meet. Those suitably situated accepted an increased intake of day pupils, for the state system was still regarded with doubt by parents who believed that something better was available for purchase, especially for those children who had failed to pass the selection test for entrance to a grammar school.

In due course the economy revived, and investment in education was seen to be of first importance in providing for one's children, on whose behalf many parents continued to make great sacrifices. When building restrictions were

Chess Team, winners of London Schools League and British Chess Federation's Shields, 1947; L.W. Barden, Captain

---

* Attempts had been made in the eighteen-eighties to establish a second winter game. At different times hockey and lacrosse had attracted a few players, but until adequate playing-fields could be provided and a permanent competent coach appointed to the staff, such experiments were doomed to failure.

relaxed, most independent schools constructed additions to serve the new emphasis on science and other practical subjects, and to provide better accommodation generally. These new buildings were usually the result of appeals to old boys and charitable trusts; parents also contributed through increased fees, which included an allocation towards such capital investment.

Socialist Policy

But over all the public schools was cast the shadow of a socialist government's avowed determination eventually to abolish fee-paying education of any kind. All Labour manifestos included this intention with their general policy – already being vigorously pursued – of nationalising transport, industry, power, banks and any other activity that formed the basis of the economy. The schools were confronted with difficult decisions. Should they flounder on as best they could before submitting to inevitable expropriation, or should they fight on defiantly and, if unable to avoid capture, provide their captors with a splendid booty whose glory would live at least in record? The danger was not yet acute, for the cost to the Exchequer of funding these thousands of independent schools of all kinds would be enormous, but the danger remained for many years in the minds of most governing bodies.

Whitgift, however, appeared to be in a strong position during these immediate post-war years. Not having been evacuated, it had suffered little diminution in numbers; war damage had been minimal; there was no shortage of applicants for admission and the 'bulge' in the birthrate helped to increase demand. But there was a danger that its reputation might decline without enlargement of its buildings and the improvement of its equipment and amenities. However, the Foundation's resources and the goodwill of parents and old boys might be thought capable of going a long way towards fulfilling these needs.

Such hopes were, however, not yet capable of fulfilment. Permits for the use of scarce materials and labour were not easy to obtain, especially in private cases where any additions might still be regarded as a luxury. Even when these shortages were relieved, the money was not readily available.

Marlar's Policies

As any other new Headmaster would, Marlar made a survey of the ways he wished to improve the working of the School, but he realised that the process of improvement might be slow unless he could persuade his Governors to adopt a vigorous policy of expansion. There was little money available for renewals and extensions to buildings already proving inadequate, for although necessary retrenchment during the War had resulted in some economies, rising costs, including increased salary scales, had not been matched by increased revenue. The relinquishment of the direct grant had to be compensated for by a large increase in fees which did little towards meeting increased expenditure. Fearful of criticism for restoring the School's independent status, the Governors were chary of making a further large demand for fees, but, hopeful of an increased income from endowments within a few years, decided to wait for a while before planning any large-scale development. That the School could show itself successful in so many fields encouraged them to think that improved facilities were not yet urgent; they also regarded the buildings as still almost brand-new and therefore not in real need of improvement or addition. (Nearly half the Governors had been in office before the move to Haling Park and were loath to believe that the design they had approved of could so soon become deficient.)

Proposed Boarding House (Bagbie)

There was in fact not much that Marlar could ask for and hope to obtain speedily, for there were still stringent regulations over the licensing of any building project. Quite early on he had deplored the absence of a chapel and a boarding-house, for to him a day-school could never be quite the equal of a boarding-school in effectiveness or reputation. (The absence of any accommodation for boarders when the School moved to Haling Park had disappointed many OWs who, living abroad or at some distance, would have liked their sons to follow them.) In January 1945 one of the Governors, Captain Bruce Humfrey, had proposed that a boarding-house should be established; he received strong support from his colleagues, and a special committee to consider the matter was formed. When Marlar learned of the existence of this committee, which had not produced any findings, he pressed for action, and the Court resolved to try to secure suitable premises near the School. There were several Victorian mansions in their own grounds of an acre or more in Haling Park Road and Pampisford Road within a quarter of a mile of the School, and when the most suitable of all, Bagbie House, actually adjacent to the School premises, came on the market in January 1949, the Governors immediately decided to buy it. Its purchase would also ensure that no other building development should take place on a site that was of great value to the School. Since there was little prospect for a few years of a building permit either to convert the house or to erect other buildings, Marlar proposed that it should be used for staff accommodation and for music and art purposes.

Music

An early opportunity had arisen for Marlar to allocate to music a greater share in the curriculum. Since 1871 there had been a succession of only three 'Song Masters':* Edward Griffith (1871-99), H.L. Balfour (1899-1933) and Dr. George Oldroyd (1933-1947). The Song Master's duties had required twice-weekly visits to the School (and also to the Middle School) to teach singing to the Juniors during school hours; during one lunch-hour per week the Choir would practise under him, and on another afternoon the Orchestra, formed by Oldroyd in 1934.

Keeping musical interest alive had been a difficult struggle with so little time for teaching and for practice. During the War the Orchestra nearly succumbed altogether, although the Choir, which under Oldroyd devoted most of its time and energies to learning hymns (some of them attractive tunes of his own composition) and other pieces of a strongly religious nature, had

*It has been erroneously stated in *The History of Whitgift Grammar School* (1892), p.97, that the Founder in his Will made provision for a song-master, yet on the same page Edward Griffith is declared to have been the first of these appointments. At that time the view of the past was so nebulous that almost any piece of guess-work passed muster if expressed with apparent authority.

Bagbie House, 1959

tackled an increasingly difficult range of choral work. When Oldroyd announced his wish to retire in 1947, Marlar saw the chance of appointing a full-time musician, but the Governors could not yet be easily persuaded that such an emphasis on music was desirable. They wished to continue the existing arrangement of a part-time visiting master, so the first Director of Music, J.S. Odom, was, to begin with, required to teach Mathematics in the Junior School and some music. However, within a very short time, when he had shown how responsive his pupils were to his enthusiasm, he was permitted to give his whole time to music, and to arrange instruction in all instruments of the orchestra by a team of visiting masters during school hours. Even by the end of his first term sufficient impact had been made for the conventional form of the concert to be abandoned. Instead of the traditional deafening tumult of the Corps of Drums in conclusion, there was a performance of *Trial by Jury*, in which for the first time Choir and Orchestra joined forces with the Dramatic Society to produce something of popular appeal to an audience. This was followed by many Gilbert and Sullivan operettas produced by I.F. Smith, which were performed with verve and confidence – at first regularly but later at greater intervals – over twenty-five years. After the first run of Gilbert and Sullivan, several other operas, including Offenbach and even Mozart, were successfully attempted, and in 1966 a home-made opera was put on.

Between 1954 and 1981 the House Music

Competition provided further opportunities for boys to sing and play before an audience and also, not least important, to listen critically. In 1954 eighty boys were learning to play a musical instrument; by 1988 the number had more than doubled. These small beginnings have resulted in one of the most important departments, with four full-time music staff and a dozen or so visiting teachers, housed in one of the finest music annexes in the country.

History of Science

In 1947 a course in the History and Philosophy of Science was introduced at Whitgift for all second-year sixth-formers, in order to give them an awareness of the importance of scientific study. During the war and subsequently, the inadequacy of pre-war scientific education in Britain and the ignorance of scientific matters among arts students had been strikingly revealed. Many scientists themselves were ignorant of the development even of their own speciality. Few historians understood any science; fewer scientists had any interest in history. At a time of great expansion in the study of science at the universities, certain senior members of the School staff thought that a knowledge of the history of science might appeal to inquiring minds and form a valuable element in general education.

These thoughts, initiated by A.H. Ewen, C.T. Prime and H.E. Parr, anticipated the 'Two Cultures' debate between C.P. Snow and F. Leavis in 1959.

In 1952 Cambridge introduced a syllabus for a GCE O-level paper for Sixth Forms, and Whitgift provided all eight candidates from the third-year Sixth, six of whom were successful. For a few years the paper attracted increasing, yet still small, numbers from other schools as well, but the experiment never became a great success, owing to the problems of staffing, lack of suitable text-books, the resistance of pupils to studying a subject that encroached upon the time they were willing to devote to their main subjects, and perhaps most importantly, the lack of support from school science staffs.

An account of the experiment, by A.H. Ewen, is given in *History of Science*, Vol. II, 1963.

O.W.A. Day

In 1948 increased importance was given to Old Boys' Day, which had remained much in its same form since it had been established forty years before to coincide with the annual cricket match between the School and an Old Whitgiftian XI. This match had been virtually the only attraction, apart from the opportunity of meeting one's contemporaries, other OWs and former masters, but

'HMS Pinafore', 1948

Memorial Service, OWA Day 1958

it was obvious, from the numbers that attended in 1947 after an absence of so many years, that this could be an occasion to make much of, when many Old Boys could be encouraged to compete at a variety of sports as well as to see old friends. A strange and inexplicable custom had arisen whereby wreaths were laid on the War Memorial on Founder's Day. Marlar suggested that a far more appropriate day for this ceremony would be OWA Day, so on the last Saturday in June 1948 proceedings began with a Commemorative Service at the War Memorial, and wreaths were laid on behalf of OWs, the Governors and the School; a marquee for tea was erected below the Terrace, three cricket matches were played, the Range was open for a shooting competition for all-comers, and the OW Cricket Club held a Ball in the evening. From these changes have developed the elaborations of OWA Day at the present time. Swimming, fencing and tennis contests between School and OW teams were introduced, together with exhibitions of various kinds, musical interludes, Beating Retreat by the Corps of Drums, and a barbecue, at first organised by the Scouts. After Saturday morning school was abandoned in 1974, and boys' attendance was no longer compulsory, a number of changes took place, not all on account of this alteration. Although for some years seven simultaneous cricket matches were played, there came a time when fewer OW cricketers could be found to play, for the commitment of the OWCC and other clubs to league cricket meant that fixtures arranged for them had to be fulfilled on OWA Day. However, boys and parents became more involved, at first through a Junior School v Parents' match, and later, after the formation of the Whitgift School Association (WSA), by parents' participation in fund-raising activities (including the barbecue) on Puntabout, and in providing tea for several hundred people in the Andrew quadrangle.

Innovations

Other ways of infusing *esprit de corps* were the encouragement of competitive sport and the formation of new clubs and societies, especially in the middle part of the School.

The increase in numbers since the School had left North End had resulted in such an overcrowding of the five Houses that administration had become unwieldy, and fewer boys had the chance of representing their House; in September 1950 a new House—Andrew's, named after the begetter of the House system—was formed. At the same time the Junior Houses: 'A', 'B' and 'C', were given more evocative names: Ash, Beech and Cedar.

The General Certificate of Education

At the Prize-Giving ceremony in March 1949 Marlar expressed his anxiety about the effects of the forthcoming changes in the external public examinations; the old School Certificate examination, which gave, through the obtaining of credits in certain subjects, exemption from university Matriculation, would in 1951 yield to the General Certificate of Education, to be taken at three levels: 'O'—Ordinary; 'A'—Advanced; 'S'—Scholarship. By the regulations no boy would be permitted to sit for any paper before the age of sixteen. Now it was perfectly evident, through previous results in the School Certificate examination, that many boys below this age would have no difficulty at all in passing several of these papers. Indeed, in 1948 out of twenty-three candidates from the 'fast stream' form, Remove AI, twenty-one had obtained matriculation exemption; their average age was fifteen years two months; not one of them would have been allowed to sit in 1950, when the lower age-limit would first be imposed. After some frustration and misgivings on the part of such boys, a broadened curriculum was drawn up, and specialisation delayed for a year. When after a few years the age restriction was removed, no great alteration was made to this more enlightened course, and indeed a more sensible balance of non-specialist studies in the Sixth Form has ever since been insisted upon.

The Cold War

Each year was offering opportunities for development, which Marlar took advantage of when he could, but 1950 was over-shadowed by the 'cold war' and the Russian blockade of Berlin, which was relieved only by the RAF and the USAAF flying in supplies. National anxiety was aroused over the possibility of conflict with our former ally, so preparations were made once more for state schools in the metropolitan area to be evacuated, but independent schools were left to make their own arrangements. Marlar negotiated successfully with the Headmaster of Christ's Hospital for Whitgift's reception there if the necessity should arise.

Unveiling of World War II Memorial by Major-General W.S. Tope CB, CBE (OW), 29 May 1949

Academic Standards

A little after this time, however, some criticism was levelled at the School's decline in academic achievement. Although there had been a 'fast stream' for many years, there had never been a deliberate selection at an early age of boys to be crammed for the Scholarship stakes; but open awards were becoming harder to win, and the good results of 1949 were not being repeated. It looked, too, as if things might be getting worse. In 1953, out of the top twenty candidates in the entrance examination, no fewer than fourteen had withdrawn to accept scholarships or free places in other schools; these were all potential university scholars. Two years before, the fees had been raised, by almost fifty per cent, to £75 per annum, which was still below what many independent London schools were charging. Yet this expenditure was found by many parents hard to justify, when the education provided by direct-grant and local grammar schools seemed to be little, if anything, inferior.

The Butler Act had resulted in the establishment of many more secondary grammar schools, while the founding of new universities, the promise of more to come, and the financial support given to students, encouraged the state grammar schools to expand their sixth forms and enlarge their horizons, so that the predicted threat to the independent schools seemed to be a real one.

Marlar had very definite views about how his school should develop to meet this challenge. In a memorandum to the Governors dated November 1953 he refers bitterly to financial stringency and to the loss of the best candidates. A fee-paying school, he said, if it was to survive, must offer more than an LEA or a direct-grant school. Whitgift, having received no additions or improvements worth mentioning since it had been built nearly a quarter of a century before, could not be satisfied with the status of a glorified grammar school, and parents wanted to feel they were buying something more than just a name. At present he could find that the only advantages that the School enjoyed were its beautiful situation, the goodwill of many Old Boys, and the loyalty and efficiency of its Staff. To enhance its reputation, the Governors must be prepared to spend money in ways that would increase the School's efficiency and its attractions. He proposed that more entrance scholarships should be awarded to attract potential scholars, who would set the intellectual pace and later achieve academic distinction; well-qualified staff must be attracted by a generous salary scale (in some instances the Whitgift scale had actually fallen below Burnham), and there must be an increase in the staff-to-pupil ratio, so that numbers in forms could be generally reduced. He also recommended that school projects, such as a survey of a part of Iceland by a team of botanists, biologists and geologists, should receive a subsidy, but his most expensive requirements were additional buildings. At many other schools generous scholarships were being awarded to attract boys of high academic potential, salary scales were increased, and building schemes were put in hand. Much of the cost, if it could not be found from appeals to Old Boys or to other sources of funds, was passed on to parents by raising the fees, without any noticeable opposition or falling-off in numbers. Although he desired a chapel and a boarding-house, for at this time Marlar believed the School's prosperity would lie in its development on the boarding side, he thought that these were not now essential for success, so priority should be given to the improvement of existing, and the provision of new, teaching facilities. These were becoming increasingly urgent, owing to the steadily rising numbers in the Sixth Form. Marlar therefore recommended the construction of a separate Junior School, which would release other accommodation, besides removing the problems involved in running a school with an age-range of ten to nineteen years; he also desired a music school, a swimming-pool, and squash and tennis courts. Also very important was the provision of living accommodation for young masters, who were finding it increasingly difficult to afford to buy anywhere to live.

Sir James Marshall

By this time, James Marshall, as Chairman of the Governors, was approaching the height of his power and authority. His services to local government, which included not only his work for Croydon, but also the development of the New Town of Crawley, had been acknowledged with a

Sir James Marshall, DL, JP

knighthood in the Coronation Honours. He had first been elected to the Council in 1928, had been Mayor of Croydon in 1945 and was now Leader of the Council. As a Whitgift Governor since 1931 and especially since being elected Chairman in 1945, he had not only assumed much of the responsibility for day-to-day administration* but he had also achieved a dominance over many of the other Governors, who were over-awed by his mastery in negotiation, his skill in dealing with complex matters, and his ruthlessness with opponents. Few of them were able to devote as much time and energy to the Foundation's affairs as he could (although his knowledge of educational matters was far from profound). They were content to allow him considerable freedom of decision and action in matters in which they were comparatively unpractised, and they dutifully approved most of the Committees' reports.

Together with his fellow Tory Councillors, Marshall strove to reduce the borough's expenditure and to maintain a stable rate, but he unnecessarily extended these principles to the conduct of the Schools' finances, hoping to gain the approval of Whitgift parents by restraining increases in fees at a time of considerable inflation. Year after year he would reiterate his policy at Prize-Giving, not always, one felt, after consultation with the Headmaster or with his colleagues, but with the intention of presenting a *fait accompli*. There were other interests also, to whose advantage this policy was directed. Several members of the Court of Governors were also Croydon councillors. In accordance with the Foundation's Scheme, now amended by the Ministry of Education after Whitgift's relinquishment of the direct grant, the Croydon Education Committee were paying the fees of the 10% of pupils who were admitted through the 11+ examination. At Whitgift Middle 50% were admitted and paid for; their fees at £27 per annum in 1952 were the lowest of any direct grant school in the country. It was cheaper for Croydon to send its rate-payers' children to either school than to provide places at its own schools.

In 1969 private preparatory schools, including the Whitgift Junior School, acquired the right to enter their pupils for the Croydon 11+ examination, and a high proportion of the allocation came to be admitted from these schools.

The two Schools between them were in fact absorbing every year over £20,000 of the Foundation's income in general subsidy of fees at a time when the money could have been invested in those new buildings and other requirements that Marlar had listed. Many Whitgift parents were aware of the position that, through being under-funded, the School was becoming run-down when it should have been expanding its facilities. Parents would have accepted an earlier substantial increase in fees, which now had to be suddenly marked up. Some prospective parents, unaware of the extent of the subsidy, gained the impression that a cheap school provided merely a cheap education, and consequently turned their attention elsewhere.

A committee of Governors, with Marshall as Chairman, examined Marlar's recommendations and agreed (a) to raise the fees by 20%, which still did not bring them to parity with the other public day schools of the London region, (b) to offer a very few more scholarships and partial remissions of fees, (c) to appoint additional masters and (d) to improve the salary scale. As for additional

---

* For instance, he would not allow Marlar to appoint an assistant porter unless the applicant was interviewed by Marshall himself, another Governor and the Clerk.

buildings, the Governors were prepared, until more detailed proposals could be drawn up, to provide masters' accommodation (from which they would draw an income), a swimming-pool (which they had intended to provide, it will be remembered, in 1934) and squash-courts (financed largely by a bequest and an appeal). They were, however, already committed to heavy expenditure at the Middle School, whose scope was expanding, whose Sixth Form was increasing in numbers, and which could no longer be content with the unimproved condition of the buildings they had taken over little more than twenty-five years before. However, the Governors directed that a general plan for future development at Haling Park should be produced. Such a plan was not prepared for some years. Marlar made further recommendations, but his request for professional assistance in design was ignored.

Whitgift Middle School becomes Trinity School

The year 1954 was important for both Schools. The Middle School was now taking a still higher proportion of the gifted boys from the primary schools, and its fees had been pegged at a figure rather less than half those at Whitgift. Under its new Headmaster, O.C. Berthoud, appointed in succession to H.S. Clayton in 1952, it was making rapid academic progress. With the growth of its Sixth Form, further accommodation was becoming essential. During the next four years additions at North End included Biology and Chemistry laboratories, a Gymnasium, Common Rooms, extra class-rooms, and internal improvements to the older buildings.

However appropriate the name of the Middle School may have appeared when it was introduced in 1882, it had for a long time been a source of confusion. Many people who were not precisely informed were aware that there were two 'Whitgift' schools. When Whitgift Grammar School dropped the term 'Grammar' the difference was made no clearer. For a good many years a degree of confusion had been regarded by some who had attended the Middle School as not altogether unacceptable, and to be able to say that one had been to 'Whitgift' without specifying which 'Whitgift' gave a mistaken impression that was not always unintended. But within a few years of moving to North End there grew a desire on the part of many Old Boys of Whitgift Middle and others connected with that school to find some more distinctive name. One suggestion was that 'Modern' should replace 'Middle'; in such a way Bedford Modern School was distinguished from what used to be called Bedford Grammar School, and there would be no change of initials. There were some who would have liked to take up the discarded 'Grammar', for that was the sort of school it had become; but to do so would obviously cause greater confusion. There was an understandable desire to keep the Founder's name in the title, but no solution could be found until John Bell, Second Master at WMS 1949-54, looking back to the Founder's establishment of his Hospital of the Holy Trinity, suggested the name of 'Trinity School of John Whitgift'. This solution pleased everyone, Governors, Old Boys and parents alike; those connected with Whitgift School were also pleased, for explanations about the difference between the two schools would become increasingly unnecessary, especially when Trinity School should become just that, *tout court*.

Trinity School could now, from September 1954, go forward unobscured by any shadow cast by Whitgift School; its academic record, evidenced by excellent examination results and an increasing number of university scholarships, justified its claim to be regarded with equal favour with Whitgift School when the provision of amenities, equipment and other advantages of the Founder's endowment was under consideration. For example, at the suggestion of Dr. A. Sandison, Chairman of the Schools Committee and himself a graduate of the College, a 'Whitgift' Exhibition was established at Trinity College, Cambridge, intended to be held by a boy from each school in alternate years, but later made available annually to boys from both schools.

General Inspection 1954

Like Andrew and Gurner before him, Marlar realised that his plans for the School's future would be more likely to receive approval from the Governors if he could produce support from high educational authority, so he was pleased

Whitgift School

when the Ministry of Education proposed to conduct a General Inspection in November 1954, the first since 1930. In their Report Her Majesty's Inspectors supported Marlar (to whom they referred as 'a man of stature, respected yet approachable, a good judge of men, and possessed of forethought and statesmanship') in all his requirements and indeed suggested more for the Governors' consideration. The chief need was for more staff to enable sixth-form teaching to be done in smaller groups. Secondly, whereas equipment was generously provided and well maintained in most departments, the buildings were inadequate in many respects: the Library was far too small; the Art department must have more room to expand its diverse undertakings; the Music department deserved accommodation of its own; Geography and Biology needed specialist rooms, the provision of which would release other space; there was a shortage of Sixth-Form rooms, of cloak-rooms and changing-rooms; an additional gymnasium was desirable. Most of these inadequacies had arisen because of the great increase in the size and interests of the Sixth Forms, which had created demands for resources, that had not been thought of a quarter of a century before, when the buildings were designed. Marlar was much encouraged by a personal letter from the Chief Inspector, D.F. Harrop:

> I may say that we thought the whole organisation and curriculum of the School reflected what we felt was your own liberal philosophy of education. To my mind the day Public School is perhaps the best combination of enlightenment with traditional high standards of achievement, and we felt that under your guidance Whitgift was maintaining and strengthening its position among such schools.

Marlar was able to reaffirm his contention ('The Governors have heard all this from me *ad nauseam*') that the School was working with grossly inadequate resources, and he was emboldened to propose a still more ambitious scheme for coherent development, a scheme that thirty years later was only in part completed, but which in the meantime had come to be regarded as not far-reaching enough. His repeated requests for a more liberal provision of entrance scholarships to thwart the loss of promising candiates met with little response; half a dozen meagre awards did little to stem the flow, when more generous offers were available elsewhere.

New Building 1955-61

One small addition to the premises that was in no way part of these planned extensions, but which has greatly improved the appearance of the Main Quadrangle, was the construction there of the Memorial to S.O. Andrew, in the form of a pool and fountain with a paved surround and rose-beds, designed by John Stammers, FRIBA (OW). The Memorial was subscribed to by hundreds of his former pupils and was opened in June 1955 by one of them, Lord Tedder.

Each of the next six years was marked with some addition to the amenities or the buildings of the School. In March 1956 Archbishop Fisher dedicated the organ in Big School. In October Whitgift Court, in Nottingham Road, a block of ten maisonnettes for masters of both schools, was ready for its first occupants. In September 1957 a new wing, with excellent Biology laboratories on the ground floor, and Geography rooms on the first floor, was completed, part of the cost being defrayed by the Industrial Fund

Unveiling of Andrew Memorial by Lord Tedder, June 1955

for the Advancement of Science Teaching in Schools, which also contributed to the extensions at Trinity. In 1958 the Masters' Common Room was enlarged and the redecoration of Big School completed with the inscription on the panelling of the names of Benefactors, Head Masters and Captains of the School. In 1959 work was started on the long-awaited swimming-pool, and the Inner Quadrangle was turned into a Botanical Garden, to take the place of what had hitherto existed in the old walled garden of Haling House, where the pool was being built. At this time Marlar invited subscriptions towards the building of squash-courts on a site near the pool, a plan which had been initiated with a legacy from the mother of an OW, Mrs. S.M. Mounsey, and generously supported by the Governors. In April the pool was opened. No expense had been spared to make it unrivalled in any other school in the country; not only was it superbly engineered, but its design, décor and setting gave it an exceptional beauty that is seldom found in a building of that kind.

In March 1961 the four squash-courts, conveniently situated next to the pool changing-rooms, were declared open by Mrs. Marlar.

Retirement

Before this date—in July 1960—Geoffrey Marlar had announced his intention to retire the following July, when he would be sixty and would have spent fifteen very busy years at Whitgift, a length of time he was heard to say was exactly right for any Headmaster; less would not allow a man to achieve all he wanted to; more might lead to stagnation. Certainly the School's reputation had increased greatly under him; many additions had been made to its amenities with the aid of the rapidly growing value of the Foundation's assets under the skilful management of the Governors with Sir James Marshall at their head. He knew the need for development would not cease, but there were good reasons why a pause must precede the next series of additions to be put in hand.

Interior of Swimming Pool, 1960

The Staff, 1961

L. to r., Back row: R.H. Jones, Nicholas, Gillard, Williams, Branston, Samy, Bell, Clay, Abbott, Savage, Nichols, R.J. Jones, H.A.C. Evans, Shotton, Felix, *Middle row*: Glynne-Jones, Parsons, Whyte, Chester, Edge, Smith, Yeo, Naftel, Odom, Tolman, Schad, Taggart, Lydall, Kennedy-Cooke, Etherington, Kennedy, Lewis, Axton, Scott, *Front row*: Worsell, Percy, Stothard, Kelly, Prime, Parr, Ewen, Marlar, Holden, Hobbs, I.A. Evans, Clifford Lewis, Hussey, Thomas, Russell

Appraisal

Marlar was interested in the 'all-rounder'. He mistrusted the 'clever devils'* who regarded school—and the world—as places to equip themselves for self-advancement, who took no interest in athletic and other school activities, but whose immediate horizons were bounded by a precocious intellectualism in some narrow field. Academic talent, to gain full respect, must be accompanied by the qualities of humanity, honour and modesty. He had himself the great gift of getting on well with all kinds of people. His manner was friendly but never familiar. What he said he meant, and his actions were free from deviousness. Yet he could employ subtlety and diplomacy in dealing with his Governors, who came round to supporting him in many of his ventures, such as the encouragement of music, the swimming-pool, the squash-courts and the organ.

Of all the Headmasters up to his time Marlar was perhaps the one best known to Whitgiftians, past and present, to parents and to people connected with other schools; he was not a desk man, but preferred to be out and doing, meeting others, talking to boys, finding out what interested them, understanding his Staff, whether academic or domestic. His obvious and unfeigned interest in others and his willingness to discuss what was of importance to them lent him both respect and authority. He was the same to all men; at ease with the mighty, he was equally unaffected when discussing the state of the playing-fields with the head groundsman. He got the best out of people because they knew he was interested in what they were doing, and they were pleased to work for him, but he would not tolerate inefficiency or slackness, and no one was ever in doubt that he was in command.

One of Marlar's chief concerns was the wellbeing of his staff, academic and domestic. He reasonably assumed that, like himself, any man appointed to Whitgift would be prepared to give of his time and effort beyond the basic calls of duty. For example, his introduction in 1952 of a tutorial system met with general acceptance. His attempts to obtain a fair and generous renumeration for his staff and to provide good living accommodation, working conditions and pension rights were not always matched with readiness in the Governors' responses. Reluctant to promote his own interests in these respects, he sometimes found himself overlooked; for instance, his own salary failed to keep pace in proportion to assistants' pay, and Headmaster's expenses and contingency funds were never adequately provided.

* This term was used by the Dean of Westminster (the Very Revd. A.C. Don, KCVO) during his address on Founder's Day 1947. It seems to derive from the Duke of Wellington's warning: 'If you educate children without religion you will produce a race of clever devils.'

Geoffrey Marlar and his wife, whose help and support for his aims and principles had been indispensable, retired to live in Eastbourne, where they were already well known, Mrs. Marlar being a native of the town. She had been an admirable headmaster's wife, showing a personal but tactful interest in all School staff, with insight and easy confidence; she was a gracious hostess at School functions, and was much liked and respected by members of the teaching staff and their families. She was also well known in the town of Croydon, being a Justice of the Peace. At Eastbourne they both followed with keen interest the cricket at the Saffrons ground, especially when their son Robin was playing for Sussex. Marlar became involved with local education and was pleased to accept an invitation to join the Governing Body of his old school, Brighton College. He died at Eastbourne at the age of 77.

Numerous tributes were paid to him by staff, old boys and others:

Above all it is by his humanity and his power to inspire respect and affection that he will be remembered – qualities that spurred a desire to excel. Even-tempered and so on good terms with all, he was no mere dictatorial figure-head. He could administer a well-deserved rebuke without incurring resentment; discipline there was, but it was acceptable; a high standard of behaviour was expected by him, but it was a standard one therefore approved of. As a speaker he displayed a light felicity of expression that captivated his audience, whether they were boys, parents or old boys – and those old boys who had preceded him were among those who held him in the warmest affection. (*The Times*)

His policy was to leave his heads of departments a completely free hand in their own affairs, and I was always happy in the confidence he showed me . . . It suited me to run my department in my own way, with a very competent team of men . . . It was Marlar's great strength as a headmaster that by his personal qualities he maintained cordial relations with those under him and encouraged them to do their best work. (H.E. Parr, Chief Mathematics Master, 1937-62, Second Master 1962-65).

. . . I was closely influenced by my Headmaster, who encouraged me more than any young man has a right to expect. He encouraged, he praised, and he allowed me to get on with the job of running the School at boy-level without interference. I always knew he was there to approve or reprimand, but we always wanted not to let him down. Because he placed trust in us we responded to that trust, and this was to influence my own career. He helped me to realise what can be achieved in headmastering, and I suppose, in my wilder thoughts I wanted to emulate him. (I.D.S. Beer, Head Prefect 1948-49, Headmaster successively of Ellesmere, Lancing and Harrow.)

He showed us many qualities, but perhaps the most telling one was the happy knack of treating boys as their different ages demanded, on their way through adolescence up the School. It takes a delicate touch of understanding to time correctly the shift from 'teaching the boy' to 'letting the young man emerge', but it was a touch that Geoffrey Marlar had. He stood unashamedly for standards of decency and honesty; he told us to read widely; he supported enterprise . . .; he had real compassion. (J.D.A. Evans, Head Prefect 1954-55).

12. M.J. Hugill 1961–70

A Second Attempt

In response to notices of the vacancy for Headmaster that were inserted in various papers, considerably fewer applications were received than might have been expected. Some potential applicants may have been deterred by the low salary offered, but others may not have been aware of the vacancy, for the customary circular giving details of the appointment was not sent to the headmasters of HMC schools for posting in their common-rooms. Having interviewed half-a-dozen candidates, the Governors recommended three for Archbishop Fisher's selection, but he rejected them all and required the vacancy to be re-advertised. At this second attempt an even less numerous but a stronger field emerged.

Appointment

Archbishop Fisher appointed Michael James Hugill, Headmaster of a maintained grammar school in Lancashire. Educated at Oundle and King's, Cambridge, he was by training a mathematician and by further inclination a man of aesthetic and cultural sensibility with a particular interest in music. Like Gurner in one respect, he was critical of the restrictions on personal freedom which they both associated with the public-school system. Throughout his time he endeavoured to liberalise outlooks at the School, encouraging an appreciation and a love for the finer things of life. He fully supported Marlar's policy of modernisation and extension, of reducing the size of classes, and of broadening the curriculum, such as had been evidenced by the recent introduction of Russian, and of the study of Economics in the Sixth Form.

First Impressions

Delivering his first report at the Annual Prize-Giving in 1962, Hugill recalled his first impressions of Whitgift as 'a thoroughly civilized school' for he had arrived at a time when it seemed to be on the crest of a wave. Academic and athletic achievement were impressive. In 1961 there had been eleven winners of state scholarships to the universities, the most since 1952, when there were twelve, a figure achieved again in 1962, after which date they were discontinued. The usual half-dozen university awards had also been gained. The rugby XV of 1961 was outstanding. Such ambitious productions as *The Winter's Tale* and *The Magic Flute* had received acclaim. He thought 'the balance was right'.

On his arrival at Whitgift in September 1961, Hugill may have been impressed by the scale of the buildings and by the pleasantness of their surroundings, but within a few weeks he became aware of significant deficiencies, of which he had been given general warning by Marlar. Some of these were due to the inadequacies of the buildings, such as had been dilated upon by his predecessor; others were the result of years of neglect through refusal to spend money on minor but necessary renewals or improvements. The state of decoration in many parts of the School was, as Hugill reported, 'depressingly poor'.

Another persistent problem that confronted him was the under-funding that dominated the School's budget, especially in respect of the payment of staff, both academic and ancillary. No sooner was some concession granted for an improved salary scale in order to attract good staff, than the new scale was seen to leave underpaid a good many masters with some few years of service. The same position had existed in

M.J. Hugill, MA

Marlar's time. The scales allotted to secretarial, technical and domestic staff were similarly inadequate, being below those offered to LEA schools. It was small wonder that good staff were difficult to find, retain or replace.

The Governors were quite willing to accede to some of Hugill's minor requests – those which could no longer be deferred, and those that could be satisfied by means of only a small outlay. In this way he obtained the gradual replacement of old-fashioned lighting by fluorescent tubes (which were more economical); an increase in the Library fund to provide a few more recently published books; the appointment of part-time fencing and squash instructors to relieve men (Henry Maslin and Eric Hall) who, while not being members of the PE staff, had taken on these sports in addition to their time-tabled work and other outside activities; and a grant to the rugby XV towards the expenses of their tour in Ireland. A good case was made out for the establishment in 1963 of two new Houses, Brodie's and Ellis's, even if the appointment of two new Housemasters did mean a slight increase in the salaries bill; another Junior House was also formed, named Oak. The Governors also approved the payment of half expenses to masters who attended professional courses or who represented the School at educational conferences during the holidays. These trifling sums did little to placate Hugill; but he was discouraged from undertaking any greatly revised budgetary estimate which might involve a considerable increase in fees.

Stagnation

The response to major requests remained negative. Hugill's reiteration of demand for Marlar's more generous entrance scholarships was mainly ignored, and in consequence a steady flow of high-quality candidates continued to filter away to other schools who were glad to offer them more attractive terms or even completely free education. Such lack of concern for quality – after all, there was no difficulty in *filling* the school – led to disappointment in Sixth-form achievement later on. The Governors remained unperturbed that each year seven or eight of the top ten candidates were being lost.

The years-old unsatisfied need for more buildings also went unheeded. Larger numbers in the Sixth Forms, due to greater expectations of following further education at university or elsewhere,* were encouraged by the greatly expanding provision of places at the old and at the new universities, and by the more readily available financial help from the state. A heavy strain was imposed upon teaching space. The biology laboratories and the geography rooms constructed in 1957 had done no more than slightly relieve this increasing pressure. The introduction of Business Studies and Economics in the Lower Sixth further induced boys to stay on for 'A' levels, even if they were not all contemplating university. Without increased space, these classes were becoming too crowded. At the beginning of Hugill's first term, the cricket pavilion and two rooms at Haling Cottage were turned over for temporary class-room use; a little later the Orderly Room was partitioned for a similar purpose, but Hugill's request for a temporary building in the unused garden of Bagbie House (itself occupied by art and music classes) was turned down. There was even some discussion about making use of the Squash-courts.

* In 1938 the university population was about 50,000; twenty years later it had doubled. The upgrading of technological and other colleges to university level and the foundation of a dozen new universities over a further thirty years have increased the numbers of full-time students reading for a degree to over 440,000 (1988).

Trinity School and Shirley Park

In January 1961 the Governors announced their intention to rebuild Trinity School at Shirley Park. Finance would be required for this venture, rather than for extensions at Haling Park. The move was a logical sequence to events that had been started by the Town and Country Planning Bill of 1947 after which Croydon became one of the first towns in England to produce a Town Planning Scheme for the re-development of its obsolescent centre. This Scheme, which allocated the whole of the North End-George Street-Wellesley Road-Poplar Walk rectangle to business purposes, and a site of about the same area in the Park Hill residential zone for the then Whitgift Middle School to move to, was regarded at the time by most people as an academic exercise undertaken by the Town Hall staff, but it quite suddenly became evident that some of its proposals were very likely to be realised. The Croydon Development Plan which, somewhat modified, received approval from the Minister of Town and Country Planning in 1954, had been created by a small group of members of the Council of the Borough of Croydon, led by Sir James Marshall. The Plan did not make much headway until 1959, when the completion of a large office-block, Norfolk House, on the site of the old Public Halls in George Street, proved to meet a need, for many large London business firms were becoming interested in removing their offices to Croydon, where already the erection of several more blocks of offices had been started. In February 1959 the Governors were encouraged by this successful development to contemplate realising the value of the North End site, for they had learnt of the possibility of buying the remaining portion of Shirley Park, less than two miles due east of North End, as a site for Trinity School. Negotiations were swiftly conducted, and the 24-acre site (considerably larger and more easily accessible than the one at Park Hill proposed in the plan), including the eighteenth-century mansion, which was then in use as a hotel, was purchased for £87,500. The low price reflected the scheduled restrictions on the property and the fact that the previous owner had received compensation on that account. In exchange for this outlay and the cost of a new building and of landscaping the grounds, the Governors received the freedom to negotiate with a development company an unhampered site in the middle of Croydon, scheduled for the most profitable type of exploitation and worth several million pounds.

Over the next four years resources were husbanded and plans prepared. The additional buildings that during the past few years had been provided at both schools had been paid for out of income, but the construction of a new school costing approximately £1,500,000 was financed mainly from reserves and from capital payments made by the company (Ravenseft Properties Ltd.) developing the North End site. The architect of the recent additions at both schools, George Lowe, FRIBA, had received his first commission in December 1953 and was now given responsibility for the design of the new school. He was urged to consult all those who would be directing its teaching and administration; in this way it was hoped to create a design that would meet the requirements of all departments and of up-to-date teaching methods. The school is of reinforced-concrete construction clad in Portland stone and presents an impressive frontage. The interior is spacious and dignified and lacks little in the way of modern equipment. A large and handsome Assembly Hall forms the core of the building, and an octagonal, two-storeyed Library is a most striking feature. The Foundation Stone was laid by Archbishop Ramsey on 8 June 1964, and the new School, which was first occupied in September 1965, was officially opened by Field-Marshal Lord Alexander of Tunis on 5 May 1966. Since that time extensive additions have been made in the form of extra laboratories, lecture-rooms and classrooms, increased accommodation for music, art and technical studies, and a Sixth Form Centre. A sports hall is now about to be constructed.

Reasons for Delay

Once Shirley Park had been purchased, the Governors adopted the policy that no other major work should be undertaken until Trinity's new school was complete. Yet the problem of accommodation could have been partly solved years before, if only the inhibiting policy on fees had been abandoned. The almost perennial statement by the Chairman that there would be no increase, or only a very small one, in the fees induced despair in the hearts of those who were aware of both the purpose and the effect of this ingratiating announcement.

Not only was building at Haling Park at a standstill, but maintenance was being intolerably neglected. A few classrooms were grudgingly redecorated, but roofs, floors, metal windows, electrical wiring, plumbing and heating were by now in acute need of attention or replacement.

Concessions

Eventually, early in 1964, Hugill was called to a Governors' meeting, where he was informed that sufficient funds were about to become available to allow plans for a Music School, a new Library and Sixth Form Unit, a Masters' Dining Room, and cottages for ground staff to be prepared. To these desirable amenities were added the three-storey wing and the locker-rooms which form Cedar Court, and with which, in fact, the new work was to begin. Thinking he was being given his head, George Lowe proposed an overall plan for comprehensive development of the parade-ground area, but this was never discussed further. A succession of piecemeal and unco-ordinated extensions were ingeniously fitted on to the existing structure. In the long run, from this delay a better contrived plan has been realised a quarter of a century later; but that is a long time in the history of any go-ahead school.

Cedar Court

In spring 1966 work started in Cedar Court, which hitherto had been hemmed in by a range of unsightly bicycle sheds, the demolition of which opened up a dignified and pleasant area that had been unimaginatively treated by the original architects. The first section to be completed was a suite of locker-rooms for the Lower Sixth forms, which enabled the lower corridors to be cleared of their clumsy obstructions; secondly, the kitchens were rebuilt, the Dining-hall enlarged and acoustically improved, and a Dining-room added for the Staff. The next stage was the construction of a three-storey wing on one side of Cedar Court, containing

Cedar Court, 1967

offices for Heads of Departments and rooms for other purposes, a Language Laboratory and ancillary accommodation, and a new Prefects' Room. Two large Sixth-Form Common-rooms, and half a dozen studies to be shared by senior boys were constructed but were later converted to form the Economics and Business Studies Department. These were all occupied by January 1967. It had been intended to proceed with the Library and follow with the Music School, but because of limits set by Government to the cost of building developments, the completion of both these two projects was forbidden, for their estimated cost had been exceeded in the terms of the contract. The less expensive building was proceeded with, and the construction of the Library was indefinitely postponed. Moreover, the funds that had been allocated would not now be available, for they were required for other purposes.

The Music School

Having established a very active department under John Odom, Marlar had thought that for the time being the staff of visiting masters was strong enough, although his recommendation that the Governors should provide a music block indicated greater importance for the subject in the future. Hugill was not at all satisfied. In 1962 he appointed another full time musician (John Hastie, who started, however, by teaching some Junior English as well), and in view of the progressive decay by neglect of Bagbie House, he pressed for the provision of better accommoda-

The Music School

tion for music teaching, which at last met with the Governors' approval.

Hugill paid the greatest attention to the details of the design and construction of the Music School, which he felt should be unsurpassed at any other school in its suitability for the encouragement of a supreme cultural activity. On 15 May 1968 the Music School was officially opened by David Willcocks, at that time Director of Music of King's College, Cambridge, and President of the Royal College of Organists. (Both Hugill and Odom were also King's men). A concert was given, for which Martin Dalby had been commissioned to compose a piece for Chorus and Orchestra, entitled *Forecast of Mechanical Inventions*. For the first part of the concert the large audience was accommodated in Big School, and then proceeded to the Music Hall in two groups, for each of which the musicians performed separately while the other viewed the rest of the new building.

The Music School has proved to be one of the greatest assets the School possesses, providing on a lavish scale facilities for teaching, practising and performing the full range of orchestral instruments. The Music Hall, a noble room with excellent acoustic properties, can seat an audience of three hundred. Regrettably the sound-proofing system of the entire building was defective and had to be improved at considerable expense. Unfortunately too, the Hall was designed without any provision for film-projection; neither was there easy means for blacking-out. It would have

The Music School, interior

been still more useful if better back-stage facilities and means of access to the platform had been provided. A gallery would have been another useful adjunct; there was plenty of room. Unhappily, use of the Hall except as a musical auditorium had been perversely discouraged in the architect's brief. Nevertheless, it has filled a long-felt need, not only on the part of musicians, but also of lecturers, demonstrators and others who perform before a medium-sized audience.

Other Projects

Further *desiderata* were an Art School, extra laboratories and a Sports Hall. The Library having been indefinitely postponed, it was now regarded as of less urgency than these new projects.

When in 1967 a professional survey of the 1931 buildings was at last conducted, a sorry state of affairs was revealed. A programme of urgent repairs was put in hand, to be followed by a very extensive and thorough schedule of restoration, redecoration and minor improvements, at a cost that would result in another postponement of new building.

Further space for art and science was found by converting the art-room into another chemistry laboratory and by constructing a temporary building on the Parade Ground to house the whole of the Art Department, which became better able to cater for a wider range of activites. Bagbie House, already vacated by the Music Department, was now, in Summer 1969, no longer required. Too derelict for conversion to any other purpose (it had been rejected as a nucleus for a boarding-house), it was demolished, and eventually, in 1978, an all-weather hockey pitch and tennis-courts were laid out on its grounds.

Academic Developments

Hugill was not battling all the time for new buildings. He continually strove to develop the integration of related subjects, and to improve the content and methods of teaching, in which there had been many challenging innovations.

A year after his arrival he established a new Sixth Form group which, under T.E. Savage, studied Economics for Examination at 'A' Level, together with perhaps History, Mathematics, a language or, later on, Business Studies. This course gave an opportunity to many who had decided to go in for business or commerce, either straight from school or after taking a degree. Before long many professions such as law and accountancy would accept only entrants who had graduated. The expansion of these studies at the universities and polytechnics has been matched by their popularity at the School, largely due to lively and enterprising teaching.

In his own subject of mathematics Hugill was content to leave Parr to continue his own successful methods, and when the 'new maths' came to the fore they discussed its introduction into the syllabus. Parr produced his own text-books to cover the new approach, supported warmly by I.F. Smith and J.R. Shelley, both of whom eventually succeeded to the post of Chief Mathematics Master. In the 1960s Whitgift scientists were pioneers in the 'Nuffield Project', a new concept in science teaching promoted by the Nuffield Foundation. Morris Thomas, Chief Chemistry Master, was one of the originators of this experiment, for which he designed the new laboratory cum lecture-room that was converted from the old art room. Here, after demonstrating the classical scientific method of investigation, he would invite a class to test a hypothesis by devising an experiment of their own, leading to a solution and the propounding of a theory: learning by discovery. Another development during Hugill's time was the language laboratory, together with a studio equipped with audio-visual aids. This was taken up enthusiastically by most of the modern-languages staff, but it was found that a great deal of expensive maintenance of

The Language Laboratory, 1967

equipment was necessary, and that after classes' initial interest in the use of the mechanism had evaporated, boredom often supervened. Within a dozen years the laboratory was dismantled.

Hugill encouraged members of the staff to attend conferences and courses during the holidays. After some protest from staff that they were still expected to pay for preparing themselves in their own time for greater efficiency on the School's behalf, the 50% subsidy from the Governors was increased to 100%. Now in-service training has come to be accepted as a necessity by both sides.

The End of Blomfield's Buildings, 1965

The impending demolition of the North End buildings had possibly dismayed more those Old Whitgiftians who had known them before 1931 than the Old Mid-Whitgiftians who had been educated there since that date. The Inspectors' criticism in 1903 of the gloominess of the 1871 building had, despite attempts to brighten the walls, become all the more valid in the course of fifty years, for the additions of 1906 were now also distinctly old-fashioned and expensive to maintain, and the whole was increasingly hemmed in by commercial development. Several sentimental pilgrimages were conducted over the buildings before they were demolished, and on 23 April 1964 one great ceremonial occasion was arranged in Big School, which for the last time accommodated an Old Whitgiftians Dinner (the previous one there having been held in 1931, just before the move to Haling Park), at which the room was filled to capacity with two hundred and fifty diners. A photographic record of the buildings was made, and certain decorative features were preserved, including the statuette of the Founder and the Foundation Stone with its contents, other stonework from the Tower, and many of the window-ledges from Big School, inscribed with the names of Brodie's sixth-formers. These were transferred to Haling Park, where they joined other relics, including the Fountain from the Cloisters and the 1914-18 War

Trinity School, North End, 1961, aerial view

M.J. Hugill 1961–70

Demolition, September 1965

Memorial that had been removed in 1931; the bell that had summoned so many thousands of boys to school was claimed by Trinity School.

The commercial speculation was timed to a nicety. In 1964 the Government had imposed restrictions upon office development, but plans for the Whitgift Centre had already been passed. A little later, perhaps, Blomfield's Victorian Big School and Tower might have been scheduled as a building of architectural importance. That this commercial precinct should be called after the Founder was deplored by many, who felt that his name had been cheapened and debased. Hitherto the name 'Whitgift', if it was not associated with its most distinguished bearer, had connoted scholastic or charitable references, but now it came to be linked in the public mind almost solely with the market-place.

Games

Not by any means an enthusiastic games-player himself, Hugill yet encouraged, through members of his staff, a whole-hearted attention to excellence in that respect, and it was during his time that several sports at Whitgift attained their highest standards.

The House Championship, when it was started in 1904, partly to provide opportunities of undertaking competitive sport by those who did not aspire to school teams, was decided by an increasingly complicated points system, whereby the various major and minor sports were allocated different, theoretical values. With the addition of so many new activities, any judgment of overall superiority by a particular House became nugatory, so in 1966 the Championship Shield was awarded (to Smith's) for the last time. Nevertheless, the Houses have continued to compete for their order of places in the different sports.

Rugby

In 1954 Gerwyn Williams, who had played full-back thirteen times for Wales and had captained London Welsh and Middlesex, had been appointed by Marlar to the Physical Education staff; he had the task of reorganising rugby coaching throughout the School, and his methods were amply vindicated within a few years. In 1961, for the first time, the First XV beat all their opponents. The fixture-list was now much stronger than it had ever been, and wins over Dulwich and Cranleigh were amply confirmed by a successful tour against prominent Irish schools. In fact the XV was one of the strongest school teams in the country that year.

To such an extent was enthusiasm generated, not merely by success, but also by the quality of

Winners of Public Schools Sevens, 1967
L. to r.: Nesbitt, Freter, Paterson, Saville, Skeen, Bloxham, Malempré

247

Unbeaten First XV, 1961
L. to r., Back row: McCall, Miller, Carter, Hislop, Gerwyn Williams Esq, Moyle, Brackstone, Hill, Oddy,
Front row: Bowden, Councell, Spanswick, Wilkinson (Capt.), Kibble, Souster, Eustace, *Inset*: Aitken

play, that several hundred boys regularly paid to be conveyed in a fleet of coaches to away matches, outnumbering the home supporters on the touchlines. Their presence at home matches was even more overwhelming.

Extracts follow from a staff reporter's account in *The Observer* of 19th November, 1961 of the game against KCS:

This was no ordinary game of Rugby – indeed, one may rarely see the like again. Whitgift were quite magnificent. Irrepressible, dominant, superbly creative . . . they produced 11 tries as good as anyone would see at any level of the game.

Whitgift have already been praised this season . . . but . . . they could never have attained the heights of this game.

'Unbeatable', some have said. Maybe not quite. But undoubtedly only a superb side could lower their flag. And I doubt if any school side could produce a matching variety of the orthodox and the basic, both marked by pure ecstasy of movement.

It was a glorious exhibition. From push-over tries reminiscent of the Springboks, to full-scale sweeping three-quarter movements from the Barbarian repertoire, they hardly put a foot wrong. Their team-work and co-ordination were first-class . . .

Their victims were UCS, Christ's Hospital, St. John's, Leatherhead, Douai, Brighton, Monmouth, KCS, Beaumont, Cranleigh, Dulwich, Blackrock and Royal Belfast.

Of the XV M.D.G. Wilkinson (Captain) later played for London District and Surrey, B.R. Councell for Sussex, J.E. Spanswick for Surrey, and G.C. Eustace for the Royal Navy; R.F. Kibble played on occasion for Oxford University.

From this time onwards Whitgift rugby enjoyed a higher reputation, supported by the comparable and sustained success of the Old Whitgiftian Rugby Football Club, whose members continued to benefit from the coaching they had received at school. After reaching the final of the Rosslyn Park Schools Seven-a-Side Competition in 1966, the Whitgift Seven and Williams achieved their greatest ambition when they won it the following year. Two years later at the University match at Twickenham there was an OW on each side (C.D. Saville, Cambridge, and J.L. Cooke, Oxford), and before retiring from coaching the First XV, Williams saw another, A.J. Wordsworth, gain his blue for Cambridge in 1973 and go on to win an England cap.

Modern Tetrathlon

A sport initiated in the sixties was Modern Tetrathlon. The excellent facilities that existed at the School for cross-country running, shooting, fencing and swimming, which go to make up this exacting individual sport, seemed to John Felix and Henry Maslin (in charge of fencing in succession to H. Bennett) to be worth exploiting, and in 1963 Whitgift won, for the first time, the Inniskilling Cup, open to public-school teams. For a dozen years, while Felix and Maslin were in charge, Whitgift enjoyed almost a monopoly of this trophy, and many exponents of the sport represented their university, their branch of the services or their country.

Swimming

Swimming also flourished. With the advantage of the new pool, C. Murray, a skilled instructor, not only of beginners, but also of school teams, improved swimming standards so much that no boy, unless he was forbidden on medical grounds from entering the water, left the School unable to

Inniskilling Cup, Modern Tetrathlon, 1967
L. to r., Back row: H.J. Maslin Esq, Bairstow, Barr, Hughman, J. Felix Esq, *Front row*: Francis, Seear, Hieatt

Bath Club Cup, 1967
L. to r.: Campion, Clark, Nesbitt, Snell

swim. In 1966, for the first time since 1925, the Bath Cup was won again. Gerwyn Williams was the Master i/c Swimming.

1967 was something of an *annus mirabilis* for the games-players: the 'Sevens' competition was won, and the Inniskilling and Bath Cups were both retained. These results rather overshadowed those of other sports which, however, usually maintained a creditable standard.

Music and Drama

While Hugill could safely leave certain school activities in other hands, he turned his attention to encouraging individual fulfilment among boys with talent in music, drama and the arts. All three were combined in 1966 in an unusual venture, an opera, *Mara*, composed and written by two members of the staff, J.A. Hastie and R.B. Kennedy, to which a hundred and fifty boys contributed in various ways. *Mara* was favourably reviewed in the Musical press, and *The Times* recommended it as an example to other schools. But this production and some others – revivals, for instance, of forgotten operas of long ago, were not greatly popular, for audiences were now more sophisticated than their predecessors of sixty years before, who had no knowledge of sound, film and television. Gilbert and Sullivan had given much pleasure on both sides of the curtain in the Whitgift productions that started in 1947, and it was difficult to persuade performers and audiences that the Savoy operas were in some way inferior to *Mara* and *Raymond and Agnes, or The Bleeding Nun*.

Drama in schools had become an activity undertaken frequently and extensively as an outlet for creativity, self-expression and aesthetic experience, concepts that had acquired a label of approval. The tradition at Whitgift established by Ewen in 1928 was strengthened by the interest of collaborators in his productions, and after the war it was revived by Maurice Etherington and others. A series of Shakespearian productions reached a very high standard, and Etherington's *Hamlet* of 1960, with Martin Jarvis as the Prince, was worthy of the great praise that it was accorded. By the mid-sixties two main productions were put on annually: a straight play, usually by Shakespeare or another classical author, and a musical. The improved facilities for music resulted in a better supply of singers and of instrumentalists, who were able to give more varied and more ambitious performances at the concerts. The stage producer was usually John Branston; John Odom or one of his assistants, for the musical staff had greatly expanded, directed the orchestra and the singers; the stage-sets were designed by Henry Maslin, assisted by Cyril Worsell and Dai Lewis, Heads of Handicraft, and executed by art and handicraft enthusiasts. Developments in lighting and sound effects also involved more boys in these technicalities, and the general standards of production were high indeed.

From these experiences during Marlar's and Hugill's time emerged a number of OWs who took up careers in the entertainment media. Among the most successful were Guy Woolfenden, Director of Music for the Royal Shakespeare Company, Martin Jarvis, versatile radio, television and West End actor, and Mark Shivas, producer and head of drama in BBC television.

Trinity becomes Independent 1968

The new Trinity School provided accommodation that was in many instances superior to that at Haling Park, and it became clear that Whitgift would now have a very formidable rival indeed, although the location of the new school on the eastern side of the town tended to separate more distinctly the catchment areas of pupils for the two schools. In February 1968 the Governors announced that in August Trinity would relinquish the direct grant and become an independent school. This decision was not intended merely to raise the school's status, already greatly enhanced by the move into its new sumptuous premises. It was made in the face of the government's threat to take over all the direct-grant schools, and it cost the Foundation many thousands of pounds in annual subsidy, but the income from the development of the Whitgift Centre was now increasing so rapidly that the Governors felt they could afford to fight off the threat to the Foundation's independence by divesting themselves of any tie with state control of education. One result of this action, which now provided the Foundation with a second independent school of apparently equal status and in competition with the other, was the bewilderment of parents of prospective pupils who were now given the option of paying fees at Whitgift two-and-half times those at Trinity. Parents of boys already at Whitgift felt they had been hard done by.

Further improvements and additions at Haling Park were put in hand, and the scale of fees at both schools was frozen. By this course the

Martin Jarvis as Hamlet, 1960

Aerial view of Trinity School, 1970

Governors thought they might widen the field from which pupils were drawn. At Trinity fifty per cent of the pupils continued to be accepted on the results of the eleven-plus examination, their fees being paid by the LEAs of Croydon and Surrey. Demand for fee-paying places in both schools was becoming so great that only one applicant in four at Whitgift could be successful, and at Trinity the proportion was even smaller, partly on account of the fewer places. This state of affairs raised the academic standards but it caused much frustration and disappointment among other candidates and their parents, whose alternatives were other independent day-schools less conveniently situated, boarding-schools or the local secondary schools. A number of private secondary schools expanded to meet this general demand for independent education.

Marlar's policy of expansion, which Hugill enthusiastically espoused, seemed to be bearing fruit. The additional buildings and the increased reputation of the School were attracting good quality candidates for admission; fewer were declining places to go elsewhere, and there was an improvement in academic standards: 'O' and 'A' Level results were better, and the number of awards won at the universities was increasing, there being nine in 1966, the best since 1949.

Haling Park Road Properties

After the purchase of Bagbie House in 1949, a number of other properties in Haling Park Road and adjoining the School grounds came on the market. They comprised houses with inconveniently large back gardens, parts of which together could have been absorbed into the School grounds and thereby used to make up the deficiency in playing-fields. These properties were sometimes offered for first consideration to the Governors who to begin with were not interested and let slip many such opportunities. It was not until 1967 that this policy was modified and certain properties – but not all that were offered – were purchased. The prospect that within the indefinable future some extra space might be found to supplement deficiencies received a severe reverse when in October 1969 the news was heard that the Governors intended to demolish Haling Cottage and erect old people's housing on the whole site. Whereas such demolition had been regarded by members of the staff as quite possible, for the house was much dilapidated, no one had imagined that the considerable area between North and South Fields would be used for anything except school purposes. Hugill had of course not been consulted, but protests were made by the Common Room, and for some time the danger seemed to recede, until an even more damaging proposal was made to take over the greater part of South Field. But any plans for such building there or at Haling Cottage were shortly to be withdrawn and kept in reserve.

The Whitgift Charities Act, 1969

During the previous few years the Foundation's improved financial circumstances had rendered much of its organisation, established under the Scheme of 1915, with subsequent amendments, difficult to administer and, in modern conditions, obsolete. The Scheme of 1915 had been formulated by the Board of Education mainly to make use of the Foundation's resources for the provision of education; but in 1969 the situation had changed. The introduction of free secondary education for all had encouraged use of the state-provided system, and the Department of Education and Science, the successor to the Ministry of Education, was no longer so concerned with the direction of an independent educational foundation. In addition, the welfare state and the provision by the local council of homes and hospitals for old people had shown up the Whitgift Hospital's premises in their primitive inadequacy. Moreover, the limitations placed by the Schemes upon the amount of the Foundation's income to be allocated to eleemosynary purposes were manifestly inequitable at this time of greatly increased costs but enormously increased revenues.

The Governors' actions in removing Trinity's name from the direct-grant list had been designed

Whitgift School was here. The Whitgift Centre, 1967

Haling Cottage, 1965

to free the Foundation from the restrictions embodied in the direct-grant regulations. These included the strong representation on the Governing Body of Croydon Council nominees, whose chief commitment was to local political advantage (although a number of them were Old Whitgiftians). Another restriction was the answerability to the Department of Education and Science. Labour governments' threats to destroy independent education aroused a determination to avoid if possible the risk of take-over or dissolution. As long as one of the Schools received the direct grant, the Governors remained all the more vulnerable, and so did both schools.

In order to meet these changes and challenges, to ease the problems of administration, and to preserve the Foundation's assets in the event of legislation to annex independent schools to the State, the Governors decided that they should seek wider powers to administer their endowments. These powers could be acquired only through a private Act of Parliament. By the Whitgift Charities Act of 1969 the Governors became a corporate body. Among the powers they now possessed were those to build additional almshouses for old people and, if it was thought desirable, to convert the existing Hospital into a museum, to provide more schools for boys or girls or for both boys and girls, to provide new administrative accommodation, and to extend their charitable functions in such ways as might be approved by the Charity Commissioners or by Government. Among the consequences of the Act was the necessity for an official seal (ever since the old corporation of the Warden and Poor had been dissolved in 1881, no seal had been required), and the Governors therefore decided that a grant of arms should be taken out by the Whitgift Foundation, a course of action they had many times previously been urged to take, but which might earlier have been hard to justify financially.*

Dr. Cecil Prime

1969 was further marked by the retirement in July of Dr. Cecil Prime. He was one of Gurner's young appointments in the first year at Haling Park. A botanist chiefly, he had many publications and many promising pupils to his credit. He became Chief Biology Master in 1949 and developed his department so successfully that it became one of the most estimable in the School. At least a score of his pupils became professors or readers in various biological sciences in universities, or directors of research institutes, throughout the world; among them were four Fellows of the Royal Society. In addition, numerous medical practitioners learnt their early science in his Sixth Form.

Problems of Administration

There were many burdensome responsibilities that Hugill called upon members of the staff to share. Years beforehand Marlar had put a strong case for the appointment of a domestic bursar or administrative officer to organise and undertake the School's non-academic management so that the teaching staff could get on with their main task of instructing and looking after boys. The Governors refused, saying that the Clerk to the Foundation was in charge of administration and could be referred to in difficulties; his function covered the collection of fees and the payment of bills for the Schools, as instructed by the Court,

---

* Appendix VI deals with the heraldry of the Founder and the Whitgift Foundation.

so no further need for a bursar existed. Because of the Clerk's remoteness from the scene, many of the incidental responsibilities of day to day management were imposed upon members of the staff, already fully enough engaged in teaching and related duties. Thus in 1967 one man was assigned the complete survey of the buildings in order to recommend what decorations and repairs should be carried out; his report, which condemned the obvious state of neglect, resulted in the inspection at last by a qualified surveyor. Another man had to concern himself with the quality and efficiency of the catering, although he had no control of the catering staff. Another was put in charge of the Library, being responsible for the ordering, cataloguing, issuing and security of books. The Chief Physics Master, being unsupported by adequate technical staff, acted as technician in the Language Laboratory. The supervision of a large ground staff devolved upon one of the Housemasters. All these diverse responsibilities could have been borne by specialists such as were normally employed in a public school.

That such a system – or lack of one – persisted for so long, despite repeated pleas – was due to the obstinacy of the Chairman of the Governors, whose repressive hand has already been alluded to, and whose dominance over his colleagues remained for too long unchallenged.

Second Masters and Discipline: Harold Parr

In all his involvements Hugill was loyally supported and wisely advised by his Second Master, Harold Parr, who had succeeded A.H. Ewen when the latter retired in 1962. Head of Mathematics from 1936 until his retirement in 1965, Parr was renowned in the academic mathematical community for his series of textbooks which were in use throughout the country and in many other commonwealth countries. He kept these up to date, rewriting them to accommodate all the vagaries of teaching requirements, through integrated studies, decimalisation and 'modern maths'. Through his associations with the universities he was able not only to ensure that his pupils were kept abreast of changing conditions for college entrance and scholarships, but also to keep himself ahead of competitors in his own speciality of school mathematical publications. Parr was steeped in Whitgift lore, experienced in all vicissitudes of the Gurner era and of war-time, and was aware of the attitudes of the Governing Body and the Old Whitgiftian Association. His and Hugill's common interest in mathematics, in music and in liberal politics was helpful to their mutual understanding. To some extent Parr became the Headmaster's mouthpiece in communication with the staff, for Hugill was reluctant to risk confrontation, dispensing with regular staff meetings, which he felt were time-wasting and which presented him with bewildering and conflicting claims for attention, with complaints and unwanted advice. Parr's tact and good humour were often able to relax tension and settle minor disputes.

On retirement Parr was succeeded by A.T. Parsons, whose calm, detached manner concealed a very keen awareness of what was going on in the School and a determination to control any disregard of the somewhat relaxed discipline that Hugill was satisfied with. At first Hugill had tried to present himself as a stern disciplinarian, a trait quite foreign to his character, for his reticence had none of the cold, unfeeling aloofness that denotes the true despot. Parsons was no despot either, but he was held in great awe; his quiet, deliberate intervention in any disruption or breach of rules, whether slight or severe, resulted in an immediate return to orderliness and decorum. Disciplinary matters were mainly left to him. When the Common Room expressed its opinion that the observance of School rules was becoming slack, Parsons pointed out that the remedy was in the staff's own hands as individuals. Prefects were themselves finding it difficult to impose a discipline that was now unsupported by powers of punishment. Over the years their responsibilities and authority had been gradually eroded, in accordance with the changing attitudes towards punishment itself. When in the past the prefects were drawn from the minority of senior boys who formed the Sixth Form, they enjoyed the general respect of the rest of the School, but now that there were so many others of their own age, they were less easily recognised and hence less readily submitted to. Marlar was following the general trend when he vetoed their use of the cane, and prefects' punishments, meted out at the twice-weekly prefects' courts established in

Andrew's time, were now not so much feared, being milder and cumbersome to administer, and inviting disregard instead of submission. Moreover, the increasing cult of the individual, with wider limits to what was regarded as tolerable – not only in school but in the world outside – was encouraging young people to defy any imposition of what were seen as unreasonable sanctions.

The Protest Movement

The late 1960s were the era of youthful protest. Radical politics, anarchic philosophies, revolutionary attitudes, defiance of authority and violent demonstrations, accompanied by a contempt for traditional stability and tolerance, were now manifest in many of the universities and had in varying degrees penetrated the schools. Whitgift escaped most of the excesses that were reported elsewhere, but a few unpleasant incidents occurred: the War Memorial was disfigured, minor wanton damage was done to the buildings and the grounds, deliberate rudeness was attempted, but open defiance seldom became manifest. Such blatant disturbances as have been alluded to were the actions of a very small group of undistinguished boys in the Lower VIth, quite unrepresentative of the School at large. There were a good many more who felt they could best assert their independence of mind by allowing their hair to grow long and untidy. One boy returned to School after the summer holidays with a full beard. This was certainly unusual, but as the School Rules contained no reference to hairy faces, nobody in authority took much notice and the beard remained, neat like the wearer's head of hair.*

Resignation

Hugill had been happy to see a number of Marlar's projects carried out (increased provision for scholarships, improved salary and wages scales, a wider interest in music and drama, greater attention to the improvement and maintenance of the buildings) and a few additions, including some that were not on Marlar's agenda, such as the Masters' Dining Room and Cedar Court, but he was thwarted in many of his own plans. The new Library had been indefinitely postponed; the temporary Art block was likely to remain for many years; science laboratories were still inadequate; new changing accommodation was essential. The expense of necessary repairs after years of neglect had eroded the sums of money set aside for additional buildings. Although he still had little difficulty in extracting moderate sums for minor amenities, such as a harpsichord, minibuses, projects and expeditions, and extra office staff, there was an atmosphere of stagnation. There had been several occasions when interference from the Chairman and other Governors with decisions that should rightly have been the Headmaster's on his own territory, became intolerable. Hugill had been nine years at Whitgift, where he felt that in the circumstances he could do little more; he now fancied a change of scene, so in July 1969 he tendered his resignation as from 31st August 1970. Thereupon he returned to class-room teaching, which he much preferred to the administration and control of a large school, going first to Keele University and later to Westminster, where he joined the Mathematics department. Here he had the stimulus of teaching a highly intelligent sixth form, and of working in the company of congenial colleagues; moreover, living in the heart of London offered the artistic, literary and cultural attractions he had had little time to enjoy.

Résumé

Michael Hugill's Headmastership had coincided with a period of major changes in education, including the broadening of the curriculum and a closer relationship between pupil and teacher. Being well disposed to such developments, he did not always find it easy to introduce innovations that seemed to some to be at variance with the School's customs and traditions. For instance, he reduced the power of the games committee in forming policy and in controlling house sport, preferring a less rigid organisation of the complex system of athletic and sporting activities. Having himself undergone a good deal of compulsory games playing at school, he believed that if boys were given a choice of such

---

*A group photograph of 1879 shows a boy in 5A wearing a chin-fringe, such as would sometimes be worn by a countryman. He too was probably flouting convention.

activities few would experience inadequacy and few would opt out.

He possessed a rich and sensitive imagination, revealed in his approach to architectural topics, in dealing with personal problems of boys and of staff, and more publicly in his occasional participation in stage performances put on by the Common Room for Christmas entertainment. At these events he was glad to drop the somewhat austere and detached manner that he thought appropriate for a headmaster, but which cloaked an essentially friendly and even mischievous lightheartedness. A wilful quirkiness manifested itself in the occasional unpredictable, even wrong-headed, decision intended apparently to defy convention. Whereas one gained the impression that he often found difficulty in making up his mind when confronted by conflicting interests, there were times when he reached decisions that seemed perverse and impulsively directed against the establishment. In 1965 the newly appointed headmaster of a projected comprehensive school in Grimsby, the Founder's birthplace, informed Hugill as a matter of courtesy that the local authority proposed to name it 'Whitgift School'. The Governors had already been at pains to get such a name withdrawn from a projected new school in the Hounslow area (where any association with the Founder must have been minimal), but Hugill, instead of pointing out to the other Head the confusion that would inevitably arise in some people's minds, and the problems that had formerly existed over the identities of the two schools of the Whitgift Foundation, gave the proposal his blessing. The Governors, who had not been made aware of this new school's existence, were less than delighted. So far, no confusion of identity between the two Whitgift Schools has come to our notice, but we now have to be careful to refer to ourselves as 'Whitgift School, Croydon'.

He was always sympathetic towards undertakings that offered a challenge or that broadened scope for activity and initiative. His 'Yes, let's do that!' encouraged many boys and members of staff to undertake projects that could be innovative and demanding. Such a one was *Mara*. On another occasion, in 1966, he broadmindedly supported a plan conceived by a junior member of the staff to raise funds to endow a Buddhist shrine in Sri Lanka. After adverse comment appeared in a daily paper, the Chairman of the Governors cancelled the project as a quite unsuitable undertaking by a school founded by an Archbishop of the Church of England.

Hugill worked tirelessly in planning for the future. Many of his proposals bore fruit, and his nine years at Whitgift brought not only a great improvement in the condition of the buildings but also numerous valuable additions. He constantly urged better use of facilities for games, while new methods of teaching, including the 'new maths', audiovisual aids, the installation of the language laboratory and the better provision for cultural subjects were his endless preoccupation. When he left he could look back with satisfaction at much progress in liberating those cultural subjects in which he was chiefly interested, and upon all of which – music, painting, drama and literature – he could express himself as a critic of experience and respected authority.

A former colleague, R. Glynne-Jones, supplies a characteristic memory of him in social mood:

He was the most charming guest imaginable at a dinner or a party, witty, endlessly varied in topics of conversation, superb with children. His greatest gift, it seemed to me, was for informal public speaking, especially those brilliant cameos he would produce with apparent nonchalance when saying goodbye to members of the staff. He would perform twice, once in Big School and again in the Common Room. I remember one summer end-of-term when six colleagues had to be thanked and applauded. Every one of the twelve speeches was exactly appropriate, spiced with wit and quotation and anecdote, all perfectly level with the two different audiences, and with never the slightest hint of repetition or redundancy.

One of Hugill's last actions before he left was to extract from the Schools Committee a recommendation that priority for any major development at either school should be the provision of a new Library at Whitgift, to be followed by better accommodation for music at Trinity. Alas, the Court did not accept this recommendation, and the Library was not started until 1989.

13. David Raeburn and Great Expectations

The Governors take Advice

In considering their appointment of a new Headmaster, the Governors decided to avoid the embarrassments that had attended their previous decisions in 1960. They thought it expedient to invite someone experienced in the selection of academic staff to advise them. Sir Robert Birley had been successively Headmaster of Charterhouse and Eton. He had been in 1942 a member of the Fleming commission on the Public Schools, and many of his former pupils had been appointed to Headmasterships. After retiring from Eton he achieved further respect in the educational sphere for his interest in universities throughout the world, many of which had conferred honorary degrees upon him. Any recommendation of his would carry great weight, not only with the Governors, but also with Archbishop Ramsey, who was not so ready as Fisher to assess the abilities of men presented for his selection. Indeed he warmly approved of the proposal to enlist Birley's help.

D. A. Raeburn

The outcome was an appropriate one, in the appointment of David A. Raeburn, who had been at Charterhouse under Birley, and a scholar at Christ Church, Oxford, where he gained a first class in Honour Moderations before proceeding to Greats. After two years of national service in the Royal Army Educational Corps he decided to take up teaching upon the advice of John Garrett, who invited him to join the staff of Bristol Grammar School. They shared an interest in drama, and when Mr. Raeburn moved on to his next post at Bradfield, he grasped the opportunity to direct two of their traditional productions of Greek plays. This love for drama, and particularly for Greek drama, has been maintained throughout his career. After a period as Senior Classics Master at Alleyn's School, he obtained his first headship at Beckenham and Penge Grammar School (later Langley Park School for Boys) in 1963. Having taught for twelve years in South London day schools, he had acquired some knowledge of Whitgift's reputation. He had a good deal of sympathy with 'progressive' aims in education, and brought with him a desire to popularise the School.

D.A. Raeburn, MA

Hugill, who would have preferred to preside over a greater formality among staff and boys, especially at official events, liked to preserve a calm aloofness, quite charmingly relaxed on private social occasions. But Raeburn immediately encouraged a much less formal relationship between himself, the staff and senior boys, through a natural and unforced friendliness, exampled by a generous use of christian names. He had the great advantage of being a family man with three young children. His wife, Mary Faith, supported him strongly in this friendly approach and in her hospitality at Haling Cottage.

Many progressive ideas had been adopted in the state schools, such as 'child-centred' learning, free activity, non-streaming, discovery methods, group teaching and open plan teaching spaces; these he was prepared to introduce by degrees in the Junior School, especially if a new building could be provided for it. One change that did soon take place was the removal of the master's dais in order to bring teacher and taught into less formal contact. None of the others was in fact taken up.

The Political Threat

In the 1960s Labour governments had been determined to integrate the public schools into the state system. If Whitgift was to be taken over, Raeburn was determined to be at the head of an efficient and well-equipped institution. The Public Schools Commission set up in 1965 to advise on this step had issued the 'Newsom' Report in 1968, which recommended only partial co-operation through providing some assisted places in the boarding schools. The Commission was thereupon instructed to turn its attention to independent and direct-grant day schools, which could be more easily integrated. In 1970 the 'Donnison' Report was issued, which revealed a division of opinion among the members of the Commission, not all of whom were in favour of integration.

Anthony Crosland, Secretary of State for the Department of Education and Science, although educated at Highgate, was a determined enemy of independent schools and of selective education of any kind; his parliamentary bill to improve comprehensive schooling was intended to be followed by a take-over of all public schools. However, the election of 1970 supervened, a Conservative government was formed under Edward Heath, and Margaret Thatcher was appointed Secretary of State, so Crosland's proposals were scrapped. Nevertheless, the danger to independent education remained, and the prospect of integration had only receded, not disappeared.

In the late 1960s the comprehensive ideal that had at first seemed a perfect solution to the difficulties imposed by the 11+ examination was already seen by many to be flawed. There was fear of domination by left-wing administrators and teachers, many of whom regarded their schools more as vehicles for social engineering than as centres of scholastic endeavour. Much disquiet had been aroused among parents and conservative academics over the decline in elementary achievement attributed to 'child-centred' teaching. The neglect of 'standard' grammatical English and of formal numeracy, together with the egalitarianism associated with comprehensive education, provoked the publication of a series of 'Black Papers', the first of which was issued in 1969 at a time when 'student power' was protesting against any kind of coercive dogmatism or imposition of traditional values, customs, behaviour and methods of teaching. It should be stated that the more extreme of these papers were not entirely congenial to some members of the Whitgift staff.

Sir James Marshall deposed

In September 1970 the signs were propitious. Within a few weeks of the announcement of Raeburn's appointment the greatest impediment to progress and independence of action was removed. On 6 March 1970 Sir James Marshall who, after twenty-four years as Chairman of the Court, expected his annual re-election to that office to be approved with the usual formality, was astounded to be confronted with strong opposition. Among certain members of the governing body there was a growing realisation that a new style of management must be introduced; so far, independent expression of opinion had received little backing, for Marshall had surrounded himself with enough supporters to render any questioning of his proposals and decisions nugatory. But recent tactful lobbying and discussion had brought to common purpose a group who were confident of defying Marshall's power.

R. D. Marten

R. D. Marten, Captain of the School in 1926 and a Governor since 1955, was a member of the firm (Marshall, Liddle and Downey) which, as the successor of Messrs. Drummond, still acted as solicitors to the Foundation. He had acquired a thorough understanding of the Foundation's business and was the chief mover in the rebellion, being supported by the Bishop of Croydon and other members of the Court who, being uninvolved in local government, did not regard themselves as committed to Marshall's philosophy.

The Archbishop had already suggested to Marshall that he should retire, a suggestion that was promptly rejected. The Court now told him that this year there would be no unopposed re-election, and he must no longer expect to run things entirely his own way. With a bad grace he submitted to being one of two candidates, the other being Marten. A full Court was present except for one member. The officers having retired from the Sixth Form Common Room at Whitgift where the meeting was held, fourteen governors cast their votes. The result was even; the absentee was likely to have voted for Marshall, who rather than cast his own extra vote in favour of himself, as he was entitled to do, decided to have nothing more to do with his colleagues and departed, relinquishing the Chairmanship to Marten. The official record may imply otherwise, but Marshall has related his own version. Nevertheless, the Court passed a warm vote of thanks to him for his services of nearly forty years as a Governor and twenty-five as Chairman. They expressed their appreciation of his acumen in acquiring Shirley Park for Trinity School, and in the development of the Whitgift Centre, which was contributing so much to the resources of the Foundation and to the benefit of both Whitgift and Trinity Schools. All this is undoubtedly true; it needed boldness to step in and bid for Shirley Park in anticipation of endorsement from the Court. Marshall had little doubt that if this authorisation had not been given he would have been able to obtain planning permission for development of a different kind on his own behalf.

A 10-year Plan

The combination of a new Chairman and a new Headmaster, each willing to examine his own and the other's responsibilities in a more relaxed, yet more investigative association, led to free discussion and ambitious ideas for development. Fully aware of the greater freedom to make use of the Foundation's increasing wealth in consequence of the Whitgift Act, Marten encouraged Raeburn to contemplate a programme of complete modernisation of the School's facilities. It seemed that the developments urged by Marlar twenty years before might at last be realised.

These formed the basis of Raeburn's '10-year plan' submitted to the Court in November 1970, two months after his arrival. He reiterated the necessity for a separate Junior School block, more science laboratories, an enlarged Library, a Sports Hall, more office and common-room space, Sixth form seminar rooms and improved sanitary and changing accommodation. He also desired a drama workshop and more flexible teaching areas for junior work to conform with the latest ideas in educational practice. He pointed out the inadequacy of the playing-fields, despite the apparent extensiveness of the school grounds. An immediate requirement for the general well-being and efficiency of the School was the renewal of class-room furniture, much of it by this time, like certain corners of the building, dingy and depressing.

He drew the attention of the Governors to the desirability of establishing a notional economic fee chargeable to parents who could afford it, but granting remission to those who might find it difficult to meet. Endowment income would then be released for capital expenditure. With a careful rein on estimates, combined with help from OWs, this policy should enable the School to provide more of what parents were expecting.

The first step towards deciding on what should have precedence was, he suggested, an inspection by the Department of Education and Science. This manoeuvre, adopted also by Andrew, Gurner and Marlar soon after their appointment, was approved immediately by the

Governors, and a prompt invitation was submitted to the Department. The Inspectors were to be specifically requested to advise on how the premises could best be brought up to date in order to fulfil the needs of the future.

DES Inspection

The Department sent a team of seven advisers, led by Mr. R. H. Adams, to visit the School during the last week of October 1971. Discussions were held between them and members of the staff about objectives, curriculum, methods of teaching, general organisation and probable future developments.

Instead of a formal Report from the Inspectorate, an 'Agreed Record of Discussions' was issued, and presented to the Schools Committee on 21 January 1972. This document included useful suggestions from the Inspectors, in particular concerning the teaching of English and of languages, the development of art and technical studies, and the co-ordination of games and physical education. Many departments were greatly hampered by the inadequacy of their space and equipment. Emphasis was given to the necessity for far better accommodation before the work of the School could be reorganised to cater for the abilities of the pupils and to take advantage of the qualities of the staff.

The Inspectors readily acknowledged the attractiveness of the School's setting in woodland and parkland slopes, and the character and style of its buildings. Recognising the importance of not further encroaching upon the grounds, they were confident that additions could be made without much loss of open space. 'Although the additions already made had met specific needs, the deficiencies,' they said, '... may sound formidable.' The first consideration was the Library, which was thought possible of extension in its position in the centre of the main building. Art and Design needed a complete reorganisation and should be combined with Technical Studies. There was a great need for expanded science facilities, more generous office accommodation, a Sports Hall and a new Junior School wing. The desirability of Raeburn's proposals for administrative and domestic improvements was also confirmed.

Provided that finance could be made available, a condition that the Inspectors understood was not insurmountable, the programme might, they thought, be completed within five years, during which time the development could be so phased as to make disturbance minimal, although necessarily continuous.

A final recommendation was the appointment of a full-time Administrative Officer.

In addition to these proposals, David Raeburn pressed again for the adaptation of the Concert Hall for multi-purpose use, the conversion of Sixth Form studies into seminar rooms, the provision of an all-weather games area for hockey and tennis, the refurnishing and decoration of Big School and the stage, and improvements to the Masters' Common Rooms.

The Governors' response was prompt in support. They would consult the section of the Department of Education and Science that advised in such matters, and confer with Headmaster, staff and boys, so that when an architect was appointed, he would receive a clear and comprehensive brief.

Innovations of the 1970s

A good many internal developments unrelated to the question of extensions were now taking place.

One of Raeburn's first exercises in good public relations was an invitation to the headteachers of preparatory and primary schools from which candidates for admission had regularly come, to attend a meeting where they could learn more about the School, its organisation and what it offered. Some primary-school heads were known to be unwilling to advise their pupils to seek places at an independent school, but they were warmly invited to attend nevertheless. Three years later a similar opportunity of inspection was given to parents of prospective pupils, when they and their sons were conducted in groups on a tour of the buildings and its surroundings; this became an annual event, and must have resulted in some increase in the number of applicants.

Early in 1971 a Xerox 3600 photocopying machine was installed, one of the first such devices in any school; it amply justified itself, simplifying and expediting teaching and administration in a manner that is now commonplace. In

June 1972 a second-hand, obsolete but valuable ICL 1500 computer was offered to the School for nothing but the cost of collection and installation; this offer was gladly taken up. A General Studies course was provided for the Lower Sixth, in order to complement the programmes of specialist 'A' level work. The fees continued to go up, but not yet to the economic level proposed. Instead of the Annual Prize Giving in 1972 an 'open evening' was instituted at which 'International Thinking' was the theme; this departure from custom lasted for only a couple of years. Parents were encouraged to make greater contact with their sons' housemasters and other members of the staff. Talks and conferences were laid on to help pupils in their personal problems and relationships. The salary scales were once again reconstructed. The Cricket XI went on tour to Holland.

But no news was heard about the new buildings; the promised discussions were not held. Minor repairs and improvements were carried out; the Concert Hall was given black-out curtains; some classroom furniture was renewed, but there was no evidence of further action on the part of the Governors over the developments that they had appeared so eager to put in hand.

Another move in prospect: Croham Hurst Golf Course

Suddenly the reason was made clear. In early October 1972 rumours were heard that the Governors intended to seek planning permission to sell Haling Park for housing development, and to rebuild the School on the Croham Hurst golf course. This was Foundation freehold land the lease of which was due to expire in 1973. The Governors gave notice of their intention to the local planning authority in December 1972, followed by a Statement of Case on 31 January. That the proposal had been under discussion for some while was evident, on account of its complexity. The golf course, of a total area of 112 acres, had been reserved under the Town Planning regulations as a private open space used for recreational purposes, but the Governors applied for permission to use most of the land for establishing what would be virtually three schools: the new Whitgift, a school for girls, and a combined Sixth Form College to include the older pupils from the other two schools. Altogether about 1500 pupils would be accommodated there. In addition there would be constructed a complex of dwellings for up to 150 old people, and a new administrative centre for the

Croham Hurst Golf Club

Whitgift School

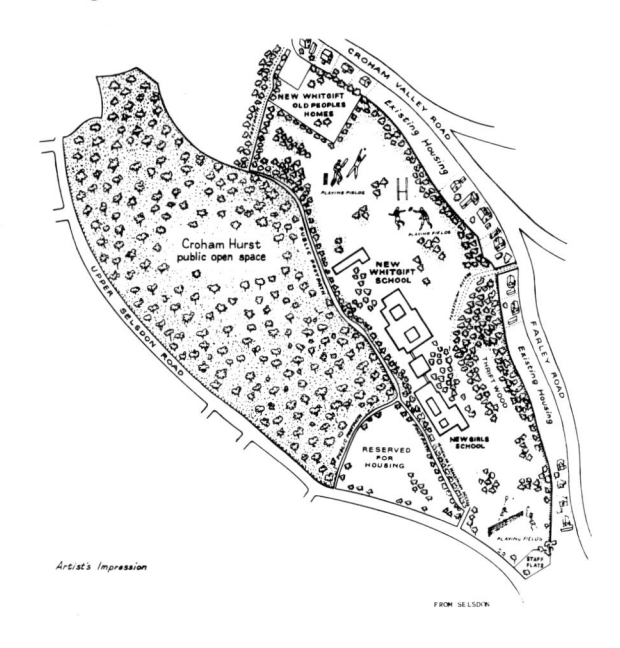

Proposed lay-out for School at Croham

Foundation. A further proposal was to allocate 14 acres to private housing, the sale of which would supplement the proceeds from the sale of Haling Park, a necessary condition for the undertaking. Thus the area would receive an influx of about 2000 people in daily occupation, not counting the occupants of the new private houses. It was to be a new kind of Whitgift Centre.

The granting of planning permission would depend on the balance of benefits to the community at large, calculated on (a) an improvement in educational facilities, as against the loss of the green acres at Haling Park; (b) the provision of much-wanted housing, against the loss of a recreational area enjoyed by golfers from well beyond the confines of Croydon; (c) the effect such development would have on the already congested roads in the area, and the delays to traffic using them, together with ecological and environmental objections; (d) the ability of the Whitgift Foundation to underwrite the whole of the massive project without jeopardising its immediate and future commitments. But the weight of the case was based upon the claim that the Foundation would be unable to perform its functions fully without undertaking this development.

At first sight the concept had its attractions for those with the interests of the School at heart. Such a large area of pleasant, undulating land would provide a superb position for an up-to-date school to replace one that, after forty years of hard use and some degree of neglect, was in need of considerable renewal and extension. Several years would elapse for plans to be prepared and buildings to be erected, but such delay would be tolerable if a superb improvement were to result.

The Chairman, R. D. Marten, the prime instigator of the whole scheme, exerted fully his powers of persuasion to influence public opinion and the views of the School, the Common Room and the Old Whitgiftian Association. Two prominent OWs had been engaged respectively as Counsel to prepare a Statement of Case in seeking planning permission and as Public Relations Officer.

The introduction of partial co-education, possibly by incorporating Croham Hurst Girls' School, which was independent, and Old Palace Girls' School, which was on the Direct Grant list, within the proposed new complex, was thought necessary to validate the Governors' desire to extend their educational aims by the move. Old Palace, which had flourished in the ancient building that had once been John Whitgift's favourite residence, seemed to deserve special attention; the premises they were proud to occupy were nevertheless not ideally located or adequately equipped. The school was also under threat of losing its status. The Labour Party in opposition having announced its intention of abolishing the Direct Grant list, Old Palace might have to choose between joining the state system (which might reject it on account of the deficiencies of its premises) and becoming independent. The Governors of both the girls' schools were eager that they should come under the Foundation's aegis. Marten was a strong supporter of co-education, which he had chosen for his own children.

The Governors thought that compulsory purchase of non-productive land such as Croham Hurst Golf Club for municipal housing was possible under a Labour government, but this action might be circumvented by offering another area, i.e. Haling Park, to the GLC or to the Regional Hospital Board, which might build there a replacement for Croydon General Hospital. Neither of these possibilities would have raised as much money as a sale to speculative developers interested in meeting the demand for high-class housing.

There was also the need for more playing-field space, which could be met only at the Croham Hurst site, especially as it seemed likely that the Brighton Road was to be widened by taking a strip of both North and South Fields, an area of land that could ill be spared.

These assertions were seen to be mainly red herrings and had little effect in stifling opposition which was strengthened by the linking of numerous residents' associations, the members of the Golf Club and groups of individuals, who adopted the slogan 'Keep Croydon green; say "no" to the Whitgift scheme'. The views of Sir James Marshall, now in dignified but not silent retirement, may have become discredited within the Foundation, but they had retained a good deal of respect in local government circles. He pronounced himself fully against it.

The 'Greens' wanted the Golf Course to be included in the Green Belt. Dissenting Governors made their views clear; Digby Weightman thought it neither financially nor economically sensible to destroy a first-class building only forty years old and replace it with something in many respects inferior; Robert Coatman deplored the destruction of yet another open space in order to realise its capital value, only for the Foundation to be confronted with financial stringency for years ahead.

In July 1973, *The Croydon Advertiser* which, in its traditional role of opponent to the power of the Whitgift Foundation, had consistently fostered opposition to the scheme, suddenly experienced a change of heart as the outcome of an interview between Marten and the editor. Marten was determined that the move should take place. It was now time for him to persuade all those who had resisted to withdraw their opposition.

He revealed to *The Advertiser* how conscience-stricken the Governors were, not to have done more in the past for old people or for the education of girls; they wished the areas designated for housing to accommodate the less affluent; they hated to displace the golfers, but hoped to buy some suitable land for them not far away in the Green Belt. Perhaps after all Haling Park might go to the Hospital Board, which was no bad thing. If the improvements at Haling Park, costing £1m, were to be put in hand, the Foundation's resources would be greatly strained, the fees could no longer be subsidised, and fewer scholarships and bursaries could be awarded. But above all, this problem of additions to the School would be solved by the move, for, according to Marten, the inspectors of the DES had had some harsh things to say: 'The 40-year-old classrooms were completely out of date; the sports facilities were heavily criticised, and there was a lack of art, metalwork and woodwork facilities.'

'There was no question of withdrawal of recognition by the DES,' commented the editor, 'but the report was clearly a blow to Croydon's prestige independent school.'

Marten's statements contained so many exaggerations, innuendoes and distortions of fact that a shadow was cast over the School's reputation. The gravity of the charges, which if they had been true, would have reflected badly upon the Governors themselves for their neglect, was completely illusory. Nothing in the agreed record of discussion between the Inspectors and the representatives of Whitgift could be described as 'harsh'; the class-rooms required only refurnishing and redecorating; the existing sports facilities were in fact commended, but extensions were desirable; there was no great *lack* of art, metalwork and woodwork facilities, but there was need for more.

This report did not endear Marten to members of the School who knew the truth and the reasons for delay in implementing the long-expected improvements. Whatever the result of the town-planning application, many years would elapse before Whitgift could hope to be adequately accommodated. There was, moreover, the prospect of co-education and a change of status if the School should move. Greater difficulty of access might also be a grave disadvantage.

There were further misgivings about the quality of the proposed new buildings and their equipment, for the expressed intention of the Governors was to spend no more than £3m on the whole of the new accommodation for 1500 pupils and the old people's homes. This sum, only twice the cost of Trinity seven years before, did not include the expense of landscaping the undulating terrain for playing fields, and Marten's admission that cheaper materials and a lower standard of design would have to be employed led to dismay, intensified when he declared, 'If Whitgift does not move, Whitgift is finished.'

The statement made by Marten to *The Advertiser* was quickly followed by a publicity campaign that presented the Governors' case in an attractive guise. After some initial doubts, David Raeburn gave his qualified support. Croham Hurst School, having been invited to become associated as the girls' school in the project, was eager to become involved. The Governors of Old Palace School, who had been approached over a possible merger with Croham Hurst, had expressed reservations, and did not so definitely commit themselves.

On 8th November 1973 the Croydon Planning Authority rejected the Foundation's application on the grounds of its being detrimental to the environment, of being inconvenient of access and of contributing to road congestion. The Foundation notified its intention to appeal to the Department of the Environment; a public enquiry was forecast for summer 1974, and a date for the appeal to be heard was projected for January 1975. Before these could take place, however, the Foundation withdrew. The financial viability of the scheme, if it had really existed without a crippling lien on the future, had now collapsed owing to rising building costs, the fall in land value including that of Haling Park and the threat to charitable status imposed upon all independent schools by the new Labour Government. The whole project had been a great waste of time and money; worst of all, the School's buildings and consequently its efficiency had been disparaged.

During the seven years since the Music School was completed at Haling Park in 1967 nothing permanent had been added. Yet there had been continuous activity; the Governors had been unwilling to call a halt to all improvement. Conversions were contrived in many departments so that new uses could be given to old premises. Temporary buildings were erected. Some of the overdue repairs and replacements were patched up. The Governors' promises that the £1m extension scheme would go ahead if the Croham Hurst project fell through were now expected to be realised.

Stagnation again

Yet these promises, so readily made when the Governors were hatching their plans for the move, now seemed to be remarkably difficult of fulfilment. The income from the Whitgift Centre was being eroded by inflation; the cost of building was shooting up; no real effort had yet been made to pitch the fees at an economic level at either Whitgift or Trinity. More and more defects were becoming apparent in the heating, electrical, gas, water and sanitary systems, so that a large sum of money, at least £350,000, would have to be found for these renewals and replacements before any £1m extension could be considered. And of course, there were still decisions to be made and plans to be prepared. To tide over the problem, more temporary buildings were erected to relieve the pressure on accommodation. These were to serve for fifteen years.

Moreover, at Trinity School grave defects in design and structure were being revealed. Roofs were leaking, decorative panels were falling off, walls were coming apart, and the basement was subject to flooding. Not only did all these demand immediate attention, but extra accommodation was also required to make up for deficiencies in the original plans, at one time thought to be unstinting in design, to meet the demands of an expanding curriculum.

The Need for better Old People's Accommodation

The interests of the brethren and sisters had also to be considered. Under the Schemes of 1881 and 1915 only a small proportion of the Foundation's income had been allocated for eleemosynary purposes, a limitation that the Whitgift Charities Act of 1969 had been partly designed to remove. A number of Governors were particularly concerned that this element of their responsibility should no longer be neglected, and they very properly demanded a thorough internal reconstruction of the ancient Hospital buildings, so that each resident should be given more space, a kitchen area, private bathroom and lavatory accommodation, central heating, a new electrical installation for light and power, and intercom services in case of emergency. Every worn part of the building was to be renewed. These improvements, costing nearly £1m and taking five years to complete, were declared open by Her Majesty the Queen on 21 June 1983. In addition, it was urged that a site

Her Majesty the Queen at Whitgift Hospital, 21st June 1983

must be found for the generous provision of sheltered housing for many more old people; because of the increased space per head the number of residents at the Hospital had been halved, there now being room for only 18. The site favoured in Hugill's time for such a development had been the grounds of Haling Cottage, but the loss of such a valuable area of potential playing-field space had been strongly opposed by the Common Room. However, when the proposals for the move to Croham Hurst Golf Club were made, the possible loss of Haling Cottage and grounds became irrelevant. One of the reasons advanced for the move to Croham Hurst had been the inadequacy of the grounds at Haling Park, and the failure in 1931 to acquire the Whitgift Avenue site had been referred to by Marten as a loss that could at last be compensated for by the move. In view of this acknowledged lack of space it was now thought that the Haling Cottage project would be rejected, and some other site decided upon.

The National Economy

In 1975 under the Wilson government the national economy was rapidly weakening; dollar reserves were diminishing; inflation rose to 25%; salaries had to go up; so did fees, but not yet to the extent that had been regarded as necessary to cover running expenses and the replacement of services. The Houghton Report and the Clegg

David Raeburn and Great Expectations

award on teachers' salaries made any forecast of the scale of fees at the beginning of the school year in 1975 an uncertain piece of guesswork; a 35% increase was eventually decided upon. A study of the financial position did not encourage hope; there would be a budgeted deficit of £84,000 on the School account for the year ending August 1976.

End of Direct Grant Schools

In January 1975 Reg Prentice himself, whose invitation to be the Guest of Honour at the revived Prize-Giving in the previous November had aroused some criticism, announced, as Secretary of State for Education and Science, the phasing-out of the Direct Grant with effect from September 1976. Loss of charitable status for independent schools was not far off. (Prentice quickly regretted his action, which was the result of his then readiness to support his party. He held his post in the Cabinet for only fifteen months, and the abolition of the Direct Grant did not come into force until his successor, Shirley Williams, was in office. Prentice crossed the

The Rt. Hon. Sir Reg Prentice

floor of the House in October 1977.) In the event, not all that was forecast occurred. Direct Grant schools were given the option of submitting to LEA control or of taking the risks of independence. Until these individual decisions were made, the effect upon existing independent schools was uncertain. Whilst Direct Grant schools taken over by the LEAs might lose some pupils to independent schools, those that chose independence were taking a risk of disaster. By and large, these schools remained successful, retaining pupils and attracting a sufficient number of new ones for whom parents were prepared to pay increased fees.

During the eight years that had elapsed since independence was chosen for Trinity, the Governors had forgone grants to a total of several hundred thousand pounds, which they had replaced during most of this time from endowment income, for the Trinity fees and the LEA places had been maintained (apart from small fee increases on account of inflation) at their former levels. In the year 1971–72 Trinity's fees were subsidised by more than 75%; Whitgift's by nearly 60%.

Raeburn's persistence

David Raeburn did not give up. Already, before the Governors pulled out of the Croham Hurst venture, he had been drawing up a schedule of requirements at Haling Park in order to cover such an eventuality. In February 1975 he presented the Governors with his proposals, based on the HMI recommendations, for a scheme of phased development that could be completed in about six years, provided that finance and the will were not lacking.

Sir Hugh Wilson PPRIBA

George Lowe, the architect of the 1960s extensions at Whitgift and of the new Trinity School at Shirley Park, having retired, the Governors appointed Sir Hugh Wilson to design and supervise all building that was to be undertaken by the Foundation: the internal reconstruction of the Hospital, the additions to Trinity, the proposed development at Croham Hurst and, if that should prove abortive, the projected old people's homes and the new buildings at Whitgift. Sir Hugh had already been engaged, as a leading consultant in town-planning, to advise on the layout of the Croham Hurst site. His quick appreciation of the Governors' requirements made him a clear choice for appointment as their general architect. His feasibility study, with plans to add to and to adapt the buildings at Haling Park according to Raeburn's brief, had already been on display at the 'open evening' in November 1973. This was a somewhat ironic exercise during the height of the Croham Hurst crisis, but formed a basis for later consideration. The first phase of the plan comprised reconstruction for better use of much of the existing non-teaching areas, followed by the building of a Junior School base and a Sports Hall. The next phase would be the reconstruction of the Library and improvements to Big School. Finally, consideration would be given to the construction, to begin in 1980, of new buildings for science, and for art, design and technology, which Raeburn foresaw would be the major requirements of forward-looking schools during the last decade of the century. But Sir Hugh's plans, even for the first phase alone, were likely to be costly, and had to give way to urgent needs that could no longer be deferred. These were the renewal of services, the provision of better fire-protection and the restoration of many parts of the structure after years of hard wear and decay. But Raeburn nevertheless urged immediate expenditure on capital developments before any corporation tax should be imposed upon educational foundations. Perhaps an appeal for funds could be addressed to Old Whitgiftians. By this time it was summer 1975.

The Five-day Week

In 1974 public disruptions were affecting the life of the nation at large. The miners' strike had already resulted in a shut-down of industry, with a limit of three working days per week to conserve fuel and power. In February the School temporarily abandoned Saturday morning attendance. This surrender of teaching time was not peculiar; many other day-schools, including the maintained sector, had already adopted a five-day week during the previous twenty-five years. Trinity had done so in 1957. In January 1972 the Common Room had received for discussion a tentative proposal from two members that

Saturday morning school should be discontinued, but the motion was withdrawn and not put to the vote. The Headmaster and the Common Room were not then in favour of a change which would, they thought, result in more losses than gains.

The temporary abandonment was received with mixed feelings. For most people, pupils and staff, the loss of Saturday morning school resulted in a gain in leisure and freedom of choice of action at the week-end. The pros and cons of a permanent adoption of the shorter week were warmly argued. If the traditional inter-school matches were to be played on Saturdays, and no other course was considered possible, a special attendance at School would be necessary for the players and for those who wished to support them. Members of the staff who had already accepted an extension of their hours of duty in coaching or supervising games would continue to be involved. If one had to attend morning school, to stay on for the afternoon was a not unreasonable, if perhaps a somewhat reluctant, sequel; to many of those involved, boys and staff, it was an acceptable, even welcome obligation.

Certain members of the staff who were in favour of the change declared that they could see an opportunity to allocate Saturday morning to voluntary but enthusiastic attendance at those activities, so liberally provided for and encouraged at the School, for which time could only with difficulty be found during the week; societies, swimming, individual games such as squash and fives, CCF, Scouts, excursions, community service, field-work, the language laboratory, or even extra tuition. Other marginal advantages, which had not been greatly ventilated earlier, were less tangible or less credible; parents would relish their sons' closer participation in family life (so that their weekend activities were not held up by waiting for morning school to finish), or older boys could take the opportunity to engage in part-time employment, thereby introducing themselves profitably to the world of work. (How this accorded with the attractions of family life, with making good use of School facilities or with the concept of loyalty to the School and its obligations was not explained. Many parents were, and still are, very happy to interest themselves in their sons' activities at School on Saturday afternoons.)

Boys, parents and staff were invited to express their preference. The outcome was inevitable; who would for long opt out from greater ease? A clear majority was in favour of the five-day week, which was permanently adopted in September 1974. When everyone else is content with shorter hours, to be obliged to report for duty on Saturday mornings (which used to be the common practice in offices and other places of work until the 1950s) would eventually have aroused resentment.

Realists foresaw some decline in the enthusiasm for representative games, in the number of spectator supporters, and in considerable neglect of the hitherto amply used amenities at the School. In point of fact, this decline and this neglect have not been greatly manifest. The variety of activities undertaken on Saturdays, in the morning and in the afternoon, has increased, largely on account of the enthusiasm and dedication of members of the staff who continue to give up much of their spare time for necessary coaching, refereeing, supervising and accompanying school teams. Parents and Old Boys have also frequently given help.

The School Advisory Committee

Two important organisations were formed in 1975 and 1976; the School Advisory Committee and the Whitgift School Association. The former was set up to help in the framing of the complicated Annual Budget and in the allocation of expenditure between running expenses, provision of bursaries, repairs and replacements and also of capital investment in buildings and equipment. It had become customary to blur the distinction between repairs, replacements and new work. Service technology was developing fast, new sources and uses of power were in competition, and specialist advice was becoming more and more desirable. The Advisory Committee (there was also one for Trinity) comprised governors, parents, masters and Old Boys, each with a valuable expertise and a commitment to offer. After close examination of problems and frank consultation with the Headmaster, the Committee, which first met on 11 October 1975, reported to the Schools Committee, who hitherto had not experienced any sifting through of enquiries, proposals and recommendations. It was made perfectly clear that the allocation of the Foundation's own resources, which were chiefly directed towards capital development, the renewal of dilapidations and the provision of scholarships and bursaries, remained solely with the Court of Governors.

The Whitgift School Association

The Whitgift School Association was mainly the outcome of a desire on the part of parents for a better understanding of the School's problems in this time of uncertainty, and of a readiness to assist in the raising of funds for expansion, which seemed as far off as ever. But because of the success of the Advisory Committee it became mainly a means of fostering a close relationship between staff, parents and others (especially Governors and Old Boys) connected with the School, and of engaging in activities to promote its pupils' welfare. A meeting was held on 25 February 1976 at which a Chairman (G. S. Galer, OW) and a Committee were elected, and a Constitution approved. The Association's primary object was 'to secure effective representation of parents' views to the Governors' and secondly 'to establish good communications among parents'.

At the first meeting, David Raeburn, who as Headmaster was inducted as President, read a paper on 'The Rôle of the Independent Sector in Education today', in which he warned his audience of the danger to the independent schools from political ideology of the left. He referred to the phasing-out of the Direct Grant, the removal of the power of the LEAs to buy places for highly intelligent pupils at independent schools and the threatened loss of charitable status. But the main points he raised were the difficulties that faced teachers in those comprehensive schools where any kind of competition or élitism was anathema, and where any inculcation of cultural or academic values was regarded as anti-social. He pointed out that independent education could still exhibit its principles of freedom and leadership as examples to the maintained system. He called upon the Association to give its support in the independent schools' battle to preserve their freedom. A lead had been given by the foundation in 1972 of National ISIS (Independent Schools Information Service).

While disclaiming that its main purpose is the raising of funds by appeal, the Association has always been active in finding money for minor additions and amenities, including £10,000 towards equipment in the new Sports Hall, curtains in Big School, a contribution to the Portrait Fund, a PA system for the Swimming Pool, support for School tours and expeditions, a scout tent, and a computer-printer for the Junior School. The social side has flourished: cheese and wine parties, soirées, supper dances, summer balls have all been successfully promoted, and in 1980 the Association was invited to combine with the OWA in providing entertainment and refreshments on OWA Day. Further projects have included the formation of Badminton, Tennis and Cricket (Honesti) clubs; a family Swimming club and a Fine Arts Society had already been in existence for a few years.

Rupert Nicholson

Towards the end of 1975 the Governors decided that a financial expert should be consulted to help the Foundation with its problems. For many years capital developments had been financed out of endowment income and treated as incidental outgoings, instead of being funded from reserves accumulated for the purpose, and of being regarded as capital assets. The prospect of great riches had for a long time been clearly perceived not far off, but too often what had become available was dissipated in subsidising fees and in paying for unanticipated renewals and replacements at the two schools. Marten approached Rupert Nicholson, OW, senior partner in one of the largest firms of chartered accountants in the country and already a member of the Schools Advisory Committee. After some weeks' study, Nicholson reported personally to the Court and made a number of recommendations, including the raising of loans and the issuing of appeals, before any major works were undertaken, for it would be several years before any growth in the Foundation's income would accrue from a large increase in rents. Nicholson's help was so much valued that he was invited to become a Governor when the next vacancy arose in March 1976. A later consequence was the setting up of a Financial and Investment sub-committee under Nicholson's chairmanship, and the appointment of professional financial advisers and assets managers.

Additions 1978–82

Another result of Nicholson's advice was the determination at last to proceed with some of the long-delayed developments, including the construction of the new Junior School base (the Ian Evans Building), which was started in March 1978 and opened for use in 1980, of a new house for the Headmaster in place of Haling Cottage, and of the Sports Hall, started in May 1980, opened by Mrs. Marlar in May 1982 and named after her late husband. This was the most considerable addition for sport since the Swimming Pool in 1969.

The construction of these three major buildings was after all financed from the Foundation's own resources, although the I. A. Evans building had been provided by the Advisory Committee from some of its own budgeted funds. Not only was great encouragement given to the Juniors and to many sporting activities, but also proof was given that the School's requirements were recognised and were approaching fulfilment. Meanwhile class-rooms, the Library, the Dining Hall and other much frequented places were being refurbished. More frequent and less conventional redecoration, improved lighting, less ponderous furniture, with curtains and carpeting in some rooms, have all contributed towards a more congenial atmosphere for learning by eliminating the dull surroundings associated with the typical school background.

Whitgift House

The decision to erect what was virtually a small village in Haling Cottage grounds was by this time accepted as inevitable. In order to stifle opposition, an even more damaging proposal had been made: to develop the greater part of South Field for the purpose, eliminating a rugby-pitch and the only permanently enclosed cricket square except for the First XI square on North Field. The acknowledged shortage of space did not now seem to matter to those who had once cast their eyes on the rolling acres of the Golf Club; neither did they consider looking any farther than the confines of Haling Park for a suitable site for the urgently needed sheltered housing for old people.

Whitgift House, as the new development has been named, was erected in two phases, and

Aerial View of Haling Park, 1982

opened by Archbishop Runcie on 1 June 1988. It consists of twenty well-appointed small flats for couples or single persons, twelve residential-care bedsit units, affording sheltered accommodation, and a full-care unit for up to thirteen people. There is a fine common room, and central catering provides meals not only for the residents but also for elderly members of a daily luncheon club which formerly met at Haling Park Cottage. There is also the Chapel of Christ the Healer and Teacher, capable of holding a congregation of up to 80, which is available for use by the School.

Haling Cottage, 1981

The School's new neighbours have been welcomed with great warmth; the School is glad to share their company and friendship. The supposition that the Founder established his Hospital for the aged and his School for the instruction of youth in close proximity in order to promote fellowship between the two extremes may not be a tenable one, but in present times a close relationship is practical and advantageous to all. Many pupils are happy in contributing towards the well-being of their elders, in the same degree as the latter are pleased to follow their juniors' activities on the playing-field or to attend their performances on the music and drama stages.

Other developments since 1970

Intake and Admissions Procedure

The number of pupils has increased from 800 to 900 overall, with 630 now in the Senior School. There has been no great change in their general social origin (professional and managerial classes) or areas of residence, but there is a higher proportion (10%) from immigrant and expatriate families.

The examination for entry at 10 or 11 is designed to test potential at least as much as attainment, the object being to identify boys of promise whether they have received special coaching or not.

In recent years there have been fewer candidates because of the reduced school-age population, but the overall quality of the intake has been maintained.

The School also admits about 20 boys each year at the age of 13 either through the Independent Schools Common Entrance Examination or through its own Scholarship examination.

Staff

The teaching staff are younger. Their turnover is slightly higher that it was twenty years ago, for there are even more opportunities for able young men to obtain posts of responsibility after good experience at Whitgift. Between 1970 and 1990, nine were promoted directly to headships or deputy headships, and over thirty to be heads of departments. In recent years more women and part-time teachers have been appointed. Recruitment is not easy, for the cost of living in the Croydon area, although relieved by the short-term availability of school rented housing, is some deterrent to applicants.

Education is now following business, industry and other professions in laying more emphasis on staff development and training. In 1985 a system of annual review was introduced which gives each member of staff the opportunity to meet his head of department and one of the management team and discuss his areas of responsibility and involvement. Staff also expect to spend a few days a year at school outside the recognised term dates for the purpose of training and discussion. Departmental meetings are more frequent, and funds are available for attendance at external courses.

Examination Results

The changes in curriculum have been in accordance with the general aims of secondary education applied to the minority of the population who aspire to tertiary education, but who share with the remainder a common core curriculum, and standards of achievement and assessment which are incorporated in the reorganised examination system. The introduction in 1988 of the General Certificate of Secondary Education, still much in dispute for its shortcomings, and of its higher equivalent at 'A' Level, has demanded different and very challenging approaches by the staff.

The average 'pass rate' (Grade C or better) at GCE 'O' Level for 1980–7 was 85%, a slight improvement on the average of 83% for 1971–9, with 27% of entries being awarded Grade A. In the first three years of the GCSE 90% were awarded Grade C or better, 42% at Grade A. Over the period the number of subjects for which boys have been entered has risen from a norm of 8 or 9 in the 1970s to an average of 11.5, with boys 'passing' in an average of 10.1 subjects in 1990. The policy has been to enter boys in all the subjects they have studied, even when their prospects of a sound grade have seemed poor.

At 'A' Level the pass-rate for 1990 was 89% compared with 75% in 1971. The average pass-rate for the period 1971–84 was 84% but a norm of 90% was established during 1985–9. The figures for 'good passes' (Grades A or B) show a similar progression during the period: 26% in 1971, 43% average for 1971–9, 47% average for 1980–4, 53% average for 1985–9. In 1988 a record 35% of entries were awarded Grade A.

The 1970s saw a steady increase in the number going on to Oxford and Cambridge, averaging 19 a year, a figure which was all but maintained in the 1980s despite the increased competition for admission from women students and the ancient universities' policy of encouraging more entries from maintained schools. 120 entrance awards were gained between 1970 and 1983, but this form of academic competition has now ceased, and the Colleges award scholarships or exhibitions to undergraduates only after they have been in residence for at least a year. A record number of 26 places was achieved by the entries for 1978 (including 13 on awards) and 1984.

Accurate total figures for those going on into higher education are hard to establish as many now take a gap year after completing their 'A' Level course and apply successfully to universities and polytechnics during that time. It is estimated that at least 85% of Sixth Form leavers now eventually go on to higher education.

Since the introduction of the GCSE even fewer boys leave school at the end of the Fifth Form year and their places are often taken by transfers from other schools.

The Fast Stream and the Upper Sixth

Until the late 1960s post-'A' Level (Upper) Sixth Forms included a number of boys who had passed from a fast-stream Remove or Fourth Form straight into the Lower Sixth at the age of 14 or 15, having taken the requisite range of 'O' Levels; they sat for 'A' Levels two years later. Many of these boys and a few others then spent a year or even two improving upon their 'A' Levels and trying for university awards. There was a tendency for those who were successful in the latter attempt to stay on for the remainder of the school year, because they were scholars or free-placers, or because the fees were low anyway, and also because there seemed to be no alternative but idleness before going to university.

The accelerated passage established by Gurner in 1933 was abolished by Hugill in 1968; it had long been recognised as leading to premature specialisation and to boredom in repetitious work. Most boys now take Mathematics and French or German before entering the Fifths, where a further range of subjects is on offer. Many boys gain passes in a total of ten or eleven subjects, and it is by no means uncommon for some to achieve 'A' grades in all of them. These achievements indicate the different requirements since 'O' Levels of the General Certificate of Education replaced the old School Certificate in 1951.

Thus it happened that upon Raeburn's arrival there was a sudden reduction in precocious membership of the Upper Sixth. Shortly afterwards he decided that those who had failed or who wished to improve upon their 'A' Levels would be better served by studying elsewhere, for retakes in the same atmosphere were not proving altogether successful.

In 1960 there had been fifty-five boys in the Upper Sixth, a figure which steadily declined over the next twenty-five years.

In 1968, when the revised procedure of Oxbridge admissions was fully adopted, the 7th-term Sixth, as it had come to be known, for its sole purpose was to seek university places at the end of the Michaelmas Term, was abolished. (The second-year Sixth had been renamed Upper Sixth in 1983).

During these twenty-five years the number of boys aged 18 at the beginning of the Michaelmas Term had fluctuated between eleven and thirty but now, in 1990, there are none. At the top of the School there used to be young men in their nineteenth or twentieth year, with 'A' Levels behind them, who had time to accept responsibility in coaching games, in House affairs and in school societies; they were prepared to attend closely to prefectorial duties and to act as exemplars to their juniors. Now the serious matter of good grades at 'A' Level is paramount in the minds of the Upper Sixth. The 'gap' year, used for travel and for work experience before university, becomes a substitute for undertaking duties at school.

Curriculum

The curriculum reflects changes in social requirements as well as different approaches to teaching. In English there has been an increase in 'creative writing', oral work and class drama. 'Classical' works have given way to more recent literature. While Shakespeare remains a staple study, Milton, Pope, Shelley and Dickens seldom get much attention below 'A' Level English specialists. Divinity has become less Bible-centred, with discussion applied to ethics and contemporary issues, i.e. social concern, rather than to theology. In History and Geography, field and project work have been developed. The Direct Method of teaching Modern Languages so insisted upon at Whitgift in the 1920s steadily lost favour. Although innovative, in that great efforts were made to instil a good native pronunciation, language study was then still based on formal expressions found in standard works of literature and a thorough understanding of grammar, rather than on everyday conversation. By the 1970s there was a greater emphasis on oral fluency, grammar was regarded as assimilable, accuracy was less desirable than making a tolerable attempt, and the requirements of modern travel and life in the community became more important than an acquaintance with the vocabulary of agricultural life or with the customs of the classroom. For a while the language laboratory proved a novel interest, but that soon waned, maintenance of equipment became expensive, and in 1979 the booths were dismantled. A simpler system was installed in 1988. Russian, which was adopted with some enthusiasm in the 1960s, dropped out for lack of demand. New boys may now choose between French and German at 11, with the option of taking up the other as well at 12. In the Lower First a language awareness course is run in Japanese and Italian.

In Classics the study of the ancient world and the appreciation of its literature have supplanted much of the old linguistic discipline. Mathematics is successfully tackled by nearly all GCSE candidates and it is studied by 60% of all A-level candidates. Further advances in technology, especially that of the sophisticated computer, have led to a development of computer studies. Statistics and Computer Studies were both time-tabled for all fourth-formers by 1980, and by 1989 second-formers were being introduced to the computer. This interest has been further stimulated by involvement in computer printing, especially of *The Whitgiftian*, the input of which is now almost entirely in the hands of boys. Social Science has flourished in the Sixth, with 'A' Level courses now being offered in Economics, Politics and Business Studies. The Natural Sciences have continued to expand, influenced by the Nuffield experiment and by a greater awareness of the economic importance of scientific studies. Syllabuses give a greater emphasis to understanding, rather than to learning facts, and also to the practical application of scientific knowledge. Links between school and industry have been forged, especially with BP plc, while field-trips have become part of the chemistry course, just as they have long been in biological studies.

Sixth Formers have always been required to devote a proportion of their time to non-examined studies, but the aims and content of these have varied considerably over the years. The opportunity to learn a new foreign language has been available. Other options have included law, music and art appreciation, and theatre studies. Practical courses in cookery and vehicle maintenance have also proved popular.

Careers Guidance

Careers advice at school was not officially available until Gurner's time. In the 1920s a boy left school when he was judged capable of taking up work by passing General Schools Certificate or Matriculation, or when he was of an age to proceed to university or to take articles under a professional man, such as a solicitor, an actuary, a chartered accountant or surveyor or, at one time, an architect.

Schoolmasters were not well qualified to advise on these matters, with the exception perhaps of choosing a college, for they had little knowledge of the commercial or industrial world. It was a boy's father who was responsible for giving or obtaining advice, for directing him into a suitable career and for providing the funds to give him his training or to see him through university. If a boy showed sufficient academic promise, someone, a head of department or the headmaster himself, might recommend a university course; a place in the Science Sixth would presuppose some decision upon a professional career.

Among Gurner's innovations was the appointment of a Careers Master, the first being E. F. Bentley, who combined the post with that of

The Old Library, 1990

Head of English. Apart from being a man of independent means and a sophisticate in literary and social circles in London's clubland, he seems to have had few advantages over other members of the staff in his qualifications for giving careers guidance. In 1946 he was succeeded by A. H. Ewen, who combined the job with that of Second Master. By this time Ewen had consolidated his position as an authority on all philosophical matters. He set up a Careers Committee, comprising himself and three or four Heads of Department, who were available to be consulted. In 1959 Dick Glynne-Jones took over, the committee was dissolved, and he established headquarters in a classroom converted for the purpose, where boys could consult a variety of sources of information. Although he relinquished the post in 1963, he returned twenty years later to an already much developed department.

Over the 1970s and 1980s counselling and information about courses in higher education and employment opportunities assumed growing importance in independent schools generally. Although not all boys found they were able to make their decision on a career before leaving school, a perspective of possibilities could help in the motivation of their school work. Career considerations, no less than boys' abilities and interests, were an important factor in the crucial choice of 'A' Level subjects. In the Sixth Form, careful research was needed to ensure that boys applied to the right university or polytechnic and for the appropriate degree course.

In due course more of the teaching staff and many parents became involved in careers guidance, and Careers is now an established department whose head occupies a prominent place in the School's hierarchy. The new extension contains, next to the Library, a larger, purpose-designed, Careers Centre, which includes a well equipped office, computerised records and an interview room.

Boys are encouraged to give thought to their future careers as early as the Third or Fourth Form through 'insight into industry' courses. Fifth Form boys receive a careers interview based on interest questionnaires and sometimes aptitude tests before they make their provisional 'A' Level choices. The department arranges a period of work experience for all boys after they have completed their GCSE exams in June. In the Sixth Form boys are given a course on self-presentation in written applications or interviews and are required to complete a personal careers project. In their final year they are formally interviewed by a panel, which Raeburn has usually chaired himself, on their applications for higher education or other plans.

For many years the department has arranged an annual 'conversazione', at which boys can meet and talk to a group of advisers, mostly Old Whitgiftians and parents, about a wide range of careers. Seminars on particular careers are also conducted at the OW Clubhouse.

The Arts

The temporary Art building of 1969 and its successor of 1988 provided more space for a wider range of activities, with greater provision for three-dimensional work and for photography; these developments, now combined with those of Craft, Design and Technology, will enjoy greater possibilities when these become fully integrated in the new Design complex.

Music

The variety of music played and the number of groups of players have vastly increased under the direction of Robert Vincent, who succeeded John Odom when the latter retired in 1980. Nearly a third of all boys are learning to play a musical instrument. The First Orchestra is supported by many other groups, which may be started, dissolved and re-formed: the Dance Band, the Jazz-Rock group, the Woodwind Ensemble, the Big Band, the String Orchestra. Although a Parents' Choral Society was formed in 1982, the School Choir itself lapsed for a short while because of the sheer conflict of demands made upon the time of young singers. The greatest peaks of achievement have been *Carmen* (1986), producer Roland Polastro, and, for the second time *The Magic Flute* (1988), producer David Raeburn; Robert Vincent directed in both productions, and the cast were joined by talented singers from Croham Hurst and Old Palace girls' schools, who greatly enhanced the quality and enjoyment of the operas.

Drama

Drama has also flourished over the period. The task of directing the main annual play was usually taken in turns by Raeburn himself and John Branston, whose productions were often toured abroad in Germany after performance in Big School. The choice of play has included several works by Shakespeare, but boys have also had the opportunity to act in Sophocles, Sheridan, Ibsen and several modern playwrights. Girls are now brought in from outside to play the female roles, again most commonly from Croham Hurst or Old Palace. In Big School regular use is made of a large apron extension, and an elaborate computerised lighting system has been installed. Though productions have been of a high standard, the hall is a large one to fill, and audiences today are less easy to attract.

After the Marlar Hall was opened in 1982, the former gymnasium was converted into a drama studio with a dual function. It is mainly used by a specialist teacher for informal classwork in drama, now established as part of the English Department's syllabus, with the aim of developing imagination and communication skills. It has also been designed to accommodate performances before small audiences of about two hundred. These can be given either with tiered seating on three sides or more conventionally at one end. A number of productions have been put on, including German plays, others sponsored by the History department, and Junior School pantomimes. A house drama competition has also been introduced, for which the studio affords an excellent setting.

Games and Sport

The Sports Hall

The Marlar Sports Hall, unmatched for the wide range of activities that it can accommodate, has provided opportunities not only to practise skills under cover in wet weather (cricket nets, hockey, tennis) but also to introduce new games, such as badminton, basket-ball and table tennis. It is much more suitable than the old 'Salle' for fencing matches. There is also a weight-training room for building up the strength of those who need remedial exercise or who wish to improve their stamina.

A wider choice in games and athletic activity has been made available, especially for the less gifted, and many of the 'minor' sports have flourished. Under 'games' must be included chess, which has been enjoying a revived popularity, and bridge, also played competitively. Success throughout this wide diversity of opportunity is difficult of fulfilment. For schools with limited facilities it is possible to concentrate all resources upon perhaps one winter and one summer game. The results may be a very consistently high standard of achievement; but the unathletically gifted can be either ignored or used as practice-objects for the better endowed: bodies for scrums to shove against, or fielders for throwing the ball back, with no chance of trying out another game.

It is not easy to find coaches for some of the 'minor' sports; the Colleges of Physical Education cannot teach their students to excel at all games. Among class-room teachers versatile athletes are increasingly hard to come by; nevertheless, the contribution made by such men continues to be outstanding. Visiting coaches have been engaged for cricket, fencing, tennis, squash, athletics and badminton, but fives and shooting remain difficult to cover.

With the provision of the renewed all-weather hockey-pitch, hockey has become popular and is played with enthusiasm as it is now at many other public schools. As the main game during the Lent term, it acquired in 1981 the status of a 'major' sport with the appropriate insignia. The quality of Whitgift hockey is illustrated by the invitations extended on two occasions to the School XI to play at Lord's immediately before the University match, by the number of recent blues, and by the achievement of the Old Whitgiftian HC in winning in 1988 and 1989 the Glenfarclas Cup for inter-Old Boy hockey. The game that Bob Schad set well on its feet in 1950 has continued its success under Brian Griffiths (Oxford and Wales). M. D. Featherstone (1961–68) became Whitgift's first hockey international.

Tennis, squash, fencing, swimming, athletics and golf, in which individual achievement is dominant, have been taken up with enthusiasm by more boys, perhaps at some expense to rugby and cricket, for the 'minor' sports are now

Whitgift School

Hockey First XI, 1989
L. to r., Back row: Morris, Morton, Shelley, Sutherland, Holt, Ellson, Ward,
Front row: Ohadi, Purcell, Davies, T. Griffiths (Capt.), S. Griffiths, Stubbs.
Played 32, won 18, Drew 10, Lost 4

encouraged all the year round, instead of being concentrated upon during the Lent term only. Several more distinguished performers, including 'blues' at rugby, cricket, hockey, athletics, cross-country, golf, fives, modern pentathlon and fencing were produced during the 1980s.

In 1988 the distinction between 'major' and 'minor' sports was abolished, and traditional first team representative colours may now be awarded to members of all teams with an approved fixture-list.

But Modern Tetrathlon, in which Whitgift excelled during the 1960s and 1970s, has been dropped, and competitive swimming for the Bath Cup is not so eagerly pursued, possibly because training demands great dedication and expenditure of time in monotonous swimming of many lengths along 25 metres of water.

Shooting is another minority sport that has declined in importance. The miniature range is well used, but the closure of open ranges at Woldingham and Westcott some years ago left Bisley as the only venue for practice. Regular shooting at 200 and 500 yards on an open range requires an expenditure of time in travel that is hard to justify. Moreover the difficulty of finding an experienced coach, absolutely necessary for effective practice, or anyone else prepared to spend the occasional weekend supervising at the ranges during the summer has resulted in the disappearance of Whitgift teams from competition for the Ashburton Shield, well over a century after their first appearance. In Victorian times open-range shooting was not only encouraged because of the need for military marksmanship, but it was also a fashionable activity connected with country gentlemen's sport on moor and mountain-side. These inducements have lost their relevance today, when weapon-training is based on different kinds of fire-arms.

The altered ethos of games

Success in team games may not now be pursued with as much zeal as in the 1950s. Diversity of opportunity, together with the emergence of professional attitudes and dominance, combined with public tolerance of bad

David Raeburn and Great Expectations

manners and violence in many kinds of sport and games, have diminished the ideal of sportsmanship. The pressure of examinations has reduced the esteem in which public school sport used to be held. The summer term, much shortened now by the early date at which GCSE and 'A' levels begin and end, leaves little time for upper school cricket, which flourished in those days when matriculation was the final academic aim, if any, of many players. The leading daily papers now overlook public school sport almost entirely; even results of Oxford and Cambridge matches are only briefly reported, and the schools the players attended are seldom printed against their name. School prestige is no longer chiefly calculated from the list of opponent schools and from the success of football and cricket teams in matches against them. In schools where academic and creative success is given priority, a category in which the most reputable public schools may now be found, there is no place for the solely athletic achiever.

These considerations, however, serve as small consolation for the many defeats inflicted by Trinity School upon Whitgift teams during the past few years.

The Sports Hall

Fencing, 1989
L. to r., Back row: Dunnett, S. McFarlane, Glancy, Fisher, *Middle row*: Patrick, Everett, Mahtani, Yeabsley, McDermott, Hewlett, Gee, *Seated*: Milla, Potts, F. McFarlane, K. Smith Esq, Fletcher, Toosy, Stafford-Bull, G. Allen, F. McCombie, *Kneeling*: D. McCombie, A. Allen

The Services, Adventure Training and Outdoor Pursuits

In 1974 the Combined Cadet Force celebrated the centenary of its formation as the Cadet Company of the 1st Volunteer Battalion of the Queen's (Royal West Surrey) Regiment. During a hundred years there had been many developments following the changing patterns of warfare. The Cadet units of the nineteenth century concentrated on drill and musketry, and wore the conventional service dress uniform of the day. The army's experiences in the Boer War led to a number of realistic changes, including the adoption of khaki in 1901, and still greater concentration on rifle-shooting. At Whitgift the establishment of the Corps of Drums in 1905, and the regular route-marches, field-days and camps at Aldershot, qualified the unit to become one of the new Officers' Training Corps in 1908, following the government's plans for defence in the inevitable war with Germany. The part played by former members of the OTC in the two World Wars needs no further description here.

In September 1940 OTCs, junior section, were disbanded, and from them were formed the Junior Training Corps, which embraced also cadet corps unconnected with school organisations. Now that conscripted service in the ranks was required from all candidates for a commission, school OTCs became unnecessary. In 1941 an Air Section was set up, and in 1948 a Naval one. In 1949 these and the original Army section were more closely united as the Combined Cadet Force. From this time on, after undergoing basic instruction in the Army section, cadets had a choice of three arms to serve in, but in 1964 new War Office regulations required the normal period of service to be reduced to three years, although a number of NCOs could be retained for administrative and instructional purposes. There was a consequent reduction in numbers by a third. In the following year the Whitgift Naval section was disbanded because it had become impossible to find an officer to take over. Further reductions in the total period of service have been made and the time formerly given to field-days is now concentrated in longer training weekends. Emphasis is now given, not to drill and formal military exercise, but to adventure training and other outdoor pursuits. The CCF invariably

Combined Cadet Force, 1983

receives high commendation from the inspecting officers. Membership of the Cadet Force has never been absolutely compulsory as there has always been a let-out on conscientious grounds but parents have been urged to allow their sons to join; for a while the School Scout Troop provided an alternative activity. Not more than two or three Whitgiftians a year go into the Services.

The Scout Troop (71st Croydon), founded with Gurner's support in 1930 by E. S. Roberts, was disbanded in 1982 after some years of uncertainty. No replacements could be found to succeed E. Shotton, Cecil Prime, C. F. Tolman and others who between them gave many years of enthusiastic service as Scoutmasters. The Duke of Edinburgh's Award Scheme has to some extent replaced it. Other non-military outdoor pursuits have included climbing, canoeing and orienteering. Under the inspiration of Frank Pattison, a Cycle-touring Club flourished for some years and their exploits reached the Guinness Book of Records.

Community Service

Before the end of the 19th century many public schools had set up 'missions' in the poorer parts of London and other big towns. Gurner's 'Boys' Club' in Pitlake, Croydon, was something of this kind. After World War II such activities nearly all died out, although there remained a strong desire to help those in a less privileged condition.

Many independent schools started up community service units in the later 1960s. It was felt to be educationally valuable in itself for young people to be helping and establishing relationships with the old, the handicapped or those in adversity. The schools were also sensitive to the charge of being socially divisive and wished to demonstrate a concern for others outside their gates.

At Whitgift a group had been formed in 1963 to help with such tasks as teaching spastic children to swim in the school pool or tending gardens for old people. The variety of projects undertaken and the number of boys involved were subsequently increased when time was found during the school day within the framework of Sixth Form 'minority time'. Examples included the visiting of patients in mental hospitals and teaching games at local primary schools. Latterly, excellent work was done at a primary school in the East End where boys were able to get to know and help children from deprived homes.

At Haling Park itself the school several times operated a special-needs play scheme for handicapped children during the summer holidays in collaboration with the Croydon Social Services department. Groups of boys have had regular contact with the residents at Whitgift House and the lunch club at Haling Park Cottage when that was in operation.

During the 1980s the school adopted 'Crisis' as a charitable concern that it particularly wished to support and raised more money by sponsorship than any other organisation through the annual pilgrimage from Canterbury to London undertaken by upwards of fifty boys.

Time is the main limiting factor in the School's programme of community service. It has never been undertaken as a compulsory alternative to games or the CCF, as in some other schools.

Discipline

Raeburn laid emphasis upon the importance of self-discipline, rather than the observance of a rigid rule-book. Like his predecessor, he would have preferred an easy-going regime altogether; with fewer named transgressions, there would be fewer offenders. Unfortunately, young people prefer to go their own way and like to experiment by challenging or even defying authority. (Hugill once remarked, 'If only boys would always be reasonable!') Corporal punishment has long since been abandoned almost everywhere, either by edict or consensus. Raeburn conceded that Whitgift boys, like others of their age or upbringing, were influenced by the pop culture of their generation and lacked the 'social gloss' (or 'mannerly polish'?) of their predecessors. It is difficult to estimate the influence of pop music and of its practitioners, with their protest songs, their loose morals and their uninhibited lifestyle, upon the successive generations of adolescents everywhere since the early 1960s. No record is easily found of the number of boys who have been 'removed at the headmaster's request', but this final sanction has not often been invoked. A marked alteration takes place during the boys' progress through the Sixth Form, when adolescence is officially left behind.

Religious observance

A problem Raeburn acknowledged was that of school worship. Although Whitgift had been founded largely to foster adherence to the Anglican faith, such an imposition of dogma has long been abandoned, and the School does not now acknowledge any official link with the Church of England, although the Archbishop of Canterbury remains its Visitor.

As recently as the 1930s, if not later, the majority of Whitgift families attended church on Sundays; the daily service at School on week-day mornings was for most boys a natural extension of their religious observance. In the 1920s and 1930s an important minority, which included numerous boys in senior rugby and cricket teams, belonged to the Christian Union and the Crusaders, and a fair number of these eventually took holy orders or otherwise committed themselves to Christian service as missionaries, doctors and evangelists abroad. But by the 1960s the daily routine of a collect, a reading by a prefect from the *Old* or *New Testament* and the singing of a hymn from *The Public School Hymn Book* was for many the only opportunity they had of participating in a religious service and of listening to the language of the *Authorized Version* and to the words of the *Book of Common Prayer*. Today this experience is denied them, for even when readings are given and prayers are offered, it is not as a rule the traditional, rhythmical phrases that are heard, but more mundane renderings in the colloquial tongue. Already in Hugill's time there was a display of strong feeling against compulsion to attend the daily act of worship, and Raeburn has said, 'The role of Christian worship in schools is difficult to determine and to get right in these secular times.' Liberal religious views have to be acknowledged; many boys are now of an alien faith or have been brought up with no religious belief at all, and a mute display of scepticism is no suitable accompaniment to even a nominal act of worship. In consequence Assembly has often been an almost entirely secular occasion with talks by staff or boys upon matters of personal concern or objects of charitable giving and community service. Only as a means of gathering the School together to give some sense of community, to convey information and instruction in sundry School matters, and occasionally to admonish or even praise, can Assembly be justified to many minds. The whole School now meets twice a week in Big School, and the Juniors meet separately in the Music School Hall on two other days. On the other hand, the Chapel at Whitgift House exists as a place of retreat for solitude and contemplation. Communion is celebrated there once or twice a term for members of the School.

Scholarships, Assisted Places and Bursaries

Ever since the Governing Body was constituted under the Chancery Scheme of 1856, it has been concerned with the just interpretation of the Founder's Statutes, in which Whitgift expressed his intention that poor children of Croydon should be educated free. With some misunderstanding of his wishes, the Governors erected and financed the 'Poor' School, which opened in 1858 for this purpose.

When the revived Whitgift School was opened in 1871, the Governors hoped that after a very few years it would pay its own way. A few scholarships giving exemption from fees were offered for competition annually, but they were tenable for only a year, so that successful candidates, usually from within the School, if they wished to retain their awards, had to compete again. These scholarships were the reward of merit rather than for the relief of need and were not competed for by boys from the Poor School. By the year 1876 a dozen were on offer, but they were then discontinued, for the School's expenses were still exceeding its income, the Poor School's subsidy was increasing yearly, and the Foundation's deficit was mounting. With the closure of the Poor School in 1881 its subsidy was discontinued, and the Middle School, which opened the following year, was charging fees, so it was thought reasonable to offer scholarships to Middle School boys for them to proceed to the Grammar School with remission for school life of the difference in fees. In a very few years these too were discontinued, because of the lack of interest on the part of members of the Middle School, who were satisfied with their own more utilitarian curriculum. The opportunity was then taken to establish, in commemoration of the Queen's Golden Jubilee in 1887, 'Victoria' open scholarships on much the same lines as those offered in the early 1870s, renewable yearly in competition. After many changes in conditions, these continue to be awarded, but in a much modified form at the end of the Third Form year to a few boys who hold no other award. They may be regarded as incentive prizes for they cover only a small remission of fees. From time to time benefactors have financed other scholarships and exhibitions, but it was not until the Direct Grant Scheme started in 1920 that free places became numerous, amounting to 10% of the intake and funded by the Grant itself, until it was relinquished in 1945.

In addition, a more generous allocation of scholarships is now on offer for excellence in the annual entrance examination and for achievement in Common Entrance. These awards may provide up to half remission of fees and in some cases may be supplemented by the bursary scheme.

Between 1945 and 1976, twelve places per year were allocated to the Croydon Education Committee in compensation for the loss of places that had been taken up under the Direct Grant Scheme. These were paid for by Croydon at the nominal rate of fees on behalf of boys who had passed the 11+ examination for secondary schools at a standard acceptable to the

Headmaster. At first the places were tenable only by boys from Croydon primary schools, but in 1951, when they became known as 'Special' places, they were made available to boys from preparatory schools and later to those who, being already in the Whitgift Junior School, went in for and passed the Croydon 11+ examination at a sufficiently high level.

The Foundation subsidy, amounting in 1950 to more than the fee itself, also benefited the LEA, a fact that Sir James Marshall was proud of drawing to the attention of Croydon Council. In 1965 as a consequence of the enlargement of the Borough of Croydon to include Purley, Sanderstead, Coulsdon and other areas, within the newly-formed Greater London Council, many more candidates qualified for this privilege based on achievement rather than need. These and their predecessors were no longer limited to 'the poorer sorte' of the Founder's Statutes.

In 1977 the LEA was compelled by law to relinquish this favour, but by this time the Governors' new policy of establishing an economic scale of fees had resulted in a four-fold increase over the previous five years, from £198 to £840 p.a. When Trinity relinquished the Direct Grant in 1968, the Foundation made up the shortfall, amounting to a basic £45,000 p.a. for several years, so that the disparity in fees between the two schools was for a while maintained.

The Governors' acceptance in the early 1970s that fees at both schools should eventually be increased to a notional figure covering running costs had been difficult to implement without causing hardship to parents who had already been budgeting for some degree of subsidy, or without deterring those who could not now contemplate sending their sons to either school. Both schools – despite Marten's allegations of deficiencies – were very well accommodated and equipped and were now of equal, independent status. It was hard to justify a fee at Trinity that was only a third of that of Whitgift. The solution, however difficult to impose, was by degrees to raise the full fees for new boys at both schools to an economic level, and to offer generous bursaries to boys who, although of high academic potential, could not otherwise aspire to admission. In 1976 the Trinity fees were set at £630 p.a., a ten-fold increase over five years. These increases proved embarrassing to a number of families, and a system of partial remissions was introduced for those already in the Schools and for a proportion of new boys as well.

For many years such remissions of School fees had been sparely granted to parents who through some crisis found themselves unable to meet their sons' expenses, and a few boys have had to leave to go to another school on this account. With the charging of an economic fee, the Governors were able to establish a regular bursary scheme out of endowment income. A ceiling was set on the total amount which could be remitted in the way of new scholarships and bursaries, calculated on the equivalent of a dozen full or 25 half-remissions yearly. In practice it has been rare for all these bursaries to be taken up, and there may well be boys of merit who, although being eligible for remissions, do not sit the entrance examination.

When in 1981 the Conservative government provided Assisted Places in independent schools, both Schools joined the scheme, Whitgift accepting annually 15 pupils in the Junior School and up to 5 in the Sixth Form.

In 1990 35% of pupils were receiving some reduction in their fees through scholarships awarded for high academic merit, through government-assisted places, or through Foundation bursaries. There is a further large subsidy that all pupils enjoy, represented by the heavy capital investment in land, buildings and equipment that in other schools has often to be funded through additions to the fees or by raising money through appeals.

The Management Team

In his survey of the 1970s, Raeburn included a forecast of what might happen as the result of general external trends, and what might be required to meet the School's needs through redeployment of existing resources and provision of new buildings.

In the first place he envisaged the establishment of a management team that would work towards agreed ends, based on his own vision of the future, already partly outlined soon after his arrival at Whitgift in 1970. This delegation of responsibilities, without which a headmaster's burden would become intolerable, was in accordance with good principles of organisation and had been adopted in large comprehensive schools and in some independent schools.

The team, or inner cabinet, that Raeburn had in mind was to comprise, under himself, two administrative partners, namely a Deputy Headmaster and a Senior Master, who were to be Peter Trevis and Anthony Ridley respectively. They would bear and exercise their individual responsibilities in certain fields, and would to some extent share the duties recently undertaken by the Second Master, A. T. Parsons, who intended to retire at the end of the summer term 1980.

Parsons had filled his post with dedication and efficiency but was now looking forward to shedding the often irksome duties of a second-in-command and to getting absorbed in other pursuits, for he was in very active good health. He had acquired a deep understanding of the interplay of personalities that formed the corpus of school life: boys, teaching and domestic staff, as well as Governors and parents. He was held by everyone in great respect, indeed awe, being a consistent but quiet disciplinarian who always made his own position clear. His responsibilities included ensuring that the School Rules were not only observed but also respected for the reason that they were necessary for the well-being of the community, not because of some traditional but whimsical custom. During Raeburn's sabbatical term at Cambridge in 1980, Parsons had ensured the continued smooth running of the whole complicated mechanism. He nevertheless maintained an inflexible opposition to certain proposed innovations.

Other members of the management team were to be co-opted *ad hoc*, such as the Chief Master of the Junior School, the Careers Master, the Chairman of the Common Room, the senior Housemaster, and the Captain of the School. The Clerk to the Governors, with whom the Headmaster was frequently in consultation anyway, could also be invited to give his advice.

The School Administrative Officer

But one of the most important associates would be the School Administrative Officer. This post so strongly recommended by Marlar in the 1950s and by the HMI in 1971 was at last created in 1977. Major A. McDowell relinquished his duties as Permanent Staff Instructor to the CCF to take up his new position. His manifold new duties had been undertaken in the past by various members of the teaching staff as additional responsibilities, sometimes acknowledged by a small addition to their salary.

Because of their desultory, fragmented and part-time nature, these duties had tended to be performed when the main demands on a man's time permitted, but there were occasions when urgent matters took precedence and teaching was interfered with. The system was also uneconomic. But now the Administrative Officer would be involved in all matters concerning routine maintenance, supervision of the cleaning contracts, control (but not appointment) of the domestic staff, liaison with caterers and with surveyors and builders over repairs programmes and any hindrance arising therefrom. He was also concerned with supplies of furniture, the control and upkeep of school vehicles and the photocopying machines, fire precautions and the numerous events of consequence that might arise on premises that during the day contained over one thousand very active people.

Building Plans 1982

Raeburn's proposals, now he had established his management team, were still mainly to do with building developments. The very generous additions that had recently resulted from the Governors' own determination, stimulated by Raeburn's persistent advocacy, to redeem their promises made when the move to the Croham Hurst Golf Club site was being pursued ten years before, went a long way towards their fulfilment, but the swift advance in technology, especially in electronics, now made it imperative to lengthen the schedule of requirements.

Meeting with an encouraging response from the Governors, he did not underpitch his proposals. There was an urgent need for more teaching space for the natural sciences, involving the replacement of the temporary buildings, and the provision of more preparation rooms and multipurpose laboratories to enable the provision of specimens and the erection of apparatus to be performed unhurriedly by the technicians.

By the end of 1982 the Governors decided that they were in a position to encourage Raeburn's hopes by appointing a Building Committee, consisting of the Chairman of the Schools Committee (I. P. Shaw), the Chairman of the Advisory Committee (R. W. Coatman) and Professor John Dougill, who would weigh up Raeburn's submissions and offer their comments. Meanwhile, Senior HMIs in Craft, Design and Technology, Physical Education, and English were invited to give their advice. The PE Inspector was much impressed with the recently opened Sports Hall, which gave an indication to the other Inspectors of the scale of development proposed. Raeburn and Anthony Ridley had been working hard on a brief for the Architect, Sir Hugh Wilson, who had produced an outline scheme that met with general approval from members of the staff concerned with Science, with Art and Technology and with the Library. Extensive building work would create a great disturbance in adjacent areas. The continued use of temporary buildings (the Art Block since 1969, and Science Annexes since 1974) would have to be accepted but later sacrificed when they made way for new development. Such disruptions, it will be remembered, had been cited as a good reason for a move in 1972.

Another Postponement

A few months later, however, enthusiasm was damped by the announcement that the new development must be delayed for an estimated eighteen months, soon to become two years. Reasons were plentiful: reviews of rents from the Whitgift Centre were not yet complete; the Whitgift House complex had to be finished; further works at Trinity were to be started in 1985; and before any additions could be built at Whitgift School, many costly renovations were necessary there.

Necessary Renovations

These were truly formidable: the complete renewal of the water, gas, electricity, central heating and telephone services; the replacement of the water-treatment plant in the Swimming Pool and of the ventilation system in the Rifle Range; the completion of a fire protection system, including alarms, smoke-detectors and self-closing fire-resistant doors, that had been insisted on by the Fire Service, but which had nevertheless been deferred on account of the uncertainty of the building's future; the replacement of the organ in Big School and of the railings in Brighton and Nottingham Roads, which had either been removed for scrap forty years before or had rusted away; the renewal of the all-weather hockey-pitch, which had not proved as durable as had been hoped; and much minor restoration of the fabric. Many of these had been overdue since the 1960s, and only temporary or makeshift treatments had been applied. All were now urgent, but few could be carried out simultaneously by reason of cost or logistics. They would be a severe drain on resources, and the disturbance involved, followed by that of new building, would be hard to endure. However, the new delay meant that no opinion need go unheard, no decision need be hurried, no plans need be ill-considered.

The Character of the New Building

In July 1985 Sir Hugh Wilson suddenly died, before much progress had been made with his plans, or the general architectural style of the new structure decided upon. A senior partner in his firm, Mr. William Armstrong, who had been involved with Sir Hugh in the preparation of the feasibility study and who was already well acquainted with requirements, was invited to complete the scheme, and he promptly submitted a number of proposals for the elevations and in particular for the lay-out of the Library and the Computer Centre, which met with the approval of the Building Committee. It took another twelve months for the plans to be completed and accepted, so that in June 1986 a contract was signed, and enabling works for the building were begun. These in themselves were extensive and necessarily disruptive, involving the adaptation of laboratories, the removal of old temporary buildings and the erection of new, the breaking through of walls and the preparation of a large works-area. Not until May 1988 could the main works be started, but these proceeded with systematic steadiness, fortunately unimpeded by bad weather during the exceptionally mild winter of 1988–89. By July 1989 the external structure was complete and ready for the installation of internal fitments. In September 1990 the School took possession, and on 7 November the New Building

The new building under construction, 1988

was officially opened by Baroness Platt of Writtle, CBE, DL, F.Eng.

The results are superb. Provision has at last been made for nearly all the requirements proposed by a succession of Headmasters and supported by HMI in 1971, together with the rapidly changing needs of more recent years. In addition, the interior of the building, which includes 5000 square metres of floor space on two levels, has been so designed that partition walls may be removed or repositioned to suit developments in teaching practice that may come about in the years to come.

It had been agreed at the outset by all parties that the appearance of the new building should blend in scale, character and texture with the old, which was dignified, distinctive and matchable, but there would be no slavish adherence to the unique 1920s style. Because other major additions such as the Swimming pool (1960), the Music School (1968) and the Sports Hall (1982) were free-standing, these had been treated in a rather different manner, especially as their purposes did not so readily lend them to the same decorative treatment as the old. The Junior School block (1980), being a reconstruction of an existing building, had been designed to match. They are all unpretentious buildings of interest and individuality.

The additions made to the original structure—the laboratories and geography department of 1957, and the extensions on the northern side made in the 1960s—were not so accordant as they might have been, but were sympathetically designed in brick with stone dressings.

The elevations of the Wilson-Armstrong block are more impressive, incorporating compatible style and texture of brick and stone with window details similar to those that have given distinction to Leathart and Granger's elevations. Yet it is clearly a contemporary building, displaying a use of the round arch and the pitched roof that have returned to architectural design after years of stark functionalism and brutalism, happily unrepresented at Haling Park.

The North-West Wing of the new building, 1990

The new block has the additional virtue of overcoming the ineffectiveness of the original design where it petered out in the narrow corridors and single-storey inexcrescences on its western side. The corridors have been widened, and the single-storey buildings have been either razed or bridged over. The importance of providing easy access between the old and the new was recognised from the beginning; this has been achieved at the cost of VAT on the whole venture, which would not have been imposed on any freestanding edifice at the time it was started.

The South-West perspective of the new building, 1990

Whitgift School

Art, Craft, Design and Technology

In the early years of the twentieth century, Art and Handicraft had been introduced as general subjects in the lower part of the school, not with any idea of training hands for employment, but as part of an all-round exercise for brain and hand. The artist was then regarded as a possibly unconventional yet acceptable member of society, and the first full-time Art Master (E. M. Carter, a gifted free-hand draughtsman), appointed in 1905, was welcomed as a member of the academic staff, but the worthy master in charge of handicraft, B. J. Lilly, taught the skills of the carpenter and joiner, and consequently enjoyed a lower esteem. After a couple of years' instruction in the woodwork shop, there might be to show for one's pains nothing more practical or ornamental than a wooden toothbrush-rack. Upon Lilly's retirement in 1926, a more widely trained expert was appointed in the person of J. E. C. Robinson, whose place on the teaching staff was never to be questioned; already many members of the staff had deplored the insult that Lilly, through the social prejudices of the time, had been subjected to. Robinson taught metalwork and mechanical drawing, as well as woodwork, in the new workshops at Haling Park and he had an assistant. Carter's successor, Frank Potter, had to make do with a smaller Art Room than the 'Drawing School' at North End, but he took a much wider interest in modern art movements than Carter (who may never have mentioned with approval the term 'impressionism' in front of a class) and introduced painting in oils and a wider range of other skills; he encouraged many boys to become architects, and a few others went to art school, including the Slade.

After World War II there was a steady rapprochement between the arts and crafts, but the departments remained physically apart. Whereas Potter had been able to employ the occasional student-teacher or part-timer to help in studio work, his joint successors, Henry Maslin and Bob Brown, could provide a much wider range of interest and instruction, at first in Bagbie House and later in the temporary but more spacious Art block, which included modelling, sculpture, pottery, engraving, hand-printing, silk-screen work, photography and other skills, such as the three-dimensional use of paper and plastics. The Craft section, under Cyril Worsell and Dai Lewis, were now not so much concerned with training in the elementary use of traditional tools, as with the intelligent use of machines and new materials, and in the solving of problems in construction by studying the properties and use of materials the product would be made of. In this objective the two departments were as one, and it would be clearly to the advantage of both if they were united. The plans of the Craft, Design and Technology area were drawn up with this end in view. The skills developed here will not only be of practical use to those who wish to follow a career in technology, but will also give insight into the needs of modern industry for those whose lives are surrounded and supported by the exercise of the skills of such specialists.

Computer Studies

Another swift and far-reaching development has been that of data-processing. When the first computer was installed at the School in 1972, almost a whole room in the Maths Department was given up to house the hardware alone, with a terminal or two in a corner. Successive developments in computer technology resulted in a doubling of the total space, but the hardware became so much more compact that over 25 terminals could be housed in two rooms. Provision in the new building has more than doubled again, there being 28 in the word-processing department attached to the Library and others in the computer workshop and at various convenient locations.

In 1991 computer studies are introduced to second-formers; many boys are enthusiastic, possess their own machines and draw up programmes for a variety of purposes at school or at home. This vitally important department, set up by Bill Boyd, has been keenly supported not only by the Mathematics Department but also by others who have found a knowledge of computing skills essential in their own disciplines. The late John Yeo, of the Biology Department, became a dedicated expert and devised programmes for solving many school administrative problems, including especially the complex processing of entrance exam results. The

Department of Design and Technology makes particular use of computers.

Word-processing, printing and desk-top publishing are off-shoots of computer studies, and *The Whitgiftian*, the *School Roll*, the termly *Calendar* and programmes are now type-set at school, providing greater opportunities for boys in a variety of activities.

Technical and Ancillary Staff

In all educational establishments, schools, colleges and universities, graduate teachers' time is now regarded as too valuable to be spent in the daily care of implements, instruments and apparatus in which much money has been invested. The preparation of botanical and zoological specimens, the construction and erection of laboratory glassware and other apparatus, the cutting-up of timber and metal, the sharpening and lubricating of tools in the workshops, the making ready of materials for art classes, and repairs to the wiring of electronic equipment can no longer be left to an unskilled 'lab-boy' or to a busy member of the teaching staff. A hundred years ago there was one part-time, casual laboratory assistant, replaced in 1905 by George Etches, who doubled as instructor to the Drums and Fifes of the OTC; otherwise masters arranged their own apparatus, cared for their own appliances, made ready their own pieces of wood or paper, such was the simplicity of equipment in those days. Now each practical department has its own technical staff, many of them very well qualified, with a diploma and sometimes a degree. Other departments also benefit from paid assistance in the interest of efficiency. Consequently the Library has its own qualified Librarians; part-time and temporary *assistants* are employed for Modern Languages; the Director of Music confides the allocation of instrumental instruction among teachers and pupils to his secretary, who records emoluments due; TV and radio programmes are recorded on video and tape; the Careers Master's secretary deals with a voluminous correspondence with individuals and business firms, university offices and professional bodies, in order to give him more time for personal involvement with those who seek his advice.

For these increased numbers the academic Common Room has become not only too small; it is inappropriate. Many of the ancillary staff, and also an increasing number of the teaching staff, are ladies. A ladies' common-room or rest-room has become a necessity; so has a common-room for the technicians, whose work is concentrated in the new building and those parts of the old that are situated adjoining it.

The Library and Archives

The new Library is a completely new area, centrally located, and accessible from every quarter. It will maintain its character as a reference and general lending library, leaving the existing departmental and junior libraries to cater for special needs. Its word-processing section is used by pupils in setting-up their own work or for printing copy for *The Whitgiftian*.

The Library incorporates the Archival Department, which has expanded by degrees from its unofficial origins in the 1950s through a series of larger but still temporary premises. The department benefits from its proximity to reference works, a conservation room and working areas where researchers may pursue their studies. The fire-proof Store contains the School and Foundation muniments and records, Whitgiftiana and memorabilia of many kinds. It has become a valuable resources centre, for its position and its wealth of material at the bookish heart of the School encourages historical enquiry, much of which has so far originated from researchers unconnected directly with the School. Indeed a number of these have contributed to our knowledge of our own history.

As recently as the 1980s it was unusual for a school, even one that had been in existence for hundreds of years, to possess a systematically preserved archive in which ancient records were cared for and new items regularly accessed and listed. Eton and Winchester at least had carefully preserved their records of the past in secure places supervised by a full-time archivist, but a survey made in 1980 of a score of public schools founded in the 16th or 17th century revealed a pitiable state of neglect. A haphazard collection of material may have existed under no official protection or control. Perhaps an over-worked Librarian or a volunteer enthusiast, an old boy or

The Language Laboratory, 1990

retired member of the staff with no paid assistance, accepted responsibility.

Fortunately the Governors of the Whitgift Foundation had appreciated the value of what remained of their ancient muniments and subsequent records. Much material was securely and methodically preserved already, the Ancient Muniments having been examined and calendared in 1934 by Clarence C. Paget, FSA. During World War II these documents were evacuated for safety to Sir James Marshall's house at Woldingham. In 1968 many of the surviving ledger-books and minute-books of the 17th, 18th and 19th centuries were rebound and microfilmed.

Seeking advice from the Historical Manuscripts Commission in 1981, the Governors accepted an offer to send an official to examine what they possessed and to advise on its preservation, description and indexing. Dr. Olney, an Old Mid-Whitgiftian, recommended that a professional archivist should be engaged to devise a system, classify, list and index the material that was scattered in various repositories at the Whitgift Hospital, the solicitor's office, the surveyor's office and of course at the School, where the embryo department was set up.

It was sadly confirmed, when the archivist, Miss Kate Chantry, started work, that maintenance of the records had been greatly neglected in the 18th and 19th centuries. From time to time some careless Schoolmaster, whose responsibility it was to maintain the records, had failed in his duty. Towards the end of the 18th century the record, sketchy at the best of times, becomes irregular, no doubt owing to destruction by the rascally Dr. John Rose in order to conceal his defalcations. After the appointment of the Governing Body in 1856 a new Minute Book was started which recorded the Governors' deliberations until 1871. This valuable record and many others of the time have vanished, but fortunately the void has been partly filled from the files of the Endowed Schools Commissioners and the Charity Commissioners in the Public Record Office (ED27).

The Archives are now kept more methodically, although the labour of comprehensive cataloguing and indexing of so much material of importance is unlikely ever to be adequately performed. But in years to come, when another hand is prepared to tackle a fresh survey of the School's history, the reference material of more recent date should be found reasonably intact among the records preserved in the Archives.

The Background of Educational Politics of the 1970s and 1980s

During the two decades between 1970 and 1990 education was subject more than ever before to stresses arising from theoretical,

Library Reading Area, 1990

economic, ideological and, above all, political dispute. The tripartite and the tertiary systems have been in turn encouraged, criticised, expanded, reorganised, generously provided for, neglected, deprived of funds. The independent sector has been reviled, threatened, emulated, praised, liberated. Battles have raged over parity of esteem; over the merits of grammar schools and comprehensive schools; tradition and progress; prescriptive standards and a common culture; discipline and permissiveness; clarity in communication and freedom of expression; examination and assessment; facts and discovery methods. The 'Black Papers' on Education continued to express feelings of dismay over the increasing rejection of methods that had stood the test of time, but which were seen by some to put the needs of an élite before those of the majority.

In 'The Great Debate' of 1978, initiated by James Callaghan, the objects of education, rather than the means of imposing state education on all, were presented for consideration to Labour politicians, but the debate never came to much, for his party never took it up. Themes included the purposes of education in society; was it to be a preparation for working, for leisure and for

West Window, Sixth Form Design, 1990

Biology Laboratory, 1990

living in society, or even for making social changes? What was the place of religion? Should it continue to be taught? Should doctrine give way to social 'caring'?

Other themes included the need for skills to be developed in order for Britain to compete with other industrialised nations, or to harmonise with the EEC; the importance of languages, mathematics, and science, and the best methods of teaching them; the teaching of English, whether as a technique of communication or for the pleasure of reading and writing; changing attitudes towards sport in the world at large and at the schools; the increased influence of television as a means of instruction or distraction; the external examination structure and the requirements for university entrance; the advent of the computer; the independence of the adolescent, with 18 the age of majority (1969); the increased expectations of girls at school and women at university and better provision for their instruction; the difficulties in recruiting teachers of the right calibre and the problems of rewarding them; the declining school-age population. All these and many other considerations have been the concern of those responsible for organising education, and not least the headmasters and headmistresses of independent schools, each one of which has had its own peculiar problems and sometimes advantages. Whitgift has been no exception. These considerations have set a constant challenge to those whose main concern has been the value of instruction to the individual, who can thereby not merely attain success and fulfilment of purpose, but also contribute to society by his sense of responsibility and achievement.

Callaghan showed a realistic concern for the quality of education, for he and others of his party had come to understand that the egalitarianism of the left was depriving our country of the skills, the knowledge and the ambition that were required if Great Britain was to compete with other industrial nations. The condemnation of independent education became less vituperative and its destruction less important, for it was clear that further taxation would have to be imposed to pay for a solely state system.

The Independent Schools Information Service (ISIS), founded in 1972, had been devoting much energy to the protection of independence whenever it was threatened, especially just before the election in May 1979 of a Conservative government and before its re-election in June 1982, at times when, to placate the left-wing extremists, the Labour manifesto was pitched at its most immoderate and included the threat of making any private payment for education unlawful.

The economic prosperity that arose during the long period of Conservative government through the 1980s enabled many more parents to send their children to independent schools, a good many of which, such as Marlborough and Rugby, have become fully co-educational after introducing the experiment in the Sixth Forms.

Many of Sir Keith Joseph's desired reforms involving the duties of teachers were thrust through by his successor, Kenneth Baker, in his Education Reform Act of 1989. These reforms took up many of Callaghan's points, themselves the planks of Conservative principles, with the purpose of establishing a more ordered and consistent frame of education for the country, more in line too with independent practice.

Declining School-age Population

The continuous decline in numbers of the school-age population has already resulted in the closure of many schools in the state sector; any marked reduction in the number or size of classes in large or scattered buildings became uneconomic. This problem will have to be faced by independent schools as well, especially if they fall behind in providing the buildings, equipment or teaching that are needed. Any hope of continuing development must rest on a flourishing economy and a supportive attitude from government. The Labour party abominated the Assisted Places Scheme as divisive and opposed to the comprehensive ideal, but the scheme greatly helped many independent schools to keep their numbers up with an intake of selected pupils whose fees were assured. Prompt and ambitious decisions had to be made. Whitgift could not hope to take a much larger share of the diminishing numbers of bright pupils; the School must be prepared to provide opportunities for the less academic, whose talents might find realisation in more practical studies, which would be all the more important, for the highest intellects as well as those of more modest abilities, to meet the demands of world-wide competitive industry. These considerations would be the basis of any planning for the remaining years of the twentieth century. There is as yet little sign of any diminishing standards among our own intake.

Reputation

In the eighteen-seventies, under Brodie, Whitgift School was fighting to establish itself in an era of uncertainty of aims; in the early years of the present century, under Andrew, it was striving successfully to acquire a high reputation as a day-school of the first grade; in the nineteen-thirties, under Gurner, it was issuing a challenge to the boarding schools; twenty years later, under Marlar, it was a successful rival; in the nineteen-nineties it fears no comparison with any other school, even of the highest academic and cultural standards. The reasons for the present situation are manifold. In the first place, its buildings and equipment, and the quality and ratio of its academic staff are all comparable with, if not superior to, what may be found elsewhere. Secondly, the School enjoys a more than local reputation, and the achievements of its Old Boys prove that they have suffered no disadvantage in attending Whitgift. Thirdly, parental attitudes are now more liberal and sympathetic towards the concept of day-school education; the social admixture, if indeed it is ever noticed, is no longer so displeasing to them; many parents are not now so prepared to dismiss their children from home for the greater part of the year, realising that such segregation from family life is not necessarily in children's best interests, especially when they reach sixth-form age and expect release from restrictions that are becoming irksome and even humiliating; except for co-educational schools a day-school offers more opportunities for companionship with the other sex; modern educational theory approves the foundation of character through the encouragement of the individual rather than of the type; the decline in religious observance has reduced the importance in parents' eyes of the chapel-centred life at a boarding-school, while Whitgift, being a Church of England foundation, although not giving doctrinal instruction, is felt to provide a Christian moral background. Finally, there is the undoubted advantage of value for one's money, combined with the solution of a difficulty that all but the affluent must experience in finding the money for a son's education.

The School's growing reputation has been reflected in the much greater distances that pupils now travel to reach it. In the nineteenth century nearly every boy lived within walking distance; a hundred years later the proportion may be about five per cent (of these who could walk, many of course do not). The 'commuter belt' stretches to the south coast; residential development in Surrey and Sussex enjoys convenient connections by rail and road with South Croydon, so that ten per cent of boys now live over ten miles from the School, almost entirely in the southern sector.

Another aspect of the School's reputation is the increased knowledge of it overseas. A varying number at any one time of sons of temporary residents from abroad—members of international firms, representatives sent by other governments, academics and other professional people on protracted visits—may be at the School, some for two or three years only, others for the remainder of their school life. When they go back home many of them value their experiences in English education, retain their friendships and preserve an interest in the School's fortunes, maintaining contact through membership of the OWA and by reading *The Whitgiftian*. Then there are the frequent exchanges of pupils with schools in Europe, of staff with Commonwealth teachers, tours abroad by drama parties, rugby, cricket and hockey teams, by groups with cultural, career and adventurous interests; all these have contributed to the School's repute in other lands for high standards of achievement and of civilized endeavour in many fields.

Retirement of D.A. Raeburn

In October 1989 David Raeburn submitted his resignation to the Court of Governors to take effect from the end of the school year in July 1991, when the latest extensions would have been opened and occupied for a full school year. He could now experience the satisfaction of seeing through, after many frustrations, the completion and occupation of the most ambitious series of building construction at the School since 1931. This was the chief material result of the plans for the future of Whitgift that he had conceived twenty years before upon his appointment as Headmaster. His expectations must have been fulfilled beyond his wildest dreams.

His successor is to be Dr. Christopher A. Barnett, educated at The Cedars School, Leighton Buzzard, and Oriel College, Oxford,

Dr. C.A. Barnett

General Art Studios, 1990

where he was an Exhibitioner. He read History, graduating in 1974, and proceeded to D.Phil. in 1981. After lecturing in the Department of Economics, Brunel University, from 1975 to 1977, he was appointed Head of History at Bradfield in 1978. From 1987 to 1991 he has been Second Master at Dauntsey's School, Devizes.

Reflections

A considered appraisal of David Raeburn's work and of his personal impact on Whitgift will in due course be given by his former pupils and members of his staff.

Like many of his recent predecessors he arrived at an opportune moment for the intro-

Engineering Workshop, 1990

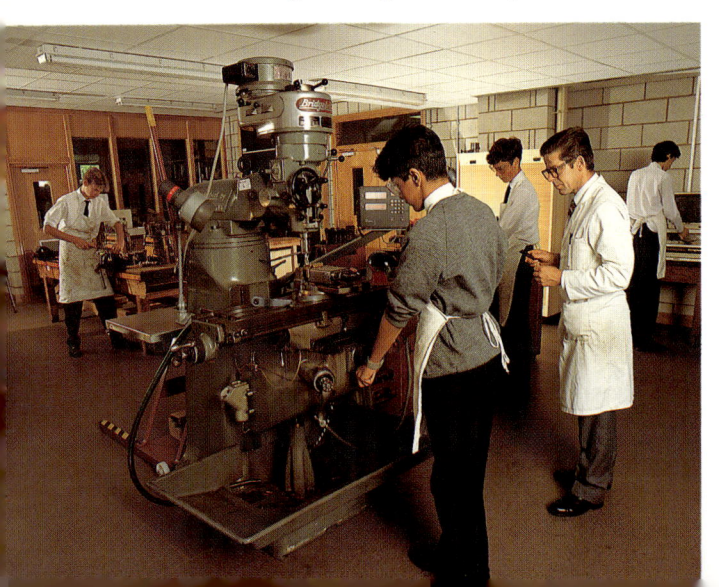

duction of new principles, new attitudes, new practices, new activities and, above all, of new buildings. Even if some valued traditional customs have had to be modified or even abandoned on that account, an enormous net gain has resulted.

David Raeburn has not limited himself to a narrow concern for the School alone. Apart from following the cultural interests expected in a man of his education and background, he has for long been active in educational and academic circles. He has been prominent in the Headmasters' Conference, having been a member of several sub-committees and in 1985 Chairman of the London Division. As Treasurer of the HMC from 1984 to 1989 he consolidated its finances and promoted the training of Heads and other staff. He also drew up new guide-lines for membership of the Conference and for maintaining links with the Secondary Heads' Association, of which he has been a member for nearly 30 years. Another important interest was his governorship of Port Regis Preparatory School.

An advocate of the continued teaching of Classics, he directed for many years the annual summer school in Ancient Greek, run by the Joint Association of Classical Teachers. He was for three years Chairman of the London branch of the Classical Association and has written many papers and given many lectures on classical subjects; he was Chairman of the Classics Committee of the now defunct Schools Council. He has been willing to travel in order to increase his knowledge of educational problems and their solution, having been a Walter Hines Page Scholar in the USA in 1978, a visitor to Australia in 1982 and 1986, to Israel in 1987 and to China in 1988. As a Schoolmaster Fellow at Jesus College, Cambridge, in 1980, he was invited by the University Greek Play Committee to direct Euripides' *Elektra* in the original Greek and Sophocles' *Women of Trachis* in 1983.

His chief delight seems to be in the combination of classical studies with drama. As a play-producer he has always been in his element, and every production of his has given pleasure to performers and audience alike. His greatest achievements have been in Shakespeare and in Greek tragedy, the latter at Bradfield, Verona and Cambridge, in Australia and at Whitgift, given in

Aerial View, 1990

the original tongue, the rhythmical cadences of which, even in the ears of a barbarian audience, have carried conviction and conveyed poetic emotion.

In retirement, in Sussex, he hopes to find opportunities for following these interests and will no doubt continue to observe, and perhaps record, the activities of the few thousand OWs who have passed through his hands during his long and distinguished period of office as Headmaster of Whitgift.

The Education of Girls

In his Statutes and in his will the Founder referred to the pupils of his School as 'scholars'; he used 'children' in referring to their eligibility for admission. By avoiding the use of the term 'boy' he did not intend that girls should also be included in 'children'. 'Boy' was used either familiarly or as a term of disapproval, often combined with an opprobrious epithet: 'peevish boy', 'saucy boy', 'whining schoolboy'.

The education of girls in grammar was not generally regarded as suitable, as has already been pointed out (see footnote, p. 39).

Old Palace School

The Chancery Scheme of 1856 makes specific mention only of 'boys', a word which by then had lost its pejorative sense, but not of 'girls', and the Governors' proposed amendment of 1869 also mentions only 'boys'.

The first references to the possible education of girls under the Whitgift Foundation occurs in the Endowed Schools Commissioners' first draft scheme of 1870: 'When the Trust property increases so as to admit of the establishment of a Girls' School on a sufficiently large scale, a supplementary Scheme for its regulation shall be passed...'

The adopted Scheme of 1881 is less explicit: 'As soon as the income of the Foundation is... sufficient... a Scheme for extending to girls the benefits of the endowment... may be made.'

Already, in November 1874, before any later scheme than that of 1856 had become lawful, the Governors, at the suggestion of their Chairman (The Vicar of Croydon, the Revd. J. G. Hodgson), had considered the possibility of establishing a 'Lower Middle Class Girls' School with fees at about £4 per head' but, there being no available building, they decided that 'such a scheme was not possible of fulfilment', for 'it was not advisable in the present state of Finance to attempt to provide a Room for a Girls' School'.

In 1884 the Croydon High School for Girls was founded in buildings on the opposite side of Wellesley Road to Whitgift. In December 1888 Hodgson's successor, the Revd. J. M. Braithwaite, proposed that it was 'desirable that the Court should make arrangements for the foundation of scholarships for girls.' It is to be assumed that these would have been tenable at the High School. A resolution referred the matter to the Schools Committee, but no entry on the subject appears in the Committee's minutes.

As has already been explained (page 179), the establishment of independent secondary schools for girls allowed the Governors to concentrate their resources on boys' education.

The amended Scheme of 1915 repeated much of the 1881 wording, but the Whitgift Charities Act of 1969 enlarged the scope of the Foundation: 'The Governors may... provide... one or more additional schools for boys or girls or both boys and girls.'

The Croham Hurst proposals of 1972 allocated an important position to girls, but it was not until April 1990 that more definite steps were announced for them to be placed under the Whitgift aegis. A plan was prepared after discussion between the two Governing Bodies, for the Old Palace School, whose academic reputation had been greatly enhanced in recent years, to become part of The Whitgift Foundation, which would help to provide new buildings and improve the condition of the old.

1970–90 A Headmaster's Personal Retrospect
by David Raeburn

As I approach my retirement in 1991, Freddie Percy has paid me the great compliment of inviting me to add my own review of twenty years as Headmaster of Whitgift to his own account of this period in the school's history. I have been delighted to do this, though I am conscious that it will be for others to judge the school's work and development under myself from a longer-term viewpoint.

Whitgift well suited both my social inclinations and my previous career. Although I had myself been to a boarding-school as a boy, I had cast my professional lot in day-school education by the time I was 30. Two of the three schools where I had worked as a Classics master were Direct Grant schools, which appealed to me particularly because many of the pupils attended either free or on reduced fees. It always seemed to me wrong that the finest education in Britain should be the preserve of children whose parents could afford it. I had greatly enjoyed a brief spell in the boarding sector at Bradfield but had found the attitudes encouraged there too limited and exclusive. I would have agreed with Ronald Gurner that day-schools had advantages in their own right and found room in their time-tables not only to achieve high academic standards but to do much else outside the classroom.

Seven and a half years as the headmaster of a maintained school proved an ideal preparation for my life's main task at Whitgift. Beckenham and Penge Grammar School was not far from Croydon and made me familiar with the local social background. Apart from the chance to acquire an excellent grounding in all the many aspects of a headmaster's task, I had a special opportunity to learn about the design and layout of school buildings, as I was responsible for planning the new purpose-built grammar school at Langley Park to which the school moved from Penge in 1969. Above all, I discovered a great deal about the management of change. Modern buildings called for modern staff attitudes and I encouraged my colleagues to re-examine their aims and methods critically in the light of contemporary trends. This resulted not only in a more thoughtful approach but in improved results in almost all departments.

The move to Whitgift was in many ways a natural progression. I was of course sympathetic to the terms of the Founder's Statutes which provided for the education of certain selected 'children of the poorer sorte', while charging fees to more affluent parents. It was also important to me to be joining a school with historic Anglican affiliations and so, by implication, a commitment to Christian principles. I had some inkling of the Foundation's resources but could not know until I started what a wealth of opportunities lay in store.

I found a school securer in its standards, both in work and behaviour, than the one I had left. It was altogether a more self-confident institution, with the strength of a longer and more unbroken tradition behind it. On the other hand, I thought it a less exciting school than Langley Park where there had been more youth on the staff. The Whitgift common room struck me as highly dedicated and unsparing of their time but I sensed a collective reluctance to experiment and innovate. The senior boys were generally assured and polite but more aloof, less spontaneous than my Beccehamians, Among some of the more forthcoming ones there was an under-current of discontent with 'the system', but this was the time when long-haired rebellion was rife among students both at universities and in sixth forms.

There was much, then, that from my earliest weeks I wanted to do and to see changed, but I knew that I should be unwise to rock a sturdy boat on what was then a stormy sea in schools generally. In any case, changes that had worked well at Beckenham might not be appropriate to Whitgift, even in circumstances which appeared similar. I sensed, therefore, that I must bide my time and seize my opportunities for change as they arose, above all in the staff appointments that I made, whether from inside or outside the school. In time I reckoned that the school would become a more forward-looking and outward-looking institution.

I was none the less able at my first Prizegiving in October 1970, to formulate the general aims and objectives that I wanted to set the school and myself. With hindsight, these were so much the bedrock of my philosophy that they are worth summarising here, as a point of reference for what follows.

1. Whitgift stood for quality in academic work, games and the arts and I hoped to maintain its standards of all-round excellence.
2. At the same time the education offered must be relevant to future leaders in the 21st century. Times were changing at an accelerating pace and the right balance must be struck between the old and the new, the traditional and the experimental.
3. To keep abreast of the times, much work was needed to improve the buildings but, with the resources of the Whitgift Foundation behind it, I thought that the school might well have 'a unique contribution to make to the life of the nation', offering opportunities unsurpassed anywhere else in the country.
4. Those opportunities, however, should not be restricted to children of parents who could afford to pay for them.
5. Finally, I hoped that Whitgift could continue to promote Christian values in this secular, technological age. The loyalty which the school inspired should not be an exclusive one and should be complemented by service to the outside community.

The following year, we celebrated the centenary of the school's revival under Robert Brodie. His vision of a Whitgift which stood comparison with the great boarding schools, I argued, was now fulfilled. In the programme of modernisation that we were already contemplating we could lay the foundations for the next hundred years in the school's development. 1971 was also the year of Britain's decision to join the European Economic Community. In this context I repeated Brodie's crucial point that the quality of the school would depend ultimately not on the buildings but on the attitudes of the boys themselves and the spirit in which they entered their adulthood. Whitgift's aim, I said, must be to produce responsible citizens of Britain, Europe and the world, committed to improving the lot of mankind.

From philosophy I turn to practice and attempt to describe the school's development over twenty years, as I see it, in academic work and achievement, co-curricular activities, resources and ethos as a community. At the same time I record the help and support I received in my challenging task.

From the outset I was clear that, as at Langley Park, new or improved buildings had to be accompanied by new approaches in the classroom. The Group Visit of HMI in late 1971 was ostensibly a consultation on how best to develop the school buildings, but I used the occasion for a very full review of the whole curriculum and incorporated this in my brief for the Inspectors. While the Visit had the result of endorsing the building programme I had in mind, no less important was the stimulus it gave to fresh thinking among the teaching staff. Thus began the process of evolutionary change, subject by subject, that I hoped for and is described in further detail by Percy on pages 272–9. This, reinforced by external factors such as the change from Ordinary Level to the G.C.S.E., helped the teaching and learning in the school gradually to become more thoughtful, imaginative and interesting.

In due course I asked my Heads of Departments to produce their own prospectuses, which were not so much syllabuses or schemes of work to be followed by their own specialist colleagues as statements of aims which could be of interest and value to colleagues in other departments. I thought it vital that no teacher's horizons should be limited to the bare requirements of an examination syllabus. He should be clear what he hoped would be left with his pupils in the way of concepts, skills, attitudes and values, once their detailed knowledge had begun to fade. I also believed that boys can benefit greatly from inter-departmental co-operation and cross-referencing between different subjects. This is much more easily said than done, but the departmental prospectuses were a way of encouraging it and creating a climate in which it might be possible.

It was a great advantage, to my mind, that the school's age-range ran from 10 to 18, without a major break at 13. During their Junior School years boys are at their most enthusiastic and receptive; this was the time to develop their curiosity and interest in learning for learning's sake. It was noticeable that those who joined the school at 13 after having their efforts directed towards the 'passing' of the Common Entrance Examination (or scoring high marks in it) were very often less self-motivated in adolescence than those who had been grounded in our Junior School with its broader and more stimulating curriculum and methods.

Early on I wondered whether we were right to admit half of our junior entry at the age of 10 rather than have all come in at 11. Certainly this was useful as a pre-emptive bid for some very bright boys. I concluded that it was educationally justified if the course and opportunities offered were at least as good as, preferably better than, those available to the same children elsewhere. The Lower First Form curriculum today, while still aiming to establish sound foundations, is unusually adventurous.

In the Senior School, from the ages of 13 to 16, I tried to keep the curriculum as broad as possible, with strict avoidance of premature options which could limit a boy's choice of 'A' Level subjects in the Sixth Form. This policy had already been introduced by Hugill and Parsons, and I made only a few variations over the years to the basic structure which they established. In essence we maintained a core curriculum right through to 16 and avoided a time-tabling pattern in the Fourth and Fifth Forms which could lead to unbalanced individual curricula and early closing of options.

A major stimulus to our work in this area of the school was given by the new common system of examining at 16 plus which eventually replaced the G.C.E. Ordinary Level. By 1985 it was clear what was going to be involved. The syllabuses would be more thoughtfully conceived, there would be a stronger emphasis on understanding rather than factual memory, and the assessment would be based on coursework as well as on a written examination. In one way this involved little change on our side, as the reforms were in the spirit of the approach which I had encouraged from the outset and was now well established.

The problem was the increased workload on the pupil. Could we maintain our heavy programme of examined subjects in the Fifth Form, already bursting at the seams? All boys were now taking the three separate Sciences, and there were further pressures to enable more to do practical or creative subjects in addition. I was determined too that Classics should still be taught to some, not only for its intellectual benefits but for cultural reasons. The education of our future citizens must include the transmission of our past heritage alongside more obviously 'useful' or 'relevant' subjects.

My deputies and I decided that we should not be daunted but maintain the full curriculum as it was and wait to see what happened. The outcome was a major advance on what we had ever managed to produce at 'O' Level. This was not, I am sure, because less was in the event demanded of the boys. In some respects, notably the coursework, more was demanded. They had to work harder and for longer, and the new methods of assessment brought out the best in more of them. The results were thus a fair measure of their greater collective achievement. They also represented a huge effort on the part of the staff who, apart from the teething problems inevitable in a new exam system, had all the burdens of marking and moderating a huge volume of coursework.

I had always hoped to see a major reform of the Sixth Form curriculum before I retired, so that my philosophy of breadth and balance could be extended right to the top of the school. Ever since I became a Headmaster I regarded the basic pattern of three 'A' Level subjects as too constricting and felt that university entrance requirements were taking priority over the general educational needs of the 16–18 age group. While narrow specialisation certainly suited a few, there were many others, including some of the very ablest, who were neither ready nor willing to limit their field of study and decide on options which could affect their university courses and even their whole future careers. Furthermore, it always seemed to me wrong for bright students today to be allowed to abandon mathematics, cease learning a foreign language or concentrate on subjects which required no extended communication in written English.

Some things could be done to alleviate the situation. Firstly, we were at pains to accommodate combinations of 'mixed' 'A' Levels. Mathematics was on offer to Arts and Science students alike and was often chosen by well over half of all candidates. Physics could sometimes be taken with History, Business Studies or a Modern Language. Biology and Geography were another possible pair. We aimed to be as flexible as we could, though each year there were always a few boys whose particular wishes could not be met.

Secondly, there was the often reviewed programme of non-examined or additional studies, some of which were taken at 'AO' Level in the Lower Sixth. This at least allowed boys the opportunity for some further language study or to develop their cultural interests. The difficulty was that active response on the boys' side varied greatly and 'minority time' studies inevitably assumed a lower priority as 'A' Levels drew closer. Some of the most successful courses were purely practical ones, like Cookery or Vehicle Maintenance, which the boys could enjoy as a relaxation from their main studies.

From the middle 1960's onwards there were various proposals to broaden the Sixth Form curriculum by making four or five subjects the norm instead of three, but all of these foundered on opposition from the universities whom it suited to have their students prepared to a higher level of attainment than they would have been in other countries. Pressure for change mounted, however, in the 1980s from the maintained schools and the more progressive wing in the independent sector to which I myself subscribed. This was backed by such bodies as the Confederation of British Industry, the Engineering Council and the Committee of University Vice-Chancellors themselves. The result was that the government introduced the Advanced Supplementary Level to encourage greater breadth. An 'AS' Level was to count as half an 'A' Level, with half the content to be studied in half the time, but with no diminution in the level of difficulty or sophistication demanded from the candidate.

Despite considerable reservations over the basic 'AS' Level concept, I decided to introduce it at Whitgift as soon as the new courses became available. I thought it was better than nothing, and accommodated it within the additional studies framework, so that boys could choose to do an extra examined subject alongside their 'A' Levels. Over half of the Lower Sixth year in 1987 embarked on a course but under 40% eventually sat the exam. A 100% pass-rate was a pleasing result, but 'AS' Level cannot be a final answer. I have little doubt that a curriculum of about five equal subjects will eventually be introduced, though several years too late for me to have implemented.

Despite my disappointment over the Sixth Form curriculum, I remain well content with the school's academic results. The 'A' Level statistics during the late 1980s were spectacularly good and put Whitgift in the very top flight of HMC schools in this respect. I made a point of interviewing virtually every boy during his Upper Sixth year, usually to discuss his university application, and this gave me the chance to assess the intellectual climate and outlook which lay at the end of our whole seven or eight year couse. The main qualities I looked for were liveliness of mind, a readiness to argue, fluency of communication and a willingness to go on learning. These were either there or developing fast in the young men I met. Whitgiftians continue to mature well at their universities, not having been intellectually exhausted at school.

I took a special interest in the progress of boys' applications to Oxford and Cambridge. It was an important part of our prospectus that we aspired to academic excellence and could challenge the gifted high-flier as well as could any of our rival schools. Over the 1970s the average number of Whitgiftians going on to the ancient universities rose quite markedly (see Percy for the figures) and we all but maintained the same level during the 1980s against much stiffer competition. One of the delights of Christmas time was to learn the results, one by one, as they came in from the different colleges, and count up the awards and places gained. Much of the excitement of the exercise was lost when the admissions system changed and there were no more post-'A' Level examinations. Entrance awards were abolished and the league tables went out. Most of Cambridge's offers and some of Oxford's were now conditional on the highest grades at 'A' Level, so that it became much harder to count one's chickens.

To some extent I regretted the changes, not least because there was no longer any need for a 'seventh term' Sixth Form and we lost the benefit, though only for some ten weeks, of between twenty and thirty mature pupils at the top of the school. The old system, however, certainly favoured independent school candidates, as maintained schools could not spare the resources to offer special post-'A' Level tuition. Moreover, Oxbridge awards had been the ultimate status symbol for too long. There are many more important criteria by which schools, even the most highly academic, should be judged, and our society's passion for pecking-orders is no good thing.

This links with an important question of school organisation: how were teaching groups best composed? We had to make sure that our high-fliers were fully stretched whilst preventing the remainder, all well above average in ability, from suffering in morale or self-esteem by comparison. We avoided any streaming of forms by general ability and, where 'setting' in certain subjects such as Mathematics and languages was essential, we found ways of blurring the pecking-order where we could, to avoid suggesting that we held low expectations of any. This policy evidently paid off in a reduced fall-out rate at 16 plus during the late 1980s.

In any event, boys may be talented in ways other than academic. They could also achieve conspicuous success on the games field, through adventure training or in the arts. All these activities were means to the building up of self-confidence, and success in one could be carried over to another. In time I came to call them 'co-curricular' rather than 'extra-curricular' activities as they were an integral part of the service we offered parents for their sons.

Though games are no longer a religion as they once were in our independent schools, sport remains an extremely important part of Whitgift life and involves a high proportion of the staff outside their classroom duties. Percy gives the facts of the school's development in this sphere and also comments on the altered ethos of games. The aim is still to play games as well and as hard as they can be played, but victory is not all. I was naturally delighted when our best sportsmen (and there were many very good ones) achieved success and honour for the school in their fixtures. I was equally concerned that games should be part of every Whitgiftian's education for leisure and that each boy could discover and develop some form of skill in physical recreation which he could take with him from school into adult life.

The question arose quite early on, and was indeed raised with the Inspectorate in 1971, whether internal games should still be run through the houses or entrusted to the Physical Education department as part of the time-tabled curriculum. Should priority be given to house spirit with the strong involvement of many enthusiastic staff and senior boys, or should the emphasis be more on boys' choosing as individuals from a variety of options with the help of more expert coaching? HMI were critical of the existing sheme, which they thought lacked co-ordination and catered poorly for the 'varying interests, needs and abilities of adolescent boys'. Furthermore, we were under-using our resources by concentrating our internal games on the Wednesday 'half-holiday'. Educationally I had no doubt that the HMI were right, but the house system was strong and this was a highly sensitive issue. Parsons warned me that I should alienate a large number of my colleagues if I changed the arrangements. Before long, however, we did introduce time-tabled games for the Junior School who then went into lessons on Wednesday afternoons. Reform in the Senior School did not come until 1984, two years after the opening of the Marlar Hall, when it became obvious to the Housemasters that our organisation was poorly geared to the best use of our facilities and that we could offer a better deal to the average and below-average games player through a wider system of options. The programme became the responsibility of the PE department, working in co-operation with the Housemasters, and has been altogether much more effective.

Apart from the spread of co-education, the most significant development in independent

The Library, 1990

schools during my professional lifetime has been the growth in the importance of the arts. A fresh balance of prestige has been struck between academic work, sport and culture and this, I am sure, has made our schools more civilised and creative places. Whitgift had already moved some way in this direction under my predecessor and it naturally accorded with my personal interests to see the arts developed further during my time and to play my own part in this development through directing some of the plays and operas. This also gave me the chance to get to know and to work with many of the boys in a way which would not otherwise have been easy for me as headmaster.

In the operas I had the pleasure of serving two gifted directors of music, and in all my produc-

Design Graphics Facility, 1990

tions I enjoyed the skilful collaboration of our imaginative art department which often designed the costumes as well as the scenery to fit my conception. From individual boys there were many memorable acting performances and artistic flair was also to be found among the stage and lighting crews.

Games, music and drama were only part of the school's co-curricular programme. I thought our programme of adventure training and outdoor pursuits through the CCF and other organisations an important antidote to the comforts of South London suburbia. I was glad to keep a period in the CCF virtually compulsory, since its educational purposes were well conceived by the officers, and the Ministry of Defence grant provided an important subsidy to this aspect of our service. Apart from the training weekends and various camps, there were innumerable trips and expeditions, mostly in the holidays, whether of a cultural or recreational nature. Keen to encourage an international outlook, I strongly supported journeys as far afield as Russia and the USA, besides our annual programme of exchanges and study visits in France and Germany. It was a special source of pride that a team of Whitgift boys was selected to represent the UK at the European Youth Parliament in 1990. Finally, there was the community service scheme which I would have extended if there had been any time in the week left.

Such a rich education could never have been offered without substantial financial backing. Over my first five years the school's fee income covered barely half of what the service cost to provide. There were major drawbacks, however, to such a generous subsidy. First, too much of the Foundation's income was being used to fund running expenditure, leaving little left for improving the school buildings. Though fees after 1970 began to rise, the increases were rapidly overtaken by the inflation which followed the oil crisis of 1973. Secondly, the system was not very businesslike. Budgeting was tentative, there was very little control of expenditure, and the school lacked defined limits within which to operate. Staff tended to regard the Foundation's purse as a bottomless pit and my heads of department were a little resentful when I required them, if only as a discipline, to submit reasonably accurate estimates of their requirements for the following academic year. Then if I required money for any special project, the outcome was unpredictable; it depended more on my powers of persuasion and the mood of the Governors than on the availability of funds within an annual budget. Finally, when the crunch came, there was a serious problem of public relations when parents' expectations of the fee levels had to be confounded.

In 1975 the Foundation was forced into a complete review of its financial arrangements for running its two schools. The immediate outcome was the setting up of the Whitgift Advisory Committee as a group responsible for the school's annual budget and for recommending fee levels. Apart from its fee income, the school was to receive a specified annual grant from which it had to meet any general subsidy to the fees, remissions by way of scholarships and bursaries and also (for the time being) all capital improvements to the school buildings except the replacement of services.

The results were wholly beneficial. At last we knew where we stood and staff were willing to accept financial disciplines and constraints. Priorities could be determined within the limits of the resources allocated to us and I was able to plan for the future and make the case for improvements, one by one. Within a very short while we succeeded in raising the fees to an economic level. This came as a shock to the parents, but in 1976 I was able to use the newly-formed Whitgift School Association as a medium of communication between them and the Governors. Despite some initial resentment, the dust settled when it was appreciated that the school was now managing its finances in an efficient and businesslike way and that there was a real intention of modernising the facilities.

Percy has related the long saga of the school building developments, starting with the 'shopping list' that I drew up within weeks of my arrival and culminating with the completion of the new extension in 1990. It was in this last massive project that I had a unique opportunity to resolve the needs of Science, Design Technology and Art in an integrated solution which would encourage a flow of ideas and co-operation between the three departments concerned. As the 1980s progressed, the message from industry and government alike grew ever clearer: our

Sixth Form Design Studio, 1990

education generally must be better geared to the application of theory to the solution of practical problems. Craft, Design & Technology was not a subject to be followed merely by the less academically able, for practical work could make no less demands on the intelligence and had essential links with both Science and Art. The opportunity to express these links in the design and layout of our new building was one well worth fighting for, even it if meant a further wait. It was very stimulating to work with Hugh Wilson over the feasibility study, and his sudden death was a devastating blow. In the event, however, his successor Bill Armstrong came up with an even better plan which incorporated the

Word Processing Facility, 1990

new Library within the total design and eventually placed the computer centre in the most appropriate relationship to other departments. There was also space left to provide an additional room for Geography and a proper base for Divinity, so that even the spiritual domain was not neglected.

I have to confess that at the outset I had no idea of the vast cost of this project, although I knew that to be architecturally worthy of our 1931 buildings it would not be cheap. Equally I had no idea that it would be on such a huge scale, more or less doubling the volume of the main building. In Percy's words, my expectations certainly were fulfilled beyond my wildest dreams. I believe that the building surpasses anything else of its kind in the country and that it opens up exceptional opportunities for the school's development in the future.

Even more important, though, than Whitgift's buildings is its staff. No school could offer a service of such richness and variety without a highly dedicated team of men and, more recently, women too. I have had the great good fortune to work with a number of teachers of exceptional flair and scholarship, but the hallmark of the Whitgift Common Room has been and remains its commitment to the boys' total development. Almost all contributed enthusiastically to co-curricular activities and were often involved in these at weekends or during the holidays. All were also asked to respond to the fresh demands of the GCSE and other developments on the academic front and rose to these challenges manificently.

Singling out names would be invidious in a narrative of this kind, even of those who, like Percy, gave a professional life-time to the service of the school. It would be wrong, however, not to refer to three men with whom I had to work most closely. Bert Parsons was my Second Master for my first ten years and, although he and I were very different personalities, I knew I could always rely on him to implement my requests with great efficiency, to give me the benefit of his sharp-thinking and practical mind and to keep the discipline of the school on an even keel. With Peter Trevis as Deputy Headmaster and Anthony Ridley as Senior Master and Director of Studies, I was able to set up a pattern and style of management which were more congenial to me and also made for an easier flow of communication with and from the Common Room. Working in a team with these two gifted schoolmasters was one of the very special pleasures of my career and I shall always be infinitely grateful for their personal loyalty and practical support in the school's development. Trevis helped the atmosphere to grow more mellow and sympathetic. Not only was he a very capable administrator but he was always sensitive to the complexities in the many human problems which arise in a school, whether of discipline, pastoral welfare or relationships. Ridley's brief was to do with the curriculum and its time-tabling, the administration of all examinations and the development of our resources, whether of staff or buildings. He played a major part in preparing the detailed brief for the new extension and, if the concept was mine, he with the architects must take the chief credit for its execution. Like Trevis, he was not only the most thorough and conscientious of administrators, he was invariably alive to the human factors implicit in any practical decision and approached every task with flexibility and tact.

I must also pay grateful tribute to the non-teaching staff, the various backstage workers who receive none of the limelight but without whom the performance cannot go ahead. Many problems were alleviated when the Foundation gave me an Administrative Officer based at the school and I was very well served by two capable ex-servicemen. I am bound to name Pat Dawson-Taylor who, throughout my time at the school, successfully combined the three roles of Headmaster's personal secretary, admissions registrar and school office manager. I was exceptionally lucky to have had a most efficient aide with an excellent memory, whose work for me was always completed accurately and to the highest standard. Only headmasters can know how much they depend on their secretaries. Without ever fussing me, Pat ensured that I was able to contend with the pressures of a very demanding routine.

To judge from Percy's history, I think I was also uniquely fortunate in the support I received from the Governors of the Whitgift Foundation. Though Sir James Marshall presided at my appointment, it was some relief to me that he was deposed from the chairmanship before I took up office. He had sent for me from Langley Park to a private meeting at which he told me that, although he never interfered in the school's discipline, the answer to Whitgift's problems lay in my making the boys cut their hair to a conventional length. I had already burnt my fingers over this peculiarly sensitive point of contemporary student fashion and had no intention of inaugurating my new headship with a confrontation on an issue of this kind. I thanked Sir James for his interest, expressed my gladness that he left the discipline in the Headmaster's hands and asked to reserve my position until I had assessed the total situation for myself. I none the less left this meeting with a sinking heart and was extremely glad to learn a little while later that I should be working under another Chairman.

It was very encouraging to learn that Dick Marten was eager to see Whitgift developed, ready to rethink the policy over fees and holding forward-looking ideas of his own. He was particularly keen for me to develop a closer association with Croham Hurst School, but whether he already had in mind the grand scheme for moving Whitgift to a new site alongside a Foundation girls' school I could not say. Certainly I had no inkling of the idea until the spring of 1972, well after the HMI Group Visit and its subsequent report. When I first learned of it, I felt that the wind had been taken out of my sails just as it was beginning to blow, but I saw the positive advantages of the plan, and the prospect of building another completely new school was not unattractive. It was no disappointment to me, however, when the project eventually collapsed. Relationships with the two girls' schools involved would have been complicated and difficult, and I thought that a single coeducational school under one head would be a sounder concept than the official proposal for two single-sex schools side by side with a joint Sixth Form. In the end, of course, we were able to develop Whitgift on its beautiful and much more accessible site at Haling Park. Dick Marten, however, was very sad when his cherished plan collapsed, and it needed a new Chairman to get the wind at Haling Park blowing afresh.

Rupert Nicholson's invaluable strengths were his understanding of the Whitgift Foundation's wealth and his ability to plan and sponsor development in a long-term perspective. It was this that eventually enabled me to get things done and to develop the school buildings to a Rolls-Royce standard. In the late 1970s, eager to see a sports hall on its way, I took the initiative and formed a committee to plan an inexpensive building and finance it by public appeal to parents, OWs and others with the help of professional fund-raisers. After we had done all the preparatory work and were ready to go ahead, Rupert Nicholson refused approval. Thank goodness he did, for we should have erected an ugly building on the parade ground, so pre-empting the site of our noble extension. He was also right on financial grounds. The Foundation might be temporarily short of cash, but its permanent wealth robbed any public appeal of credibility. Nicholson was not going to have pressure put on parents, many of whom were in any case struggling to meet the fees, by fund-raisers who would pocket a substantial proportion of the proceeds for themselves. I therefore waited a little longer for the sports hall and chose a better site overlooking Puntabout. The Governors did us proud with a building which is still the envy of other schools in the south-east. The Advisory Committee had funded the Ian Evans Building by annual instalments out of the grant, but the Marlar Hall was paid for by the Foundation quite separately. I asked the WSA to contribute £10,000 towards its equipment, to show appreciation. Even this took a lot of time and effort on the parents' side and was the full extent of their involvement.

To Rupert Nicholson too I owe the decision to go ahead with the new extension. When the quantity surveyors produced some projected estimates, some of the Governors were anxious and questioned the cost-effectiveness of the design. It was Nicholson who persuaded them it could be done if we waited one more year. Thank goodness again that he did. To have gone back to the drawing board would have set us back another five years and we could not have continued to improvise in our old accommodation for that long. As it turned out, the opening of the new extension proved a great climax to Nicholson's chairmanship.

There were three other Governors to whom I owed a particular debt. Digby Weightman chaired the Advisory Committee when it was first set up and gave me a great deal of encouragement when progress in improvements seemed rather slow. He was succeeded by Robert

Coatman who was deeply concerned for the school's buildings and brought his own expertise as a quantity surveyor to their discussion. He showed a keen eye for detail in the annual budget, while never failing to support my overall approach and line of argument. In his role as Committee Chairman he was extremely skilful in the conduct of intricate agenda and in ensuring that the various interests represented had their say. I owed most, however, to the Chairman of the Schools' Committee, Peter Shaw. He was sympathetic to my educational philosophy from the outset and with him I could discuss every detail of the school's business, including problems with colleagues and difficult matters of discipline. He was a frequent visitor to the school who made it his business to get to know as many of the staff as possible and even some of the senior pupils. For his ready ear and encouragement, together with his profound interest in the school's progress and development, I am eternally grateful.

I enjoyed a most happy and fruitful collaboration with two Clerks to the Foundation, most of my time with Michael Barnes until his health forced him to retire and he was succeeded by Raymond Smith. With two schools under their control, it would have been easy for the Foundation and its Clerks to impose a certain uniformity in their management or to play Whitgift and Trinity off against one another. Instead they accepted that they had two good but different schools, whose success depended on their Headmasters' being allowed the independence and freedom of action to reach their own decisions and make their own recommendations in the light of each school's character and circumstances. Looking back over twenty years, I realise anew how fortunate I was to be serving the Whitgift Foundation with its excellent resources and to have received the moral as well as the financial backing to put my educational ideas into practice.

I come finally to the most important and subtle aspect of a headmaster's role, his responsibility for the ethos of his school and quality of its life as a community. Under this general heading come the pastoral framework, relationships with parents, discipline and also the place which religion assumes in the total scheme of values.

In one important respect I probably departed from the thinking of my predecessors, certainly down to Marlar. By my time the ideals of a 'public school' education had grown somewhat tarnished by the connotations of exclusiveness, snobbery and social divisiveness. Percy refers to the various attacks from the Labour left and, apart from my own doubts of conscience, I was bound to be sensitive to these. My aim, therefore, was that Whitgift should be an outstandingly good school according to the finest contemporary educational criteria. Brodie's hopes had already been realised, and it was now irrelevant to be thinking about social cachet or playing in the right league. Above all, I felt the school must never claim a monopoly of virtue in its pupils' education. Where such a climate might inspire loyalty, it could lead to complacency on the part of the staff and either arrogance or hostility in the minds of the boys.

I therefore saw the school's independence essentially as a means of achieving the excellence to which we aspired. Later in the 1970s I advanced a political argument to justify the existence of an independent sector within the current national context (see Percy pp. 288–90), but this had no bearing on my wish, in Percy's phrase, to 'popularise' the school and avoid all sense of exclusiveness.

This wish lay behind my own recommendation to the Governors, after a general referendum, that we should change to a five-day week. Saturday morning school was regarded by some as a point of superiority which I did not feel was justified in the reality. I had little doubt that the balance of educational advantage lay in its abandonment and was glad to use a timely opportunity, for which I had waited, to bring Whitgift more into line with most other local schools, including Trinity.

Another point where day-schools like Whitgift had imitated the public boarding school was in the development of a strong house system. What should be the role of houses in a day-school context? I felt that 'house spirit' could be a mixed blessing if it meant that a boy was thought a good and loyal citizen if he was a keen games-player, but a selfish individualist if he preferred to play the violin in the orchestra, act in the play or just to be painting quietly in the Art room. What to me was important was that each boy should feel he mattered as an individual within the wider school community, that all his worthwhile interests were appreciated, and that his progress was being carefully monitored by several staff who knew him well at any given time.

It was this that determined the gradual shift in emphasis that I encouraged in the house system. Today it is not so much an end in itself as an important means of pastoral supervision. While form teachers have the responsibility for monitoring a boy's academic progress in any given year, the housemasters' role is to provide continuity and watch each boy's personal development through his participation in non-academic activities, however organised, whether in or outside the school. The house system still provides a basis for corporate activities, by no means all in sport, but care must be taken to ensure that a boy's house commitments are compatible with his other ones and that competitions involve those whose needs are not otherwise catered for. It also offers valuable opportunities for responsibility to some below the level of school prefectship.

This point of evolution took some time. It proved rather easier to change the school's relationships with its parents who I found had been kept rather at arm's length. Each year, from my first intake, I stressed to new parents that education was a matter of partnership and co-operation between home and school and that our communication needed to be as free as we could make it. This resulted quite soon in an increase in the number of evenings when parents came up to the school to discuss their sons' progress with the staff who taught them.

At Beckenham I had discovered the great value of a Parents' Association in cementing school-home relationships, but found that in this matter again I had to bide my time as the common room feared the tail might wag the dog. The ostensible motive behind the formation of the Whitgift School Association in 1976 was to set up a channel of communication between parents and governors over fees. In the event, it soon became what it is today, an active and supportive body which contributes admirably, notably on OWA Day and at other social functions which often involve the staff as well. There has never been any question of its interfering in the curriculum or the day-to-day running of the school.

I was also convinced that it would help our relationship with parents if we could sometimes make our facilities available to them as well as to their sons. Today parents, and former parents sometimes, can belong to the Arts and Scientific Societies. They have access to the Swimming Pool on two evenings a week, to the Marlar Hall for Badminton and keep-fit sessions and to the tennis courts.

'Good discipline' means several different things in the life of a school. I always believed that an orderly classroom ultimately depended on interesting teaching. With regard to behaviour in and outside the school at large, boys need to know that there are limits they may not transgress, but rules and sanctions, though indispensable, seemed to me less effective than caring supervision and an atmosphere of trust which stressed commonsense, thoughtfulness for others and regard for the school's reputation. Intelligent boys from supportive homes (as most of ours were) could usually be relied on to respond to this approach and gradually to acquire the self-control they would need as adults.

When I came, I found that some masters were still making quite frequent use of the cane for classroom offences, although it was no longer a punishment usable by boys. I had never approved of corporal punishment but found it wiser to discourage caning rather than actually to prohibit it. In time it dwindled to the point of disappearance. Hardly anyone, I think, regretted it in the long run and staff-pupil relationships were undoubtedly better without it.

If boys went astray, I was always inclined to ask why and often found a reason in terms of home difficulties or even boredom in the classroom. This, I know, made me a demanding taskmaster for those colleagues who felt less personally secure. Yet I firmly believed that boys as they mature should learn to do the right thing for the right reason rather than as a matter of blind conformity. Of course I was sometimes let down, but not very often. Whitgift gets less than its fair share of disciplinary difficulties. By and large I found the boys sensible, orderly and responsive to appeal. Not much could be wrong when staff told me how much they had enjoyed taking them on trips outside school and how their good behaviour had received favourable comments in places where they were staying—something, surely, of an acid test. That said, no headmaster can ever afford to be complacent over discipline, as social influences can suddenly prove subversive.

Throughout my twenty-one years the Prefects continued to play an important part in the smooth running of the school. When vesting them with their authority, I always emphasised their positive role in setting an example and representing the school well on public occasions. I wanted them to be efficient but not officious in the performance of their duties. Towards the end of my time we arranged a weekend training seminar at which the Prefects were asked to share their early experiences of authority and examine the meaning of leadership in today's society, with tact and understanding as cardinal elements. Most of the Prefects I appointed exercised their authority very responsibly in exchange for little privilege. Some of my School Captains and Vice-Captains were really outstanding in the tone they set for the rest of the pupil community.

In 1989 I was led to re-examine the sense in which Whitgift could claim to be a Christian school. In co-operation with local organisations, including the Croydon Council of Churches, we had accommodated a multi-faith celebration at the school, and some staff felt that this compromised our traditional Christian stance. Where the boys themselves were concerned, I had to accept that many of them, perhaps a majority, came from families which did not subscribe actively to any religion at all, while there was a substantial group of devout believers of non-Christian faiths among our Asian pupils. Percy describes the problems of school worship today. Despite these, I believed that the school would be poorer if it ceased to meet for our twice-weekly Assemblies. Here I felt it important from time to time to acknowledge the existence of other faiths, although we continued to sing traditional Christian hymns and to invoke the Trinity in our prayers.

Difficult as this might be, I was clear that Christian values should inform Whitgift's life as a community. Its hallmarks should be friendliness, understanding, mutual tolerance and, wherever possible, forgiveness. If the relationships in the school are good, the environment will be conducive to learning and the growth of self-confidence as the boys pass from childhood through adolescence to young adulthood. It always pleased me particularly when parents said they had chosen Whitgift because of its friendly atmosphere. This was to me at least as importance as our academic and other achievements. Indeed I believed it to be the key to all the rest. If we have not 'charity', we are nothing.

This brings me on finally to the boys for whom the school exists. Socially they provide a fair cross-section within the middle socio-economic groups. Some come from low-income families but these are unlikely to be children of manual workers. This raises the question whether the high-grade academic course we offer is now too forbidding for 'children of the poorer sorte' and whether the time has not come once again to ask how the Founder's wishes can best be carried out in today's changing context.

All that is speculative. Over other things I am more sure. My happiest hours as Headmaster were those that I was able to spend with the boys themselves, particularly as a teacher of Classics or Divinity in the classroom, or in rehearsal for my dramatic productions. I do not think that Whitgift produces a distinctive type (at least I hope it does not) but, to generalise, I found the boys enthusiastic, responsive to challenge and encouragement, self-assured as they came through the school, though in a natural way that was pleasantly free from 'side'. Today's Whitgiftian likes to feel identified with his generation as a whole and, although he is proud of his school and values the confidence it has given him, he is unlikely to flaunt his loyalty in a particularly assertive way. At university he is as much at ease with those who have come from maintained school backgrounds as with those who have been to other independent schools. Over twenty years I have counted myself privileged to be working with and for him.

Towards the end of my time, I came to feel that we had sold our Upper Sixth form leavers short at the end of their school days by sending them off with virtually no ceremony after they had finished their 'A' Level exams. Some rite of passage was needed, better than the unruly lapse into childish behaviour which sometimes characterised their last day at school. I therefore introduced a graduation ritual when boys in their parents' presence each received a leaving certificate from the Chairman of the Governors. I used the occasion to give a valedictory address in which I revoiced the hope of my first Prizegiving speech, that each one would use the opportunities that his education at Whitgift had given him not merely to feather his own nest but to tackle problems and promote happiness in human society at large. I also thought it right, in a world where family values are so insecure, to wish those young men success and stability in their future home relationships.

There is thus a valid sense in which my headmastership admits of no appraisal for many years to come. I cast my bread upon the waters in faith and hope. The outcome will only be seen in the lives and personal fulfilment of the three thousand and more Whitgiftians for whom it was my very happy lot to care.

About the Author

F.H.G. Percy was born at Colchester in 1911. He entered Whitgift School in 1922, and left in 1930, by which time he was Captain of the School, of Rugby and of Cross's House. From 1930 to 1934 he was at Oriel College, Oxford, receiving his BA in 1933 (he proceeded MA in 1959).

He taught at Southwell, Notts, and Stafford from 1934 to 1937, playing Rugby for Notts, Lincs and Derby in the 1935–36 season, and for Staffordshire in 1936–37.

He was appointed by Ronald Gurner to teach French and English at Whitgift in 1937, and after War Service from 1940 to 1945, as a Captain in the Royal West Kent Regiment, he returned to the School in 1946. He was Master in charge of Rugby from 1949 to 1954, and Housemaster of Cross's from 1949 to 1966. He retired in 1976, the year in which his *History of Whitgift School* (the first edition of this book) was published. Having established the Whitgift School Archive, he took on the responsibilities of School and Foundation Archivist in his retirement, a position which he still holds.

Freddie Percy has always played an active part in the OWA. He was Captain of the Old Whitgiftian RFC in 1939, and would undoubtedly have continued for longer in that position had it not been for the interruption of the Second World War. He was Honorary Secretary of the OWA from 1953 to 1975, and its President from 1975 to 1976.

His interests are by no means limited to Whitgift matters. His recreations include the study of the fine arts, both at home and abroad, listening to classical music, and of course, reading a wide range of English literature.

He was married in 1940 to Mollie Robin. They had three children, Valerie (who sadly died in 1988), Antony and Michael. Both Antony and Michael are OWs.

It was with great reluctance that Freddie Percy agreed that I might write and include this personal note in his book. He felt that it had no place in a history of the School, and additionally was embarrassed by the thought that readers would look upon it as an exercise in self-advertisement (the last thing in fact that Freddie could be accused of). I am certain that all those who enjoy the book will share my belief that it would not have been complete without a few brief details about the author, and will be glad that my persuasion was finally effective.

M.R.L.

Appendix I
Schoolmasters and Head Masters

Schoolmasters and Chaplains

1. AMBROSE BRYGGES 1600–1

B. *c.*1552; MA, University unknown. *Appointed by Archbishop Whitgift 31 March 1600*, aged 48. *Left 24 June 1601.* Rector of Sutton, Surrey, 29 December 1600 (successor appointed 22 March 1603). No more of him is known, except that Francis Terrell, citizen and grocer of London, who gave a market-house to the town of Croydon, forgave in his will (PCC Dorset, 30 March 1609) 'Ambrose Brigges, sometime Schoolmaster at the free school at Croydon, such moneye as owed me'.

2. JOHN IRELAND 1601–6

B. *c.*1575; of Westmorland. Ed. at Westminster and Christ Church, Oxford; BA 1595; MA 1599, at which time he described himself as 'head of a school'. *Appointed by Archbishop Whitgift, 24 June 1601*, aged 27; *resigned 4 July 1606*, Bur. St. Margaret's, Westminster, 27 September 1607. He left £3 to the poor of the Hospital.

3. ROBERT DAVIES 1606–16

B. *c.*1580; of Denbigh. Ed. at Christ Church, Oxford; BA 1602. Usher at Westminster. *Appointed by Archbishop Bancroft 4 July 1606*, married, aged 27. *Dismissed 28 June 1616.* In his nuncupative will (PCC 76 Meade, 21 June 1618) he mentions his brother Ryce, his only daughter Margaret, and his brother-in-law William Ireland, of Croydon (a relative of John Ireland?).

4. WILLIAM NICOLSON 1616–29

B. 1 November 1591, at Stratford St. Mary, Suffolk, s. of Christopher Nicolson, Clothier. Ed. at Magdalen College School and Magdalen College, Oxford; BA 1611; MA 1615; Chaplain 1616. Vicar of Shoreham, Sussex (a college living) 1614. *Appointed by Archbishop Abbot 3 July 1616*, aged 24. *Resigned 1629.* Rector of Llandeilo, co. Carmarthen, 1626; Archdeacon of Brecknock 1644, later deprived. In 1648 established with Jeremy Taylor a successful private school at Newton Hall, Carmarthen. Bishop of Gloucester 1661. M. first, Jane —, who d. 1619; second, 1620 Elizabeth Brigstocke, widow (née Heighton), of Croydon, who d. April 1663. Died 5 February 1671/2. In his will (PCC 47 Eure) he left a sum of money to his old parish at Llandeilo to put children to a trade or profession, his heir being his step-grandson, Owen Brigstocke. If he had any children, they do not seem to have survived him. He published: i. *A Plain Exposition of the Catechism of the Church of England, enjoined to be learned by every child . . .* , 1655 (reprinted several times, it was in frequent use in schools and was known as 'Nicolson's Paraphrase'). ii. *An Apology for the Discipline of the Ancient Church*, 1659. iii. *A Plain Exposition of the Apostles' Creed*, 1661. iv. *An Easy Analysis of the Whole Book of Psalms*, 1662. See *DNB*.

5. JOHN WEBB 1629–48

B. *c.*1603, s. of Thomas Webb, of Wallington, Surrey. Ed. at Croydon under Nicolson (?) and Magdalen Hall, Oxford; BA 1624; MA 1628. *Appointed by Archbishop Abbot 4 May 1629*, aged 26. In November 1624 his mother, Bridget Webb, was a party with William and Elizabeth Nicolson and several members of the Brigstocke family in a lawsuit (Chancery Proceedings Ser. II 378/20). M. first, Janet —, who d. June 1637; second, Sarah —, who survived him and m. Richard Holford; she d. 1660. He had ten children. *Died 16 April 1648*, in possession of real estate, including lands at Sutton, valued at over £1200 (will PCC 81 Essex); executors were 'my loving friends Sir John Evelyn of Godstone . . . and Richard Holford of Croydon'.

309

Appendix I

6. NORIS WOOD 1648–51

B. *c*.1618. Ed. at Charterhouse and Trinity College, Cambridge; BA 1640. Usher at Charterhouse 1634–47 ('removed on marriage'). *Appointed by E. Corbitt, Minister of Croydon, and John Rawlinson, Rector of Lambeth, 14 June 1648*, aged 30. *Resigned March 1650/1* on his appointment to Leicester Grammar School, where in November 1651 new decrees for the conduct of the school on Puritan principles were prescribed. Headmaster of Charterhouse, February 1654/5; resigned June 1662 as unwilling to subscribe to the oath required by the Act of Uniformity; there is no further record of him.

7. THOMAS DAY 1651–62

B. *c*.1616, s. of Edmund Day of Marston, Lincs. Ed. at Magdalene College, Cambridge, and Christ's; BA 1637, MA 1640. *Appointed by Sir William Brereton, Bt., 24 March 1650/1*, aged 34. Apparently *resigned September 1662* as unwilling to subscribe to oath required by Act of Uniformity. Later history unknown.

8. JOHN PHILIPS 1662–8

B. *c*.1602, s. of John Philips of Middlesex. Ed. at New College, Oxford; BA 1624; MA 1627. First Under-Master, Merchant Taylors' School, November 1627. Suspended for insubordinate behaviour, January 1637/8, and later dismissed. A man of this name was Headmaster, St. Saviour's School, Southwark, June 1638 to January 1643/4. His occupation between this date and his *appointment by Archbishop Juxon 29 September 1662*, aged 60, is unknown. *Died 6 August 1668*.

9. WILLIAM CROWE 1668–75

B. 1616, s. of William Crowe, rector of Barnby, Suffolk. Ed. at his father's school at Barnby, and at Caius College, Cambridge (his father's old college); scholar 1633; BA 1637; MA 1639. Vicar of Mutford, Suffolk, 1648–54. Unsuccessful nominee to Cambridge University Librarianship 1668. *Appointed by Archbishop Sheldon 4 December 1668*, aged 52. *Committed suicide; bur. at Croydon 11 April 1675*. Publications: i. *An Exact Collection or Catalogue of our English Writers on the Old and New Testament . . . 1663*. ii. *Elenchus Scriptorum tam Graecorum quam Latinorum . . . 1672*. See *DNB*.

10. JOHN SHEPHEARD 1675–81

B. 1643, s. of John Shepherd of Cheselbourne, Dorset, Ed. at Wadham College, Oxford (Scholar); BA March 1664; ordained priest 1664; admitted curate of 'Stypleton', Dorset, June 1664; Rector of Caterham, Surrey, 1667. *Appointed by Archbishop Sheldon 17 April 1675*, aged 31. *Resigned 11 June 1681*. Chaplain to William Gulston, Bishop of Bristol, 1678–9; Rector of Sanderstead, February 1678/9; Rector of Oxted, Surrey, September 1681 (held with Sanderstead). M. first, 23 September 1675, Joan Atwood of Sanderstead, who d. 25 November 1679; second, about 1682, Ellen French of Croydon, who d. March 1702/3. He was bur. at Sanderstead 3 June 1705. His son, Atwood Sheppard, b. November 1678, bur. at Sanderstead February 1714/15.

See *Notes & Queries for Somerset & Dorset*, Vol. XXX, September 1979, 'John Shepheard, Master of Whitgift School when John Oldham was Under-Master.' – Professor Harold F. Brooks. (Shepheard made a number of changes in the spelling of his surname. When he subscribed to the Oath of Supremacy in June 1664 he signed as John Shepherd. When appointed Master in 1675, he had become John Shepheard, but upon his induction to the Rectory of Sanderstead in 1679 he changed his signature once more – to John Sheppard, a spelling he continued to use until his death. These changes may have been made in order to distinguish himself from other John Shepherds or Shepards, with whom he might have been confused.)

11. JOHN CAESAR 1681–1712

B. *c*.1655, son of John Caesar, of Reed, Herts. Ed. at Hitchin and Christ's College, Cambridge; BA 1673. *Appointed by Archbishop Sancroft 11 June 1681*, aged 26. Vicar of Croydon, January 1688/9. Chaplain to Scroop, 4th Earl of Bridgewater (see Alumni), before 1708. M. —; children who survived were Julius and Charles (see Alumni), Susannah. *Resigned late 1711*. Died Croydon 10 March 1719/20. Publications: i. *Sermon preached at Croydon Assizes 10 March 1707/8*, 1708. ii. *Sermon preached at Guildford Assizes 14 July 1708*, 1708. Unpublished letters to Archbishop Sancroft in Bodley: Letters Rawl. 59, 100–101.

12. HENRY MILLS 1712–42

B. *c*.1674, s. of Nathaniel Mills, of Wells, Somerset. Ed. at Wells Cathedral School (?) and

Trinity College, Oxford; BA 1694; MA 1698. Schoolmaster Wells Cathedral School, 1699. Prebendary of Dinder, Somerset, June 1702. Elected Headmaster Highgate School, January 1712 (post declined). *Appointed by Archbishop Tenison 11 April 1712*, aged 38. M. first, —, by whom he had a daughter, Mary (who m. 11 October 1736 Rev. William Agat); second, 2 April 1714, Hannah Hervey, who survived him, by whom he had at least six children. Rector of Merstham, Surrey, February 1723/4. *Died Croydon 11 April 1742.* Will PCC 125 Trenley. Publications: i. *A Full Answer to Mr Pillonnière's Reply to Dr Snape*, 1718. ii. *An Essay on Generosity*, 1732. iii. *Pueritiae Formandae Artifex*, 1741. A MS book of notes for sermons is in Bodley: MS Rawl. Sermons 237.

13. SAMUEL STAVELEY 1742–51

Bapt. 3 September 1718 at Sherborne Abbey, Somerset. Ed. at Sherborne School (?) and Emmanuel College, Cambridge; organist; BA 1741; MA 1747. *Appointed by Archbishop Potter 19 June 1742*, aged 23. *Resigned 26 August 1751.* Chaplain to East India Co., arriving at Fort St. George, Madras, June 1752, where he kept a vestry school from August 1753 to June 1762, when he went as Chaplain to Fort William, Calcutta; here he died in October 1762. Unmarried? In his will, dated December 1758, he left all his property to his two sisters, Ann and Elinor Staveley, of Sherborne. Letters to Warren Hastings in B.L. Add. MS 29132.

14. JOHN TAYLOR LAMB 1751–74

B. *c.*1726 at Ditchling, Sussex, son of William Lamb, clerk. Ed. at a private school at Streatham and St. John's College, Cambridge; BA 1750. Usher and Fellow of Dulwich College, 2 August 1751. *Appointed by Archbishop Herring 3 September 1751*, aged 25. Vicar of Leysdown, Sheppey, Kent, 1757–61; Rector of Keston, Kent, 1761–74. M. Mary —, who survived him; three sons: John, William, Thomas (all admitted to St. Paul's School after their father's *death in 1774*). Will PCC 149 Hargrave, pr. April 1774.

15. JAMES HODGSON 1774–1801

B. *c.*1750, s. of Rev. James Hodgson, Rector of Humber, co. Hereford. Ed. at Charterhouse and Christ Church, Oxford; BA 1770; MA 1773. In 1771 ordained deacon as curate to his father's church, where he succeeded as rector. *Appointed by Archbishop Cornwallis 14 June 1774*, aged 24. Rector of Keston, Kent, same date. M. first, 1774, Jane, dau. of Rev. Richard Coke, of Lower Moor, Hereford, who d. February 1790; issue: James, John Richard, Jane, Francis; of these only the last survived their father (see Alumni). M. second, Winifred —, by whom he had a daughter, Elizabeth. Rector of Southrepps, near Cromer, Norfolk; Rector of Barwick in Elmet, near Leeds, February 1799. *Resigned March 1801.* Died at Barwick October 1810. Will PCC 599 Collingwood. Unpublished correspondence: B.L., Liverpool Papers (Add. MSS 38225–38473 passim).

16. JOHN ROSE 1801–12

B. *c.*1755, s. of John Rose, of Lambeth, gent. Ed. at Merchant Taylors' School (Head Scholar 1770) and St. John's College, Oxford (scholar); BA 1776; MA 1785. Third Under-Master, M.T.S., 1779; Second Under-Master 1783; First Under-Master 1785. Rector of St. Martin's, Outwich, 1795. Resigned from M.T.S. 1797. *Appointed by Archbishop Moore 1 April 1801*, aged 45. DD Lambeth 1808. *Resigned 9 July 1812.* Defendant in legal action taken by Brethren and Sisters of the Whitgift Hospital November 1813. President, Sion College, London, 1814, 1815. M. Ann —, who d. 1819, with issue at least nine children. Died May 1821. Will PCC 519 Mansfield. Publications: i. *A Quarter of an Hour before Dinner, or, Quality Binding*, a farce, 1788. ii. *The Prisoner*, a musical romance, 1792. iii. *Caernarvon Castle, or, The Birth of the Prince of Wales*, an opera, 1793. MS play: *The Family Compact*, 1792 (MS Larpent (Huntington Coll.)). See also: *Proceedings & Evidence (in the case of) The Rev. John Rose, DD, . . .* , 1813.

17. JOHN COLLINSON BISSET 1812–43

B. 1785, s. of Alexander Bisset, of Croydon, schoolmaster. Ed. his father's school (?) and St. Edmund Hall, Oxford; BA 1808; MA 1819. *Appointed by Archbishop Manners-Sutton 29 July 1812*, aged 27. Curate of Addington, Surrey. Vicar of Addington 1820. *Resigned February 1843.* Vicar of Leysdown, Kent, February 1843. Died 1852.

Appendix I

18. GEORGE COLES 1843–65

B. 16 November 1798, s. of William Coles, West India Merchant of London and his wife Ann Godwin. Ed. at Eton and Peterhouse, Cambridge; BA 1821; MA 1824. Curate of Croydon 1823; priest-in-charge, later vicar, of St. James's, Croydon, 1829–65. *Appointed by Archbishop Howley 20 March 1843*, aged 42. Moved to Dorking 1863, where *he died 22 January 1865*. M. his first cousin Elizabeth, d. of Thomas Coles of St. Mary Abchurch, and his wife Elizabeth Fenning; issue at least four children.

Head Masters

19. ROBERT BRODIE 1871–1902

B. 15 April 1840 in Lincoln's Inn Fields, 5th s. of Peter Bellinger Brodie, barrister-at-law. Ed. at Charterhouse and Balliol College, Oxford; Trinity College (scholar); 1st class, Hon. Mods 1860; 1st class, Greats 1863. Assistant Master Charterhouse and Sherborne School. Senior Student Christ Church 1864; Tutor in residence 1866–70. *Appointed by Archbishop Tait January 1871*, aged 30. M. 15 February 1871, Emma B. Moseley; four sons (O.W.s) and one daughter. *Retired 19 December 1902*. Died 9 December 1925.

20. SAMUEL OGDEN ANDREW 1903–27

B. 8 January 1868 at Lees, near Oldham, Lancs., s. of Samuel Andrew and his wife Mary Ogden. Ed. at Manchester Grammar School and Oriel College, Oxford (scholar); 1st class, Hon. Mods 1888; 1st class, Greats 1890. Studied psychology at Universities of Berlin and Tübingen. Sixth-form Master Llandovery College 1892; Headmaster Hulme Grammar School, Oldham, 1895. *Appointed by Archbishop Frederick Temple to take office in January 1903*, aged 35. M. Lilian Pullinger; one son (O.W.), two daughters. *Resigned July 1927*. Died 10 April 1952. Publications: i. *Greek Prose Composition*, 1902. ii. *Geometry, an Elementary Treatise in the Theory and Practice of Euclid*, 1903; 3rd edition, revised, 1916. iii. *Practical Arithmetic* (with A. Consterdine), 1905. iv. *Lingua Latina* (general editor with W. H. D. Rouse), 1912. v. *Praeceptor, a Master's Book for Lingua Latina*, 1913. vi. *Gawaine and the Green Knight, a modern version in the original metre*, 1929. vii. *Translation of Homer's Iliad, Bk XXIV, Hector's Ransoming*, 1934. viii. Ditto, *The Wrath of Achilles*, 1938. ix. *Syntax and Sytle in Old English*, 1940. x. *Postscript on 'Beowulf'*, 1948. xi. *Translation of Homer's Odyssey*, 1948, xii. *Translation of Homer's Iliad* (with M. J. Oakley, etc.), 1955.

Master

21. STANLEY RONALD KERSHAW GURNER 1928–39

B. 23 January 1890, 2nd s. of Walter Gurner. Ed. at Merchant Taylors' School and St. John's College, Oxford (scholar). 1st class, Hon. Mods. 1910; Aegrotat, Greats 1912. Assistant Master, Haileybury, Clifton and Marlborough, 1912–14. Served in Great War (as Major) 1914–18, wounded, MC, mentioned in dispatches. Housemaster Marlborough 1918; Headmaster, Strand School, London, 1920; Head Master King Edward VII School, Sheffield, 1926. *Appointed by Archbishop Davidson July 1927, to take office January 1928*, aged 37. Adopted title of *Master*, 1931. M. 1920, Rosalie Leila, dau. of Thomas Romer, Senior Master of the Court of Chancery; one adopted son. *Committed suicide 16 May 1939*. Publications: i. *War's Echo*, poems, 1917. ii. *The Day-Boy*, a novel, 1924. iii. *For Sons of Gentlemen*, a novel (under pseudonym of 'Kerr Shaw'), 1926. iv. *C3*, a novel, 1927. v. *The Riven Pall*, a novel, 1929. vi. *Pass at Ypres*, a novel, 1930. vii. *Day Schools of England*, 1930. viii. *Reconstruction*, a novel, 1931. ix. *I Chose Teaching*, autobiography, 1937. x. *We Crucify! (Imaginary Minutes of the Sanhedrin, based on scriptural classes at Whitgift School)*, 1939.

Headmasters

22. GERALD EDWARD HAROLD ELLIS, 1939–46

B. 17 December 1878, in Wellington, New Zealand, s. of Edward Ellis, MD. Ed. at Epsom College and Lincoln College, Oxford; 1st class, Hon. Mods. 1899; Greats 1901. Assistant Master, Epsom, Felsted and Bradfield, 1901–3. Assistant Master, Whitgift, 1903; Housemaster of Ellis's House (later Smith's) 1909; of Cross's 1909–46; Second Master 1922; Acting Head Master, Michaelmas Term 1927 and May to July 1939.

Appointed by Archbishop Lang July 1939, aged 60. Adopted title of *Headmaster*. *Retired July 1946*. M. 1909, Gladys Magdalen, dau. of Rev. S. J. Rowton; no children. Died 7 August 1967.

23. EDWARD ALFRED GEOFFREY MARLAR 1946–61

B. 2 January 1901, s. of J. F. Marlar. Ed. at Brighton College and Selwyn College, Cambridge; History Tripos Pt. I; Law Tripos; LLB. Senior History Master, Dunstable Grammar School, 1922; Senior History and Sixth-form Master, Worksop College, 1927; Headmaster, Moulton Grammar School, Lincs, 1934; Headmaster, King Edward VI School, Lichfield, 1937. Major in Home Guard, War of 1939–45; MBE 1944. *Appointed by Archbishop Fisher September 1946*, aged 45. *Retired July 1961*. M. 1924, Winifred Stevens; one son, one daughter. Died 24 April 1978.

24. MICHAEL JAMES HUGILL 1961–70

B. 13 July 1918, in Edinburgh, s. of Rear-Admiral R.C. Hugill, CB, MVO, OBE. Ed. at Oundle and King's College, Cambridge (exhibitioner); Maths Tripos 1939; MA 1943. War service 1939–46 in RN (Lt.-Com.) After a short period in industry, Mathematics Master, Stratford Grammar School, London, 1947; Senior Maths Master, Bedford Modern School 1951; Headmaster, Preston Grammar School, Lancs. 1957. *Appointed by Archbishop Fisher September 1961*, aged 43. *Resigned July 1970*. Mathematics Master, Westminster School. 1972–86. Unmarried. Publications: *Advanced Statistics*, 1985.

25. DAVID ANTONY RAEBURN 1970–91

B. 22 May 1927, at Hampstead, eldest s. of Walter A. L. Raeburn, QC. Ed. at Charterhouse and Christ Church, Oxford (scholar); 1st Class, Hon. Mods. 1947; Greats 1949. National Service 1949–51; Temporary Captain RAEC. Assistant Master, Bristol Grammar School 1951; Bradfield College 1955; Senior Classics Master, Alleyn's School 1958. Headmaster, Beckenham and Penge Grammar School (later Langley Park School for Boys) 1963. FRSA 1969. *Appointed by Archbishop Ramsey September 1970*, aged 43. M. 1961, Mary Faith Hubbard; two sons (OWs), one daughter. *Retired July 1991*.

26. CHRISTOPHER ANDREW BARNETT 1991 –

B. 1 February 1953, in Epping, s. of Peter A. Barnett. Ed. at the Cedars School, Leighton Buzzard, and Oriel College, Oxford (exhibitioner); BA (Hons) Modern History 1974; MA 1978; DPhil 1981; Lecturer, Dept. of Economics, Brunel University 1975–77; Head of History, Bradfield College 1978–87; Second Master, Dauntsey's School, West Lavington 1987–91. *Appointed by Archbishop Runcie September 1991*, aged 38. M. 1976, the Hon. Laura Miriam Elizabeth Weidenfeld; three sons, one daughter.

Appendix II
Alumni 1600–1800

* These attributions are conjectural, but good circumstantial evidence exists for including them.

Under Robert Davies, 1606–16

JENNEY, Thomas. S. of Ambrose, of Eltham, Kent. B. Bexwall, Norfolk. Caius College, Cambridge, 1611. D. before 1621 (?).

DALENDAR, Henry. S. of Sir William, of Buckland, Surrey. B. 1601. Caius College, Cambridge, 1617. Rector of Headley, Surrey, sequestered 1645; of Wisborough Green, Sussex, 1657. Will: Chichester 22/95, pr. 14 Jan 1661/2.

*BROME, Thomas. S. of George, of Croydon, gent. Christ Church, Oxford, 1615, aged 18. Serjeant-at-Law, d. 27 July 1673; of Basinghall Street and Tuppenham, Kent.

Under William Nicolson, 1616–29

VAUGHAN, Richard. S. of Richard, MP. Comptroller of the Household of the Prince of Wales; Baron Vaughan of Mullingar 1621, Earl of Carbery 1628. B. *c.* 1602. Kt. 1626. MP 1624–29. Gray's Inn 1638; Baron Vaughan of Emlyn (in the English peerage) 1643. Lieutenant-general royal army in Wales; Lord Lieutenant of the Marches 1660. Three times married. D. 1686. DNB. Portrait at Carmarthen Museum; copy at School.

PERCY, Henry, Y.S. of Henry, ninth Earl of Northumberland. B. *c.* 1603. Christ Church, Oxford 1624. MP Marlborough 1629; Master of the horse to Prince of Wales 1639; Captain and Governor of Jersey 1640; Baron Percy of Alnwick 1643. D. unm. 1659. DNB. Portrait at Petworth (Van Dyck); copy at School.

*STYLE, William. S. of William, of Langley in Beckenham Kent. B. 1603; Queen's College, Oxford 1618; Inner Temple 1618. Writer on legal and other matters. D. 1679. DNB. Portrait in Tate Gallery.

*STYLE, Richard. S. of William of Langley. B. 1603. Twin (?) brother of William. BA, St. John's College, Cambridge 1625. D. Cambridge 1625.

*CAREW, Francis, S. of Nicholas, of Beddington, Surrey. University College, Oxford, 1619, aged 16. Inner Temple, 1620. MP Haslemere, 1624. Kt. February 1624/5. Bur. April, 1649.

*WEBB, John. S. of Thomas, of Beddington, Surrey. Magdalen Hall, Oxford, 1621, aged 18. Schoolmaster, Croydon, 1629–48.

*STYLE, George. S. of William of Langley. B. 1604. Queen's College, Oxford 1618; Inner Temple 1621. Bro of William and Richard.

*BRIGSTOCKE, John. S. of Robert, of Croydon, yeoman, whose widow, Elizabeth, née Heighton, m. 1620 William Nicolson. Bapt. October 1604. M. 1625 Mary Bowen, of Llechdwny, co. Carmarthen. D. Kidwelly, 1640.

*CAREW, Nicholas. S. of Nicholas, of Beddington, Surrey. University College, Oxford, 1621. Inner Temple 1622.

*CAREW, George. S. of Nicholas, of Beddington, Surrey. University College, Oxford, 1624, aged 19.

KEMP, Bartholomew. E. s. of Bartholomew, gent. of Croydon and London. Caius College, Cambridge, 1622, aged 16. Scholar 1622–9. Cousin of John Viell and John Smith, *q.v.*

SMITH, John. S. of William, merchant, of London. Caius College, Cambrige, 1623, aged 16. Cousin of Bartholomew Kemp and John Viell, *q.v.*

VIELL, John. S. of Abraham, of London. Scholar, Caius College, Cambridge, 1622, aged 15. Usher and Fellow of Dulwich College, 1628; Schoolmaster 1630. Cousin of Bartholomew Kemp and John Smith, q.v.

*BARCROFT, Charles. S. of John, merchant taylor, of London Bridge and Croydon. Pembroke College, Oxford, 1626, aged 17.

*CAREW, Edmund. S. of Nicholas, of Beddington, Surrey. University College, Oxford, 1624, aged 17. Inner Temple, 1637. Bur. September 1654.

*CAREW, Oliver, S. of Nicholas, of Beddington. Peterhouse, Cambridge, January 1625/6. D. 1670, aged 63.

*KEMP, William. S. of Bartholomew, of Croydon. Queens' College, Cambridge, 1624, aged 16. Bro. of Bartholomew, q.v.

COOKE, Richard. S. of Richard, mercer. B. All Saints', Thames St., London. Sidney Sussex College, Cambridge, 1624/5, aged 16. Ordained 1635; curate of Haslemere, Surrey, 1662.

HATTON, Richard. S. of Sir Robert, Kt., Steward to Archbishop Abbot. B. Tottenham, Middlesex. Sidney Sussex College, Cambridge, 1623, aged 14. Gray's Inn 1619. Kt. January 1644/5.

*STYLE, Thomas. S. of William of Langley. B. 1610. Christ Church, Oxford, 1632; DCL 1666. Bro of William, Richard and George. D. 1677.

*HOWARD, Charles. 5th s. of Charles, Lord Howard of Effingham and First Earl of Nottingham. B. at Haling, Croydon, December 1610; Kt. 1624; BA Christ Church, Oxford 1627; succeeded his half-brother, 2nd Earl, 1642; d.s.p. Mortlake 1681, bur. Reigate, earldom becoming extinct.

PALMER, Henry. S. of Sir Henry, Kt. Bapt. Bekesbourne, Kent, April 1611. Sidney Sussex College, Cambridge, 1629. Gray's Inn 1631. Kt. February 1641/2. Comptroller of Royal Navy. D. 1659.

*WYVELL, Marmaduke. S. of Marmaduke. B. 1611. Trinity College, Cambridge, 1626. Inner Temple 1628. D. Croydon, 2 January, 1678. Will: PCC King 39 (1679).

*HAMDEN, John. S. of John, of Croydon, priest. Corpus Christi College, Oxford, 1630/1, aged 18. D. 8 September 1636. MI in college chapel.

*TONSTALL, Henry. E. s. of Sir John, of Addiscombe, Croydon, Kt. Queen's College, Oxford, 1628, aged 16. Gray's Inn 1631. D. August 1650. (Sir John Tonstall was Gentleman-Usher and Esquire to Queen Anne, consort of James I. In 1621 he was appointed by Archbishop Abbot to receive the resignation of Robert Jenkins, Warden of the Hospital of the Holy Trinity.) See also *Addiscombe Place* in *Croydon Homes of the Past*, by C. G. Paget; publ. Croydon Libraries, 1937.

*WYVELL, Duke. S. of Marmaduke Wyvell, of Croydon (who was 2nd s. of Sir Marmaduke Wyvell, of Constable Burton, Yorks.). Captain in Royalist army; Commissioner for surrender of Boarstall House, June 1646.

*TONSTALL, Frederick. 2nd. s. of Sir John (as above). Queen's College, Oxford, 1628, aged 14. Rector of Caldbeck, Northumberland, and Canon of Carlisle, 1640.

Under John Webb, 1629–48

*FINCH, William. S. of John, priest, of Croydon. Corpus Christi College, Oxford, 1631, aged 18. D. September 1636.

*LEIGH, Wolley. S. of Francis, of Addington, Surrey. Queen's College, Oxford, 1631, aged 18. D. 1642.

*LEIGH, Francis. 2nd s. of Francis, of Addington. Queen's College, Oxford, 1631, aged 16. Inner Temple 1633.

DALYSON, John. 5th s. of Sir Maximilian Dalyson, of Halling, Kent. B. 15 August 1620. Trinity College, Cambridge, 1637. Of St. Anne's, Blackfriars, when he d. 14 December 1642. Will: PCC Campbell 127. (See Arch. Cant. Vol. XV, pp. 386 ff. and Kent Archives U790 AI.)

DALYSON, Spencer. 6th s. of Sir Maximilian (see above). Survived his brother John.

*HARBEY, Clement. 2nd s. of Sir Thomas, Kt. of Wallington, Surrey. Cousin of Carews. Emmanuel College, Cambridge, 1635. Inner Temple 1638. Kt. April 1669.

Appendix II

TUBBE, Henry. S. of John, 'Captain beyond the sea'. B. Southampton, 1618. St. John's College, Cambridge, June 1635. Tutor in household of Earl of Thanet 1652–4. Poet and miscellaneous writer. Benefactor. (Literary remains: B. L. Harleian MS 4126; *Meditations Divine and Morall*, 1659; *Works edited by G. C. Moore Smith, Clarendon Press*, 1915; article by W. D. Hussey, *Whitgiftian*, December 1955).

GARDINER, Onslow. E. s. of Christopher, of Haling, Croydon. B. 1622. Sidney Sussex College, Cambridge, March 1638/9. D. 1658. (See: C. G. Paget, *Croydon Homes of the Past*, 1937).

GARDINER, Christopher. 2nd s. of Christopher, of Haling. B. 1624. Magdalen Hall, Oxford, October 1640. D. 1662. (See: Paget, *op. cit.*) Will: PCC Laud 107.

SWALE, George. s. of Christopher, DD. of Hurstpierpoint, Sussex. Sidney Sussex College, Cambridge, April 1637, aged 17. Inner Temple 1639.

*SWALE, Edward. S. of Christopher, DD. of Hurstpierpoint, Sussex. Trinity College, Cambridge, 1639. Gray's Inn January 1645/6. D. September 1660. Will: PCC Nabbs 257. (George and Edward Swale were cousins of the Wyvells and of Sir Solomon Swale, the Royalist; their father had been tutor to Prince Henry, s. of James I.) (See: Sussex Arch. Coll. Vols. 9, 11, 22, 25, 38.)

BEST, Henry. S. of Aaron, of Croydon. B. *c.* 1622. Emmanuel College, Cambridge, 1646. Middle Temple December 1647. Will: PCC Mico 71, 1666. (His father, Aaron, was guardian of John Brigstocke). (See Aaron Best's will: PCC Sadler 83, 1634.)

HARVEY, Daniel. Bapt. Nov. 1631. S. of Daniel, of London and Coombe, Croydon (brother of William, the physiologist). Caius College, Cambridge, November 1646, aged 15. MP for Surrey 1660. Kt. May 1660. Ambassador to Turkey, 1669–72. D. Constantinople, August 1672. Will: PCC Eure 136. (See S. P. Dom.; Geoffrey Keynes: *Life of William Harvey*, 1966, etc.) Portrait (Sir Peter Lely) at School.

Under Noris Wood, 1648–51

BISHOP, Zacharias. D. August 1650. (Croydon Parish Register: 'Bordar at Mr Woods at the Skool, bur.')

*CAREW, Nicholas. S. of Sir Francis, of Beddington. Lincoln College, Oxford, 1651. MP Gatton, 1664–81. Kt. D. January 1687/8.

SILLS, Christopher. S. of Richard, of Croydon. A member of the household of the Tonstall family, of Addiscombe. B. *c.* 1637. Rector of East Donyland, Essex, in 1677. M. Penelope, dau. of Henry Tonstall (*q.v.*)

NOKES, William. S. of Bartholomew, merchant, of St. Stephen's, Coleman St., London. St. John's College, Cambridge, May 1651. Rector of St. Olave's, Silver St., London. (See Matthews, *Calamy Revised.*)

*WEBB, John. S. of John Webb, schoolmaster, of Croydon, Bapt. December 1635. Magdalen Hall, Oxford, 1651. Usher of Magdalen School 1656–7. Vicar of Basingstoke 1659–61.

Under Thomas Day, 1651–62

*BOARDE, William, S. of John, of Croydon. Bapt. November 1637. Wadham College, Oxford, December 1653.

PRICE, John. S. of Thomas, of Esher, Surrey. St. John's College, Cambridge, April, 1657. Inner Temple, 1656.

Under John Philips, 1662–8

None traced.

Under William Crowe, 1668–75

None traced.

Under John Shepheard, 1675–81

*JOYNER, Valentine. S. of Christopher, of London and (?) Croham, Croydon (tenant of the Hospital of the Holy Trinity). Magdalen Hall, Oxford, July 1676, aged 18. Inner Temple 1677. Bur. Temple Church, March 1681/2. Will: PCC Cottle 45.

*JOYNER, Thomas, Yr. br. and heir of Valentine. Of St. Bennet Fink, London, 1713.

*JOYNER, William. Yst. br. of Valentine. Magdalen Hall, Oxford, June 1679, aged 18. Inner Temple 1683.

*ATWOOD, Harman. S. of Harman, of Sanderstead and Westminster. St. John's College, Oxford, November 1679.

*CASTLEMAN, Jonathan. S. of Paul, of Croydon. B. Camberwell. B.N.C. Oxford, April 1679, aged 16. Inner Temple, 1681.

*CASTLEMAN, Paul. S. of Paul, of Croydon; b. there. B.N.C. Oxford, 1679, aged 13. Inner Temple 1681.

*CAREW, Francis, S. of Nicholas, of Beddington. Magdalen College, Oxford, July 1680, aged 16. D. September 1689.

BLESE, Henry. Name in Oldham's papers, Bodl. Rawl. Poet. 123. 1680.

MORE, Edward. Name in Oldham's papers. 1680.

RICH, Elias. Name in Oldham's papers. S. & h. of Sir Peter Rich, Sheriff of London 1682, Master of Saddlers' Company, a timber-merchant and gunpowder manufacturer. Master of Saddlers' Co., 1703.

Under John Caesar, 1681-1712

*CAREW, Nicholas, Of Beddington. Christ Church, Oxford, March 1685/6, aged 17. D. January 1721/2.

*MELLISH, George. S. of Henry, turkey merchant, of Sanderstead; bapt. December 1669. B.N.C. Oxford, June 1687. Middle Temple 1687. D. November 1693.

EGERTON, Scroop. 4th, but 1st surviving s. of 3rd Earl of Bridgewater. B. August 1681, St. Giles, Cripplegate. Succeeded father, March 1700/1. M. Elizabeth, 3rd dau. of John Churchill, Duke of Marlborough. Created Marquess of Brackley and Duke of Bridgewater, June 1720. D. January 1744/5. See Bernard Falk: *The Bridgewater Millions*, 1942. Portrait at School on loan from Duke of Sutherland.

FREDERICK, John. 1st s. & h. of Thomas Frederick, of Downing St. Westminster, and of St. Olave's, London. B. March 1677/8, St Olave's. Grandson of Sir John Frederick, Lord Mayor of London, 1661-2. Sidney Sussex College, Cambridge, November 1695. Created Bart. June 1723. D. October 1755. Portraits at Fine Art Museum, Ghent.

*SHEPHEARD, Atwood. S. of John Shepheard, Schoolmaster 1675-81. B. November 1678. Distiller. D. February, 1714/5.

*PEMBERTON, John. S. of John Pemberton, of Croydon, who was a frequent witness of John Caesar's signature, etc. in the ledger Books. B. Croydon, August 1684. Bookseller and stationer in Fleet St., London 1709-death, July 1739.

*CAREW, Nicholas. S. of Sir Francis, of Beddington. B. February, 1786/7. St. Catharine's College, Cambridge, April 1703. MP Haslemere. Created Bart. 1714. D. Beddington, March 1726/7.

*ATWOOD, John. S. of George, of Sanderstead, Merton College, Oxford, April 1705, aged 17. Inner Temple 1723. D. 1759.

*ATWOOD, Thomas. S. of George, of Sanderstead. Merton College, Oxford, July 1707, aged 17.

CAESAR, Julius. S. of John Caesar, Schoolmaster. B. 1690. Of Doctors' Commons; Deputy registrar for Archdeaconry of Surrey, 1762. D. May 1763. (Pusey Deposition).

COOKE, Edward. S. & h. of John Cooke, of St. Jago de la Vega, Jamaica. D. August 1716. Will PCC Whitfield 168. (Pusey Deposition.)

DABERON, Thomas. S. of Edward (?), of Croydon. (Pusey Deposition.)

KNAGGS, Thomas. S. of Thomas, of Newcastle, and Lecturer of St. Giles-in-the-Fields, London. B. Newcastle, March 1690/1. Emmanuel College, Cambridge, July 1708. D. in College; bur. July 1709. (Pusey Deposition.)

PARKER, John. Probably s. of John, citizen and mercer of London and Waddon Court, Croydon. M. Beersheba Bowyer, of Selsdon Court, Croydon, May 1708. D. June 1740. (Pusey Deposition.)

PHILP, Mathias. Of Jamaica. Council of Jamaica, 1738. D. before July 23, 1746, of Westmoreland Parish. (Pusey Deposition.)

PHILP, Verney. Bro. of Mathias. Of Jamaica.

Appendix II

Council of Jamaica, 1738. D. before March 1769. (Pusey Deposition.)

PUSEY, William. S. of John, of Jamaica. Council of Jamaica 1718–28. Claimant to estate of Pusey in Berkshire. In jail, 1728 (for debt?); a bankrupt. Last heard of in 1738. (Pusey Deposition; PRO Town Depositions C24, Bundle 1446/65).

ROBERTS, Philip. Of Jamaica. (Pusey Deposition.)

TURNER, Arthur. (Pusey Deposition.)

CAESAR, Charles. 2nd s. of John, Schoolmaster. An officer in the Royal Navy. M. Susannah Rose, of Croydon. D. about 1756.

Under Henry Mills, 1712–42

ANDREWS, William. S. of James, of Wedmore, Somerset. Magdalen Hall, Oxford, June 1718, aged 18. Translator of *Life and Letters of Pascal* (1744). See Lathbury: *History of the Non-jurors*, 1845; B.L. Add. MS 38480 (letters to William Draper). (Verses on the Peace.)

BAGG, Richard. (Verses on the Peace.)

BUSH, William. Possibly s. of William, a barber-surgeon of Croydon, 1710. (Verses on the Peace.)

BUSHEL, Thomas. (?) S. of Robert, of Cleeve, Worcs. Oriel College, Oxford, June 1715, aged 16. (Verses on the Peace.)

DRAPER, William. S. & h. of William, of Addiscombe Place, Croydon. Grandson of John Evelyn, the diarist. B. May 1698. St. John's College, Oxford, August 1716 (?). For correspondence see B.L. Add. MS 38464, 38480; Papers of Smyth and Ashton Court (Bristol Records). D. 1759. (Verses on the Peace.)

GAY, Thomas. S. of Robert, of St. Andrew's, Holborn, FRS, Treasurer of Christ's Hospital, MP for Bath. Hart Hall, Oxford, January 1718/9, aged 18. Middle Temple May 1725. D. September 1752. (Verses on the Peace.)

GLYNN, William. Possibly a member of the family of Sir John Glynne, LCJ 1655, whose daughter and two grandsons married into the Evelyn family. (Verses on the Peace.)

GREENWAY, Randolph. Of Thavies Inn, Lyford, Berks, and Chertsey, Surrey. D. July 1754. Bur. Richmond. Will: PCC Pinfold 198. (Verses on the Peace.)

HALE, Edward Biss. E. s. of Gabriel, of Alderley, Gloucs., who was grandson of Sir Matthew Hale, LCJ 1676. B. 1697. Lincoln's Inn January 1715/6. D. 1762. (Verses on the Peace.)

HALE, Matthew. S. of Gabriel (above). B. *c.* 1699. Partner in the Old Bank, Bristol, that opened in 1750. D. April 1764. (Verses on the Peace.)

HEATHFIELD, John. S. of John, brewer, of Croydon, and Crewses, Warlingham, Surrey. B. 1698. M. Mary, dau. of Thomas White, of Shipley, Sussex. JP for Surrey. D. November 1776. Will: PCC Bellas 462. (Verses on the Peace.)

KING, Edward. (Verses on the Peace.)

SMYTH, John, S. & h. of Sir John, Bt. of Long Ashton, Somerset. B. 1699. Removed to Winchester, St. John's College, Oxford, October 1717. Succeeded father as 3rd Bt. May 1726. DCL, May 1729. Sheriff of Somerset 1732–3. M. March 1728/9. Ann Pym, of Oxford. D.s.p. July 1741. Will: PCC Spurway 213. (See Smyth Papers of Ashton Court at Council House, Bristol; Liverpool Papers B.L. Add. MS 38480). (Verses on the Peace.) Portrait at Long Ashton.

SMYTH, Hugh, Y. s. of Sir John (as above). B. 1704. Proceeded to Taunton School. St. John's College, Oxford, February 1721/2. D. August 1735.

TENISON, Thomas. O. s. of Edward, of Lambeth, Archdeacon of Carmarthen, etc., later Bishop of Ossory, 2nd cousin of Archbishop Tenison, whose godson Thomas was. B. 1700. Proceeded against his will from Whitgift to Sevenoaks School, from which he ran away to sea. Clare College, Cambridge, 1716. LLB 1721; LLD 1726. Fellow of Trinity Hall, 1725–28. Inner Temple, November 1721. Ord. September 1726. Vicar of Lydd, R. of Chiddingstone, Kent, and Archdeacon of Carmarthen, 1727–42. Chancellor of Diocese of Oxford 1734–42. Prebendary and Commissary of Canterbury 1739–42. M. 1st, dau. of Dr. John Potter, Bishop of Oxford, later Archbishop of Canterbury, who d. 1729; 2nd, dau. of — Smith, of Nottingham. D. May 1742; bur. Canterbury Cathedral. (Verses on the Peace.)

WIGAN, William. Probably y. s. of William Wigan, V. of Kensington and Chaplain in Ordinary to William & Mary. Alive in 1741. (Verses on the Peace.)

BEMPDY, — S. of — Bempdy, of Pall Mall. Mentioned by Pillonnière.

TAYLOR, — Mentioned by Pillonnière.

*GRESHAM, Marmaduke. S. & h. of Sir Charles, Bt. of Titsey, Limpsfield, Surrey. Bapt. July 1700, Mortlake, Surrey. Succeeded father as 4th Bt. March 1718/9. M. November 1724, Anne, dau. of William Hoskins of Barrow Green, Oxted. D. at Bath January 1741/2.

*CHAPMAN, Robert. S. of William, of Croydon, a proctor of Doctors' Commons. University College, Oxford, May 1720, aged 16. BCL 1727; DCL 1736.

*LOVELACE, Nevill, 6th Baron Lovelace of Hurley. S. of John, 4th Baron, Governor of New York, 1708–9. B. c. 1708. Succeeded brother (who d. two weeks after their father), May 1709. Their mother dau. of Sir John Clayton, of Godstone, etc. B. 1708. Gentleman of the Bedchamber 1725. D. unm. July 1736, when barony became extinct.

ASHBY, George, B. Clerkenwell, 1724. Proceeded to Westminster and to Eton. St. John's College, Cambridge, October 1740. Fellow, 1756. R. of Hungerton, Leics., 1754; of Twyford, 1759. President, St. John's College, 1769–75. Antiquary. D. June 1808. (See *DNB*.)

Under Samuel Staveley, 1742–51

None traced.

Under John Taylor Lamb, 1751–74

LAMB, John Taylor. E. s. of John Taylor. Aged 14 in 1774, when admitted to St. Paul's School. Trinity College, Cambridge, May 1777. R. of Upper Hemsley, Yorks. D. January 1828.

LAMB, William. S. of John Taylor, aged 10 in 1774 on admission to St. Paul's School.

LAMB, Thomas, S. of John Taylor. Aged 8 in 1774 on admission to St. Paul's School.

Under James Hodgson 1774–1801

APTHORPE, Frederick. S. of Rev. East, V. of Croydon, and R. of St. Mary-le-Bow. Jesus College, Cambridge, April 1795, aged 17: scholar 1796. Ord. September 1801. Prebendary of Lincoln, 1802–53; V. of Bicker, Lincs., 1803–53, etc. D. August 1853.

HODGES, Henry. S. of Thomas Hallett, of Hensted Place, Benenden, Kent. Proceeded to Harrow. B. July 1779. Trinity College, Cambridge, September 1796. V. of Benenden, etc; of Frittenden, 1805–37. D. July 1837.

HODGES, John. S. of Thomas Hallett (as above). At school 1792–3. Proceeded to John Bettesworth's Naval Academy, Chelsea. May have d. shortly after.

HODGES, Francis. S. of Thomas Hallett (as above). B. May 1782. Proceeded to Harrow in 1792. Midshipman on H.M.S. *Nonpareil*. D. of fever in West Indies, 1800 or 1801. (Twysden Papers, Kent Archives, Maidstone: U47 C13.)

JENKINSON, Charles Cecil Cope. Y. s. of Charles, 1st Lord Hawkesbury and Earl of Liverpool B. May 1784. Served in Navy between ages of 9 and 13. Coached by James Hodgson 1798–1801. Christ Church, Oxford, April 1801. MP Sandwich 1807–12, Bridgnorth 1812–18, East Grinstead 1818–28. Parliamentary Under-secretary for the Home Department, 1807; Under-secretary of State for War and the Colonies, 1809; Lord Steward of the Household, 1841; PC. Succeeded half-brother as 3rd Earl of Liverpool, December 1828. GCB 1845. D. October 1851 at his seat, Buxted Park, Sussex. (See *DNB*; Liverpool Papers, BL.) Portrait in possession of Earl of Liverpool; copy at School.

HODGSON, Francis. S. of James, Schoolmaster. B. Croydon, November 1781. Proceeded to Eton, July 1794, scholar. King's College, Cambridge, February 1800. Fellow of King's 1803–15; Assistant master at Eton, 1807. Ord. 1814. V. of Bakewell, Derbys., 1816–36; Archdeacon of Derby, 1836–40. Provost of Eton, 1840–52. Author of translations and poems. D. December 1852, at Eton. (See *DNB; Memoir by his son, Rev. J. T. Hodgson*, 1878; Liverpool Papers, B.L.)

Appendix III
A Select and Varied List of 100 OWs since 1871

	left		*died*
Sir James Berry, FRCS, FSA	1876	President, Royal Society of Medicine	1946
J W H Thompson, MP	1877		1959
Gilbert Marks	1878	Art Nouveau Silversmith	1905
William Webb	1879	Garden City Pioneer	1930
Sir Henry Berney, ARIBA, DL	1879	Architect	1953
Sir Gilbert Walker, FRS	1881	Meteorologist	1958
Lt Col G P Mills, DSO	1882	Pioneer sporting cyclist and motorist	1948
W M Geldart, CBE	1885	Vinerian Professor of Law. Fellow of All Souls', Oxford	1922
F H Carr, PhD, CBE	1889	Chairman, British Drug Houses	1969
Maj-Gen Rt Hon Sir Frederick Sykes, GCSI, GCIE, GBE, KCB, CMG, MP	1891	Chief of Air Staff 1918–19; Governor of Bombay 1928–33	1954
A R Hinks, FRS	1892	Astronomer	1945
Leon Quartermaine	1893	Shakespearian and West End Actor	1967
Revd H F Davidson	1894	Notorious Rector of Stiffkey	1937
A Talbot Smith	1895	Represented England at Shooting. 'Punch' Artist	1971
A V-M Sir Alfred Iredell, KBE, CB	1896	Director, RAF Medical Services	1967
Sir Newman Flower	1896	Chairman of Cassells Ltd.	1964
VFS Crawford	1897	Cricketer; played as a schoolboy for Gentlemen v. Players	1922
Harcourt Williams	1897	Shakespearian Actor and Producer (Old Vic)	1957
J B Densham	1898	Olympic Hurdler 1908	1975
Walter H Godfrey, CBE, FRIBA	1898	Architect, Director of National Buildings Record	1961
H E Evans, QC	1900	Solicitor-General, New Zealand	1970
Sir Ronald Bowater, Bt.	1902	of Bowaters, Ltd.	1945
Robert Keable	1905	Novelist and Benefactor	1927
Basil Dean, CBE	1905	Stage Producer and Director	1978
Sir Dudley Bowater, Bt.	1905	succeeded brother	1972
D Ll Hammick, D. Phil, FRS	1906	Vice-Provost, Oriel College, Oxford	1966
Sir Bernard Carr, CMG	1907	Colonial Service	1981
Marshal of the RAF Lord Tedder, GCB	1909	Deputy Supreme Commander of Allied Exped. Forces 1944; Chief of Air Staff 1946–49	1967
Maj-Gen W S Tope, CB	1909	Col Commandant REME	1962
Sir James Marshall	1912	Governor 1931 and Chairman, Whitgift Foundation 1945–70	1979
Instr Rear Admiral Sir William Bishop KBE, CB	1917	Director, Naval Education Service	

Appendix III

Name	left		died
Sir Walter Chiesman, MD	1918	Medical Adviser to the Treasury	1970
Richard de la Mare	1920	Chairman & President, Faber & Faber Ltd	1986
Sir Allan Walker, QC	1924	Sheriff Principal, Lanark	
Revd P W P Brook	1924	Cambridge University and England rugby	
Lord Diplock, PC, QC	1925	Lord of Appeal in Ordinary	1986
T C Skeat, FBA	1926	Keeper of MSS, British Museum Library	
Maj-Gen M H P Sayers, OBE	1927	Pathologist to the Army	
Sir Gordon Whitteridge, KCMG, OBE	1927	Ambassador to Afghanistan	
K H Jackson, FBA, DLitt, CBE	1928	Professor of Celtic Studies, U of Edinburgh	1991
Eric Barker	1929	Radio, TV and Film Comedian	1990
E E D Tomlin	1930	Whitgift's only Rowing Blue	1956
J M Howard, MP	1930	PPS to Mr. Edward Heath	1982
B E Nicholson	1930	England and British Lions rugby	1985
David Whitteridge, DM, FRS	1931	Professor of Physiology, Oxford	
Robert Dougall, MBE	1931	TV Newscaster	
Lord Trend, PC, GCB, CVO	1932	Secretary of the Cabinet, Rector of Lincoln College, Oxford	1987
A R Smith	1932	England Fencing	
E W F Tomlin, CBE	1932	Writer on Philosophy and other subjects	1988
J L Harkness, OBE	1935	Rose-grower	
Gp Capt John Cunningham, CBE, DSO, DFC, DL	1935	Night-fighter pilot RAF	
S V Peskett	1936	Principal, Royal Belfast Academical Institute	
E J Hewitt, PhD, FRS	1936	Agronomist	
A V-M J C T Downey, CB, DFC, AFC	1937		
Rear Adm P G La Niece, CB, CBE	1937	Port Admiral, Portsmouth	
P G Williams	1937	England Fencing	
Rt Revd J W Roxburgh	1939	Bishop of Barking	
M F Turner	1940	Cambridge University and England rugby	
Rear Adm A J Monk, CB	1940	Port Admiral, Rosyth	
Rt Hon Sir Reg Prentice, MP	1940	Minister of Education 1975	
Sir Robert Boyd, FRS	1941	Professor of Physics UCL; Director of Mullard Space Lab.	
D L Kerr, MP	1941	Former Chairman of War on Want	
J P Wild, PhD, FRS	1941	Radio-physicist	
Sir Bryan Roberts, KCMG, QC	1942	Colonial Service; Stipendiary Magistrate	
Lt Col C C Mitchell, A & SH, MP	1943	"Mad Mitch", cmdg British forces in Aden 1967	
D M Dixon, CVO	1944	Oxford U. Athletic Club President; Hon Sec, Commonwealth Games Federation 1989	
R I Kidwell, QC	1944	Advocate	
Rt Revd M R J Manktelow	1945	Bishop of Basingstoke	
Lord Wedderburn of Charlton, PC, FBA, QC	1945	Professor of Commercial Law, LSE	
Leonard Barden	1947	Joint British Chess Champion 1954	
Bernard Crick, PhD	1947	Professor of Politics, London; writer.	
Ian Caldwell	1948	International (Walker Cup) Golfer	

Appendix III

	left		*died*
Rt Hon Sir Michael Mann	1948	Lord Justice of Appeal	
I D S Beer	1949	Headmaster, Harrow School; Cambridge U and England rugby	
B D Harrison, PhD, FRS	1949	Plant virologist	
R Subba Row, CBE	1950	Cambridge U and England Test Cricketer, Chairman TCCB	
J R McAulay, QC	1951	Advocate	1987
C C B Norwood, MP	1951		1972
Sir David Hancock, KCB	1952	Perm. Sec., Dept. of E and S	
Liam Hudson	1952	Professor of Psychology, Edinburgh; writer	
S B O Cranmer	1952	Olympic Miniature Rifle Shooting 1952	
Rt Revd C O Buchanan	1953	Bishop of Aston	
J R S Adams	1954	A Judge on the South Eastern Circuit	
P R Grant, PhD, FRS	1955	Ecologist	
K S Rokison, QC	1955	Advocate	
Mark Shivas	1956	Head of Drama, BBC	
Guy Woolfenden	1956	Composer; Director of Music RSC	
C C D Lindsay, QC	1957	Advocate	
Sir Peter Michael, CBE	1957	Chairman UEI	
Andrew Patience, QC	1960	Advocate	
Martin Jarvis	1960	Actor	
Roger Freeman, MP	1961	Minister of State, Dept. of Transport	
Sir Peter Bowness, CBE	1961	Chairman, GLC Residuary Body	
M P Hassell, PhD, FRS	1961	Ecologist	
G N Tope, MP	1961		
Peter Hedges	1965	International (Walker Cup) Golfer	
J L Cooke, QC	1966	Advocate, Oxford U rugby	
MD Featherstone	1968	Headmaster, Ryde School; Oxford U and England Hockey	
A J Wordsworth	1972	Cambridge U and England rugby	
Duncan Bridge	1976	England Badminton	

(Readers may wish to submit their own candidates for inclusion in this list)

Appendix IV
Chairmen of the Governors

1. REV. JOHN GEORGE HODGSON, elected Chairman, 2 April 1855

Vicar of Croydon. *Ex-officio* Governor under new Scheme, which was not sanctioned until 1st August 1856, although Governors had been appointed by Archbishop Sumner in April 1855. B. 1812. Ed. Westminster and Trinity College, Cambridge. Resigned July 1879 on removal from Croydon. Died 24 May 1888.

2. RT. REV. EDWARD WYNDHAM TUFNELL 9 January 1880

Vicar of Croydon. *Ex-officio* Governor 20 September 1879. Elected Chairman on first appearance at Court. B. 1815. Ed. Eton and Wadham College, Oxford; Fellow 1839–67. Rector of Basingstoke 1846–57; of Marlborough 1857–9; Bishop of Brisbane 1859–75; Vicar of Croydon 1879–82; of Felpham, Sussex, 1882. Resigned on removal from Croydon, June 1882.

3. ALFRED CARPENTER, MD 5 January 1883

Appointed Governor by Archbishop Tait 4 May 1868. B. 1825. Ed. Moulton Grammar School, Northants, and St. Thomas's Hospital; MRCS 1851; MD 1859. Medical Adviser to Archbishops of Canterbury 1860–92. President B.M.A. 1878–81. Author of *Principles and Practice of School Hygiene*, 1887. Died 27 January 1892.

4. SAMUEL LEE RYMER 5 February 1892

Appointed Governor by Archbishop Tait 4 May 1868. B. 1832, Plymouth. Ed. privately at Charlton King's. Dental Surgeon. Started practice in Croydon 1852; helped to found British Dental Association. JP. A founder of *Croydon Guardian* 1877. Died at his residence, Pevensey, Wellesley Road, 7 March 1909, aged 76.

5. REV. LEONARD HENRY BURROWS 1 April 1909

Vicar of Croydon. *Ex-officio* Governor July 1904. B. 1858. Ed. Charterhouse and New College, Oxford. Resigned June 1909, on appointment as Suffragan Bishop of Lewes (1909–14); Bishop of Sheffield 1914–39; DD. Died 6 February 1940, aged 82.

6. SIR FREDERICK (THOMAS) EDRIDGE 1 July 1909

Appointed Governor by Archbishop Benson 15 February 1892; resigned 7 January 1901; re-appointed by Archbishop Davidson 1 January 1906. B. 1843. Ed. Marlborough. Of the Hudson Bay Company. M. 1867, Elizabeth Sarah, dau. of J. M. Eastty, of Wellesley House, Croydon, a Governor. JP, DL, Kt. 1896. of Bramley Croft, Haling Park Road, South Croydon. Resigned 20 September 1919. Died 3 October 1921, aged 78. See Benefactors (Appendix IV).

7. EDWARD WILLIAM GRIMWADE 2 October 1919

Appointed Governor by JPs for Croydon Division 18 November 1899. Deputy Chairman from 1917 during incapacity of Sir Frederick Edridge. B. 1836 at Harleston, Norfolk. Ed. privately at Chelmsford. Shipper to Australia. Of Croham House, South Croydon. Died 15 March 1920, aged 83.

8. HOWARD HOULDER 1 April 1920

Appointed Governor by Archbishop Frederick Temple 4 February 1901. B. Camberwell 1858. Ed. privately at Denmark Hill and at Amersham Hill, Reading. Ship-broker and ship-owner (Howard Houlder & Partners). Mayor of Croydon 1916–18. JP, DL. Of Heathfield, Addington. Resigned 7 February 1924, on bankruptcy. Died at Rustington, Sussex, 8 October 1932, aged 73.

Appendix IV

9. ALBERT JAMES CAMDEN FIELD 7 February 1924

Appointed Governor by Croydon Council 9 November 1916; by Archbishop Davidson 14 August 1920. B. 1865. Surveyor; came to Croydon 1889; retired from business 1907. From 1910 devoted himself to local public affairs. Mayor of Croydon 1925–27. JP. Of Avondale Road, South Croydon. Died at Albourne, Sussex, 26 December 1936, aged 71.

10. FRANCIS ALLEN 7 January 1937

Appointed Governor by Archbishop Davidson 31 October 1919. B. 1865. Solicitor. MBE, JP. Of Haling Cottage, South Croydon. Resigned 4 January 1945. Died 3 February 1945, aged 79.

11. SIR JAMES MARSHALL 4 January 1945

Appointed Governor by Croydon Council 24 November 1931; by Archbishop Lang 5 January 1937. B. 1894. Ed. Whitgift. JP, DL, Kt. 1953. Mayor of Croydon 1945. Of Whistler's Wood, Woldingham, later of The Rose Walk, Purley. Resigned 6 March 1970. Died 20 February 1979, aged 84.

12. RICHARD DENDY MARTEN 6 March 1970

Appointed Governor by Archbishop Fisher 10 June 1955. B. 1907. Ed. Whitgift. Solicitor LLB, JP (Messrs. Marshall, Liddle & Downey, Croydon). Of Storrington, Sussex. Resigned March 1979; elected Governor Emeritus. Died 5 March 1987, aged 79.

13. EDWARD RUPERT NICHOLSON 23 March 1979

Elected co-optative Governor 12 March 1976. B. 1909. Ed. Whitgift. FCA, Senior partner, Peat, Marwick, Mitchell. Of Banstead, Surrey. Resigned March 1991.

14. IVAN PETER SHAW 22 March 1991

Appointed Governor by Archbishop Fisher 8 July 1957; Chairman, Schools Committee 1968–91. B. 1914. Ed. Whitgift (School Captain) and Magdalen College, Oxford; Stanhope Prize 1935; 1st Class Hons, Modern History 1936; MA 1942. Lecturer, King's College London 1937–52; Secretary 1952–77; Fellow 1957. War Service, Captain I Corps 1940–45. Trustee, City Parochial Foundation (London) 1958–88. Of Shirley, Croydon.

Govenors in the Audience Chamber, 1984

Appendix V
Benefactors

(This list refers only to those whose benefactions were of benefit to Whitgift School.)

1599 JOHN BOYS, Steward to the Founder, and a lawyer at the Middle Temple, gave the Casements and Glazing of the Schoolhouse at a cost of £11. 13s. 10d.

1600 DR. WILLIAM PRITHERGH, an advocate of Doctors' Commons, gave two houses in Northampton, which were sold by the Foundation in 1920 for £4800, the proceeds going towards the first purchase of the Haling Park lands.

1600 EDWARD BARKER, Registrar of the High Commission, gave a rent charge of £6. 13s. 4d. per annum for 1000 years on a house in St. Paul's Churchyard. His wife, SUSAN BARKER, gave £40 to purchase land.

1614 RICHARD AND JANE STOCKDALE gave property in Butcher Row (now Surrey Street), Croydon.

1655 HENRY TUBBE, OW 1628–35, gave forty shillings to buy books for the use of the School.

1707 RALPH SNOW, Treasurer and Registrar to successive Archbishops of Canterbury, who died aged 94, bequeathed £300 to trustees, who purchased lands at Mitcham.

1880–91 STEPHENSON CLARKE, of Croydon Lodge, gave between 1880 and his death in 1891 a number of exhibitions to be held at the School, as well as contributing to extensions of the School buildings. He bequeathed £1000 to establish a Leaving Exhibition.

1880 ROBERT AMADEUS HEATH (Baron Heath), a Governor 1855 until his death in 1882, gave many valuable books to the School Library; made numerous benefactions, some in conjunction with Stephenson Clarke; additions to the Headmaster's House, support for the Rifle Corps, Exhibitions, etc. The 'Heath' Leaving Exhibition derives from a fund collected in his memory.

1885 MRS. ADA BERRY gave £100 for annual prizes in Mathematics in remembrance of the education received by her three sons at the School (Sir James Berry, 1872–6, E. E. Berry, 1872–6, A. Berry, 1872–6).

1888 JOHN SPURRIER WRIGHT, of Duppas Hill, Croydon, bequeathed £2000 to establish Leaving Exhibitions and Prizes.

1890–1901 HENRY JOHN GOSCHEN, of Heathfield, Addington, a Governor 1882–1900, gave numerous exhibitions to the School, open to outside candidates.

1892 JOHN PELTON, father of W. F. Pelton, OW 1872–8, gave £20 to form the nucleus of a university exhibition fund, to be known as 'The Town Scholarship Fund'. This sum was to be invested at compound interest until the Governors should decide to release the interest for exhibition purposes. The original sum was invested in $2\frac{1}{2}\%$ Consols. The Fund amounted in 1974 to a nominal figure of £382 and a market value of £195.

(In 1892 the Governors resolved that a Benefactors' Board should be placed in Big School, which should bear the names of those whose benefactions were of the value of £100 or more; in 1957 this figure was raised to £250. It is now £2000.)

Appendix V

1910–19 SIR FREDERICK EDRIDGE, of Bramley Croft, South Croydon, a Governor 1892–1901 and 1905–19, Chairman 1909–19, presented between 1910 and 1914 a Cricket Pavilion, Fives-Courts, O.T.C. Orderly Room, Changing Rooms, and the Gallery in Big School (all at North End), and £1980 for a Leaving Exhibition and Prizes. He bequeathed, under certain conditions, £5000 to establish Leaving Exhibitions for boys intending to take Holy Orders.

1917 WALTER LIONEL PAINE, Assistant Master 1910–14, killed in action, June 1915, bequeathed £1000 to establish a Leaving Exhibition. His father, G. W. Paine, also gave £77 to establish Prizes in his memory.

1920 WALTON F. TURNER, a Governor 1917–44, provided £240 to supplement Leaving Exhibitions.

1920 ALBERT E. WATSON, Assistant Master 1881–1920, bequeathed £100 to provide Prizes in Divinity for the Junior School.

1927 ROBERT KEABLE, OW 1901–5, novelist, bequeathed £2500 to found a Scholarship in Modern History at his old College, Magdalene, Cambridge.

1939 JOHN SHIRLEY FOX, OW 1875–6, artist, who painted the portraits of Robert Brodie and S. O. Andrew in the Dining Hall, bequeathed £200 to endow an annual Prize for a paper on some archaeological or historical subject selected by the Head Master.

1941 THOMAS L. HINTON, OW 1880–2, of South Africa, bequeathed £1000 to establish a Leaving Exhibition.

1946 EDWARD JAMES CASON, OW 1874–6, bequeathed £2000 to establish a Scholarship at Keble College, Oxford, for boys desirous of taking Holy Orders in the Church of England.

1947 MISS THYRA JENSEN bequeathed £100 to establish an annual Prize for the best all-round boy in the School, in memory of her brother, Einar Rudolph Jensen, O.W. 1884–9.

1948 HOWARD HINTON, OW 1880–3, of Australia, bequeathed £2000 to establish a Leaving Exhibition.

1948 MRS. S. M. MOUNSEY, mother of Group Captain R. J. Mounsey, OBE, RAF, OW 1904–8, who died in June 1939, bequeathed a proportion of her estate for the promotion of games at the School, in memory of her son. This fund provided part of the cost of the Squash-Courts.

1950 ROBERT A. EBBUTT, OW 1911–19, a Governor 1947–57, made many gifts to the School, including the RAF Cup, the Drum-Major's Silver Mace, and Portrait-frames in the Dining Hall.

1955 DUDLEY W. A. SOMMER, OW 1913–16, gave £500 to the Head Master for him to use at his discretion; this sum was applied towards the cost of the Organ in Big School.

1956 MISS RHODA BRODIE, daughter of Robert Brodie, Head Master 1871–1902, bequeathed a sum of money to provide an annual Prize in her father's memory. This Prize is awarded to the Captain of the School.

1960 MADAME LOUISE KURTEN, mother of G. P. Kurten, OW 1898–1907, killed in action April 1918, and J. P Kurten, MC, OW 1904–11, died 1937, bequeathed a proportion of her estate to provide a Leaving Exhibition in memory of her sons.

1961 MRS. GLADYS MABEY bequeathed £1000 to establish a Leaving Exhibition in memory of her husband J. H. N. Mabey, OW 1893–98, who died of wounds in November 1917.

1963 J. H. G. GRATTAN, OW 1889–97, Professor of English at Liverpool University, bequeathed £300 for the School Library.

1965 MRS. DOROTHY GIBSON gave £250 in memory of her husband, Lt.-Col. C. H. Gibson, D.L. a Governor 1938–62. This gift has been applied to the fund to provide portraits of distinguished OWs to be hung in the Dining Hall.

1969 J. W. WHITLOCK, a Governor 1955–68, presented many valuable scientific works to the School Library.

1970 MISS CONSTANCE GROVES gave £500 in memory of her brother, J. W. M. Groves, OW 1909–17, for many years Hon. Treasurer of the OWRFC. The gift was allocated to the planting of trees on the bank by the Entrance Drive.

1971 BRYAN T. HARLAND, a Governor 1920–30, who died in 1930, bequeathed, subject to a life-interest, a sum of money to endow prizes for Divinity, which became available in this year.

1975 G. R. GILBERT, OW 1933–39, presented a sailing dinghy in memory of his son, P. G. Gilbert, OW 1966–72, who was accidentally drowned at the age of 20.

1980 PETER S. WILSON, OW 1952–58, gave £1000 towards the purchase of the portrait of Sir Daniel Harvey, OW 1641–46, by Sir Peter Lely.

1982 CYRIL SWEETT, CEng, FRICS, OW 1918–21, endowed annual prizes 'for Literature', in commemoration of his professional services in the construction of the Ian Evans Building.

1982 F. L. R. SMITH, an Old Mid-Whitgiftian, who left his residuary estate to the Whitgift Foundation for unspecified purposes. The income from the sum invested is divided equally between the two schools. In Whitgift's case it has been used for helping OWs to travel in their 'gap' year.

Appendix VI
Whitgift Heraldry

For a complete study of the subject, reference should be made to *Notes on the Right Arms of John Whitgift*, by M. H. Ouseley, in *Surrey Archaeological Collections*, Vol. LXIII, 1966, and to articles in *The Whitgiftian*, September 1967, January 1968 and Summer 1974.

A. 1. On 2 May 1577, on his appointment to the Bishopric of Worcester, John Whitgift was granted arms: Or, on a cross fleurettee azure, four bezants.

2. In June 1588, he took out a second grant, quartering the above arms with a similar design in new colours: in the 1st and 4th quarters, argent on a cross humette fleurettee sable, four bezants; in the 2nd and 3rd quarters, or on a cross humette fleurettee azure, four bezats. (This grant seems never to have been used in practice.)

3. In July 1588 he took out a further grant, in which the colours of Grant I were abandoned: Argent, on a cross humette fleurettee sable, four bezants.

4. On 22 January 1598/9 he was granted: Argent, on a cross formy fleurettee sable, five bezants or. (These arms, in some cases impaled with those of the See of Canterbury, appear on Foundation property dating from the Founder's own time and later. From about 1889 until recently the arms thus *in pale* have been used

John Whitgift's Arms, 1588

John Whitgift's Arms in a 1595 piece of stained glass

Appendix VI

Coat of Arms, Whitgift Foundation, 1971

has continued to display as its Badge a Shield with the Founder's arms as described in the grant of 1598/9.

The Motto 'Vincit qui patitur'

A motto was originally a slogan or battle-cry and formed no part of an English grant of arms, although many depictions of arms include a motto beneath.

'Vincit qui patitur' – 'He conquers who endures (or suffers)' clearly has a Christian reference, but its origin has not been traced. It is the motto of a score of families and was in use before Whitgift's time.

The only display of 'Vincit qui patitur' in connection with the Founder that has been found dating from his lifetime appears on several of his portraits; for example, at the Whitgift Hospital, at Lambeth Palace and in Cambridge University Library.

commemoratively by the Foundation and its two schools.)

B. On 28 October 1971 the Whitgift Foundation was granted arms: Argent on a Cross formy flory sable five Bezants, in the Canton a Mitre with infulae Azure stringed and garnished Or, with a Crest: on a Wreath Argent, Sable and Azure, issuant from a Coronet Or, a Lion's Gamb Argent armed Gules, holding a Cross formy flory Sable within a Chaplet of Laurel proper, Mantled Sable and Azure, doubled Argent and Or. Two Badges were also granted:

(a) A Mitre with infulae Argent stringed and garnished Azure charged with a Cross formy flory Sable thereon five Bezants, the Mitre enfiled by a Crozier Or. (Whitgift School.)

(b) A Mitre with infulae Azure stringed and garnished Or charged with five Bezants in cross and enfiled by a Cross flory Sable. (Trinity School.)

However, to avoid confusion, Whitgift School

Badge of Whitgift School

329

Appendix VII

Appendix VII
Summary of Developments at Haling Park
1921–1990

1920	Nov	Governors' offer for first Purchase: North Field and Haling Cottage, 12 acres, accepted (£10,000)
1922	July	Purchase completed
1922	Oct	Second Purchase: Haling Park Cottage and South Field.(£2,700).
1924	June	Third Purchase: site of Whitgift Court (£450)
1924	Sept	Fourth Purchase: small area near South Field (£25)
1925	Feb	Fifth Purchase: remainder of available land, 20 acres (£8000)
1930	Jan	Building commenced
1930	May	Laying of Foundation Stone
1931	July	Official Opening of School by HRH Prince George
1931	Oct	Sixth Purchase: Littleside, Edridge Field, Walled Garden & c (£10,000).
1933		Scout Hut (converted barn) and Fives Courts
1938		Outside Changing Rooms (now rebuilt)
1939		Air-raid shelters around Parade Ground etc. and beside the Miniature Range, now used by CCF
1949		Purchase of Bagbie House
1956		Whitgift Court
1957		Geography and Biology Wing
1958		Extensions to Masters' Common Room
1960		Swimming Pool, Fencing Salle
1961		Squash Courts
1965		Masters' Dining Room and New Kitchens; Porter's Bungalow
1966		Cedar Court wing: Languages, Sixth Form Rooms (later Economics and Business Studies); Prefects' Room; Ground Floor departmental offices, etc. Locker Rooms.
1967		First purchase (after Bagbie House) of a property (No. 18) in Haling Park Road
1967		Music School

Appendix VII

1969		Temporary Art Block, replacing Bagbie House and former Art Room; the latter being converted to a Junior Chemistry Laboratory
		Demolition of Bagbie House
1971		Temporary Science Labs, Lecture Rooms and Offices erected on edges of Parade Ground. Demolished 1988
1974		Temporary Common Rooms and Divinity Rooms in Cedar Court. Demolished 1990.
1978		All-weather Hockey Pitch and Tennis Courts on site of Bagbie House
1980		Maintenance and Groundsmen's Compound
		Junior School (I. A. Evans building)
1982		Marlar Sports Hall; Haling House, HMs Residence; Conversion of Gymnasium to Drama Studio
1984–88		Whitgift House constructed in three stages
1987		Second Temporary Art Block. (Removed 1990)
1988		Preparation for new Extension (Removal of first temporary Art Block and of Science buildings)
1990	May	Partial occupation (Labs) of new extension
1990	Sept	Full occupation
1990	Nov	Official Opening by Baroness Platt of Writtle

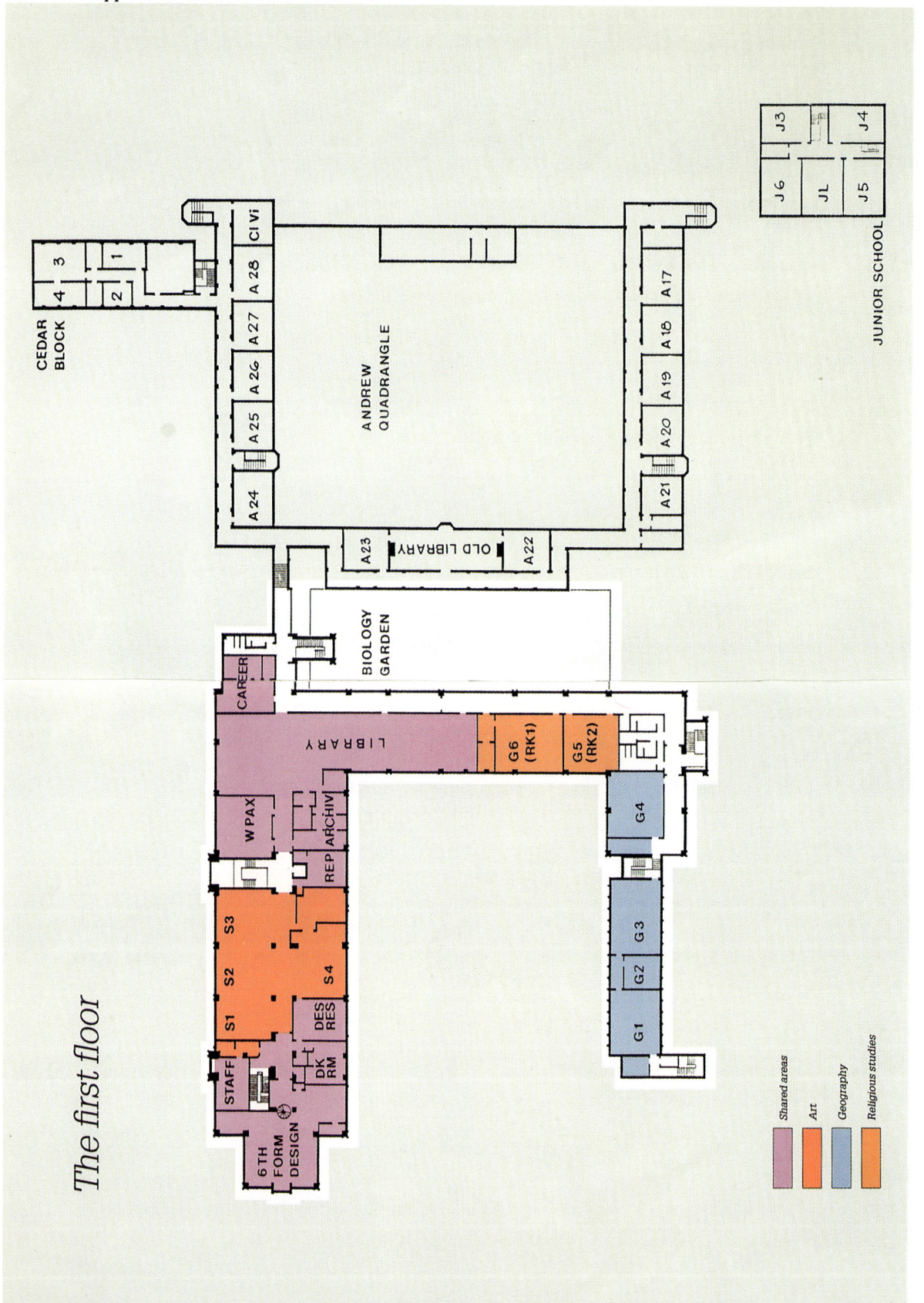

Appendix VII

The first floor

Plan of School, showing new building in colour
Key: A = classrooms, CR = common room, HM = Headmaster, J = Junior School classrooms, L = laboratories,
OP = outside pursuits store, W = workshops

Shared areas
Art
Geography
Religious studies

332

Appendix VII

The ground floor

Plan of School, showing new building in colour

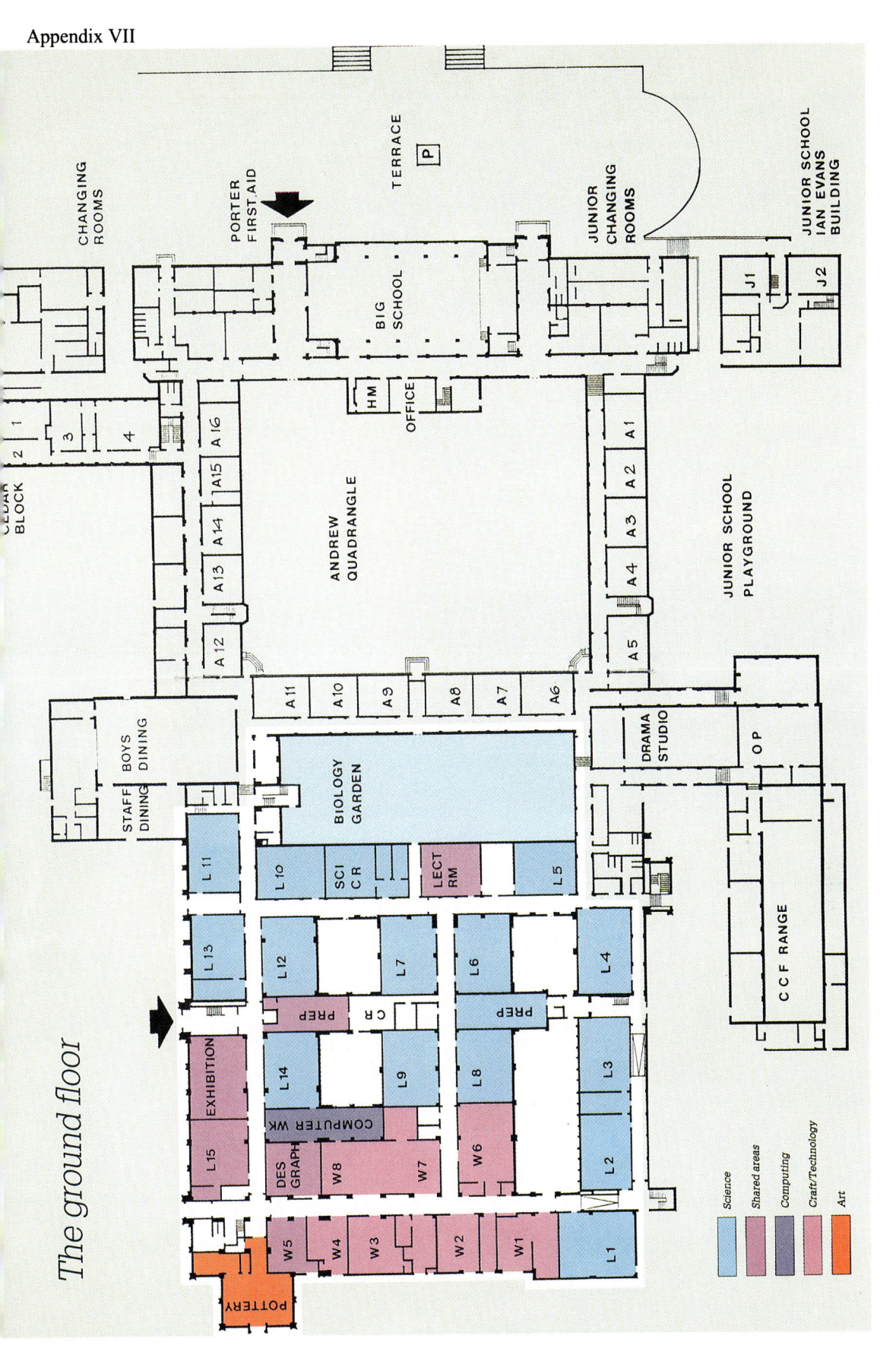

Key: A = classrooms, Des Res = Design Resources, G = Geography, J = Junior School classrooms, Rep = Reprographics, RK = religious knowledge, S = studios, WP AX = word processing annex

Appendix VIII
The Old Whitgiftian Association and affiliated Clubs and Societies

Some account has already been given of the formation of the OWA, the Rugby, Cricket and Shooting (Veterans) Clubs. Further details of the establishment of these and other Clubs, and of the extinction of some of them, seemed worthy of record. They follow in order of formation. All activity was suspended during the two World Wars.

Rugby Football: Founded 1876 as **North Park Whitgift FC**. After a couple of years 'Whitgift' was dropped from the name; having become a fully open club, it assumed the name of Croydon FC in 1879. **The Old Whitgiftian F.C.** was founded in 1901; The Croydon Club expired in 1903. (See I. S. Hubbard: *History of OWFRC Vol. I, 1901–51.*)

Cricket: Founded 1878 as **Whitgift Wanderers CC.** The first OW side that played against the School in 1874 was called 'Whitgift Past'. The Wanderers played only irregularly until 1885 but thereafter for a while a fixture list of about a dozen games per season was fulfilled. There followed a period of erratic fortunes; in 1908 the Club adopted the name of **Old Whitgiftians CC**, but it was not until the OW ground at Croham Road became available in 1930 that it had a permanent home. The Club takes part in 'The Cricketer' Cup competition. (See R. M. Horn, ed.: *History of the OWCC, 1878–1978.*)

Music: **The Whitgift Choral Union** was formed in 1880, but it expired after five years. The **OW Musical Society** was founded in 1926 but closed in 1936. A more ambitious Society was re-formed in 1955. It has had a very chequered career and has often lapsed into inactivity; a recent renaissance has taken place.

Shooting: **The Whitgift Veterans Rifle Club** was formed in 1896 to compete in the inter-Old Boys competitions at Bisley, after some years of

OWA Clubhouse, 1990

unsystematic team-raising. The Club won the aggregate Public Schools' Veterans Trophy in 1934.

The Old Whitgiftian Association, open to all OWs as a means of maintaining links with each other and the School, was formed in 1907. All members of affiliated Clubs and Societies are required to be members. A pre-payment scheme for membership is open to boys at School. The great majority join in this way.

The Whitgiftian Benevolent Society was founded in 1909 to afford relief to distressed OWs, Masters, their widows, orphans or other dependents. Generous donations from many OWs have provided the Society with an ample income. In these days of the Welfare State there are few in great need, but information about those who could be helped is always welcomed by the Honorary Secretary and other officers.

The Golfing Society was formed in 1913 and meets on several occasions annually. It provides a team to compete in the Halford-Hewitt Cup Tournament, in which it has several times reached the semi-finals.

The 'Adeste' Lodge of Freemasons was founded in 1934. A 'Whitgift' Lodge had been formed many years before, but it was open to non-Whitgiftians so a new OW Lodge – 'Adeste' – was formed. It was dissolved through lack of support in 1984.

The OW Athletic Club founded in 1938 opened to an excellent start in 1939, when it did well in the Old Boys' AA Championships and won several inter-Old Boys matches. It was re-started after World War II in 1952, but has not operated for several years.

The OW Biologists' Association formed in 1938, by pupils of Dr. Cecil Prime. Its members still meet occasionally at the School.

The Majorca Society for the fine arts, founded in 1949 and named after the London restaurant where its first meeting was held. It has been inactive for several years, although several of its founders are alive.

The OW Squash Club, founded in 1952, used to play at the Wellesley Club, Croydon, but since the opening of the School Courts in 1960, the Club has had the advantage of using them in the evenings. The Club provides a team to compete for the Londonderry Cup.

OW Prayer Fellowship, founded in 1952, meets privately, and occasionally in Whitgift House Chapel.

OW Linnaean Society (OWLS), formed in 1954 for ornithologists. Not much news of its activities has recently been published.

OW Careers Panel, formed in 1954, holds regular meetings to give advice to School leavers and others in their choice of a career.

OW Fencing Club, formed in 1956, allegedly as the revival of a pre-war club, whose activities seem to have been unrecorded, and primarily to organise a team against the School on OWA Day.

OW Lawn Tennis Club formed in 1959 to provide a team to compete in the d'Abernon Cup in which it had a few early successes and reached the final in 1963. After half-a-dozen years, with no home base, it expired. Attempts have recently been made to revive it, with use of the School courts.

OW Swimming Club, founded in 1960, after the opening of the School pool; its members meet weekly at the School and compete in swimming and water-polo matches.

OW Rugby Fives Club, not founded until 1961, although fives has been a School game since 1871. After some years of inactivity it has recently been re-started.

OW Hockey Club, the junior club of all, and at the moment possibly the most successful, was formed in 1962, as a Sunday, wandering side. Since becoming established at the OW ground in Croham Road in 1982, it has had many successes, winning the Glenfarclas Cup in 1988 and 1989.

From time to time attempts have been made to start up clubs for other purposes, including sailing, chess and bridge, but sufficient support has not been forthcoming.

Appendix IX
Bibliography

Chapter I The Founder

Manuscript and other unpublished material
Cambridge, Peterhouse: Registers.
Chelmsford, Essex Record Office: Essex Parish Registers.
Dublin, Trinity College: Catalogue of the Library of John Whitgift. (MS E.4.13; microfilm in School Archives.)
Lambeth Palace Library: MSS 178, 275, 807, 807b, 2009. (Microfilm of MSS 275, 807, 807b in School Archives.) Register of Archbishop Whitgift; Carte Misc. V., Act Books.
Lincoln, Record Office: Will of Henry Whitgift, 1552.
Oxford, Bodleian Library: Tanner MSS 77, 79, 80.
Ouseley, M.H.: Notes on the Family of Whitgift (School Archives).
Public Record Office: PCC Will Harte 45.
Sheffield, City Central Library: Wentworth Woodhouse MSS: Treatises 32.
Whitgift Foundation: Ledger Books 1599– . (Microfilm in School Archives.)

Publications
Brook, V.J.K.: *Whitgift and the English Church*, 1957.
Calendar of Close Rolls
Calendar of Patent Rolls
Charlton, Kenneth: *Education in Renaissance England*, 1965.
Clayton, H.J.: *Archbishop Whitgift and his Times*, 1911.
Collinson, Patrick: 'The Elizabethan Puritan Movement, 1967; The "nott conformytye" of the young John Whitgift' (*Journal of Ecclesiastical History*, Vol. xv, No. 2).
Dawley, Powell Mills: *John Whitgift and the Reformation*, 1954.
Fuller, Thomas: *The Worthies of England* (Ed. John Freeman), 1952.
Grimsby Parish Church Registers.
Hill, Christopher: *Economic Problems of the Church from Archbishop Whitgift to the Long Parliament*, 2nd Ed. 1963.

Historical Manuscripts Commission Reports: *Marquess of Salisbury's MSS; Lord de Lisle & Dudley's MSS; Records of Grimsby.*
Leonard, E.M.: *Early History of English Poor Law Relief*, 1965.
Macaulay, T.B., Lord: *Essay on Bacon*, 1843.
Maitland, S.R.: 'Archbishop Whitgift's College Pupils' (*British Magazine*, Vols. xxxii. xxxiii. 1847–8).
Oates, J.C.T.: *Cambridge University Library, a History*, 1988.
Paule, Sir George: *Life of John Whitgift*, 1612.
Porter, H.C.: 'Reformation and Reaction in Tudor Cambridge, 1598. The Anglicanism of Archbishop Whitgift' (*Historical Magazine of the Protestant Episcopal Church of the United States*, Vol. xxxi, 1962).
Richardson, William: *Some Useful Consumers of Waste, Adlingfleet and Whitgift*, 1989.
Calendar of State Papers Domestic.
Strype, John:*Life and Acts of John Whitgift*, 1718.
Surtees Society Publications.
Victoria County History of Lincolnshire.
Whitgift, John: *Works* (Parker Society), 1851.
Yorkshire Record Society Publications.

Chapter II Foundation

Manuscript and other unpublished material
British Library: Sloane MS 27 (photocopy in School Archives), Lansdowne MS 209.
Cambridge, Caius College: MS 694.
Croydon Public Library: Paget, C.G.: Transcripts of Court Rolls, Deeds, Wills, etc. relating to Croydon.
Lambeth Palace Library: MS 275; Registers of Archbishops Grindal and Whitgift.
Public Record Office: Chancery Proceedings Ser. ii, 378/20.
Whitgift Foundation: Archives and Muniments.

Publications
Battely, Nicholas: *Antiquities of Canterbury*, 1703.

Hobson, J.M.: *Some Early and Late Houses of Pity*, 1926.
Jordan, W.K.: *Charities of Rural England 1480–1660*, 1961; *Charities of London 1480–1660*, 1960; *Philanthropy in England 1480–1660*, 1959.
Leach, A.F.: *Schools of Mediaeval England*, 1915; 'Whitgift Grammar School' (*V.C.H. Surrey*), 1905.
Paget, C.G.: *Abstracts of Ancient Muniments of the Whitgift Foundation* (privately printed), 1934.
Simon, Joan: *Education and Society in Tudor England*, 1966; 'A.F. Leach on the Reformation' (*British Journal of Educational Studies*, Vols iii, iv), 1954–6.
Stowe, A. Monroe: *English Grammar Schools in the Reign of Queen Elizabeth*, 1908.
Watson, Foster: *The English Grammar Schools to 1660*, 1908; *The Old Grammar Schools*, 1916.

Chapter III The Seventeenth Century Grammar School, 1600–1712.

Manuscript and other unpublished material
Alnwick Castle: Accounts of Officers of the Household for Alnwick, Syon, Petworth and London: UI 1564–1686.
British Library: Add. MSS 19, 165 f.253 *et seq.*; Add. MS 5,865 f.106.
Croydon Public Library: Transcripts of Croydon Parish Registers, by W. Bruce Bannerman and others; Pedigree of Brigstocke.
Henry E. Huntington Library, San Marino, California: Ellesmere Papers.
Lambeth Palace Library: Act Books 3 and 4.
Leicester, Borough Archives: Hall Papers xiii.
London, Merchant Taylors' Company: School Lists.
Maidstone, Kent Archives Office: MSS U522 A2; U790 A1.
Oxford, Bodleian Library: C.C. Coll. MS C390; MS Wood D11; MS Rawl. Poet. 123; Tanner MSS 29, 30, 104, 127, 140, 162; MS Rawl. Letters 100; H.F. Brooks: Complete Works of John Oldham (unpublished thesis for D.Phil.: MS D.Phil. C129).
Public Record Office: Chancery Proceedings, Collins (C6) 259/69, 210/33. Whittington 167/86; Lay Subsidies, Hearth Tax Returns, Surrey 1673–4; Exchequer Bills & Answers Will. & Mary, Sy.8; Exchequer of Pleas—Plea Rolls 722/14 1689, 730/4 1691; PCC Wills; Two Depositions, Bundle 1446/65.
St. Saviour's Grammar School, Southwark: Governors' Minutes.
Whitgift Foundation: Archives.

Publications
Anon.: *Thomas Tenison, Memoir of his Life & Times*, 1716.

Archaeologia Cantiana: Vol. xv: Dalison Documents, 1883.
Barker, G.F.R. & Stenning, A.H.: *Records of Old Westminsters*, 1928.
Batho, G.R.: Ed.: *Household Papers of Henry Percy, ninth Earl of Northumberland* (Camden Soc.) 1962.
Bibliotheca Topographica Britannica xlvi (Case of the Inhabitants of Croydon 1673), 1787.
Brooks, Harold F. 'John Shepheard, Master of Whitgift School when John Oldham was Under-Master', *Notes & Queries for Somerset & Dorset*, Vol. xxx, Sept. 1979.
Brooks, Harold F. and Selden, Raman, eds.: *The Poems of John Oldham*, 1987.
Camden, William: *Britannia*, translated by Philemon Holland, 1610.
Charlton, Kenneth: *Education in Renaissance England*, 1965.
Cross, M. Claire: *The Free Grammar School of Leicester*, 1953.
de Sola Pinto, Vivian: *Enthusiast in Wit* (Earl of Rochester), 1962.
Dictionary of National Biography.
Draper, F.W.M.: *Four Centuries of Merchant Taylors' School*, 1962.
Erith, P.F.W.: *Brief History of Newport Grammar School*, 1950.
Falk, Bernard: *The Bridgewater Millions*, 1941.
Foster, J.: *Alumni Oxonienses*, 1891.
Fuller, Thomas: *Church History of Britain*, 1655.
Holmes, Geoffrey: *Augustan England, Professions, State and Society 1680–1730*, 1982.
Hoole, Charles: *New Discovery of the Old Art of Teaching Schoole*, 1659.
Kierney, Hugh: *Scholars and Gentlemen (Universities and Society in Pre-Industrial Britain, 1500–1700)*, 1970.
Lawrence-Archer, J.: *Inscriptions of the British West Indies*, 1875.
Lawson, John.: *A Town Grammar School through Six Centuries* (Hull), 1963.
Marshall, C.J.: *History of Cheam and Sutton*, 1936.
Nicolson, William: *An Exposition of the Apostles' Creed delivered in several Sermons*, 1661.
Oldham, John: *Compositions in Prose & Verse, with a Memoir of his Life*, Ed. by Edward Thompson, 1770; *Poetical Works*, Ed. by Robert Bell, 1854.
Oliver, V.L.: *Caribbeana*, 1910–19.
Stanier, R.S.: *Magdalen School*, 1958.
Stone, Lawrence: 'Educational Revolution in England 1560–1640' (*Past & Present* No. 28, July 1954).
Stone, Lawrence: *The Crisis of the Aristocracy 1558–1641*, 1965.
Venn, J. & J.A.: *Alumni Cantabrigienses*, 1922–54.
Vincent, W.A.L.: *The State and School Education,*

Appendix IX

1640–60, 1950. *The Grammar Schools, their continuing Tradition, 1660–1714*, 1969.

Walls, P.J.: 'The Wase School Collection' (*Bodleian Library Record*, Vol. iv, No.2, Aug. 1952).

Wase, Christopher: *Considerations regarding Free Schools*, 1678.

Wilson, H.B.: *History of Merchant Taylors' School*, 1812.

Wood, Anthony: *Athenae Oxonienses*, Ed. P. Bliss, 1813–17

Chapter IV Henry Mills, 1712–1742

Manuscript and other unpublished material
Bristol City Archives: Smyth Papers from Ashton Court.
British Library: Add. MS 38480.
Lambeth Palace Library: MS 953 (Wake's Diary); Act Books 6, 7.
Oxford, Bodleian Library: MS Rawl. Sermons 237: Christ Church Library: Wake MSS 6, 7, 8, 15, 20, 22, 27.
Public Record Office: PCC Will Trenley 125 (1742).

Publications
Anon.: *Journey through England in familiar Letters from a Gentleman*, 1732.
Aubrey, John: *Natural History and Antiquities of Surrey*, 1723.
Bangorian Controversy:
  Snape, Andrew: *Second Letter to the Lord Bishop of Bangor*, 1717.
  Pillonnière, François de la: *Answer to Dr Snape's Accusation*, 1717.
  Snape, Andrew: *Vindication of a Passage in Dr Snape's Second Letter*, 1717.
  Pillonnière, F. de la: *Reply to Dr Snape's Vindication*, 1718.
  Mills, Henry: *Full Answer to Mr Pillonnière's Reply,* 1718
  Pillonnière, François de la: *A Third Defense,* 1718
  Warder, Joseph, & Bowen, Charles: *A Vindication*, 1718.
  T . . . B . . . : *Remarks upon the Publick Advertisements concerning Mr Pillonnière*, 1718.
  Hoadly, Benjamin: *Letter to Clement Chevallier*, 1757.
Bantock, Anton: *The earlier Smyths of Ashton Court 1545–1741*, 1982.
Carpenter, Edward: *Thomas Tenison, his Life and Times*, 1948.
Clarke, John: *Education of Youth in Grammar Schools.* 1730. *An Essay on Study*, 1731.
Complete Peerage.
Daily Courant, 1717–18.

Defoe, Daniel: *Tour through England & Wales*, 1724.
Garrow, W.: *History of Croydon*, 1818.
Hans, Nicholas: *New Trends In Education in the 18th Century*, 1951.
Historical MSS Commission: *Report on MSS of the Dean & Chapter of Wells*, Vol. II.
Hollis, Christopher: *Eton*, 1960.
McDonnell, Michael: *Annals of St. Paul's School*, 1959.
Mills, Henry: *Essay on Generosity*, 1732. *Pueritiae Formandae Artifex*, 1741.
Oxford Historical Society: *Hearne's Collections*, vii.
Postboy, 1717–18.
Tate, E.W.: 'Episcopal Licensing of Schoolmasters' (*Church Quarterly Review*, Vol. clxii), 1956.
Tompson, Richard S.: *Classics or Charity, the Dilemma of the 18th Century Grammar School*, 1971.
Williams, Basil: *The Whig Supremacy 1714–60*, 1952.

Chapter V Decline, 1742–1843

Manuscript and other unpublished material
British Library: Add. MSS 29132; 34583–34592 *passim*; 38222–38580 *passim.*
Croydon Public Library: Transcript of Parish Registers; William Page: My Recollections of Croydon Sixty Years Since, 1880.
Gordon Clark, Rev. Charles P., Rector of Keston, Kent: Information contributed, 1971.
Lambeth Palace Library: Act Books 8–13;. Arch P/A Secker 22/2; VC/1D/2/5; VP/11/2/3/6; VV/IV/9/1–7.
Maidstone, Kent County Record Office: Twysden Papers U49/C13.
Public Record Office: PCC Will Mansfield 519 (John Rose); HO 107/1078 (Census 1841).
Whitgift Foundation: Archives.

Publications
Act for Improving and Extending the Benefits of Grammar Schools, 1840.
Anderson, J. Corbet: *Chronicle of Croydon*, 1882; *Croydon Inclosure Award 1797–1801*, 1889.
Annual Register, 1798.
Blakiston, Noel: 'Archives of Eton College' (*Archives*, Vol. v)
Carlisle, Nicholas: *Concise Description of the Endowed Grammar Schools of England & Wales*, 1818.
Charity Commissioners: *13th Report*, 1825; *31st Report*, 1837.
Committee on the Education of the Poor:
  Brougham, Henry, M.P.: *Letter to Samuel Romilly, M.P.*, 1818.

Anon.: *Letter to Rt. Hon. Sir William Scott*, 1818.
Ireland, Rev. J.: *Letter to Henry Brougham, M.P.*, 1819.
Knox, Vicesimus: *Remarks on the Bill to degrade Grammar Schools*, 1821.
Digest of Parochial Returns, Session 1818, Vol. ii., 1819.
Committee on the Law and Practice relating to Charitable Trusts (Nathan) Report, 1952.
Draper, F.W.M.: *Four Centuries of Merchant Taylors' School*, 1962.
Ducarel, Andrew: *Some Account of the Town of Croydon*, 1783.
Gardiner, R.B.: *Admission Registers of St. Paul's School*, 1884.
Hodgson, Rev. J.T.: *Memoir of Francis Hodgson*, 1878.
Home Office: *Abstract of Education Returns 1833*, Vol. iii, 1835.
Hyde, H.B.: *Parochial Annals of Bengal*, 1901.
Leach, A.F.: 'Schools', in *Encyclopaedia Britannica*, 11th ed., 1910.
Mack, Edward C.: *Public Schools and British Opinion 1780–1860*, 1930.
Marples, Morris: *The Romantics at School*, 1967.
Musgrave, P.W.: *Society and Education in England since 1800*, 1968.
New, Chester W.: *Life of Henry Brougham to 1830*, 1961.
Nicoll, Allardyce: *History of English Drama*, Vol. iii, 1952.
Penny, F.: *The Church in Madras*, Vol. i.
Pollard, Hugh M.: *Pioneers of Popular Education*, 1969.
Rose, Dr John: *Proceedings of Evidence against . . .*, 1812.
St. Martin, Outwich: *Parish Registers* (Harleian Society).
Sanderson, J.M.: 'The Grammar School and the Education of the Poor, 1780–1840' (*British Journal of Educational Studies*, Vol. xi, 1962).
Simon, Brian: *Studies in the History of Education 1780–1870*, 1960.
Stewart, W.A.C. & McCann, W.P.: *The Educational Innovators, 1750–1880*, 1967.
Universal British Directory, before 1795.
Wilson, H.B.: *History of Merchant Taylors' School*, 1812.
Young, William: *History of Dulwich College*, 1889.

Chapter VI The struggle for Reconstruction, 1843–1871

Manuscript and other unpublished material
Croydon Public Library: Memorial of the Inhabitants of Croydon, 1868; Reply of the Governors, 1868; Rejoinder to that Reply, 1869. Johnson, C.W.: Collection of 'Notices relating to Croydon', 2 vols.
Public Record Office: HO 107/1601 (Census 1851); RG 9/448–9 (Census 1861). Ed/27 4479–518 (Files of Charity Commissioners and Endowed Schools Commissioners relating to the Whitgift Foundation), and Ed/27, other schools.
Lambeth Palace Library: Canterbury Act Books 14, 16, 17. Tait Papers (Home) Vols. 168, 177; Tait's Diary.
National Society Library: Croydon, St. Andrew's.
Whitgift Foundation: Schoolmaster's Minutes 1812–1848.

Publications
Anderson, J. Corbett: *Croydon Old Church and the Whitgift Charity*, 1878; *The Parish of Croydon*, 1882 (Reprint of 1970).
Arnold, Ralph: *The Whiston Matter*, 1961.
Best, Geoffrey: *Mid-Victorian Britain 1851–75*, 1981
Burn, W.L.: *The Age of Equipoise*, 1964.
Cornell, W.F.: *Educational Thought and Influence of Matthew Arnold*, 1950.
Croydon Advertiser, 1869–.
Croydon Chronicle, 1856–.
Croydon Times, 1861–.
Endowed Schools Act, 1869.
Gray's Croydon Directory, 1855–.
Griffith, George: *Endowed Schools of England and Ireland*, 1864.
Marsh, P.T.: *The Victorian Church in Decline: Archbishop Tait and the Church of England 1868–1882*, 1969.
Notes & Queries, Ser. 7, Vol. ix, 1890.
Public Schools (Clarendon) *Commission Report*, 1864.
Scheme for Management of the Hospital of the Holy Trinity, Croydon, approved by the Court of Chancery, 1856; *Draft Scheme* do., prepared by the Governors, for Endowed Schools Commissioners, 1869; *Draft Scheme* do., prepared by the E.S.C.s. 1870; *Governors' Alternative Draft Scheme*, 1870.
Schools Inquiry (Taunton) Commission: *General Report*, 1868. (For Croydon, see Vol. vii, App. iv, and Vol. xi, pp. 160–2).
The Times.
Ward, Jesse W.: *Croydon in the Past*, 1883.
Warwick, Alan R.: *The Phoenix Suburb*, 1972.
Whitgift Foundation: *Statutes* (printed by S. Clouter, Croydon), 1863.

Chapter VII The Reconstructed School under Robert Brodie, 1871–1902

Manuscript and other unpublished material

Appendix IX

Lambeth Palace Library: Tait Papers (Home) Vols. 236, 241, 255; Personal Diary.
Edward Benson Papers: Vols. 8, 16, 17, 44, 64, 76, 79, 90, 102, 111, 114, 140.
Frederick Temple Papers: Vols. 7, 17, 27, 35, 39, 56.
National Society Library: Croydon, St. John Baptist and Parish Church Files.
Public Record Office: Ed/27 4483–584 (Whitgift Foundation); Ed/27, other schools; Census 1871.
Whitgift Foundation: Governors' Minutes and other Records.
Whitgift School: Archives.

Publications
Croydon Guardian 1877–, and other local papers cited in Chapter VI.
Croydon Public Library: *Readers' Index*, 1939.
Davidson, Randall: *Life of Archbishop Tait*, 1891.
Endowed Schools Act 1869, Amendments of 1873, 1874; *Report* from Select Committee, 1873, 1886, 1887.
Gosden, P.H.J.H.: 'Board of Education Act 1899' (*British Journal of Educational Studies*, Vol. xi, Nov. 1962).
History of Whitgift Grammar School, 1892.
Lowndes, G.A.N.: *The Silent Social Revolution*, 1937.
Mack, Edward C.: *Public Schools and British Opinion since 1860.* 1941.
Mangan, J.A.: *Athleticism in the Victorian and Edwardian Public School*, 1981; *'Benefits Bestowed'? Education and British Imperialism*, 1988.
Marsh, P.T.: *The Victorian Church in Decline*, 1969.
Percival, Alicia C.: *The Origins of the Headmasters' Conference*, 1969; *Very Superior Men*, 1973.
Scheme for Administration of Hospital of the Holy Trinity (E.S.Cs' Revised Draft), 1874; *Draft* do. by Whitgift Hospital and Croydon Charities Committee, 1877; *Charity Commissioners' Scheme*, approved 1881.
Scientific Instruction, Royal Commission (Devonshire) in: *6th Report: On the Teaching of Science in Public and Endowed Schools, 1875.*
Secondary Education (Bryce) *Commission Report*, 1895.
Simon, Brian: *Education and the Labour Movement 1870–1920*, 1965.
Whitgift Magazine, 1879–1904.
Who Was Who, Vol. i, 1897–1915; Vol. ii, 1916–28.

Chapter VIII S.O. Andrew, 1903–1927

Manuscript and other unpublished material

Croydon Corporation: Minutes of Education Committee 1903–27.
Lambeth Palace: Randall Davidson Papers, *passim.*
Micklewright, H.G.F.: Information communicated.
Public Record Office: Ed27/8501–7; 8516–17; Ed35/2396–401; 6049–51; Ed43/912–25; Ed109/5660–3; 5655–7 (Board of Education files on Whitgift Foundation).
Roche, Dr. J.W.: The First Half-Century of the Headmasters' Conference, 1869–1919 (Ph.D. Thesis, University of Sheffield), 1972.
Whitgift Foundation: Governors' Minutes and other Archives.
Whitgift School: Archives.

Publications
Croydon Advertiser and other local newspapers cited.
Dent, H.C.: *A Century of Growth in English Education, 1870–1970*, 1970.
The Education of the Adolescent (Hadow Report), 1926.
Mason, M.H.H. (compiler): The Book of Remembrance, 1920.
Moore, H. Keatley and Sayers, W. C. Berwick: *Croydon and the Great War*, 1920.
Public Schools Year-Book, 1908.
Read, Donald: *Edwardian England 1901–14*, 1972.
Schemes for the Administration of the Whitgift Foundation, 1904, 1907, 1915, with later Amendments.
Whitgift Magazine –1904 and *The Whitgiftian* 1905–.

Chapter IX Ronald Gurner and Haling Park

Manuscript and other unpublished material
Cecil, Hugh: Draft chapter on Ronald Gurner.
Cummings, John: Information communicated.
Gurner, Mrs. R.: Information communicated.
Micklewright, H.G.F. Information communicated.
Parr, H.E.: Information communicated.
Public Records Office: Ed27/8508–15; 9703; ED35/6052; Ed109/5663.
Whitgift Foundation: Governors' Minutes.
Whitgift School: Archives.

Publications
Consultative Committee on Secondary Education: *Report* (Spens), 1939.
Croydon Advertiser and *Croydon Times.*
Gurner, Ronald: *Day Schools of England*, 1930; *I Chose Teaching*, 1937.
Mack, Edward C.: *Public Schools and British Opinion, since 1860.* 1941.
Norwood, Cyril: *The English Tradition of Education*, 1929.

Seaman, L.C.B.: *Life in between the Wars*, 1970.
Simon, Brian: *The Politics of Educational Reform, 1920–1940*, 1974.
The Times.
The Whitgiftian.

Chapter X G.E.H. Ellis and World War II

Manuscript and other unpublished material
Chuter Ede, James: Diaries; BL Add MS 59698.
Whitgift Foundation: Governors' Minutes.
Whitgift School: Archives.

Publications
Committee on Public Schools: *Abolition of Tuition Fees in Grant-aided Secondary Schools*, 1943. *The Public Schools and the General Educational System* (Fleming Report), 1944.
Education Act (Butler) 1944.
Hansard: House of Commons Report, 11 June 1945.
Sayers, W. C. Berwick: *Croydon and the Second World War*, 1949.
The Times.
The Whitgiftian.

Chapter XI E.A.G. Marlar and Post-War Opportunities

Manuscript and other unpublished material
Lambeth Palace: Fisher Papers.
Marlar, E.A.G.: Information communicated.
Parr, H.E.: Information communicated.
Whitgift Foundation: Governors' Minutes, etc.
Whitgift School: Archives.

Publications
Boyd, David: *Elites and their Education* 1973.
Central Advisory Council for Education: *15 to 18* (Crowther Report), 1959.
Croydon Advertiser and *Croydon Times.*
Ewen, A.H.: 'A Sixth Form Course in the History and Philosophy of Science.' *History of Science, Vol. II*, 1963.
Whitgift Charities Act, 1969.
The Whitgiftian.

Chapter XII M.J. Hugill 1961–70

Manuscript and other unpublished material
Hugill, M.J.: Information communicated.
Parr, H.E.: Information communicated.
Whitgift Foundation: Governors' Minutes.
Whitgift School: Archives.

Publications
Cox, C.B. and Dyson, A.E., eds.: *Black Paper One*, 1969; *Black Paper Two*, 1969; *Black Paper Three*, 1970.
Public Schools Commission: *Reports i, Boarding Schools* (Newsom), 1968; ii, *Independent and Direct Grant Day Schools* (Donnison), 1970.
Richmond, W. Kenneth: *The Teaching Revolution*, 1967.
Rooke, Margaret Anne: *Anarchy and Apathy, Student Unrest 1968–70*, 1971.
Whitgift Charities Act, 1969.
The Whitgiftian.

Chapter XIII David Raeburn and Great Expectations

Manuscript and other unpublished material
Whitgift Foundation: Governors' Minutes.
Whitgift School: Archives.

Publications
Bamford, T.W.: *Public School Data*, 1974.
Cox, C.B. and Boyson, Rhodes: *Black Paper 1977*, 1977.
The Croydon Advertiser.
Fox, Irene: *Private Schools and Public Issues, The Parents' View*, 1985.
Lawton, Denis, ed.: *The Education Reform Act; Choice and Control*, 1989.
Rae, John: *The Public School Revolution, 1964–79*, 1981; *Too Little, Too Late?*, 1989.
Salter, Brian, and Tapper, Ted: *Power and Policy in Education; The Case of Independent Schooling*, 1985.
Saunders, Peter: *Urban Politics, A Sociological Interpretation*, 1979.
The Whitgiftian.

A *Select List* of works of more general interest or covering long periods of educational history.
Adamson, J.W.: *English Education 1789–1902*, 1930.
Archer, R.L.: *Secondary Education in the 19th Century*, 1921. (Professor Archer was on the staff at Whitgift 1900–3; to him must be attributed the frequently repeated allegation that between 1812 and 1871 there were no pupils at the School.)
Armytage, W.H.G.: *Four Hundred Years of English Education*, 1964.
Bamford, T.W.: *The Rise of the Public Schools*, 1967.
Barnard, H.C.: *Short History of English Education, 1760–1944*, 1947.
Board, Ministry, or Department of Education: numerous pamphlets.
Burgess, H.J.: *Enterprise in Education; the Church and Elementary Education*, 1958.

Appendix IX

Carpenter, Edward: *Cantuar, The Archbishops in their Office*, 1971.
Clarke, M.L.: *Classical Education in England, 1500–1900*, 1959.
Curtis, S.J.: *History of Education in Great Britain*, 1967 ed.
Davidson, Alexander: *Blazers, Badges and Boaters: A Pictorial History of School Uniform*, 1990.
Evans, Keith: *The Development and Structure of the English School System*, 1985
Gardner, Brian: *The Public Schools*, 1973
Gathorne-Hardy, Jonathan: *The Public Schools Phenomenon*, 1977.
Godfrey, Walter H. (OW): *The English Almshouse*, 1955.
Gordon, Peter: *Selection for Secondary Education*, 1980.
Griggs, Clive: *Private Education in Britain*, 1985.
Heald, Tim: *Networks*, 1983.
Honey, J.R. de S.: *Tom Brown's Universe*, 1977.
Howarth, T.E.B.: *Culture, Anarchy and the Public Schools*, 1969.
Kalton, Graham: *The Public Schools, a Factual Survey*, 1966.
Lamb, G.F.: *The Happiest Days*, 1959.
Lowe, Roy: *Education in the post-war Years*, 1988.
Maclure, J. Stuart: *Educational Documents, 1816 to the present Day*, 1986.
Newsome, David: *Godliness and Good Learning*, 1961.
O'Day, Rosemary: *Education and Society, 1500–1800*, 1982.
Seaborne, Malcolm: *The English School, its Architecture and Organisation 1370–1870*, 1971.
Seaborne, Malcolm and Lowe, Roy: *The English School, its Architecture and Organisation, Vol. II, 1870–1970*, 1977.
Simon, Brian and Bradley, Ian, eds: *The Victorian Public School: Studies in the Development of an Educational Institution*, 1975.
Stone, Lawrence: 'Literacy and Education in England 1640–1900' (*Past & Present* No. 42 Feb. 1969).
Walford, Geoffrey: *Life in Public Schools*, 1985; ed: *British Public Schools, Policy and Practice*, 1984.

Index

A-levels 232, 241, 245, 251, 261, 271, 272, 274, 276, 298–9, 306
Abbot, Archbishop 38, 51, 58
Addington 45
Addington Palace 102, 172
Addiscombe 37, 64, 91, 166, 180, 185, 205
Addiscombe Place 45, 66, 70, 80, 90, 97, 99; *100*
adventure training 278, 300
Advisory Committee 301, 303
Aldenham School 42, 105, 157
Alexander of Tunis, Field Marshal Lord 242
Allder (OW) 136
Allen, Francis (Governor) 220, 223
almshouses 33, 70
alumni 50, 152–3, 314–19, 320–22
Anderson, John Corbet 142–3, 145
Andrew, Samuel Ogden (Head Master) 163–92, 210, 213, 217, 221, 235, 236, 259, 290; *163*
Andrews, William (OW) 80
Apthorpe, Frederick (OW) 97
Archbishop Tenison's School 81, 101, 103
archives 287–8
Armstrong, William, 283, 301
Arnett, M.G. (Master) 207
Arnold, Thomas 115, 122
Art Department 166, 196, 202, 236, 245, 260, 266, 274, 286; *172, 289, 292, 300, 301*
Ashburton Shield Competition 140, 208, 276
athletics 140, 207, 225, 226, 227, 275, 276
Atkins, M.R. (OW) 169
Atwood, Harman (OW) 65, 69
Aylworth, Edward 37, 58

Bacon, Anthony 18, 20
Bacon, Francis 18, 20, 30, 48, 64, 94
Bagbie House 228–9, 241, 243, 245, 251, 286; *229*
Bagg, Richard (OW) 80
Baker, Thomas Southey (Master) 140
Balfour, H.L. (Song Master) 197, 229
Balfour Education Act 162, 169, 217
Balley, E.J. (Master) 161
  Whitgift School and its Evolution (1937) 161
Banbury School 42
Bancroft, Archbishop 22, 24, 25, 26, 27, 29, 37, 50
Bangorian Controversy 83–8
Banks, F.L. (OW) 154
Barden, L.W. (OW) 226
Baret's *Dictionarie* 49
Barnes, Michael (Clerk to the Foundation) 304
Barnett, Dr. Christopher A. (Headmaster) 291–2; *291*
Batchelar (OW) 136
Bath Cup 208, 249, 276; *249*
Beaumont College 248
Beckenham and Penge Grammar School 257, 295, 305
Beddington, 45
Bedford School 121, 124, 148, 180, 204
Bedford Modern School 146

Beer, I.D.S. (OW) 226, 239
Bell, Dr. Andrew 104
Bell, John 235
benefactors 325–7
Bennett, H. (Master) 207, 249
Benson, Archbishop 154, 155
Bentley, E.F. (Master) 273–4
Berkhamsted School 171
Bernard, Dr. Samuel 54, 59, 60
Berney, Sir Henry (OW) 152, 153, 163, 166, 183
Berry, Arthur (OW) 138
Berry, Edward (OW) 138
Berry, Sir James (OW) 138
Berthoud, O.C. (Headmaster Trinity School) 235
Best, Henry (OW) 56
Betham's School, Croydon, 32
Big School 131, 135, 139, 141, 159, 166, 183, 192, 195, 197, 198, 202, 224, 236, 237, 244, 246, 247, 260, 266, 268, 275, 283; *171*
  memorial tablet 178
  names carved on stonework 139, 246
  organ 236, 283
Birley, Sir Robert 257
Bishop, Sir William (OW) 191
Bishop's licence 32, 60, 85
Bisset, John Collinson (Schoolmaster) 103, 106–9, 110
Bisset's (Alexander) School, Croydon 101, 103
Blackheath Proprietary School 154
Blackrock College 248
Blake, William J. (Governor) 118
Blanchard, Mary 88, 106
Blese, Harry (OW) 68
Blomfield, Sir Arthur 121, 122, 166, 246–7
Blore, Rev. George 127
Blundell's School 42, 171
Board of Education (1902) 162, 168, 170, 174, 180, 185, 199, 205, 213, 217, 252
boarding houses 147–8, 228–9
books *see* library books
Borough Secondary School, Croydon 170, 172, 179, 187
Botanical Garden 237
boxing 226
Boyd, Bill (OW and Master) 286
Boys, John (Benefactor) 37
Boys' Club 198, 278–9
Bozman, E.F. (OW) 192
Bradford, John 15
Bragg brothers (OW) 225
Bragg Trophy 225
Braithwaite, Rev. J.M. (Vicar of Croydon) 294
Branston, John (Master) 250, 275
brass money 71
Brereton, Sir William 60
Brethren and Sisters 37, 38, 39, 70, 110, 264
  defy Archbishop 107–8
  distrust of the Schoolmasters 11, 64, 66, 78, 82, 84, 88, 111

343

drunkenness 52, 90
income 62, 111
litigation 102, 107–8
responsibilities replaced by Governors 116, 145
uniforms 57–8, 70
Brighton College 157, 223, 239, 248
Brigstocke, John (OW) 53, 62
Bristol Grammar School 148, 171, 204, 257
'Brodeus' 54; *55*
Brodie, Douglas (Master) 135, 161
Brodie, Robert (Head Master) 59, 127–8, 129–61, 164, 167, 169, 188, 190, 210, 223, 246, 290, 296, 304; *130, 139*
Bromley 45
Bromsgrove School 96, 127
Brook, Rev. P.W.P. (OW) 185
Brougham, Henry, M.P. 105, 108, 111, 112
Brougham Select Committee on Education 105–8
Brown, Bob (Master) 286
Bruce, W.N. 171
Bryce, James 126
Bryce Report 126–7, 131, 162, 169, 217
Brygges, Ambrose (Schoolmaster) 46–7
Budgen, John (Governor) 118, 122
Burke, Sgt-Maj. 151, 161
Burton, Rev. W. (Master) 191
Bury St. Edmund's School 62, 72
Bush, William (OW) 80
Bushel, Thomas (OW) 80
Butler Education Act (1944) 123, 191, 217–18, 220, 227–8, 233

Cadet Corps 140, 151, 161, 176; *150, 175*
Caesar, John (Schoolmaster) 69–76, 81, 82
Caesar, Julius (OW) 74
Caldwell, I. (OW) 226
Cambridge University 20, 24, 50, 298, 299; *see also* universities
  Caius College 38, 50, 63, 136
  Christ's College 60, 69
  King's College 88, 138, 240
  Pembroke Hall 15, 17, 18, 26
  Peterhouse 15, 18, 26
  Queens' College 15
  St. John's College 19, 50, 61, 74, 96
  Selwyn College 121, 223
  Sidney Sussex College 50, 57
  Trinity College 17–20, 26, 47, 50, 58, 74, 155, 235; *19*
Camden, William 50, 63; *49*
  Britannia 30, 50, 62
  Greek Grammar 48, 50, 56, 57, 73
careers guidance 273–4
Carmen 133, 141, 155
Carpenter, Dr. Alfred (Governor) 122
Carr, Sir Bernard (OW) 191
Carshalton 45
Carter, E.M. (Master) 165, 286
Cartwright, Thomas 20; *20*
Caterham 181, 205
Cecil, Dr. Hugh 212n
Cecil, Sir Robert 24
Cecil, Sir William, Lord Burghley 16, 17, 22, 23, 33; *17*
Cedar Court 243, 255; *243*
Ceppi, Marc (Master) 173
Chantry, Kate 288

chapel 228, 233, 270, 280
Chapman, John Skelton 105
Charitable Procedures Act (1812) 111
Charitable Trusts Act (1853) 111, 112
Charities Bill (1597/8) 31
Charity Commission 109, 110, 112–13, 116, 118, 119, 120, 121–3, 124, 125, 126, 141–2, 143, 144, 152, 159, 162, 253, 288
  education reform 116
  and Founder's Tomb 152
Charterhouse School 15, 44, 48, 58, 59, 97, 98, 99, 114, 120, 122, 127, 128, 129, 133, 134, 139, 141, 151, 155, 257
Chatfield, Charles (Governor) 118
Cheam School 60, 93, 94
Checquer Inn 33, 34, 35
Cheltenham College 114, 124, 146, 157, 161
chess 226, 275; *227*
Cheyne, R.J. (OW and Master) 156, 160–1
Chiesman, Sir Walter (OW) 191
Chipstead 181
Chislehurst 45
Christian Fields 36, 37
Christian Union 183, 196, 279
Christ's Hospital 129, 140, 155, 232, 248
City of London School 126, 140, 154, 180
Civil war 57
Church Road School 117, 119, 146, 148, 153, 163, 185; *119*
Chuter Ede, Lord (Governor) 218, 219
Clarendon, Lord 120, 129
Clarendon Report on Public Schools 120, 123, 124, 129, 157, 208
Clarke, John, on education 91–2
  Education of Youth 91
Clarke, Stephenson (Benefactor) 149, 155
Clavering, Essex 18, 23, 24, 26
Clayton, H.S. (Headmaster of Whitgift Middle) 188, 189, 235
Clewer, Dr. William (Vicar of Croydon) 65, 76
Clifton College 193, 194
Clinton, Lord 122, 143, 144, 145
Clot Mead 36, 117
coat of arms 253; *43, 328–9*
Coatman, Robert (Governor) 263, 283, 304
Coles, Rev. George (Schoolmaster) 110–11, 120–1; *111*
College House School, Croydon 115, 119
Collins, W.H. (Master) 161
Collinson, Dr. Patrick 18
Coloma School, Croydon 179
Combined Cadet Force 278, 300; *278*; *see also* Cadet Corps; Officers' Training Corps
commercial education 116, 119
'Commerical' School, Croydon 115, 116–28
Commission for Charities (1818) 111–12
Common Room Society 220
'Common' School 113–14, 116, 152n
community service given by boys 198, 278–9, 300
Computer Centre 283
computer studies 272, 286; *301*
concerts 133, 155, 177, 197–8, 244
Cooke, Edward (OW) 74
Cooke, J.L. (OW) 249
Cooper's *Dictionarie* 48–9

Index

Coopers' Company School 120
Cornwallis, Archbishop 97
corporal punishment *see* discipline
Corps of Drums 156, 198, 229, 231, 278, 287; *185*
Coulsdon 181, 205, 281
Councell, B.R. (OW) 248
Courlander (OW) 136
Courtney, Archbishop 32
Court of Chancery 110, 111, 112, 116, 145
Court of Governors *see* Governors
Cranleigh School 140, 154, 247
Cranmer, S.B.O. (OW) 226
Crawford, V.F.S. (OW) 154
cricket 139–40, 154, 184, 207, 222, 225, 226, 227, 230, 231, 261, 275, 276; *154, 184, 199*
Croham Hurst proposals 261–4, 265, 266, 282, 294; *261, 262*
Croham Hurst Girls' School 179, 262, 264, 274, 303
Croham Manor 37, 38, 103, 166, 185
Cross, W.E. (Master) 165, 167, 191
cross-country 207, 276
Crowe, William (Schoolmaster) 63–5, 66
  Catalogue 63
  Elenchus 63; *63*
Crowson, Paul (OW) 197
Croydon 23, 29, 33, 34, 39, 45, 108, 116, 151–2, 158, 181, 205, 242, 281; *46, 89*
  almshouses 33
  charities 106
  Memorials of the inhabitants 122–3, 143, 144
  Old Palace *see* Croydon Palace
Croydon Advertiser, The 263, 264
Croydon Chronicle, The 130, 155
Croydon Education Committee 187, 188–9, 205, 234, 280
Croydon Enclosure Act (1797) 101, 103
Croydon FC 141
Croydon Grammar School 115
Croydon High School for Boys 179
Croydon High School for Girls 170, 171, 179, 294
Croydon Hospital *see* Hospital of the Holy Trinity
Croydon Palace 33, 45, 55, 60, 88, 90, 96, 102, 262; *29*
Croydon Parish Church 26, 32, 152
'Croydon School' 50
Croydon School Board 143, 145
Croydon schools 31–2, 81, 103–4, 120, 123, 126, 130, 139, 162–3, 169, 170, 280–1; *see also* names of individual schools
Cumberland, Earl of 19, 20, 41
Cummings, J. (Master) 207
Cunningham, Group-Capt. John (OW) *217*
curriculum 91, 93, 94–5, 115, 116, 120, 123, 133, 134, 143, 145, 164, 165, 168, 174-5, 206, 241, 271–3, 296–9
  computer studies 272, 286
  Greek 31, 48, 54, 62, 92–3, 94, 123, 126, 133, 138, 145
  Latin 31, 47, 48, 62, 92–3, 94, 107, 115, 123, 125, 133, 145, 173, 174
  science 134–6, 159, 164, 230, 273
cycle-touring 278

Daberon, Thomas (OW) 74
Dacie, John (Usher) 74
Dalendar, Henry (OW) 50, 51
Dalyson, John (OW) 56, 73; *57*
Dalyson, Spencer (OW) 56

Davidson, Archbhishop 165, 166, 168, 171, 173, 178, 190, 193, 194, 200
Davies, Robert (Schoolmaster) 50–1, 52; *51*
Dawson-Taylor, Pat 302
Day, Thomas (Schoolmaster) 60–1; *60*
De Cize, Emanuel (Usher) 82, 84
Deed of Endowment 37
Deed of Foundation 37; *34*
Dingwalls 151, 204
dining hall 163, 166, 184, 202, 269
Diplock, Lord (OW) 191; *211*
Direct Grant 170, 180, 218–20, 228, 250, 252–3, 262, 265–6, 268, 280, 281
direct method 173–4, 216
discipline 129, 139, 254–5, 279, 305
Dodd, W.H. (Master) 161, 167
Domini Cricket Club 226–7; *174*
Donnison Report 258
Douai School 248
Dougill, Prof. John (Governor) 283
drama 196, 222, 229, 240, 249–50, 257, 275, 292, 300
Draper, William (OW) 80, 91
drilling 151
Drummond, John (Governor) 117, 118, 119, 122
Drummond, Patrick 108, 118
Drummond, William (Clerk to the Governors) 118, 119, 121, 122, 128, 146, 154
Drummonds (solicitors) 112, 118–19, 121, 122, 127, 141, 259
Ducarel, Dr. A.C., *History of Croydon* 113, 126
Dulwich College 44, 48, 96, 127, 140, 154, 180, 184, 220, 247
Dunboy, Lord 20
Dynewell, Anne (John Whitgift's mother) 13

Eagle, Ross 208
East India Company 96, 108
Eastbourne College 147, 154
Eastty, J.M. (Governor) 122
Ebbutt (OW) 136
Edridge, Sir Frederick (Benefactor and Governor) 156, 175–6, 182, 202, 207; *175*
education 129–30, 149–50, 217, 227, 257–8
  for commerce 116, 119
  comprehensive 123, 258
  elementary 103, 106, 130, 162
  girls' 39n, 127, 146, 179, 293–4
  politics of 228, 258–9, 268, 288–90
  secondary 123, 162, 169–72, 217
Education Act (1870) 130, 162, 169
Education Act (1899) 169
Education Act (1902) 162, 169, 170, 217
Education Act (1918) 179
Education Act (1944) 123, 191, 217–18, 220, 227–8, 233
Educational Institute, Croydon 115
Egerton, Scroop, Duke of Bridgewater (OW) 72–3; *72, 73*
Eldon, Lord, ruling on grammar schools 104, 105
Elementary Education Act (1870) 130, 162, 169
Elizabeth I 15, 17, 18, 21, 22, 23, 24–5, 29, 31, 32, 45, 50; *32*
  death 24–5; *25*
Elizabeth II, opens Hospital restoration 35, 264; *265*
Ellis, Gerald Edward Harold (Head Master) 165, 191, 194, 196, 204, 213–22, 224n, 225; *214, 221*

Elwyn, Richard 129
Enclosure Act (1797) 101, 103
Endowed Schools Act (1869) 124–5, 141
Endowed Schools Act (1874) 142
Endowed Schools Commission 124–6, 134, 141, 144, 146, 157, 288
Endowment, Deed of 37
Entrance Examination 181, 233, 270
Epsom 45
Epsom College 140
Essex, Earl of 23, 25
Etches, George (Instructor) 198, 287
Etherington, Maurice (Master) 207, 226, 250
Eton College 31, 50, 79, 83, 93, 96, 97, 108, 110, 114, 120, 139, 257, 287
Eton House School, Croydon 115
Eustace, G.C. (OW) 248
Evans, H.E. (OW) 161
Evans, I.A. (Master) 207
Evans, J.D.A. (OW) 239
Evans, John (Usher) 74
Ewelme, Oxfordshire 44
Ewen, A.H. (Master) 197, 223, 224, 230, 254, 274
examinations 150
    entrance 181, 233, 270
    external 205–6
    results 271
exhibitions 125, 138, 149, 155, 175, 179
expulsions 139

Fairfield House School, Croydon 110
Fanatics 197
Farnborough 45
'fast stream' 206, 232, 233, 271
Fearon, D.R. 113–14, 144–6
    Fearon Report on Whitgift's Foundation 113–14, 123, 144–6
Fearon, J.P. 112–13
Featherstone, M.D. (OW) 275
Feild, Nicholas 49, 51
Felix, John (Master) 249
Felsted School 32
fencing 207, 225, 226, 231, 275, 276; *277*
Finch, Daniel 109
Finche, Samuel (Vicar of Croydon) 34, 35–6, 37, 38, 41, 49, 50, 70
Fisher, Archbishop 223, 236, 240
Fisher, C.J. (Master) 165, 192, 221
Fisher Education Act 179
fives 140, 198, 207, 225, 226, 227, 275, 276
fives-courts 166, 175, 202, 207, 216; *208*
Fleming Report on public schools 218–19
Flower, John Wickham (Governor) 118
Flower, Sir Newman (OW) 161
Forster Education Act (1870) 130, 162, 169
Foundation, Deed of 37; *34*
Foundation Stone 122, 200, 246; *200*
Founder's Day 35, 155–6, 225, 231; *176*
Frazer, N.L. (Master) 173
Frederick, John (OW) 73
Freeland, Alexander (OW) 136
Friends' School, Croydon 108
Fuller, Thomas, *Church History of Britain* 60, 62
Fulnetby, Margaret 18

Galer, G.S. (OW) 268
games 139–40, 184–5, 198, 206–8, 222, 225–6, 247–9, 275–77, 299
Games Committee 225
Gardiner, Christopher (OW) 57
Gardiner, Onslow (OW) 57
Garrett, John (Master) 197, 257
Garrow, D.W., *History of Croydon* 113
Gay, Thomas (OW) 80
General Certificate of Education 232, 271–2
General Schools Certificate 181, 206, 217
Genge, E.H. (Master) 133, 134, 160, 167
George, Duke of Kent 201; *201*
Gernon, Mrs Elizabeth 79n, 81, 86
girls 39n, 126, 127, 146, 179, 261, 293–4, 303
Glenfarclas Cup 275
Glynn, William (OW) 80
Glynne-Jones, R. (Master) 256, 274
golf 226, 275, 276
Goodwin, G.P. (OW) 185
Governors 116, 117–18, 122–7, 135, 141–2, 146–7, 156, 158, 159, 164, 168, 175, 188–9, 234, 253, 258–60, 268–9, 280–1, 294, 303–4; *324*
    appointment of 122, 142, 146
    Chairmen 323–4
    governing body 117–18, 122, 145, 146–7, 180, 182, 183, 190, 196, 234
    powers 169, 181
Grammar Schools 31–2, 47–8, 61–2, 64, 94–6, 105, 115, 148
Grammar Schools Act (1840) 105, 109, 110
Grattan, J.H.G. (OW) (Benefactor) 155
Gratwick, Charles (Usher) 74
'Great Schools' 91, 105, 114, 120, 124, 131, 139, 161, 208; *see also* Charterhouse, Eton, Harrow, Merchant Taylors', Rugby, St. Paul's, Shrewsbury, Westminster, Winchester
Greek 31, 42, 48, 54, 61, 92–3, 94, 123, 126, 127, 133, 138, 145, 192
Greenway, Randolph (OW) 80
Griffith, Edward (Song Master) 133, 141, 155, 160, 229
Griffiths, Brian (Master) 275
Grimsby, Lincs 13, 14, 23, 33, 256; *14*
Grimwade, Edward William (Governor) 182
Grindal, Archbishop 15, 21, 26, 32, 144
Gurner, Ronald (Head Master) 193–212, 213–4, 223, 224n, 235, 240, 253, 254, 259, 271, 273, 278, 290, 295, 308; *194*
    and day-schools 208–9
    health 209–10
gymnasium 184, 202, 207, 236, 275; *204*

Hackney School 90, 94
Hadow Report on the education of the adolescent 191, 217
Haig-Brown, William 129, 141, 155
Haileybury College 161, 193
Hale, Edward Biss (OW) 80
Hale, Matthew (OW) 80
Haling Cottage 185, 220, 223, 241, 252, 265, 269; *253, 270*
Haling House 237; *95, 188*
Haling Manor 22, 45, 57
Haling Park 176, 178, 185–9, 197, 198, 203–4, 235, 243, 251–2, 263, 264, 330–1; *198, 203, 269, 293*
    plans for new school 199–202

new building 282–8
Haling Park Cottage 186, 270
Hall, Eric (Master) 241
Halsbury, Lord Chancellor 153
Hammick, D. Ll. (OW) 173, 191
Hampton Court Conference 25
handwriting 48
Harding, William Dutton 106, 122
Harland, Bryan T. (Governor and Benefactor) 187
Harrow School 39, 95, 96, 97, 105, 120, 124, 139, 190, 194
Harvey, Sir Daniel (OW) 54–5; *56*
Hastie, J.A. (Master) 243, 249
Hatton, Sir Christopher 22, 25
Hatton, Richard (OW) 52
Hawkins, H.H.B. (OW) 154
Hawkins, M. Rhode 119
Head Master's House 153, 223; *153*
 study 224
Head Masters 312–13 *see also* names of individual Head Masters
Headmasters' Conference 124, 171, 173–4, 208, 218, 292, 299
Heath, Robert Amadeus (Governor and Benefactor) 118, 138, 148–9, 155, 158
Heathfield, John (OW) 80
heraldry 253, 328–9
Hereford Grammar School 21, 33
Herring, Archbishop 96
Heyman, Professor J (OW) 211n
Higher Certificate 182, 206, 217
Highgate School 77, 95, 105
Hinks, A.R. (OW) 154
History of Whitgift Grammar School (1892) 51, 66, 133, 140, 152, 229n
Hoadly, Benjamin 83, 84, 88
Hobbs, R.F. (Master) 207, 208
hockey 225, 227, 245, 275, 276, 283; *276*
Hodges, Frank (OW) 98
Hodges, John (OW) 98
Hodges, Thomas Law 98; *98*
Hodgson, Christopher 102, 118
Hodgson, Francis (OW) 97, 100
Hodgson, James (Schoolmaster) 97–100, 101, 118, 129
Hodgson, Rev. J.G. (Vicar of Croydon and Governor) 112, 118, 146, 294
Holden, A.H. (Master) 224
Hollier, William (Usher) 74
Hood, Sir William (Governor) 122
Hoole, Charles, *New Discovery of the Old Art of Teaching Schoole* 60
Hospital of the Holy Trinity 24, 29, 33–6, 43; *35–7; see also* Brethren and Sisters
 Attorney-General's petition 112–13
 building 34–6; repairs 70–1
 'Commercial' School 115, 116–28
 'Common' School 113–14
 constitution 64
 Deed of Foundation 37; *34*
 Deed of Endowment 37
 disputes with tenants 65–6
 dissolution 145
 early benefactors 37
 Letters Patent 33–4, 37; *32*
 listed building 154n

purchase of site 33
reform of administration 112
religious observance 40
restoration 265
Statutes 34, 38–41, 47, 55, 64, 65–6, 70, 75, 112, 113, 118; *38, 40*
tercentenary 155 6
visitations 55–6, 63, 83, 106
House system 161, 167, 225, 232, 241, 247, 304–5
Howard of Effingham, Charles, Lord, Earl of Nottingham 22, 45, 202n; *21*
Howley, Archbishop 110, 111, 112
Hugill, Michael James (Headmaster) 240–56, 258, 271, 297; *241*
Humfrey, Capt. Bruce (Governor) 228
Hurstpierpoint College 140, 154
Hussey, W.D. (OW and Master) 54, 224
Hutton, Archbishop 96

Ian Evans Building 269, 284, 303
Independent Schools Information Service 268, 290
Ingrams, W.S. (Master) 135
Ingrams, William (Head Master of the Poor School and of Whitgift Middle School) 119, 121, 135, 145, 146, 148, 149, 185
Inniskilling Cup 249; *249*
Inns of Court 48, 115
Inspections 156, 164–5, 174, 181, 205, 235–6, 259, 296, 299, 303
Ipswich School 72
Iredell, A.V.M. Sir Alfred (OW) 161
Ireland, Dr. John (Vicar of Croydon) 102, 104, 107, 108
Ireland, John (Schoolmaster) 47, 49, 50

Jamaica 74
James I 25
Jarvis, Martin (OW) 250; *250*
Jenkins, Philip (Warden) 37
Jenkinson, Cecil, 3rd Earl of Liverpool (OW) 98–100; *100*
Jenkinson, Charles, 1st Earl of Liverpool 97, 98–100
Jenkinson, Robert Banks, 2nd Earl of Liverpool 98–9
Jenney, Thomas (OW) 50
Jones, John (Clerk to the Foundation) 187, 190
Jones, Ll.J. (Master) 165, 213, 224
Jones, Rev. G.A. (Head Master of Middle School) 185
Jones, Rev. (Usher) 84
Jonson, Ben 54
Junior School 233, 234, 258, 259, 260, 266, 269, 284, 297, 299, 303; *156, 172*
Junior Training Corps 198, 278
Juxon, Archbishop 61, 63

Keable, Robert (OW) (Benefactor) 167
Keen, Thomas (Governor) 118
Kennard (OW) 136
Kennedy, R.B. (Master) 249
Kent, George, Duke of 201; *201*
Kibble, R.F. (OW) 248
King, Edward (OW) 80
King Edward's School, Birmingham 96, 114, 122
King Edward VI School, Lichfield 223
King Edward VII School, Sheffield 193, 208
King's College, London 194
King's College School 114, 126, 140, 154, 157, 180, 220, 248

347

Whitgift School

King's School, Canterbury 124, 127
Kitchener, E.E. (Master) 165, 173, 192, 220, 221
Kitchener, F.E. 156
Knaggs, Thomas (OW) 74

Labram, G.W. (OW) 222
Laceby, Lincs. 23
Lamb, John Taylor (Schoolmaster) 96–7, 109
Lambeth Palace 14, 23, 25, 27, 29, 31, 34, 39, 63, 64, 83, 88
Lancaster College 38, 66
Lancaster, Joseph 104, 106
Lancing College 157
Lang, Archbishop 200, 213, 215
Langley Park School for Boys 257, 295
Language laboratory 243, 245–6, 254, 272; *245, 288*
Latin 31, 41, 42, 43, 47, 48, 62, 92–3, 94, 107, 115, 123, 125, 133, 145, 173, 174
Latin exercises 59, 67; *58, 68*
Laud, Archbishop 55, 57, 60
lawn tennis 140, 208, 226, 231, 245, 275
Lazenby, E. (Instructor) 207
Leach, A.F. 32, 51, 59, 75, 168, 171
Leathart and Granger 199, 202, 284
leaving age 48, 182, 272
Leeds Grammar School 105, 148, 171, 204
Leicester Free Grammar School 59
Letters Patent 33–4, 37; *32*
Lewis, Dai (Master) 250, 286
Lewis, W. Clifford (Master) 223
Leysdown, Kent 97, 109
Library 202, 236, 243, 245, 254, 255, 256, 260, 266, 269, 283, 286, 287; *132, 202, 273, 288, 300*
library books 48–9, 72, 131, 149, 155
Lilly, B.J. (Master) 286
Lily's *Grammar* 48, 92
Lincoln Deanery 23
Literary and Debating Society 196, 197
Locke, John, *Thoughts concerning Education* 91, 94
Lockett, M.V. (Master) 207
Longley, Archbishop 121, 122
Longley, Henry 122, 144, 145
Lovelace, Nevill, Lord (OW) 90
Loving, C.E. (Master) 207
Lowe, George 242, 243, 266
Lower School 125, 136, 138, 142, 143, 156, 158, 165, 166
Lyttelton, Lord 124

McCormick, Canon W.P. (Governor) 182
McDowell, Maj. A. 282
Mainwaring, C.L. (Master) 173
Makheyt's School, Croydon 32
Malleson, W.T. (Governor) 147
Malvern College 147
Manchester Grammar School 148, 171, 204
Manners-Sutton, Archbishop 102, 103, 104, 107, 109, 110
Manor House School, Croydon 115
Marks, Geoffrey (OW) (Governor) 160, 161, 190, 207
Marlar, Edward Alfred Geoffrey (Head Master) 223–39, 240, 241, 250, 251, 254, 255, 259, 290, 304; *224*
Marlar, Mrs 237, 239, 269
Marlar Sports Hall *see* Sports Hall
Marlborough College 114, 124, 146, 157, 161, 190, 193, 194, 290

Marshall, Sir James (OW) (Governor) 220, 233–5, 237, 242, 254, 255, 256, 258–9, 263, 281, 288, 302–3; *234*
Marshall, Liddle and Downey 259
Marten, Richard Dendy (OW) (Governor) 259, 262–4, 281, 303
Martin, Philip (OW) 197
Martin Marprelate tracts 22
Maslin, Henry (Master) 241, 249, 250, 286
Mason, Rev. M.H.H. (Master) 147, 161, 167, 173, 190
Masterman, C.S. 112, 113
Masterman, W.S. 112, 113
Masters' Common Room 166, 202, 220, 226, 237, 251, 256, 260, 262, 266, 267, 287, 302
Master's Dining Room 224n, 243, 255
Memorials 178, 231, 236, 247, 255; *231*
Mercers' Company 33, 80, 90
Mercers' School 15
Merchant Taylor's School 15, 32, 61, 72, 101, 120, 122, 126, 140, 146, 154, 180, 184, 193, 208
Micklewright, H.G.F. (Master) 165, 191, 196
middle class education 114–16
Middle Class School 116, 122, 125, 127, 128, 130, 139, 142, 143, 144, 146
Mill Hill School 140, 154
Miller, Rev. N.A.L. (OW) 192
Mills, Henry (Schoolmaster) 77–93, 96, 98; *85, 92*
  Bangorian Controversy 83–8
  Essay on Generosity 91, 92
  Primitiae Poetices 93
  Pueritiae Formandae Artifex 92
Mitcham 45, 74, 118
Mitcheson, R.E. 171
modern pentathlon 276
modern tetrathlon 249, 276; *249*
Monk, Rear-Admiral A.J. (OW) 211n
Monmouth School 248
Moore, Archbishop 101, 102
Morant, R.L. 171
More, Edward (OW) 68
Morgan, R.B. (Master) 165, 173
Mounsey, Mrs S.M. (Benefactor) 237
Murray, C. (Instructor) 249
Musgrave, C.S. (Master) 192, 221
music, 133, 141, 155, 177, 197–8, 216, 229–30, 236, 249, 274–5, 300
Music School 243–5, 260, 261, 264, 284; *244*

National School, Croydon 104–8, 109, 112, 116, 119–20
National Society for the Education of the Poor 104, 114, 116
Neligan, A.R. (OW) 59
new building (Haling Park) 282–8
New University School, Croydon 115
Newbold, John (Master) 198, 223
Newcastle Royal Grammar School 105
Newnham, Dr. 182
Newsom Report 258
Newton, Charles (Governor) 122
Nicholson, B.E. (OW) 207
Nicholson, Edward Rupert (OW) (Governor) 268–9, 303
Nicolson, William (Schoolmaster) 51–4; *51, 54*
Norbury 180, 205
Northampton 28, 66
North End 108, 121, 128, 130, 151, 187, 189, 199, 202, 235, 242, 246–7; *117*

North Park Whitgift FC 141
Norwood, Dr. Cyril 191, 194, 204, 209, 210
Nuffield Project 245, 272

OWA Day 230–1, 268, 305; *231*
O-Levels 232, 251, 271, 272, 298–9
Oakham School 96, 171
Odom, J.S. (Master) 229, 243, 244, 250, 274
Officer's Training Corps 176–7, 196, 198, 214, 225, 278; *187*, *201*, *208*; *see also* Cadet Corps; Combined Cadet Force
old boys 141, 152, 161; *see also* Old Whitgiftian Association
Old Palace Girls' School 179, 262, 264, 274, 294; *293*
Old Whitgiftian Association 168–9, 188, 190, 220, 262, 334–5
    Clubhouse *334*
    clubs 141, 168, 334–5
    Cricket Club 141, 168, 207, 231
    Dinner 141, 192, 246
    Hockey Club 275
    Rugby Football Club 141, 169, 207, 248
    Veterans Rifle Club 141, 168, 177
Oldham, John (Usher) 67–9, 73; *67*, *69*
Oldroyd, George (Song Master) 198, 229
Oundle School 42, 96, 157, 208, 240
Oxford University 50, 298, 299; *see also* universities
    Christ Church 47, 50, 52, 97, 127, 128, 151, 154, 257
    Magdalen College 51, 54
    Magdalen Hall 54, 57
    New College 61
    Oriel College 164, 291, 308
    Pembroke College 169
    St. Edmund Hall 67
    St. John's College 101, 193
    scholars 169
    Trinity College 77
    Wadham College 65

Page, William 108
Paget, Clarence C. 288
Paine, Walter Lionel (Master and Benefactor) 173
Palmer, A.H.G. (Master) 196
Parker, Archbishop 16, 29, 38
Parker, John (OW) 74
Parr, H.E. (Master) 196, 224, 230, 239, 245, 254
Parsons, A.T. (Master) 254, 282, 297, 299, 302
Paton, William (OW) 169
Pattison, Frank (Master) 278
Paule, Sir George 13, 20, 23, 27, 29, 41, 62, 63
Peet, William (Governor) 188, 189
Pelton, Rev. W.F. (OW) 136, 138, 139–40
Pemberton, John (OW) 90–1
Percy, Henry, Baron (OW) 52
Pereira, Rt. Rev. H.H. (Bishop of Croydon) 190
Perne, Andrew 15
Phelps, Mathias (OW) 74
Phelps, Verney (OW) 74
Philips, John (Schoolmaster) 61, 66, 193
Photographic Society 196
Pillonnière, François de la (Usher) 82, 83
    Bangorian Controversy 83–8
Platt of Writtle, Baroness 284
playing-fields 151, 159, 187, 202, 203, 207, 251–2, 259

Poor School, Croydon 36, 116, 117, 119, 125, 126, 127, 130, 135, 142, 143, 145, 146, 148, 149, 162, 280; *119*
Potter, Archbishop 96
Potter, Frank (Master) 196, 197, 286
Powell, Maurice 52
prefects 136, 175, 195, 226, 243, 254–5, 306; *226*
Prentice, Rt. Hon. Sir Reginald (OW) 211, 265–6; *265*
Price, George (Governor) 118
Price, John (OW) 61
Prime, Dr. Cecil (Master) 197, 224, 230, 253, 278
Prithergh, Dr. William (Benefactor) 38
public schools 111, 135, 157, 218, 227–8
    Clarendon report 120, 123, 124, 129, 157, 258
    criticised 120, 209
    Fleming report 218–19
    'Great Schools' 91, 105, 114, 120, 124, 131, 139, 161, 208; *see also* Charterhouse, Eton, Harrow, Merchant Taylors', Rugby, St. Paul's, Shrewsbury, Westminster, Winchester
Public Schools Commission 120, 123, 129, 157, 208, 258
Purley 181, 205, 281
Pusey, William (OW) 74

Quartermaine, Charles (OW) 161
Quartermaine, Leon (OW) 161
Raeburn, David Antony (Head Master) 257–94; *257*
    personal retrospect 295–307
Ramsey, Archbishop 242, 257, 259
Ravenseft Properties Ltd 242
Reigate 181, 205
religious observance 40, 48, 279–80, 306
Repton School 62, 157, 208, 223
Rich, Elias (OW) 68; *68*
Richmond, D.C. 145

Ridley, Anthony (Master) 282, 283, 302
Rifle-range 163, 283
Ripman, Prof. Walter 170
Roberts, Sir Bryan (OW) 211n
Roberts, E.S. (Master) 197, 278
Roberts, Philip (OW) 74
Robinson, J.E.C. (Master) 286
Roby, H.J. 141
Rochester, Earl of 68–9
Rogers, Charles (OW) 136
Roose, G.U.B. (OW) 154
Roper, S.D. (OW) 217
Rose, Dr. John (Schoolmaster) 101–3, 109, 193, 288; *102*, *103*
Rose, H.E. (OW) 138
Rouire, Jean (Usher) 84
Rouse, W.H.D. 173
Rowed, Nicholas (Writing-Master) 48
Royal Belfast School 248
rugby 140, 154–5, 184–5, 198, 207, 215, 216, 222, 225, 226, 227, 240, 241, 247–9, 275, 276; *247*, *248*
Rugby School 32, 95, 96, 105, 114, 120, 122, 124, 127, 148n, 156, 184, 290
Runcie, Archbishop 270
Ryan, A.P. (OW) 192
Ryecrofts 36, 37
Rymer, Samuel Lee (Governor) 122

St. Anthony's School 14, 96

St. Dunstan's College 154
St. John's School, Leatherhead 140, 248
St. Paul's Cross 31
St. Paul's School 14, 31, 33, 67n, 80–1, 90, 97, 120, 126, 139, 154, 157, 180, 184
St. Saviour's Grammar School, Southwark 45, 61, 63
Sancroft, Archbishop 66, 69, 70, 71, 74, 75, 76
Sandell, W.H. (OW) 154
Sanderstead 181, 205, 281
Sandford, Rev. C.W. 127
Sandison, Dr. A. 235
Saturday school 266–7, 304
Savage, T.E. (Master) 245
Saville, C.D. (OW) 249
Saward, Michael 122, 126, 127, 142
Scapula, *Lexicon* 48–9
Schad, R.C. (Master) 227, 275
scholarships 96, 125, 149, 155, 164, 169, 172, 182, 206, 233, 241, 270, 280–1
School Advisory Committee 267
school bills 19, 56, 73; *57*
School Leaving Certificate 182–3, 189, 206, 217, 232
school fees 56, 57, 73, 116–17, 138, 142, 158–9, 165–6, 170, 180, 228, 233, 234, 250, 264, 266, 280–1, 301
School of Industry, Croydon 103
school life 49, 150–1, 177–8
School Ordinances 42–4
Schoolhouse 36–7, 39, 42, 103, 104, 111, 112, 113, 116, 119, 131–2; *42, 113, 153*
 demolished 153–4
 repairs 70, 71, 97, 132
 used for National School 104–5, 107–8
Schoolmasters 55, 63–4, 104, 309–12 *see also* names of individual Schoolmasters
 disputes with tenants 65–6
 duties 39–41, 57; *40*
 paying pupils 42, 47, 48, 64, 78, 95, 102, 110
 qualifications 42
 stipend 38, 42–3, 46, 47, 59, 64, 95
 teaching 48, 64, 104–5
Schoolmaster's House 36, 37, 42–3, 46, 47, 59, 70, 71, 110, 121; *42, 43, 81*
 demolished 153–4
Schools Inquiry Commission (1864) 114, 123, 124, 131, 144
schools *see* names of individual schools; grammar schools; public schools
science 134–6, 158, 159, 164, 165, 173, 196, 230, 273
Scientific Society 196
Scouts 197, 278
seal 31; *34*
Secker, Archbishop 95, 97
Select Committee on education (1816) 106–8
Selhurst 163, 170
Selhurst Grammar School 172, 187, 191n, 205
Selhurst Grammar School for Girls 172, 179
Shaw, Peter (OW) (Governor) 197, 283, 304
Sheldon, Archbishop 63, 64, 65
Shelley, J.R. (Master) 245
Shepheard or Sheppard, John (Schoolmaster) 65–7, 68
Sheppard, R.A. (OW) 154
Sherborne School 62, 96, 129, 147
Shirley 37
Shirley Park 242; *see also* Trinity School

Shivas, Mark (OW) 250
shooting 140, 154, 207–8, 225, 226, 275, 276; *150*
Shorne, Kent 24, 26
Shotton, E. (Master) 278
Shrewsbury, Earl of 27, 41
Shrewsbury School 105, 114, 120
Sixth Form 138, 156, 158, 165, 169, 173, 174–5, 182–3, 195–6, 197, 206, 211, 230, 233, 236, 240, 243, 245, 254, 259, 260, 271–3, 274, 279, 297–8, 299, 306–7
Skeat, T.C. (OW) 191
Smith, A.H. (Master) 165
Smith, A.R. (OW) 207
Smith, H. Leslie (OW) 155
Smith, I.F. (Master) 229, 245
Smith, Raymond (Clerk to the Foundation) 304
Smyth, Sir John (OW) 78–9, 80, 81; *80*
Snape, Dr. Andrew 83, 84, 88
Snell, E.W. (Master) 165
Snow, Ralph (Benefactor) 74, 118; *75*
Society of Friends 108
Society for Promoting Christian Knowledge 81
Song Master 133, 160, 197, 229
South Norwood 163
Spanswick, J.E. (OW) 248
Speech Day 151, 216
Spencer Cup 154
Spens report on secondary education 43–4, 217
Sports Hall 245, 259, 260, 266, 268, 269, 275, 283, 284, 299, 303, 305; *277*
sports *see* games
squash 275
squash-courts 235, 237, 241
staff 133, 145, 158, 160, 165, 168, 191–2, 207, 270–1; *160, 183, 216, 238*
 Masters' Common Room 166, 202, 220, 226, 237, 251, 256, 260, 262, 266, 267, 287, 302
 Masters' Dining Room 224n, 243, 255
 pension funds 168
 salaries 134, 157, 168, 179, 205, 233, 238, 240–1
staff-to-pupil ratio 133, 145, 195–6, 233
Stammers, John (OW) 236
Stationers' Company School 120
Statute of Charitable Uses 111
Staveley, Samuel (Schoolmaster) 96
Staycross 34
Steinman, G.S., *History of Croydon* 113
Steward, Hannah 89–90
Stockdale, Richard (Benefactor) 38
Stow, John, *Survey of London* 43
Strand School, Brixton 193, 208
Strong, Dr. (Governor) 146, 147, 151, 182
Stroud Green 37
Subba Row, R. (OW) 226
Sumner, Archbishop 112, 122
Sutherland, John W. (Governor) 118
Sutton 45, 181
swimming 207–8, 225, 226, 231, 249, 268, 275, 276; *249*
swimming pool 163, 166, 202, 207–8, 235, 237, 268, 283, 284, 305; *237*
Sykes, Rt. Hon. Maj-Gen. Sir Frederick (OW) 161; *178*

Tadworth 205
Tait, Archbishop 122, 125, 126, 127, 139, 142, 144, 145, 146, 151, 156, 171

Index

Tate, E.W. (Master) 161, 167
Taunton Commission 123, 124, 134, 162, 169
Taunton School 180
technical studies 260
Tedder, Marshal of the RAF, Lord (OW) 178, 236; *225, 236*
Temple, Frederick, Archbishop 156, 159, 163, 164, 165, 172
Temple, Sir Purbeck 66, 70, 71, 74, 80
Temple, William, Archbishop 223
Tenison, Archbishop 75, 76, 77, 78, 81, 82, 83
  see also Archbishop Tenison's School
Tenison, Archdeacon Edward 88
Tenison, Thomas (OW) 80
tennis *see* lawn tennis
Teversham, Cambridgeshire 15; *17*
Thomas, Rev. J.W. (Master) 147
Thomas, R. Morris (Master) 224, 245
Thompson, Dr. Robert 66, 70
Thornton Heath 205
Thring, Edward 124, 147
Tillotson, Archbishop 75
Tolman, C.F. (Master) 278
Tomlin, Frederick (OW) 197
Tonbridge School 42, 62, 64, 121, 127, 147, 157, 204
Tounge, Kent 24
Trend, Lord (OW) 197, 211; *210*
Trevis, Peter (Master) 282, 302
Trinity School 235, 242, 247, 250–2, 256, 259, 263, 264, 266, 277, 281, 283, 304; *246, 247, 251*; *see also* Whitgift Middle School
Tubbe, Henry (OW and Benefactor) 54, 59; *59*
Turner, Arthur (OW) 74
Turner, Martin (OW) 207
Turner, Rev. H.W. (Master) 133, 134, 139, 160
Turner, Walton F. (Benefactor and Governor) 189, 199, 218

uniform 136, 195
universities 62, 64, 241n
  entrants 47, 93, 138, 182–3, 271–2
  scholarships 96, 138, 169, 206
University College, London 155
University College School 126, 154, 155, 180, 248
Upper School 125, 136, 138, 142, 143, 156, 159, 164, 165, 166
Uppingham School 32, 42, 96, 124, 127, 147, 161, 208
ushers 67, 74, 82, 84, 86; *67*

Vane, H.M. 112, 121, 141
Vaughan, Richard, Earl of Carbery (OW) 52, 53, 62; *53*
Verses on the Peace 79–80; *79*
Vincent, Robert (Master) 274
'Vincit qui patitur' 155, 329
visitations 51, 55–6, 63, 83, 88–9, 104, 106

Wake, Archbishop 83, 88–9, 90, 92
Wallington 181
Walton, Izaak, *Life of Richard Hooker* 62
war memorials 178, 231, 247, 255; *231*
Wardens 37, 40, 41, 63, 66, 107–8, 145
Warder, Joseph 85–7
Warlingham 181, 205
Warner, E.T. (OW) 154

Wase, Christopher 64
Watson, A.E. (Master) 161
Watson, Rev. H.C. (Chaplain) 121
Webb, Henry 119
Webb, John (OW and Schoolmaster) 54–8
Weightman, Digby (Governor) 263, 303
Weil, Dr. (Master) 133
Wellesley House 151, 153, 166
Wellington College 161
Wells Cathedral School 77–8
Westall, Edward (Governor) 118, 122
Westminster School 15, 32, 33, 47, 50, 67n, 93, 96, 120, 255
West Wickham 45
Wheatcroft, John (Master) 160
White, William R. (Governor) 118
Whitgift, Alice (sister of JW) 14, 15
Whitgift, Bridget (niece of JW) 26
Whitgift, Geoffrey (brother of JW) 14, 23
Whitgift, George (brother of JW) 14, 23, 24, 26
Whitgift, Henry (father of JW) 13, 15
Whitgift, Isobel (aunt of JW) 13, 14, 15
Whitgift, John (Founder) 13–30; *16, 26, 28*
  appearance 27
  Archbishop of Canterbury 21–3, 33
  arms 328; *328*
  at Cambridge 15–20
  attacked in tracts 22
  benefactions 24, 33, 60
  birth 13
  Bishop of Worcester 21, 23, 24, 33
  Canon of Ely 18
  character 18, 27–30, 155
  concern for the poor 31
  correspondence with Cecil 17
  death 25–6
  debts 17–18
  education at school 14–15
  favourite residence 262
  Fellow of Peterhouse 15
  friendship with Elizabeth I 18, 25
  Hampton Court Conference 25
  interest in education 33
  Lady Margaret Professor of Divinity 15, 18
  library 29
  Master of Pembroke Hall 17
  Master of Trinity 18, 23, 24
  Privy Councillor 22, 24, 73
  purchase of property 24, 33, 36, 37, 38
  Rector of Laceby 23
  Rector of Teversham 15
  Regius Professor of Divinity 18, 23
  religious beliefs 15–16, 18, 20–3
  Royal Chaplain 18, 25
  statuette 246; *132*
  Statutes 34, 38–41, 42, 47, 55, 64, 65–6, 70, 75, 112, 113, 116, 118, 133, 280, 295; *38, 40*
  tomb 26, 152, 225; *27, 152*
  Vice-Chancellor 20
  wealth 18, 23–4, 33
  will 26–7
Whitgift, John (grandfather of JW) 13, 15
Whitfift, John (nephew of JW) 24, 26, 50
Whitgift, John de 13

351

Whitgift School

Whitgift, Philip (brother of JW) 14, 15
Whitgift, Richard (brother of JW) 14, 23, 26, 36
Whitgift, Robert (uncle of JW) 13, 14, 15, 18
Whitgift, William (brother of JW) 18, 23, 24, 26
Whitgift, Humberside (formerly Yorkshire) 13; *14*
Whitgift Almshouse and Pension Foundation 162
Whitgift Almshouses *see* Hospital of the Holy Trinity
Whitgift Avenue 204
Whitgift Centre 108, 247, 250, 259, 264, 283; *252*
Whitgift Charities Act (1969) 252–3, 264, 294
Whitgift Charity 88, 122, 124, 141
Whitgift Court 236
Whitgift Educational Foundation 162
Whitgift Exhibition 235
Whitgift family origins 13
Whitgift Foundation 162, 169, 170, 294, 304
 governing body 145
 grant of arms 253
 income 179, 259, 300
Whitgift Grammar School 146, 147, 148, 204; *see also* Whitgift School
Whitgift heraldry 328–9
Whitgift Hospital *see* Hospital of the Holy Trinity
Whitgift Hospital and Croydon Charities Committee 143
Whitgift House 269–70, 279, 280, 283
Whitgift Middle School 121, 142, 146, 148, 149, 158, 162–3, 170, 171–2, 179, 189, 199, 205, 219, 235, 280; *119*; *see also* Trinity School
 change of name 235
 Direct Grant 180, 219–20, 266, 280, 281
 fees 234
 move to North End 189
 opened 1882 148
 purchase of Haling Park for 185–188
 war time 215
Whitgift motto 155, 329
Whitgift School
 administrative officer 253, 260, 282, 302
 alumni 50, 152–3, 314–19, 320–22
 assisted places 280–1, 290
 badge *329*
 boys admitted 132–3, 138, 142, 145, 148, 153, 158, 161, 181
 Building Committee 282–3
 buildings 70, 117, 119, 121–2, 130–2, 146, 164, 166–7, 202–3, 237, 243–4, 269, 282–8; *119*, *131*, *147*, *167*, *201*, *203*, *204*, *284*, *285*
 bursaries 281
 change of name 146, 204
 decline 94–109
 Direct Grant 180, 219–20, 266, 280, 281
 foundation 31–44
 free places 180, 219, 234
 games 139–40, 184–5, 198, 207–8, 222, 225–6, 247–9, 275–7, 299
 Head Masters 312–13
 House system 161, 167, 225, 232, 241, 247, 304–5
 Inquiry of 1878 144–6
 Inspections 156, 164–5, 174, 181, 236, 259–60, 296, 299, 303
 Junior School 233, 234, 258, 259, 260, 266, 269, 284, 297, 299, 303; *156*, *172*
 management team 281–2, 302
 modernisation 165–6
 move to Haling Park 189, 204
 move to North End 129
 plans *186*, *332*, *333*
 prefects 136, 254–5, 306; *226*
 record cards 225
 schemes of reorganisation 116–17, 141–2, 143, 144, 145, 146, 149, 162, 179, 252, 294
 School Advisory Committee 267–8, 301, 303
 Schoolmasters 309–12
 School Roll 225, 287
 societies 141, 177, 196, 197–8, 214, 232, 278, 279
 Statutes 34, 38–41, 42, 47, 55, 64, 65–6, 70, 112, 113, 116, 118, 133, 280, 295; *38*, *40*
 tercentenary 155–6
 war casualties 176, 177, 178, 217
 war-time restrictions 215–17
Whitgift School and its Evolution (Balley) 161
Whitgift School Association 231, 268–9, 301, 303, 305
Whitgift seal 31; *34*
Whitgift Veterans Rifle Club 141, 168, 177
Whitgift Wanderers CC 141, 168
'Whitgiftian' as a term 167
Whitgiftian, The 59, 140–1, 167, 173, 177, 216, 221, 225, 272, 287
Whitgift's School and National School 104–8
Whitteridge, Prof. David (OW) 211
Whitteridge, Sir Gordon (OW) 191
Wigan, William (OW) 80
Wigram, D.R. (Master) 197
Wild, Prof. J.P. (OW) 211n
Wilkinson, M.D.G. (OW) 248
Willcocks, David 244
Williams, Gerwyn (Master) 247, 249
Williams, Harcourt (OW) 161
Williams, P.G. (OW) 207
Wilmot, Edward 78
Wilson, Sir Hugh 266, 283, 301
Winchester College 31, 50, 59, 96, 120, 287
Wireless Society 196
Woldingham 181
Wood, Anthony à, *Athenae Oxonienses* 51, 52, 63
Wood, Noris (Schoolmaster) 58–9, 129
Wood Roberts, T. (Governor) 181, 188
Woodford House School, Croydon 179
Woodgate, H.G. (Master) 192
Woods, Rt. Rev. E.S. (Bishop of Croydon and Governor) 201, 207, 223; *200*
Woodside 37, 120, 121
Woolfenden, Guy (OW) 250
Worcester 21, 23
Worcester, Earl of 20, 26, 41
Wordsworth, A.J. (OW) 249
World War I 176–8
World War II 214–17
Wormeall, Christopher 34, 37, 38
Worsell, Cyril (Master) 250, 286
Wotton, James and William 74
Wright, John Spurrier (Benefactor) 155
Writing-masters 48

Yeo, John (Master) 286

Zouche, Lord 20, 26, 41